GreenWorld's

almanac

Directory

environmental

organizations

United States *1994* and Canada

Published by
GreenWorld Environmental Publications CO.

GreenWorld Environmental Publications Co.
253 A 26th Street, Suite 306
Santa Monica, CA 90402
Telephone (310) 815 8867 • Fax (310) 815 8868

To order additional copies of this book, please use the order form on page 325

ISBN 0-9640403-1-X

First Printing

Printed in Belgium by Imprimerie Campin • Rue Barthélémy Frison 13 7500 Tournai - Belgium • Coordination Eric Leconte

Printed on 100% recycled paper

acknowledgments

To you **millicent**, *all our gratitude for making this project possible.*

GreenWorld's staff would like to thank all the people who have contributed to the realization of this project including the numerous **environmental** *groups and* **organizations** *who supplied us with the information listed in this publication.*

Special thanks to **beth parke** *from the Society of Environmental Journalists,* **harriet modler** *from the Independent Writers of Southern California, environmental writer* **kathryn phillips**, **patricia campbell**, **paul john balson**, **éric leconte**, *and* **muriel bensimon** *for her precious artistic help.*

Many thanks to the **organisation** *for* **economic co-operation** *and* **development** *(State of the Environment Division), the* **northwest coalition** *for* **alternatives** *to* **pesticides**, *the* **united states energy association**, *and* **the world bank**.

introduction

 6

The publishing of GreenWorld's Almanac and Directory of Environmental Organizations is, in a way, *a tribute to all women and men of the environmental movement* in Northern America. It is a recognition of their remarkable achievements towards insuring the protection of all nature's assets essential to sustain life on Earth. The public owes thanks to the conservation and environmental organizations for many a victory on the environmental front. It is they who placed environmental issues on the agenda of government, and pushed and pulled until necessary laws were adopted to protect the resources of our land, our waters, and our air. But like any political movement in its early days, the environmental movement has yet to focus its efforts and develop a cohesive action program. *Oftentimes it appears to be a movement locked* into a variety of conflicts - with government, the business world, and within itself. This last conflict needs to be viewed from both short-range and long-range perspectives as an aberration to be corrected. For too long, a sterile face-à-face with an adversarial mood has been taking place between the so-called liberal and conservative wings of the environmental movement. The *time has come to realize certain truths*. Yes, the environment has profound political, economic, and social implications. Yes, everybody breathes the same fouled air and will suffer the consequences of irreversible assaults on Earth's natural resources. If movement members would take stock of these truths, they would take a major step toward acceptance of one another's agenda. Any historical background of the conservation and environmental movement would demonstrate *the prominent role played by grassroots organizations* in promoting at the local, state, and federal levels the landmark pieces of legislation that put the defense of environment on the political map. Some of the early groups themselves have turned into the mainstream giants within the movement. Now big and efficient players in the economic and political arenas, these vanguard groups possess the know-how, the expertise, and the clout to push for meaningful decisions. At the other end of the spectrum, we find the grassroots citizens, the foot soldiers who initiate new actions against the environmental destructors. They form the foundation of the political support and constitute the basic force to the movement's ultimate success. This is - and will always be - the prevalent order. Logic dictates that dialogue between grassroots and mainstream organizations should be pursued relentlessly, developed and coordinated until it gives rise to a powerful alliance. Under such conditions, *the entire movement will become a political force to be reckoned with nationally and worldwide*.

GreenWorld Environmental Publications, a newly established company, pledges its support in the development of a greater awareness of environmental issues, in correcting wrong perceptions, and stressing the urgent need to address them. This is an invitation to adhere to an environmental peace agreement between the various economic and social segments of society: citizens, government, commerce and industry, the environmental organizations. It is an invitation to usher in a new era where confrontation and hostility give way to common action toward a common goal: the restoration and protection of our natural habitat for the benefit of all generations to come. A more apt definition for the objectives pursued by the environmental movement would include the reassessment of present ethics and social values. There will be no exaggeration in stating that the movement is actually *in search of a new culture, a new civilization*. But will the movement be capable of creating the right conditions for such a mission? We at GreenWorld believe that the North American conservation and environmental organizations have already gone a long way in this direction. But the distance is still awesome and there are many requirements yet to be met. These are : • the involvement of the greatest possible number of citizens and voters • the commitment of the business world and industry to change their ways and to redefine their notions of profit and public interest • the need to educate against the excesses of ingrained consumerism and promote an entirely new social behavior • the sine qua non condition of bringing together the various trends of the movement for a concerted mobilization from absolutely all sectors of society. *This publication* is designed precisely to encourage a meeting of minds and hearts by offering complete knowledge about a great number of organizations. It is *a tool to bridge the gap* between environmentalists, the business community, and concerned citizens and their government. It is a tool to bring together diverse groups, *to promote understanding* of one another's motivations and objectives, and to favor the implementation of programs and cancel duplication. It is a practical tool for a variety of users: environmentally active citizens, potential members of the listed organizations and volunteers, public officials and representatives at all levels of government, natural resources managers, corporate officers, decision makers, business and industry leaders, students, professors, and scholars, philanthropists, professionals, lawyers, doctors, members of the media and communications world. GreenWorld's Almanac and Directory of Environmental Organizations *responds to the need for networking*, to act together amongst organizations, and to interact with the world outside of the movement. The publication offers a series of articles about the environmental state of affairs in different fields of heightened concern. These articles reflect preoccupations shared by many. They express our shared hopes for a general awakening to the catastrophic threats looming over the entire planet and its inhabitants. Most of all, GreenWorld's Almanac and Directory of Environmental Organizations *reflects a heartfelt call* for the leaders in all walks of life to acknowledge their responsibilities and set the appropriate course in Earth's resources management. It is an appeal for rescue that should be heeded with the corresponding sense of urgency. • THE EDITOR

greenworld

managing editor *Tarik Redjimi*

art director *Michel Maïquez*

research associates *Jeffrey Barrie*
Kynan Dunmeyer
Pascal El Grably
Soraya Greenway
Karie Ihara
Karl Kassoul
Joe Lavallee

graphic illustrations *Tarik Redjimi*
Alexandra Ross

9

authors

deborah brown *Los Angeles-based freelance writer. Her credits include creation materials for the Earth Day International Awards, the New World's Eve Foundation, the American Public Health Association and the Big Blue Foundation.*

lyn corum *Independent journalist specializing in energy. She covers the independent power industry for a variety of national publications from her office in Santa Monica, California.*

carolyn l. davis *Freelance writer living in Livermore, California with her husband and two children. She has been writing about environmental and occupational safety and health issues for the past nine years.*

david drum *Freelance journalist whose work has appeared in Barron's, the Los Angeles Times, San Francisco Chronicle, People and other publications. He is president of the Los Angeles-based Independent Writers of Southern California.*

joel grossman *Santa Monica, California, freelance writer, computer database researcher and photographer who specializes in environmental issues.*

laura l. klure *Widely published independent writer based in Riverside, California. She has a BA in biology and was a Staff Research Associate in Plant Pathology at UC Riverside.*

pamela s. leven *Former staff writer for Business Week and Investor's Business Daily. Based in Culver City, California, she is now an independent writer for a variety of local and national publications.*

athena f. lucero *Freelance writer living in Sierra Madre, California, she has worked on various transportation and environmental projects in Los Angeles.*

john vargo *Los Angeles-based playwright, poet, essayist and fiction writer. A great appreciator of nature, he is contemplating a collection of "philosophical musings" about man and his environment.*

petra yee *Information officer of the International Rivers Network in Berkeley, a non-profit organization dedicated to the preservation of rivers and watersheds. She has been an environmental writer for many years and holds a masters degree in biology from the University of Freiburg, Germany.*

directory
organizations

& almanac
articles

vities

llenges

list of **charts**

global environmental

challenges

part one

"*Humanity is at a crossroads of enormous consequences. Never before has civilization faced an array of problems as critical as the ones now faced. As forbidding and portentous as it may sound, what is at stake is nothing less than the global survival of humankind.*"

United Nations Organisation AGENDA 21
The Earth Summit Strategy To Save Our Planet

global
environmental concerns

CHAPTER 1

14

Northern America and the Environment, an Overview by the editor

LET US BEGIN WITH THE "GREENEST trade agreement ever", as the North American Free Trade Agreement has been qualified by its proponents in the American administration. It is a development that will have worldwide repercussions as a model and a precedent.
For the first time, a legal international instrument has been devised by three important neighboring countries - Canada, Mexico, and the United States of America - a whole continent, to make environmental requirements part and parcel of their economic life and trade exchanges. Three nations made themselves accountable to their people, to each other, and to the international community in the spirit of the 1992 Earth Summit in Rio de Janeiro and its environmental blueprint "Agenda 21". At last environmental problems that know no frontiers, such as transboundary pollution, will be addressed in a concrete way in their geographical dimension. The NAFTA signatories are bound to harmonize many of their laws, rules, and regulations in the environmental domain and implement mechanisms for their enforcement. Sustainable development appears high on

their agenda as well as the overall protection of natural resources, health, and well-being of their citizens.

IN NORTHERN AMERICA, as in the rest of the world, the environmental impact on public

> ## In Northern America, as in the rest of the world, the *environmental impact on public health* shows the real dimension of human tampering with nature and its resources.

health shows the real dimension of human tampering with nature and its resources. In their quest for evermore fulfilling ways of life, modern societies have created wealth, comfort, beauty, and have elevated their intellect and scientific abilities to new summits. At the same time,

incapable of measuring the boundaries of their powers, societies continue to pollute and degrade their environment in a way that is bound to substantially compromise the quality of life and the state of health. Medical advancement is constantly

defeated by an inconsiderate misuse and abuse of Earth's resources. The consequences spare no one, much less our children, the most fragile component of our societies. Children are unknowingly exposed to a string of health hazards and potential ailments

that might surface during their adult life. When these health conditions develop, they are generally difficult or impossible to cure. The present generation of parents should find this prospect sobering and take the necessary steps as citizens and voters to initiate and support corrective action by government. A case in point: the alarming effects on fetuses, infants, and children of lead, chemicals and pesticides. Children are exposed to insidious poisoning at home, school, and outside where they play. Pesticide residues are found in the vegetables and fruits that children eat, in the air they breathe, in the drinking water. Because young brains, nervous systems, and other body organs are at their most vulnerable stage of development, the immediate effects can be devastating and the long-term ones are completely unknown. Fortunately, the scientific community and government both support legislation to gradually remove dangerous chemicals and pesticides from the market. Incidents of food poisoning, another major concern for youngsters' health, has prompted a complete overhaul of inspection systems for meat, poultry, fish, and other foods. While the blame is often placed on government and industry, the danger too often starts at home. Second-hand smoke, perhaps the most avoidable health hazard, is responsible for impairing the respiratory health of hundreds of thousands of youngsters.

CHILDREN, OUR MOST PRECIOUS human resource, seem to suffer most from a culture gone awry. In addition to the assaults on their physical health, their mental health seems increasingly threatened in their homes by violence-prone radio and television programming. Man's awesome power to create an artificial environment out of the natural environment has a tendency to go overboard and be counter-productive. Man and his environment are not always in a happy symbiosis. In the field of audio-visual arts, people have used their superior aptitude to create the most stunning environment, to expand the frontiers of intellect, but while doing so, have altered the moral fabric spun over centuries of civilization. Violence and criminal behavior seem to mirror the television screen rather than the other way around and give frightening rise to generations of youngsters whose cultures draw their terms of reference from a world of make-believe and intellectual deceit.

Why single out television? Because of its presence in every household where its instant access and availability precludes a deliberate choice such as going out to a movie theater.

Children watch television the way they inhale polluted air: because it's there.

Polluters of the air waves, no more so than polluters ▶

United States

20•20 VISION
1828 JEFFERSON PLACE NW   WASHINGTON DC 20036
PHONE (202) 833 2020   FAX (202) 833 5307

Founded 1986 • *Geographic Coverage* Local, State, Regional, National, Global • *Chapters* 58 • *Individual Members* 12,000

Mission To revitalize democracy by creating persistent, strategic citizen action to persuade decision makers to protect the earth by reducing militarism and preserving the environment.

Annual Fees	Regular	Families	Sponsor	Enthusiast	Visionary
	$20	$35	$40	$75	$100

Programs Sponsors periodic regional advocacy/activist training and in-depth education on various issues. Monthly action postcard tailored to where subscriber lives, informing them of current opportunities for action and changing policy.

Publications Monthly *Legislative Update*. Monthly action alert postcard. Study *Is Anyone Listening*, surveys congressional staff on effective citizen action

For more Information Database

Who's Who PRESIDENT **LOIS BARBER** • EXECUTIVE DIRECTOR **KERRY COOKE** • LEGISLATIVE DIRECTORS **ROBIN CAIOLA**, **STEPHEN YOUNG** • LIBRARIAN **ELISABETH FROST**

ALLIANCE FOR OUR COMMON FUTURE
C/O NATIONAL PEACE FOUNDATION
1835 "K" STREET, NW, SUITE 610   WASHINGTON DC 20006
PHONE (202) 223 1770   FAX (202) 223 1718

Founded 1989 • *Geographic Coverage* National, Global • *Other Field of Focus* Human Rights & Environment • *Organization Members* 70

Mission The Alliance, a coalition of NGOs, is an interorganizational effort working to further the development of a just world community, a healthy global environment, and effective structures for peace.

ALLIANCE FOR SURVIVAL
200 NORTH MAIN STREET, SUITE M-2   SANTA ANA CA 92701
PHONE (714) 547 6282   FAX (714) 547 6322

Founded 1977 • *Geographic Coverage* Local, Regional, Global *Cooperative Partner* Statewide Network on Nuclear Waste Management • *Chapters* 2 • *Individual Members* 4,000

Mission To work to make the direct and indirect links between the issues of peace, ecology, equality, and a nuclear free future.

Annual Fees	Regular	Student/Senior
	$25	$15

Programs Past projects have included the Governor Pete Wilson "Don't Waste Our Desert" postcard campaign, high school environmental legislative network, Interior Secretary Bruce Babbitt postcard campaign; "Low-Level Radiation Isn't Low Risk" flier distribution, and support for Navajo People of Big Mountain, AZ. In 1992, the Alliance also held a candlelight vigil and street party celebrating the peace movement's role in ending the Cold War, a town hall summit on energy, and an Earth Summit garden party.

For more Information Database, Library

Who's Who PRESIDENT **JEAN BERNSTEIN** • SECRETARY **ALAN SEAMAN** • TREASURER **BOB ANDERSON** • EXECUTIVE DIRECTOR **MARION PACK**

ASHOKA: INNOVATORS FOR THE PUBLIC
1700 NORTH MOORE STREET, SUITE 1920   ARLINGTON VA 22209
PHONE (703) 527 8300

Founded 1980 • *Geographic Coverage* Global • *Chapters* 10, in

of land, air, and water, should avail themselves of basic freedoms and their constitutional base to undermine the most fundamental values.

WITH CHILDREN STILL IN MIND, one must ask how to best counteract the inertia of living patterns and lifestyles resulting from the rightful pursuit of a happiness that is spurred by the advent of guaranteed freedoms,

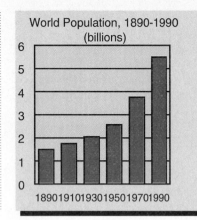
World Population, 1890-1990 (billions)

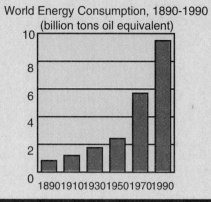
World Energy Consumption, 1890-1990 (billion tons oil equivalent)

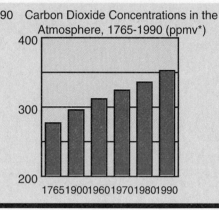
Carbon Dioxide Concentrations in the Atmosphere, 1765-1990 (ppmv*)

the US and Europe • *Individual Members* 600

Mission To find and support individuals in developing countries who are pursuing innovative projects for social change. Ashoka's investment in people yields pattern-setting changes in education, health, environmental protection, human rights, and many other fields of social concern.

Funding *Foundations* 100%

Total Income $2,300,000

Usage	Administration	Fundraising	Programs
	7%	13%	80%

Publications Occasional newsletters

Who's Who PRESIDENT WILLIAM DRAYTON • VICE PRESIDENT DEBORAH MCGLAUFLIN

CALIFORNIA LEAGUE OF CONSERVATION VOTERS
965 MISSION STREET, SUITE 705   SAN FRANCISCO CA 94103
PHONE (415) 896 5550

Founded 1972 • *Geographic Coverage* State • *Chapters* 2
Individual Members 35,000

Mission The League works in communities around the state to elect candidates, pass ballot measures, and hold leaders accountable to the environmental concerns of their constituents.

Annual Fees *Regular* $25

Programs Research on candidates which probes beneath campaign rhetoric to document and publicize each candidate's commitment to environmental protection. The League's education program communicates directly with hundreds of thousands of voters each year to fill them in on how their representatives are voting on crucial environmental issues. Each year, using background research, questionnaires and

face-to-face interviews the League gives its seal of approval to the very best environmental candidates and initiatives throughout the state. The Campaign Strength program backs the League's political endorsements with campaign expertise assisting candidates with the media, fundraising and grassroots strategies needed to win races. Campaign Skills Training Conference: Building Environmental Leadership for Tomorrow '93.

CENTER FOR GLOBAL ENVIRONMENTAL TECHNOLOGIES   PAGE 285
NEW MEXICO ENGINEERING RESEARCH INSTITUTE (THE)
UNIVERSITY OF NEW MEXICO   ALBUQUERQUE NM 87131-1376
PHONE (505) 272 7250   FAX (505) 272 7203

CENTER FOR THE STUDY OF THE ENVIRONMENT
301 EAST CARILLO STREET   SANTA BARBARA CA 93101
PHONE (805) 963 5088   FAX (805) 569 1164

Geographic Coverage Global

Mission To provide solutions to global, regional and local environmental problems by identifying ways to remove or reduce the causes of damage and to repair their effects; to develop methods for maintaining sustainable supplies of renewable resources such as fisheries, forest and wildlife.

Programs Forecasts outcomes of environmental conditions using advanced computer modeling and gathers critical environmental data not being obtained by universities, government agencies or other organizations.

Who's Who PRESIDENT DANIEL B. BOTKIN • VICE PRESIDENT MILTON HAMMER SECRETARY PHILIP THRESHER

CHARLES A. LINDBERGH FUND, INC. (THE)   PAGE 287
708 SOUTH THIRD STREET, SUITE 110   MINNEAPOLIS MN 55415-1141
PHONE (612) 338 1703   FAX (612) 338 6826

World Population Growth, World Energy Consumption, and Carbon Dioxide Concentrations in the Atmosphere

* ppmv = parts per million by volume

Source: United Nations Environment Programme 1992,
United Nations Population Division 1991,
U.S. Bureau of the Census, Report WP/91,
World Population Profile 1991

democracy, and a high-technology industrial age with its horn of plenty. One asks why the grandparents and parents of today, their minds and attitudes molded by a lifetime of indulging, are not able to alter their deeply ingrained way of living. Indeed, in the twenty years since the first Earth Day celebration, few dents have been inflicted on consumer habits. Not even the current economic downturn has encouraged a significant change. Quite to the contrary, signs of recovery show a renewed impetus towards consuming as the basic response to all economic shortcomings. Where does that leave the lofty recommendations and popular enthusiasm for a wise management of Earth's resources? We are passing more liabilities and reduced assets to the next generations. Recycling, one of the more concrete approaches, still shows modest results in view of the problem of vast waste. If grandparents and parents cannot accept a new, more restrained way of life, they can at least pave the way for their descendants by supporting the environmental agenda and working hard to create a future in an environmentally safe world. Not to do so will be unjustifiable and unforgivable. ▶

CORNELL WASTE MANAGEMENT INSTITUTE
CENTER FOR THE ENVIRONMENT

425 HOLISTER HALL   ITHACA NY 14853
PHONE (607) 255 8444

Founded 1991 • *Geographic Coverage* Global • *Other Field of Focus* Waste - Management / Disposal / Treatment / Recycling

Mission To address pressing environmental issues in their full interdisciplinary complexity through teaching, research, and outreach. Its current field of studies encompasses combustion/incineration science, biospheric chemical prospecting, social and economic consequences of climate change, cultural factors affecting developing nations, composting, water and wetlands, and sustainable agriculture.

Total Income $4,000,000

Usage	Administration	Programs
	6%	94%

Programs Water Resources Institute. Waste Management Institute. Cornell Laboratory for Environmental Applications of Remote Sensing. Work and Environment Initiative. Institute for Comparative and Environmental Toxicology. Cornell Institute for Research in Chemical Ecology.

Publication Newsletter *Environmental Update*

For more Information Library

Who's Who PRESIDENT **ROBERT BARKER**

COUNCIL FOR A LIVABLE WORLD

110 MARYLAND AVENUE, NE, SUITE 409   WASHINGTON DC 20002
PHONE (202) 543 4100   FAX (202) 543 6297

Founded 1962 • *Geographic Coverage* National, Global • *Other*

Field of Focus Pollution / Radiations • *Cooperative Partners* Peace Political Action Committee, Council for a Livable World Education Fund

Mission To combat the menace of weapons of mass destruction, including nuclear, biological and chemical weapons, and of arms sales to other governments.

Programs Council activities include working for arms control legislation, lobbying Congress and the Administration, supporting pro-peace political candidates, holding seminars, disseminating information, and working in coalition with other peace groups.

Publications Numerous fact sheets, articles, reprints

Multimedia Online information service 1-202-543-0006, gives callers status of arms control measures in Congress and recommends action to influence senators and representatives

Who's Who CHAIRPERSON **JEROME GROSSMAN** • PRESIDENT **JOHN ISAACS**

COUSTEAU SOCIETY, INC. (THE)

870 GREENBRIER CIRCLE, SUITE 402   CHESAPEAKE VA 23320-2641
PHONE (804) 523 9335   FAX (804) 523 2747

Founded 1973 • *Geographic Coverage* Global • *Other Fields of Focus* Ecosystem Protection / Biodiversity, Wildlife - Animal & Plant *Cooperative Partner* Equipe Cousteau, sister organization - France *Individual Members* 330,000 worldwide

Mission To protect and improve the quality of life for present and future generations. The Society is guided by the belief that only a well-informed public can make the best choices to provide a healthier and more productive way of life for itself and for future generations.

Annual Fees	Regular	Families
	$20	$28

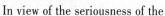

▶ IN ADDITION TO CHILDREN, large segments of our population show high vulnerability to the global environmental crises. Ethnic minorities and the economically poor are disproportionately exposed to industrial pollution, hazardous wastes, pesticides, and toxic contamination. They bear an equally disproportionate cost in terms of health.
In view of the seriousness of the

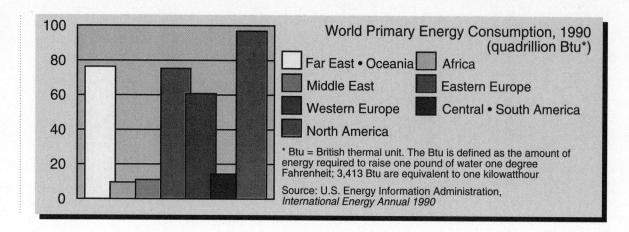

World Primary Energy Consumption, 1990
(quadrillion Btu*)

- ☐ Far East • Oceania ☐ Africa
- ☐ Middle East ☐ Eastern Europe
- ☐ Western Europe ■ Central • South America
- ☐ North America

* Btu = British thermal unit. The Btu is defined as the amount of energy required to raise one pound of water one degree Fahrenheit; 3,413 Btu are equivalent to one kilowatthour

Source: U.S. Energy Information Administration, *International Energy Annual 1990*

Funding

Membership	Educational Films & Filmstrips	Contributions & Grants
53%	25%	8.8%

Other Sources *Publishing & Royalties* 5.5% • *Other* 7.7%

Total Income $12,986,149

Usage

Administration	Fundraising	Programs	Membership Development
11.1%	9.4%	72%	7.5%

Total Expenses $14,845,372

Publications Bimonthly magazine *Calypso Log*. Reports on global environmental issues. Bimonthly educational children's magazine *Dolphin Log*. Numerous books and scientific papers

Multimedia The Cousteau Society produces 4 films each year in collaboration with Turner Broadcasting Systems

For more Information Annual Report, List of Publications

Who's Who PRESIDENT **JACQUES-YVES COUSTEAU** • VICE PRESIDENT **PAULA DiPERNA** VICE PRESIDENT SCIENCE AND EDUCATION **RICHARD MURPHY** • VICE PRESIDENT EUROPEAN AFFAIRS **HENRI JACQUIER** • CONTACT **SANDRA S. BOND**

EARTH ISLAND INSTITUTE

300 BROADWAY, SUITE 28	SAN FRANCISCO CA 94133-3312
PHONE (415) 788 3666	FAX (415) 788 7324

Founded 1982 • *Geographic Coverage* Global • *Cooperative Partners* Rainforest Action Network, International Rivers Network, Earth Island Action Group, Star Valley, Meadowcreek, Northcoast Environmental Center, Central Coast Conservation Center, Worldware, Center for Global Sustainability • *Chapters* Earth Island centers, local grassroots organizing points throughout the US • *Individual Members* 30,000

Mission To work toward the goals of conservation, preservation, and restoration of the global environment, by providing institutional support for the ideas and projects of individuals working on ecologically linked issues.

Annual Fees

Regular	Student/Senior	Contributing	Supporting	Sponsor
$25	$15	$50	$100	$250

Other Fees *Lifetime* $750

Programs Environmental Project on Central America. International Marine Mammal Project. Earth Island Energy Program. Climate Protection Institute. Endangered Species Project. Green Education and Development Fund. Mountain Alliance Fund.

Publications Quarterly *Earth Island Journal*. *The Greenhouse Gas-ette* published by The Climate Protection Institute

Who's Who PRESIDENT **CARL ANTHONY** • VICE PRESIDENT **ELISABETH R. GUNTHER** SECRETARY **ELLEN MANCHESTER** • TREASURER **DAVE McGREW** • EXECUTIVE DIRECTORS **JOHN A. KNOX, DAVID PHILLIPS** • EDITOR **GAR SMITH**

EARTH SHARE

3400 INTERNATIONAL DRIVE, NW, SUITE 2-K	WASHINGTON DC 20008
PHONE (202) 537 7100	FAX (202) 537 7101

Founded 1988 • *Geographic Coverage* National • *Other Fields of Focus* Ecosystem Protection / Biodiversity, Public / Environmental Health *Organization Members* 40

Mission To help prevent health problems arising from air, water, and toxic pollution, to preserve and conserve fresh water, marine, and land resources, and to protect biological diversity and wildlife habitat, by using public education and workplace solicitation campaigns to expand public involvement on environmental issues.

Funding *Government Support* 99%

Total Income $6,881,138

problem, the Clinton administration is looking into violations of civil rights and is planning measures to include sociological considerations in all legislation pertaining to environmental protection. The latent crises of the inner-cities and the homeless poor also call for an urgent and equivalent attitude by local authorities. The problems of the cities, the location of industrial facilities, and the creation and protection of jobs are all enmeshed with environmental impacts on human health, on air, water, and wildlife. What is needed most is a recognition of this relationship as well as the political will to find the proper balance between all these factors. In the spring of 1993, the Clinton administration assembled representatives from the lumber and related industries, leaders of environmental organizations, and officials from local governments in an effort to end the "owl versus jobs" tug of war in the Pacific Northwest. President Clinton emphasized that "the long-term economic and environmental health of the region must be what drives the administration's policy". He rebuffed the confrontation between economics and the environment and set the tone for future debates in other areas of environmental contention. "It is time to make tough decisions and redefine our forest resources policies to reflect the realities of sustainable development and environmental health", he said. What emerged was a blueprint for ecosystem management coupled with a plan to launch a national biological survey, an inventory of all plants and animals in the United States. ►

Usage	Administration	Fundraising	Programs	Other
	4.7%	4.3%	89.5%	1.5%

Programs Public Education and Information Campaign (in conjunction with The Advertising Council, and designed by DDB Needham Worldwide). Combined Federal Campaign makes outreach efforts to federal agencies to maximize donations. Holds workplace fundraising drives. Seeks corporate sponsorships.

For more Information Annual Report

Who's Who CHAIR **ERIK MEYERS** • VICE CHAIR **PAULA HAYES** • SECRETARY **ELIZABETH MCCORKLE** • TREASURER **JAY FELDMAN** • EXECUTIVE DIRECTOR **KALMAN STEIN**

EARTHWATCH
680 MOUNT AUBURN STREET, P.O. BOX 403-N   WATERTOWN MA 02272
PHONE (617) 926 8200   FAX (617) 926 8532

Founded 1972 • *Geographic Coverage* Global • *Other Fields of Focus* Environmental Education / Careers / Information / Networks, Ecosystem Protection / Biodiversity • *Cooperative Partner* The Center for Field Research • *Chapters* 6, in Melbourne, Oxford, Tokyo, Moscow, Santa Monica, and Washington • *Individual Members* 80,000

Mission To improve human understanding of the planet, the diversity of its inhabitants, and the processes that affect the quality of life on Earth. Earthwatch is a coalition of citizens and scientists working to sustain the world's environment, monitor global change, conserve endangered habitats and species, explore the vast heritage of all peoples, and foster world health and international cooperation. Earthwatch is a leader in the field of experimental education. To date, more than 3,075 students and 2,625 teachers have received career training on Earthwatch expeditions.

Annual Fees	Regular	Sponsor	Donor	Backer
	$25	$50	$100	$500

Funding	Membership	Foundations	Other
	76%	20%	4%

Usage	Administration	Fundraising	Programs	Publications & Reports
	17%	7%	64%	12%

Programs Each year Earthwatch sponsors numerous projects around the world (165 in 1993), and recruits volunteers to serve in an environmental EarthCorps. Projects include "Understanding the Earth", "Threatened Habitats", "Strategies for Survival", "Human Impacts", and "Managing the Planet".

Publication Bimonthly magazine *Eartwatch*

Multimedia Online information service 1-800-776-0188

For more Information Database, Library

Who's Who PRESIDENT **BRIAN A. ROSBOROUGH** • EXECUTIVE DIRECTOR **DAVID SILVERBERG** • EDITOR **MARK CHERRINGTON** • CONTACT **KARA A. BETTIGOLE**

ECOLOGIA
ROUTE 547, BOX 199   HARFORD PA 18823
PHONE (717) 434 2873   FAX (717) 434 2769

Founded 1989 • *Geographic Coverage* National, Central and Eastern Europe • *Focused Regions* Former USSR, Baltic states • *Cooperative Partner* Eco-Test Laboratory • *Chapter* 1

Mission To replace Cold War competition with environmental cooperation, and to offer environmental activism as a pathway to political participation and activism to citizens who have never before participated in political life, by providing information, training, and technical support to grassroots environmental groups in the former USSR, the Baltic states, and central and eastern Europe.

Annual Fees	Regular	Student/Senior	Organization	Supporting	Benefactor
	$20	$10	$30	$50	$100

► This novel approach, combined with the signing of the International Convention on Biological Diversity in December 1993, put the United States in a position of leadership.

THE COMPREHENSIVE CONSERVATION analysis conducted in the Pacific Northwest by world-class experts in hydrology, forestry, biology and socio-economics could serve as a working model and be integrated to all aid programs designed to help developing countries stem the tide of large scale destruction of habitat and loss of living species.
The tropical forests are the natural habitat of more than half the world's species. As in the Pacific Northwest, the same environmental dilemma exists on a much larger scale in tropical forests. But it should not stay that way. An international

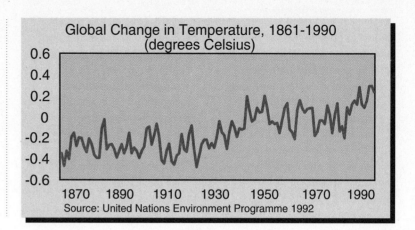

Global Change in Temperature, 1861-1990 (degrees Celsius)
Source: United Nations Environment Programme 1992

Other Fees *Lifetime* $1,000

Programs Environmental Monitoring Network, a citizens' network, provides pollution monitoring equipment and training. Chernobyl Child Program-1992 has arranged for twenty-five Ukrainian children to visit the United States for 100 days. Environmental Renaissance Project provides direct linkages between American grassroots environmental organizations and NGOs in Eastern and Central Europe and the former USSR through internships and exchanges of independent non-governmental experts. Siberian Forest Project provides equipment and personnel to measure the effects of industrial pollution upon Siberian forests. Conferences for grassroots leaders.

Publication Bimonthly newsletter *Ecologia*

Who's Who PRESIDENT RANDY KRITKAUSKY • PROGRAM DIRECTOR JOYCE LIBAL NEWSLETTER EDITOR CAROLYN SCHMIDT

ENVIRONIC FOUNDATION INTERNATIONAL, INC.
916 ST. VINCENT STREET   SOUTH BEND IN 46617-1443
PHONE (219) 233 3357

Founded 1970 • *Geographic Coverage* Global • *Chapters* 4, in Canada, Japan, United Kingdom, Turkey • *Individual Members* 50

Mission The Foundation is concerned with global environmental issues.

Who's Who PRESIDENT LEROY S. TROYER • VICE PRESIDENT ROBERT D. KUZELKA SECRETARY PATRICK HORSBURGH

ENVIRONMENTAL ACTION
6900 CARROLL AVENUE, SUITE 600   TAKOMA PARK MD 20912
PHONE (301) 891 1100   FAX (301) 891 2218

Founded 1970 • *Geographic Coverage* National • *Other Fields of*

Focus Pollution / Radiations, Waste - Management / Disposal / Treatment / Recycling • *Individual Members* 10,000

Mission Guided by the belief that a clean environment is a basic human right, Environmental Action works with grassroots groups to fight for better laws and accountability on environmental issues.

Annual Fees	*Regular* $25	*Student/Senior* $15	*Corporation* $35

Funding	*Membership* 40%	*Foundations* 60%

Total Income $1,170,000

Usage	*Administration & Fundraising* 19%	*Programs* 81%

Publications Quarterly magazine *Environmental Action*, circulation 13,000. Quarterly newsletter *Wastelines*, circulation 500

For more Information Annual Report, Library

Who's Who EXECUTIVE DIRECTOR MARGARET MORGAN HUBBARD

ENVIRONMENTAL COMMISSION OF THE DEMOCRATIC SOCIALISTS OF AMERICA
1608 NORTH MILWAUKEE, FOURTH FLOOR   CHICAGO IL 60647
PHONE (312) 384 0327   FAX (312) 702 0090

Founded 1988 • *Geographic Coverage* National, Global • *Other Fields of Focus* Human Rights & Environment, Public / Environmental Health • *Cooperative Partner* Socialist International • *Individual Members* 150

Mission To build a network of activists and intellectuals interested in the relationship of the movements for environmental sustainability and social justice.

Nature can absorb only so much of misguided human engineering. *New perceptions are emerging in the wake of recent cataclysms* **and at the prospect of impending man-made disasters.**

concerted effort could bring together representatives of developing countries, which depend on their tropical forests to foster their economic development, to meet with those of industrialized countries keen on preventing the permanent disappearance of innumerable species. Driven by a common destiny, they should draw a similar plan to preserve endangered species, to ▶

Annual Fees *Regular* $10

Funding	*Membership*	*Foundations*
	50%	50%

Total Income $2,000

Usage	*Administration*	*Fundraising*	*Newsletter Publication*
	10%	20%	70%

Total Expenses $2,000

Publication Quarterly newsletter *EcoSocialist Review*, circulation 500

For more Information Library, List of Publications

Who's Who PRESIDENT JAMES HUGHES • VICE PRESIDENT RODGER FIELD • SECRETARY ROBERT ROMAN • TREASURER EUGENE BIRMINGHAM • EXECUTIVE DIRECTOR MARK SCHAEFFER

ENVIRONMENTAL DEFENSE FUND

257 PARK AVENUE, SOUTH NEW YORK NY 10010
PHONE (212) 505 2100 FAX (212) 505 2375

Founded 1967 • *Geographic Coverage* Global • *Other Fields of Focus* Ecosystem Protection / Biodiversity, Environmental Law / Consulting *Cooperative Partners* Local non-governmental environmental groups worldwide, United Nations agencies • *Chapters* 5, in Washington, Oakland, Boulder, Raleigh, and Austin • *Individual Members* 200,000

Mission To help develop innovative, economically viable, and workable solutions to environmental problems by bringing together scientists and attorneys as well as economists and computer experts. The organization's central areas of focus currently include ozone layer depletion, acid rain, tropical rainforests, toxic waste, wetlands, global warming, recycling, Antarctica, water, wildlife, and habitats.

Annual Fees	*Regular*	*Student/Senior*	*Families*	*Supporting*	*Contributing*
	$20	$10	$35	$35	$50

Other Fees *Donor* $250 • *Patron* $500 • *Benefactor* $1,000

Funding	*Membership*	*Foundations*	*Bequests & Endowments*	*Investment Income*
	55%	36%	5%	4%

Total Income $20,226,633

Usage	*Administration*	*Programs*	*Other*
	4%	80%	16%

Total Expenses $19,536,094

Publications Monthly newsletter *EDF Letter*. Numerous publications focusing on acid rain, biotechnology, coral reefs, energy, environmental toxics, global atmosphere, solid waste, solid waste management, waste reduction, transportation, wildlife, water and wetlands

For more Information Annual Report, Database, Library, List of Publications

Who's Who EXECUTIVE DIRECTOR FREDERIC D. KRUPP • OTHER ADAM C. STERN, MARCIA ARONOFF, PAULA M. HAYES, JOEL PLAGENZ, PAUL WYCISK • CONTACT CHRIS MAGERL

ENVIRONMENTAL PARTNERSHIP FOR CENTRAL EUROPE
A PROJECT OF THE GERMAN MARSHALL FUND

11 DUPONT CIRCLE, NW, SUITE 210 WASHINGTON DC 20036
PHONE (202) 588 9018 FAX (202) 462 8097

Founded 1991 • *Geographic Coverage* Central Europe • *Chapters* 4

Mission To provide small grants to non-governmental organizations and local governments to address local environmental problems in Poland, Hungary, Slovakia, and the Czech Republic.

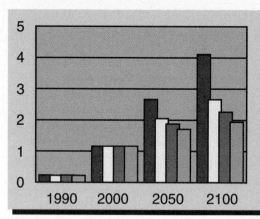

Projected Rise in Global Temperature Above Pre-industrial Times, 1990-2100 (degrees Celsius)

Scenario A
Energy supply and demand continue as they are. Deforestation continues at present rate. Partial implementation of Montreal Protocol ("business-as-usual")

Scenario B
Energy supply mix shifts towards low carbon fuels and natural gas. More energy efficiency. Deforestation reversed. Full implementation of Montreal Protocol

Scenario C
Shift towards renewable sources of energy and nuclear power in second half of next century

Scenario D
Shift towards renewable sources of energy and nuclear power in first half of next century

■ Scenario A   □ Scenario B
■ Scenario C   ■ Scenario D

Source: United Nations Environment Programme 1992

Who's Who PROJECT DIRECTOR IRMGARD HUNT • PROGRAM OFFICER MARIANNE LAIS GINSBURG

FRIENDS OF THE EARTH USA

218 "D" STREET, SE   WASHINGTON DC 20003
PHONE (202) 544 2600   FAX (202) 543 4710

Founded 1969 • *Geographic Coverage* National • *Other Fields of Focus* Atmosphere & Climate / Global Warming, Forest Conservation / Deforestation / Reforestation, Human Rights & Environment *Cooperative Partners* 51 Friends of the Earth international affiliates around the globe • *Individual Members* 50,000

Mission To eliminate the use of ozone-depleting chemicals, educate decision makers that environmental protection creates jobs, safeguard communities from toxic chemicals, stop the loss of rainforests and protect the indigenous cultures that depend on them for their livelihood, advocate environmental justice, achieve comprehensive groundwater protection and safe drinking water programs across America, pressure corporations to make environmental reforms, and change US spending, tax and trade policies to benefit the environment.

Annual Fees	*Regular*	*Student/Senior*	*Low Income*
	$25	$15	$15

Other Fees *Membership Contributions* from $50 to 1,000+

Programs Activist Program provides activist members with periodic Action Alerts about key legislative initiatives and other important activities. Health and safety programs. Environmental Justice Program. Anti-pollution Program: Challenging Corporate Polluters.

Publications Newsmagazine *Friends of the Earth* published ten times per year. Newsletters *Atmosphere* • *Community Plume* • *Groundwater News*

Who's Who PRESIDENT JANE PERKINS

GLOBAL 2000, INC.

THE CARTER CENTER
ONE COPENHILL   ATLANTA GA 30307
PHONE (404) 872 3848   FAX (404) 874 5515

Geographic Coverage Global • *Other Fields of Focus* Human Rights & Environment, Public / Environmental Health • *Chapters* The Carter Center maintains offices in Accra - Ghana, Lome - Togo, Cotonou - Benin, Khartoum - Sudan, Dar es Salam - Tanzania, Lagos - Nigeria, Islamabad - Pakistan, and Entebbe - Uganda

Mission Global 2000, Inc., draws on its inspiration from the Global 2000 Report commissioned by former US President Jimmy Carter during his administration. Projecting trends in population growth and environmental degradation into the 21st century, that report depicted a spiral of poverty, disease, hunger, and social injustice in rural areas of developing countries that could seriously threaten economic stability and world peace. The organization's goal is to help arrest this downward spiral through programs that motivate and support the governments of these countries to promote self-reliance, improve health standards, and address environmental problems.

Programs Global 2000 agricultural strategies focus on assuring village level availability of input supplies and market outlets to support farmers using new production test plot technologies. Guinea worm eradication projects focus on fully mobilizing remaining endemic African countries for the 1995 target. The organization's forest initiative focuses on policy efforts, coalition building, applied research, and public education and advocacy in the battle to save the world's dwindling forests. The broad guidelines of the program involve a triad approach: working with and listening to people and local organizations to identify forest problems and solutions; working with political leaders to identify and implement policy reforms; and establishing partnerships with Northern and Southern governments, NGOs, and private groups.

Who's Who CHAIRMAN JIMMY CARTER • EXECUTIVE DIRECTOR WILLIAM H. FOEGE ACTING ASSOCIATE DIRECTOR JOHN HARDMAN • DIRECTOR OF OPERATIONS ANDREW

▶ expand protected areas, and to promote the rehabilitation of damaged ecosystems and the sustainable use of biological resources. Ecosystem protection and management should benefit from national and international commitments to insure the perpetuation of all living species and reduce the threat of global warming. Conceivably the mere existence of ecosystems, such as forest expanses, and the increase of global warming are mutually exclusive. If this aspect is still open for debate, it is proven however that trees, because they absorb carbon dioxide, play a crucial role in abating the greenhouse effect and adverse climatic conditions. Undeniably, any further warming of the atmosphere would have destructive effects on ecosystems. The 1993 floodings by the Mississippi River provide a dramatic illustration of theory and reality. If the sudden and drastic climate changes that brought unusually heavy rain are still a matter of speculation, the building of levees to contain the overflow of rivers and of human settlements close to river beds come into question as a large-scale tampering with natural phenomena - a tampering that, in many instances, should have never taken place.

The devastating floods are responsible for new considerations to let rivers follow their natural course.

TECHNOLOGICAL PROGRESS IS meeting its limits. Nature can absorb only so much of misguided human engineering. New perceptions are emerging in the wake of recent cataclysms and at the prospect of impending man-made disasters. ▶

N. AGLE • ASSOCIATE DIRECTOR OF OPERATIONS P. CRAIG WITHERS, JR. • ASSISTANT DIRECTOR OF OPERATIONS FOR PROGRAMS BEKKI J. JOHNSON • ADMINISTRATIVE COORDINATOR MARY ROWE

GLOBE USA

409 THIRD STREET, SW, SUITE 204   WASHINGTON DC 20024
PHONE (202) 863 0153   FAX (202) 479 9447

Founded 1989 • *Geographic Coverage* Global • *Chapters* 3, in Brussels, Moscow, and Tokyo • *Individual Members* 100

Mission To provide a forum which enhances interaction between legislators, and allows legislative and parliamentary leaders from different countries to work together to forge balanced and informed policy responses to pressing environmental challenges. Global Legislators Organization for a Balanced Environment is an international organization of legislators from the United States, Japan, the European Community and the Russian Federation.

Programs Organizes two conferences yearly, at which member legislators review international developments, receive presentations on emerging environmental issues, and develop innovative approaches to environmental lawmaking for application in their respective legislatures. When members reach consensus on issues, statements of principles and guidelines for legislative action are drafted for ratification by the full membership. Members have drafted a detailed GLOBE forest convention, designed to conserve timber resources and biodiversity globally and to mitigate negative economic impacts for countries dependent on timber exports. GLOBE has also introduced legislation in US, Japanese and European parliamentary bodies to mandate environmental impact assessments of GATT proposals; pursued a ban on the dumping of radioactive materials into the sea; and promoted technologies to minimize the flow of waste into international waters.

Who's Who PRESIDENT SENATOR JOHN F. KERRY • VICE PRESIDENT CONGRESSMAN JOHN EDWARD PORTER • EXECUTIVE DIRECTOR PATRICK R. RAMAGE

GREEN PARTY OF CALIFORNIA

P.O. BOX 480578   LOS ANGELES CA 90048
PHONE (310) 314 7336

Founded 1990 • *Geographic Coverage* State • *Other Field of Focus* Human Rights & Environment • *Individual Members* 95,000

Mission To work for peace, social justice, ecology, and a democratic society. To keep members involved in the workings of government. To pursue ecological wisdom, grassroots democracy, personal and social responsibility, non-violence, decentralization, community-based economics, post-patriarchal values, respect for diversity, global responsibility, and a focus on the future.

Annual Fees *Supporting Member* $25 or more

Programs The Green Party of California has ongoing efforts to register voters, mobilize new members, campaign for ballot initiatives, monitor and lobby government, cultivate future candidates, educate the public, train new activists, build social ties and a sense of community among members. The party's "Gooperate LA" program is an effort to incorporate self-determination, sustainability, and community-based cooperative economics into all reconstruction and future development in Los Angeles.

Who's Who CORRESPONDING SECRETARY WILLIAM A. YEAGER • SPOKESPERSON KWAZI NKRUMAH

GREENPEACE, INC.

1436 "U" STREET, NW   WASHINGTON DC 20009
PHONE (202) 462 1177   FAX (202) 462 4507

Founded 1987 • *Geographic Coverage* National, Global • *Other Fields of Focus* Atmosphere & Climate/Global Warming, Ecosystem Protection / Biodiversity, Pollution / Radiations • *Cooperative Partners* Greenpeace Fund, Inc., Greenpeace International, Greenpeace affiliates worldwide • *Chapters* 4 • *Individual Members*

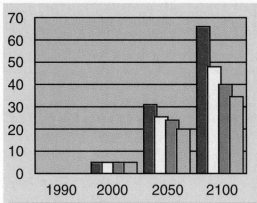

Scenario A Energy supply and demand continue as they are. Deforestation continues at present rate. Partial implementation of Montreal Protocol ("business-as-usual")

Scenario B Energy supply mix shifts towards low carbon fuels and natural gas. More energy efficiency. Deforestation reversed. Full implementation of Montreal Protocol

Scenario C Shift towards renewable sources of energy and nuclear power in second half of next century

Scenario D Shift towards renewable sources of energy and nuclear power in first half of next century

Projected Sea Level Rise Worldwide, 1990-2100 (centimeters)

■ Scenario A   □ Scenario B
■ Scenario C   ■ Scenario D

Source: United Nations Environment Programme 1992

4,000,000 worldwide

Mission To promote and advocate the protection and preservation of the environment through lobbying, educational and advocacy efforts at both the state and national levels.

Annual Fees *Regular* $30+

Funding	Contributions & Donations	Other
	98%	2%

Total Income $16,366,258 in 1991

Usage	Administration	Fundraising	Programs
	11.5%	20.9%	67.6%

Total Expenses $18,652,588 in 1991

Programs Works to protect the planet through non-violent action. Lobbying program works to strengthen laws that protect the atmosphere, conserve natural resources, and support alternative sources of energy. Provides support for local grassroots efforts to bring attention to environmental threats in communities nationwide. Ocean Ecology Campaign works to protect ocean ecosystems from rampant overfishing and other destructive fishing practices. Toxics Campaign works to put an end to the production and use of persistent, bio-accumulative toxics and toxic waste disposal methods. Nuclear Campaign works to eliminate development of new nuclear weapons by campaigning for a comprehensive nuclear test ban and a ban on plutonium production. Atmosphere & Energy Campaign works to halt the production of all ozone-destroying substances, and increase energy efficiency.

Publications Quarterly newsletter *Greenpeace*. Action alerts distributed to members of the Activist Network

For more Information Annual Report

Who's Who PRESIDENT **KAY TREAKLE** • EXECUTIVE DIRECTOR **STEVE D'ESPOSITO**

INTERNATIONAL CLEARINGHOUSE ON THE ENVIRONMENT

1601 CONNECTICUT AVENUE, NW, SUITE 301   WASHINGTON   DC 20009
PHONE (202) 387 3034   FAX (202) 667 3291

Founded 1983 • *Geographic Coverage* Former USSR • *Other Field of Focus* Environmental Education / Careers / Information / Networks

Mission To support the democratic process and efforts to improve conditions for people who live in the former USSR, with a focus on environmental issues. Through publications, environmental partnership programs, and other clearinghouse activities, the organization collects and distributes information about joint efforts addressing areas of critical need and encouraging personal initiative and democratic approaches.

Funding	Membership	Foundations
	10%	90%

Publications Quarterly magazine *Surviving Together: Cooperative Efforts to Support Civil and Sustainable Societies in Eurasia.* Handbook *Organizations Involved in Soviet-American Relations* - 1990 edition. Proceedings *Joint US - USSR NGO Conference on the Environment, March 1991*

Who's Who EXECUTIVE DIRECTOR **ELISA KLOSE**

IUCN THE WORLD CONSERVATION UNION

1400 16TH STREET, NW   WASHINGTON DC 20036
PHONE (202) 797 5454   FAX (202) 797 5461

Founded 1948 • *Geographic Coverage* Global • *Other Field of Focus* Sustainable Development / Agriculture - Environmental Technologies • *Cooperative Partners* United Nations agencies, UNESCO, FAO, United Nations Environment Programme with which it forms the Ecosystems Conservation Group, World Wildlife Fund • *Chapters*

Ozone-depleting substances are still making their way to the Earth's stratosphere, allowing increased harmful radiation towards life on the Earth's surface. Greater volumes of carbon dioxide are reaching the atmosphere, further contributing to the much-dreaded greenhouse effect, a potential for global warming and climatic upheavals. Fossil-fuel burning and global warming are "perhaps the biggest environmental threat to this planet", warned President Clinton. Fossil fuels, the foundation of the industrial and technological age and the lifeblood of most nations, threaten to choke their users. Cutting greenhouse gas emissions and reducing reliance on fossil fuels have become the standing challenge for modern societies. Meaningful policies such as energy taxes tailored to provide revenue and deter polluting practices have yet to be adopted to complement environmental laws. Today still, the best support for the enforcement of the environmental laws is litigation based on solid legislative grounds. The mere prospect of litigation can be a powerful deterrent against environmental violations. However, with the passage of time, reliance on liability and law enforcement should become less dominant, as the environmental factors find wider acceptance.

IN ORDER TO INSURE PRUDENT, responsible, and ethical management of products and processes from the point of view of health, safety, and the environment, environmental considerations must be made part of the mainstream of business practices. Many business ►

30 offices in developed and developing countries • *Organization Members* 650

Mission IUCN is a union of sovereign states, government agencies, and non-governmental organizations, working to initiate and promote scientifically based action that will establish links between development and the environment, and to provide leadership and promote a common approach for the world conservation movement, and to ensure that human use of natural resources is appropriate, sustainable, and equitable.

Funding	*Membership*	*Foundations*
	10%	90%

Total Income $45,000,000

Usage	*Administration*	*Programs*	*Other*
	8.5%	90%	1.5%

Total Expenses $42,000,000

Programs Ongoing efforts working for species conservation, responsible wetlands use, ecology, environmental strategies, forest conservation, parks and protected areas.

Publications News journal *IUCN Bulletin.* Numerous reports, booklets and updates including *United Nations List of National Parks and Protected Areas* • *Red Data Books* describe the world's threatened species. Periodicals *Red List of Threatened Animals* • *The World Conservation Strategy* and follow-up *Caring for the Earth*

Multimedia Online information service 1-800-828-1302

For more Information Annual Report, Library, List of Publications

KOMPASS RESOURCES INTERNATIONAL
1322 18TH STREET, NW, SUITE 400   WASHINGTON DC 20036
PHONE (202) 332 1145   FAX (202) 833 3705

Established 1985, incorporated as Kompass in 1989 • *Geographic Coverage* Former USSR

Mission To improve long-term relations and to foster peaceful change between the USA and the former USSR by promoting cultural, professional, scientific and other exchanges between peoples of the USA and the former USSR.

Funding	*Government Support*	*Corporations & Foundations*
	70%	30%

Total Income $483,121

Usage	*Administration*	*Programs*
	20%	80%

Total Expenses $483,121

Programs Provides administrative and technical support to the scientific community and NGOs.

Publications Monthly *Environmental Corporation Bulletin. The Directory of Environmental Groups in the Newly Independent States and Baltic Nations - 1990-92 Edition* • *Directory of Research and Natural Resources Institutions and Organizations of the Russian Far East*

Who's Who EXECUTIVE DIRECTOR **MELISSA L. STONE**

LEAGUE OF CONSERVATION VOTERS
1707 "L" STREET, NW, SUITE 550   WASHINGTON DC 20036
PHONE (202) 785 8683   FAX (202) 835 0491

Founded 1970 • *Geographic Coverage* National • *Individual Members* 35,000

Mission To change the balance of power in the US Congress to reflect the pro-environment concerns of the American public. The

League educates voters and environmental activists, and works to elect candidates to federal office who will vote to protect the nation's environment.

Annual Fees *Regular* $25

Programs Annually publishes *National Environmental Scorecard*, with environmental ratings for members of US Congress based on voting record during Congressional sessions. Provides direct and in-kind support to endorsed candidates, including media assistance, and voter education. Works with grassroots groups on voter education and training environmentalists in public debate skills.

Publications Report *National Environmental Scorecard*. Various special issue publications

For more Information Annual Report

Who's Who CONTACT NINA T. TRACY

MEMORIAL WILDLIFE FEDERATION

P.O. BOX 240   HOLLBROOK NY 11741
PHONE (516) 567 0031

Founded 1981 • *Geographic Coverage* Local, Regional, National, Global • *Other Field of Focus* Wildlife - Animal & Plant • *Individual Members* 17

Mission Environmental organization concerned with global environmental problems. Among its primary concerns are children and planet Earth, animal rescue, protection of wetland areas, clean air, global reforestation, recycling, surveys with the cooperation of both the Department of the Interior and American Indian Nations.

Annual Fees	Regular	Families
	$20	$25

Funding	Membership	Corporations
	25%	75%

Programs Environmental education programs (free). Earthwalks. Ecodefenders. Primitive technology. Life and Planet Earth. Wilderness Survival. The Deer People. Stories from the Earth. The River Series from Peter Lourie. Ancient Ways and Native Days.

Who's Who PRESIDENT STANLEY BETHIEL

NATIONAL ASSOCIATION OF ENVIRONMENTAL PROFESSIONALS

5165 MACARTHUR BOULEVARD, NW   WASHINGTON DC 20016-3315
PHONE (202) 966 1500   FAX (202) 966 1977

Founded 1975 • *Geographic Coverage* National • *Individual*

Members 3,500

Mission To promote ethical, technical competency, and professional standards in the environmental field. The Association is a multidisciplinary, non-partisan, professional association, committed to the partnership of environmental protection and economic growth. The organization's members work in all areas of air, water, noise, waste, ecology, and education.

Annual Fees	Regular	Student/Senior
	$75	$25

Total Income $500,000

Programs Peer-reviewed Certification (CEP) Program. Annual conference and exposition focusing on cutting edge issues and technologies of relevance to environmental professionals.

Publications Quarterly journal *The Environmental Professional* provides an open forum for the discussion and analysis of significant environmental issues. Bimonthly newsletter *NAEP*

Who's Who PRESIDENT KEVIN M. BURGER • VICE PRESIDENT GARY F. KELMAN TREASURER RITA C. SCHENCK • EXECUTIVE DIRECTOR SUSAN EISENBERG

SIERRA CLUB OF CALIFORNIA

923 12TH STREET, SUITE 200   SACRAMENTO CA 95814
PHONE (916) 557 1100   FAX (916) 557 9669

Geographic Coverage State • *Cooperative Partners* National Sierra Club, Sierra Club Legal Defense Fund, Sierra Club Political Committee *Chapters* 13 • *Individual Members* 185,000 of the Sierra Club's 570,000 members

Mission To lobby for environmental issues by representing the Sierra Club before the state legislature, state agencies, and the governor's office; to provide up-to-date information to members and the general public; and to train Sierra Club members in political and organizational effectiveness.

Annual Fees	Regular	Student/Senior	Supporting	Contributing
	$35	$15	$50	$100

Other Fees Lifetime $750

Publications Newsletter *Legislative Agenda*. Reports including *California Environmental Regulations: Failure to Protect?* • *California State Parks: Next on the Endangered List?*

For more Information List of Publications

Who's Who PRESIDENT DAN SULLIVAN • CONSERVATION CHAIR MARTY DAIT LEGISLATIVE CHAIR MICHAEL ENDICOTT • DEVELOPMENT CHAIR JANIE FIGEN • VICE PRESIDENT HAROLD WOOD • SECRETARY ROBIN IVES • TREASURER GEORGE SHIPWAY EXECUTIVE DIRECTOR MICHAEL PAPARIAN

and industry leaders are discovering that such policy is even more profitable because it reduces waste, health hazards and increases product appeal to consumers. Natural resource management and environmental care should no longer be pursued separately; convergence of the two should stand behind all human endeavors. It is the only way to satisfy the requirements of today's societies and of a truly sustainable development in all sectors of human activities. For the 1990s and beyond, to achieve a higher level of awareness and mobilization of all people everywhere, remains a major challenge. The educational systems have an added duty to promote a new sense of values, new behaviors and teachings specifically geared to the sensitivity of children towards the environment. Schools should create programs that unravel the complexities and mysteries of nature and nature's relationship to human activities. Children are the best hope to reshape societies - if they grow up with the appropriate knowledge and are guided by the vision of a new culture.

In support of families, schools, and universities, the national media can contribute significantly to the educational process for sustainable development. The mass media hold the power to educate, mobilize and positively influence both public opinion and government policies on environment. The quality of environmental coverage made available to the general public by the printed press, radio and television augurs well of their forthcoming role. •

The Editor

SOCIETY FOR HUMAN ECOLOGY (THE)

4512 McMurray Drive   Fort Collins CO 80525-3400
Phone (303) 226 9438

Founded 1981 • *Geographic Coverage* Global • *Cooperative Partners* International Association for Ecology, International Impact Assessment • *Individual Members* 100

Mission To promote the development of collaboration and interdisciplinary understanding of human ecology and its applications.

Annual Fees

	Regular	Student/Senior	Contributing Member	Sustaining Member
	$40	$15	$150	$1,000

Funding *Membership* 100%

Usage

Administration	Programs
85%	15%

Programs Conferences. Workshops. Symposia.

Publications Semiannual *Human Ecology Bulletin*. Books *Human Ecology • Coming of Age: An International Overview • Strategies for the Future • Steps to the Future • Research and Applications • A Gathering of Perspectives • International Directory of Human Ecologists*. Numerous other journals and monographs

For more Information List of Publications

Who's Who President **Thomas Dietz** • Vice President **Peter Richerson** Second Vice President **Robert J. Griffore** • Third Vice President **Eva Ekehorn** Treasurer **Nancy Markee** • Executive Director **John G. Taylor**

WOMEN'S ENVIRONMENT AND DEVELOPMENT ORGANIZATION

845 Third Avenue, 15th Floor   New York NY 10022
Phone (212) 759 7982   Fax (212) 759 8647

Founded 1989 • *Geographic Coverage* Global • *Other Fields of Focus* Human Rights & Environment, Sustainable Development / Agriculture - Environmental Technologies • *Cooperative Partners* Women USA Fund, Inc., World Women's Congress for a Healthy Planet, World Conference on Human Rights, United Nations Conference on Population and Development, World Conference on Women - Action for Equality, Development and Peace • *Chapters* 8 in process in Africa, Asia, Europe, Latin America, the Caribbean, the Middle East, North America, and the Pacific, to focus on regional issues

Mission The organization consists of an active and connected movement of women working for a healthy planet, to restore the earth's health, promote sustainable development, and ensure that women play a strong role in framing and implementing viable environmental policies.

Annual Fees *Regular* $15

Programs The Community Report Card project is working to organize and mobilize Women for a Healthy Planet Groups across North America. The report cards allow participants to target priority areas requiring positive change, and provide a basis for building sound environmental and development policy. The Organization also has a program to monitor Earth Summit environmental commitments, with a focus on UNCED recommendations for women. Outreach and Leadership Programs help women become policy makers as well as policy monitors. Education and Communications Program gathers and disseminates news of women's issues and activities. The Organization's Lobbying Platforms for governments, the United Nations and other intergovernmental bodies are designed to incorporate the concerns of women about the environment and development into policy making and implementation and to ensure that women are equal partners in these processes.

Publications Quarterly newsletter *News & Views*. Book *Women's Action Agenda 21* a blueprint for incorporating women's concerns about the environment and sustainable development into local, national and international decision making from now into the next century

Multimedia Video *Giving Women an Equal Say!*. Radio documentary *World Women's Congress*

For more Information Database, Library

Who's Who PRESIDENT BELLA ABZUG • EXECUTIVE DIRECTOR RACHEL KYTE • OTHER THAIS CORRAL, JOCELYN DOW, ELIN ENGE, FARKHONDA HASSAN, WANGARI MAATHAI, CHIEF BISI OGUNLEYE, VANDANA SHIVA, MARILYN WARING, MIM KELBER, LIBBY BASSETT • CONTACT CHRISTINA SECKINGER

WORLD GAME INSTITUTE

3215 RACE STREET	PHILADELPHIA PA 19104
PHONE (215) 387 0220	FAX (215) 387 3009

Founded 1972 • *Geographic Coverage* Local, Regional, National, Global • *Chapters* 3 • *Individual Members* 500

Mission To foster responsible change and leadership in a global society.

Annual Fees *Regular* $30

Programs The Institute sponsors World Game Workshops for elementary and high schools, community groups, universities and corporations. The workshops interactively involve participants while giving them an overview of the problems, resources and dynamics shaping the world.

Publications Books and reports including *A New World Map for a New World Order* • *The World Game: How It Came About* • *Remapping the World* • *The Regeneration of Africa: Resources, Needs and Capacities* • *Doing the Right Things, What the World Wants and How to Get It*. Data sheets and maps including *Vital Statistics of Spaceship Earth* • *World Game Data Sheet* • *Oil Data Sheet*

Multimedia Software *Global Data Manager™*, a dedicated spreadsheet computer program which displays over 180 variables and data - population, food, energy, education, natural resources, economics - for every country and continent in the world • *Global Recall™2.0.* • Global Data Manager Data Disks including *World Development Indicators* • *Indicators of Social Development* • *World Resources Disk 1988-89* and *1990-91* • *United Nations Energy Disks*

For more Information Database, Library, List of Publications

Who's Who PRESIDENT **MEDARD GABEL**

WORLD RESOURCES INSTITUTE

1709 NEW YORK AVENUE, NW	WASHINGTON DC 20006
PHONE (202) 662 2543	FAX (202) 638 0036

Founded 1983 • *Geographic Coverage* National, Global • *Other Field of Focus* Sustainable Development / Agriculture - Environmental Technologies • *Cooperative Partners* The Brookings Institution, The Santa Fe Institute, IUCN The World Conservation Union, United Nations Environment Programme, United Nations Development Programme, US Agency for International Development

Mission To help societies meet human needs and nurture economic growth without destroying the natural resources and environmental integrity that make prosperity possible, through a program of policy research and technical assistance designed to help governments, the private sector, environmental and development organizations, and others address these issues. Central to the Institute's work are two principal concerns: the effects of natural resource deterioration on economic development and the obstacles it poses to the alleviation of poverty and hunger in developing countries, and the new generation of globally important environmental and energy challenges now confronting both industrial and developing countries.

Funding	*Membership*	*Government Support*	*Investment Income*	*Publications*
	50.1%	23.5%	22.5%	3%

Total Income $10,442,117

Usage	*Administration*	*Programs*	*Development*
	12.5%	81.7%	5.7%

Total Expenses $10,546,747

Programs The Institute strives to build bridges between scholarship and action, bringing the insights of scientific research, economic analysis, and practical experience to political, business, and other leaders around the world. The Institute's policy research program includes the Program in Biological Resources and Institutions, Program in Economics and Population, Program in Climate, Energy and Pollution, Program in Technology and the Environment, and Program in Resource and Environmental Information. Its Center for International Development and Environment operates four main programs all aimed at capacity building: Natural Resources Management Strategies and Assessments, Natural Resource Information Management, Community Planning and NGO Support, Sectoral Resource Policy and Planning. The Institute's 2050 Project is working to define the steps needed for the transition to sustainability in the coming decades, examining the concept of sustainability in an integrated way, exploring both desirable future conditions and the transitions needed to reach them.

Publications Reference publications include biennial *World Resources Report Series* prepared in collaboration with the United Nations Environment Programme and the United Nations Development Programme • *Teacher's Guide to World Resources 1992-93* • *World Resources Cumulative Index* • *1993 Directory of Country Environmental Studies* • *The 1993 Information Please Environmental Almanac*. Numerous publications focusing on environment and development, acid rain and air pollution, agriculture and water resources, biological diversity, economics, energy, forests, global climate change and ozone depletion, industry, institutions, population, resource management, sustainable development, technology, and transportation

Multimedia Database diskettes *World Resources 1992-93* and *1993 Directory of Country Environmental Studies Companion*

For more Information Annual Report, Database, Library, List of Publications

Who's Who PRESIDENT JONATHAN LASH • VICE PRESIDENTS J. ALAN BREWSTER, JESSICA T. MATHEWS, WALTER V. REID, ROBERTO C. REPETTO, DONNA W. WISE • SECRETARY WALLACE D. BOWMAN • DIRECTOR OF COMMUNICATIONS SHIRLEY GEER • LIBRARIAN SUSAN N. TERRY

WORLDWATCH INSTITUTE

1776 MASSACHUSETTS AVENUE, NW   WASHINGTON DC 20036-1904
PHONE (202) 452 1999   FAX (202) 296 7365

Founded 1974 • *Geographic Coverage* Global • *Cooperative Partners* WGBH Boston, United Nations agencies

Mission To inform policy makers and the general public about the interdependence of the world economy and its environmental support system, and to raise public awareness of environmental threats to the level where it will support an effective public policy response. The global scope of the research topics and the integrative or interdisciplinary nature of the research distinguish the Institute's work.

Funding	*Foundations*	*Earned Income*
	35%	65%

Total Income $2,600,000

Usage	*Administration*	*Fundraising*	*Programs*
	24%	1%	75%

Programs Research results are disseminated in the form of publications, articles, television and radio interviews, talks, lectures and testimony before legislative bodies, such as the US Congress, UK House of Lords, the Brazilian Parliament, International Parliamentarians on Population and Development, and the European Parliament.

Publications Bimonthly magazine *Worldwatch*. Annual *State of the World* series published in 26 languages. Various books including *The Environmental Alert* series on specific major environmental topics • *Vital Signs* series on the trends that are shaping the earth's future. 112 Worldwatch papers published and translated to date.

Multimedia Collaboration with WGBH on *Race to Save the Planet*.

For more Information List of Publications

Who's Who PRESIDENT LESTER R. BROWN • VICE PRESIDENT BLONDEEN GRAVELY

SECRETARY REAN JANISE KAUFFMAN • RESEARCH ADMINISTRATORS CHRISTOPHER FLAVIN, SANDRA POSTEL

ALBERTA GREENS

BOX 133, STATION "M"   CALGARY AB T2P 2H6
PHONE (403) 269 2384

Founded 1990 • *Geographic Coverage* Province • *Individual Members* 60

Mission To bring environmental issues into the political arena in the province of Alberta.

Annual Fees *Regular* $10

Funding *Membership* 100%

Total Income $5,000

Usage	*Administration*	*Programs*
	75%	25%

Total Expenses $5,000

Programs Public education.

Publication Newsletter

Who's Who PRESIDENT DAVID CROWE • SECRETARY MADELEINE OLDERSHAW TREASURER PAM MUNROE

CAMROSE INTERNATIONAL INSTITUTE   PAGE 297

5061 50TH STREET   CAMROSE AB T4V 1R3
PHONE (403) 672 8780   FAX (403) 672 4331

CANADIAN EARTHCARE SOCIETY

P.O. BOX 1810, STATION "A"   KELOWNA BC V1Y 8P2
PHONE (604) 861 4788   FAX (604) 868 3718

Founded 1985 • *Geographic Coverage* Global • *Cooperative Partner* Canadian EarthCare Foundation • *Chapters* 2, in Kamloops, and Victoria

Mission Dedicated to the care and preservation of the earth's environment for future generations and for all life, through a program combining public education advocacy, and litigation.

Annual Fees	*Regular*	*Student/Senior*	*Families*	*Organization*	*Corporation*
	$25	$15	$35	$35	$100

Programs Provides environmental advice on local, provincial, national, and international issues. Storm Drain Marking Program. During "Environment Week", the Society presents displays at malls and conducts events at parks to promote environmental awareness. On "Household Hazardous Waste Day", it disseminates educational information on proper disposal and alternatives to the use of household hazardous wastes. The Society's community education activities include presentations on how to minimize human impact on ecosystems offered to all grade levels and numerous community groups. EcoArt Gallery shows environmentally conscious works by eco-aware artists. Also provides consulting services for businesses.

Multimedia *EarthNet* dataline electronic research and communication system (604) 769 5097

For more Information Database

Who's Who COMMUNICATIONS DIRECTOR **LEONARD FRASER**

CANADIAN GREENS, GREEN PARTY OF CANADA

831 COMMERCIAL DRIVE   VANCOUVER BC V5L 3W6
PHONE (604) 254 8165   FAX (604) 254 8166

Geographic Coverage National • *Chapters* 7

Mission To enhance the effectiveness of the global green movement in creating a green society by providing an evolving social and political structure that embraces, includes, and supports green values and offers itself as a voice for the broader Green Movement.

Annual Fees *Regular* $5

Programs The Green Party's platform focuses on Business and Economics; Social and Cultural issues; Farming, Fishing and Forestry; Technology; Ecology; and Government. The Sustainable Planet Savings Plan aims to invest in an active political voice to officially represent recycling, toxic waste reduction and sustainable biosystems.

Publications Provincial, territorial, regional Green Party periodicals include *BC Green Party News* • *The Greenhouse* • *The Planet Today* • *Québec Newsletter of the Green Party of Canada* • *Québec Vert* • *Greenews* • *Green Notes* • *Alberta Greens Newsletter* • *Northern Alberta Green Newsletter* • *Green Party of Canada Digest*. Local chapter Green Party periodicals include *Green City Vancouver* • *The Greenhorn* • *Greenleaf* • *Newsletter of the McMaster/Westdale Greens* • *Okanagan Greens Newsletter* • *Victoria Green News*

For more Information List of Publications

Who's Who EXECUTIVE SECRETARY **STEVE KISBY**

FRIENDS OF THE EARTH
LES AMIS DE LA TERRE
251 LAURIER AVENUE, WEST, SUITE 701   OTTAWA ON K1P 5J6
PHONE (613) 230 3352   FAX (613) 232 4354

Founded 1978 • *Geographic Coverage* National, Global • *Other Fields of Focus* Atmosphere & Climate / Global Warming, Forest Conservation / Deforestation / Reforestation • *Cooperative Partners* Friends of the Earth International, Canadian Environmental Network, Canadian Council for International Cooperation • *Chapter* 1 • *Individual Members* 10,000

Mission Friends of the Earth strives to serve as a national voice for the environment, working with others to inspire the renewal of human communities and the Earth through research, education, and advocacy.

Annual Fees	Regular	Student/Senior	Families	Corporation
	$35	$15	$35	$5,000

Funding	Membership	Corporations	Foundations	Contracts	Earned Income
	52.2%	19%	4.7%	10.5%	13%

Total Income $1,029,479

Usage	Administration	Fundraising	Programs
	17%	25%	58%

Total Expenses $1,086,833

Programs The Atmospheric Campaign is comprised of three programs: The Ozone Campaign calls on the Canadian government to ban ozone-destroying CFCs, methyl chloroform, methyl bromide and halons by 1994, most hydrochlorofluorocarbons (HCFCs) by 1995, and all HCFCs by 2000. The Climate Change and Energy Campaign calls on the Canadian government to reduce Canada's emissions of carbon dioxide from fossil fuel use by 20% from 1988 levels by 2005 through increased energy efficiency and greater use of renewable energy sources. The Global ReLeaf Programme aims to improve the environment through planting more trees in Canadian communities and maintaining existing forests. The Sustainable Agriculture and Food Campaign works to promote food systems that are nutritionally sound, socially just, economically viable and environmentally sustainable, and to mobilize consumers to use their purchasing power to affect change.

Publications Quarterly newsletter *Earth Words*, circulation 10,000. *The Global ReLeaf Action Guide*. Various reports, technical studies, brochures, fact sheets, educational kits, teachers' manuals and household guides

For more Information Annual Report, Database, Library, List of Publications

Who's Who PRESIDENT **MICHAEL ROBINSON** • VICE PRESIDENT **WENDY COOK** TREASURER **TAMARA JOHNSON** • EXECUTIVE DIRECTOR **SUSAN TANNER** • LIBRARIANS **MSCHEL GAREAU, SUZIE VINNICK** • CONTACT **JEREMY BYATT**

GAIA GROUP (THE)
2258 RAE STREET   REGINA SK S4T 2E9
PHONE (306) 352 4804

Founded 1985 • *Geographic Coverage* Regional, National, Global
Cooperative Partners Saskatchewan Eco-Network, Canadian Environmental Network • *Chapter* 1 • *Individual Members* 45

Mission To foster harmony between people and the environment. The Gaia Group promotes the use of the Gaia theory as the basis for the development of a sustainable human society.

Annual Fees *Regular* $10

Funding

Membership	*Government Support*	*Foundations*
19%	77%	4%

Total Income $2,600

Usage

Administration	*Programs*
8%	92%

Total Expenses $2,600

Programs A 5 Acre Vegetation Project. A Sustainable Clean Transportation Strategy. A Review of Uranium Mining Project Proposals in Saskatchewan.

Who's Who PRESIDENT JIM ELLIOTT

GLOBAL AWARENESS IN ACTION, INC.
GAIA

14 LES PLATEAUX	ANSE ST. JEAN PQ G0V 1J0
PHONE (418) 272 2931	FAX (418) 272 2931

Founded 1988 • *Geographic Coverage* Global

Mission To promote and contribute to a greater global awareness, to provide educational materials and papers that help people in this objective.

Who's Who PRESIDENT JEAN HUDON

GREENPEACE CANADA

185 SPADINA AVENUE, SUITE 600	TORONTO ON M5T 2C6
PHONE (416) 435 8404	FAX (416) 345 8422

Geographic Coverage Global • *Other Fields of Focus* Atmosphere & Climate / Global Warming, Ecosystem Protection / Biodiversity, Pollution / Radiations

Mission To preserve or re-create an environment in which living things, including people, can survive without threat to their lives and health.

Programs Greenpeace presently divides its efforts into five campaign areas: Atmosphere/Energy, Nuclear/Disarmament, Ocean Ecology, Tropical Rainforests, and Toxics.

HARMONY FOUNDATION OF CANADA
FONDATION HARMONIE DU CANADA

560 JOHNSON STREET, SUITE 209	VICTORIA BC V8W 3C6
PHONE (604) 380 3001	FAX (604) 380 0887

Founded 1985 • *Geographic Coverage* National, Global • *Other Field of Focus* Environmental Education / Careers / Information / Networks

Mission To encourage cooperative action on environmental issues and Canadian leadership in the global campaign; to develop environmental education programs which encompass both practical and values education for educators, the workplace, the public, and communities.

Programs The Summer Institute for Environmental Values. The Growing Up Green Programme, a project aimed at children. The GreenWorks Project, a workplace education program. The Foundation also operates a multi-sectoral training program for sustainable communities, and the Summer Institute for Environmental Values.

Publications Numerous books focusing on environmental education in the home, workplace, and the community

Multimedia Video *Positive Action for the Environment*

For more Information Database, Library, List of Publications

Who's Who PRESIDENT ROBERT BATEMAN • VICE PRESIDENT TOM AXWORTHY SECRETARY DAVID COX • TREASURER BOB VAN TONGERLOO • EXECUTIVE DIRECTOR MICHAEL BLOOMFIELD • COMMUNICATIONS COORDINATOR JANE ORION SMITH

NORTHWATCH

P.O. BOX 282	NORTH BAY ON P1B 5E6
PHONE (705) 497 0373	FAX (705) 476 2060

Founded 1988 • *Geographic Coverage* Northeast Ontario • *Cooperative Partners* Ontario Environmental Network, Canadian Environmental Network • *Chapter* 1 • *Organization Members* 22 • *Individual Members* 500

Mission To advocate the incorporation of environmental considerations into all social and economic planning and decision making in northeastern Ontario.

Annual Fees

Regular	*Organization*
$25	$40

Programs Advocacy. Policy development. Member support. Quarterly regional meetings.

Publication Quarterly newsletter

For more Information Database, Library, List of Publications

WOMEN AND ENVIRONMENTS EDUCATION AND DEVELOPMENT FOUNDATION (THE)

736 BATHURST STREET   TORONTO ON M5S 2R4
PHONE (416) 516 2600   FAX (416) 531 6214

Founded 1987 • *Geographic Coverage* Global • *Other Fields of Focus* Public/
Environmental Health, Urban Environment • *Members* 1,000 including organizations

Mission To provide a forum for communication and to conduct research on
issues relating to women in the fields of planning, health, ecology and environment, workplace design, community development, urban and rural sociology.

Annual Fees	*Regular*	*Organization*
	$21.97	$31.97

Funding	*Membership*	*Government Support*	*Foundations*
	30%	60%	10%

Programs Stop-the-Whitewash Project. WOPHE Project (Women's Perspectives on Housing and the Environment). Building Women Networks
for Sustainability Projects.

Publications *Women and Environments*, circulation 1,000. *The Rag-
Times Newsletter*, circulation 500

For more Information Library

Who's Who PRESIDENT **MARJORIE LAMB** • SECRETARY **GAYE ALEXANDER** • TREASU-
RER **LESLEY WATSON** • CONTACT **LINDA NORHEIM**

atmosphere & climate global warming

CHAPTER 2

Global Warming Stalled between Theories and Reality, by Joel Grossman

33

MASSIVE BURNING OF FOSSIL FUELS, with the subsequent release of huge amounts of greenhouse gases such as carbon dioxide, is one of the largest "uncontrolled experiments" in global atmospheric and climate modification since the Earth formed from cosmic dust some 5 billion years ago. Historical precedence for rapid global climate change comes from recent analyses of ancient Greenland ice cores and sediments from large extraplanetary objects. Studies focused on huge volcanic eruptions that may have blotted out the sun, cooling the earth and causing massive species extinctions in bygone eras. However, due to the sheer complexity of the systems and feedback loops that control atmospheric changes and global climate, scientists are divided as to the scale, direction and eventual consequences of burning fossil fuels and releasing greenhouse gases. But there is no disagreement about the rising concentrations of carbon dioxide and other greenhouse gases in the atmosphere. Recent evidence from bore-hole temperature readings, oxygen isotope ratios in glacial ice cores, tree-line migration to higher levels, and glacial retreat indicate that global

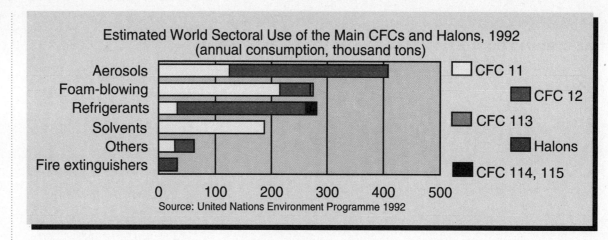

Estimated World Sectoral Use of the Main CFCs and Halons, 1992
(annual consumption, thousand tons)

Source: United Nations Environment Programme 1992

warming may already have started.

THERE ARE MANY POTENTIAL consequences of an enhanced greenhouse effect from massive carbon dioxide and greenhouse gas releases: rising temperatures, violent storms, species extinctions, cancers from deleterious ultraviolet light wavelengths penetrating the ozone hole, drought in some interior areas, and flooding of coastal areas from rising sea levels. Carbon dioxide is not the only greenhouse gas of concern. Trace gases (methane, chlorofluorocarbons, bromines, and nitrous oxide) - though present in only parts per million (ppm), billion (ppb) or trillion - pack enormous power; molecule for molecule, they are

chemically active and, in contrast to the other more inert and abundant atmospheric gases (carbon dioxide, nitrogen, oxygen, and argon) can destroy the stratospheric ozone layer. Among the greenhouse gases, only water vapor is more abundant than carbon dioxide, which is already up over 25 percent from 280 ppm in 1850 to over 350 ppm today. With over 6 billion tons of carbon injected into the atmosphere annually from fossil fuel burning and deforestation, carbon dioxide levels are rising 0.4 percent per year. Along with water vapor and other trace greenhouse gases, carbon dioxide absorbs infrared radiation and bounces it back to Earth, creating the warming greenhouse effect. While some greenhouse effect is essential to

prevent the earth from entering another Ice Age, there is real concern that an enhanced greenhouse effect from human activities could lead to excessive global warming. Thus, scientists stress the need to cut global production of carbon dioxide and other greenhouse gases to prevent excessive warming.

HOWEVER, CURBING CARBON DIOXIDE output is not simple because the world economy still depends on energy from fossil fuel combustion. There are also economic and population pressures to cut forests that absorb carbon dioxide. Fortunately, the amount of energy needed to produce a unit of gross national product is declining: the US economy ►

▶ grew 40 percent between 1973 and 1985 with no increase in energy consumption. Thus, holding down carbon dioxide emissions may be compatible with making better use of energy and raw materials in an expanding economy. Nevertheless, with an atmospheric residence time of over 100 years for carbon dioxide, it will take generations for any cutbacks in carbon dioxide production to have an impact. Even the Climate Change Action Plan, proposed by the United States as fulfillment of the 1992 Rio de Janeiro Earth Summit Climate Convention, merely stabilizes carbon dioxide emissions near 1990 levels. Canada, which produces about 2 percent of global greenhouse gases, has a similar goal of stabilizing carbon dioxide and greenhouse gas emissions at 1990 levels. Many other factors also affect the outcome of adding carbon dioxide and other greenhouse gases to the atmosphere. For example, the oceans play a major role in global climate change that we are just beginning to understand. Sulfate aerosols from sulfur dioxide emissions have a mitigating cooling effect. Some scientists even go so far as to predict a decline in solar irradiance in the next century that will counteract the warming effects of greenhouse gases. As a further complication to projections, many physical factors, such as cloud cover, don't fit easily into computer models of climate change, but they can moderate the greenhouse effect. Equally difficult to calculate are the effects of living carbon sinks like marine biota, soil microbes, and land plants. These can sequester carbon when factors

---

United States

ACID RAIN FOUNDATION, INC. (THE)

1410 VARSITY DRIVE   RALEIGH NC 27606
PHONE (919) 737 3311

Founded 1981 • *Geographic Coverage* Global • *Other Field of Focus* Pollution / Radiations • *Cooperative Partners* North Carolina Department of Natural Resources and Community Development, The North Carolina Wildlife Resources Commission

Mission To foster greater understanding of global atmospheric issues by raising the level of public awareness, supplying educational resources, and supporting research. The Foundation's main areas of concern include acid rain, the global atmosphere, recycling and forest ecosystems.

Annual Fees *Regular* $35

Funding	Membership	Government Support	Programs
	3%	53%	44%

Programs Education. Development. Marketing. Conference. Symposia. Expert referral service.

Publications Various books including *The Acid Rain Resources Directory* • *International Speakers Bureau* • *International Directory of Acid Deposition Researchers* • *Acid Rain in Minnesota* • *Acid Rain in North Carolina.* Curriculum materials developed for 3rd grade through high school

Multimedia Computer information retrieval system. Audio-visual library

For more Information Library

Who's Who PRESIDENT HARRIET S. STUBBS

CENTER FOR CLEAN AIR POLICY

444 NORTH CAPITOL STREET, SUITE 602   WASHINGTON DC 20001
PHONE (202) 624 7709   FAX (202) 508 3829

Founded 1985 • *Geographic Coverage* State, National • *Other Fields of Focus* Energy - Alternative / Renewable Energies, Transportation Systems / Impacts / Alternatives • *Chapter* 1 office in the Czech Republic

Mission To protect air purity and reduce noxious emissions through legislative activity.

For more Information List of Publications

Who's Who CHAIR GOVERNOR TONY EARL • EXECUTIVE DIRECTOR NED HELME CONTACT JANET-ANN GILLE

CLIMATE INSTITUTE

324 FOURTH STREET, NE   WASHINGTON DC 20002-5821
PHONE (202) 547 0104   FAX (202) 547 0111

Founded 1986 • *Geographic Coverage* Global • *Chapters* 2 *Organization Members* 50 • *Individual Members* 5,000

Mission To advance public understanding of global warming produced by the enhanced greenhouse effect and of strategies to avert atmospheric ozone depletion, by serving as a bridge between the scientific community and decision makers.

Annual Fees	Regular	Student/Senior	Patron
	$95	$20	$1,000

Funding	Membership	Corporations	Foundations
	10%	5%	85%

Total Income $1,400,000

Usage	Administration	Fundraising	Programs
	10%	5%	85%

Programs Municipal Briefings on Climate Change in North American Cities. National Action Plan Development for Eight Asian Nations. Envi-

such as temperature and nutrients are not limiting.

ADDING TO THE COMPLEXITY of the global warming puzzle are the trace greenhouse gases (methane, nitrous oxide, chlorofluorocarbons, and ozone), which absorb infrared radiation much better than carbon dioxide, and contribute more to global warming on a molecule-for-molecule basis. For example, ▶

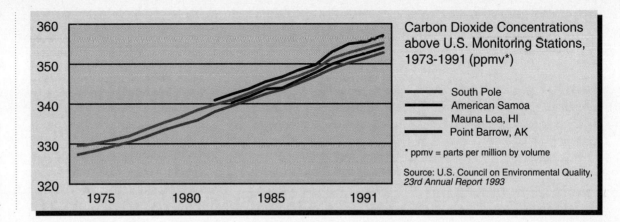

Carbon Dioxide Concentrations above U.S. Monitoring Stations, 1973-1991 (ppmv*)

——— South Pole
——— American Samoa
——— Mauna Loa, HI
——— Point Barrow, AK

* ppmv = parts per million by volume

Source: U.S. Council on Environmental Quality, *23rd Annual Report 1993*

ronmental Refugee Study. Sponsors a series of conferences on preparing for climate change.

Publications Bimonthly newsletter *Climate Alert*. Proceedings of the Second North American Conference on Climate Change: *Coping With Climate Change*. Other publications include *Global Change and Cities* • *The Arctic and Global Change* • *Report of the International Workshop on Framework Convention and Associated Protocols: A Non-governmental Perspective*

For more Information Annual Report

Who's Who PRESIDENT JOHN C. TOPPING, JR. • VICE PRESIDENT DANIEL E. POWER III SECRETARY NANCY C. WILSON • TREASURER JOHN BOND • PUBLICATIONS CHAIRMAN MARK GOLDBERG

ENVIRONMENTAL INFORMATION NETWORKS PAGE 253
119 SOUTH FAIRFAX STREET   ALEXANDRIA VA 22314
PHONE (703) 683 0774   FAX (703) 683 3893

FRIENDS OF THE EARTH USA   PAGE 22
218 "D" STREET, SE   WASHINGTON DC 20003
PHONE (202) 544 2600   FAX (202) 543 4710

GREENPEACE, INC.   PAGE 23
1436 "U" STREET, NW   WASHINGTON DC 20009
PHONE (202) 462 1177   FAX (202) 462 4507

INDUSTRY COOPERATIVE FOR OZONE LAYER PROTECTION
2000 "L" STREET, NW, SUITE 710   WASHINGTON DC 20036
PHONE (202) 737 1419   FAX (202) 296 7442

Founded 1989 • *Geographic Coverage* National, Global • *Coope-*

rative Partners US Environmental Protection Agency, Center for Global Change, Energy International Agency, Sweden Environmental Protection Agency • *Organization Members* 14 corporate organizations and 18 affiliates

Mission To work for the protection of the stratospheric ozone layer by working to encourage the prompt substitution of safe, environmentally acceptable, non-proprietary alternatives (substances, processes and technologies) for current industrial CFC solvents; to act as an international clearinghouse for information on CFC alternatives; and to work with private, national, and international trade groups, organizations, and governmental bodies to develop the most efficient means of generating, gathering, and distributing information on CFC alternatives.

Annual Fees	*Associate*	*Supporting*	*Sustaining*	*Full Member*
	$2,000	$5,000	$10,000	$18,000

Funding *Corporations* 100%

Usage	*Programs*	*Information Support*
	50%	50%

Publications Five technical manuals on phasing out the use of ozone depleting solvents *Manual of Practices to Reduce and Eliminate CFC 113 Use in the Electronics Industry* • *Aqueous and Semi-Aqueous Alternatives for CFC 113 and Methyl Chloroform Cleaning of Printed Circuit Board Assemblies* • *Conservation and Recycling Practices for CFC 113 and Methyl Chloroform* • *Eliminating CFC 113 and Methyl Chloroform in Precision Cleaning Operations* • *Alternatives for CFC 113 and Chloroform in Metal Cleaning*

Multimedia Database *OZONET* donated to United Nations Environment Programme, created by Northern Telecom Ltd. provides solvent users with the information they need in their daily tasks and decision making processes

Who's Who PRESIDENT DAVID CHITTICK • VICE PRESIDENT ART FITZGERALD • TREA-

the 310 ppb of nitrous oxide in the atmosphere, mostly from natural sources, traps heat 250 times more than carbon dioxide and persists for 170 years. Methane molecules, which trap heat 25 times more than carbon dioxide and persist for about 10 years, are present in the atmosphere at over 1,800 ppb and increasing at a 1.1 percent annual rate from oil and natural gas production, bacterial fermentation, increased cattle and rice farming by an expanding human population, and other sources. Another concern is the fact that highly reactive long-lived molecules, such as chlorofluorocarbons already released may be destroying the ozone layer well into the next century, despite reduced production under the Montreal Protocol. Though chlorofluorocarbons replacements like hydrochlorofluorocarbons are less destructive to the ozone layer, they may also have to be eliminated in favor of safer alternatives. Environment Canada and the provinces are working with companies to recover and recycle chlorofluorocarbons and other ozone-depleting substances. The US Climate-Wise Program will complement the Global Change Research Program and Section 1605(b) of the Energy Policy Act of 1992, under which companies voluntarily report reductions in greenhouse gases. The American premise is that innovative ways of reducing greenhouse gases will be invented if the government establishes broad goals and allows individuals to devise the means and technologies to achieve those goals. The search for solutions to these global problems has only just begun. •

Joel Grossman

SURER **Cynthia Pruett** • Executive Director **Susan F. Vogt** • Contact **Allison Morrill**

NATIONAL CENTER FOR ATMOSPHERIC RESEARCH

P.O. Box 3000, 1850 Table Mesa Drive   Boulder   CO   80307-3000
Phone (303) 497 8600   Fax (303) 497 8610

Founded 1960 • *Geographic Coverage* Global • *Organization Members* 60 universities

Mission To conduct research related to the atmosphere. Currently, the Center's research is concentrated in four main areas: storms and other similar-sized weather phenomena, climate, the chemistry of the atmosphere, and the sun.

Funding	*Government Support*	*Other Contracts*
	92%	8%

Total Income $87,488,000

Usage	*Administration*	*Programs*
	7%	93%

Total Expenses $87,488,000

Programs Atmospheric Chemistry Research Program performs research on the impacts of smog, acid rain, and increasing carbon dioxide and other trace gases on the atmosphere. The Climate and Global Dynamics Research Program constructs computer scenarios of past and present climates to project possible future weather and climate conditions. The Mesoscale and Microscale Meteorology Research Program looks at how the atmosphere is organized to produce fronts and jet streams, how severe storms develop and die, how radiation is absorbed and reflected by cloud particles, how variations in the shape and character of land surfaces affect the weather, the ways air mixes, and other fundamental processes. The Sun and the Earth Research Program concentrates on the various parts of the solar anatomy, from its thermonuclear core to its far-flung atmosphere, while considering the sun's effects on earth.

Publications Numerous technical notes and books focusing on atmospheric chemistry, climate and global dynamics, environmental and societal impacts of atmospheric phenomena, high altitude observations, mesoscale and microscale meteorology

For more Information Annual Report, Database, Library, List of Publications

Who's Who Executive Director **Robert Serafin**

US CLIMATE ACTION NETWORK

1350 New York Avenue, NW, Suite 300   Washington   DC   20005
Phone (202) 624 9360   Fax (202) 783 5917

Founded 1989 • *Geographic Coverage* Global • *Other Field of Focus* Environmental Education / Careers / Information / Networks *Chapters* 6, in Nairobi - Kenya, Dhaka - Bangladesh, Jakarta - Indonesia, Santiago - Chile, London - UK and Brussels - Belgium

Mission To promote governmental and individual action to limit human induced climate change to ecologically sustainable levels. In pursuit of this goal, the objectives of the Network are to coordinate information exchange on international, regional and national climate policies and issues, to formulate policy options and position papers on climate-related issues, and to undertake further collaborative action to promote effective non-governmental organization involvement in efforts to avert the threat of global warming.

Publication *Climate Action Network Directory*

For more Information Database, Library

Who's Who Coordinator **Andrew Gettelman**

Canada

ENVIRONMENT CANADA
ATMOSPHERIC ENVIRONMENT SERVICE

4905 DUFFERIN STREET   DOWNSVIEW ON M3H 5T4
PHONE (416) 667 4551

Geographic Coverage North America • *Cooperative Partner* World Meteorological Organization • *Individual Members* 3,000 volunteers

Mission The basic services provided by Atmospheric Environment Service are publicly funded in order to ensure the safety of Canadians and the security of their property, to contribute to the efficiency of the economy, and to help safeguard environmental quality. They include the maintenance of huge data files to answer questions on climatic extremes and normals, the monitoring of ice and iceberg motions to protect ships and drill rigs in the Arctic and Atlantic, and the monitoring and prediction of the movement of atmospheric pollution to help safeguard environmental quality. The Service also performs research on major aspects of acid rain, toxic air pollutants, the high level ozone layer, and anticipated changes in climate produced by an increasing greenhouse effect.

Programs Air Quality programs, to advise the government and industrial decision makers on such key issues as acid rain, toxic chemicals and climatic change. Research and Development program to develop new instrumentation for forecasting and monitoring. World Weather Watch Programme makes use of data observing networks, modern communications and standardization of weather data.

Publications Fact sheets including *The Ozone Layer* • *The Impacts of Global Warming* • *Drought* • *Climate Change and Variability* • *Tornadoes* • *Weather Satellites* • *Environmental Implications of the Automobile.* Environmental indicator bulletins

For more Information Database

FRIENDS OF THE EARTH   PAGE 30
LES AMIS DE LA TERRE
251 LAURIER AVENUE, WEST, SUITE 701   OTTAWA ON K1P 5J6
PHONE (613) 230 3352   FAX (613) 232 4354

GREENPEACE CANADA   PAGE 31
185 SPADINA AVENUE, SUITE 600   TORONTO ON M5T 2C6
PHONE (416) 435 8404   FAX (416) 345 8422

ecosystem protection biodiversity

CHAPTER 3

Biodiversity, a Global Responsibility, by Joel Grossman

ECOSYSTEMS, SPECIES, AND GENE pools are sustainable biological resources - capital assets that help feed the world, relieve suffering, protect the environment, and benefit humanity in other ways. The Convention on Biological Diversity that emerged from the 1992 Rio de Janeiro Earth Summit recognized the seriousness and the irreversible continuing loss of our biodiversity capital assets that have been caused by ecosystem and habitat destruction, pollution, over-harvesting, and non-native species introductions. All the earth's ecosystems interact. For that reason, the Earth Summit participants emphasized the international nature of ecosystem protection. For example, the loss of forest ecosystems, whether in Canada, the United States or the tropics, results in increasing rapid runoff of rainfall, of soil erosion and of flooding; it also accelerates local and global climate changes that affect other ecosystems and global biodiversity. Ecosystem protection and conservation of biodiversity involves protecting all types of natural habitats.

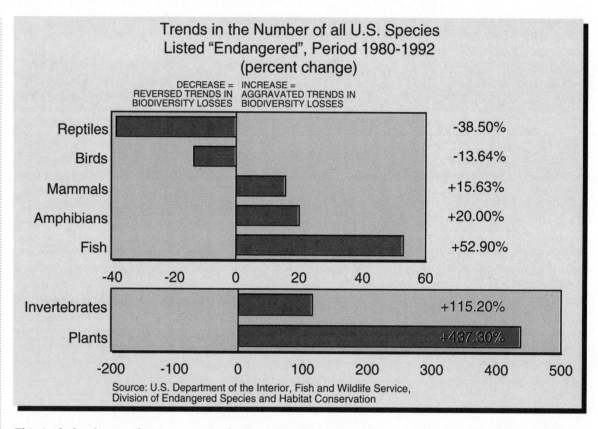

Trends in the Number of all U.S. Species Listed "Endangered", Period 1980-1992 (percent change)

DECREASE = REVERSED TRENDS IN BIODIVERSITY LOSSES   INCREASE = AGGRAVATED TRENDS IN BIODIVERSITY LOSSES

Reptiles	-38.50%
Birds	-13.64%
Mammals	+15.63%
Amphibians	+20.00%
Fish	+52.90%
Invertebrates	+115.20%
Plants	+437.30%

Source: U.S. Department of the Interior, Fish and Wildlife Service, Division of Endangered Species and Habitat Conservation

This includes forests, deserts, grasslands, wetlands, coral reefs, rivers, lakes, oceans, and mountains. Despite good intentions of well-meaning citizens, the creation of zoos, botanical gardens, gene banks, and germplasm repositories do not substitute for conserving broad expanses of natural habitats. In fact, even a patchwork of isolated reserves and geographically fragmented natural habitats the size of continental-shelf islands is insufficient to stop the loss of biodiversity.

SPECIES EXTINCTION RATE is estimated at 20 percent within 50 years. In the case of small specialized habitats like ridge tops, ancient lakes, and desert springs, habitat loss may mean the more immediate extinction of species. A major cause of extinctions is the burgeoning human population. Humans appropriate between 20 and 40 percent of the solar energy resources trapped by land plants and create a threat to ecosystems and biodiversity. "There is no way that we can draw upon the resources of the planet to such a degree without drastically reducing the state of most other species", says Pulitzer Prize-winning Harvard University biologist E. O. Wilson. Scientists have identified and described approximately 1.4 million species. Another 5 million to 30 million more remain uncategorized and unknown. The genetic code of each species is a repository of up to 10 billion bits of information, an irreplaceable resource accumulated over thousands or millions of years by natural selection. With each extinction, this rich genetic legacy shrinks - along with the possibility of humankind's future potential for health, wealth and survival. For example, 25 percent of US pharmacy prescriptions, which are valued at about $8 billion, contain active ingredients from green plants. Amazingly, the healing and food potential of wild plants has barely been tapped. Quinoa, amaranth and other obscure ancient American plants rescued from oblivion are helping diversify North American farms. Only a handful of fragile sources of germplasm now exist that can lead to the development of high-yielding staple crops resistant to pestilence.

These are genes from corn ancestors growing wild in only a precious few patches in Mexico, weedy wild wheat relatives clinging to survival in remote Middle Eastern deserts, and potatoes grown by only a handful of native farmers high in the Andes Mountains.

THOUGH LESS VISIBLE THAN endangered mammals and harder to value than crop ▶

United States

ALLIANCE FOR THE WILD ROCKIES

P.O. Box 8371   Missoula MT 59807
Phone (406) 721 5420   Fax (406) 721 9917

Founded 1988 • *Geographic Coverage* US northern Rockies, Canadian southern Rockies • *Other Fields of Focus* Natural Resources / Water Conservation & Quality, Wildlife - Animal & Plant • *Chapters* 2 *Organization Members* 450 • *Individual Members* 4,500

Mission To protect and preserve the Wild Northern Rockies.

Annual Fees	Regular	Student/Senior	Organization	Corporation	Donor
	$15	$5	$25	$25	$100

Funding	Membership	Foundations	Contributions & Special Events
	33%	44%	23%

Total Income $127,217

Usage	Administration & Fundraising	Programs
	22%	78%

Programs Ecosystem defense. Legislative action.

Publication Newsletter *The Networker*

Who's Who PRESIDENT PAUL FRITZ • VICE PRESIDENT LIZ SEDLER • EXECUTIVE DIRECTOR MIKE BADER

AMERICAN LITTORAL SOCIETY

Sandy Hook   Highlands NJ 07732
Phone (201) 291 0055

Founded 1961 • *Geographic Coverage* National • *Other Field of Focus* Natural Resources / Water - Conservation & Quality • *Coope-* *rative Partners* The Watershed Association of the Delaware River, The Coast Alliance, The Barrier Island Coalition, The Society of Wetland Scientists, Monitor, Clean Ocean Action • *Chapters* 7 regional offices *Individual Members* 9,000

Mission To promote a better understanding of the littoral zone (the shore, adjacent wetlands, bays, and rivers) and of the value of marine life and habitats, and to provide a unified voice advocating the protection of coastal marine life.

Annual Fees	Regular	Student/Senior	Families	Organization
	$25	$15	$25	$30

Other Fees *Foreign* $35 • *Sustaining* $50 • *Supporting* $100 *Sponsor* $250 • *Donor* $500

Funding	Membership	Foundations	Contracts	Trips & Sales	Other
	81%	3%	8%	6%	2%

Total Income $745,000

Usage	Chapters	Salaries & Payroll Tax	Main Office	Printing & Publications	Other
	36%	40%	8%	9%	7%

Total Expenses $980,000

Programs Organizes citizen coastal water quality monitoring programs. Educational program publishes information on the impacts of stormwater runoff on wildlife habitats. World's largest volunteer fish tag-and-release program. Legal program sues municipalities to protect the public's right to access shores and beaches. Lobbies in state legislatures and in Congress for the implementation and enforcement of laws to protect the coast. Sponsors a field trip program through which members can visit coastal areas.

Publications Quarterly magazine *Underwater Naturalist*. Quarterly newsletter *Coastal Reporter*. Books *The Whalewatcher's Handbook* • *The Seaside Reader*

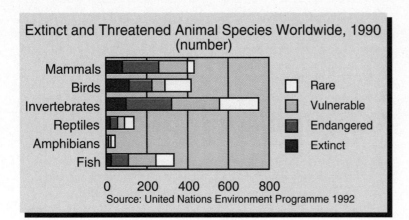

Extinct and Threatened Animal Species Worldwide, 1990 (number)

Mammals
Birds
Invertebrates
Reptiles
Amphibians
Fish

Rare
Vulnerable
Endangered
Extinct

0   200   400   600   800

Source: United Nations Environment Programme 1992

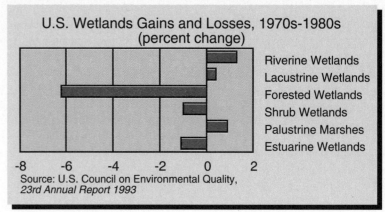

U.S. Wetlands Gains and Losses, 1970s-1980s (percent change)

Riverine Wetlands
Lacustrine Wetlands
Forested Wetlands
Shrub Wetlands
Palustrine Marshes
Estuarine Wetlands

-8   -6   -4   -2   0   2

Source: U.S. Council on Environmental Quality,
23rd Annual Report 1993

For more Information Annual Report

Who's Who PRESIDENT **D. W. BENNETT**

AMERICAN OCEANS CAMPAIGN

725 ARIZONA AVENUE, SUITE 102   SANTA MONICA CA 90401
PHONE (310) 576 6162   FAX (310) 576 6170

Founded 1987 • *Geographic Coverage* Global • *Other Field of Focus* Natural Resources / Water - Conservation & Quality • *Chapters* 2 *Individual Members* 1,000

Mission To protect the vitality of the coastal waters, estuaries, bays, wetlands and deep oceans of America and the world, by educating the public and local, state, federal and international decision makers on the need to stop abusing the marine environment. The organization is committed to strong grassroots support and scientific information as the key ingredients to making public policy.

Annual Fees	*Regular*	*Student/Senior*	*Friend*	*Sponsor*	*Patron*
	$25	$25	$50	$75	$250

Funding	*Membership*	*Corporations*	*Foundations*	*Other*
	40%	6.5%	15.5%	38%

Total Income $480,000

Usage	*Administration*	*Fundraising*	*Programs*
	11%	15.5%	73.5%

Total Expenses $460,000

Programs Volunteer program, Kids Club.

Publication Quarterly newsletter *Splash*

For more Information Annual Report

Who's Who PRESIDENT **TED DANSON** • VICE PRESIDENT **CASEY COATES-DANSON** SECRETARY **MARIE RYAVEC** • TREASURER **CONNIE MISSISSIPPI** • EXECUTIVE DIRECTOR **ROBERT H. SULNICK**

ANTARCTIC AND SOUTHERN OCEAN COALITION

P.O. BOX 76920   WASHINGTON DC 20013
PHONE (202) 544 2600

Founded 1979 • *Geographic Coverage* Regional • *Focused Region* Antarctica, southern Atlantic Ocean • *Cooperative Partner* The Antarctica Project • *Organization Members* 270

Mission The organization is a coalition of non-governmental organizations dedicated to preserving the environment and ecosystems of Antarctica and the Southern Ocean.

Publication Periodical *ECO*

ANTARCTICA PROJECT (THE)

P.O. BOX 76920   WASHINGTON DC 20013
PHONE (202) 544 2600

Founded 1982 • *Geographic Coverage* Regional • *Cooperative Partners* The Antarctic and Southern Ocean Coalition, The International Union for Conservation of Nature and Natural Resources • *Organization Members* 270 • *Individual Members* 300

Mission The Antarctica Project is dedicated to the full and permanent environmental protection of Antarctica. It works to develop and advance protection concepts to this end, monitors treaty meetings, and serves as secretariat to the Antarctic and Southern Ocean Coalition.

Annual Fees	*Regular*	*Student / Senior*	*Patron*
	$30	$20	$100

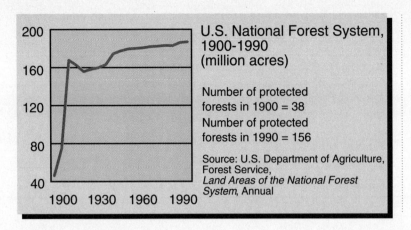

U.S. National Forest System, 1900-1990 (million acres)

Number of protected forests in 1900 = 38
Number of protected forests in 1990 = 156

Source: U.S. Department of Agriculture, Forest Service, *Land Areas of the National Forest System*, Annual

▶ germplasm, the biodiversity of less glamorous birds, reptiles, amphibians, fish, invertebrates, and microorganism species is integral to maintaining healthy ecosystems. By the time that small animals, invertebrates, or plant species become endangered, the larger animals and many higher plants have often vanished. Hence, the whole ecosystem is often severely degraded, possibly even near total collapse and in urgent need of protection. It is argued that every animal and plant in an ecosystem, no matter how small, has value - even if that value is not immediately obvious. For example, scientists observing the community of 2 million species of insects are discovering new pollinators, predators, and parasites ▶

Funding	Membership	Foundations	Other
	20%	70%	10%

Usage	Administration	Fundraising	Programs
	20%	10%	70%

Programs To educate the public and decision makers about the values of Antarctica. Monitoring of international and scientific meetings. Development of protection concepts. Serves as secretariat to international coalition of environmental organizations.

Publication Quarterly newsletter *The Antarctica Project*

Who's Who COUNSEL JAMES BARNES • DIRECTOR BETH MARKS

APPALACHIAN MOUNTAIN CLUB

5 JOY STREET   BOSTON MA 02108
PHONE (617) 523 0636

Founded 1876 • *Geographic Coverage* Regional • *Other Field of Focus* Natural Resources / Water - Conservation & Quality • *Chapters* 11 *Individual Members* 55,000

Mission To promote the protection, enjoyment and sound management of the mountains, rivers, and trails of the Northeast. The Club's current areas of concern include forest protection, Federal Energy Regulatory Commission dam relicensing, environmental education, trail maintenance, air quality research, and local involvement of members in conservation projects.

Annual Fees	Regular	Student/Senior	Families
	$40	$25	$65

Funding	Membership	Foundations	Facilities	Programs
	24.9%	13.7%	44.4%	6.3%

Other Sources *Publications* 7.3% • *Investment Income* 3.4%

Total Income $8,257,000

Usage	Administration	Fundraising	Programs	Facilities
	12.5%	3.9%	22.3%	39.2%

Other Usage *Member Services* 15.9% • *Publications* 6.2%

Programs Volunteer Trail Conservation Corps-Leadership Training for Urban Youth Leaders Program. Outdoor recreation and backcountry safety workshops. Northern Forest Project.

Publications Monthly magazine *AMC Outdoors*. Journal *Appalachian*. Children's books. Trail and river guides. Trail maps. *Country Walk* series. *How-to* Recreation Guides

For more Information Annual Report

Who's Who PRESIDENT PRESTON H. SAUNDERS • SECRETARY JOHN G. CASAGRANDE • EXECUTIVE DIRECTOR ANDREW J. FALENDER

ARAL SEA INFORMATION COMMITTEE   PAGE 103
1055 FORTH CRONKHITE   SAUSALITO CA 94965
PHONE (415) 331 5122   FAX (415) 331 2722

ARCTIC TO AMAZONIA ALLIANCE   PAGE 61
P.O. BOX 73   STRAFFORD VT 05072
PHONE (802) 765 4337

BAYKEEPER,
A PROJECT OF THE SAN FRANCISCO BAY-DELTA
PRESERVATION ASSOCIATION   PAGE 104
BUILDING A, FORT MANSON   SAN FRANCISCO CA 94123-1382
PHONE (415) 567 4401   FAX (415) 567 9715

BIOREGIONAL PROJECT (THE)
H.C.R. 3, BOX 3   BRIXEY MO 65618
PHONE (417) 679 4773

Founded 1982 • *Geographic Coverage* Global

Mission To support the development of the bioregional movement. To promote bioregionalism and ecologically-based systems to deal with all human needs.

Funding	Foundations	Other
	50%	50%

Usage	Administration	Fundraising	Programs
	10%	25%	65%

Who's Who SECRETARY DAVID HAENKE

CENTER FOR ALASKAN COASTAL STUDIES

P.O. BOX 2225   HOMER AK 99603
PHONE (907) 235 6667

Founded 1981 • *Geographic Coverage* Local, State • *Other Field of Focus* Natural Resources / Water - Conservation & Quality • *Individual Members* 500

Mission To increase awareness, knowledge, and understanding of Alaska's marine environment by providing educational programs and encouraging research with emphasis on the Kachemak Bay area; to advocate protection of habitats and responsible stewardship of Alaskan coastal and marine resources.

Annual Fees	Regular	Student/Senior	Families	Corporation	Supporting
	$25	$10	$40	$500	$100

Other Fees *Lifetime* $1,000

Programs The Center delivers educational programs to over 1,500 students and visitors every year. Kachemak Bay Natural History Tours. The Center also sponsors the annual Kachemak Bay Coastwalk to gather baseline data and monitor the shores of Kachemak Bay.

Publication Quarterly newsletter

For more Information Database

CENTER FOR MARINE CONSERVATION

1725 DESALES STREET, NW   WASHINGTON DC 20036
PHONE (202) 429 5609   FAX (202) 872 0619

Founded 1972 • *Geographic Coverage* National, Central America • *Focused Countries* USA, Caribbean Islands • *Other Fields of Focus* Natural Resources / Water - Conservation & Quality, Wildlife - Animal & Plant • *Cooperative Partners* Jointly establishing the International Marine Conservation Network in cooperation with World Wildlife Fund and IUCN The World Conservation Union *Chapters* 4 • *Individual Members* 110,000 worldwide

Mission To protect marine wildlife and their habitats, prevent over-exploitation, and conserve ocean and coastal resources through policy research, science-based advocacy, education, regional citizen coalitions, and interaction with governments and industries, with an emphasis on sustainable fisheries, prevention of solid waste pollution, conservation of species, and management of marine protected areas in US waters and, increasingly, in other countries.

Annual Fees *Regular* $20

Funding	Government Support	Contributions / Grants & Bequests	Other
	8%	87%	5%

Total Income $7,877,672

Usage	Administration	Fundraising	Programs	Membership Development
	3%	16%	71%	9%

Total Expenses $5,762,790

Programs International Beach Cleanup Campaign. Citizen Pollution Patrol Program. Marine Debris Action Plan. Clean Ocean Campaign. Storm Drain Stenciling Campaign. Sea Grassroots Activist Program. International Marine Conservation Network helps governments, industries, and conservation NGOs work together.

Publications Quarterly newsletters *Marine Conservation News* • *Sanctuary Currents*. Semiannual *Coastal Connection* updates beach cleanup activities. Numerous reports and books on marine fisheries, sewage treatment, coastal cleanup and marine wildlife. Children's literature and classroom activity sets

Multimedia Slide show *Whales* • *Sea Turtles* • *Marine Debris and Entanglement* • *The Turtle Excluder Device* • *The Archie Carr Sea Turtle Refuge*. Video *Inherit the Sea: America's Marine Sanctuary*

For more Information Annual Report, List of Publications

Who's Who CHAIRMAN ANTHONY A. LAPHAM • VICE CHAIRMAN CAMERON H. SANDERS • PRESIDENT ROGER E. MCMANUS • SENIOR VICE PRESIDENT FOR MANAGEMENT MICHAEL L. FRANKEL • VICE PRESIDENT DEVELOPMENT ROBERTA ROSS TISCH • VICE PRESIDENT PROGRAMS R. GARY MAGNUSON • VICE PRESIDENT MEMBERSHIP ANNE MARIE GROSS • SECRETARY CECILY M. MAJERUS • TREASURER EDITH LEDBETTER • PUBLIC INFORMATION OFFICER REBECCA S. MACKAY

CENTER FOR NATURAL LANDS
MANAGEMENT, INC.   PAGE 88
3228 WINDSOR DRIVE   SACRAMENTO CA 95864-3827
PHONE (916) 481 6454   FAX (916) 485 8911

COAST ALLIANCE, INC.   PAGE 106
235 PENNSYLVANIA AVENUE, SE   WASHINGTON DC 20003
PHONE (202) 546 9554   FAX (202) 546 9609

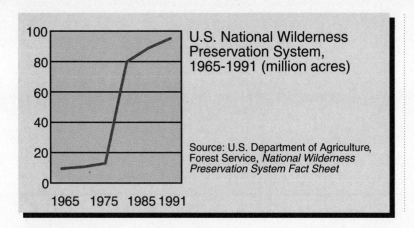

U.S. National Wilderness Preservation System, 1965-1991 (million acres)

Source: U.S. Department of Agriculture, Forest Service, *National Wilderness Preservation System Fact Sheet*

that can replace chemical pesticides as biological pest control agents. Even microbial biodiversity has its role, though we know little about it. Microorganisms such as fungi - often taken for granted as fermenting agents for beer, bread, cheese and antibiotic drugs - are also essential symbionts that enhance soil quality and growth and protect against plant disease. Only 69,000 of the 1.5 million species of fungi believed to exist have even been identified and described by scientists. Endangered microbes get sadly little attention.

The dreaded smallpox virus is a notable exception and its few remaining specimens are the center of a scientific debate that challenges our notions of biodiversity. Namely, should a species deemed ▶

COASTAL SOCIETY (THE)

P.O. Box 2081   GLOUCESTER MA 01930-2081
PHONE (508) 281 9209

Founded 1975 • *Geographic Coverage* National, Global • *Other Field of Focus* Natural Resources / Water - Conservation & Quality *Organization Members* 150 • *Individual Members* 150

Mission To promote the better understanding and sustainable use of the earth's coastal resources, by serving as a forum for coastal resource professionals and individuals.

Annual Fees	Regular	Student/Senior	Non-US	Institution
	$25	$12.50	$27.50	$35

Funding	Membership	Corporations
	25%	75%

Total Income $40,000

Usage	Administration	Programs
	15%	85%

Programs Biennial conferences. Occasional special meetings. Provides information on careers and volunteer programs. Note: The Coastal Society is a volunteer organization with very limited capability to provide individualized career counseling.

Publication Quarterly bulletin *The Coastal Society*

Who's Who PRESIDENT **MARGARET DAVIDSON** • PRESIDENT-ELECT **DAVID SMITH** • SECRETARY **GARY MAGNUSON** • EXECUTIVE DIRECTOR **THOMAS E. BIGFORD**

CONSERVATION INTERNATIONAL

1015 18TH STREET, NW, SUITE 1000   WASHINGTON DC 20036
PHONE (202) 429 5660   FAX (202) 887 5188

Founded 1987 • *Geographic Coverage* Latin America, North America, West Africa, Southeast Asia • *Focused Countries* Botswana, Canada, Indonesia, Madagascar, Papua New Guinea, the Philippines • *Other Field of Focus* Human Rights & Environment • *Cooperative Partners* The Bolivian National Academy of Sciences, The Bolivian Institute of Ecology, Center for Conservation Studies at the University of San Carlos *Chapters* 1 in Portland, OR, 11 in foreign countries • *Individual Members* 10,000

Mission To conserve ecosystems, biological diversity, and the ecological processes that support life on earth, with special emphasis on building local capacity. Temperate and tropical rainforest conservation, and indigenous people rights are the organization's main areas of focus.

Annual Fees	Regular	Families
	$35	$30

Funding	Membership	Corporations	Foundations
	7%	5%	88%

Total Income $9,821,536

Usage	Administration	Fundraising	Programs
	10%	6%	84%

Programs Marketing development communications. Scientific programs. Conservation biology. Conservation economics. Gender and social policy. Legislative affairs.

Publications Quarterly newsletter. Other publications include *Lessons from the Field* • *Communication and Environment Series*

Who's Who CHAIRMAN **PETER SELIGMANN** • PRESIDENT **RUSSELL A. MITTERMEIER**

CONSERVATION TREATY SUPPORT FUND

3705 CARDIFF ROAD   CHEVY CHASE MD 20815
PHONE (301) 654 3150   FAX (301) 652 6390

44

Founded 1991 • *Geographic Coverage* Global • *Cooperative Partners* United Nations Environment Programme - Caribbean Environment Programme, International Whaling Commission, US Fish and Wildlife Service - International Program, Convention on International Trade in Endangered Species (CITES)

Mission To further the conservation of wild natural resources by providing direct support to international treaties designed to support these goals, particularly, the Convention on International Trade of Endangered Species and the Convention on Wetlands of International Importance.

Total Income $559,000

Publications *CITES Brochure* outlines the largest international conservation agreement. *CITES Endangered Species Coloring Book* aims to educate children aged 7 to 12 about the worldwide variety of animals and plants

Multimedia Videos *Wetland World* (13 min.) • *CITES Video* describes how the 118-nation Endangered Species Treaty helps conserve thousands of animal and plant species on the verge of extinction

Who's Who PRESIDENT GEORGE A. FURNESS, JR. • VICE PRESIDENT FREDERICK E. MORRIS • VICE PRESIDENT INTERNATIONAL JOHN C. GOLDSMITH • SECRETARY LINDA E. MANNHEIM • TREASURER FAITH T. CAMPBELL

COUSTEAU SOCIETY, INC. (THE)   PAGE 17
870 GREENBRIER CIRCLE, SUITE 402   CHESAPEAKE VA 23320-2641
PHONE (804) 523 9335   FAX (804) 523 2747

DEFENDERS OF WILDLIFE   PAGE 136
1244 19TH STREET, NW   WASHINGTON DC 20036
PHONE (202) 659 9510   FAX (202) 833 3349

DELTA WATERFOWL FOUNDATION
NORTH AMERICAN WILDLIFE FOUNDATION
102 WILMOT ROAD, SUITE 410   DEERFIELD IL 60015
PHONE (708) 940 7776   FAX (708) 940 3739

Founded 1911 • *Geographic Coverage* North America • *Other Field of Focus* Wildlife - Animal & Plant

Mission To work for the preservation of wetlands and the waterfowl and wildlife dependent upon them.

Annual Fees	Regular	Sustaining	Patron	Patron Advisory Council
	$50	$100	$500	$1,000

Funding	Contributions	Restricted Funds & Endowment
	84%	9%

Other Sources *Net Investment Income & Unrestricted Funds* 7%

Total Income $1,807,729

Usage	Administration	Fundraising	Programs	Other
	15%	11%	57%	17%

Total Expenses $1,775,521

Programs Principal project is the Delta Waterfowl and Wetlands Research Station in Manitoba, where various research projects are conducted by graduate students. NAWF has also begun to supplement its research program with active attempts to implement programs to benefit wildlife in wetland areas, including the Adopt A Pothole Program, the Wild Duck Rearing and Release Program, and the Prairie Farming Program.

Publications Bimonthly newsletter *Delta Waterfowl Report*. Handbooks include *Canvas Back of Minnedosa* • *Managing Your Duck Marsh*. Over 500 research papers

For more Information Annual Report, Library, List of Publications

Who's Who PRESIDENT P. A. W. GREEN • VICE PRESIDENT DANIEL W. LEBLOND TREASURER PETER P. HUFF • EXECUTIVE VICE PRESIDENT CHARLES S. POTTER, JR. CONTACT BONNIE R. ZAMBOS

DESERT FISHES COUNCIL
P.O. BOX 337   BISHOP CA 93514
PHONE (619) 872 8751

Founded 1970 • *Geographic Coverage* North America • *Other Field of Focus* Wildlife - Animal & Plant • *Individual Members* 500

Mission To preserve the biological integrity of North America's desert aquatic ecosystems and their related faunas and floras.

Annual Fees	Regular	Student/Senior	Patron
	$15	$5	$25

Funding *Membership* 100%

Total Income $10,000

Publications Proceedings of annual symposium

Who's Who PRESIDENT JOHN N. RINNE • SECRETARY EDWIN P. PISTER

DUCKS UNLIMITED, INC.   PAGE 107
1 WATERFOWL WAY   MEMPHIS TN 38120
PHONE (901) 754 4666   FAX (901) 753 2613

EARTH SHARE   PAGE 18
3400 INTERNATIONAL DRIVE, NW, SUITE 2-K   WASHINGTON DC 20008
PHONE (202) 537 7100   FAX (202) 537 7101

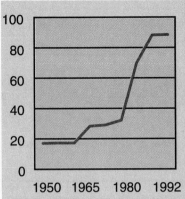

U.S. National Wildlife Refuge System, 1950-1992 (million acres)

Number of protected refuges in 1950 = 246
Number of protected refuges in 1992 = 485

Source: U.S. Department of the Interior, Fish and Wildlife Service, *Lands Under the Control of the Fish and Wildlife Service*, Annual

(y-axis: 0, 20, 40, 60, 80, 100; x-axis: 1950, 1965, 1980, 1992)

► undesirable also be protected from extinction? The issue may be more than academic, as the genetic code of the few remaining laboratory cultures might one day prove useful.

MEANWHILE, THERE IS AN URGENCY to protect existing ecosystems and natural habitats before the Earth's biodiversity dwindles to the point of becoming a museum exhibit for what once was a treasure chest of genetic information and biological potential. Though not as rich in species diversity as the tropics, North America has a rich natural heritage needing protection. Canada's unique natural heritage includes almost 20 percent of Earth's wilderness (excluding Antarctica) and freshwater, 10 percent of the forests, ►

EARTHWATCH
PAGE 19
680 MOUNT AUBURN STREET, P.O. BOX 403-N   WATERTOWN MA 02272
PHONE (617) 926 8200   FAX (617) 926 8532

EFFIE YEAW NATURE CENTER
PAGE 107
P.O. BOX 579   CARMICHAEL CA 95609
PHONE (916) 489 4918   FAX (916) 489 4983

ELKHORN SLOUGH FOUNDATION
P.O. BOX 267   MOSS LANDING CA 95039
PHONE (408) 728 5939   FAX (408) 728 1056

Founded 1982 • *Geographic Coverage* Local • *Other Field of Focus* Natural Resources / Water - Conservation & Quality • *Cooperative Partners* The Nature Conservancy, California Department of Fish and Game, National Oceanic and Atmospheric Administration *Chapter* 1 • *Organization Members* 150 • *Individual Members* 1,000

Mission To develop and support research, education, and conservation programs in the Elkhorn Slough wetlands and watershed, and promote sound resource management in the Central Coast of California.

Annual Fees	Regular	Student/Senior	Families
	$15 to 25	$10	$35

Other Fees *Lifetime* $400

Funding	Membership	Government Support	Foundations	Sales, Activities & Other
	5.5%	57.9%	12.6%	24%

Total Income $244,994

Usage	Administration	Fundraising	Programs	Support
	10%	2%	81%	7%

Total Expenses $244,000

Programs Research on erosion/sedimentation in wetlands. Habitat restoration of degraded uplands. School programs. Exhibit design. Media relations.

Publications Newsletter published three times per year. Two books published. Pamphlets, media spots and scientific publications

For more Information Database, Library, List of Publications

Who's Who PRESIDENT **ANNE FRASSETTE** • VICE PRESIDENT **JIM VAN HOUTEN** • SECRETARY **DIANE COOLEY** • TREASURER **WILL SMITH** • EXECUTIVE DIRECTOR **MARK SILBERSTEIN**

ENVIRONMENTAL DEFENSE FUND
PAGE 21
257 PARK AVENUE, SOUTH   NEW YORK NY 10010
PHONE (212) 505 2100   FAX (212) 505 2375

FRIENDS OF THE EVERGLADES
101 WESTWARD DRIVE, OFFICE 2   MIAMI SPRINGS FL 33166
PHONE (305) 888 1230

Founded 1969 • *Geographic Coverage* Local • *Other Field of Focus* National Parks - Land Use / Conservation / Acquisition *Cooperative Partner* National Everglades Coalition • *Chapter* 1 *Organization Members* 50 • *Individual Members* 5,000

Mission To promote harmony between people and the natural environment, and to work for the protection and restoration of the Everglades as a laboratory for that coexistence.

Annual Fees	Regular	Organization
	$1	$25

Funding	Membership	Corporations	Foundations
	15%	10%	75%

Total Income $23,000

Usage	Administration	Fundraising	Programs
	10%	2%	88%

Total Expenses $23,000

Programs The Joan and Hy Rosner Environmental Education Project. The Dade TOXICS Project. The Environmental Information Service. Environmental Leaders Roundtable. Safe Energy Committee. Everglades Mercury Project. Environet. Ongoing programs on Everglades repair, wetlands protection, drinking water and groundwater protection, wildlife habitat restoration, public lands protection, coral reefs, hurricane debris, recycling and water pollution abatement.

Publications Newsletter *Everglades Reporter* published whenever possible. Books *The Nature of Dade County, A Hometown Handbook* (Spanish version is available) • *The Dade County Environmental Story* • *Lake Okeechobee: A Lake in Peril* • *Who Knows The Rain? Nature and Origin of Rainfall in South Florida* • *The Book of Twelve for South Florida Gardens*

For more Information Database, Library, List of Publications

Who's Who PRESIDENT **NANCY CARROLL BROWN** • VICE PRESIDENT **JOETTE LORION** SECRETARY **SHARYN RICHARDSON** • TREASURER **JOYCE FLANAGAN** • EXECUTIVE DIRECTOR **JOE PODGOR** • DIRECTORS **SANDE HAYNES, MABEL MILLER, HY ROSNER, JOAN ROSNER, JIM WELLINGTON**

GLACIER INSTITUTE (THE)
PAGE 89
P.O. BOX 7457
KALISPELL MT 59904
PHONE (406) 756 3837

GRAND CANYON TRUST
PAGE 109
THE HOMESTEAD, ROUTE 4, BOX 718
FLAGSTAFF AZ 86001
PHONE (602) 774 7488
FAX (602) 774 7570

GREAT LAKES UNITED
STATE UNIVERSITY COLLEGE AT BUFFALO
CASSETY HALL, 1300 ELMWOOD AVENUE
BUFFALO NY 14222
PHONE (716) 886 0142

Founded 1982 • *Geographic Coverage* North America • *Focused Region* Great Lakes, St. Lawrence River Basin • *Other Field of Focus* Natural Resources / Water - Conservation & Quality • *Chapter* 1, in Canada • *Organization Members* 195 • *Individual Members* 10,000

Mission To work for the restoration, conservation and protection of the Great Lakes - St. Lawrence River Basin ecosystem by serving as an information exchange and forum to support groups working on this issue.

Annual Fees	Regular	Organization
	$20	$100

Funding	Membership	Foundations	Other
	90%	5%	5%

Total Income $248,451

Usage	Administration	Fundraising	Programs	Other
	19%	1%	77%	3%

Total Expenses $295,889

Programs At annual meeting, adopts resolutions on issues of water quality, hazardous and toxic substances, atmospheric deposition, regulation of levels and flows, fish and wildlife management, energy development and distribution, land quality and land use practices, navigation issues, and public support for Great Lakes ecosystem research, education, and management. The organization's representatives attempt to participate in policy formation and implementation around these issues.

Publications Quarterly newsletter *The Great Lakes United*. Quarterly *Bulletin of Pollution Prevention* . Numerous publications focusing on restoration, conservation and preservation of the Great Lakes and St. Lawrence River Basin ecosystem

For more Information Annual Report, List of Publications

Who's Who PRESIDENT **DICK KUBIAK** • VICE PRESIDENT **SARAH MILLER** • SECRETARY **DORREEN CAREY** • TREASURERS **JEANNE JABANOSKI, FRED L. BROWN** • EXECUTIVE DIRECTOR **TERRY YONKER** • CONTACT **ROBERT WAPPMAN**

GREATER ECOSYSTEM ALLIANCE
P.O. BOX 2813
BELLINGHAM WA 98227
PHONE (206) 671 9950
FAX (206) 671 8429

Founded 1988 • *Geographic Coverage* Regional • *Focused Region* Washington state, British Columbia • *Organization Members* 25 *Individual Members* 500

Mission To protect wilderness and diversity in areas of Washington state and lower British Columbia, by focusing on large natural areas, particularly watersheds and greater ecosystems (e.g., the Greater North Cascades Ecosystem) with a program of research, education, litigation, and legislation.

Annual Fees	Regular	Student/Senior
	$25	$15

Other Fees *Lifetime* $200

Funding	Membership	Foundations	Other
	20%	70%	10%

Total Income $100,000

Usage	Administration	Fundraising	Programs
	25%	10%	65%

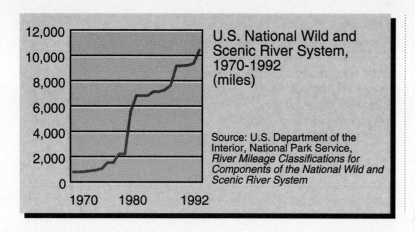

U.S. National Wild and Scenic River System, 1970-1992 (miles)

Source: U.S. Department of the Interior, National Park Service, *River Mileage Classifications for Components of the National Wild and Scenic River System*

▶ and 24 percent of the planet's remaining wetlands. However, with one acre of wilderness disappearing every 15 seconds, Canada cannot create new marine and national and provincial parks, ecological reserves, wildlife management areas, and migratory bird sanctuaries fast enough.

Fewer than 10 percent of Canada's 434 unique natural regions and ecosystems are represented among the parks and protected areas.

The Canadian Council of Ministers of the Environment approved an action plan linking preservation of biodiversity to sustainable human settlements. Canada's Green Plan makes natural ecosystems and protected areas integral components of sustainable development ▶

Programs Regional Biodiversity Initiative. North Cascades International Parks/Greater North Cascades Ecosystem. Works for grizzly bear recovery, lynx protection, ancient forest protection.

Publications Quarterly journals *NorthWest Conservation* • *News & Priorities*. Book *Cascadia Wild*

Multimedia Video *The Biodiversity Revolution*

Who's Who PRESIDENT **PAULA SWEDEEN** • VICE PRESIDENT **GREG MILLS** SECRETARY **GEORGE DRAFFAN** • EXECUTIVE DIRECTOR **MITCH FRIEDMAN** OTHER **MICHELLE SPANGBERG, LILIAN FORD, VALERIE THOMPSON, WILLIAM B. HENKEL**

GREATER YELLOWSTONE COALITION

P.O. BOX 1874 BOZEMAN MT 59771
PHONE (406) 586 1593 FAX (406) 586 0851

Founded 1983 • *Geographic Coverage* Regional • *Other Field of Focus* National Parks - Land Use / Conservation / Acquisition *Chapter* 1 • *Organization Members* 90 • *Individual Members* 4,800

Mission To preserve and protect the Greater Yellowstone Ecosystem and the quality of life it sustains, by working to ensure the successful blending of wildland protection and sustainable development. The organization's mission includes the preservation of wildlife, maintenance of biodiversity, geothermal protection, ecosystem management, wildland protection, watershed protection, development of national parks, and mitigation of hardrock mining. Threatened and endangered species such as the grizzly bear and the bald eagle are of special concern.

Annual Fees	Regular	Student/Senior	Organization	Supporting
	$25	$15	$25 to 50	$50

Other Fees *Sustaining* $150 • *Contributing* $300 • *Patron* $500 *Donor* $1,000

Funding	Membership	Corporations	Foundations	Annual Meeting, Interest & Other
	45%	2%	50%	3%

Total Income $747,544

Usage	Administration	Fundraising	Programs
	14%	14%	72%

Total Expenses $742,968

Programs The majority of the organization's yearly program plan is committed to saving habitat for endangered species such as grizzly bears, bald eagles, whooping cranes, and other wildlife. Legislative campaigns. Limited internship program.

Publications Quarterly journal *Greater Yellowstone Report*. *EcoAction* alerts. Brochure *Inside Greater Yellowstone*. Book *Environmental Profile of the Greater Yellowstone Ecosystem*. Report *Sustaining Greater Yellowstone: A Blueprint for the Future*

For more Information Annual Report

Who's Who PRESIDENT **GRETCHEN LONG GLICKMAN** • VICE PRESIDENT **LAMAR EMPEY** • SECRETARY **ALBERT ANDREWS, JR.** • EXECUTIVE DIRECTOR **ED LEWIS** • PROGRAM DIRECTOR **LOUISA WILCOX** • COMMUNICATIONS ASSOCIATE **BOB EKEY** • MEMBERSHIP AND DEVELOPMENT DIRECTOR **KEN BARRETT** • ASSOCIATE PROGRAM DIRECTORS **JEANNE-MARIE SOUVIGNEY, BART KOEHLER** • OTHER **DENNIS GLICK, LANG SMITH, BERT HARTING** • CONTACT **VALORIE DRAKE**

GREENPEACE, INC. PAGE 23

1436 "U" STREET, NW WASHINGTON DC 20009
PHONE (202) 462 1177 FAX (202) 462 4507

HUBBS • SEA WORLD RESEARCH INSTITUTE

1700 SOUTH SHORES ROAD SAN DIEGO CA 92109
PHONE (619) 226 3870 FAX (619) 226 3944

Founded 1963 • *Geographic Coverage* Global • *Other Field of Focus* Natural Resources / Water - Conservation & Quality • *Organization Members* 10 • *Individual Members* 120

Mission To study the world's biota and natural resources, with emphasis on marine and coastal environments. The Institute's fields of expertise include aquaculture, bioacoustics physiology, conservation biology (Leatherback Sea Turtles), and marine mammal studies.

Annual Fees *Regular* $25

Funding	Grants for Individual Products	Membership	Foundations	Other
	80%	3%	3%	14%

Usage	Administration	Fundraising	Programs	Other
	15%	5%	50%	30%

Who's Who VICE PRESIDENT DON KENT • EXECUTIVE DIRECTOR FRANK A. POWELL, JR. RESEARCH COORDINATOR PAMELA K. YOCHEM • CONTACT KATY KOSTER

INTERNATIONAL MOUNTAIN SOCIETY

P.O. BOX 1978	DAVIS CA 95617
PHONE (916) 752 8330	FAX (916) 752 9592

Founded 1980 • *Geographic Coverage* Global • *Cooperative Partners* United Nations University, IUCN The World Conservation Union, International Geographical Union • *Organization Members* 600 *Individual Members* 500

Mission To protect mountain environments the world over, by networking with natural scientists, social scientists and development institutions.

Annual Fees	Regular	Student/Senior	Organization
	$36	$22	$76

Publication Quarterly scholarly journal *Mountain Research & Development*

For more Information List of Publications

Who's Who PRESIDENT JACK D. IVES • VICE PRESIDENT BRUNO MESSERLI • SECRETARY ROGER BARRY • EDITOR PAULINE IVES

INTERNATIONAL SOCIETY FOR THE PRESERVATION OF THE TROPICAL RAINFOREST (THE)   PAGE 78

3931 CAMINO DE LA CUMBRE	SHERMAN OAKS CA 91423
PHONE (818) 788 2002	FAX (818) 990 3333

JESSIE SMITH NOYES FOUNDATION

16 EAST 34TH STREET, 22ND FLOOR	NEW YORK NY 10016
PHONE (212) 989 4369	FAX (212) 689 6549

Founded 1947 • *Geographic Coverage* Regional

Mission To prevent irreversible damage to the natural systems upon which all life depends, and strengthen individuals and institutions committed to protecting natural systems and ensuring a sustainable society.

Funding *Endowment* 100%

Total Income $3,983,228

Usage	Administration	Grants Paid
	15%	85%

Total Expenses $4,431,489

Programs Makes grants primarily in areas of environment and population. Components of the program are Water and Toxics, Sustainable Agriculture, and Population and Reproductive Rights.

Publication Guidelines brochure

For more Information Annual Report

Who's Who CHAIR NICHOLAS JACANGELO • PRESIDENT STEPHEN VIEDERMAN TREASURER EDWARD TASCH • PROGRAM OFFICERS JAMIE FELLNER, VICTOR DE LUCA, JAEL SILLIMAN

LEAGUE TO SAVE LAKE TAHOE (THE)   PAGE 113

989 TAHOE KEYS BOULEVARD, SUITE 6	SOUTH LAKE TAHOE CA 96150
PHONE (916) 541 5388	FAX (916) 541 5454

LIGHTHAWK

P.O. BOX 8163	SANTA FE NM 87504-8163
PHONE (505) 982 9656	FAX (505) 984 8381

Founded 1979 • *Geographic Coverage* North America, Central and South America • *Other Field of Focus* Forest Conservation / Deforestation / Reforestation • *Cooperative Partners* Since its inception, LightHawk has flown almost 300 different conservation and citizen's groups from Alaska to Central and South America • *Chapters* 3 *Organization Members* 100 • *Individual Members* 3,500

Mission To bring the power of flight to conservation programs and to design and carry out creative environmental campaigns. The concept behind LightHawk is both straightforward and visionary: if more people could fly and see mankind's abuses of the land, better awareness and land management decisions would likely follow.

Annual Fees	Regular	Student/Senior	Supporting
	$35	$25	$100

Other Fees *Flight Member* $500 • *President's Flight Member* $1,000

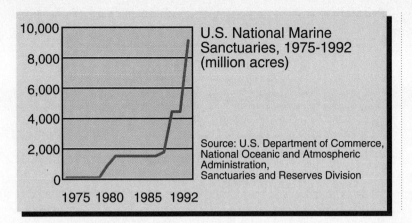

U.S. National Marine Sanctuaries, 1975-1992 (million acres)

Source: U.S. Department of Commerce, National Oceanic and Atmospheric Administration, Sanctuaries and Reserves Division

strategies.

In the United States, economic development and private-property rights often clash with the Endangered Species Act and ecosystem protection efforts. The National Biological Survey to inventory species exemplifies the slow and deliberate US approach to ecosystem protection. Nonetheless, it is now clearly evident that humans control the fate of other species. How we manage our ecosystems today will determine our planet's future. It is hoped that decision makers will make their determinations based on studies and appreciation of species, gene pools, ecosystems and the benefits of biodiversity. •

Joel Grossman

Funding

Membership	Foundations	Other
43%	55%	2%

Total Income $1,654,636

Usage

Administration	Fundraising	Programs
7%	3.8%	89.2%

Total Expenses $1,618,995

Programs LightHawk flies members of Congress, leaders from partner conservation groups, media representatives, business leaders and scientists over and into endangered forests, to see firsthand the lands and practices in question, in the belief that attitudes, and thus decisions, can change quickly once the problem is clearly seen in what LightHawk refers to as "conversion experiences". Policy reform for public lands. Scientific research programs. Protected areas planning and management in Latin America.

Publication Quarterly newsletter *LightHawk, The Environmental Air Force*

For more Information Database, Library

Who's Who President **William Parish** • Vice President **Joan Bavaria** • Secretary **Richard Barn** • Treasurer **Jim Roush** • Executive Director **Robert Harrill** Librarian **Julia Bergen** • Contact **Diana Stephens**

MANOMET BIRD OBSERVATORY

P.O. Box 1770
Phone (508) 224 6521

Manomet MA 02345
Fax (508) 224 9220

Founded 1969 • *Geographic Coverage* Global • *Other Field of Focus* Wildlife - Animal & Plant

Mission To conserve and manage natural systems throughout the Americas for the benefit of wildlife and human populations; to conserve bird diversity and natural habitats; to improve management of marine resources; to promote stewardship of coastal and wetland habitats; to foster sustainable use of tropical and temperate forests; and to train and educate environmental resource managers, science teachers, and students.

Annual Fees

Regular	Student/Senior	Supporting	Sustaining
$25	$15	$50	$100

Other Fees *Benefactor* $250 • *Special Friend* $500 • *Manomet Associate* $1,000

Total Income $1,933,911

Total Expenses $1,912,074

Programs The Observatory has a number of research programs, including terrestrial programs, wetlands programs, marine programs and endangered species programs. It also offers a number of educational programs, including a field biology program for graduate students, and an environmental education program to improve science education in schools. The organization's Birder's Exchange Program provides basic research equipment to groups involved in identifying and protecting bird habitats.

Publication Periodical *MBO Quarterly*

For more Information Annual Report, Library

Who's Who President **William S. Brewster** • Vice President **Mrs. Jeptha H. Wade** • Secretary **Anne Gamble** • Treasurer **Hanson C. Robbins** • Director of Development **Karen A. Haglof**

MARINE FORESTS SOCIETY

P.O. Box 5843
Phone (714) 675 7729

Balboa Island CA 92662

Founded 1986 • *Geographic Coverage* California, France • *Other*

50

Field of Focus Forest Conservation / Deforestation / Reforestation
Organization Members 600

Mission To demonstrate the potential of marine sciences and technologies to develop life in the sea, replacing losses in terrestrial biomass, through the plantation of underwater forests for the enhancement of the sea.

Annual Fees *Regular* $25

Funding	*Foundations*	*Other*
	95%	5%

Total Income $45,000

Usage	*Administration*	*Fundraising*	*Programs*
	25%	3%	72%

Programs Local groups of volunteer divers have started the plantation of 50 marine forests.

Publication *The Marine Foresters Journal*

Who's Who   PRESIDENT **RODOLPHE STREICHENBERGER** • VICE PRESIDENT **ROY LAY**
SECRETARY **RANDOLPH BROWN**

MONO LAKE COMMITTEE   PAGE 114
P.O. BOX 29   LEE VINING CA 93541
PHONE (619) 647 6595

NATIONAL AUDUBON SOCIETY (THE)
700 BROADWAY   NEW YORK NY 10003-9562
PHONE (212) 979 3000   FAX (212) 979 3188

Founded 1886 • *Geographic Coverage* National, Global • *Other Field of Focus* Wildlife - Animal & Plant • *Chapters* 13 • *Individual Members* 600,000

Mission To conserve and restore natural ecosystems, focusing on birds and other wildlife for the benefit of humanity and the earth's biological diversity.

Annual Fees *Regular* $35

Funding	*Membership*	*Foundations*	*Earned Income & Interest*
	26%	39%	27.6%

Other Sources *Sale of investments* 4.8% • *Royalties* 2.6%

Total Income $43,814,989

Usage	*Administration*	*Fundraising*	*Programs*	*Membership Development*
	9%	10%	70%	11%

Total Expenses $43,460,191

Programs Protecting the Arctic National Wildlife Refuge from oil development. Assisting concerned citizens to protect wetlands in their communities. Mapping the ancient forests of the Pacific Northwest and lobbying for legislation that will create an ancient forest reserve system. Fighting water developments on the Platte River that would disrupt river flows and endanger wildlife. Fighting for a strengthened Endangered Species Act. Protecting important habitat for migratory birds. Solving the country's solid waste crisis. Lobbying for population policies that recognize the limits of natural resources. A campaign to encourage utilities to switch to solar energy. Improving the environment of the Everglades ecosystem.

Publications Bimonthly magazine *Audubon*, circulation 481,000. Book *Familiar Birds of North America*. Activist tool kits. Brochures

Multimedia Slide shows featuring Audubon's High Priority Campaigns. Video *The Endangered Species Act: A Commitment Worth Keeping* (8 min.)

For more Information Annual Report, Database, Library

Who's Who   PRESIDENT **PETER A. BERLE** • VICE PRESIDENT **MARY JOY BRETON**
VICE PRESIDENT EDUCATION **MARSHAL T. CASE** • VICE PRESIDENT PUBLIC AFFAIRS **GRAHAM COX** • VICE PRESIDENT SCIENCE INFORMATION **SUSAN RONEY DRENNAN** • VICE PRESIDENT PLANNING AND DEVELOPMENT **SUSAN PARKER MARTIN**
VICE PRESIDENT MEMBERSHIP **ASA ORSINO** • VICE PRESIDENT PUBLICATIONS **MICHAEL W. ROBBINS**

NATIONAL SPELEOLOGICAL SOCIETY, INC.   PAGE 278
2813 CAVE AVENUE   HUNTSVILLE AL 35810-4431
PHONE (205) 852 1300   FAX (205) 851 9241

NATIONAL WILDLIFE FEDERATION   PAGE 144
1400 16TH STREET, NW   WASHINGTON DC 20036
PHONE (202) 797 6800   FAX (202) 797 6646

NATURE CONSERVANCY (THE)   PAGE 94
1815 NORTH LYNN STREET   ARLINGTON VA 22209
PHONE (703) 841 5300

NEW JERSEY AUDUBON SOCIETY   PAGE 145
P.O. BOX 125, 790 EWING AVENUE   FRANKLIN LAKES NJ 07417-9982
PHONE (201) 891 1211

NORTHERN ALASKA ENVIRONMENTAL CENTER
218 DRIVEWAY   FAIRBANKS AK 99701
PHONE (907) 452 5021   FAX (907) 452 3100

Founded 1971 • *Geographic Coverage* State, Regional • *Other Field of Focus* Natural Resources / Water - Conservation & Quality

Individual Members 1,100

Mission To promote the preservation and sound management of interior and Arctic Alaska, a vast area of streams and rivers, 3,200 miles of coastline, and 293,000 square miles of largely pristine lands. The Center monitors industry's impact on the environment and reviews environmental regulations and environmental impact statements. Mining, forestry, and oil field development are the organization's main areas of concern.

Annual Fees	*Regular*	*Student/Senior*	*Families*	*Donor*	*Friend*
	$30	$25	$35	$100	$250

Other Fees *Corporation* $300 • *Lifetime* $1,200

Funding	*Membership*	*Foundations*	*Other*
	10%	71%	19%

Usage	*Administration*	*Fundraising*	*Programs*
	12%	12%	75%

Programs The Center operates Camp Habitat, an environmental summer day camp for kids. It also offers unpaid internships throughout the year.

Publications Quarterly journal *The Northern Line*. Special reports, and action alerts

Who's Who PRESIDENT **JUNE WEINSTOCK** • VICE PRESIDENT **CARL ROSENBERG**

PROGRAMME FOR BELIZE
C/O MASSACHUSETTS AUDUBON SOCIETY

208 SOUTH GREAT ROAD   LINCOLN MA 01773
PHONE (617) 259 9500

Founded 1987 • *Geographic Coverage* Central America • *Other Field of Focus* Natural Resources / Water - Conservation & Quality *Cooperative Partners* Massachusetts Audubon Society, The Nature Conservancy International Program

Mission The program was established when the government of Belize invited conservation organizations to participate in the country's efforts at linking development and conservation in satisfactory and efficient ways. The program carries out research projects designed to investigate the system of biodiversity and the thoughtful use of natural resources. All funds are devoted to the purchase and protection of property in northwestern Belize.

Publication Semiannual newsletter

Who's Who PRESIDENT **JAMES HYDE** • EXECUTIVE DIRECTOR **MRS. A. JOY GRANT**

PROJECT REEFKEEPER

2809 BIRD AVENUE, SUITE 162   MIAMI FL 33133
PHONE (305) 858 4980   FAX (305) 858 4980

Founded 1988 • *Geographic Coverage* North America, Middle East, Pacific, Southeast Asia • *Focused Regions* Coral reef areas the world over • *Other Field of Focus* Natural Resources / Water - Conservation & Quality • *Cooperative Partner* American Littoral Society *Chapters* 3, in Puerto Rico, Hawaii, and Mexico

Mission To protect coral habitats and preserve their biological diversity, by providing a comprehensive program of coral reef environmental protection through policy analysis, grassroots organization, public awareness, agency monitoring, and issue advocacy.

Annual Fees	*Regular*	*Organization*	*Corporation*
	$25	Free	$100+

Other Fees *Reef Friend* $100 • *Reef Sponsor* $250 • *Reef Guardian* $500 • *Reef Champion* $1,000

Funding	*Membership*	*Corporations*	*Grants*
	14%	3%	83%

Total Income $144,000

Usage	*Administration*	*Fundraising*	*Programs*
	10%	10%	80%

Total Expenses $144,000

Programs The Project has created coral reef protected areas in Texas, Florida, Hawaii, Puerto Rico, Japan, Thailand, Jamaica, and the US Virgin Islands. It has worked for offshore oil leasing exclusions for coral reef areas in the Florida Straits, Gulf of Mexico, and US Caribbean. Wir mesh fish trap ban - Florida, Texas, US Virgin Islands. Coral habitat protection from dredging and beach renourishment smothering - Florida, Hawaii, St. Lucia. Coral collection prohibition - Puerto Rico, US Virgin Islands, Jamaica, Malaysia, Thailand. Nutrient pollution reduction - Florida, Puerto Rico, Hawaii.

Publications Quarterly newsletter *Reef Alert!*. Bimonthly journal *Reef-Keeper Report*. Books including *Public Recommendations for Development of a Management Plan for the Florida Keys National Marine Sanctuary* - Vol. I & Vol. II • *Public Recommendations for Biological Resources Management in the Florida Keys National Marine Sanctuary* • *The Case for Marine Fisheries Reserves in Fisheries Management: Executive Digest* • *Nominating Coral Reef National Marine Sanctuaries*

For more Information Annual Report, Database, Library, List of Publications

Who's Who SECRETARY **LADISLAO DURANZA** • TREASURER **KATHRYN ARBUTHNOT** EXECUTIVE DIRECTOR **ALEXANDER STONE** • CONTACT **SANDY WENZEL**

RARE CENTER FOR TROPICAL CONSERVATION

1529 WALNUT STREET   PHILADELPHIA PA 19102
PHONE (215) 568 0420   FAX (215) 568 0516

Founded 1973 • *Geographic Coverage* Central America • *Focused Region* The Caribbean • *Individual Members* 1,800

Mission To develop and implement innovative programs that protect endangered tropical habitats and ecosystems. These programs are developed by RARE Center's staff and volunteer board of trustees, which includes conservationists, scientists, and business people with broad experience in tropical America. Programs are always implemented in partnership with government agencies and conservation groups in host countries.

Annual Fees *Regular* $30

Total Income $454,829

Usage	Administration	Fundraising	Programs
	17%	8%	75%

Total Expenses $449,872

Programs Conservation education programs work to change attitudes by appealing to national pride, reaching people through the endangered national bird whose survival depends primarily upon habitat protection. Conservation Biology Program helps Latin American conservationists compile data to evaluate existing nature reserves and enhance their protection. Forest Fragment Conservation.

Publications Quarterly newsletter *RARE Center News*. Materials for distribution to the organization's programs in the Caribbean and Central America

Multimedia Computerized Mapping System *CAMRIS* helps local organizations display data on migration patterns and habitat distribution in a way that clearly shows decision makers how they can protect biological resources

For more Information Annual Report

Who's Who PRESIDENT **ROGER F. PASQUIER** • VICE PRESIDENT **JOHN E. EARHART** SECRETARY **JAMES PLYLER** • TREASURER **OWEN P. MCCAFFREY** • EXECUTIVE DIRECTOR **JOHN GUARNACCIA** • DIRECTOR OF ADMINISTRATION AND MEMBERSHIP **CHRISTINE A. PSOMIADES**

REEF RELIEF

P.O. BOX 430   KEY WEST FL 33041
PHONE (305) 294 3100   FAX (305) 293 9515

Founded 1986 • *Geographic Coverage* Local • *Other Field of Focus* Natural Resources / Water - Conservation & Quality • *Cooperative Partner* Reef Relief Environmental Education Center

Mission To preserve and protect the living coral reef of the Florida Keys. Reef Relief supports educational and reef management programs essential to the continued vitality of this biologically diverse marine eco-system.

Annual Fees	Regular	Contributing	Sponsor
	$20	$100+	$500+

Programs Reef Relief designs and implements programs and materials to increase awareness of the importance of the living coral reef, installs and maintains reef mooring buoys for public use to eliminate the need to drop anchors on living coral, encourages regional water quality improvements to reduce pollution from sewage and agricultural run-off, supports a permanent moratorium on off-shore oil development in the Florida Keys and a national energy policy based on renewable energy.

Publications Quarterly newsletter *Reef Line*, circulation 5,000. Brochures *Reef Relief* • *Florida's Coral Reef Ecosystem*

For more Information Database, Library, List of Publications

Who's Who PRESIDENT **BRUCE ETSHMAN** • VICE PRESIDENT **WILLIAM KUYPERS** TREASURER **GARYANNE KIMBERLING** • EXECUTIVE DIRECTOR **DEEVON QUIROLO**

RIVER WATCH NETWORK   PAGE 119

153 STATE STREET   MONTPELIER VT 05602
PHONE (802) 223 3840   FAX (802) 223 6227

RIVERS COUNCIL OF WASHINGTON   PAGE 119

1731 WESTLAKE AVENUE, NORTH, SUITE 202   SEATTLE WA 98109-3043
PHONE (206) 283 4988

SAVE OUR SHORES

P.O. BOX 1560   SANTA CRUZ CA 95061
PHONE (408) 462 5660   FAX (408) 462 6070

Founded 1980 • *Geographic Coverage* Local • *Focused Region* Californian central coast • *Other Field of Focus* Natural Resources / Water - Conservation & Quality • *Cooperative Partners* Center for Marine Conservation, Friends of the Sea Otter • *Chapter* 1 • *Members* 1,400 including organizations

Mission Save Our Shores (SOS) is a grassroots marine conservation group dedicated to preserving the ecological heritage of California's central coast, particularly the Monterey Bay National Marine Sanctuary. The organization has led the effort to curtail and prohibit human activities which threatened the Californian coast, including defending California's coast from offshore oil drilling, and was instrumental in the designation of the Monterey Bay Marine Sanctuary.

Annual Fees	Regular	Student/Senior	Corporation	Associate	Sustaining
	$35	$15	$100	$100	$500

Other Fees *Lifetime* $1,000

Funding

	Membership	Government Support	Foundations
	18%	2%	80%

Total Income $59,140

Total Expenses $56,670

Programs Marine Sanctuary Watch, a citizen's watchdog program. Classroom Education Project, a slide show which travels to grades 6-12 throughout Santa Cruz County. Marine Fleet Program, an offshoot of sanctuary watch, reports sanctuary violations. SOS also trains volunteers to make educational presentations to the public and community groups about the marine environment and its protection. Additionally, SOS works with other environmental groups to inform the public about marine issues.

Publications Quarterly newsletter. Brochures and pamphlets

Multimedia Online information service 1-800-974-6737. Video *The Worlds Below*

For more Information Database

Who's Who PRESIDENT ANNE ROWLEY • TREASURER MICHAEL DELAPA • EXECUTIVE DIRECTOR VICKI NICHOLS • CONTACT LAURA MCSHANE

SCENIC HUDSON, INC.   PAGE 119
9 VASSAR STREET   POUGHKEEPSIE NY 12601
PHONE (914) 473 4440   FAX (914) 473 2648

SIERRA CLUB
730 POLK STREET   SAN FRANCISCO CA 94109
PHONE (415) 776 2211   FAX (415) 776 0369

Founded 1892 • *Geographic Coverage* North America, Global *Other Fields of Focus* Global Environmental Concerns, Natural Resources / Water - Conservation & Quality, Sustainable Development / Agriculture - Environmental Technologies • *Cooperative Partners* Sierra Club Legal Defense Fund, Sierra Club Political Committee, Sierra Club Foundation • *Chapters* 58, and 403 groups • *Individual Members* 570,000

Mission To promote conservation of the natural environment by influencing public policy decisions - legislative, administrative, legal and electoral. Sierra Club seeks to explore and protect the ecosystems of the earth, to educate and enlist the general public, to protect and restore the quality of the natural and human environment.

Annual Fees

Regular	Student/Senior	Supporting	Contributing
$35	$15	$50	$100

Other Fees *Lifetime* $750

Funding

Membership	Foundations	Book Sales	Advertising	Royalties
38.5%	32%	9.2%	8.2%	3.5%

Other Sources *Outings* 5.4% • *Reimbursements* 3.2%

Total Income $50,575,700

Usage

Administration	Fundraising	Programs	Membership Development
14%	11%	59.4%	15.6%

Total Expenses $52,183,000

Programs Works on hundreds of conservation issues - local, regional, national and international - but prioritizes national conservation campaigns in two-year cycles corresponding to the sessions of the US Congress. Great Lakes Ecosystem Program coordinates efforts in nine states and Canada to take a unified approach to the Great Lakes ecosystem. Florida Everglades' Protection Program focuses on the restoration of the Kissimmee River. Greater Yellowstone Program works to reintroduce wolves into the ecosystem and protect the habitat of the imperiled grizzly bear population. Critical Ecoregions Program works for the survival of endangered ecological regions throughout the United States and Canada. International and Population Programs with other NGOs to seek solutions to global problems such as ozone depletion, deforestation, and population pressures. Lobbying programs. A media team coordinates press conferences and media blitzes nationwide. Legal program. Political program evaluates candidates seeking office and makes endorsements based on their environmental record.

Publications Bimonthly magazine *Sierra*, circulation 500,000. *National News Report* published 24 times per year. Newsletters reporting local environmental news and Club events. 28 new books and 10 children's titles were published in 1991. The Fall 1991 list included *Hidden Dangers: Environmental Consequences of Preparing for War* • *Chemical Deception: The Toxic Threat to Health and the Environment* • *Olympic Battleground: The Power Politics of Timber Preservation* • *Amazonia*

For more Information Annual Report, Database, Library, List of Publications

Who's Who PRESIDENT PHILLIP BERRY • VICE PRESIDENT EDGAR WAYBURN • SECRETARY ANTHONY RUCKEL • TREASURER ANN POGUE • EXECUTIVE DIRECTOR MICHAEL FISCHER • DIRECTOR OF PUBLIC AFFAIRS JOANNE HURLEY • EDITOR-IN-CHIEF SIERRA MAGAZINE JONATHAN KING

SIERRA CLUB SOUTHWEST   PAGE 120
515 EAST PORTLAND STREET   PHOENIX AZ 85004
PHONE (602) 254 9330   FAX (602) 258 6533

SOCIETY FOR ECOLOGICAL RESTORATION (THE)
1207 SEMINOLE HIGHWAY   MADISON WI 53711
PHONE (608) 262 9547   FAX (608) 262 9547

Founded 1987 • *Geographic Coverage* Global • *Cooperative Part-*

ners UW Arboretum, The Nature Conservancy, Center for Plant Conservation of St. Louis • *Chapters* 4 • *Organization Members* 100 *Individual Members* 1,800

Mission To facilitate communication among restorationists, encourage research into restoration, promote awareness of the value of restoration, contribute to public policy discussions related to restoration, develop public support for restoration and restorative management, and recognize those who have made outstanding contributions to restoration. The Society is an international membership organization of professionals and others engaged or interested in the repair and ecologically sensitive management of ecosystems.

Annual Fees	*Regular*	*Student/Senior*	*Organization*	*Contributing*	*Sustaining*
	$64	$54	$160	$160	$250

Funding	*Membership*	*Corporations*	*Foundations*	*Conferences*
	47%	13%	1%	39%

Total Income $219,130

Usage	*Administration*	*Fundraising*	*Programs*
	19%	11%	70%

Total Expenses $214,271

Programs Yearly conference (two in 1992). Various symposia by the Society for Ecological Restoration Central and its chapters.

Publications Quarterly newsletter *SER News*. Quarterly peer reviewed scientific journal *Restoration Ecology*. Semiannual *Restoration and Management Notes*, published by the University of Wisconsin Press and distributed to SER members by special arrangements

Multimedia Conference audiotapes

For more Information Database, List of Publications

Who's Who PRESIDENT ANDRE CLEWELL • VICE PRESIDENT NIKITA LOPOUKHINE SECRETARY JOHN RODMAN • TREASURER WILLIAM HALVORSON • EXECUTIVE DIRECTOR DONALD FALK • LIBRARIAN ROBIN KURZER

SOUTH SLOUGH NATIONAL ESTUARINE RESERVE

P.O. BOX 5417   CHARLESTON OR 97420
PHONE (503) 888 5558

Founded 1974 • *Geographic Coverage* Regional • *Focused Region* Washington state, Oregon, California • *Other Field of Focus* Natural Resources / Water - Conservation & Quality • *Cooperative Partners* Friends of South Slough Reserve, National Estuarine Research Reserve System

Mission To promote awareness about the ecological and economic values of estuaries, through an integrated program of research and education about estuaries from the Washington coast to Northern California.

Annual Fees	*Regular*	*Student/Senior*	*Families*	*Corporate Sponsor*
	$15	$10	$25	$500

Other Fees *Lifetime* $250

Programs Education (Interpretive Center, guided walks along the trails, field trips, workshops). Research (ongoing monitoring of the estuary's biological and ecological components, field laboratory). Recreation. Stewardship. Volunteers. Non-profit friends group. The South Slough Estuary Study Program.

Multimedia Slide shows and film presentations

THRESHOLD, INC.
INTERNATIONAL CENTER FOR ENVIRONMENTAL RENEWAL
DRAWER CU   BISBEE AZ 85603
PHONE (602) 432 7353

Founded 1972 • *Geographic Coverage* Africa, Asia, Latin America, Pacific Basin • *Chapters* 4

Mission Threshold's Environmental Crisis Fund is designed to dispatch fund quickly and directly to projects, preferably those formed by local environmental action and study groups, which seek to protect critically-endangered ecosystems. The organization also emphasizes building coalitions of like minded groups to resolve environmental issues.

Annual Fees	*Regular*	*Supporting*	*Patron*
	$25 to 75	$100 to 300	$500

Programs Asian, African, Pacific Basin and Latin American tropical forest protection. Pesticide spraying in Third World countries. Coastal, Estuarine and Coral Reef Ecosystems Conservation. Temperate, Rainforests, and Redwoods Conservation. Acid Rain Reduction. Elimination of Ocean Pollution. Wilderness and Natural Area Protection. Currently starting Eco-Action Training & Geography-of-Hope Programs. Works to disseminate information on the global environmental crisis through all available media.

Multimedia Asian tropical forest video *Seeds of Hope*

Who's Who CHAIR JOHN P. MILTON • VICE CHAIR GEORGE A. BINNEY • ADMINISTRATIVE OFFICER CADO DAILY • PROGRAM DEVELOPMENT COORDINATOR DEBORA JOY ELLIOTT

UPPER MISSISSIPPI RIVER CONSERVATION COMMITTEE

4469 48TH AVENUE COURT   ROCK ISLAND IL 61201
PHONE (309) 793 5800

Founded 1943 • *Geographic Coverage* Regional • *Other Field of Focus* Natural Resources / Water - Conservation & Quality • *Individual Members* 200

Mission To promote the sound use and management of Upper Mississippi River natural resources. The Committee is concerned with human induced impacts (e.g., navigation) and the long-term health of the Upper Mississippi River ecosystem.

Funding *Government Support* 100%

Programs Ongoing activities in the areas of fish, wildlife, recreation, water quality and law enforcement.

Publications Bimonthly newsletter *UMRCC*. Proceedings of annual meeting

Who's Who PRESIDENT **BILL BERTRAND** • COORDINATOR **JON DUYVEJONUK**

WALDEN FOREVER WILD, INC.

P.O. BOX 275   CONCORD   MA   01742
PHONE (203) 429 2839

Founded 1980 • *Geographic Coverage* Local • *Other Field of Focus* Natural Resources / Water - Conservation & Quality

Mission To change the State Walden Pond Reservation from a swim-recreation park to a nature preserve-type sanctuary. The organization is concerned with forestry, ecology, and the degradation of the Walden Pond environment as witnessed in, for example, the erosion of paths from wrong use and abuse, or the destruction of natural plant life by careless visitors.

Annual Fees *Regular* $10

Programs Annual Walden Pond Bay Meeting at end of May. Currently suing the state of Massachusetts for wrong use and abuse of Walden.

Publications Quarterly newsletter *Voice of Walden*. Pamphlets including *Walden Facts* • *The Walden Loon* • *Henry David Thoreau: How Great a Son of Concord* • *Fish, Fishing and Scuba Studies at Walden* • *Use and Abuse of Walden* • *Walden Ecology*

Who's Who CHAIRMAN **MARY P. SHERWOOD** • TREASURER **SARAH CHAPIN**

WETLANDS PRESERVE

161 HUDSON STREET   NEW YORK   NY   10013
PHONE (212) 966 5244   FAX (212) 925 8715

Founded 1989 • *Geographic Coverage* National, Global • *Other Field of Focus* Natural Resources / Water - Conservation & Quality *Cooperative Partners* Earth First!, Earth Island Institute, Rainforest Action

Network, Save America's Forests • *Organization Members* 6 • *Individual Members* 250

Mission The organization is a grassroots support center dedicated to providing information on wetland issues.

Programs Direct Action Campaign, to stop government and corporate destruction of the earth's environment.

For more Information Database, Library

Who's Who EXECUTIVE DIRECTOR **JAMES HANSEN** • CONTACT **COLIN COOGAN**

WHITTIER AUDUBON SOCIETY   PAGE 152

6231 GREGORY AVENUE   WHITTIER   CA   90608-0548
PHONE (213) 691 9251

WILDERNESS SOCIETY (THE)   PAGE 97

900 17TH STREET, NW   WASHINGTON   DC   20006-2596
PHONE (202) 833 2300   FAX (202) 429 3958

WILDLIFE CONSERVATION SOCIETY (THE)   PAGE 153

C/O NEW YORK ZOOLOGICAL SOCIETY
185TH STREET & SOUTHERN BOULEVARD   BRONX   NY   10460
PHONE (212) 220 5100

WOODLANDS MOUNTAIN INSTITUTE

MAIN & DOGWOOD STREETS, P.O. BOX 907   FRANKLIN   WV   26807
PHONE (304) 358 2401

Founded 1972 • *Geographic Coverage* Regional, National, Global

Mission To advance mountain cultures and preserve mountain environments from an Appalachian and Himalayan base by promoting worldwide partnerships that create innovative and sustainable solutions to mountain problems.

Funding	*Foundations*	*Other*
	93%	7%

Total Income $1,432,289

Usage	*Administration*	*Fundraising*	*Programs*
	9%	2%	89%

Total Expenses $1,546,430

Programs Leadership Training Process for the state of Virginia. Community Schools. Mount Everest Ecosystem Conservation Program, which has recently opened two new nature preserves - the Makalu Barun Conservation Project in Nepal and the Qomolangma Nature Preserve in China's Tibet Autonomous Region - demonstrating how local people can assume a management role in conservation.

Publications Various reports. Bookchapters

Who's Who PRESIDENT **D. JANE PRATT**

WORLD BIRD SANCTUARY

P.O. BOX 270270   ST. LOUIS MO 63127
PHONE (314) 938 6193   FAX (314) 938 9464

WORLD WILDLIFE FUND
PAGE 156

WWF
1250 24TH STREET, NW   WASHINGTON DC 20037-1175
PHONE (202) 293 4800   FAX (202) 293 9211

Canada

ALBERTA SPELEOLOGICAL SOCIETY
PAGE 281

BOX 2474   JASPER AB T0E 1E0
PHONE (403) 234 8829

ARCTIC INSTITUTE OF NORTH AMERICA (THE)
UNIVERSITY OF CALGARY
2500 UNIVERSITY DRIVE, NW   CALGARY AB T2N 1N4
PHONE (403) 220 7515   FAX (403) 282 4609

Founded 1945 • *Geographic Coverage* Regional • *Cooperative Partners* University of Calgary's Northern Students' Association, the Northern Studies Group • *Organization Members* 700 • *Individual Members* 1,500

Mission To advance the study of Canada's North through the natural and social sciences, as well as the arts and humanities; and to acquire, preserve and disseminate information on physical and social conditions in the North.

Annual Fees

	Regular	Student/Senior	Organization	Corporation
	$40	$25	$85	$2,000

Other Fees *Lifetime* $400

Funding

	Membership	Government Support	Corporations
	6.7%	29.7%	9%

Other Sources *University of Calgary* 20.5% • *Field stations & user fees* 9% • *Other* 25.1%

Total Income $1,512,035

Usage

	Administration	Programs
	24.7%	75.3%

Total Expenses $1,429,197

Programs The Institute's Research and Research Facilities Programme comprises field research stations, sponsored and supported research associates, northern fellowships, scholarships and grants, contributions to learned, public and private sector conferences. The Database Programme is organized within the Arctic Science and Technology Information system. The Networking Programme is designed to facilitate dialogue and co-operation between scholars and lay people.

Publications Quarterly journal *Arctic*. Quarterly newsletter *Information North*. Reports, conference proceedings. Komatik series of monographs including *Gathering Strength* • *Crossroads to Greenland: 3000 Years of Prehistory in the Eastern Arctic* • *Back from the Brink: The Road to Muskox Conservation in the Northwest Territories*

Multimedia The Arctic Science and Technology Information System is an automated database in which over 33,000 abstracts on the Canadian Arctic are easily accessible to the public through QL Systems Ltd. and National Information Services Corporation's *Arctic and Antarctic Regions* CD-ROM

For more Information Annual Report, Database, Library

Who's Who CHAIR **CYNTHIA C. HILL** • VICE CHAIR **RANDALL G. GOSSEN** EXECUTIVE DIRECTOR **MIKE ROBINSON** • ASSOCIATE DIRECTOR **GERALD J. THOMPSON**

CANADIAN ARCTIC RESOURCES COMMITTEE
1 NICHOLAS STREET, SUITE 412   OTTAWA ON K1N 7B7
PHONE (613) 236 7379   FAX (613) 232 4665

Founded 1971 • *Geographic Coverage* Regional • *Individual Members* 5,000

Mission To bring an independent and critical but constructive perspective to environmental, economic, constitutional, and other issues in the Canadian North. The Committee bridges the gap between North and South, between aboriginal and non-aboriginal communities, and works to build consensus around issues to facilitate change.

Annual Fees

	Student/Senior	Sustaining
	$15	$30

Other Fees *Lifetime* $500

Publications Quarterly journal *Northern Perspectives*. Books and monographs focusing on various environmental issues related to the Canadian North

For more Information List of Publications

Who's Who PRESIDENT **NIGEL BANKES** • VICE PRESIDENT **LINDSAY STAPLES** TREASURER **TOM YARMON** • EXECUTIVE DIRECTOR **TERRY FENGE**

GreenWorld's Almanac & Directory '94   Part One   **56**

CANADIAN CENTRE FOR BIODIVERSITY

CANADIAN MUSEUM OF NATURE

P.O. Box 3443, Station "D" Ottawa ON K1P 6P4
Phone (613) 990 8819 Fax (613) 990 8818

Founded 1991 • *Geographic Coverage* Global • *Individual Members* 1,000

Mission To discover and communicate knowledge about biodiversity on Earth.

Funding	Membership	Government Support	Corporations
	5%	90%	5%

Publications Quarterly bulletin *Global Biodiversity*. Book *Canada Country Study on Biodiversity*

For more Information Database, Library

Who's Who Senior Biodiversity Advisor **Don E. McAllister** • Program Officer **Noel Alfonso**

GREENPEACE CANADA

PAGE 31

185 Spadina Avenue, Suite 600 Toronto ON M5T 2C6
Phone (416) 435 8404 Fax (416) 345 8422

HUNTSMAN MARINE SCIENCE CENTRE

Brandy Cove Road St. Andrews NB E0G 2X0
Phone (506) 529 1200 Fax (506) 529 1212

Founded 1969 • *Geographic Coverage* National • *Other Field of Focus* Natural Resources / Water - Conservation & Quality • *Organization Members* 20 universities

Mission To enhance knowledge and provide the leadership necessary to achieve understanding and effective management of coastal environments, through a program of research and education.

Annual Fees	Regular	Families	Benefactor	Supporting Corporation
	$30	$50	$100	$500 to 1,999

Funding	Membership	Contracts & Grants	User Fees	Other
	8%	61%	23%	8%

Total Income $1,728,007

Usage	Administration	Programs
	38%	62%

Total Expenses $1,883,650

Programs The Centre operates a number of academic and research programs, including Summer field courses, a resident research program, a year-round visiting research program, a specimen supply service for researchers and educational institutions, a consulting service in the marine sciences, provision of facilities, and organization of workshops and conferences. Aquaculture Programme. The Atlantic Reference Centre, operated with the Department of Fisheries and Oceans, maintains and contributes new material to a historically significant and unique zoological/botanical museum collection of aquatic organisms. Public Education Programme.

Publications Quarterly newsletter *Huntsman Marine Science News*. Technical reports and books

For more Information Annual Report, Library

Who's Who President **Michael D. B. Burt** • Executive Director **John H. Allen**

OCEAN RESOURCE CONSERVATION ALLIANCE

ORCA

Box 1189 Sechelt BC V0N 3A0
Phone (604) 885 7518 Fax (604) 885 2518

Founded 1986 • *Geographic Coverage* Province, National, North America • *Focused Region* Western North America • *Other Field of Focus* Natural Resources / Water - Conservation & Quality • *Cooperative Partner* Marine Environmental Consortium • *Chapters* 2 *Individual Members* 335

Mission The Alliance focuses on research and information sharing about the environmental and socio-economic effects of the artificial rearing and manipulation of fish, with emphasis on its effects on wild salmon and other fish.

Annual Fees	Regular	Families
	$6	$10

Funding	Foundations	Travel Support from Government
	75%	25%

Total Income $9,000

Usage	Administration & Programs	Transportation
	75%	25%

Programs Scientific research.

For more Information Database, Library

Who's Who Executive Director **Teri Dawe**

OCEAN VOICE INTERNATIONAL, INC.

2883 Otterson Drive Ottawa ON K1V 7B2
Phone (613) 990 2207 Fax (613) 521 4205

Founded 1987 • *Geographic Coverage* Global • *Focused Countries*

The Philippines, Canada, Maldives, Indonesia • *Other Field of Focus* Natural Resources / Water - Conservation & Quality • *Cooperative Partners* IUCN The World Conservation Union, Haribon Foundation for Conservation of Natural Resources, Canadian Environmental Network, World Wildlife Fund, Indonesian Forestry Department, Canadian Wildlife Service, Canadian Museum of Nature, Le Centre de Données sur le Patrimoine Naturel du Québec - The Data Centre on the Natural Heritage of Québec • *Organization Members* 10 *Individual Members* 120

Mission To conserve the diversity of marine life, to protect and restore marine environments and enhance the quality of life and income of those who harvest marine resources, through a program which includes providing education, sponsoring and engaging in projects to train people to use environmentally sound marine resource harvesting methods, and sponsoring, engaging in, and sharing marine life research.

Annual Fees

Regular	Student/Senior	Families	Organization	Library
$25	$15	$30	$50	$50

Other Fees *Corporation* $250 • *Associate* $100 • *Sponsor* $1,000 *Patron* $3,000

Funding

Membership	Foundations	Donations & Publication Sales	Other
14%	61.5%	22%	2.5%

Total Income $58,196

Usage

Administration	Fundraising	Programs
11%	3%	86%

Total Expenses $39,369

Programs The Green School Checklist Programme evaluates how environmentally friendly the school activities and courses are. The Netsman Project assists in the training of aquarium fish collectors in the Philippines to use small environmentally friendly monofilament nets. The Guides to Selected Fishes of the Maldives Programme helps developing countries create, enhance or monitor ocean-based activities such as mariculture and fisheries. SSC Coral Reef Fish Specialist Group. Development of Coral Geographic Information Map, a new method used to compare and analyze sets of mapped geographic information.

Publications Quarterly bulletin *Sea Wind*. Books including *Shiraho Coral Reef and the New Ishigaki Island Airport, Japan* • *Guide to Selected Fishes of the Maldives* • *Rare Fishes of Québec*. Booklet *How Green Is Your School*

For more Information Database, Library

Who's Who PRESIDENT **DON E. MCALLISTER** • VICE PRESIDENT **GARY SPILLER** SECRETARY **NOEL ALFONSO** • EXECUTIVE DIRECTOR **PHYLLIS KOFMEL** • DIRECTORS **JAIME BAQUERO, ANDREW L. HAMILTON, JOANE LAUCIUS, ANGUS MCALLISTER, KERRY ANN SHEEHAN, MAXINE SUDOL**

ONTARIO SOCIETY FOR ENVIRONMENTAL MANAGEMENT

PAGE 299

136 WINGES ROAD, UNIT 15   WOODBRIDGE ON L4L 6C4
PHONE (905) 850 8066   FAX (905) 850 7313

RAWSON ACADEMY OF AQUATIC SCIENCE (THE)

1 NICHOLAS STREET, SUITE 404   OTTAWA ON K1N 7B7
PHONE (613) 563 2636   FAX (613) 533 4758

Founded 1978 • *Geographic Coverage* National • *Other Field of Focus* Natural Resources / Water - Conservation & Quality • *Cooperative Partners* Resources Future International, Inc., Environment Canada, Department of Fisheries and Oceans, National Round Table on Environment and Economy, Canadian Water and Wastewater Association *Organization Members* 300 • *Individual Members* 50

Mission To develop and promote policies and programs to protect Canada's aquatic ecosystems.

Annual Fees

Regular	Organization
$35	$160

Funding

Government Support	Corporations	Foundations	Other
55%	32%	8%	5%

Total Income $1,221,660 in 1991

Total Expenses $1,154,996 in 1991

Programs Numerous scientific, policy studies, and education/information programs including Hudson Bay/James Bay Bioregion Study, Mine Environment Neutral Drainage review, New Directions Group, and consulting for the Experimental Lakes Area facility of the Department of Fisheries and Oceans.

Publications Bimonthly *Canadian Water Watch*. Various papers series and reports including *Towards an Ecosystem Charter for the Great Lakes-St. Lawrence* • *Canadian Water Exports and Free Trade* • *Rafferty Alameda: An Assessment of the Agreement Between Canada and the United States for Water Supply and Flood Control in the Souris River Basin* • *Greenprint for Canada: A Federal Agenda for the Environment* • *An Economic Study of the Environment Laboratory Service Industry Sub-Sector in Canada*

For more Information Annual Report, Library, List of Publications

Who's Who PRESIDENT **DIXON THOMPSON** • DIRECTORS **RON WALLACE, MICHAEL HEALEY, PATRICIA LANE, TED HAMMER, MAXWELL COHEN** • LIBRARIAN **JAMIE LINTON**

WILDLIFE HABITAT CANADA

7 HINTON AVENUE, NORTH, SUITE 200   OTTAWA ON K1Y 4P1
PHONE (613) 722 2090   FAX (613) 722 3318

Founded 1984 • *Geographic Coverage* North America • *Other Field of Focus* Wildlife - Animal & Plant

Mission Dedicated to working with private citizens, governments, non-government organizations, and industry to protect, enhance and restore the great variety of habitats across Canada. The organization provides financial support for conservation and enhancement programs, communication and education projects, and research and graduate scholarship programs.

Funding

Habitat Conservation Stamp Programme	*Project Contributions*
87%	5.5%

Other Sources *Print & other program royalties* 4.5% • *Interest* 3%

Total Income $3,443,326

Usage

Administration	*Fundraising*	*Programs*	*Communications*
3.2%	5.7%	81.4%	9.7%

Total Expenses $3,354,996

Programs The organization's Conservation Projects include Agricultural Landscape, Coastal Landscape, Forested Landscape, Northern Landscape, and Urban Landscape. Provincial Conservation Initiatives. Habitat Conservation Stamp Programme.

Publications Various publications focusing on wildlife and habitat issues

For more Information Annual Report, Library

Who's Who PRESIDENT TOM BUELL • VICE PRESIDENT MERRILL PRIME • SECRETARY NESTOR ROMANIUK • EXECUTIVE DIRECTOR DAVID J. NEAVE • CONTACT DORIS GOODWIN

human rights & environment

CHAPTER 4

An Injustice Calling for Redress, by John Vargo

A PERVASIVE NOTION THROUGHOUT the world's environmental communities is that the creatures of the Earth have a birthright to live in a clean, unmolested habitat as nature intended.

The idea that all species exist within nature's rules of genetics and surroundings has matured into general acceptance since the 19th century when Charles Darwin first proposed it to a reluctant scientific community. Implicit in this understanding is that humans are also endowed with the same birthright.

The evolution of the 20th century has brought about unprecedented international concern by the industrialized nations for the basic rights of humans throughout the world. We implemented rules for war at the Geneva Convention and exercised them at Nuremberg. We instituted international relief efforts for victims of tragedy. We expressed outrage and put forth political measures in support of those unjustly jailed. The demonstration of our capacity to be moved by the horrors of our own creation suggests that we understand, deep within our moral composition, the most elemental of human rights.

Human beings, like any other creature on the planet, have the right to exist in a clean unmolested environment.

> ## The demonstration of our capacity to be moved *by the horrors of our own creation* suggests that we understand, deep within our moral composition, the most elemental of human rights.

IN NORTH AMERICA, WHERE THE "great experiment" of freedom was born and nurtured, we consider this concept almost sacred. It is here that humans have bestowed upon themselves the right to live as they choose. And though challenges to this idea continually emerge, most people living within the boundaries of the United States and Canada feel a solemn dedication to protect the powers endowed by their constitutions.

Still, most will concede that enormous work lies ahead. Centuries of atrocities against humans are not easily eliminated with good ideas and correcting the problems is widely considered a necessity. Until recently, however, such work has not been the province of environmental organizations. There is vast common ground between environmental concerns and human rights. By definition, environmental interests include where humans will live; what particles are in the air they breathe; what has seeped into the water they drink; and what has been absorbed into their food supply. At highest risk are people of limited income with little representation who find themselves incapable of preventing the encroachment of industry into their living areas. Uncontrolled toxic waste sites pepper rural and suburban areas across North America; most urban waste sites are located in poverty level neighborhoods. A Louisiana area along an 80-mile stretch of the Mississippi River has earned the dubious nickname "Cancer Alley". Communities living around the mills and refineries built there suffer from an extraordinarily high incidence of cancer and other ailments. Some babies are stillborn, others live with deformities. The indigenous wildlife and domestic farm creatures produce horrible genetic mutations.

To people living near toxic sites, the issue is as much about race as it is about environment. Minorities dominate most of the areas around dump sites. Examples and statistics strongly suggest that proposed dump sites are targeted for areas heavily populated by minorities. But until recently, organized opposition by minorities against environmental hazards has been conspicuously absent.

There exists a long-standing mistrust among various racial and ethnic groups that presents a tremendous hurdle to building a united front. Most environmental organizations concede that they have paid little attention to the issue of race and the environment. To them, environmental protection has an implicit benefit to the human race. And many minority activists would concede that, until recently, environment, as defined in general ecological terms, has been a predominantly "white" issue. Progress is being made. Many major environmental organizations are offering their support to people subjected to pollution. Minority groups, tending to find themselves closest to toxic sites, are realizing that they need to contribute their numbers and other resources to environmental causes or they risk becoming irrelevant in the fight for a cleaner, better world.

In October 1991, the First National People of Color Environmental Leadership summit was held in Washington, DC, sponsored by the Commission for Racial Justice. Delegates adopted ▶

United States

ALLIANCE FOR OUR COMMON FUTURE
PAGE 15
C/O NATIONAL PEACE FOUNDATION
1835 "K" Street, NW, Suite 610   Washington DC 20006
Phone (202) 223 1770   Fax (202) 223 1718

ARCTIC TO AMAZONIA ALLIANCE
P.O. Box 73   Strafford VT 05072
Phone (802) 765 4337

Founded 1987 • *Geographic Coverage* Global • *Other Field of Focus* Ecosystem Protection / Biodiversity • *Organization Members* 200 • *Individual Members* 2,300

Mission To facilitate intercultural work on environmental and indigenous rights issues, and to seek models of non-industrial alternatives to development. The Alliance's current areas of focus include multicultural communication, collaboration, and education, forest regeneration, indigenous links, community economic development, and organizational training.

Annual Fees	*Regular*	*Foreign*	*Patron*
	$25	$35	$100

Funding	*Membership*	*Corporations*	*Foundations*
	80%	5%	15%

Total Income $60,000

Usage	*Administration*	*Fundraising*	*Programs*
	15%	10%	75%

Programs New England Tropical Forest Project. Rubber Tapper and Maple Sugar Tapper Link. Sustainable Forestry Program. Conferences. Cultural Center.

Publication Quarterly newsletter *Arctic to Amazonia Alliance Report*

Who's Who President Erik van Lannep • Vice President Kim Rheinlander Secretary Petey Becker

BALTIMORE JOBS IN ENERGY PROJECT
PAGE 236
28 East Ostend Street   Baltimore MD 21230
Phone (410) 727 7837   Fax (410) 539 2087

CENTER FOR ALTERNATIVE MINING DEVELOPMENT POLICY
210 Avon Street, Suite 9   La Crosse WI 54603
Phone (608) 784 4399

Founded 1977 • *Geographic Coverage* Lake Superior region - Michigan, Wisconsin, Minnesota • *Cooperative Partners* Wisconsin Resources Protection Council, Environment Mining Network

Mission To provide information and technical assistance to Indian and non-Indian communities faced with large-scale mining and energy development in the northern Great Lakes region of the United States.

Publications Pamphlet *Land Grab: The Corporate Theft of Wisconsin's Mineral Resources.* Book *Plunder!*

Multimedia Video *The New Resource Wars*

For more Information Library

Who's Who Executive Director Al Gedicks

CONSERVATION INTERNATIONAL
PAGE 43
1015 18th Street, NW, Suite 1000   Washington DC 20036
Phone (202) 429 5660   Fax (202) 887 5188

> *Where humans reside*, **whether near a radioactive waste dump in the outskirts of a desert or an incinerator in the inner city, their environment, their** *living conditions, are vital concerns.* **Environment is everywhere.**

ENVIRONMENTAL COMMISSION OF THE DEMOCRATIC SOCIALISTS OF AMERICA   PAGE 20
1608 NORTH MILWAUKEE, FOURTH FLOOR   CHICAGO IL 60647
PHONE (312) 384 0327   FAX (312) 702 0090

FRIENDS OF THE EARTH USA   PAGE 22
218 "D" STREET, SE   WASHINGTON DC 20003
PHONE (202) 544 2600   FAX (202) 543 4710

GLOBAL 2000, INC.   PAGE 22
THE CARTER CENTER, ONE COPENHILL   ATLANTA GA 30307
PHONE (404) 872 3848   FAX (404) 874 5515

GREEN PARTY OF CALIFORNIA   PAGE 23
P.O. BOX 480578   LOS ANGELES CA 90048
PHONE (310) 314 7336

HUMAN RIGHTS WATCH
485 FIFTH AVENUE   NEW YORK NY 10017-6104
PHONE (212) 972 8400   FAX (212) 972 0905

Founded 1978 • *Geographic Coverage* Global • *Cooperative Partner* International Helsinki Federation - Vienna, Austria • *Chapters* 5

Mission To monitor on a sustained basis the human rights practices of some 60 governments around the world, and to work to stop any abuses of these rights. Human Rights Watch is the largest US-based international human rights organization.

Annual Fees	*Regular*	*Participating*	*Contributing*	*Sustaining*
	$20	$30	$50	$120

Other Fees *Director's Circle* $500 • *Leadership Circle* $1,000

Programs Human Rights Watch employs a staff of professional inves-

tigators - lawyers, journalists and regional experts - to collect timely, accurate and comprehensive information about human rights practices. The organization also devotes substantial energies to shaping US foreign policy, and seeks to harness the economic and moral power of the US government as a force for the protection of human rights. The organization is composed of five regional organizations - Africa Watch, Americas Watch, Asia Watch, Helsinki Watch, and Middle East Watch - plus the Fund for Free Expression. Americas Watch works to protect rainforests and the rights of indigenous peoples.

Publications Quarterly newsletter *Human Rights Watch. Annual Review* summary of the organization's *World Report* surveying human rights conditions in more than sixty countries. Annual *Human Rights Watch in the News* contains a selection of press clippings about the organization and its action

For more Information Annual Report, Database, Library, List of Publications

Who's Who PRESIDENT **ROBERT L. BERNSTEIN** • VICE PRESIDENT **ADRIAN DEWIND** • EXECUTIVE DIRECTOR **KENNETH ROTH** • WASHINGTON DIRECTOR **HOLLY J. BURKHALTER** • ASSOCIATE DIRECTOR **GARA LAMARCHE** • CALIFORNIA DIRECTOR **ELLEN LUTZ** • PRESS DIRECTOR **SUSAN OSNOS** • COUNSEL **JEMERA RONE** • OPERATIONS DIRECTOR **STEPHANIE STEELE** • DEVELOPMENT DIRECTOR **MICHAEL LONGFELDER**

INSTITUTE FOR FOOD AND DEVELOPMENT POLICY
398 60TH STREET   OAKLAND CA 94618
PHONE (510) 654 4400   FAX (510) 654 4551

Founded 1975 • *Geographic Coverage* Global • *Focused Regions* Pacific, Latin America, Africa • *Organization Members* 1,000 *Individual Members* 17,000

Mission Dedicated to contributing to bringing about a better life for the hungry and oppressed of the world.

▶ guidelines and creed for a fight against environmental racism and for basic human rights. Such organization was crucial, not just to raise concerns over deadly pollution that plagues minority communities, but to become a major force by broadening the base of environmental awareness and bringing the voting power of minorities to environmental causes. Some grassroots minority groups have created alliances with major environmental organizations such as the National Toxics Campaign and Greenpeace. They have gained minority representation and voices on boards of directors. This is an effort to highlight a specialized agenda and galvanize potent relationships with organizations that are always looking for added muscle. Organizations whose mission statements link human rights and the environment offer support in two ways. First, they provide assistance to victims of environmental hazards through organization and counseling. Second, they take the battles to the courtrooms to halt toxic progressions through litigation. The scope of environmental issues has widened dramatically in recent years. Along with the rights of plants and beasts comes the rights of humans. What is good for the air, the land, and the water is good for people. And where humans reside, whether near a radioactive waste dump in the outskirts of a desert or an incinerator in the inner city, their environment, their living conditions, are vital concerns. Environment is everywhere. •

John Vargo

Annual Fees	Regular	Organization	Corporation	Sustaining
	$30	$100	$100	$100

Other Fees *Patron* $500 • *Major Donor* $1,000

Funding	Membership	Foundations	Publication Sales	Royalties & Honoraria
	20.5%	56%	20%	2.5%

Total Income $615,538

Usage	Administration	Programs	Membership & Development
	10.5%	77.5%	12%

Total Expenses $576,199

Programs The Institute sponsored the First Annual San Francisco Environmental Film Festival in January '93. Democracy and Development Project. Cooperative project in Thailand with several Thai non-governmental organizations, looking at the Thai experience in export-led industrialization and the impact it is having on the quality of life in that formerly largely rural society.

Publications New releases include *Dragons in Distress: Asia's Miracle Economies in Crisis* • *Trading Freedom: How Free Trade Affect Our Lives, Work and Environment.* Various publications focusing on global poverty issues

Who's Who PRESIDENT **ANN EVANS** • VICE PRESIDENT **MERCEDES LYNN DE URIARTE** SECRETARY **STEVE HELLINGER** • TREASURER **CROSBY MILNE** • EXECUTIVE DIRECTOR **WALDEN BELLO**

LABOR COMMUNITY STRATEGY CENTER PAGE 195

3780 WILSHIRE BOULEVARD, SUITE 1200   LOS ANGELES CA 90010
PHONE (213) 387 2800   FAX (213) 387 3500

RAINFOREST ACTION NETWORK PAGE 81

450 SANSOME STREET, SUITE 700   SAN FRANCISCO CA 94111
PHONE (415) 398 4404   FAX (415) 398 2732

RAINFOREST ALLIANCE PAGE 81

65 BLEECKER STREET   NEW YORK NY 10012-2420
PHONE (212) 677 1900   FAX (212) 677 2187

SOUTHWEST ORGANIZING PROJECT

211 10TH STREET, SW   ALBUQUERQUE NM 87102
PHONE (505) 247 8832   FAX (505) 247 9972

Founded 1981 • *Geographic Coverage* Regional • *Cooperative Partner* Southwest Network for Environmental and Economic Justice *Chapter* 1 • *Individual Members* 100

Mission To empower the disenfranchised in the Southwest to realize racial and gender equality and social and economic justice.

Annual Fees *Regular* $24

Publications Quarterly magazine *Voces Unidas*, circulation 9,000. Book *Five Hundred Years of Chicano History in Pictures. Environmental Justice* booklets

For more Information Database, Library, List of Publications

Who's Who PRESIDENT **SOFIA MARTINEZ** • TREASURER **ROGER MCNEW** • EXECUTIVE DIRECTOR **JEANNE GOUNA**

SOUTHWEST RESEARCH AND INFORMATION CENTER PAGE 267

105 STANFORD, SE, P.O. BOX 4524   ALBUQUERQUE NM 87106
PHONE (505) 262 1862   FAX (505) 262 1864

SYNERGOS INSTITUTE (THE)

100 EAST 85TH STREET   NEW YORK NY 10028
PHONE (212) 517 4900   FAX (212) 517 4815

Founded 1986 • *Geographic Coverage* Global • *Focused Regions* Asia, Africa, Latin America • *Cooperative Partners* The Roda Viva Partnership - Brazil, Ghanaian Association of Private Voluntary Organizations in Development - Ghana, Fundación Grupo Esquel - Ecuador, Associaçao Para o Desenvolvimento da Comunidade - Mozambique, South North Development Initiative

Mission Dedicated to overcoming poverty by bringing together rich and poor to develop collaborative approaches addressing the causes and conditions of poverty. The Institute believes that to achieve lasting solutions, concerned groups must jointly identify the causes of poverty and together create and implement solutions.

Programs The organization's vision of collaborative approach covers a broad spectrum, including Multiparty Development Partnerships, Endowed National Foundations for Community Development and Community-to-Community Linkages to Overcome Poverty.

For more Information Annual Report

Who's Who CHAIR **MICHAELA WALSH** • PRESIDENT **PEGGY DULANY** • EXECUTIVE DIRECTOR **S. BRUCE SCHEARER** • DEVELOPMENT AND COMMUNICATIONS ASSISTANT **ANDREW S. DUPREE**

TONANTZIN LAND INSTITUTE

P.O. BOX 40182   ALBUQUERQUE NM 87916
PHONE (505) 256 0097

Founded 1982 • *Geographic Coverage* Regional • *Focused Region* Southwest • *Other Field of Focus* Natural Resources / Water -Conservation & Quality • *Organization Members* 65

Mission To protect, preserve, and defend the land, water, and human rights of indigenous peoples. The Institute's current field of focus consists of organizing community advocacy with traditional communities throughout the Southwest.

Funding	*Membership*	*Foundations*
	25%	75%

Total Income $200,000

Usage	*Administration*	*Fundraising*	*Programs*
	35%	5%	60%

Publication Periodical *Tribal Survival*

Who's Who PRESIDENT **ABBY MOQUINO** • VICE PRESIDENT **BEN TAFOYA** • SECRETARY **TUPAC ENRIQUE**

WOMEN'S ENVIRONMENT AND DEVELOPMENT ORGANIZATION   PAGE 27

845 THIRD AVENUE, 15TH FLOOR   NEW YORK NY 10022
PHONE (212) 759 7982   FAX (212) 759 8647

Canada

ADVOCACY GROUP FOR THE ENVIRONMENTALLY SENSITIVE   PAGE 268

1887 CHAINE COURT   ORLEANS ON K1C 2W6
PHONE (613) 830 5722   FAX (613) 834 6699

VALHALLA SOCIETY (THE)   PAGE 127

BOX 224   NEW DENVER BC V0G 1S0
PHONE (604) 358 2333   FAX (604) 358 7950

population demographic aspects

CHAPTER 5

Population Growth, Environmental Decline, by David Drum

MORE THAN 5 BILLION HUMAN BEINGS inhabit the face of the Earth and our numbers increase by the minute. Increases in population put enormous stress on the environment simply because more people means more mouths to feed, more products, and more services to provide. Since 1970, the world's population has increased by 43.2 percent while the supply of arable and permanent cropland has increased only by 4.8 percent. Human fertility now produces two additional people each second, swelling our numbers by 70 million each year. With the human life span lengthened by medical science, the human race now grows at a slow but alarming rate of about 2 percent per year. The World Bank projects that our present global population of 5.4 billion will expand to 12 billion by late in the next century. In *Saving the Planet*, Lester Brown, Christopher Flavin and Sandra Postelin make the case that 12 billion people will drastically overload natural ecological life support systems, which are already collapsing in many under-developed countries. No matter where a child is born, each new arrival forces us to stretch the resources and capabilities of this planet further than ever before.

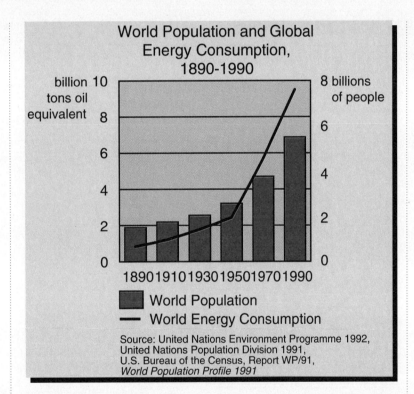

World Population and Global Energy Consumption, 1890-1990

Source: United Nations Environment Programme 1992, United Nations Population Division 1991, U.S. Bureau of the Census, Report WP/91, *World Population Profile 1991*

THE US POPULATION OF 249 MILLION is currently increasing by 2 million per year; Canada's population of 26.5 million increases about 250,000 per year. Much of the increase comes from women born during the "Baby Boom" years after World War II. More comes from immigration into both countries, a trend which will surely continue because citizens of poorer countries are drawn to higher living standards. Compared with most of the world, the United States and Canada are not densely populated. The United States has 49 people per square mile, Canada has seven per square mile, mostly clustered along the US border. But in Singapore, 11,562 people are packed into each square mile. Serious environmental consequences result from uncontrolled population growth, whether in North America or elsewhere. Consumption depletes fresh water supplies, soil fertility, and marine and plant life. It contributes to air and water pollution and creates mountains of solid wastes. Population control is a more obvious concern in developing countries, but the richer societies consume a wildly disproportionate share of the world's finite resources.

THUS, POPULATION INCREASES in the United States and Canada amplify the stress on the environment. It has been estimated that one American produces 342 times more stress on the environment than one Indonesian. The United States alone consumes 30 percent of the world's raw materials. Canada also consumes a disproportionate share simply because Canadian citizens can afford to do so. Richer societies also spend more money on food, contributing to the depletion of the planet's finite supply of precious farmland. The average North American uses an estimated five times more agricultural resources than the average Indian, Nigerian, or Colombian. This is because wealthier societies consume more complex food products such as meat and milk, which are more costly to produce than staples like rice and grain. Billions of tons of precious topsoil in North America are also lost each year due ▶

to improper farming practices by farmers driven to produce greater and greater quantities of food for burgeoning populations.

POPULATION PRESSURES ARE CAUSING precious US farmland to be lost to urban development at a rate estimated at 3 million acres per year. As populations increase, municipalities sprawl into suburbs, simultaneously increasing land area and decreasing farmland. To create suburbs, developers must build roads, sewer systems, and other amenities, using great quantities of resources in the process. Rich societies consume more natural resources such as water. Average daily per capita water use is 188 gallons in the United States and 142 gallons in Canada - about 10 times average daily usage in India. The United States and Canada rank second and fourth as water consumers in the world. Over the past 100 years, world population growth has paralleled growth in industrialization, energy consumption, and accumulations of carbon dioxide in the atmosphere. Some 150,000 Canadian lakes, particularly in industrial provinces, have been polluted by acid rain, their waters fouled by a combination of vehicle emissions and industrial activity across the border. The rate at which people use water in North America has increased much faster than population growth. While the US population increased 50 percent between 1950 and 1980, withdrawals of water from lakes, streams, and underground aquifers increased 150 percent. Water is abundant in North America, but such withdrawals cannot continue indefinitely because the supply of

---

United States

INTER-AMERICAN PARLIAMENTARY GROUP ON POPULATION AND DEVELOPMENT

902 BROADWAY, 10TH FLOOR	NEW YORK NY 10010-6089
PHONE (212) 995 8860	FAX (212) 995 8853

Geographic Coverage North America, Latin America

Mission To improve the quality of life in the Western hemisphere by promoting just and coherent population and development policies; to increase awareness in the countries of the Americas of the close relationship between population and development; to create awareness about the need to reach a balance between the utilization of resources and the protection of the environment; and to promote the formation of national committees of parliamentarians dedicated to improving population and development policies. The Group is a membership organization open to legislators from all countries in the Americas which have a body of elected representatives.

Total Income $78,352

Usage	Programs	Other
	95%	5%

Total Expenses $78,352

Programs Regional Population Education and Communications Program. The Western Hemisphere Conference of Parliamentarians on Population and Development, Quito, Ecuador, 1990.

Publications Quarterly newsletter. Monthly bulletin. Various other publications including *Family Planning and the Health of Mothers and Children* • *High Infant Mortality and the Plight of Street Children: Special Problems in Latin America and the Caribbean* • *Population Policy in Latin America and the Caribbean* • *Women in Latin America and the Caribbean: The Invisible Half* • *Population Growth and the Environment*

Who's Who PRESIDENT SENATOR BLANCA ESPONDA • SECRETARY BRUCE HALLIDAY, M.P. • TREASURER BENJAMIN CRUZ • EXECUTIVE DIRECTOR HERNAN SANHUEZA SENIOR ADVISER FRANCISCO DI BLASI • CONTACT ALEJANDRA MAGLIOLI

JOHN HOPKINS CENTER FOR COMMUNICATION PROGRAMS

111 MARKET PLACE, SUITE 310	BALTIMORE MD 21202-4024
PHONE (410) 659 6301	FAX (410) 659 6266

Geographic Coverage Global • *Cooperative Partner* Population Communication Services

Mission To provide an accurate, authoritative overview of important developments in population, family planning, and related health areas through the publication of *Population Reports*.

Funding	Population Communication Services	Population Information Program
	60%	21%

Other Sources *Family health services* 12.5% • *Subcontracts* 4%

Total Income $13,333,970

Usage	Administration	Programs	Subagreements & Subcontracts	Other
	13%	47%	30%	10%

Total Expenses $13,333,970

Programs Population Information Program. Population Communication Services. AIDS and AIDSCOM. Workshops and conferences.

Publication Quarterly fact sheet *Population Reports*, circulation 100,000 (85% to developing countries)

Multimedia *Population Communication Services* co-produced with Televisi Republik Indonesia 3. Videos by Indonesia's leading filmmakers *Tasi* • *Oh Tasi* • *Lost Child (Anak Hilang)* • *Procession (Arak-Arakan)*. POPLINE CD-ROM, a computerized collection of over 200,000 citations with abstracts

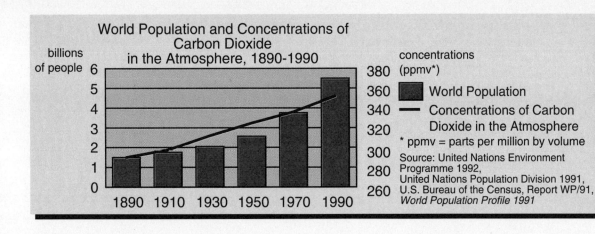

World Population and Concentrations of Carbon Dioxide in the Atmosphere, 1890-1990

billions of people

concentrations (ppmv*)

■ World Population

— Concentrations of Carbon Dioxide in the Atmosphere

* ppmv = parts per million by volume

Source: United Nations Environment Programme 1992, United Nations Population Division 1991, U.S. Bureau of the Census, Report WP/91, *World Population Profile 1991*

fresh water is finite. By the year 2000, the US Water Resources Council estimates that water supplies will be "severely inadequate" in almost 15 percent of US water supply regions. The industrial use of water, timber, minerals, and other natural resources creates great quantities of waste. Each day, the average American creates 3.3 pounds of solid waste, much of which consists of packaging. ▶

For more Information Annual Report, Database, Library

Who's Who DIRECTOR CENTER FOR COMMUNICATION PROGRAMS PHYLLIS T. PIOTROW EDITOR AND DEPUTY DIRECTOR POPULATION INFORMATION PROGRAM WARD RINEHART MANAGING EDITOR STEPHEN M. GOLDSTEIN • CONTACT MERRIDY R. GOTTLIEB

MORRISON INSTITUTE FOR POPULATION AND RESOURCE STUDIES

HERRIN LABS, ROOM 467, STANFORD UNIVERSITY   STANFORD CA 94305-5020
PHONE (415) 723 2300

Founded 1986 • *Geographic Coverage* Global, Southeast and Northeast Asia • *Focused Countries* China, India • *Cooperative Partners* Population Research Institute of Xi'an Jiaotong University - China, N. I. Valivov Institute of General Genetics of the Russian Academy of Sciences - Moscow, Russian Federation, Hoover Institute, Food Research Institute

Mission To support research and education on the interconnected global issues of population growth, its effects on the environment, the pressure on natural resources, and the capacity of many nations to achieve sustainable economic development.

Funding *Foundations* 100%

Usage	Administration	Programs
	13%	87%

Publications Current readings *Population and Resources in a Changing World.* Numerous academic papers

Who's Who PRESIDENT MARCUS W. FELDMAN • EXECUTIVE DIRECTOR JEAN DOBLE

POPULATION ACTION INTERNATIONAL

1120 19TH STREET, NW, SUITE 550   WASHINGTON DC 20036-3605
PHONE (202) 659 1833   FAX (202) 293 1795

Founded 1965 • *Geographic Coverage* Global

Mission To work for a better quality of life for present and future generations, by working for universal access to high quality voluntary family planning and health services, for the empowerment of individuals, especially women, to make their own reproductive choices, and for the early stabilization of world population size. Population Action works to meet these goals through a program which includes research, public education, and advocacy.

Annual Fees	Friend	Sustaining	Sponsor	Patron	Benefactor
	$100	$250	$500	$1,000	$5,000

Total Income $3,042,000

Usage	Administration	Fundraising	Publications & Media
	13%	7%	31.3%

Other Usage *Education & Liaison* 14.3% • *Population & Environment* 11.7% • *Library & Computer Services* 7.6% • *Special Projects* 11.8% • *Other* 3.3%

Total Expenses $3,233,000

Programs Works to focus attention on key changes that need to take place in the family planning programs of India and China (two countries that contribute a third of the 92 million people added to world population each year). Working to persuade USAID and the government of India to go forward with a major new family planning project; this $300 million project marks the arrival of the "priority country" programming direction long advocated by the organization as the best way to achieve real demographic progress. Helping to convince the US Food and Drug Administration to approve the injectable contraceptive Depo-Provera, after more than 20 years of success abroad.

Publications Population policy information sheets. Booklets focusing on population and demographic issues. *Country Study* series. Full color wall charts and briefing papers

► The average Canadian creates 3.7 pounds per day - many times more than citizens of Third World nations. Crowded urban population centers create stress on residents and the environment and lead to a lower overall quality of life.

ATTEMPTS TO SLOW POPULATION growth through strategies such as family planning and population control "strike at the very structure, functioning, and behavior of society

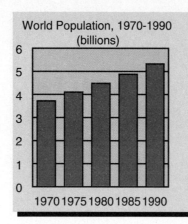

World Population, 1970-1990 (billions)

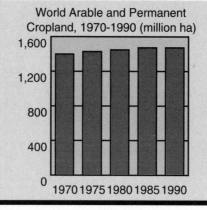

World Arable and Permanent Cropland, 1970-1990 (million ha)

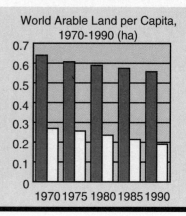

World Arable Land per Capita, 1970-1990 (ha)

Multimedia Reaches an audience of 500 million people worldwide via TV, radio, and the print media

For more Information Annual Report, Database, Library, List of Publications

Who's Who PRESIDENT J. JOSEPH SPEIDEL • VICE PRESIDENTS SHARON L. CAMP, CATHERINE CAMERON • SECRETARY PHYLLIS TILSON PIOTROW • TREASURER WILLIAM C. EDWARDS • DEVELOPMENT DIRECTOR PATRICIA L. McGRATH • LIBRARIAN ANNE MARIE AMANTIA • CONTACT PATRICIA SEARS

POPULATION COMMUNICATION

1489 EAST COLORADO BOULEVARD, SUITE 202   PASADENA CA 91106
PHONE (818) 793 4750   FAX (818) 793 4791

Founded 1977 • *Geographic Coverage* Global • *Focused Countries* Bangladesh, Brazil, Egypt, India, Indonesia, Mexico, Nigeria, Pakistan, the Philippines, Thailand • *Cooperative Partners* InterAction, Global Tomorrow Coalition, American Public Health Association • *Chapter* 1

Mission To communicate population messages to national leaders. The organization's primary concern is the impact of population on the environment and the problems associated with the environmental cost of achieving population stabilization.

Programs In collaboration with Earth Day events, Population Communication has prepared kits and educational materials linking population and the environment. It has initiated a Statement on Population Stabilization which has been signed by more than fifty heads of government.

For more Information List of Publications

Who's Who PRESIDENT ROBERT W. GILLESPIE

POPULATION COMMUNICATIONS INTERNATIONAL

777 UNITED NATIONS PLAZA, SUITE 7-C   NEW YORK NY 10017-3521
PHONE (212) 687 3366   FAX (212) 661 4188

Founded 1985 • *Geographic Coverage* Global • *Focused Countries* Mexico, India, Kenya, Tanzania, Brazil, the Philippines

Mission To work towards a reduction in current trends towards rapid population growth through the use of entertainment mass media (particularly soap operas) to promote the desirability of smaller family size, and the use of family planning and open family communications; to enhance the status of women and their control in the family planning process.

Funding *Contributions* 99.6%

Total Income $1,155,842

Usage	Administration	Fundraising	Programs
	4%	13%	83%

Total Expenses $1,248,589

Programs Development of soap opera programs in developing countries such as Mexico, India, Kenya, Tanzania, Brazil, and the Philippines, to enhance the status of women, model open family communications and promote family planning.

For more Information Annual Report

Who's Who PRESIDENT DAVID O. POINDEXTER • EXECUTIVE VICE PRESIDENT WILLIAM N. RYERSON • SENIOR VICE PRESIDENT RODNEY SHAW • DIRECTOR OF DEVELOPMENT CHARLES S. C. CLEMENT • ADMINISTRATIVE ASSISTANT KATHY GASKINS

POPULATION COUNCIL (THE)

1 DAG HAMMARSKJOLD PLAZA   NEW YORK NY 10017
PHONE (212) 339 0500

Founded 1952 • *Geographic Coverage* Global • *Focused Regions* Especially less developed countries • *Cooperative Partners* International Planned Parenthood Federation, The World Bank, United Nations Population Fund, United Nations Development Programme, World Health

A. 1970-1990:
World population increased by 43.2%

B. 1970-1990:
World area of arable land increased by 4.8%

C. Consequence:
Area of arable land per head of population fell by 28.6% in the developing countries and 12.5% in the developed countries

■ Developed Countries

□ Developing Countries

Source: United Nations Environment Programme 1992,
United Nations Population Division 1991,
U.S. Bureau of the Census, Report WP/91,
World Population Profile 1991

and challenge many of the fundamental tenets upon which our social and economic systems are based, including the pursuit of superaffluence among the rich and the desire for large families among the poor", Brown has written. Nonetheless, growth rates have begun to slow in several countries. Thirteen European countries have already achieved population equilibrium, a numerical balance between births and deaths. Birth rates in North America are dropping. Since 1960, reports the United Nations Population Fund, birthrates in all regions of the developing world have dropped from an average of 6.1 births per woman to 3.9 births.
Even China's once exploding population is close to equilibrium. But the world's population continues to increase.
The world population needs to be stabilized at 8 billion within the next 40 years, Brown and his co-authors believe. That is a number that can be supported by the Earth's finite resources. This means births and deaths must be in perfect equilibrium, an event which has never happened. Despite many developments, stabilizing the world's population at an optimum level remains a race against time and against ourselves. •
David Drum

Organisation, United Nations Children's Fund, Mexico's National Council for the Prevention and Control of AIDS, UNICEF • *Chapters* 17, in Kenya, Zimbabwe, Senegal, Burkina Faso, Mali, Mexico, Bolivia, Brazil, Honduras, Peru, Thailand, Bangladesh, India, Indonesia, Pakistan, the Philippines, and Egypt

Mission To apply science and technology to the solution of population problems in developing countries, through social and health science programs and research (such as research on contraceptive development and introduction), publications and public information, and fellowships and awards in the population sciences.

Funding	Membership	Interest, Net Gains, Fees & Publications Sales
	70%	30%

Total Income $44,129,504

Usage	Administration	Programs
	15.1%	84.9%

Total Expenses $40,208,726

Programs Sponsors various scientific studies and programs related to population issues in numerous countries, including family planning programs, maternity and children's health programs. Provides publishing and technical services to all Council staff and programs. Sponsors seminars and workshops.

Publications Periodicals Population and Development Review • *Studies in Family Planning*. Pamphlets *Quality/Calidad/Qualité: Celebrating Mother and Child on the Fortieth Day* • *Tunisia Postpartum Program* • *Man/Hombre/Homme: Meeting Male Reproductive Health Care Needs in Latin America* • *The Bangladesh Women's Health Coalition* • *By and For Women: Involving Women in the Development of Reproductive Health Care Materials*. Numerous scientific publications dealing with population issues

Multimedia CD-ROM database available to researchers

For more Information Annual Report, Database, Library, List of Publications

Who's Who Chair Mc George Bundy • President George Zeidenstein • Vice Presidents George F. Brown, John Bongaarts, C. Wayne Bardin • Secretary Shirley M. Alexander • Treasurer Donald J. Abrams • Head Office of Communications Ethel P. Churchill • Editor Studies in Family Planning Julie K. Reich • Librarian H. Neil Zimmerman

POPULATION INSTITUTE (THE)

107 Second Street, NE   Washington DC 20002-7396
Phone (202) 544 3300   Fax (202) 544 0068

Founded 1969 • *Geographic Coverage* Global • *Chapters* 3, in Brussels - Belgium, Colombo - Sri Lanka, Kuala Lumpur - Malaysia

Mission Concerned with bringing the world's population into balance with its resources and environment, creating population stability and enhancing the quality of life. The Institute is dedicated to convincing the leaders of developing nations that they must balance their populations with their resources, and to encouraging the leaders of industrialized countries to help developing nations achieve this goal.

Funding	Contributions & Grants	Capital Campaign	Other
	80%	18%	2%

Total Income $1,729,992

Usage	Administration	Fundraising	Programs
	13%	8%	79%

Total Expenses $1,440,076

Programs Community Leaders Program, designed to develop a strong network of community leaders and train them in the international population field. Public Policy Division, responsible for monitoring all legislation that deals specifically or indirectly with population issues. Information, education, and communication programs. International programs, and participation to major international conferences and meetings.

Publications Bimonthly newsletter *Popline*, circulation 63,000. Books *The Nairobi Challenge, Global Directory of Women's Organizations Implementing Population Strategies • Gaining People, Losing Ground: A Blueprint for Stabilizing World Population*

Multimedia Video *Silent Explosion* (20 min.). Audiotapes *Population and Global Survival: A Vision for the Nineties • Regional Power Kegs: Chartering U.S. Security in an Exploding World*

For more Information Annual Report, List of Publications

Who's Who PRESIDENT **WERNER FORNOS** • CHAIR **JOYCE W. CRAMER** • VICE CHAIR **JOAN KRAUS COLLINS** • SECRETARY **STEPHEN KEESE** • TREASURER **VAN CRAWFORD** • PUBLIC POLICY ASSISTANT **ANDREA JOHNSTON**

POPULATION REFERENCE BUREAU, INC.

1875 CONNECTICUT AVENUE, NW   WASHINGTON DC 20009-5728
PHONE (202) 483 1100   FAX (202) 328 3937

Founded 1929 • *Geographic Coverage* Local, Regional, National, Global • *Cooperative Partners* Center for Applied Research on Population and Development - Mali, Academy for Educational Development, US Agency for International Development, United Nations agencies, Decision Demographics, Inc., a wholly owned subsidiary organized in 1983 *Organization Members* 1,184 • *Individual Members* 2,737

Mission To inform and educate people about population issues. The organization provides accurate and up-to-date information about population trends and their implications for public officials, educators, business leaders, and other audiences concerned about US and world affairs. The organization communicates population information to a wide audience through press outreach and media appearances by its staff.

Annual Fees	Regular	Student/Senior	Educator	Library
	$45	$25	$30	$55

Other Fees *Non-profit organization* $55 • *For-profit organization* $200

Funding	Membership	Foundations	Government Contracts
	4%	23%	53%

Other Sources *Sales of Publications* 8% • *Investments* 5% • *Decision Demographics, Inc. (subsidiary)* 7%

Total Income $3,400,000

Usage	Fundraising	Programs	Other
	2.5%	87.6%	9.9%

Total Expenses $3,450,000

Programs International programs - many of the Bureau's international activities in 1992 focused on Africa. International population policy communications. US population seminar series. Visiting scholars program

Publications Monthly newsletters *Population Today • Population Bulletins*. Annual fact sheets *World Population Data • US Population Data*. Handbooks. Policy reports. Resources for teachers

For more Information Annual Report, Library, List of Publications

Who's Who PRESIDENT **BARBARA BOYLE TORREY** • VICE PRESIDENT **CARY DAVIS** SECRETARY **COLETTE THOMAS** • OTHER **CARL HAUB, CAROL J. DEVITA, JACKI MAJEWSKI, ALENE H. GELBARD, MARTHA FARNSWORTH RICHE** • LIBRARIAN **LALLIANZUALI H. MALSAWMA**

POPULATION RESOURCE CENTER

15 ROSZEL ROAD   PRINCETON NJ 08540
PHONE (609) 452 2822   FAX (609) 452 0010

Founded 1975 • *Geographic Coverage* Global • *Chapter* 1, in Washington

Mission The Center works to ensure that decision makers have the most current, complete, and carefully researched demographic information available, by analyzing population trends and their potential impact, and presenting options for action.

Funding	Corporations	Foundations
	20%	80%

Total Income $711,920

Usage	Administration	Fundraising	Programs
	20%	15%	65%

Programs Youth at Risk: The Role of Family Structure. International Migration: Cross Border Issues. The Changing American Family: The Economic Consequences. Demographic Trends in the Middle East. Population Trends in Mexico. Population and Environment: A Collision Course.

Publications Numerous executive summaries including *The Demographics of Aging America • The Changing American Family • America's Baby Boomlet • Demographic Profile of India • The 1990 Census*. Population environment booklets *Putting the Piece Together • Baby Boomers*

For more Information List of Publications

Who's Who FOUNDER **HENRY L. MCINTYRE** • CHAIR **OSCAR HARKAVY** • SECRETARY **EDNA M. FRIEDMAN** • PRESIDENT **JANE S. DE LUNG** • DIRECTOR WASHINGTON OFFICE **SHELLEY E. KOSSAK**

POPULATION-ENVIRONMENT BALANCE

1325 "G" STREET, NW, SUITE 1003   WASHINGTON DC 20005-3104
PHONE (202) 879 3000   FAX (202) 879 3019

Founded 1973 • *Geographic Coverage* National • *Organization Members* 1,000 • *Individual Members* 4,000

Mission To encourage population stabilization in the US, to encourage a responsible immigration policy for the US, and to promote increased funding for contraceptive research and availability. The organization is a grassroots membership organization dedicated to educating the public about the impacts of population growth on the environment.

Annual Fees	Regular	Student/Senior	Sustaining
	$25	$15	$100

Funding	Membership	Foundations
	66%	33%

Usage	Administration	Fundraising	Programs
	23%	3%	74%

Programs Public education, advocacy, media campaigns, and publications.

Publications *Balance Report* • *Have You Heard* • *BALANCE Data.* Action alerts. Brochure

Who's Who PRESIDENT VIRGINIA ABERNETHY • VICE PRESIDENT DAVID DURHAM

ZERO POPULATION GROWTH, INC.
1400 16TH STREET, NW, SUITE 320   WASHINGTON DC 20036
PHONE (202) 332 2200   FAX (202) 332 2302

Founded 1968 • *Geographic Coverage* Global • *Cooperative Partner* Zero Population Growth of Canada, Inc. • *Chapters* 22, nationwide • *Individual Members* 50,000

Mission To further the achievement of a sustainable balance between the Earth's population, its environment, and its resources, by seeking to raise awareness of the environmental, social, and economic impacts of population growth, in the USA and worldwide. The Association's central areas of concern presently include the status of women, sustainable development, environmental protection, energy and transportation, family planning, maternal and child health, and reproductive rights.

Annual Fees	Regular	Student/Senior
	$20	$10

Funding	Membership	Foundations
	80%	20%

Total Income $1,900,000

Usage	Administration	Fundraising	Programs
	11%	9%	80%

Programs Action Alert Network. Media Targets. Roving Reporter. Newswatch. Speakers Network. Population Education Trainers Network.

Publications Bimonthly *The ZPG Reporter*. Quarterly newsletter *ZPG Backgrounder* designed for teachers. Book *USA by Numbers*. Special reports including *Planning the Ideal Family* • *Abortion in America* • *Children's Stress Index* • *Environmental Stress Index* • *Urban Stress Test*. Numerous teaching materials, and fact sheets focusing on population issues

Who's Who PRESIDENT KATHERINE JANEWAY • VICE PRESIDENTS KENNETH BILBY, THOMAS KRING, JOHN LAZARUS, MAURA O'NEILL • SECRETARY MARY SINGLETARY EXECUTIVE DIRECTOR SUSAN WEBER

Canada

ZERO POPULATION GROWTH OF CANADA, INC.
P.O. BOX 113   AJAX ON L1S 3C5
PHONE (416) 487 2619

Geographic Coverage National, Global • *Cooperative Partner* Zero Population Growth, Inc. - USA

Mission To establish a population policy for Canada based on the sustainable environmental and economic potential of the country; to develop awareness of the strong linkages between human numbers, human activity, the environment and human well-being; to make it clear that Canada is no longer an untapped frontier capable of accommodating a larger population but a nation with a declining environment that must now work toward long-term solutions for its environmental and economic problems.

Annual Fees *Regular* $20

Publications Various fact sheets focusing on population issues, including *World Foodland Map* • *Economics and the Environment* • *Economic Impact of Population Growth* • *Economic Impact of Immigration on the Canadian Economy* • *Linkages: Does Canada Need More People?* • *Canadian Population and Immigration* • *Population Growth and Urban Problems*.

the **earth** and its natura

resources

part two

"All resources –

food, water, air,

minerals, energy –

are finite, and there

are limits to the

growth of all living

systems.

These limits

are finally dictated

by the finite size of

the earth and the

finite input

of energy from

the sun."

Third Law of Ecology

forest conservation deforestation, reforestation

CHAPTER 6

Before the Last Tree Falls, by John Vargo

SOME ENVIRONMENTAL ISSUES CARRY the burden of immediate global crisis. Combating such problems requires extraordinary international cooperation and definitive political leadership, for they threaten to lead to widespread disaster in the foreseeable future. Deforestation is one of those issues. Reports illustrating the devastation are becoming sadly familiar. Areas of tropical rainforest that are larger than many countries are disappearing annually. But the scope of forest decimation is much more dramatic when one looks at the true losses. Species are becoming extinct at a rate 1,000 times faster than any time in the last 65 million years. Atmospheric changes resulting from forest loss accelerates the destruction. Deforestation directly contributes to massive erosion and the losses to genetic study and future medicinal benefits are incalculable. An often-used example is the Pacific yew, an endangered species which provides taxol, a chemical base for a cure for some types of cancer. Declining genetic diversity, which historically has caused crop failures, is another result of forest destruction. Every second of the day, it is claimed, an acre and a half is lost. Ancient tropical forests are disappearing at roughly 27,000

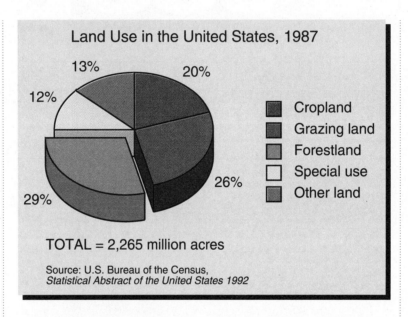

Land Use in the United States, 1987

13% · 20% · 12% · 29% · 26%

- Cropland
- Grazing land
- Forestland
- Special use
- Other land

TOTAL = 2,265 million acres

Source: U.S. Bureau of the Census,
Statistical Abstract of the United States 1992

square miles a year. An additional 27,000 square miles are either partially cleared or damaged. Rainforests in South America, Madagascar, and the Far East are critically threatened and Brazil is most severely deforested. Some experts conservatively predict that, at the current rate of deforestation, the world's remaining rainforests will be gone within 20 to 40 years, taking with them all the life that thrived there. Unchecked population growth is cited as one of the main reasons for the loss of rainforests. People make excessive demands on land: rainforests offer quick, short-term profits for impoverished peoples; they

promise debt-ridden countries immediate sources of funds from exploitation of minerals. The need for more pasture lands for livestock also cuts into the forests.

FORESTS ABSORB MASSIVE AMOUNTS of carbon dioxide from the air. Therefore, a direct relationship exists between the forests and the amount of carbon dioxide in the air. In fact, the burning of wood in forest clearing adds to the carbon dioxide content in the atmosphere. And the problem of too much carbon dioxide causes other damaging consequences. Historic and scientific evidence show atmospheric carbon dioxide

facilitates global warming through an enhanced greenhouse effect - the trapping of the sun's infrared rays. Seemingly minor temperature changes can cause dramatic, global changes in the climate. The global Ice Age temperature is estimated to be only a few degrees colder than today's temperatures. Disappearing tropical rainforests also disrupt the hydrological cycle. These forests trap and store moisture, evaporate water into the air, and emit gases that promote rainfall. Fewer rainforests mean less humidity and less rainfall and more arid conditions. The deciduous forests of North America are also at risk. Despite efforts at reforestation - the planting of seedlings in denuded areas - the practice is not proving to be a sufficient remedy. Many replanted forests are replacing hardwoods with monoculture coniferous woods and wildlife are finding it difficult to return and adjust to the new environments. The lists of causes of deforestation and the effects of deforestation on the environment has motivated leaders of industrial nations to address the problem. But hopes of a treaty at the Earth Summit in Rio de Janeiro in June 1992 were lost to debate.

EFFORTS TO PRESERVE, CONTROL AND manage the world's remaining forests continue. The Earth Summit did open a dialogue between nations on a problem that is truly international. Deforestation was addressed and the various nations agreed to a "statement of principles" regarding forests. In British Columbia, a few Native American tribes have signed or proposed treaties to protect some forests, specifically areas they claim to be sacred to their heritage. But the British ▶

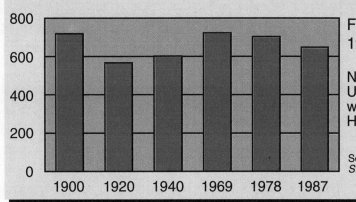

Forestland in the United States, 1900-1987 (million acres)

Note: The total land area of the United States increased in 1959 with the addition of Alaska and Hawaii as states

Source: U.S. Bureau of the Census, *Statistical Abstract of the United States 1992*

United States

ASSOCIATION OF FOREST SERVICE EMPLOYEES FOR ENVIRONMENTAL ETHICS

P.O. Box 11615   Eugene OR 97440
Phone (503) 484 2692

Founded 1989 • *Geographic Coverage* National • *Other Field of Focus* Sustainable Development / Agriculture - Environmental Technologies • *Chapters* 8 • *Organization Members* 500 • *Individual Members* 10,500

Mission To forge a socially responsible value system for the Forest Service based on a land ethic which ensures ecologically and economically sustainable resource management. The Association's central areas of focus presently include national forests conservation, public land management, biodiversity, grazing, and old growth forests conservation.

	Regular	Foreign	Sustaining	Advocate	Patron
Annual Fees	$20	$35	$50	$100	$500

	Membership	Foundations	Other
Funding	39%	58%	3%

Total Income $682,278

	Administration	Fundraising	Programs
Usage	9%	19%	72%

Total Expenses $655,479

Programs Public education program disseminates information through publications and speaking engagements. Chapter organizing and development. Legal support for protecting integrity and ethics of forest service employees. Monitoring for employees of environmental, wildlife and natural resource agencies.

Publications Bimonthly newspaper *Inner Voice*. Informational brochures and handouts. Action alert *Activist*. Reports on special projects

For more Information Annual Report

Who's Who President **Dave Iverson** • Vice President **Dan Heinz** • Secretary **Terry Fairbanks** • Executive Director **Jeff DeBonis** • Other **Richard Fairbanks, Cynthia Reichelt, Walt Rule**

COMMITTEE FOR NATIONAL ARBOR DAY

P.O. Box 333   West Orange NJ 07052
Phone (201) 731 0840

Founded 1936 • *Geographic Coverage* National • *Chapters* 25 *Organization Members* 6 • *Individual Members* 25

Mission To establish the last Friday in April as National Arbor Day.

Funding *Foundations* 100%

Programs Arbor Day programs on the last Friday in April.

Publications *Arbor Day Past and Present* • *National Arbor Day Review*

Who's Who President **Harry J. Banicer** • Vice President **Pat Banker**

EAST BAY CONSERVATION CORPS

1021 Third Street   Oakland CA 94607
Phone (415) 891 3900

Founded 1983 • *Geographic Coverage* San Francisco Bay communities • *Other Field of Focus* Urban Environment

Mission The Corps is a non-profit work and education organization serving the East San Francisco Bay communities. The East Bay Conservation Corps is a new slant on an old idea; during the Great Depression in the 1930s, President Franklin Roosevelt created the Civilian Conservation

Columbia provincial government makes few restrictions on logging and the result is a clear-cut so large that it can be seen in photos taken from space. The treatments applied to the problem by the various North American organizations are diverse. Some take a firm posture, calling a halt to domestic logging and international rainforest decimation. Others believe in wise policies that would preserve and maintain forest acreage while still reaping economic benefits. Many environmental groups concerned with the world's forests focus on the underlying causes because they recognize that complex problems require complex solutions. These organizations sponsor programs of education, replanting, alternative sources of income, management of livestock pastures and the other factors which impact on clear-cutting and

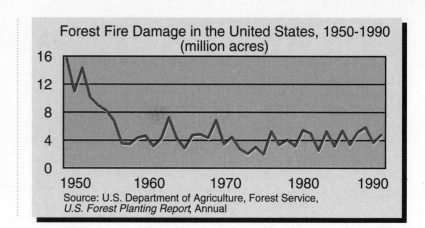

Forest Fire Damage in the United States, 1950-1990 (million acres)

Source: U.S. Department of Agriculture, Forest Service, *U.S. Forest Planting Report*, Annual

Corps, putting three million people to work on the land. They planted 1.3 billion trees, renovated entire neighborhoods, and built Camp David, the presidential retreat. Today's Corps still focuses on land and forest conservation and restoration projects.

Programs Land conservation projects all over the East Bay, from clearing trails to planting dune grass, refurbishing day care and emergency shelters to construction of playgrounds in low-income neighborhoods.

Who's Who CHAIRMAN JOHN A. NEJEDLY • VICE CHAIRMAN ROBERT G. SPROUL, III SECRETARY ROBERT EMMETT DOYLE • EXECUTIVE DIRECTOR JOANNA L. LENNON

ECOFORESTRY INSTITUTE USA (THE)

P.O. BOX 12543   PORTLAND OR 97212
PHONE (503) 287 7252   FAX (503) 287 5130

Geographic Coverage North America • *Cooperative Partner* The Ecoforestry Institute of Canada • *Chapter* 1

Mission To provide ecologically sound alternatives to the current industrial forestry practices which for short-term gain destroy biodiversity and most other values of natural forests as well as rural communities. The Institute supports preservation of ancient and natural forests. It encourages restoration of plantation tree farms to natural forest status and recognizes that humans need to use forests in a variety of ways. These needs can be met in the long-run only if practices are consistent with the needs of forest ecosystems.

Annual Fees	Regular	Sustaining	Advocate	Patron
	$20	$50	$100	$500

Programs Demonstration forests and research programs. Develops certification systems for raw materials and secondary products. Provides community outreach through conferences, videos and publications. Provides training and certification programs for education of ecoforesters. Offers research grants and scholarships. Helps community watershed and land trusts set up ecoforestry programs. Helps groups in other countries to set up Ecoforestry Institute affiliates.

ELM RESEARCH INSTITUTE

ELM STREET   HARRISVILLE NH 03450
PHONE (603) 827 3048   FAX (603) 827 3794

Founded 1967 • *Geographic Coverage* National • *Organization Members* 650 cities and colleges

Mission To combat Dutch Elm disease and restore Elm trees to the American landscape.

Annual Fees	Regular	Organization	Corporation	Sustaining
	$25	$50	$50	$50

Other Fees *Charter* $100 • *Town / City* $300 to 1,500 depending on community size

Programs The Institute's "Johnny Elmseed" project distributes disease-resistant American Liberty Elm trees (a hybrid developed by the Institute for its ability to resist Dutch Elm Disease) to communities and college campuses across the country.

Publications Periodical newsletter *Elm Leaves*. Report *Conscientious Injectors Report*

Multimedia Online information service 1-800-FOR-ELMS

Who's Who EXECUTIVE DIRECTOR JOHN P. HANSEL

FOREST ECOSYSTEM RESCUE NETWORK (THE)

7781 LENOX AVENUE   JACKSONVILLE FL 32221

Founded 1983 • *Geographic Coverage* Global • *Other Field of Focus* Environmental Education / Careers / Information / Networks *Chapters* 3, in Canada, New Zealand, and Mexico • *Members* 100 including organizations

Mission To resist the destruction of forests and eventually restore forests to health. Historically, the Network has focused primarily on the threat

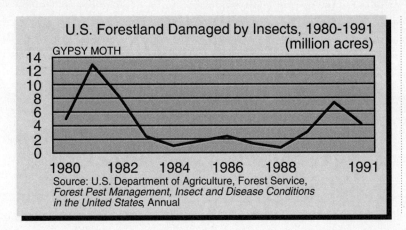

U.S. Forestland Damaged by Insects, 1980-1991
(million acres)

GYPSY MOTH

Source: U.S. Department of Agriculture, Forest Service, *Forest Pest Management, Insect and Disease Conditions in the United States*, Annual

burning. They work with local people and governments to stem the temptation to harvest the forests. Some groups simply purchase land, acre by acre, to make it private and unavailable to the local "harvesters". Others make their mission in planting trees and replanting forests. They celebrate the tree and its symbol of life, and sponsor nurseries and tree-planting forays to replenish what has been lost. Through these groups comes Arbor Day, the planting of seedlings of appropriate species in cleared areas, and other methods of bringing attention to the worldwide problem of deforestation.

Whatever methodology is applied, the common goal is to stem the forest destruction and promote replenishment.

STILL, THE AMOUNT OF DAMAGE is enormous. Much of the lost ▶

posed by pollution to temperate forests, but also actively supports protection of both temperate and tropical forests from the threat of overcutting.

Annual Fees

Regular	Individual non-US	Local Chapter	National Chapter
$16.50	$18	$25	$50

Funding *Membership* 100%

Usage *Programs* 100%

Programs Tree Bank (Genetic Rescue) Program seeks to insure the genetic diversity of tree species which are at risk. Fate of Our Forests Conferences, is a call for a set of simultaneous, worldwide conferences where people meet in their own regions to decide what they can do to save and restore forests.

Publications *Robin Newsletter* • *Forest Activist*

FOREST HISTORY SOCIETY

701 VICKERS AVENUE
PHONE (919) 682 3919
DURHAM NC 27701

Founded 1946 • *Geographic Coverage* North America, Global *Cooperative Partners* Duke University, American Forest Council, American Forestry Association, National Forest Products Association, Society of American Foresters, Western Timber Association

Mission To better understand the critical relationships between human beings and the world's forests by exploring the history of timber, water, soil, forage, fish and wildlife, recreation, scenic values, and the people who lived on the land.

Annual Fees

Regular	Corporation	Library Subscription	Institution
$30+	$150+	$45	$50

Total Income $341,000

Total Expenses $443,000

Programs Carl A. Weyerhaeuser Library Program. Alvin J. Huss Archival Program. Ongoing efforts in research and publication, reference and referral services, conferences, awards, and fellowships.

Publications Quarterly journal *Forest & Conservation History*. Quarterly newsletter *The Cruiser*. Numerous books, brochures and pamphlets published in cooperation with trade and university presses

Multimedia Computer information. Films

For more Information Annual Report, Database, Library

Who's Who PRESIDENT **HESTER TURNER** • VICE PRESIDENT **PETER J. MURPHY** • SECRETARY **HAROLD K. STEEN** • TREASURER **LUTHER E. BIRDZELL** • LIBRARIAN **CHERYL OAKES**

FOREST TRUST

P.O. BOX 519
PHONE (505) 983 8992
SANTA FE NM 87504
FAX (505) 986 0798

Geographic Coverage Regional, National, North America • *Cooperative Partner* Practitioners' Network

Mission To protect forests and foster productive relationships between human and natural communities. The Trust challenges traditional forest management philosophies and provides resource protection strategies to grassroots environmental organizations, rural communities, and public agencies. The Trust also provides land stewardship services to owners of private lands of significant conservation value.

Funding

Membership	Foundations	Fees for Services	Other
44%	5%	45%	6%

Total Income $588,000

Usage by Program *Community Forestry* 38% • *Land Stewardship*

forests, especially in tropical regions, is gone forever - and with them the ability of the land to sustain a forest that has been hurt by soil erosion. Trees are being felled or lost to pollution and acid rain with increasing rapidity. Species are disappearing at an alarming extinction rate. The atmosphere continues to collect carbon dioxide, methane, and other harmful chemicals. Time has become as much an enemy as unchecked population growth and poverty. Every day wasted means thousands more acres are lost and environmental disaster is that much closer. The battle for the world's forests is not just to preserve natural wildlife habitats, or the lifestyles of indigenous peoples, or the beauty and grandeur of the areas. It is a battle to keep one dominant species from extinction: human beings. •

John Vargo

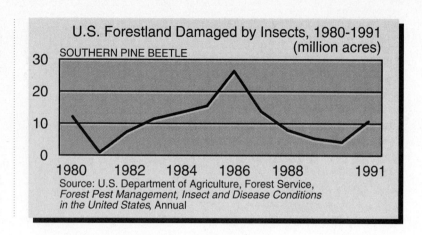

U.S. Forestland Damaged by Insects, 1980-1991 (million acres)

SOUTHERN PINE BEETLE

Source: U.S. Department of Agriculture, Forest Service, *Forest Pest Management, Insect and Disease Conditions in the United States*, Annual

---

37% • *National Forests* 18% • *General Program* 6% • *Land Trust* 1%

Total Expenses $571,000

Programs National forest program responds to complex federal forest management issues. Land trust program protects private forest and range lands through conservation easements, land acquisition and management. Stewardship program provides services to absentee landowners.

Publications Periodicals including newsletter *Forest Trust Quarterly Report* • *Quarterly Grassroots Network News* • *Monthly Practitioner Newsletter*. Directory of forest-based rural development practitioners 1993. Other publications include *Working Session 1993: Restructuring the Timber Economy* • *Biennial Report*. Numerous papers, research reports, and workshop manuals

For more Information Annual Report, List of Publications

Who's Who EXECUTIVE DIRECTOR **HENRY H. CAREY** • PROJECT MANAGER LAND STEWARDSHIP PROGRAM **STEPHEN GRANT**

FRIENDS OF THE EARTH USA   PAGE 22
218 "D" STREET, SE   WASHINGTON DC 20003
PHONE (202) 544 2600   FAX (202) 543 4710

INTERNATIONAL SOCIETY FOR THE PRESERVATION OF THE TROPICAL RAINFOREST (THE)
3931 CAMINO DE LA CUMBRE   SHERMAN OAKS CA 91423
PHONE (818) 788 2002   FAX (818) 990 3333

Founded 1983 • *Geographic Coverage* Global • *Focused Countries* Brazil, Peru, Costa Rica, Venezuela, Ecuador • *Other Field of Focus* Ecosystem Protection / Biodiversity • *Chapters* 3 • *Individual Members* 9,000

Mission To conserve tropical forest areas through park implementation and species preservation; to work directly at governmental and village levels to crea-

te awareness of the importance of environmental stewardship for future generations; to help local people set up sustainable cooperatives and cottage industries within the framework of their cultural heritage; to promote the use of the Society's Peruvian research camp to enhance understanding of the rainforest's biodiversity; to promote "Managed Educational Conservation Tourism" which provides local people with revenue from ecotourism, demonstrating to both visitors and inhabitants the importance of preserving these natural resources.

Annual Fees	*Regular*	*Student/Senior*	*Organization*	*Corporation*	*Families*
	$25	$20	$35	$35	$30

Other Fees *Lifetime* $100

Funding	*Membership*	*Corporations*	*Foundations*
	30%	20%	50%

Usage	*Administration*	*Programs*
	10%	90%

Programs Preservation of the Amazon River Dolphin (PARD) Program. Three scientific and "ecotourist" camps on the Yarapa river in Peruvian Amazon. Establishment of the Yarapa River Communal Preserve in Peru. Tropical hardwood ban for Los Angeles City use.

Publications Newsletter *Amazon Frontline*. Book *Tropical Rainforest - A World Survey of Our Most Valuable and Endangered Habitat with a Blueprint for its Survival*

Multimedia Videos

For more Information Database

Who's Who PRESIDENT **ARNOLD NEWMAN** • SECRETARY **ARLENE NEWMAN** • EXECUTIVE DIRECTOR **ROXANNE KREMER** • LIBRARIAN **RANDALL JOHNSTON**

INTERNATIONAL SOCIETY OF TROPICAL FORESTERS
5400 GROSVENOR LANE   BETHESDA MD 20814
PHONE (301) 897 8720

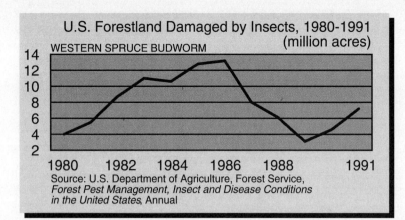

U.S. Forestland Damaged by Insects, 1980-1991 (million acres)

WESTERN SPRUCE BUDWORM

Source: U.S. Department of Agriculture, Forest Service, *Forest Pest Management, Insect and Disease Conditions in the United States*, Annual

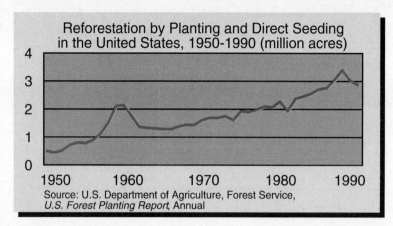

Reforestation by Planting and Direct Seeding in the United States, 1950-1990 (million acres)

Source: U.S. Department of Agriculture, Forest Service, *U.S. Forest Planting Report*, Annual

Founded 1950 • *Geographic Coverage* Global • *Chapters* 7
Individual Members 2,200

Mission To promote tropical forest conservation the world over.

Funding	Membership	Government Support	Foundations
	56%	27%	17%

Total Income $45,000

Usage	Administration	Fundraising	Programs
	33%	2%	65%

Publications Quarterly newsletter *ISTF News* (available in English, Spanish and French)

For more Information Database, Library

Who's Who PRESIDENT **WARREN T. DOOLITTLE** • VICE PRESIDENT **SANGA SABHASRI** SECRETARY **MARILYN HOSKINS** • TREASURER **RODOLFO SALAZAR** • EXECUTIVE DIRECTOR **HOWARD HEINER** • LIBRARIAN **JAMES CLARK**

LIGHTHAWK   PAGE 48
P.O. BOX 8163   SANTA FE NM 87504-8163
PHONE (505) 982 9656   FAX (505) 984 8381

MARINE FORESTS SOCIETY   PAGE 49
P.O. BOX 5843   BALBOA ISLAND CA 92662
PHONE (714) 675 7729

NATIONAL ARBOR DAY FOUNDATION
100 ARBOR AVENUE   NEBRASKA CITY NE 68410
PHONE (402) 474 5655   FAX (402) 474 0820

Founded 1971 • *Geographic Coverage* National • *Individual Members* 1,000,000

Mission The National Arbor Day Foundation is dedicated to tree planting and environmental stewardship.

Annual Fees	Regular	Introductory
	$15	$10

Funding	Membership	Other
	58%	42%

Total Income $14,934,274

Usage	Administration	Fundraising	Programs
	10%	3%	87%

Programs Trees Conservation Program, Tree City USA, Tree for America, Celebrate Arbor Day.

Publications Periodicals *Tree City USA Bulletin* • *Arbor Day*

Who's Who PRESIDENT **JIM LEUSCHEN** • VICE PRESIDENT **MRS. LEE A. CRAYTON, JR.** SECRETARY **GARY HERGENRADER**

NATIONAL TREE SOCIETY, INC. (THE)
P.O. BOX 10808   BAKERSFIELD CA 93389
PHONE (805) 589 6912

Founded 1989 • *Geographic Coverage* Global • *Chapters* 6
Organization Members 100 • *Individual Members* 1,000

Mission To preserve the balance of the Earth's biosphere by planting and caring for trees. The Society's work focuses on the goal of establishing nurseries in every state to supply the vast number of trees needed to replace the millions destroyed annually and to offset man's ever increasing use of combustion. The Society also fosters research related to trees and is developing a specialized library focusing on the earth's biosphere.

Annual Fees *Regular* $36.50

Funding	Membership	Corporations	Foundations
	5%	5%	90%

Total Income $98,807

Usage	Administration	Fundraising	Programs
	2%	10%	88%

Programs Tree planting

Publication Newsletter *TreeNews*

For more Information Library

Who's Who PRESIDENT GREGORY W. DAVIS • VICE PRESIDENT DAVID POLLEI SECRETARY JOHN BO

NATIVE FOREST COUNCIL

P.O. BOX 2171   EUGENE OR 97402
PHONE (503) 688 2600   FAX (503) 461 2156

Founded 1988 • *Geographic Coverage* National • *Cooperative Partners* National Wildlife Federation, The Wilderness Society, Defenders of Wildlife, Western Ancient Forest Campaign, Earth Island Institute, World Resources Institute, LightHawk, Friends of the Earth, Animal Welfare Institute, Protect our Woods, Heartwood, Oregon Natural Resources Council, Public Forest Foundation • *Organization Members* 130 *Individual Members* 2,000

Mission To preserve the remaining five percent of America's native forests. The Council's primary goal is to stop logging on publicly owned lands where the vast majority of native forests remain. It has committed itself to preserving and protecting all remaining native forests on public lands, to restricting all logging to the 95% of the nation's forests already logged, to restoring the native biodiversity of logged public lands, and to advocating for economic assistance for timber communities and workers.

Annual Fees *Regular* $35

Usage	Administration	Fundraising	Programs	Marketing
	11%	3%	82%	4%

Programs National media campaign to alert the public about the forces behind the destruction of their forests. Coalition building and networking with other organizations. Active participation in conferences and public speaking engagements.

Publication Newspaper *Forest Voice* focusing on National Forests issues

For more Information Library

Who's Who PRESIDENT DAVID FUNK • SECRETARY VICTOR ROZEK • TREASURER GEORGE HERMACH • EXECUTIVE DIRECTOR TIM HERMACH • CONTACT PHIL NANAS

NEW ENGLAND FORESTRY FOUNDATION

238 MAIN STREET   CAMBRIDGE MA 02142
PHONE (617) 864 4229

Founded 1944 • *Geographic Coverage* Regional • *Focused Region* New England • *Individual Members* 800

Mission To counter the deterioration of New England's unique forest resources due to fragmentation and lack of management by promoting forest land stewardship, responsible forestry practices, multigenerational forest landplanning, and environmental education.

Annual Fees *Regular* $30

Funding	Membership	Investments
	60%	40%

Total Income $130,000

Programs Annual Field Day in July; other field days scheduled throughout the year.

Publication Periodical *Timberline*

Who's Who PRESIDENT WILLIAM A. KING • VICE PRESIDENT G. MONTGOMERY LOVEJOY III

NEW FORESTS PROJECT

731 8TH STREET, SE   WASHINGTON DC 20003
PHONE (202) 547 3800   FAX (202) 546 4784

Founded 1982 • *Geographic Coverage* Global • *Focused Regions* Developing countries • *Other Field of Focus* Sustainable Development / Agriculture - Environmental Technologies • *Cooperative Partners* Solar Box Cookers Northwest, The Katalysis Foundation, Organization for the Development of Women's Enterprise, National Association of Peasant Farmers for Land - Guatemala, International Association for the Study of Common Property • *Chapter* 1 regional training center in Guatemala

Mission To promote self-help solutions for rural poverty and deforestation. To help individuals plant multipurpose, fast-growing, nitrogen-fixing trees by providing them with free seeds and technical information. Reforestation, sustainable rural development, community forestry, and agroforestry are the organization's main areas of focus.

Funding	Foundations	Contributions	Contracts & Fees	Other
	18.5%	71%	9%	1.5%

Total Income $1,126,094

Usage	Administration	Fundraising	Programs
	20%	8%	72%

Total Expenses $1,154,970

Programs World Seed Program, which aims to distribute tree seeds, planting materials and assistance, training aids, and on-site technical training in Africa, Asia, and Latin America. In 1990, the Project initiated a Regional Demonstration-Training Center in Guatemala. The Project has also begun new programs in the former USSR (e.g., the Armenia Tree Project).

Publications Quarterly newsletter *New Forests News*. Various books from the Board of Science and Technology for International Development of the National Academy of Sciences focusing on forestry, agriculture and small-scale development

Multimedia Filmstrips from World Neighbors (available in English, Spanish or French)

For more Information Annual Report

Who's Who DIRECTOR **STUART CONWAY** • PROJECT COORDINATOR **JESSICA GOLDBERGER**

PROTECT OUR WOODS
P.O. BOX 352   PAOLI IN 47454
PHONE **(812) 678 4303**

Founded 1985 • *Geographic Coverage* Local, State • *Cooperative Partners* Hoosier Environmental Council, Environmental Fund for Indiana, IN Karst Conservancy, Lost River Conservation Association, Partners in Flight, IN Forest Resource Coordinating Committee • *Individual Members* 800

Mission To protect the forests, wildlife, rivers, caves, farms, and rural communities of southern Indiana through the use of biological and economic research, education, and litigation.

Annual Fees	Regular	Families
	$20	$35

Funding	Membership	Foundations	Sales & Interest
	83%	9%	8%

Total Income $11,607

Usage	Administration	Fundraising	Programs	Other
	1%	9%	85%	5%

Programs Hoosier National Forest Project. Lost River Project. Anderson River Project. Little Pigeon Creek Project. TVA Biomass Waste/Energy Project. Patoka River Project. Ongoing efforts in the areas of sustainable forestry, military forests, and land use planning.

Publication Quarterly newsletter, circulation 5,000

For more Information Library

Who's Who PRESIDENT **JOHN MAIER** • VICE PRESIDENTS **ALISON COCHRANE, JEANNE MELCHIOR** • SECRETARY **KATH KLAWITTER** • TREASURER **ANNE TANGEMAN** • EXECUTIVE DIRECTOR **BOB KLAWITTER**

RAINFOREST ACTION NETWORK
450 SANSOME STREET, SUITE 700   SAN FRANCISCO CA 94111
PHONE **(415) 398 4404**   FAX **(415) 398 2732**

Founded 1985 • *Geographic Coverage* Global • *Focused Regions* Tropical regions worldwide • *Other Field of Focus* Human Rights & Environment • *Cooperative Partners* World Rainforest Movement, Friends of the Earth Malaysia, Rainforest Information Centre • *Chapters* 150 *Individual Members* 35,000

Mission To preserve the world's rainforests through activism on issues including the logging and importation of tropical timber, cattle ranching in rainforests, the activities of international development banks, and the rights of indigenous rainforest peoples. Sponsors letter writing campaigns, boycotts, and demonstrations, conducts grassroots organizing in the USA, builds coalitions, and collaborates with other environmental, scientific, and grassroots groups. Works to educate the public about the effects of tropical hardwood logging, and promotes ecologically sound plantations.

Total Income $1,250,000

Publications Monthly bulletin *Action Alert*. Quarterly *World Rainforest Report* in conjunction with Friends of the Earth Malaysia and Rainforest Information Centre. Books *Wood User's Guide* • *Amazonia: Voices From the Rainforest* • *Corporate Greed and Human Need* • *Striving for Balance in Papua New Guinea*. Fact sheets.

Multimedia Online information service 1-800-989-RAIN

For more Information Library, List of Publications

Who's Who EXECUTIVE DIRECTOR **RANDALL HAYES** • CONTACT **CAMILLA FOX**

RAINFOREST ALLIANCE
65 BLEECKER STREET   NEW YORK NY 10012-2420
PHONE **(212) 677 1900**   FAX **(212) 677 2187**

Founded 1987 • *Geographic Coverage* Global • *Other Field of Focus* Human Rights & Environment

Mission To conserve the world's endangered tropical rainforests, by developing and promoting economically viable and socially desirable alternatives to tropical deforestation. The Alliance works in concert with local peoples to develop forests products and businesses that offer long term stable income for native people.

Annual Fees	Regular	Student/Senior
	$25	$15

Programs Banana Project. Timber Project. Smart Wood Certification Program. Amazon Rivers Project. Catalysts Grant Program.

Publication Newsletter *The Canopy*

Who's Who EXECUTIVE DIRECTOR **DANIEL R. KATZ**

SAVE AMERICA'S FORESTS

4 LIBRARY COURT, SE   WASHINGTON DC 20003
PHONE (202) 544 9219

Founded 1990 • *Geographic Coverage* National • *Organization Members* 303 groups, 72 corporations

Mission Save America's Forests is a coalition of groups, businesses, and individuals working to pass national laws protecting forest ecosystems.

Annual Fees	Regular	Student/Senior
	$25	$15

Funding	Membership	Foundations
	85%	15%

Publications Quarterly newsletter *DC Update*, circulation 12,000. Book *Citizens Action Guide*. Periodic action alerts and fax action alerts.

Who's Who DIRECTORS **CARL ROSS**, **MARK WINSTEIN**

SAVE THE RAINFOREST, INC.

604 JAMIE STREET   DODGEVILLE WI 53533
PHONE (608) 935 9435

Founded 1988 • *Geographic Coverage* Africa, Central America, Southeast Asia • *Cooperative Partners* The Nature Conservancy, World Wildlife Fund, The Monteverde Conservation League, Cultural Survival, The International Council for Bird Preservation, The International Children's Rainforest Network, Children's Carbon Dioxide Challenge Coalition • *Members* 15,000 including organizations

Mission To involve schools from around the USA in projects that educate people about the rainforest. To provide opportunities for students and teachers to actively campaign for rainforest conservation.

Funding	Corporations	Foundations
	5%	95%

Total Income $482,000

Usage	Administration	Programs
	15%	85%

Publication Book *Teachers Guide to Environmental Action* including information on rainforests, resource lists, speaker lists, descriptions of conservation projects schools can support and descriptions of two-week rainforest ecology courses that are available for teachers and high school students each summer.

Who's Who PRESIDENT **BRUCE CALHOUN** • SECRETARY **JACK HARRISON**

SAVE-THE-REDWOODS LEAGUE

114 SANSOME STREET, ROOM 605   SAN FRANCISCO CA 94104
PHONE (415) 362 2352   FAX (415) 362 7017

Founded 1918 • *Geographic Coverage* National • *Cooperative Partners* California State Park Commission, National Park Service

Mission To rescue from destruction representative areas of America's primeval forests; to purchase Redwood groves by private subscription; to foster and encourage a better and more general understanding of the value of the primeval Redwood, Sequoia and other forests of America as natural objects of major interest to present and future generations, and to support reforestation and conservation of the country's forest areas.

Annual Fees	Regular	Contributing	Sustaining	Patron
	$10	$25	$50	$500

Other Fees *Lifetime* $100 • *Associate Founder* $2,500 • *Founder* $5,000

Publications Quarterly bulletin *Save-the-Redwoods League*. Guide *California Redwood Parks and Preserves*

Who's Who PRESIDENT **BRUCE S. HOWARD** • VICE PRESIDENT **R. A. L. MENZIES** TREASURER **WILLIAM P. WENTWORTH** • EXECUTIVE DIRECTOR **JOHN B. DEWITT** • ASSISTANT SECRETARY **MARY A. ANGLE-FRANZINI**

SOCIETY FOR THE PROTECTION OF NEW HAMPSHIRE FORESTS

54 PORTSMOUTH STREET   CONCORD NH 03301-5400
PHONE (603) 224 9945   FAX (603) 228 0423

Founded 1901 • *Geographic Coverage* State • *Chapter* 1 • *Individual Members* 10,000

Mission To promote conservation and sound management of resources through land protection, management, education and advocacy.

Annual Fees *Regular* $26

Programs School programs. Tree Steward Program. Land Steward Program. Tree Farm.

Publication Bimonthly magazine *Forest Notes*, circulation 20,000

For more Information Library

Who's Who PRESIDENT **PAUL O. BOFINGER** • EXECUTIVE DIRECTOR **ROBERT TROWBRIDGE** • CONTACT **RICHARD OBER**

TREEPEOPLE   PAGE 196

12601 MULHOLLAND DRIVE   BEVERLY HILLS CA 90210
PHONE (818) 753 4600   FAX (818) 753 4625

TREES FOR LIFE

1103 JEFFERSON   WICHITA KS 67203
PHONE (316) 263 7294   FAX (316) 263 5293

Founded 1984 • *Geographic Coverage* Global • *Focused Countries* Guatemala, India, Nepal, USA • *Foreign Chapters* 2, in Austria, and Canada • *Organization Members* 1,500 • *Individual Members* 5,000

Mission To assist in the worldwide planting of fruit trees, which protect the environment and provide a self-renewing source of nutrition for people in need. The program is now operating in India, Guatemala, and Nepal with affiliate offices in Austria and Canada. To date, more than 14 million trees have been planted, and plans call for the planting of 100 million fruit trees during this decade.

Annual Fees Any gift qualifies

Funding	Corporations	Foundations	Donors	Merchandising	Other
	19%	22%	30%	22%	7%

Total Income $304,049

Usage	Administration	Fundraising	Programs
	17%	15%	68%

Programs Project Trees For Life includes a tree adventure planting kit and educational materials for elementary students designed to promote ecological awareness, to encourage the planting of trees, and to teach the relationship between trees and hunger in the world. Since 1987 more than one million children in the US have participated in this program.

Publications Semiannual *Life Lines* • *Update*

Who's Who PRÉSIDENT BALBIR S. MATHUR • SECRETARY DAVID KIMBLE • TREASURER VICTOR KLAASEN

TREES FOR TOMORROW, INC.   PAGE 250

P.O. BOX 609
611 SHERIDAN STREET   EAGLE RIVER WI 54521
PHONE (715) 479 6456

VEGETARIAN SOCIETY (THE)   PAGE 280
SAVE THE RAINFOREST ACTION COMMITTEE
P.O. BOX 34427   LOS ANGELES CA 90034
PHONE (310) 281 1907

WORLD WILDLIFE FUND   PAGE 156
WWF
1250 24TH STREET, NW   WASHINGTON DC 20037-1175
PHONE (202) 293 4800   FAX (202) 293 9211

ASSOCIATION FORESTIÈRE DU BAS-ST-LAURENT ET DE LA GASPÉSIE, INC.
BAS-ST.-LAURENT AND GASPÉSIE FORESTRY ASSOCIATION, INC.
378 AVENUE DE LA CATHÉDRALE   RIMOUSKI PQ G5L 5K9
PHONE (418) 723 3161   FAX (418) 723 3161

Founded 1940 • *Geographic Coverage* Local, Province • *Cooperative Partners* Association Forestière Québécoise, Inc. - Québec Forestry Association, Inc., Canadian Forestry Association • *Chapter* 1 • *Individual Members* 300

Mission To promote the preservation of forests, to inform the public about their important role, to motivate the population to take an active part in the preservation of forests, to promote the thoughtful use of all natural resources as a basic principle for human welfare, and to collaborate with other groups sharing the same philosophy.

Annual Fees	Regular	Organization
	$31.16	$58

Programs Conferences. Tree and Forest Week. Golf tournament

For more Information Library

Who's Who PRESIDENT BERNARD LAUDRY • VICE PRESIDENTS EUGENE LAUDRY, PIERRE BERTHELET • SECRETARY JULIE BUJOLD

ASSOCIATION FORESTIÈRE QUÉBÉCOISE, INC.
QUÉBEC FORESTRY ASSOCIATION, INC.
175 RUE ST JEAN, 4EME ETAGE   QUÉBEC PQ G1R 1N4
PHONE (418) 529 2911   FAX (418) 529 3021

Founded 1939 • *Geographic Coverage* Province • *Cooperative Partners* Canadian Forestry Association, Québec Forest Industries Association Ltd., Association Forestière du Bas-St-Laurent et de la Gaspésie, Inc. - Bas-St.-Laurent and Gaspésie Forestry Association, Inc., Ordre des Ingénieurs Forestiers du Québec - Québec Society of Forest Engineers, Club 4H Québec • *Chapters* 11 • *Organization Members* 100 *Individual Members* 4,000

Mission To conserve and protect Québec trees and forests.

Annual Fees	Regular	Student/Senior	Families	Organization	Corporation
	$30	$20	$20	$300	$2,000

Other Fees *Lifetime* $300

Funding	Membership	Government Support	Corporations
	10%	40%	50%

Programs Remarkable Trees Programme (Programme Arbres Remarquables). Tree and Forest Week (Semaine de l'Arbre et des Forêts). Forest Camps (Camps Forestiers).

Publication Bimonthly review *Forêt Conservation*, circulation 6,000

For more Information Database, Library

Who's Who PRESIDENT SERGE LEBLANC • VICE PRESIDENT DANIELLE DUSSAULT • EXE-CUTIVE DIRECTOR LOUISE BRIAND

CANADIAN INSTITUTE OF FORESTRY

151 SLATER STREET, SUITE 1005   OTTAWA ON K1P 5H3
PHONE (613) 234 2242   FAX (613) 234 6181

Founded 1908 • *Geographic Coverage* National, North America
Cooperative Partners International Union of Societies of Foresters, International Union of Forest Research Organizations • *Chapters* 22
Organization Members 55 • *Individual Members* 2,400

Mission To advance the stewardship of Canada's forest resources through leadership and public awareness, to increase the knowledge of the organization's members, and to cooperate with other forestry organizations in Canada and around the world.

Annual Fees	Regular	Student	Retired	Organization	Corporation
	$120	$30	$38	$250	$250

Funding	Membership	Corporations	Subscriptions & Advertising Sales
	80%	10%	10%

Total Income $350,000

Usage	Administration	Fundraising	Programs	Chapters	Other
	25%	5%	45%	15%	10%

Total Expenses $350,000

Programs The Institute's "Sustainable Forests: A Canadian Commitment" program works in conjunction with federal and provincial ministers responsible for forests and members of the Canadian forest community to maintain and enhance the long-term health of Canadian forest ecosystems for the benefit of all living things, while providing environmental, economic, social, and cultural opportunities for the benefit of present and future generations. Annual conference and business meetings. Technical conference. National continuing education program.

Publications Bimonthly journal *The Forestry Chronicle*, circulation 3,000. Monthly newsletter. Pamphlets including *Policy Statement on Sustainable Development* • *Statement on Acid Rain* • *Careers in Forestry*. Report *Sustainable Forests, A Canadian Commitment*

For more Information Annual Report, Database, Library

Who's Who PRESIDENT A. A. ROTHERHAM • VICE PRESIDENTS PETER MURPHY, HAP OLDHAM • TREASURER R. J. BOURCHIER • EXECUTIVE DIRECTOR CHRISTOPHER A. LEE

CONSULTING FORESTERS OF
BRITISH COLUMBIA   PAGE 232
890 WEST PENDER STREET, SUITE 600   VANCOUVER BC V6C 1K4
PHONE (604) 687 5500   FAX (604) 687 1327

ECOFORESTRY INSTITUTE OF CANADA (THE)
P.O. BOX 5783, STATION "B"   VICTORIA BC V8R 6S8
PHONE (604) 592 8333   FAX (604) 595 8265

Geographic Coverage North America • *Cooperative Partner* The Ecoforestry Institute USA • *Chapter* 1

Mission To provide ecologically sound alternatives to the current industrial forestry practices which for short-term gain destroy biodiversity and most other values of natural forests as well as rural communities. The Institute supports preservation of ancient and natural forests. It encourages restoration of plantation tree farms to natural forest status and recognizes that humans need to use forests in a variety of ways. These needs can be met in the long-run only if practices are consistent with the needs of forest ecosystems.

Annual Fees	Regular	Sustaining	Advocate	Patron
	$20	$50	$100	$500

Programs Demonstration forests and research programs. Develops certification systems for raw materials and secondary products. Provides community outreach through conferences, videos and publications. Provides training and certification programs for education of ecoforesters. Offers research grants and scholarships. Helps community watershed and land trusts set up ecoforestry programs. Helps groups in other countries set up Ecoforestry Institute affiliates.

FRIENDS OF NATURE CONSERVATION SOCIETY
P.O. BOX 281   CHESTER NS B0J 1J0
PHONE (902) 275 3361

Founded 1954 • *Geographic Coverage* Global • *Focused Countries* Canada, New Zealand, USA • *Other Field of Focus* Natural Resources / Water - Conservation & Quality • *Cooperative Partner* Canadian Nature Federation

Mission To maintain the balance of nature, with particular concern for the world's fast disappearing old growth forests.

Annual Fees *Regular* $30

Who's Who EXECUTIVE SECRETARY MARTIN R. HAASE

FRIENDS OF THE EARTH   PAGE 30
LES AMIS DE LA TERRE
251 LAURIER AVENUE, WEST, SUITE 701   OTTAWA ON K1P 5J6
PHONE (613) 230 3352   FAX (613) 232 4354

TREEmendous SASKATCHEWAN FOUNDATION, INC.

Box 400   Prince Albert SK S6V 5R7
Phone (306) 763 2784   Fax (306) 953 2360

Founded 1990 • *Geographic Coverage* Province • *Cooperative Partners* Prairie Farm Rehabilitation Administration, Provincial Tree Nursery, Save Our Soils Programme, Scouts Canada, Souris Basin Development Authority, Urban Parks Association, Tree Plan Canada

Mission To provide the opportunity for all citizens of Saskatchewan to participate in improving the quality of the environment through participation in tree planting and tending activities, and environmental awareness programs; to expand tree planting and tending activities presently undertaken in the province of Saskatchewan; to expand awareness and understanding of the importance of trees to the province's natural, rural, and urban environment.

Programs Recent TREEmendous projects have ranged from the planting of a single tree to over 40,000 trees in a single project. The "Power 99FM Plants A Forest Project" sets itself the goal of planting one tree for every man, woman and child in Prince Albert and the surrounding area. In the Foam Lake Adopt-A-Tree Programme, organizations and individuals were invited to come out and pick up a tree or trees to plant in the community or in private yards. The Central Canada Potash Mine Colonsay Project resulted in the planting of over 10,000 seedlings.

For more Information Annual Report, Library

Who's Who President **Thomas H. Ballantyne** • Secretary **Carol Adams** Other **Marie Grono, Del Phillips, Larry Schlosser**

national parks land use, conservation, acquisition

CHAPTER 7

The Land and Its Resources : A Public Trust, by John Vargo

ONE OF THE EARLIEST AND STRONGEST ecological programs in North America has been the job of staking out, establishing and protecting national parks. Since 1872 when the Yellowstone Act was instituted, champions of preservation gazed in awe at the grandeur of nature. "It was like lying in a great solemn cathedral", President Theodore Roosevelt recalled in 1903 about camping among the redwoods with naturalist John Muir. To Muir, the wilderness was "the face of all Heaven". With Theodore Roosevelt installed in the White House, conservationists had a powerful ally. President Roosevelt displayed a capacity for rejoicing over nature, and a tendency for showing anger when these areas were marred, desecrated and pillaged. In 1906 he signed the Antiquities Act which allowed for the preservation of historic and scenic sites by executive order. By the end of his tenure as President, Roosevelt had doubled the number of national parks.

DESPITE SUCH A STRENGTH ROOTED in history and government protection, national parks have never been without threat. Early dangers to the parks came from speculators, logging, railroad and

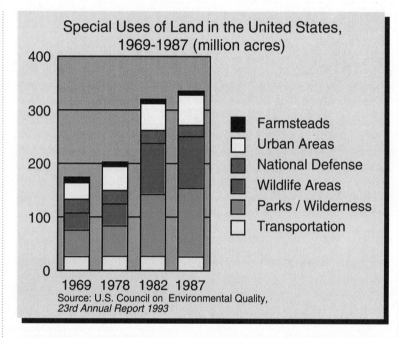

Special Uses of Land in the United States, 1969-1987 (million acres)

Legend:
- Farmsteads
- Urban Areas
- National Defense
- Wildlife Areas
- Parks / Wilderness
- Transportation

1969 1978 1982 1987

Source: U.S. Council on Environmental Quality, *23rd Annual Report 1993*

mining interests, and the ever-encroaching westward expansion. Today, profit still appears to drive many of the immediate dangers: housing tracts and shopping malls line parks borders like the skyscrapers girding New York's Central Park. But a potentially lethal danger comes from the very people who love the parks. In 1920 over one million people visited the national parks in the United States. By 2010 park authorities expect over a half billion visitors to have passed by their gates. Among the people who

appreciate and respect nature's gifts will be consumers, generating tons of garbage (25 tons daily in Yosemite alone), trampling through the delicate brush, plucking and trading artifacts and, even, poaching. In the Florida Everglades, the number of wading birds has diminished by 90 percent since the 1930s. Despite the grizzly bear's place of prominence on the California state flag, not a single specimen can be found running wild in the Golden State. Air pollution from distant cities hovers like a heavy gray pall

over many parks. Human fecal waste leaches into groundwater. Industrial waste seeps into wetlands. Without safe wildlife corridors, creatures following the paths nature has ingrained in their brains often stray unwittingly into established communities with results usually more tragic for the animal.

AREAS WITHOUT A FEDERAL protection designation are facing problems even more dire. Millions of acres of rangeland are threatened with desertification as a result of overuse. Wetlands are being developed. Tons of nutrient-rich topsoil are disappearing from mismanaged farmlands by erosion, gone forever to rest as silt on the bottom of the Gulf of Mexico. Vast areas of forests have been stripped bare, leaving bald, undulating hilltops as a testimony to the efficiency of industry. Strip mining has created massive dust bowls in the Earth, repositories for toxic pools of water that collect inside. To the credit of industry, many of these problems are being addressed. Replanting efforts are replacing trees where earlier generations were felled. Mining companies are wary of the devastation stripping can cause and are designing new techniques for extracting minerals. New efforts are underway to replace what is lost to erosion. Notably, the term "wise use" has entered the language to define the conciliatory meeting ground for negotiation between those sworn to protect the Earth and those whose livelihood relies upon the harvesting of its riches. But, almost as soon as its inception, the "Wise Use Movement" was deemed synonymous with "anti-environment" practices. Debate complicates efforts to use, then mend the land. Does the planting of saplings in logged areas replace lost habitat? Should logging continue on public land? How much emphasis must be given to endangered species, such as the spotted owl, when their habitats are slated for clear-cutting or development?

Regardless of their positions on these issues, organizations dedicated to our national parks and land conservation almost unanimously advocate and foster education in wilderness for better understanding and appreciation of the environment. Most also stress on-going scientific research in protected lands, not only to gauge the damage done by our continuous assaults on the Earth, but to facilitate discovery, to increase our knowledge of remaining species, to enhance our relationship and dependence upon nature.

To many groups whose focus is land use, stewardship and preservation are important elements in their investments. They feel it is important to maintain the natural beauty and habitat of unprotected lands while still providing access ▶

United States

ACRES, INC.

2000 NORTH WELLS STREET   FORT WAYNE IN 46808
PHONE (219) 422 1004

Founded 1960 • *Geographic Coverage* State • *Organization Members* 10 • *Individual Members* 400

Mission The organization is dedicated to protecting the best remaining natural areas in Northeast Indiana. The natural areas are open to the public for education, scientific study, and enjoyment.

Annual Fees	Regular	Student/Senior	Families	Patron
	$15	$10	$25	$100

Programs Annual Tree Day. Annual members dinner. Sponsors numerous hikes. Work days. Programs for school groups, clubs, and organizations.

Publication Quarterly brochure *ACRES*

Who's Who PRESIDENT TED HEEMSTRA • VICE PRESIDENTS JAMES M. BARRETT, ETHYLE BLOCH, BOB WEBER • SECRETARY JANE DUSTIN

ADIRONDACK COUNCIL (THE)

P.O. BOX D-2   ELIZABETHTOWN NY 12932-0640
PHONE (518) 873 2240

Founded 1975 • *Geographic Coverage* Local • *Cooperative Partners* Association for the Protection of the Adirondacks, Natural Resources Defense Council, The Wilderness Society, National Parks and Conservation Association

Mission Dedicated to the protection, preservation, and enhancement of the Adirondack Park for future generations.

Annual Fees	Regular	Sustaining	Sponsor	Patron
	$25	$50	$100	$250

Other Fees *Benefactor* $500 • *Friend* $1,000 • *Guardian* $5,000

Funding	Individual Contributions	Foundations	Other
	69%	24%	7%

Total Income $1,254,913

Usage	Salaries & Related Expenses	Postage & Printing	Other
	49.5%	16%	15.5%

Other Usage *Professional Services* 10% • *Communications* 9%

Total Expenses $1,256,699

Programs Public education. Legislative lobbying. Legal action when necessary. Monitoring Park protection efforts and prodding state government. Mobilizing public opinion when major threats and opportunities arise.

Publications Quarterly newsletter *Adirondack Council*. Report *State of the Park 1993*. Conference proceedings on Managing Growth and Development. *Adirondack Wildguide - a natural history guide to the Adirondack Park*

For more Information Annual Report

Who's Who PRESIDENT PETER BORRELLI • VICE PRESIDENTS KIM ELLIMAN, THOMAS D. THATCHER • SECRETARY DEAN L. COOK • TREASURER JOHN L. ERNST • EXECUTIVE DIRECTOR TIMOTHY J. BURKE • ADMINISTRATOR DONNA BEAL

APPALACHIAN TRAIL CONFERENCE

WASHINGTON & JACKSON STREETS, P.O. BOX 807 HARPERS FERRY WV 25425
PHONE (304) 535 6331

Founded 1925 • *Geographic Coverage* Regional • *Other Field of Focus* Quality of Life / Outdoor Activities • *Cooperative Partners*

► to responsible industry. They believe a common ground may be established for common good - a sound balance between industry and nature, access with strictly limited harm. Some are dedicated to agricultural research to better utilize land, such as farms and ranches, already designated for food production. They hope to preserve the remaining feet of topsoil, prevent erosion, and halt ►

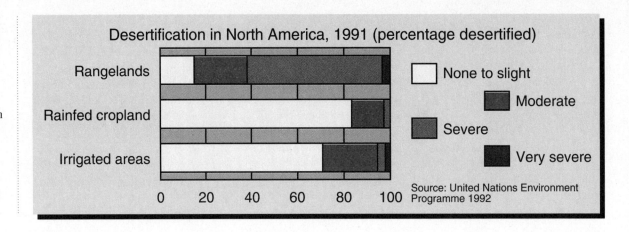

Desertification in North America, 1991 (percentage desertified)

Rangelands

Rainfed cropland

Irrigated areas

None to slight

Moderate

Severe

Very severe

0 20 40 60 80 100

Source: United Nations Environment Programme 1992

National Park Service, Trust for Appalachian Trail Land • *Organization Members* 165 • *Individual Members* 22,450

Mission To promote, maintain, and manage the Appalachian Trail and associated lands.

Annual Fees	Regular	Student/Senior	Families
	$25	$18	$30

Other Fees *Lifetime* $500 to 750

Funding	Membership	Government Support	Corporations	Foundations	Sales	Endowment
	26.5%	20%	5%	15.5%	27%	6%

Total Income $1,898,266

Usage	Administration	Fundraising	Programs
	15.3%	6%	78.7%

Programs Neighborhood Greenway-Crew Program active in bridge and shelter construction, trail relocation, trail assessment, technical support, and information service.

Publications Various magazines including *Appalachian Trailway News* published 5 times per year • Bimonthly *The Register* • Semiannual *Trail Lands*. Official Appalachian Trail guidebooks

For more Information Annual Report

Who's Who CHAIR MARGARET C. DRUMMOND • VICE CHAIRS DAVID FIELD, CLAUDE R. EPPS, JR., SARA DAVIS • SECRETARY COLIN T. TAIT • EXECUTIVE DIRECTOR DAVID N. STARTZELL

CENTER FOR NATURAL LANDS MANAGEMENT, INC.

3228 WINDSOR DRIVE   SACRAMENTO CA 95864-3827
PHONE (916) 481 6454   FAX (916) 485 8911

Founded 1990 • *Geographic Coverage* National • *Other Field of*

Focus Ecosystem Protection / Biodiversity • *Cooperative Partner* The Nature Conservancy • *Chapters* 4

Mission To manage natural resource conservation lands in perpetuity for the public trust and in accordance with the intent and purpose for which they have been dedicated; to protect biological diversity; to ensure biologically sound mitigation projects by working with governmental agencies and the development community; to promote the values of resource conservation and biodiversity through public awareness and education; and to encourage public involvement and volunteerism in resource conservation.

Annual Fees	Regular	Student/Senior	Families	Organization	Corporation
	$35	$25	$50	$50	$1,000+

Other Fees *Associate* $100 • *Sustaining* $250 • *Charter* $1,000

Funding	Membership	Government Support	Corporations	Foundations	Contract Work
	20%	20%	10%	30%	20%

Total Income $150,000

Usage	Administration	Fundraising	Programs
	25%	5%	70%

Total Expenses $150,000

Publication Quarterly newsletter *Perpetuity*

For more Information Database, Library

Who's Who PRESIDENT KENT A. SMITH • VICE PRESIDENT BRENDA PACE • EXECUTIVE DIRECTOR SHERRY TERESA • ASSOCIATE DIRECTOR PETER H. BLOOM

COALITION TO PROTECT ANIMALS
IN PARKS AND REFUGES

PAGE 135

P.O. BOX 26   SWAIN NY 14884-0026
PHONE (607) 545 6213

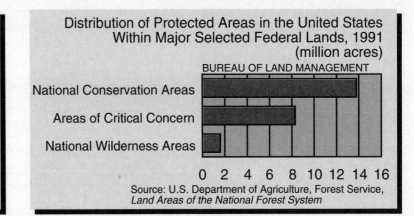

U.S. National Park System, 1900-1992 (million acres)

Number of protected parks in 1900 = 17

Number of protected parks in 1992 = 362

Source: U.S. Department of the Interior, National Park Service, *Areas Administered by the National Park Service, Information Tables,* Annual

Distribution of Protected Areas in the United States Within Major Selected Federal Lands, 1991 (million acres)

BUREAU OF LAND MANAGEMENT

National Conservation Areas

Areas of Critical Concern

National Wilderness Areas

Source: U.S. Department of Agriculture, Forest Service, *Land Areas of the National Forest System*

CONTINENTAL DIVIDE TRAIL SOCIETY — PAGE 275

P.O. Box 30002   BETHESDA MD 20824-0002

PHONE (301) 493 4080

EAST BAY REGIONAL PARK DISTRICT — PAGE 275

CRABE COVE VISITOR CENTER

ROBERT CROWN MEMORIAL STATE BEACH

1252 McKAY AVENUE   ALAMEDA CA 94501

PHONE (510) 521 6887

FEDERATION OF WESTERN OUTDOOR CLUBS — PAGE 276

512 BOYLSTON AVENUE, EAST, SUITE 106   SEATTLE WA 98102

PHONE (206) 322 3041

FLORIDA TRAIL ASSOCIATION, INC. — PAGE 276

P.O. Box 13708   GAINESVILLE FL 32604-1708

PHONE (904) 378 8823

FRIENDS OF THE EVERGLADES — PAGE 45

101 WESTWARD DRIVE, OFFICE 2   MIAMI SPRINGS FL 33166

PHONE (305) 888 1230

GLACIER INSTITUTE (THE)

P.O. Box 7457   KALISPELL MT 59904

PHONE (406) 756 3837

Founded 1983 • *Geographic Coverage* Local • *Other Field of Focus* Ecosystem Protection / Biodiversity

Mission The Glacier Institute provides field classes which examine Glacier National Park and the surrounding ecosystem's cultural and natural resources while increasing public awareness of management policies, resource issues, and research efforts.

Funding	*Foundations*	*Course Fees*
	25%	75%

Usage	*Administration*	*Programs*
	10%	90%

Total Expenses $90,000

Programs Field classes. Internships.

Who's Who PRESIDENT **W. A. BLOOD** • VICE PRESIDENT **BRACE HAYDEN** • SECRETARY **JOHN H. BRUNINGA III**

GOLDEN GATE NATIONAL PARK ASSOCIATION

BUILDING 201, FORT MASON   SAN FRANCISCO CA 94123

PHONE (415) 776 0693

Founded 1981 • *Geographic Coverage* National • *Cooperative Partner* National Park Service • *Chapter* 1 • *Individual Members* 8,000

Mission Dedicated to supporting and protecting America's national parks.

Annual Fees	*Regular*	*Student/Senior*	*Families*	*Corporation*
	$25	$20	$35	$1,000

Funding	*Membership*	*Foundations*	*Program Income*
	8%	38%	54%

Total Income $4,000,000

Usage	*Administration*	*Fundraising*	*Programs*
	19%	10%	71%

Total Expenses $3,700,000

Programs Education/interpretation. Wildlife research. Habitat restora-

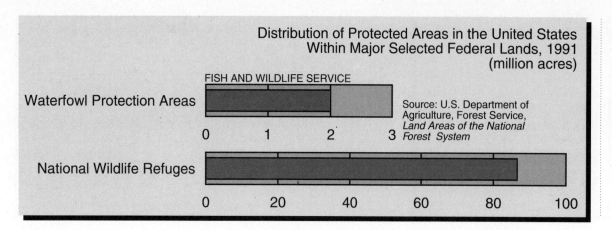

Distribution of Protected Areas in the United States
Within Major Selected Federal Lands, 1991
(million acres)

FISH AND WILDLIFE SERVICE

Waterfowl Protection Areas

0   1   2   3

Source: U.S. Department of Agriculture, Forest Service, *Land Areas of the National Forest System*

National Wildlife Refuges

0   20   40   60   80   100

▶ desertification. Others, citing the devastating destruction that has already occurred, believe a hands-off policy is the only remedy for an ailing environment. Some organizations use their funds to purchase large tracts of land before corporations or developers gain control. The deeds to these lands are held in trust, that they will never be sold for development of any kind, ensuring that the land will remain unmolested and the

tion. Park site improvements. Park planning.

Publications Quarterly newsletter. Books on Alcatraz, Fort Point, Muir Woods, Marin Headlands and Lands End. Numerous trail and subject guides

For more Information Database, Library, List of Publications

Who's Who PRESIDENT **TOBY ROSENBLATT** • VICE PRESIDENT **SHARON WOO** • TREASURER **MARK PERRY** • EXECUTIVE DIRECTOR **GREG MOORE** • DEVELOPMENT DIRECTOR **NANCY RATZESBERGER**

GRAND CANYON TRUST   PAGE 109
THE HOMESTEAD, ROUTE 4, BOX 718   FLAGSTAFF AZ 86001
PHONE (602) 774 7488   FAX (602) 774 7570

GREAT SMOKY MOUNTAINS INSTITUTE AT TREMONT
ROUTE 1, BOX 700   TOWNSEND TN 37882
PHONE (615) 448 6709

Founded 1969 • *Geographic Coverage* Regional • *Other Field of Focus* Natural Resources / Water - Conservation & Quality • *Cooperative Partner* Great Smoky Mountain National Park • *Individual Members* 2,000

Mission To provide programs that will increase the awareness, appreciation, and understanding of the natural and cultural resources of the Great Smoky Mountain National Park and promote appropriate stewardship of these resources.

Annual Fees *Individual program fees vary from $64 and up*

Total Income $500,000

Usage	Administration	Programs
	20%	80%

Programs Offers naturalist weekends, educator workshops, backpacking adventures, nature photography, cultural explorations, summer camps, school groups, Elderhostel, 3-Day Intensives.

Publication Guide *Trashers Guide: Connecting People and Nature*

Multimedia Audiotape *I Love the Earth*

Who's Who PRESIDENT **MARTAN OATES** • VICE PRESIDENT **VERNON McCURRY** SECRETARY **DAVE SCANLON**

GREATER YELLOWSTONE COALITION   PAGE 47
P.O. BOX 1874   BOZEMAN MT 59771
PHONE (406) 586 1593   FAX (406) 586 0851

ISAAC W. BERNHEIM FOUNDATION
BERNHEIM ARBORETUM AND RESEARCH FOREST   CLERMONT KY 40110
PHONE (502) 543 2451   FAX (502) 543 2331

Founded 1929 • *Geographic Coverage* Regional • *Focused Regions* Midwest and South • *Cooperative Partners* Kentucky Department of Education, Kentucky Department of Tourism, Kentucky Environmental Protection Agency • *Organization Members* 200 • *Individual Members* 1,250

Mission To promote land protection and conservation.

Annual Fees	Regular	Families	Organization	Corporation
	$25	$35	$100	$250

Total Income $987,000

Total Expenses $1,065,000

Programs Horticulture. Environmental education. Natural history. "Recycle, Reduce, Reuse" Program. Organic mulching. Art in Nature - Flora & Fauna.

creatures living there will always have a place. Associations dedicated to land use and the protection of national parks understand the fragility of the natural balance. By observing what we have preserved, we can better understand what we have lost in lands long ago given away to "progress". We can see how the elimination of a single species, or the introduction of a non-indigenous one, can ▶

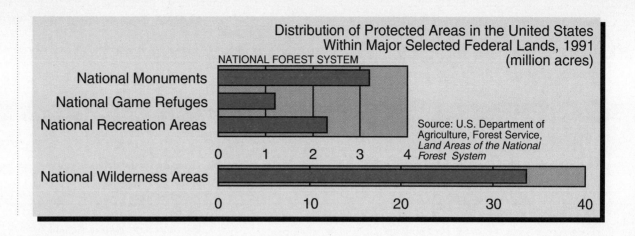

Distribution of Protected Areas in the United States Within Major Selected Federal Lands, 1991 (million acres)

NATIONAL FOREST SYSTEM

Source: U.S. Department of Agriculture, Forest Service, *Land Areas of the National Forest System*

Publications Quarterly newsletter *The Peddler*, circulation 2,800. Catalog of plants

For more Information Library

Who's Who PRESIDENT BOYCE F. MARTIN • VICE PRESIDENT MS. LEE COCHRAN • SECRETARY L. SHAPIRA • EXECUTIVE DIRECTOR C. K. MCCLURE MANAGER OF OPERATIONS CARL SUK • DIRECTOR OF EDUCATION GAYLE WEINSTEIN • DIRECTOR OF RESEARCH VARLEY WIEDMAN • CONTACT MS. LEIGH RAQUE

IZAAK WALTON LEAGUE OF AMERICA (THE) PAGE 112

1401 WILSON BOULEVARD, LEVEL B   ARLINGTON VA 22209-2318
PHONE (703) 528 1818   FAX (703) 528 1836

JOSHUA TREE NATIONAL MONUMENT

74485 NATIONAL MONUMENT DRIVE   29 PALMS CA 92277
PHONE (619) 367 4528   FAX (619) 367 6392

Founded 1936 • *Geographic Coverage* Local • *Cooperative Partner* United Nations Man and Biosphere Programme

Mission To promote conservation and protection of the Joshua Tree National Monument.

Funding *Government Support* 100%

For more Information Database, Library, List of Publications

Who's Who SUPERINTENDENTS DAVID E. MOORE, WILLIAM TRUESDELL, ROBERT L. MOON

LAND INSTITUTE (THE)   PAGE 293

2440 EAST WATER WELL ROAD   SALINAS KS 67401
PHONE (913) 823 5376   FAX (913) 823 8728

LAND TRUST ALLIANCE

1319 "F" STREET, NW, SUITE 501   WASHINGTON DC 20004-1106
PHONE (202) 638 4725   FAX (202) 638 4730

Founded 1982 • *Geographic Coverage* National • *Chapter* 1, in New York • *Organization Members* 620 • *Individual Members* 300

Mission To strengthen the land trust movement and ensure that land trusts have the information, skills, and resources they need to save land. One of the organization's missions consists on acting as the voice for land trusts in Washington, DC.

Annual Fees	Regular	Organization	Land Protector	Land Conservator
	$35	$100	$100	$500

Other Fees *Trustee of the Land* $1,000

Funding	Membership	Foundations	Publications & Workshops	Interest
	55%	29%	14%	2%

Total Income $650,201

Usage	Administration	Fundraising	Programs
	8%	15%	77%

Total Expenses $692,996

Programs Provides information services for a fee, produces and distributes publications, and holds an annual conference, "The National Rally", which educates and brings together land conservationists.

Publications Quarterly professional journal *Exchange*. Quarterly newsletter *LTA Landscape*. Brochure *Land Trust.* Various books including *Lessons from the States: Strengthening Land Conservation Programs through Grants to Non-profit Land Trusts* • *Starting a Land Trust* • *1991-1992 National Directory of Conservation Land Trusts* • *Preserving Family Lands* • *Developing a Land Conservation Strategy: Handbook for Land Trusts* • *Creative Land Development: Bridge to the Future*

► detrimentally affect the other creatures in a food chain. And how that effect, in turn, plays upon the rest of nature. They comprehend the direct link between humans and the environment. Hidden in the physiology of other species are medical treatments, diagnostic capabilities, and a potential wealth of cures. Moreover, there is the production of oxygen upon which our daily existence depends. Because of the dedication of our enterprising ancestors, many of North America's grand wonders are preserved and available for our enjoyment. Now that the fight to protect the environment seems more urgent, even the small wonders clinging to life in less breathtaking milieux must receive careful attention. •

John Vargo

Multimedia Videos *Land Trusts in America: Guardians of the Future* (VHS) • *For the Common Good: Preserving Private Lands with Conservation Easements*

For more Information Annual Report, Library, List of Publications

Who's Who PRESIDENT JEAN HOCKER • VICE PRESIDENT CHARLES H. COLLINS SECRETARY STEPHEN SMALL • TREASURER ROBERT MYHR • CHAIRPERSON PETER STEIN ASSOCIATE DIRECTOR KATHY BARTON • INFORMATION CENTER MANAGER SUSAN DORAN

LAND UTILIZATION ALLIANCE

P.O. BOX 1259   STOCKTON CA 95201
PHONE (209) 467 7554   FAX (209) 467 7553

Founded 1988 • *Geographic Coverage* Local • *Focused Region* Central California Valley • *Other Field of Focus* Natural Resources / Water - Conservation & Quality • *Organization Members* 60 • *Individual Members* 3,000

Mission To promote, support and encourage reasonable urban growth, the preservation of agricultural land, restoration and protection of the environment and natural resources, and the best quality of life for the urban and rural dweller, through a program of research and education.

Annual Fees

Regular	Student/Senior	Organization
$15	$5	$50

Programs Spring Forum, focuses on land use issues and provides means for working out solutions to growth problems.

Publication *LUA Newsletter*

For more Information Library

Who's Who PRESIDENT LINDA LINDBERG

MAINE COAST HERITAGE TRUST

167 PARK ROW   BRUNSWICK ME 04011
PHONE (207) 729 7366

Founded 1970 • *Geographic Coverage* State

Mission To protect land essential to the character of Maine, particularly its coastline and islands.

Annual Fees *Regular* $30

Publications Newsletter. Technical bulletins

For more Information Annual Report

Who's Who PRESIDENT JAMES J. EPSY, JR. • VICE PRESIDENT CAROLINE PRYOR

MARIN CONSERVATION LEAGUE   PAGE 113

35 MITCHELL BOULEVARD, SUITE 11   SAN RAFAEL CA 94903
PHONE (415) 472 6170

NATIONAL ASSOCIATION OF STATE PARK DIRECTORS (THE)

126 MILL BRANCH ROAD   TALLAHASSEE FL 32312
PHONE (904) 893 4959

Founded 1962 • *Geographic Coverage* National • *Individual Members* 50

Mission To promote and advance the state park systems of America, to provide a common forum for the exchange of information regarding state park programs, to take collective positions on those issues which affect state park programs, to encourage the development of professional leadership in the administration of state park and recreation programs, and to establish and maintain a working relationship with other agencies involved in park and recreation programs.

Annual Fees *Regular* $400

Funding *Membership* 100%

Total Income $20,000

Usage

	Administration	Programs
	40%	60%

Publication *Annual Information Exchange*

Who's Who PRESIDENT DALE R. BREE • VICE PRESIDENT EDWARD J. KOENEMANN SECRETARY DAVID L. KLEIZENICKER

NATIONAL PARK FOUNDATION

1101 17TH STREET, NW, SUITE 1102   WASHINGTON DC 20036
PHONE (202) 785 4500   FAX (202) 785 3539

Founded 1967 • *Geographic Coverage* National • *Cooperative Partner* National Park Service

Mission To help meet the needs of the country's 367 National Park sites.

Funding	Corporations	Foundations	Other
	47.8%	15.5%	36.7%

Total Income $5,937,794

Usage	Administration	Programs
	9.4%	90.6%

Programs Parks as Classrooms Program links schools and Parks to provide hands-on learning experiences. Easy Access Park Challenge works to increase accessibility to the Parks for people with disabilities. $2.4 million in grants to support educational and preservation programs in the National Park system.

Publications Book *The Complete Guide to America's National Parks.* Newsletter

For more Information Annual Report

Who's Who CHAIRMAN **BRUCE BABBITT** • VICE CHAIRMAN **JAMES R. HARVEY** • PRESIDENT **ALAN A. RUBIN** • DIRECTOR OF COMMUNICATIONS **JANE McQUEEN**

NATIONAL PARKS AND CONSERVATION ASSOCIATION

1776 MASSACHUSETTS AVENUE, NW   WASHINGTON DC 20036-1904
PHONE (202) 223 6722   FAX (202) 659 0650

Founded 1919 • *Geographic Coverage* National • *Individual Members* 280,000

Mission Dedicated to defending and improving America's national park system and informing Americans about this national heritage.

Annual Fees	Regular	Student/Senior	Contributing	Defender	Supporting
	$25	$18	$35	$50	$100

Other Fees *Guarantor* $250

Programs Establishing new parks such as Mesa Verde, Great Basin, Everglades, Cape Cod, and 47 million acres of Alaskan parklands. Stopping the National Rifle Association from opening the parks to hunting and trapping. Halting the construction of potentially damaging dams and stopping raids on other park water resources in the Grand Canyon and Dinosaur National Monument. Protecting wildlife - especially endangered species - many of which are dependent on park habitats.

Publication Bimonthly magazine *National Parks*

For more Information Annual Report

Who's Who PRESIDENT **PAUL C. PRITCHARD** • DIRECTOR OF CONSERVATION PRO-

GRAMS **WILLIAM J. CHANDLER** • DIRECTOR OF DEVELOPMENT **JESSIE A. BRINKLEY** DIRECTOR OF PUBLICATIONS **SUE E. DODGE** • DIRECTOR OF COMMUNICATIONS **KATHY WESTRA**

NATIONAL RECREATION AND PARK ASSOCIATION

2775 SOUTH QUINCY STREET, SUITE 300   ARLINGTON VA 22206-2204
PHONE (703) 820 4940

Founded 1966 • *Geographic Coverage* National • *Other Field of Focus* Quality of Life / Outdoor Activities • *Cooperative Partners* Nearly 60 affiliated state and regional associations *Chapters* 5

Mission To advance parks, recreation, and environmental conservation efforts that enhance the quality of life for all people.

Programs Fuel for Fitness Nutrition Program. Healthy Strides National Walking Program. Exercise the Right Choice to Thirty Days of Family Fun.

Publications Periodicals *Recreation and Parks Law Reporter* • *Therapeutic Recreation Journal* • *Job-Opportunities Bulletin* • *Journal of Leisure Research.* Books including *Parks and Recreation.* • *Recreation... Access in the 90s* • *Park Practice Program* • *Friends of Parks and Recreation*

Who's Who PRESIDENT **JOSEPH O'NEILL** • EXECUTIVE DIRECTOR **R. DEAN TICE**

NATIONAL WILDLIFE REFUGE ASSOCIATION

10824 FOX HUNT LANE   POTOMAC MD 20854
PHONE (301) 983 1238

Founded 1975 • *Geographic Coverage* National • *Other Field of Focus* Wildlife - Animal & Plant • *Members* 925 including organizations

Mission To preserve and enhance the integrity of the National Wildlife Refuge System as the nation's most important network of diverse and strategically located habitats set aside in perpetuity for the benefit of fish, wildlife, and plants. The Association works to accomplish its mission through advocacy, dissemination of information, and assistance to the National Wildlife Refuge System.

Annual Fees	Regular	Student/Senior
	$20	$15

Funding	Membership	Foundations	Other
	24%	73%	3%

Total Income $52,838

Usage	Administration	Programs
	18%	82%

Publication Quarterly newsletter *Blue Goose Flyer*

Who's Who President **Richard R. Rodgers** • Vice President **Hans Neuhauser** Secretary **Lawrence S. Smith**

NATURE CONSERVANCY (THE)

1815 North Lynn Street   Arlington VA 22209
Phone (703) 841 5300

Founded 1950 • *Geographic Coverage* National, Global • *Focused Regions* Latin America, North America, Pacific, Southeast Asia • *Other Fields of Focus* Ecosystem Protection / Biodiversity, Natural Resources / Water - Conservation & Quality • *Chapters* 50 state chapters *Organization Members* 678 • *Individual Members* 708,000

Mission To preserve plants, animals, and natural communities that represent the diversity of life on Earth by protecting the lands and waters they need to survive. To save ecologically significant lands, the organization first identifies significant natural areas that need to be set aside, then protects those areas through gift, purchase, cooperative agreements, landowner education, or by assisting or advising government.

Annual Fees	Regular	Contributing	Supporting
	$25	$35	$50

Funding	Membership	Sales of Land	Gifts of Land	Other
	44.3%	33%	12.9%	9.8%

Total Income $274,909,000

Usage	Administration	Fundraising	Programs	Membership Development
	7.4%	5.9%	83.7%	3%

Total Expenses $216,197,000

Programs Manages more than 1,300 preserves and other natural areas through restoration techniques such as prescribed burnings, reforestation, fencing, and the removal of alien species. The Conservancy's Pacific Program is working to identify and protect threatened areas in Indonesia, Melanesia, and Micronesia. In Latin America, the Conservancy's Conservation Program works to help provide infrastructure, community development, professional training and long-term funding for legally protected but under-funded areas throughout the continent. Total acres protected in the US since 1953: 6.9 million. Outside the US: 20 million.

Publication Bimonthly magazine *Nature Conservancy*

For more Information Annual Report

Who's Who Chair **John C. Sawhill** • Vice Chairs **Daniel P. Davison, Sherry F. Huber, John G. Smale** • Secretary **Orie L. Loucks** • Treasurer **Robert L. Mitchell** • Contact **John W. Humke**

NEW ENGLAND TRAIL CONFERENCE

33 Knollwood Drive   East Longmeadow MA 01028
Phone (413) 525 7052

OPEN SPACE INSTITUTE, INC.

145 Main Street   Ossining NY 10562
Phone (914) 762 4630   Fax (914) 762 4595

Founded 1974 • *Geographic Coverage* State • *Other Field of Focus* Natural Resources / Water - Conservation & Quality • *Cooperative Partners* Concerned Citizens for Open Space, Conservation Partnership, Croton Arboretum and Sanctuary, European Recycling Workshop, No Time to Lose, Save our Streams, Schodack Area Land Trust, Stewart Park and Reserve Coalition, Sustainable Development Institute, Westchester Wildlife

Mission To provide public access to resources, and protect open spaces and important landscapes for public use, by working with local and state governments, other non-profit organizations, and individuals, and by providing technical and organizational assistance to citizen groups concerned with specific land use problems. The Institute has successfully protected thousands of acres of land in the state of New York.

Funding	Membership	Foundations	Interest	Preservation Management
	5.2%	72.8%	9.4%	12.6%

Total Income $1,042,757

Usage	Administration	Fundraising	Programs
	7%	4%	89%

Total Expenses $1,034,038

Programs Citizen Action Program. Various sponsored projects and educational programs. Land Acquisition Program.

For more Information Annual Report, Library

Who's Who Chair **John H. Adams** • Vice Chairs **Katherine O. Roberts, J. Matthew Davidson** • Secretary **Patricia F. Sullivan** • Treasurer **Edward A. Ames** • President **Christopher J. Elliman** • Executive Vice President **Peter R. Borrelli** • General Counsel **Robert K. Anderberg** • Project Manager **Ik Icard** Contact **Caroline A. Woodwell**

PARTNERS IN PARKS

4916 Butterworth Place, NW   Washington DC 20016
Phone (202) 364 7244

Founded 1988 • *Geographic Coverage* National • *Cooperative Partners* Arnold Air Society, Colorado Native Plant Society, Rocky Mountain National Parks • *Chapter* 1

Mission To strengthen and expand the research and resource management programs in national parks, to establish long-term partnerships between the park managers and those who would contribute their time and skill to studying and protecting the natural and cultural environment, and to develop a constituency for parks which will speak knowledgeably and passionately about the parks' value as part of America's national heritage.

Funding *Foundations* 100%

Total Income $13,000

Programs Volunteer projects in national parks.

Publication *Partners for Research and Resource Management*

For more Information Annual Report

Who's Who PRESIDENT **SARAH G. BISHOP** • SECRETARY **DAVID KIKEL** • CONSULTANT **LINDA FRAZIER** • WRITERS **RUSSELL CAHILL, ROBERT CAHN, PATRICIA CAHN**

PUBLIC LANDS FOUNDATION
P.O. BOX 10403   MCLEAN VA 22102
PHONE (703) 790 1988

Founded 1985 • *Geographic Coverage* National • *Chapters* Regional representatives in each Western state • *Individual Members* 800

Mission To work for the proper use, protection, and professional management of the lands administered by the Bureau of Land Management (BLM). The Foundation's objectives are to foster effective management of the public lands and the natural resources under BLM management, to encourage optimum implementation of the Federal Land Policy and Management Act of 1976, to foster professionalism among employees, and to support the utilization of the professional career employees throughout BLM, including the top management positions.

Annual Fees	*Regular*	*Organization*
	$10	$10

Other Fees *Lifetime* $150

Funding	*Membership*	*Foundations*
	80%	20%

Usage	*Administration*	*Programs*	*Chapters*
	15%	80%	5%

Programs Congressional testimony. Presentations in various public forums. Conducts and sponsors studies and workshops needed to analyze public land issues.

Publications Newsletter *The Public Lands Monitor*. Position statements and analytical reports

Who's Who PRESIDENT **GEORGE LEA** • SECRETARY **JAME O'CONNOR** • DIRECTORS **DEAN STEPANEK, MEL SHILLING, BLANCHE SKINNER, GLEN COLLINS, VINCE HEEKER, NEAL MORCK, JOE DOSE**

QUAIL RIDGE WILDERNESS CONSERVANCY
25344 COUNTY ROAD 95   DAVIS CA 95616-9735
PHONE (916) 758 1387   FAX (916) 758 1316

Founded 1989 • *Geographic Coverage* Local • *Other Fields of Focus* Natural Resources / Water - Conservation & Quality, Wildlife - Animal & Plant • *Cooperative Partners* University of California's Natural Reserve System, California State Department of Fish and Game, Bureau of Land Management • *Individual Members* 250

Mission Dedicated to wilderness preservation, the promotion of biological diversity, native habitat research, and education about environmental stewardship. Currently working for the protection of a near pristine peninsula located on Lake Berryessa in northern California, the scope of the Conservancy will eventually broaden to include other wild areas in need of protection. Its work favors a preventive approach to wilderness preservation by focusing on acquisition of untouched wilderness areas as sites for carefully controlled research projects on native biota.

Annual Fees	*Regular*	*Student/Senior*	*Families*	*Sustaining*	*Benefactor*
	$35	$25	$50	$75	$100

Funding	*Membership*	*Foundations*	*Loans*	*Interest & Dividends*	*Other*
	11%	69%	5.5%	5.5%	9%

Total Income $46,557

Usage	*Administration*	*Programs*	*Other*
	5%	78%	17%

Total Expenses $96,529

Programs Monthly guided walks on Quail Ridge Ecological Reserve. CalTrans Adopt-A-Highway Program, developed to sow seeds and plant bulbs along segments of state highways. Educational programs for grades schools.

Publications Semiannual newsletter *Quail Ridge Monitor*. Trail guides. The organization has its brochure available in Spanish and in Chinese

Multimedia Video *Guardian of the Future*

For more Information Annual Report

Who's Who PRESIDENT **FRANK W. MAURER, JR.** • VICE PRESIDENT **STEPHEN SOUZA** SECRETARY **LENORA TIMM** • DIRECTORS **GERALD DICKINSON, MILDRID REIS, ANN ROSENTHAL, EDITH VERMEIJ**

RAILS-TO-TRAILS CONSERVANCY   PAGE 279
1400 16TH STREET, NW, SUITE 300   WASHINGTON DC 20036
PHONE (202) 797 5400   FAX (202) 797 5411

ROCKY MOUNTAIN NATURE ASSOCIATION

ROCKY MOUNTAIN NATIONAL PARK   ESTES PARK CO 80517
PHONE (303) 586 3565

Founded 1931 • *Geographic Coverage* Local • *Other Field of Focus* Natural Resources / Water - Conservation & Quality

Mission To promote environmental education, to preserve and protect natural treasures, to purchase land for wildlife and wilderness, and to prepare the park for the future. The organization's focus is on Rocky Mountain National Park.

Annual Fees	*Regular*	*Families*	*Supporting*	*Contributing*
	$15	$25	$50	$100

Other Fees *Lifetime* $1,000

Programs Assists with natural history education through the development of interpretive publications for visitors. Major contributor to improvement projects like the Kawuneeche Visitor Center, the Moraine Park Museum renovation and Lily Lake Visitor Center exhibits. Supports research projects such as Wolverine and Lynx population studies, Black Bear ecology, Bighorn Sheep in the Never Summer Range, and exotic plant population studies. Helped purchase 56 acres of land to expand park boundaries near Lily Lake. Junior Ranger program teaches children about the environment. Field seminars.

Publications Quarterly newsletter. Various books on Rocky Mountain National Park including books for young people. Backcountry guides including *Rocky Mountain National Park Classic Hikes and Climbs* • *A Family Guide to Rocky Mountain National Park* • *Rocky Mountain National Park Hiking Trails* • *A Climbing Guide to Colorado's Fourteeners*

Multimedia Various videos including *Rocky Mountain High* • *The Colorado: Secrets at the Source* • *World of the Beaver* • *Wild Voices, Quiet Waters* • *Desert Song*

For more Information List of Publications

SOCIETY FOR RANGE MANAGEMENT

1839 YORK STREET   DENVER CO 80206
PHONE (303) 355 7070

Founded 1948 • *Geographic Coverage* Global • *Focused Countries* Canada, Mexico, USA • *Chapters* 22 • *Organization Members* 23 *Individual Members* 5,427

Mission To promote and enhance the stewardship of the earth's rangelands and rangeland resources to meet diverse human needs based upon science and sound policy, through scientific research, public policy development, and the training of range managers in the art and science of range management.

Annual Fees	*Regular*	*Student/Senior*
	$45 to 50	$22 to 39

Funding	*Membership*	*Other*
	41%	59%

Total Income $538,000

Usage	*Administration*	*Programs*
	30%	70%

Publications *Journal of Range Management and Rangelands*. Other periodicals published bimonthly on an alternating basis including texts and reference materials

Who's Who PRESIDENT GARY B. DONART • VICE PRESIDENT DAVID A. FISHBACH

TRUST FOR PUBLIC LAND

116 NEW MONTGOMERY STREET   SAN FRANCISCO CA 94105
PHONE (415) 495 4014

Founded 1972 • *Geographic Coverage* National • *Chapters* 12

Mission To protect public land as a living resource for present and future generations.

Funding	*Foundations*	*Other*
	75%	25%

Total Income $16,941,000

Usage	*Administration*	*Fundraising*	*Programs*
	9%	3%	88%

Programs New York City Land Project. California Releaf Program. National Land Counselor Program. Cities Initiative. Historic preservation. Waterfront Heritage Program.

Publications Quarterly magazine *Land on People*. Regional newsletters

Who's Who PRESIDENT MARTIN J. ROSEN • VICE PRESIDENT RALPH BENSON

TRUSTEES OF RESERVATIONS (THE)

572 ESSEX STREET   BEVERLY MA 01915-1530
PHONE (508) 921 1944

Founded 1891 • *Geographic Coverage* State • *Chapters* 5 *Organization Members* 200 • *Individual Members* 11,800

Mission To conserve for public use and enjoyment properties of exceptional scenic, historic, and ecological value in Massachusetts. Land conservation in Massachusetts, including open spaces, cultural landscapes, and historic structures is the organization's main area of focus.

Annual Fees	*Regular*	*Student/Senior*	*Families*
	$35	$25	$50

Funding

	Membership	Foundations	Reservation Receipts	Investment Income
	10%	20%	39%	31%

Total Income $5,200,000

Usage

	Administration	Fundraising	Programs	Other
	10%	6%	81%	3%

Programs Ecology programs (focusing on shorebird protection, dune restoration, Lyme disease and deer management, forestry). Public events. Land conservation through acquisition or deed restrictions.

Publications Quarterly newsletter *Special Places*. Guide *A Guide to the Properties of the Trustees of Reservations: How to Find and Enjoy Seventy-Two Very Special Places in Massachusetts*. Various interpretative brochures, and booklets

For more Information Annual Report

Who's Who CHAIRMAN **NORTON Q. SLOAN** • VICE PRESIDENTS **PETER MADSEN, SUSANNE PHIPPEN** • EXECUTIVE DIRECTOR **FREDERIC WINTHORP, JR.** • DEPUTY DIRECTOR FOR PUBLIC INFORMATION **LISA McFADDEN**

VOYAGEURS REGION
NATIONAL PARK ASSOCIATION

119 NORTH FOURTH STREET, SUITE 302-C   MINNEAPOLIS MN 55401
PHONE (612) 333 5424

Founded 1965 • *Geographic Coverage* Local • *Cooperative Partners* Saint Croix National Scenic River Way, Mississippi National River and Recreation Area, National Park Service • *Organization Members* 15 • *Individual Members* 450

Mission To preserve the natural, recreational, and historic resources of Voyageurs National Park in accordance with the park's enabling legislation; to encourage and promote public awareness of the same; to be a friend to other National Park Service-managed lands in the region.

Annual Fees

	Regular	Families	Supporting	Sustaining
	$15	$30	$50	$100

Funding

	Membership	Foundations
	27%	73%

Total Income $55,000

Usage

	Administration	Fundraising	Programs
	44%	10%	46%

Programs Activities in National Park Service-managed lands. Sponsors biannual membership meetings. Provides opportunities to meet with National Park Service (NPS) officials. Organizes work parties with the NPS.

Publication Quarterly newsletter

Who's Who CHAIRMAN **ALLAN DAVISSON** • PRESIDENT **JOE KOTNIK** • VICE PRESIDENT **MICHAEL PUNTO** • SECRETARY **NANCY ALBRECHT** • EXECUTIVE DIRECTOR **JENNIFER HUNT**

WILDERNESS SOCIETY (THE)

900 17TH STREET, NW   WASHINGTON DC 20006-2596
PHONE (202) 833 2300   FAX (202) 429 3958

Founded 1935 • *Geographic Coverage* National • *Other Field of Focus* Ecosystem Protection / Biodiversity • *Cooperative Partners* Many, including Everglades Coalition, Ancient Forest Alliance, Greater Yellowstone Coalition, Alaska Coalition, Northern Forest Alliance • *Chapters* 13 • *Individual Members* 300,000

Mission To advocate the protection and sound management of federal public lands and other natural landscapes. The Wilderness Society works on the conservation of biological diversity and promotes development of a land ethic.

Annual Fees

	Regular	Student/Senior	First-Year & Low-Income	Friend
	$30	$15	$15	$50

Other Fees *Associate* $100 to 500 • *Advocate for Wilderness* $1,000

Funding

	Membership	Foundations	Development Contributions	Other
	57%	15%	16%	12%

Total Income $16,820,000

Usage

	Administration	Fundraising	Programs	Recruitment
	10%	9%	75%	6%

Total Expenses $16,480,000

Publications Quarterly magazine *Wilderness*. Newsletters *Wild Fish* • *New Voices* • *Green Fire*. Various reports and studies

For more Information Annual Report

Who's Who COUNSELOR **GAYLORD NELSON** • PRESIDENT **GEORGE T. FRAMPTON** • EXECUTIVE VICE PRESIDENT **GRANT P. THOMSON** • OTHER **SUSAN KASLOW, ROSEANN LEWIS, CATHERINE HABERLAND** • VICE PRESIDENT CONSERVATION **KARIN P. SHELDON** • VICE PRESIDENT RESOURCE PLANNING AND ECONOMICS **MARK SHAFFER** • VICE PRESIDENT MEMBERSHIP DEVELOPMENT **REBECCA WODDER** • VICE PRESIDENT PUBLIC AFFAIRS **MARY F. HANLEY** • EDITOR **T. H. WATKINS**

YELLOWSTONE ASSOCIATION FOR NATURAL
SCIENCE, HISTORY & EDUCATION, INC. (THE)   PAGE 252

P.O. BOX 117   YELLOWSTONE NATIONAL PARK WY 82190
PHONE (307) 344 7381

YOSEMITE ASSOCIATION

P.O. Box 545   Yosemite National Park   CA   95389
Phone (209) 379 2646

Geographic Coverage Local

Mission To support Yosemite National Park through a program of visitor services, publications, and membership activities. The focus of the Association's support is research, scientific investigation, education, and environmental programs.

Annual Fees	*Regular*	*Supporting*	*Contributing*	*Sustaining*
	$20	$35	$50	$100

Other Fees *Lifetime* $500 • *Lifetime Participating* $1,000

Funding	*Membership*	*Publication Sales*	*Other*
	8.3%	75%	16.7%

Total Income $2,257,320

Usage	*Administration*	*Publication Costs*	*Membership Development*	*Other*
	15.2%	63.2%	6%	15.6%

Total Expenses $1,869,745

Programs Outdoor courses and trips. Operation of the Ostrander Ski Hut. Co-sponsorship of the Yosemite Art Activity Center. Sponsorship and orientation of the Yosemite Theater which offers interpretative programs to augment those presented by the National Park Service. Film Assistance Program which provides support and guidance for film, video, and photographic crews on location in Yosemite. Field Seminars on Winter Ecology, Spring Wildflower, History Seminars. Botany, Geology, Astronomy, and Natural History Seminars. Birding Seminars. Native American Seminars. Photography Seminars. Drawing, Painting & Language Arts.

Publications Quarterly journal *Yosemite*. Various brochures, trail guides and other publications focusing on natural history, geology, art and photography

Multimedia Videos and audiotapes about the Park

For more Information Annual Report, Library, List of Publications

Who's Who President STEVEN P. MEDLEY • Secretary ANNE STEED • Seminars Coordinator PENNY OTWELL • Membership Coordinator HOLLY WARNER • Editor YOSEMITE GUIDE BRIDGET MCGINNISS

YOSEMITE FUND (THE)

155 Montgomery Street, Suite 1104   San Francisco   CA   94104
Phone (415) 434 1782   Fax (415) 434 0745

Founded 1985 • *Geographic Coverage* Local • *Cooperative Partner* National Park Service

Mission To provide private funding for projects and programs of lasting benefits to Yosemite National Park.

Annual Fees	*Donor*	*Supporting*	*Contributing*	*Protector*
	$25	$50	$100	$1,000

Publication Semiannual newsletter *Approach*, *The Journal of the Yosemite Fund*

Who's Who President ROBERT C. OTTER • Executive Director ROBERT C. HANSEN • Administrative Assistant ANN J. WALKER

YOSEMITE NATIONAL INSTITUTE   PAGE 252

Golden Gate National Recreation Area, Building 1033   Sausalito CA 94965
Phone (415) 332 5771

YOSEMITE RESTORATION TRUST

116 New Montgomery Street   San Francisco   CA   94105
Phone (415) 543 9062

Founded 1990 • *Geographic Coverage* Local • *Cooperative Partner* National Park Service

Mission To ensure implementation of the General Management Plan for Yosemite to the maximum extent feasible, with primary focus on the role of the concessionaire. The Trust is currently focusing on the upcoming concession contract, the visitor use management for the park, the concessionaire and employee housing planning, and transportation within the park.

Funding	*Membership*	*Government Support*	*Foundations*
	5%	10%	85%

Total Income $273,298

Who's Who Chairpersons WILLIAM ALSUP, ROBERT O. BINNEWIES • Secretary JOAN REISS • Executive Directors DONALD S. GREEN, JUDITH KUNOFSKY

Canada

ALBERTA RECREATION, PARKS AND WILDLIFE FOUNDATION   PAGE 280

10405 111th Street, Harley Court Building   Edmonton AB T5K 1K4
Phone (403) 482 6467   Fax (403) 488 9755

BRUCE TRAIL ASSOCIATION   PAGE 281

P.O. Box 857   Hamilton ON L8N 3N9
Phone (905) 529 6821   Fax (905) 529 6823

CANADIAN PARKS PARTNERSHIP

501 Salem Avenue, SW   Calgary AB T3C 2K7
Phone (403) 244 6067   Fax (403) 244 1842

Geographic Coverage National

Mission To strengthen and increase support of Canada's park system, protecting them now and in the future.

Programs Canadian Parks Partnership Environmental Education Programme helps people develop a better understanding of Canada's natural heritage and an enthusiastic commitment to its preservation. Program and service support for cooperating associations in national parks and national historic sites. National education and outreach programs. Community Foundation to provide seed money through the Parks Fund for programs in parks and sites in partnership with cooperating associations focusing on Interpretation/Education programs, Environmental Citizenship programs, Heritage and Environmental Research, Heritage and Environmental Restoration.

Publication Quarterly bilingual newsletter *Partners - Partenaires*

Who's Who CHAIR LILIAN TANKARD • VICE CHAIR DAVE DAY • SECRETARY ERIKA ALEXANDER • TREASURER SYLVIA WORRALL • EXECUTIVE DIRECTOR JOCELYNE DAW

NATURE CONSERVANCY OF CANADA

110 EGLINTON AVENUE, WEST   TORONTO ON M4R 2G5
PHONE (416) 932 3202   FAX (416) 932 3208

Founded 1963 • *Geographic Coverage* National • *Chapters* 2

Mission Dedicated to preserving biological diversity through purchasing and protecting ecologically significant natural areas and places of special beauty and educational interest.

Annual Fees *Regular* $25

Funding	Membership	Government Support	Corporations	Foundations	Other
	49.6%	17.5%	6.6%	23%	3.3%

Total Income $1,686,472

Usage	Administration	Property-Related Expenses
	53.7%	26.5%

Other Usage *Canadian National Conservation Data Centre* 19.8%

Total Expenses $1,178,518

Programs Ongoing land acquisition program - properties acquired in 1992 include Herring Island, PEI; Ile au Citron, PQ; Big Creek Marsh, ON; Ausable River Gorge, ON; Dorcas Bay, ON; Tall Grass Prairie, MB; Northern Fescue Prairie, AB; Read Island, BC; and Munroe's Island, NS. Creation of the Mount Broadwood Heritage Conservation Area, Canada's largest private conservation project in 1992. Natural Land Donations Programme.

Publication Quarterly newsletter *The Ark*

For more Information Annual Report

Who's Who PRESIDENT WAYNE WRIGHT • VICE PRESIDENTS WILLIAM E. SCHWARTZ, ROBERT S. CARSWELL • EXECUTIVE DIRECTOR JOHN EISENHAUER NATIONAL PROJECTS DIRECTOR AMANDA JONES • PUBLIC RELATIONS DIRECTOR SHERI-LYNN ARMSTRONG

NATURE TRUST OF BRITISH COLUMBIA (THE)

100 PARK ROYAL SOUTH   WEST VANCOUVER BC V7T 1A2
PHONE (604) 925 1128   FAX (604) 926 3482

Founded 1971 • *Geographic Coverage* Province • *Other Field of Focus* Natural Resources / Water - Conservation & Quality • *Chapters* 2 *Individual Members* 12

Mission Dedicated to the conservation of plants, animals, and natural habitats of significance in British Columbia by protecting the lands and waters critical for their survival.

Total Income $4,059,083

Total Expenses $3,771,049

Programs Pacific Estuary Conservation Programme. South Okanagan Critical Areas Programme. Vancouver Island Wetland Management Programme. British Columbia Conservation Data Centre. Vancouver Island Marmot Recovery Programme.

Publication Semiannual newsletter *Natural Legacy*, circulation 3,800

Who's Who CHAIRMAN G. EDWARD MOUL • VICE CHAIRMAN EDWARD D. H. WILKINSON • SECRETARY HELEN N. TORRANCE • EXECUTIVE DIRECTOR L. RONALD ERICKSON

natural resources
water conservation & quality

CHAPTER 8

North America's Troubled Waters, by Petra J. Yee

THE EARTH'S NATURAL RESOURCES are becoming increasingly limited and fragile. At the same time as valuable top soil is being lost, once productive croplands suffer from waterlogging and salinization caused by poor irrigation practices. Forests spared by loggers' saw wither from the effects of atmospheric pollution, as the wildlife they once supported faces extinction. Land and water development close in farther of what remains of natural habitats. Beyond its importance as the lifeblood of all living things on the planet, the planet's water is perhaps our most demanded resource. As demands grow for consumption, irrigation, and energy production, this lifeblood is increasingly threatened.

IN SUMMER 1993, the midwestern United States and its people were exposed to the worst flood in American history as the Mississippi River rose mightily over its banks, flooding homes, freeways, and whole communities. In December 1993, the US Congress signed the North American Free Trade Agreement (NAFTA) between the United States, Canada, and Mexico to remove trade barriers. Though

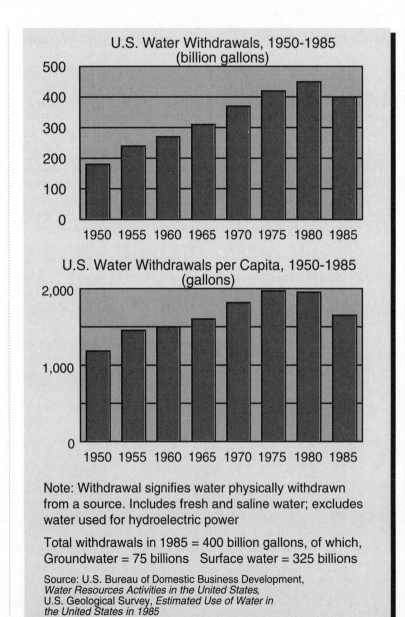

U.S. Water Withdrawals, 1950-1985 (billion gallons)

U.S. Water Withdrawals per Capita, 1950-1985 (gallons)

Note: Withdrawal signifies water physically withdrawn from a source. Includes fresh and saline water; excludes water used for hydroelectric power

Total withdrawals in 1985 = 400 billion gallons, of which, Groundwater = 75 billions   Surface water = 325 billions

Source: U.S. Bureau of Domestic Business Development, *Water Resources Activities in the United States*, U.S. Geological Survey, *Estimated Use of Water in the United States in 1985*

seemingly unrelated, the two events illustrate the mistakes in past American water policy and the future of North American water development. The failure of the multi-million-dollar Mississippi River levee system, designed to straighten the river and protect the communities along its banks, is an example of American water development in the 20th century. Starting early in the 1900s, the Bureau of Reclamation and the Army Corps of Engineers embarked on a dam building, channelization and river-control program to divert massive amounts of irrigation water for agriculture, urbanization and industrial development. Rivers such as the Mississippi, the Columbia in the Pacific Northwest, the Snake in Idaho, and the Kissimmee River in Florida were dredged, channelized and restricted by earthen embankments or put behind dams. Many of these projects came as a result of old-fashioned pork-barrel politics.

THE CONSEQUENCES OF THIS extensive water development are dire. Natural riparian and aquatic habitats were replaced by concrete channels. Reservoirs flooded over canyons of

spectacular beauty and submerged native American settlements and burial grounds. Dams wiped out entire species of fish. Reservoirs accumulated agricultural contaminants and toxins, forever altering the river's ecology downstream from the dam. Structural interference with American rivers has diminished the nation's wetlands. Eighty percent of wetlands lost between 1955 and 1975 stemmed from irrigated agricultural production. Illinois wetlands were diminished by 85 percent, Missouri's by 87 percent, and Iowa's by 89 percent. Of the original 20 million acres of wetlands along the Mississippi River, only two million remain. One third of the nation's endangered and threatened species depend on these wetlands for their habitat. Dams and channels were erected under the rationale of providing flood control, water supply, and large amounts of hydroelectricity. But, as the Mississippi River showed in a dramatic way in the summer of 1993, the plan did not work. Despite the structural flood control measures on American rivers, flood damage has more than doubled in the past 60 years.
Critics, such as the Berkeley-based International Rivers Network, suggest that the US government reorient its flood control options away from constructing more physical barriers and towards flood management measures, such as zoning.

RECKLESS IRRIGATION PRACTICES, increased industrial pollution, inefficient water use, and shifting precipitation patterns due to a global warming ▶

United States

ACTION FOR NATURE, INC.

300 Broadway, Suite 300   San Francisco CA 94133
Phone (415) 421 2640   Fax (415) 922 5717

Founded 1982 • *Geographic Coverage* National, Global • *Individual Members* 100

Mission To foster a love and respect for nature through personal action.

Annual Fees *Regular* $25

Funding	Membership	Corporations	Foundations	Special Events
	27.3%	18.2%	27.3%	27.2%

Total Income $2,750

Usage	Administration	Programs
	25%	75%

Programs Producing a book of young people's environmental success stories from around the world.

Publications Children's environmental books

For more Information Library

Who's Who PRESIDENT EVELYN DE CHETALDI • SECRETARY MARY M. GRIFFIN-JONES • TREASURER DAVID YAMAHAWA • CONTACT BERYL KAY

ALLIANCE FOR THE WILD ROCKIES

PAGE 39
P.O. Box 8371   Missoula MT 59807
Phone (406) 721 5420   Fax (406) 721 9917

AMERICAN CANAL SOCIETY, INC.

809 Rathton Road   York PA 17403
Phone (717) 843 4035

Founded 1972 • *Geographic Coverage* National • *Other Field of Focus* Quality of Life / Outdoor Activities • *Individual Members* 800

Mission To encourage the preservation, restoration, interpretation and usage of the numerous canals of the United States; to cooperate with individual canal societies for action on threatened canals, or in the absence of local canal societies to act as a focal point for action; to provide for the exchange of general canal information.

Annual Fees	Regular	Sustaining	Patron
	$14	$20	$40

Other Fees *Lifetime* $150

Publications Quarterly bulletin *American Canals*. Book *Picture-Journey Along the Pennsylvania Main Line Canal*. Other publications include *The Best from American Canals* • *American Canal Guides* • *1993 Canal Boat Construction Index*

Who's Who PRESIDENT WILLIAM E. TROUT III • VICE PRESIDENTS WILLIAM E. GERBER, WILLIAM J. MCKELVEY, JR. • SECRETARY CHARLES W. DERR

AMERICAN GROUNDWATER TRUST

6375 Riverside Drive   Dublin OH 43017
Phone (614) 761 2215   Fax (614) 761 3446

Founded 1975 • *Geographic Coverage* National

Mission To initiate and promote public education programs and information activities that will lead to the optimal utilization and protection of America's groundwater resources.

Funding *Foundations* 100%

102

Programs Scholarship program. Lectures.

Publications Quarterly newsletter *POINTS*. Public information brochures

Multimedia Online information service 1-800-423-7748

Who's Who PRESIDENT **KENNETH L. KIRK** • VICE PRESIDENT **JERRY E. COOK** SECRETARY **RICHARD E. SCHRAMM** • TREASURER **WALTER STOCKERT** • EXECUTIVE DIRECTOR **KEVIN B. MCCRAY** • PROGRAM DIRECTOR **ANDREW STONE**

AMERICAN LITTORAL SOCIETY   PAGE 39
SANDY HOOK   HIGHLANDS NJ 07732
PHONE (201) 291 0055

AMERICAN OCEANS CAMPAIGN   PAGE 40
725 ARIZONA AVENUE, SUITE 102   SANTA MONICA CA 90401
PHONE (310) 576 6162   FAX (310) 576 6170

AMERICAN PUBLIC WORKS ASSOCIATION   PAGE 199
106 WEST 11TH STREET, SUITE 1800   KANSAS CITY MO 64105-1806
PHONE (816) 472 6100   FAX (816) 472 1610

AMERICAN RIVERS
801 PENNSYLVANIA AVENUE, SE, SUITE 400   WASHINGTON DC 20003
PHONE (202) 547 6900   FAX (202) 543 6142

Founded 1973 • *Geographic Coverage* National • *Chapters* 2

Mission To help protect and restore America's river systems and to foster a river stewardship ethic in the United States.

Annual Fees *Regular* $20

Funding	Membership	Foundations	Other
	57.3%	33%	9.7%

Total Income $1,610,083

Usage	Administration	Fundraising	Programs
	7.2%	15.8%	77%

Total Expenses $1,703,608

Programs Actively monitors current river issues throughout the country. Works for hydropower policy reform. Works for protection of endangered species, particularly salmon. Works for Western water allocation and instream flow protection.

Publication Quarterly newsletter *American Rivers*

Who's Who PRESIDENT **KEVIN J. COYLE** • DIRECTOR **LORRI BODI** • MEMBERSHIP

DIRECTOR **MARY-ELLEN KIRKBRIDE** • DIRECTOR OF COMMUNICATIONS **RANDY SHOWSTACK**

AMERICAN RIVERS MANAGEMENT SOCIETY
P.O. BOX 621911   LITTLETON CO 80162-1911
PHONE (614) 265 6460

Founded 1988 • *Geographic Coverage* National • *Other Field of Focus* Quality of Life / Outdoor Activities • *Chapters* 6

Mission To advance the professional field of river management by providing river managers, researchers, and interested individuals with a forum for sharing information about the appropriate use and management of river resources; to promote the protection and management of river resources in order to provide continued opportunities for high quality recreation experience; and to foster a holistic understanding of river basin management. The Society continues to build its organization with a broad base of interest and expertise in all aspects of river management, including an ecosystem approach to recreational use, water quality, riparian zone health, and watershed management.

Annual Fees	Student/Senior	Organization	Professional	Friend of ARMS
	$20	$50	$30	$100

Other Fees *Lifetime* $300 • *Research Supporter* No Minimum

Publication Newsletter

Who's Who PROGRAM DIRECTOR **CAROLINE TAN**

AMERICAN WHITEWATER AFFILIATION
P.O. BOX 85   PHOENICIA NY 12464
PHONE (914) 688 5569

Founded 1961 • *Geographic Coverage* National, Global • *Focused Countries* Canada, Chile, New Zealand, USA • *Other Field of Focus* Quality of Life / Outdoor Activities • *Organization Members* 100 *Individual Members* 3,000

Mission To protect and preserve whitewater rivers and to promote whitewater recreation.

Annual Fees	Regular	Families	Attainer and Club Affiliate	Patron
	$20	$30	$50	$100

Funding	Membership	Foundations	Other
	37%	18%	45%

Total Income $118,410

Usage	Administration	Fundraising	Programs
	9.5%	2.5%	88%

Total Expenses $98,245

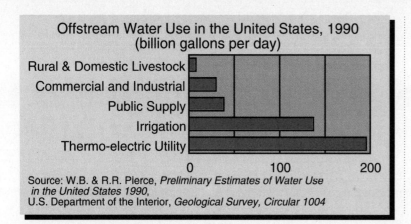

Offstream Water Use in the United States, 1990
(billion gallons per day)

Rural & Domestic Livestock	
Commercial and Industrial	
Public Supply	
Irrigation	
Thermo-electric Utility	

0   100   200

Source: W.B. & R.R. Pierce, *Preliminary Estimates of Water Use in the United States 1990*,
U.S. Department of the Interior, *Geological Survey, Circular 1004*

▶trend have all turned water into a scarce resource. The water table in the Avra Valley near Casa Grande has fallen by 100 meters after 50 years of farming. Cities like Tucson, where people depend on groundwater for their entire water supply, face the threat of losing all water by the end of the century. American rivers and watersheds face another threat: they are loaded with domestic wastewater, industrial effluents and land-use runoff, and leachings from mine tailing and solid waste dumps. The United States and Canada are among the top water-consuming nations on a per-capita basis. Overpumping the Ogallala Aquifer, which stretches from South Dakota to Northwest Texas and supplies 30 percent of American groundwater for irrigation, has led to a drop ▶

Programs National Regional Coordination Network. Annual Ocoee Rodeo and Gauley River Festival helps fund expanding conservation efforts. Public education on river conservation and safety. Assistance to local river activists.

Publications Bimonthly magazine *American Whitewater*. Books International *Scale of Whitewater Difficulty* • *AWA Safety Code* • *Nationwide Whitewater Inventory* • *The Rivers of Chile*

Who's Who PRESIDENT RISA SHIMODA CALLAWAY • VICE PRESIDENT MAC THORNTON • SECRETARY ANITA ADAMS

ANITA PURVES NATURE CENTER

1505 NORTH BROADWAY AVENUE   URBANA IL 61801
PHONE (217) 384 4062

Founded 1979 • *Geographic Coverage* Local

Mission To promote the sound stewardship of the natural environment by fostering appreciation, understanding, and responsible use of the earth. The Center is a facility of the Urbana Park District.

Total Income $190,000

Usage	Administration	Programs
	20%	80%

Programs Hands-on display area featuring seasonal exhibits, live animals, and local natural history information. Classroom and meeting space. Teacher Resource Center. Prairie Demonstration Garden. Topical environmental programs. Field trips. Workshops. Day camps. School tours.

Publication Quarterly newsletter *Nature Watch*

Who's Who STAFF OFFICERS JUDY MILLER, DEB DIPIETRO, PATTI SHAVER, JEAN GRAVES, STACY MCDADE, LYNETTE BAKER

APPALACHIAN MOUNTAIN CLUB   PAGE 41
5 JOY STREET   BOSTON MA 02108
PHONE (617) 523 0636

ARAL SEA INFORMATION COMMITTEE

1055 FORTH CRONKHITE   SAUSALITO CA 94965
PHONE (415) 331 5122   FAX (415) 331 2722

Founded 1990 • *Geographic Coverage* National, Central Asian Republics • *Focused Regions* Uzbekistan, Karakalpakstan, Turkmenistan, Tajikistan, Kyrgyzstan, southern Kazakhstan • *Other Field of Focus* Ecosystem Protection / Biodiversity • *Cooperative Partner* Union to Defend the Aral and Amu Darya - Nukus, Karakalpakstan • *Organization Members* 4 - 1 in USA, 3 in Central Asia • *Individual Members* 30

Mission To assist the NGOs of Central Asia change existing water use of the Amu Darya and Syr Darya rivers to give priority to water for people, and to restore damaged fish and wildlife environments, including the Aral Sea. The Committee believes that making the Aral region productive again, for man and nature, can be instructive for ecosystem restoration problems worldwide.

Annual Fees	Regular	Student/Senior
	$25	$15

Funding *Foundations* 100%

Total Income $5,300

Programs The Committee's Restoring Central Asia's Waters project is working to educate Central Asians about the technical and political aspects of managing water in a desert environment, with the eventual goal of restoring and protecting the water systems and land resources of Central Asia.

Publication Book How *The Silk Road Turned Into a Cotton Highway*

For more Information Database, Library, List of Publications

Who's Who PRESIDENTS **W. EDWARD NUTE, YUSUP KAMALOV** • EXECUTIVE DIRECTOR **WILLIAM T. DAVOREN** • OTHER **NANCY LUBIN, OLEG TSARUK, ANDREY ZATOKA**

BASS ANGLERS SPORTSMAN SOCIETY®, INC.

P.O. Box 17900	MONTGOMERY AL 36141-0900
PHONE (205) 272 9530	FAX (205) 279 7148

Founded 1967 • *Geographic Coverage* Japan, South Africa, USA, Zimbabwe • *Chapters* 46 state federations • *Individual Members* 550,000

Mission To promote full adherence to all conservation codes, to demand adequate water standards and legal enforcement of existing regulatory standards, to detect and report any polluter and call public and political attention to the crime, and to encourage research and study on waters.

Programs In 1991 and 1992, the Reauthorization Coalition worked toward reauthorization of the Clean Water Act through the National Clean Water Act. Bassin' Buddy® Club. Bass Fishing Information Service. Rubbermaid®-Bassmaster®-CastingKids® Program.

Publications Magazines *Bassmaster published ten times per year* • *Southern Outdoors Magazine* • *B.A.S.S. Times* • *Fishing Tackle Retailer Magazine* • *Fishing and Our Environment. Guides Anglers Guide to Environmental Action* • *Freshwater Artificial Recif* • *A Guide to the Construction of Freshwater Artificial Reefs*

Multimedia *The BASSMASTERS* TV show

Who's Who PRESIDENT **ROY SCOTT** • ENVIRONMENTAL DIRECTOR **AL MILLS** • EDITOR **DAVE PRECHT** • CONTACT **MARGARET CLEVELAND**

BAYKEEPER,
A PROJECT OF THE SAN FRANCISCO BAY-DELTA PRESERVATION ASSOCIATION

BUILDING A, FORT MANSON	SAN FRANCISCO CA 94123-1382
PHONE (415) 567 4401	FAX (415) 567 9715

Geographic Coverage Local • *Other Field of Focus* Ecosystem Protection / Biodiversity

Mission To protect, preserve and enhance the resources and health of the ecosystems and communities in the Bay-Delta region, through a high visibility, on-the-water, grassroots enforcement program that seeks to detect, investigate and deter violations of environmental laws that protect water quality.

Publication Quarterly newsletter *BayKeeper Log*

Multimedia Online information service 1-800-KEEPBAY

Who's Who PRESIDENT **HAL KRUTH** • SECRETARY **GREGORY THOMAS** • TREASURER **WILL SIRI** • EXECUTIVE DIRECTOR **MICHAEL HERZ** • ASSOCIATE DIRECTOR **JOHN PAYNE** FIELD COORDINATOR **SCOTT ROUILLARD** • DEVELOPMENT CONSULTANT **MARSHA MATHER-THRIFT** • ADMINISTRATIVE ASSISTANT **SHEHNAZ ATCHA**

CALIFORNIA WILDERNESS COALITION

2655 PORTAGE BAY EAST, SUITE 5	DAVIS CA 95616
PHONE (916) 758 0380	

Founded 1976 • *Geographic Coverage* State • *Other Field of Focus* Wildlife - Animal & Plant • *Organization Members* 50 • *Individual Members* 100

Mission To promote the preservation and protection of wildlands in California.

Annual Fees	Regular	Student/Senior	Organization	Corporation	Sustaining
	$25	$15	$30	$50	$35

Other Fees *Lifetime* $500

Funding	Membership	Foundations
	85%	15%

Total Income $43,000

Usage	Administration	Fundraising	Programs	Grants to Groups
	25%	5%	60%	10%

Programs Research. Conferences and scoping meetings.

Publication Monthly newsletter *Wilderness Record*

For more Information Database, Library

Who's Who PRESIDENT **MARY SCOONOVER** • VICE PRESIDENT **ALAN CARLTON** SECRETARY **STEVE EVANS** • TREASURER **WENDY COHEN** • EXECUTIVE DIRECTOR **JIM EATON**

CENTER FOR ALASKAN COASTAL STUDIES PAGE 42

P.O. Box 2225	HOMER AK 99603
PHONE (907) 235 6667	

CENTER FOR CITIZEN INITIATIVES
ENVIRONMENTAL PROGRAM

3268 SACRAMENTO STREET	SAN FRANCISCO CA 94115
PHONE (415) 346 1875	FAX (415) 346 3731

Founded 1983 • *Focused Region* Former USSR • *Other Field of Focus* Pollution / Radiations • *Cooperative Partner* Socio-Ecological Union - Moscow, Russian Federation

Mission To collaborate with environmentalists in the former USSR on

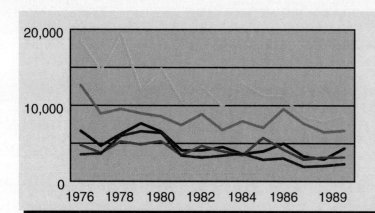

**Estimated Phosphorus Loadings
to the Great Lakes, 1976-1989
(metric tons)**

- Lake Erie
- Lake Ontario
- Lake Michigan
- Lake Huron
- Lake Superior

Source: Great Lakes Water Quality Board, *Great Lakes Water Quality Surveillance Subcommittee Reports to the International Joint Commission, United States and Canada*, Biennial

▶ in groundwater supplies. While the United States - and especially its midwestern and southwestern states - is suffering from restricted water supply and several year-long droughts, Canada seems to have an abundance of this much-desired resource. Ambitious plans to use water as a means of trade to be exported to the United States have long been the subject of discussion. Canada has ▶

local, regional and national issues, primarily Lake Baikal, nuclear weapons production, water quality, and energy efficiency.

Total Income $350,000

Programs Land-use Planning. Lake Baikal Basin Activist Collaboration at Nuclear Weapons Production Sites. US and FSU St. Petersburg Water Quality and other regional issues (dioxins, etc.). Energy Efficiency Strategies for FSU.

Publications Program newsletters published approximately quarterly. Book *Sustainable Land-Use Planning in the Lake Baikal Basin*

For more Information Database

Who's Who PRESIDENT SHARON TENNISON • VICE PRESIDENT DALE NEEDLES CONTACT SOPHIA CHEN

CENTER FOR MARINE CONSERVATION   PAGE 42

1725 DESALES STREET, NW   WASHINGTON DC 20036
PHONE (202) 429 5609   FAX (202) 872 0619

CENTER FOR THE RESTORATION OF WATERS@ OCEAN ARKS INTERNATIONAL, INC.

1 LOCUST STREET   FALMOUTH MA 02540
PHONE (508) 540 6801   FAX (508) 540 6811

Founded 1981 • *Geographic Coverage* National, Global • *Chapter* 1
Individual Members 3,500

Mission To resolve water pollution problems through ecological knowledge, by working in support of the emerging field of ecological engineering, which the Center's members believe will become the predominant technological approach for providing society with the necessary sustainability to meet its needs in the coming century. A specific goal of the Center is to bring non-polluting, innovative Living Machine technolo-

gies into the mainstream for consideration as sustainable alternatives to conventional technologies, through a combined program of education, communication, public advocacy, and scientific demonstration.

Annual Fees	Regular	Canadian	Student/Senior	Families	Foreign
	$30	$35	$15	$50	$40

Other Fees *Supporting* $100 • *Patron* $1,000

Funding	Membership	Government Support	Foundations
	10%	50%	40%

Total Income $885,000

Usage	Administration	Fundraising	Programs
	20%	10%	70%

Total Expenses $898,000

Programs Has developed a biological family of technologies for purifying wastewaters to high quality standards without using chemicals or creating large amounts of toxic sludge, by using ecologically engineered pond and marsh ecosystems seeded with hundreds of life forms. Offers a range of courses combining the applied ecological sciences of design and engineering with an ethic of stewardship. Providence Solar Aquatics Research Facility. Flax Pond Remediation Project. Maryland Demonstration Facility.

Publication Newspaper *Annals of Earth* published three times per year

For more Information Database

Who's Who PRESIDENT JOHN H. TODD • VICE PRESIDENT NANCY JACK TODD SECRETARY JAMES MICHAEL SHAW • LIBRARIAN LESLEY IAMELE • CONTACT KERRY SULLIVAN HAYES

CHULA VISTA NATURE CENTER   PAGE 237

1000 GUNPOWDER POINT DRIVE   CHULA VISTA CA 91910-1201
PHONE (619) 422 2481   FAX (619) 422 2964

CLEAN WATER ACTION, INC.

1320 18TH STREET, NW   WASHINGTON DC 20036-1811
PHONE (202) 457 1286   FAX (202) 457 0287

Founded 1971 • *Geographic Coverage* National • *Chapters* 28
offices in 13 states • *Individual Members* 1,000,000

Mission To work for clean and safe water at an affordable cost, control
of toxic chemicals, non-burn solutions to the garbage crisis, and the protection of US national natural resources by lobbying full time, and by
organizing and working with citizen coalitions to achieve strong laws
and their enforcement.

	Regular	Organization	Corporation	Sustaining
Annual Fees	$24	$40	$40	$60

Programs War on Waste Program, a Clean Water Action coordinated coalition of 600 organizations, works to promote recycling, halt new incinerator
construction and protect communities from unsafe waste disposal technologies.
Wetlands program seeks to prevent wetlands from being opened up to for-profit private interests. Toxics Program seeks better testing and treatment of drinking water.

Publications Periodic newsletter *Clean Water Action News*. Numerous
publications focusing on water, wetlands, solid waste, toxics and general environmental issues

For more Information List of Publications

Who's Who MANAGING DIRECTOR SUE M. SERGENT

COAST ALLIANCE, INC.

235 PENNSYLVANIA AVENUE, SE   WASHINGTON DC 20003
PHONE (202) 546 9554   FAX (202) 546 9609

Founded 1979 • *Geographic Coverage* National • *Other Field of
Focus* Ecosystem Protection / Biodiversity

Mission To educate the public about the need to protect the nation's
four coasts: Pacific, Atlantic, Great Lakes and Gulf of Mexico.

Publications Books *And Two It By Sea*. Reports including *Storm on the
Horizon: The National Flood Insurance Program* • *Using Common Sense
to Protect the Coasts* • *Threats to Human Health and the Environment
from Contaminated Sediments*

For more Information List of Publications

Who's Who PRESIDENT SARAH CHASIS • VICE PRESIDENT ANDREW PALMER • EXE-
CUTIVE DIRECTOR BETH MILLEMANN

COASTAL SOCIETY (THE)   PAGE 43

P.O. BOX 2081   GLOUCESTER MA 01930-2081
PHONE (508) 281 9209

COLORADO MOUNTAIN CLUB (THE)   PAGE 274

710 10TH STREET   GOLDEN CO 80401
PHONE (303) 279 5643   FAX (303) 279 9690

COLORADO RIVER STUDIES OFFICE

BUREAU OF RECLAMATION

P.O. BOX 11568, 125 SOUTH STATE STREET   SALT LAKE CITY UT 84147
PHONE (801) 524 4099   FAX (801) 588 4099

Founded 1905 • *Geographic Coverage* State

Mission The Bureau is responsible for the Glen Canyon Environmental
Studies and Glen Canyon Dam Environmental Impact Statement.

Who's Who CONTACT KATE O'HARE

CONSERVATION AND RESEARCH FOUNDATION (THE)

P.O. BOX 3420   KANSAS CITY KS 66103-0420

Founded 1953 • *Geographic Coverage* Global

Mission To promote the conservation and enlightened use of the earth's
renewable natural resources, to encourage related research in the biological sciences, to deepen understanding of the intricate relationships between people and the environment that supports them, and to address the
problem of overpopulation by promoting methods of limiting human fertility.

	Foundations	Trust Fund	Other
Funding	33%	49%	18%

Total Income $85,351

	Administration	Programs
Usage	5%	95%

For more Information Annual Report

Who's Who PRESIDENT RICHARD H. GOODWIN • SECRETARY MARY G. WETZEL

COUNCIL FOR A GREEN ENVIRONMENT

1330 21ST STREET   SACRAMENTO CA 95814
PHONE (916) 442 7195   FAX (916) 442 7198

Founded 1991 • *Geographic Coverage* State • *Other Field of
Focus* Urban Environment

Mission The Council is a coalition of Californians dedicated to conserving water, and formed to implement an ongoing public information
campaign promoting the benefits of a green environment.

Program Public Education Campaign to promote the benefits of a
green urban environment.

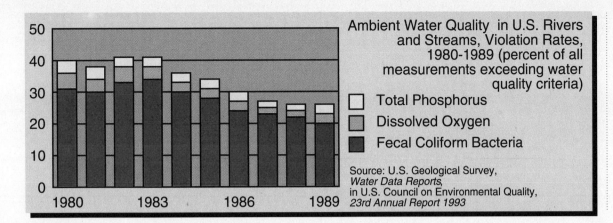

Ambient Water Quality in U.S. Rivers and Streams, Violation Rates, 1980-1989 (percent of all measurements exceeding water quality criteria)

☐ Total Phosphorus
▨ Dissolved Oxygen
■ Fecal Coliform Bacteria

Source: U.S. Geological Survey, *Water Data Reports,* in U.S. Council on Environmental Quality, *23rd Annual Report 1993*

►shown a passion for diverting large amounts of water and in fact, has diverted more water from one river basin to another than any other country in the world.

The approval of NAFTA by the US Congress raised the issue of water transfer between the three countries. Critics claim that the agreement does not protect Canada's water as a resource. ►

Publication Brochure *Guilt Free Gardening*

For more Information Database

Who's Who PRESIDENT MILES ROSEDALE • VICE PRESIDENTS MIKE KUNCE, DAVE STRAUS • SECRETARY RICHARD ROGERS • TREASURER JAMES JOSEPH

DUCKS UNLIMITED, INC.

1 WATERFOWL WAY	MEMPHIS TN 38120
PHONE (901) 754 4666	FAX (901) 753 2613

Founded 1937 • *Geographic Coverage* North America, including Mexico • *Other Fields of Focus* Ecosystem Protection / Biodiversity, Wildlife - Animal & Plant • *Individual Members* 500,000

Mission To develop, preserve, and maintain waterfowl habitat throughout North America and to educate the public on waterfowl management and wetlands conservation.

Annual Fees	Regular	Student/Senior	Patron
	$20	$5	$200

Total Income $58,700,000

Usage	Administration	Fundraising	Programs
	5%	19%	76%

Publication Magazine *Ducks Unlimited*

Who's Who PRESIDENT DONALD ROLLINS • VICE PRESIDENT MATTHEW B. CONNOLLY, JR. • SECRETARY BILL L. WILLSEY

EAST-WEST CENTER
PROGRAM ON ENVIRONMENT

1777 EAST-WEST ROAD	HONOLULU HI 96848
PHONE (808) 944 7265	FAX (808) 944 7298

Founded 1960 • *Geographic Coverage* Asia and the Pacific region *Other Field of Focus* Sustainable Development / Agriculture - Environmental Technologies

Mission To improve management of natural resources and the environment in Asia and the Pacific, by investigating how environmental factors influence human welfare, how human activities are changing the environment, how such environmental change can be controlled or mitigated, and how societies can best respond to unavoidable changes.

Programs Renewable Resources Management Program. Environmental Risk and Development Program. Institutions and Environmental Management Program.

Publications Numerous books, journal articles, reports and papers

For more Information Library, List of Publications

Who's Who PRESIDENT A. TERRY RAMBO • SECRETARY FANNIE LEE KAI • EXECUTIVE DIRECTOR MARGARET WHITE • SENIOR EDITOR HELEN TAKEUCHI

EFFIE YEAW NATURE CENTER

P.O. BOX 579	CARMICHAEL CA 95609
PHONE (916) 489 4918	FAX (916) 489 4983

Founded 1976 • *Geographic Coverage* Local • *Other Field of Focus* Ecosystem Protection / Biodiversity • *Cooperative Partner* American River Natural History Association • *Individual Members* 720

Mission To provide opportunities for the visitor that will promote awareness, appreciation, understanding, and enjoyment of the natural and cultural resources of the Sacramento Region, and to promote awareness and understanding of human interdependence within a finite ecosystem and of the need to conserve its resources and protect its quality.

Annual Fees	Regular	Student/Senior	Families	Contributing
	$15	$10	$25	$50

Other Fees *Sponsor* $100 • *Sustaining* $250 • *Patron* $500

Funding	Membership	Government Support	Corporations	Foundations
	67%	22%	1%	10%

Total Income $315,691

Usage	Administration	Fundraising	Programs
	10%	5%	85%

Total Expenses $315,691

Programs The Center's Educator Workshops and Project WILD (K-12) help provide educators with tools to develop in others an awareness and knowledge of wildlife and environmental issues resulting in informed and responsible decisions and behaviors. Native California Skill Seminars include Nature Area Tours; Aquatic Ecosystems (Living In Water, Aquatic Interactions, Aquatic Invertebrates, Pond & River Communities, Dipping Into Creeks, Dip Kits); Animal Interactions (Sensational Senses, Amazing Salmon, Things That Slither - Reptiles and Amphibians, Fur, Feathers & Scales - The Vertebrates, Beaks, Claws, and Jaws - Animal Adaptations, Feathers and Flight - The Birds, Species in Danger - Reptiles and Amphibians, Animals Without Backbones - The Invertebrates); Pioneer Life; Frontier Ranch Life; and Maidu Indian Life.

Publications Books including *Dipping Into Creeks* educator's packet designed primarily for elementary and middle school teachers • *Creek Life and Creek Ecology* developed by the Sacramento chapter of the Urban Creeks Council • *The Outdoor World of the Sacramento Region* local field guide to the plants and animals commonly found along the American River Parkway

For more Information Library, List of Publications

Who's Who DIRECTORS SUE WITTORFF, DOUG GRANT

ELKHORN SLOUGH FOUNDATION   PAGE 45

P.O. BOX 267   MOSS LANDING CA 95039
PHONE (408) 728 5939   FAX (408) 728 1056

FRIENDS OF THE RIVER

FORT MASON CENTER, BUILDING C   SAN FRANCISCO CA 94123
PHONE (916) 442 3155

Founded 1973 • *Geographic Coverage* State • *Chapters* 3 • *Individual Members* 10,000

Mission To protect free flowing rivers in the state of California.

Annual Fees	Regular	Student/Senior
	$30	$20

Funding	Membership	Corporations	Foundations	Other
	11%	35%	31%	23%

Total Income $817,703

Usage	Administration	Fundraising	Programs	Membership
	8%	17%	67%	8%

Programs Southern California Benefit Action. Membership services. Phonebank. Annual conference. River Trips Program.

Publication *Conservation Update*

Who's Who EXECUTIVE DIRECTOR TOM MARTENS • ASSOCIATE DIRECTOR LINDA CLOUD

GLOBAL RIVERS
ENVIRONMENTAL EDUCATION NETWORK
G.R.E.E.N.

216 SOUTH STATE STREET   ANN ARBOR MI 48104
PHONE (313) 761 8142   FAX (313) 761 4951

Founded 1989 • *Geographic Coverage* National, Global • *Chapters* 35 • *Members* 1,800 including organizations

Mission To provide a means for the exchange of data, information and ideas between people, schools and communities interested in studying and improving local and global water quality through hands-on monitoring and local problem solving. G.R.E.E.N. originated with a water quality monitoring project involving high school students in the Great Lakes region. G.R.E.E.N. is now composed of programs involving thousands of students in Africa, Asia, Europe, Latin America, North America and Oceania.

Annual Fees	Regular	Student/Senior	Corporation	Group
	$25 to 30	$20	$1,000	$150

Other Fees *Lifetime* $500

Publications Quarterly *GREEN* Newsletter. Educational materials *Field Manual for Water Quality Monitoring: An Environmental Education Program for Schools* • *Investigating Streams and Rivers* • *Water Studies for Younger Folks* • *Directory of Green Participants* • *Lesson Plans for a 15-Day Water Quality Project* • *Cross-Cultural Partners Activities Manual* • *Water Curriculum Materials*

Multimedia *G.R.E.E.N. Video* focusing on the concepts of watershed, river uses, river issues and the specific concerns of people within watersheds (8 min.)

For more Information Database, Library, List of Publications

Who's Who EXECUTIVE DIRECTOR MARE CROMWELL

GRAND CANYON TRUST

THE HOMESTEAD, ROUTE 4, BOX 718   FLAGSTAFF AZ 86001
PHONE (602) 774 7488   FAX (602) 774 7570

Founded 1985 • *Geographic Coverage* Regional • *Other Fields of Focus* Ecosystem Protection / Biodiversity, National Parks - Land Use / Conservation / Acquisition • *Cooperative Partner* Bureau of Land Management • *Individual Members* 5,000

Mission To conserve the natural and cultural resources of the Colorado Plateau. The organization advocates an ecologically responsible and sustainable balance between resource use and preservation, along with the protection of areas of beauty and solitude where people may find relief from the pace of civilization. The Trust fosters and assists efforts of individuals, groups, communities, and governments - local, tribal, state, and federal - to achieve this balance. To these ends the Trust employs science, economics, resource management, education, communication, and law.

Annual Fees

Regular	Associate	Defender	Protector
$25	$35	$50	$100

Other Fees *Guardian* $250 • *Patron* $500

Funding

Membership	Foundations	Donated Legal & Consulting Services
52.3%	36.5%	7.4%

Other Sources *Interest & Other Income* 3.7%

Total Income $626,710

Usage

Administration	Fundraising	Programs
9.1%	13.6%	77.3%

Total Expenses $632,844

Programs Clean Air Program, which in 1991 reached an agreement with the Navajo Generating Station near the Grand Canyon to reduce sulfur dioxide emissions by 90% by 1992. Vital Natural Systems Program, to make Glen Canyon Dam operate in a manner that protects Colorado River's downstream natural resources. Helped establish Western States Riparian Council, composed of ranchers, environmentalists, and resource managers. Community Initiatives Program encourages communities on the Colorado Plateau to incorporate resource conservation and environmental protection into local decisions and actions. Colorado Plateau Resources Monitoring Program.

Publication Quarterly newsletter *Colorado Plateau Advocate*

For more Information Annual Report, Database, Library

Who's Who PRESIDENTS STEVEN SNOW, EDWARD M. NORTON • TREASURER HANSJÖRG WYSS • EXECUTIVE VICE PRESIDENT JIM RUCH • EXECUTIVE DIRECTOR TOM JENSEN • DIRECTOR OF ADMINISTRATION FRAN JOSEPH • MEMBERSHIP COORDINATOR ALICE JOHNS • OTHER NANCY PANLENER, STEPHANIE ACHEY, TONY SKRELUNAS, RICK MOORE, WILL BUCHANAN

► "The combination of an international trend toward the treatment of water as a commodity and the establishment of a continental water market through NAFTA leads inexorably toward the international trading of water", concludes a study by the Ontario-based Rawson Academy of Aquatic Science Consequences.
The study examined the results of exporting large amounts of water across country borders, such as the introduction of parasites and bacteria into drainage basins, and reduced streamflow in affected estuarine and marine ecosystems.
The group concluded that the social costs for the dislocation of entire communities would be enormous; those most affected by the flooding ►

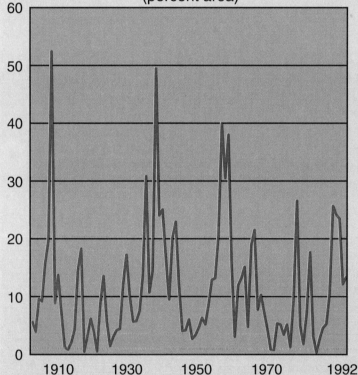

Severe to Extreme Drought in the Conterminous United States, 1896-1992 (percent area)

Note: The Palmer Drought Severity Index (PDSI) is used to measure long-term drought and wet conditions. The PDSI is calculated for each climate division in the conterminous United States. This chart presents the percent area of the country experiencing severe to extreme long-term drought conditions

Source: U.S. Department of Commerce, National Oceanic and Atmospheric Administration, National Climatic Data Center

Chapter 8 • Natural Resources • Water Conservation & Quality

GREAT LAKES UNITED
STATE UNIVERSITY COLLEGE AT BUFFALO

CASSETY HALL, 1300 ELMWOOD AVENUE   BUFFALO NY 14222
PHONE (716) 886 0142

GREAT SMOKY MOUNTAINS
INSTITUTE AT TREMONT

ROUTE 1, BOX 700   TOWNSEND TN 37882
PHONE (615) 448 6709

HAWAII
NATURE CENTER

2131 MAKIKI HEIGHTS DRIVE   HONOLULU HI 96822
PHONE (808) 955 0100   FAX (808) 955 0116

HEAL THE BAY
1640 FIFTH STREET, SUITE 112   SANTA MONICA CA 90401
PHONE (310) 394 4552   FAX (310) 395 6878

Geographic Coverage Local • *Other Field of Focus* Pollution / Radiations • *Individual Members* 12,000

Mission To make Santa Monica Bay and Southern California's coastal waters safe and healthy for people and for marine life through a combination of research, education, public outreach, and advocacy programs.

Annual Fees	Regular	Supporter	Benefactor
	$25	$50	$100

Programs Gutter Patrol Program is working to develop and test a community action program where thousands of individuals throughout Southern California can help end the pollution of beaches and coastline by taking action to stop storm drain pollution at its source. The Gutter Patrol is a type of "neighborhood watch" program that involves the participants in educational activities, including painting a new symbol on the pavement throughout Southern California with a warning sign informing people that there is "No Dumping", and that "This Drains To The Ocean".

Publications Bimonthly newsletter *Heal The Bay*, circulation 12,000. Educational papers

Multimedia Online information service 1-800-HEAL-BAY

Who's Who EXECUTIVE DIRECTOR **ADI LIBERMAN** • EDITOR **TONI POGUE**

HUBBS
SEA WORLD RESEARCH INSTITUTE

1700 SOUTH SHORES ROAD   SAN DIEGO CA 92109
PHONE (619) 226 3870   FAX (619) 226 3944

INTERNATIONAL ASSOCIATION
FOR ENVIRONMENTAL HYDROLOGY
P.O. BOX 1088   ALEXANDRIA VA 22313
PHONE (703) 683 9768   FAX (703) 683 6137

Founded 1991 • *Geographic Coverage* National, Global

Mission To speed international communication among scientists and professionals working in environmental hydrology, encourage effective communication across all countries and between all disciplines that relate to water and the environment, and promote links between the scientific community and practicing environmental hydrologists and water professionals.

Annual Fees	Regular	Student/Senior	Organization	Corporation
	$96	$48	$175	$175

Publications Quarterly *Journal of Hydrology*. Monthly *Environmental Hydrology Report*

Who's Who PRESIDENT **ROGER PEEBLES** • VICE PRESIDENT **PATRIZIA PIASTRA**

INTERNATIONAL EROSION
CONTROL ASSOCIATION
P.O. BOX 4904,
1485 SOUTH LINCOLN   STEAMBOAT SPRINGS CO 80477-4904
PHONE (303) 879 3010

Founded 1972 • *Geographic Coverage* Global • *Chapters* 6
Individual Members 660

Mission To serve as a global resource for environmental education and information exchange. The Association represents, leads, and unifies a diverse group of people worldwide who share a common concern for the causes, prevention, and control of erosion.

Annual Fees	Regular	Student/Senior	Corporation	Emerald
	$75	$35	$225	$500

Funding	Membership	Corporations
	60%	40%

Total Income $285,000

Usage	Administration	Programs
	40%	60%

Programs Offers short courses, conferences, scholarships, standards.

Publications Quarterly *Report*. Proceedings from the Annual Conference. Directories of members, products and services

Who's Who PRESIDENT **ERIC SCHERER** • VICE PRESIDENTS **TONEY DRIVER, MARC THEISEN** • SECRETARY **GARY OSENDORF**

INTERNATIONAL RIVERS NETWORK

1847 BERKELEY WAY
PHONE (510) 848 1155

BERKELEY CA 94703
FAX (510) 848 1008

Founded 1986 • *Geographic Coverage* Global • *Organization Members* 500 • *Individual Members* 800

Mission To save the world's rivers and watersheds. The organization is a network of NGOs, experts, activists, engineers, and academics on water issues. The current field of focus consists of a critical look at multilateral development banks and their funding of destructive, large-scale hydroelectric development.

Annual Fees	Regular	Organization	Institution
	$30	$50	$100

Funding	Membership	Foundations
	20%	80%

Total Income $300,000

Usage	Administration	Programs
	20%	80%

Programs Internships and volunteer programs (research interns, editorial, media, information, development).

Publications Quarterly *World Rivers Review* • *BankCheck*

Who's Who PRESIDENT PHIL WILLIAMS

INTERNATIONAL WILDERNESS LEADERSHIP FOUNDATION

211 WEST MAGNOLIA
PHONE (303) 498 0303

FORT COLLINS CO 80521
FAX (303) 498 0403

Founded 1974 • *Geographic Coverage* Global • *Focused Countries* Australia, Namibia, Norway, South Africa • *Other Field of Focus* Wildlife - Animal & Plant • *Individual Members* 5,000

Mission To assist in the protection of wilderness and wildlife internationally, by providing environmental education, training, and experience.

Annual Fees	Regular	Student/Senior	Patron
	$20	$15	$100

Funding	Membership	Corporations	Foundations
	15%	50%	35%

Total Income $500,000

Usage	Administration	Fundraising	Programs
	10%	5%	85%

and diversions would be indigenous peoples. With water supplies running low in the United States, agencies such as the Bureau of Reclamation and the Army Corps of Engineers are shifting their focus from dam-building and channel dredging to energy conservation and environmental restoration. The costs for this new path will be high. In 1989, the Army Corps of Engineers proposed a $220 million program to return Florida's Kissimmee River, which was channelized in 1971, to its natural state.

In Washington state, two important dams are being decommissioned and taken down in the hope of restoring the Pacific Northwest's once booming salmon fisheries. In October 1993 a plan was developed by conservation ►

Precipitation Index for Western United States, 1896-1992 (standardized Z-score)

Note: To produce the standardized Z-score, the annual precipitation for each climate division in the U.S. is first standardized by gamma distribution, then weighted by area to calculate a regional precipitation index. The regional values are averaged to calculate a national mean standardized precipitation index. As indicated in the chart, the western region has been consistently dry (negative values) since the 1986-87 rainy season

Source: U.S. Department of Commerce, National Oceanic and Atmospheric Administration, National Climatic Data Center

Programs Wilderness Experience Program. Cheetah Conservation Fund - Namibia. Wilderness Leadership School - South Africa. Touch the Earth - North America. The World Wilderness Congress - Norway.

Publications Newsletter *The Leaf*. Books *Wilderness Management* • *For the Conservation of Earth* • *South African Passage: Diaries of the Wilderness Leadership School* • *The Highest Use of Wilderness: Using Wilderness Experience Programs to Develop Human Potential*. Proceedings of the 2nd, 3rd, and 4th World Wilderness Congress (WWC)

For more Information List of Publications

Who's Who PRESIDENT **VANCE MARTIN** • VICE PRESIDENT **CHERRI BRIGGS** • SECRETARY **ROBERT CLEAVER**

112

IZAAK WALTON LEAGUE OF AMERICA (THE)

1401 WILSON BOULEVARD, LEVEL B   ARLINGTON VA 22209-2318
PHONE (703) 528 1818   FAX (703) 528 1836

Founded 1922 • *Geographic Coverage* National • *Other Fields of Focus* National Parks - Land Use / Conservation / Acquisition, Wildlife - Animal & Plant • *Chapters* 400 local chapters and 21 state divisions *Individual Members* 53,000

Mission To protect and maintain wildlife in all its aspects; to work with Congress, foresters, government agencies, ranchers and timber companies to protect water quality and wildlife on America's heavily used public forests and rangeland; to help protect national parks, forests, wilderness areas and other lands from unsound development; to support tough controls on acid rain and airborne toxics; and to promote the outdoor experience and public access to national parks.

Annual Fees	Regular	Student/Senior	Families	Supporting
	$20	$5	$30	$50

Other Fees *Lifetime* $250 • *Master* $100 • *Associate* $250 *Sustaining* $500 • *Patron* $1,000

Funding	Membership	Foundations	Other
	40%	56%	4%

Total Income $2,036,838

Usage	Administration	Fundraising	Programs
	15.5%	7.5%	77%

Total Expenses $2,074,694

Programs The Save Our Streams Program involves groups and citizens in hands-on stream adoption projects that include regular monitoring, streambank restoration and learning about water pollution laws. The Wetlands Watch Program promotes wetland protection by encouraging people to identify, adopt and protect these wildlife nurseries. Uncle Ike Youth Education Program, operating at the chapter level, exposes youngsters to their natural surroundings and help builds a pool of strong

conservation leaders for the future. Outdoor Ethics Program works to reduce poaching, trespassing and other illegal and inconsiderate outdoor activities. Several regional conservation programs, including Soil Conservation Program in the Midwest, Chesapeake Bay Program, Public Lands Restoration Task Force in Oregon.

Publications Quarterly newsletters *Outdoor Ethics* • *Splash*. Newsletter of the Save Our Streams Program. Quarterly magazine *Outdoor America*

For more Information Annual Report, Library

Who's Who PRESIDENT **CHARLES WILES, JR.** • VICE PRESIDENT **SAMUEL GIBBONS** SECRETARY **MELVIN SNEED** • TREASURER **FRANCIS SATTERLEE** • EXECUTIVE DIRECTOR **MAITLAND SHARPE** • MEDIA ASSISTANT **JOAN REINERTSON** • LIBRARIAN **MARY FUCHS**

LAKE ERIE NATURE AND SCIENCE CENTER   PAGE 244

28728 WOLF ROAD   BAY VILLAGE OH 44140
PHONE (216) 871 2900

LAKE MICHIGAN FEDERATION

59 EAST VAN BUREN, SUITE 2215   CHICAGO IL 60605
PHONE (312) 939 0838

Founded 1970 • *Geographic Coverage* Regional • *Focused Region* Lake Michigan Basin • *Chapters* 3 • *Organization Members* 50 *Individual Members* 4,000

Mission To improve and maintain water quality in the Lake Michigan Basin, to promote sound plans for shoreline management, and to increase lake appreciation through education. Citizen advocacy on water quality issues, such as toxic pollution, pollution prevention, wetlands protection, and contaminated sediments are the organization's main areas of expertise.

Annual Fees	Regular	Student/Senior	Organization
	$20	$10	$30

Funding	Membership	Corporations	Foundations	Other
	10%	12%	45%	33%

Total Income $361,700

Usage	Administration	Fundraising	Programs
	7%	2%	91%

Programs Adopt-A-Beach Program works to clean shores. Other ongoing programs are working on the issues of pollution prevention, wetlands protection, household pollution prevention, and nuclear waste.

Publications Numerous guides and handbooks including *A Citizen's Guide: Cleaning up Contaminated Sediment* • *The Great Lakes in my World: An Activities Workbook for Grades K-8* • *Wetlands and Water Quality: A Citizen's Handbook for Protecting Wetlands* • *Guide to Non-*

Toxic Cleaners: Recipes for a Clean Home and a Cleaner Environment • The Effectiveness of the U.S. Army Corps of Engineers in Requiring, Monitoring & Enforcing Wetland Mitigation in the Great Lakes Basin • Great Lakes Lakefills: A Survey of Federal, State & Municipal Laws, Policies & Regulations in the United States

LAND UTILIZATION ALLIANCE

PAGE 92

P.O. BOX 1259 — STOCKTON CA 95201
PHONE (209) 467 7554 — FAX (209) 467 7553

LEAGUE TO SAVE LAKE TAHOE (THE)

989 TAHOE KEYS BOULEVARD, SUITE 6 — SOUTH LAKE TAHOE CA 96150
PHONE (916) 541 5388 — FAX (916) 541 5454

Founded 1965 • *Geographic Coverage* Local • *Other Field of Focus* Ecosystem Protection / Biodiversity • *Individual Members* 4,200

Mission To preserve the environmental balance, scenic beauty, and recreational opportunities of the Lake Tahoe Basin.

Annual Fees	Regular	Student/Senior	Patron	Sponsor
	$35	$15	$100	$500

Funding *Membership* 100%

Usage	Administration	Fundraising	Programs
	25%	15%	60%

Publication Quarterly newsletter *Keep Tahoe Blue*

Who's Who PRESIDENT **STEPHEN BRANDENBURGER** • SECRETARY **STEPHANIE MOOERS**

MARIN CONSERVATION LEAGUE

35 MITCHELL BOULEVARD, SUITE 11 — SAN RAFAEL CA 94903
PHONE (415) 472 6170

Founded 1934 • *Geographic Coverage* Local • *Other Field of Focus* National Parks - Land Use / Conservation / Acquisition

Mission To protect and conserve Marin County's environment, as well as enhance its natural landscape, by educating citizens and community leaders, building alliances with diverse groups to promote common environmental goals, and supporting sound planning for Marin's future welfare.

Annual Fees	Regular	Student/Senior	Corporation	Supporting	Contributing
	$25	$10	$100	$50	$100

Funding	Membership	Foundations	Investment Income	Other
	14%	55%	26.3%	4.7%

Total Income $253,705

▶ groups to restore the Florida Everglades, its water quality and natural water flow. Exciting changes in American domestic water policy, when viewed in the context of global water issues, could serve as a catalyst for a comprehensive approach to watershed management worldwide. Non-structural methods of flood control are needed outside the US borders.

Water conservation, particularly in the industrial and agricultural sectors, will - and must - become second nature as we move into the 21st century, into an era of climate change and water redistribution. By then, the value of water - liquid gold - will surely increase. •

Petra J. Yee

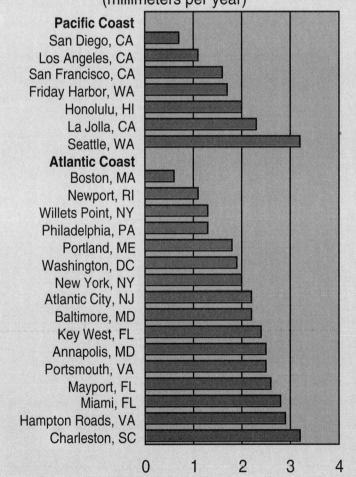

Sea Level Trends for Selected Coastal Areas in the United States, 1930-1980 (millimeters per year)

Source: Douglas, B.C., "Global Sea Level Rise", Journal of Geophysical Research, 96(C4), April 1991, in U.S. Council on Environmental Quality, 23rd Annual Report 1993

114

Usage	Administration	Programs
	40%	60%

Total Expenses $222,913

Programs Atmospheric Pollution Program, presented public forums on how human activity is changing the earth's atmosphere, with emphasis on ozone depletion and the greenhouse effect. Coastal Preservation Program. Educational programs. Hazardous wastes programs.

For more Information Annual Report

Who's Who EXECUTIVE DIRECTOR KARIN URQUHART • PUBLIC EDUCATION COORDINATOR KAY SLAGLE • FINANCIAL DEVELOPMENT COORDINATOR NANCY NORELLI CONTACT DEE WELTE

MISSISSIPPI RIVER REVIVAL

P.O. BOX 14702   MINNEAPOLIS MN 55414-0702
PHONE (612) 339 4142   FAX (612) 631 8238

Founded 1982 • *Geographic Coverage* Regional • *Cooperative Partners* National River Networks, Mississippi Support Networks *Chapters* 8 • *Organization Members* 20 • *Individual Members* 1,300

Mission To support efforts dedicated to the protection, preservation, and improvement of the Mississippi River.

Annual Fees	Regular	Families
	$25	$35

Funding	Membership	Corporations	Foundations	Other
	25%	25%	25%	25%

Usage	Administration	Fundraising	Programs	Chapters
	30%	5%	60%	5%

Programs River cleanups. Provides education and information on river problems.

Publications Annual newsletter. Local chapter publications

For more Information Database, Library

Who's Who PRESIDENT D. ALLEN • VICE PRESIDENT SOL SIMON • SECRETARY JOHN ELWARD • EXECUTIVE DIRECTOR ROGER AIKEN

MONO LAKE COMMITTEE

P.O. BOX 29   LEE VINING CA 93541
PHONE (619) 647 6595

Founded 1978 • *Geographic Coverage* Local • *Other Field of Focus* Ecosystem Protection / Biodiversity • *Cooperative Partners*

Mono Lake Foundation, Mono Lake Information Center • *Chapter* 1, in Los Angeles

Mission To save Mono Lake from excessive diversion of water from its tributary streams. Seeks a solution that will meet the real water needs of Los Angeles and protect the natural ecosystem of the lake.

Annual Fees	Friend	Supporting	Advocate
	$25	$35 to 50	$100

Funding	Membership	Foundations	Information Center Sales Program
	68%	15%	9%

Other Sources *Recovery of Attorney's Fees* 6% • *Interest & Other* 2%

Total Income $1,034,093

Usage	Administration	Fundraising	Programs	Information Center Sales Program
	12%	19%	62%	7%

Total Expenses $955,157

Programs Mono Basin Workshops. Natural History Canoe Tours.

Publications Quarterly newsletter. Books including *Plant Communities of the Mono Basin* • *Roadside Geology of the Eastern Sierra* • *Mono Lake Guidebook*

For more Information Annual Report

Who's Who CHAIRS SALLY GAINES, ED GROSSWILER • SECRETARY TOM SOTO TREASURER DAVE PHILLIPS • EXECUTIVE DIRECTOR MARTHA DAVIS

NATIONAL ASSOCIATION OF CONSERVATION DISTRICTS

P.O. BOX 855   LEAGUE CITY TX 77574-0855
PHONE (713) 332 3402   FAX (713) 332 5259

Founded 1946 • *Geographic Coverage* National • *Cooperative Partners* National Conservation District Employees Association, National Association of State Conservation Agencies, US Department of Agriculture, National Watershed Coalition, Grazing Lands Conservation Initiative, National Wetlands Conservation Alliance, Crop Residue Management Alliance • *Organization Members* 3,000 conservation districts *Individual Members* 7,000

Mission Guided by the philosophy that conservation decisions should be made by local people, with technical and funding assistance provided by federal, state, and local governments, the Association works to provide information and support services to assist the nearly 3,000 Conservation Districts across the United States in the conservation, orderly development, and sound use of natural resources. Active in governmental affairs, the organization monitors the actions of federal and state governments as they pertain to soil and water conservation. It offers a number of services and products that are designed especially for conservation districts and professional conservation workers.

Annual Fees

Regular	Supporting	Contributing	Affiliate
$35	$10	$60	$100+

Funding

Membership	Operations, Income & Interest	Special Projects
81%	14%	5%

Total Income $1,629,021

Usage

Administration	Programs	Meeting Expenses
19%	71%	10%

Total Expenses $1,745,817

Programs The Association's Office of Policy and Programs lobbies Congress and federal agencies, analyzes and summarizes policy and program information for use by districts, and sponsors leadership training programs. The Association also provides printing and public relations services. The Conservation Technology Information Center and Urban and Community Conservation Information Center provide the media and public with conservation information. Farming for Maximum Efficiency Program. Soil and Water Stewardship Week. The Growing Into the 21st Century Symposium focuses on sustainable farming practices. Conservation Awards Program. National Conservation Poster Contest.

Publications Newsletters *Tuesday Letter* • *Forestry Notes* • *Watershed News*. Analytical white papers. Catalog of products and services

Multimedia Slide shows. Videos

For more Information Annual Report, List of Publications

Who's Who PRESIDENT GERALD B. DIGERNESS • VICE PRESIDENT GERALD L. VAP SECRETARY WILLIAM D. LANGE • EXECUTIVE VICE PRESIDENT ERNEST C. SHEA • DIRECTOR OF ASSOCIATION SERVICES RON FRANCIS

NATIONAL COALITION FOR MARINE CONSERVATION

5105 PAULSEN STREET, SUITE 243   SAVANNAH GA 31405
PHONE (912) 354 0441   FAX (912) 354 0234

Founded 1973 • *Geographic Coverage* National • *Other Field of Focus* Wildlife - Animal & Plant

Mission The Coalition is composed of fishermen and environmentalists working together to conserve fish and protect the marine environment. Its goals are to restore fish populations to healthy levels, to promote sustainable use policies that balance commercial, recreational, and ecological values, to eliminate wasteful fishing practices, to improve the scientific understanding of fish and their role in the marine ecosystem, and to preserve coastal habitat and water quality.

Publications Quarterly newsletter *NCMC Marine Bulletin*. Bimonthly

Currents, a summary of the organization's staff news and activities

For more Information List of Publications

Who's Who PRESIDENT CHRISTOPHER M. WELD • VICE PRESIDENT CHARLES H. JOHNSON • SECRETARY JOHN W. HEYER • TREASURER SANDRA T. KAUPE • EXECUTIVE DIRECTOR KENNETH A. HINMAN • PROGRAM DIRECTOR CARL H. PAULSEN

NATIONAL MARINE EDUCATORS ASSOCIATION

P.O. BOX 51215   PACIFIC GROVE CA 93950
PHONE (408) 648 4841   FAX (408) 372 8471

Founded 1978 • *Geographic Coverage* National, Global • *Other Field of Focus* Natural Resources / Water - Conservation & Quality *Chapters* 15 • *Organization Members* 100 • *Individual Members* 1,100

Mission To inform the public about the world of water - both fresh and salt. The organization's current main focus consists on developing marine and aquatic educational programs.

Annual Fees

Regular	Student/Senior	Families	Corporation
$40	$20	$60	$250

Other Fees *Lifetime* $500

Funding *Membership* 100%

Usage

Administration	Programs
25%	75%

Publications Quarterly newsletter *NMEA News*. *The Journal of Marine Education* published three to four times per year

Who's Who PRESIDENT JOHN DENDO • SECRETARY PAM STRYKER • TREASURER VALERIE CHASE

NATIONAL POND SOCIETY

P.O. BOX 449   ACWORTH GA 30101
PHONE (404) 975 0277   FAX (404) 975 0222

Founded 1989 • *Geographic Coverage* National • *Organization Members* 200 • *Individual Members* 3,000

Mission To promote pond keeping and wildlife around the pond.

Annual Fees

Regular	Corporation
$24	$36

Publication *Pondscapes Magazine*

For more Information Database, Library

Who's Who PRESIDENT KARLA SPERLING • VICE PRESIDENT ALAN SPERLING

116

NATIONAL WATER CENTER

ROUTE 3, BOX 716   EUREKA SPRINGS AZ 72632
PHONE (501) 253 9755

Founded 1979 • *Geographic Coverage* Regional • *Cooperative Partners* Municipality of Eureka Springs, Senior Women's Advisory Group on Sustainable Development to the Executive Director of the United Nations Environment Programme • *Organization Members* 50 *Individual Members* 1,200

Mission To promote clean water advocacy and stewardship, and meta-ecological research.

Annual Fees *Regular* $10

Funding *Publication Sales* 100%

Usage *Programs* 100%

Programs Symposia

Publications Journal *Aqua Terra*. Book *We All Live Downstream: A Guide to Waste Treatment That Stops Water Pollution*

Who's Who PRESIDENT BARBARA HARMONY • VICE PRESIDENT JACQUELINE FROEUITT SECRETARY JODIE VANDERWALL

NATURAL RESOURCES CONSERVATION WORKSHOP

UNIVERSITY OF ARIZONA

BIOLOGICAL SCIENCES DEPARTMENT, EAST 325   TUCSON AZ 85721
PHONE (602) 621 7269

Founded 1981 • *Geographic Coverage* State • *Organization Members* 10 • *Individual Members* 35

Mission The organization focuses on renewable natural resources, ecosystem management, rangelands, forests, wildlife and fisheries, watershed management, and landscape architecture.

Annual Fees *Regular* $200

Funding	*Membership*	*Foundations*	*Other*
	60%	30%	10%

Total Income $7,000

Usage *Programs* 100%

Who's Who CONTACT JOHN STAIR

NATURAL RESOURCES COUNCIL OF AMERICA

801 PENNSYLVANIA AVENUE, SE, SUITE 410   WASHINGTON DC 20003
PHONE (202) 547 7553

Founded 1946 • *Geographic Coverage* National • *Organization Members* 80

Mission To foster cooperative efforts among its members to promote adoption of public policies to further protect the environment. The Council is a group of national and regional organizations concerned with the conservation and sound management of the nation's natural resources.

Funding	*Membership*	*Foundations*	*Special Programs*	*Investments*
	25%	25%	25%	25%

Usage	*Administration*	*Programs*	*Other*
	30%	20%	50%

Programs CRT Lunches (conservation round table).

Publication Monthly newsletter *NRCA News*

Who's Who PRESIDENT J. MICHAEL McCLOSKEY • VICE PRESIDENT WILLIAM H. BANZHAF • SECRETARY KEVIN COYLE • TREASURER NORMAN A. BERG • EXECUTIVE DIRECTOR ANDREA J. YANK • OTHER KEITH A. ARGOW, DAVID G. BURWELL, ALAN FRONT, T. DESTRY JARVIS, SUSAN WEBER

NATURE CONSERVANCY (THE)   PAGE 94

1815 NORTH LYNN STREET   ARLINGTON VA 22209
PHONE (703) 841 5300

NORTH AMERICAN LAKE MANAGEMENT SOCIETY

1 PROGRESS BOULEVARD, BOX 27   ALACHUA FL 32615-9536
PHONE (904) 462 2554   FAX (904) 462 2568

Founded 1980 • *Geographic Coverage* North America • *Chapters* 16 *Individual Members* 2,200

Mission To promote the understanding, protection, restoration, and management of lakes, ponds, and reservoirs.

Annual Fees	*Regular*	*Organization*	*Corporation*	*International*	*Library*
	$25	$35	$250	$35	$75

Other Fees Lifetime $750 • *Sustaining* $500

Programs Annual international symposia. Regional workshops. Technical assistance. The Society wrote and published the *Lake & Reservoir Restoration Guidance Manual* for the US Environmental Protection Agency. Expertise Data Bank.

Publications Journal *Lake & Reservoir Management*. Magazine *Lake Line*. Book *The Lake Management Guide*. NALMS publishes additional books, surveys and other material to meet members' needs

Multimedia Video and slide program *Lakes: What They Are and How*

to Care for Them. NALMS distributes a series of software in 5.25" IBM-compatible diskettes focusing on lake management and engineering

Who's Who President **Eugene Welch** • President-elect **Bruce Wilson** • Secretary **Carol Jolly**

NORTHCOAST ENVIRONMENTAL CENTER

879 9th Street   Arcata CA 95521
Phone (707) 822 6918   Fax (707) 822 0827

Founded 1971 • *Geographic Coverage* Local • *Focused Region* Northwestern California • *Chapter* 1 • *Organization Members* 12 *Individual Members* 4,500

Mission To help focus and coordinate the combined efforts of local conservation organizations and concerned people on environmental quality in Northwestern California.

Annual Fees	Regular	Student/Senior	Families	Organization	Sustaining
	$20	$15	$30	$250	$100

Other Fees *Lifetime* $400

Funding	Membership	Corporations	Foundations	Sales
	50%	5%	10%	35%

Total Income $210,000

Usage	Administration	Fundraising	Programs
	8%	5%	87%

Total Expenses $205,000

Programs The Center's phone referral provides an "information clearinghouse" about meetings, outings, or whom to contact for help with environmental problems, locally or nationally. Community events. Workshops. Speaking engagements. Arcata Community Recycling Center. Launch of "Adopt-A-Beach Program".

Publications Newsletter *ECONEWS* published 11 times per year. Various educational publications including reprints on current issues and profiles of North Coast wildlife and plants

Multimedia Radio broadcast *ECONEWS Report*, 30-minute weekly radio program on KHSU-FM

For more Information Database, Library

Who's Who President **Larry Glass** • Vice President **Andy Aranes** • Treasurer **Felicia OldFather** • Executive Director **Tim McKay** • Editor **Sid Dominitz**

NORTHERN ALASKA ENVIRONMENTAL CENTER   PAGE 50
218 Driveway   Fairbanks AK 99701
Phone (907) 452 5021   Fax (907) 452 3100

NORTHWEST RENEWABLE RESOURCES CENTER

1411 Fourth Avenue, Suite 1510   Seattle WA 98101
Phone (206) 623 7361   Fax (206) 467 1640

Founded 1984 • *Geographic Coverage* Regional

Mission Founded by leaders of industry, Indian tribes, and environmental groups, the Center is dedicated to cooperative problem solving of disputes over natural resources and environmental policy, by providing conflict assessment, mediation, facilitation, and training in dispute resolution and cross-cultural communications. Among the issues the Center has focused on are forest practices, water, habitat, solid waste, growth management, and fisheries management.

Funding	Membership	Government Support	Corporations	Foundations
	15%	18%	1%	42%

Other Sources *Fees for Services* 20% • *Other* 4%

Usage	Administration	Programs	Other
	24%	16%	60%

Publications Quarterly newsletter. Books *A Short Course on Tribal/County Intergovernmental Coordination* • *Living with Eagles: Status Report and Recommendations* • *Land Consolidation Handbook*

Who's Who President **James Waldo**

OPEN SPACE INSTITUTE, INC.   PAGE 94
145 Main Street   Ossining NY 10562
Phone (914) 762 4630   Fax (914) 762 4595

PASSAIC WATER COALITION
246 Madissonville Road, NE   Basking Ridge NJ 07920
Phone (201) 766 7550

Founded 1969 • *Geographic Coverage* Local • *Focused Region* Passaic River Basin • *Organization Members* 100 • *Individual Members* 2,000

Mission To serve the people, governments, and businesses of the Passaic River Basin as an advisor on water, land, resource management, and public health. The organization's goals emphasize careful resource management in the Passaic River Basin and include improvement of water quality, enhanced water supply management, natural flood control, public ownership of flood hazard areas, watershed management, riverfront restoration, and others.

Annual Fees	Regular	Student/Senior	Patron
	$15	$10	$50

Publication *Passaic River Review*

For more Information Library

PIEDMONT ENVIRONMENTAL COUNCIL

28-C Main Street, Box 460	Warrenton VA 22186
Phone (703) 347 2334	Fax (703) 349 9003

Founded 1972 • *Geographic Coverage* Local

Mission To preserve the traditional character and visual order of the countryside, towns, and villages of the northern Piedmont region of Virginia, and to help provide for orderly economic progress sensitive to conservation of its land, water, air and other natural resources.

Annual Fees	Regular	Student/Senior	Organization	Corporation
	$25	$15	$100	$1,000

Other Fees *Patron* $100 • *Special* $1,000+

Usage	Administration	Programs	Membership Development
	15.7%	75%	9.3%

Publication Monthly newsletter *The Newsreporter*

For more Information Annual Report

Who's Who President **Robert T. Dennis** • Director of Planning Services **Josephine F. de Give** • Field Officers **John Gleason, Blair Lawrence** • Office Manager **Karen H. Haworth**

PROGRAMME FOR BELIZE
PAGE 51

C/O MASSACHUSETTS AUDUBON SOCIETY

208 South Great Road	Lincoln MA 01773
Phone (617) 259 9500	

PROJECT REEFKEEPER
PAGE 51

2809 Bird Avenue, Suite 162	Miami FL 33133
Phone (305) 858 4980	Fax (305) 858 4980

QUAIL RIDGE WILDERNESS CONSERVANCY
PAGE 95

25344 County Road 95	Davis CA 95616-9735
Phone (916) 758 1387	Fax (916) 758 1316

QUÉBEC-LABRADOR FOUNDATION

ATLANTIC CENTER FOR THE ENVIRONMENT

39 South Main Street	Ipswich MA 01938
Phone (508) 356 0160	

Founded 1961 • *Geographic Coverage* Regional • *Focused Region* Northern New England, Eastern Canada • *Other Field of Focus* Quality of Life / Outdoor Activities • *Chapters* 3

Mission To improve the quality of life and environment for persons living in rural areas of eastern Canada and northern New England through programs that promote natural resource conservation and leadership training, with a focus on environmental education, wildlife research, habitat management, international training fellowships, and technology transfer.

Funding	Membership	Corporations	Foundations	Other
	15%	3%	50%	32%

Total Income $1,300,000

Usage	Administration	Fundraising	Programs
	13%	12%	75%

Programs Community services. Scholarships. River conservation. Sustainable community development/training. Wildlife research. International training (professionals). Environmental education and outreach.

Publications *Nexus*. Newsletters. Ecological handbook series. Occasional papers. Program reports

For more Information Annual Report

Who's Who President **Lawrence B. Morris** • Vice Presidents **Kathleen A. Blanchard, Thomas F. Horn**

REEF RELIEF
PAGE 52

P.O. Box 430	Key West FL 33041
Phone (305) 294 3100	Fax (305) 293 9515

RIVER NETWORK

P.O. Box 8787	Portland OR 97207-8787
Phone (503) 241 3506	Fax (503) 241 9256

Founded 1988 • *Geographic Coverage* National • *Other Field of Focus* Environmental Education / Careers / Information / Networks *Cooperative Partner* American Rivers, Inc.

Mission To support grassroots river conservation groups in America.

Funding	Membership	Foundations	Land Acquired
	15.6%	5.8%	77.7%

Total Income $1,523,838

Usage	Administration	Programs
	3%	97%

Total Expenses $671,051

Programs The River Leadership Program develops and supports leaders in river protection. The River Clearinghouse provides needed information to river conservationists throughout the country. The Riverlands Conservancy works with local people to save critical riverlands for wildlife and recreation.

Publications Quarterly newsletter *River Voices*. Other publications include *River Wealth* • *River Wise*

Multimedia Online information service 1-800-423-6747. Database *Directory of River Information Specialists - DORIS*

For more Information Annual Report

Who's Who PRESIDENT TOM MACY

RIVER WATCH NETWORK

153 STATE STREET   MONTPELIER VT 05602
PHONE (802) 223 3840   FAX (802) 223 6227

Founded 1987 • *Geographic Coverage* National, Global • *Focused Countries* Hungary, Mexico, USA • *Other Field of Focus* Ecosystem Protection / Biodiversity • *Individual Members* 6,000 volunteers

Mission To bring people together to monitor, restore, and protect rivers.

Annual Fees *Regular* $25

	Membership	Government Support	Corporations	Foundations	Service Fees
Funding	15%	5%	5%	55%	20%

Total Income $350,000

	Administration	Fundraising	Programs
Usage	10%	10%	80%

Total Expenses $350,000

Programs 37 programs in 13 American states, Mexico (Rio Grande), and the Danube River in Hungary.

Publications Semiannual newsletter. Books *Water Quality Reports for Various Rivers* • *Guides to Sampling and Analysis for Various Water Quality Parameters*

For more Information Database, Library

Who's Who PRESIDENT HENRY T. BYRNE • VICE PRESIDENT WILLIAM E. STETSON III EXECUTIVE DIRECTOR JOHN M. BYRNE • CONTACT NANCY LIGHT

RIVERS COUNCIL OF WASHINGTON

1731 WESTLAKE AVENUE, NORTH, SUITE 202   SEATTLE WA 98109-3043
PHONE (206) 283 4988

Founded 1984 • *Geographic Coverage* State • *Other Field of Focus* Ecosystem Protection / Biodiversity • *Individual Members* 700

Mission To lead an expanding grassroots effort to preserve and protect rivers in Washington state.

Who's Who PRESIDENT RON GREGG • VICE PRESIDENT DENNIS CANTY • SECRETARY DOUG FINLAYSON • TREASURER WALT NORTH • EXECUTIVE DIRECTOR JOY HUBER

ROCKY MOUNTAIN NATURE ASSOCIATION   PAGE 96

ROCKY MOUNTAIN NATIONAL PARK   ESTES PARK CO 80517
PHONE (303) 586 3565

SAVE OUR SHORES   PAGE 52

P.O. BOX 1560   SANTA CRUZ CA 95061
PHONE (408) 462 5660   FAX (408) 462 6070

SAVE SAN FRANCISCO BAY ASSOCIATION

1736 FRANKLIN STREET   OAKLAND CA 94612
PHONE (510) 452 9261   FAX (510) 452 9266

Founded 1961 • *Geographic Coverage* Local • *Individual Members* 24,000

Mission To protect and restore the natural and recreational values of the largest estuary on the West Coast. The Association is currently working on wetland protection, water diversion, and the restoration of the Bay and its surrounding habitats.

Annual Fees *Regular* $1

	Membership	Corporations	Foundations	Other
Funding	80%	2%	12%	6%

Total Income $457,219

	Administration	Fundraising	Programs
Usage	12%	8%	80%

Programs Active volunteer program which includes office work, letter writing campaigns, shoreline work parties, and various special projects.

Publication Quarterly *Bay Watcher*

Who's Who PRESIDENT TRISH MULVEY • VICE PRESIDENT DON WEDEN • SECRETARY POLLY SMITH

SCENIC HUDSON, INC.

9 VASSAR STREET   POUGHKEEPSIE NY 12601
PHONE (914) 473 4440   FAX (914) 473 2648

Founded 1963 • *Geographic Coverage* Regional • *Other Field of Focus* Ecosystem Protection / Biodiversity • *Cooperative Partner* The Cousteau Society, Inc. • *Individual Members* 5,000 supporters

Mission To preserve, restore, and enhance the ecological, scenic, historic, and recreational resources of the Hudson River, and to broaden understanding and appreciation of the natural beauty and historic importance of the Valley to the nation. To accomplish these goals, Scenic Hudson works on many fronts and with many interests - local officials, public agencies, legislators, developers, and environmental groups.

Annual Fees	Regular	Supporting	Friend	Sponsor	River Champion
	$15	$25	$50	$100	$175 to 1,000

Funding	Membership	Corporations	Foundations	Benefits
	21%	2%	45%	18%

Other Sources *Merchandise Sales, Conferences, Interest & Other* 14%

Total Income $1,101,247

Usage	Administration	Fundraising	Programs
	7%	8%	85%

Total Expenses $1,177,934

Programs Saving Open Space Program works to save lands that are significant to the spectacular natural panorama of the Hudson River. Hudson River Valley Greenway. Safeguarding the riverfront. Fighting for clean air and water. Protecting a historic legacy. Legislative action.

Publication *Scenic Hudson News*

For more Information Annual Report

Who's Who CHAIRMAN ALEXANDER E. ZAGOREOS • PRESIDENT ROBERT H. BOYLE • SECRETARY JUDITH M. LA BELLE • TREASURER B. HARRISON FRANKEL EXECUTIVE DIRECTOR KLARA B. SAUER • ASSISTANT EXECUTIVE DIRECTOR BARBARA C. MURPHY

SIERRA CLUB
PAGE 53
730 POLK STREET
SAN FRANCISCO CA 94109
PHONE (415) 776 2211
FAX (415) 776 0369

SIERRA CLUB SOUTHWEST
515 EAST PORTLAND STREET
PHOENIX AZ 85004
PHONE (602) 254 9330
FAX (602) 258 6533

Geographic Coverage North America • *Other Field of Focus* Ecosystem Protection / Biodiversity • *Cooperative Partners* National Sierra Club, Sierra Club Legal Defense Fund, Sierra Club Political Committee, Sierra Club Foundation

Mission To promote conservation of the natural environment by influencing public policy decisions, to explore and protect the ecosystems of the earth, and to protect and restore the quality of the natural and human environment.

Annual Fees	Regular	Student/Senior	Supporting	Contributing
	$35	$15	$50	$100

Other Fees *Lifetime* $750

Programs International and Population Programs with other NGOs to affect solutions to global problems such as ozone depletion, deforestation, and population pressures. Lobbying Programs. A Media Team coordinates press conferences and media blitzes across the country. Legal Program. Political Program to evaluate candidates for office and make endorsements based on their environmental record.

Publication Monthly newsletter *Canyon Echo*

Who's Who PRESIDENT SHARON GALBREATH • VICE PRESIDENT TOM SLABACK • SECRETARY KAREN AMACKER • TREASURER ROY EMRICK • CONTACT STACY CLAWSON-DAMP

SOIL AND WATER CONSERVATION SOCIETY
7515 ANKENY ROAD, NE
ANKENY IA 50021-9764
PHONE (515) 289 2331
FAX (515) 289 1227

Founded 1945 • *Geographic Coverage* National, Global *Cooperative Partners* Agricultural Research Service, Cooperative Extension, The Freshwater Foundation, Natural Resources Council of America, Natural Resources Work Group, Water Quality 2000 *Chapters* 120 • *Individual Members* 11,000

Mission To support conservation efforts by bringing together over 11,000 professionals and lay persons from a broad range of backgrounds, and supporting them in their conservation efforts.

Annual Fees	Regular	Student/Senior	Spouse Member	Contributor	Sustaining
	$44	$12.50	$12	$30	$70

Other Fees *First-Time Member* $30

Programs The Society's programs foster communication among disciplines and institutions - communication necessary to achieve focused land and water management. It creates wide-ranging forums to identify and analyze land and water management problems and to formulate workable recommendations in response to those problems.

Publications *Conservogram Newsletter*. Bimonthly *Journal of Soil & Water Conservation*. Books *Soil Conservation for Survival* • *Conservation Policies for Sustainable Hillslope Farming*. Environmental Adventures, instructional materials for 9 to11-year-old students. *Natural Resource Policy Catalog*, lists the official policy positions of 45 conservation and agricultural organizations

Multimedia Online information service 1-800-THE-SOIL

For more Information Database, Library, List of Publications

Who's Who PRESIDENT CAL PERKINS • VICE PRESIDENT GARY STEINHARDT • EXECUTIVE VICE PRESIDENT DOUGLAS M. KLEINE • WASHINGTON REPRESENTATIVE NORMAN BERG • CONTACT KAREN HOWE

SOUTH SLOUGH NATIONAL ESTUARINE RESERVE PAGE 54

P.O. Box 5417   CHARLESTON OR 97420
PHONE (503) 888 5558

SOUTHERN UTAH WILDERNESS ALLIANCE

1471 SOUTH 1100 EAST   SALT LAKE CITY UT 84105-2423
PHONE (801) 486 3161   FAX (801) 486 4233

Geographic Coverage Local, State • *Cooperative Partners* Utah Wilderness Coalition, Community Shares - Utah • *Chapters* 2

Mission To further the sound management of public lands on the Colorado River Plateau and the protection of the Southern Utah Wilderness through a program of administrative involvement, legislation, litigation, and education.

Annual Fees *Basic Dues* $25

Funding	Membership	Foundations	Appeals	Sales
	30%	51%	11%	8%

Total Income $652,107

Usage	Administration	Fundraising	Programs	Membership Development
	13%	1.7%	45.3%	40%

Total Expenses $570,894

Programs The Alliance sponsors the Utah Wilderness Cosponsor Drive, an effort to get Congress to co-sponsor H.R.1500 which proposes to designate 5.7 million acres of Utah's wildlands as officially protected wilderness. The Imagine Wilderness Program is a slide show tour displaying some of the most beautiful places in southern Utah, designed to target critical congressional districts. The Planned Gift Program helps provide critical funding to programs to save canyon country.

Publications Quarterly newsletter. Action-oriented bulletins. Books including *Wilderness at the Edge: A Citizen Proposal to Protect Utah's Canyons and Deserts* • *How Not to Be Cowed* • *Utah's Unprotected Wilderness: Places You Can Save*

For more Information Annual Report, List of Publications

Who's Who CHAIR BERT FINGERHUT • VICE CHAIR JANET ROSS • SECRETARY RAY WHEELER • TREASURER MARK RISTOW • EXECUTIVE DIRECTOR BRANT CALKIN • ASSOCIATE EXECUTIVE DIRECTOR SUSAN TIXIER • MEMBERSHIP DIRECTOR AMY O'CONNOR

TENNESSEE CITIZENS FOR WILDERNESS PLANNING

130 TABOR ROAD   OAK RIDGE TN 37830
PHONE (615) 482 2153

Founded 1966 • *Geographic Coverage* State • *Other Field of Focus* Wildlife - Animal & Plant • *Individual Members* 400

Mission To promote the care of Tennessee's natural environment, by working together with government representatives to define the issues, to clarify the interrelationship of aesthetic, economic, scientific, and other relevant factors, and to help in the comprehensive planning needed for the preservation of optimum areas of wild land and waters.

Annual Fees	Regular	Student/Senior	Sustaining	Contributing
	$15	$10	$30	$60

Other Fees *Lifetime* $200

Funding	Membership	Foundations
	90%	10%

Total Income $10,708

Programs Annual March for Parks. Trail maintenance on 4 separate trails (walking and canoe). Annual meeting.

Publication Newsletter published 5 to 6 times per year

Who's Who PRESIDENT JENNY FREEMAN • VICE PRESIDENT DAVID ADLER • SECRETARY MAUREEN CUNNINGHAM

TONANTZIN LAND INSTITUTE   PAGE 64

P.O. Box 40182   ALBUQUERQUE NM 87916
PHONE (505) 256 0097

UPPER MISSISSIPPI RIVER
CONSERVATION COMMITTEE   PAGE 54

4469 48TH AVENUE COURT   ROCK ISLAND IL 61201
PHONE (309) 793 5800

WALDEN FOREVER WILD, INC.   PAGE 55

P.O. Box 275   CONCORD MA 01742
PHONE (203) 429 2839

WATER ENVIRONMENT FEDERATION

601 WYTHE STREET   ALEXANDRIA VA 22314-1994
PHONE (703) 684 2400   FAX (703) 684 2492

Founded 1928 • *Geographic Coverage* Global • *Cooperative Partners* Environment Canada, Association of Boards of Certification, Water Environment Research Foundation • *Chapters* 64 member associations, 3 corresponding associations, 7 operator associations • *Individual Members* 40,000

Mission To enhance and preserve water quality worldwide, through the provision of education and technical services. The Federation guides technological developments in water quality and provides members and the public with the latest information on wastewater treatment and water quality protection.

Annual Fees	Regular	Student/Senior
	$75	$20

Funding	Membership	Other
	40%	60%

Total Income $3,000,000

Programs Over 1,500 members serve on committees ranging from non-point source pollution to government affairs and public education.

Publications Magazines *Water Environment and Technology* • *Operations Forum* • *The Safety Bulletin*. Newsletters *Federation Highlights* • *The Bench Sheet* • *The Job Bank* • *Water Environment Regulation Watch*. Numerous books and brochures. 80 technical publications including *Manuals of Practice*

Multimedia Audio-visual training courses

Who's Who PRESIDENT CHARLES SORBER • VICE PRESIDENT MICHAEL R. POLLEN CONTACT LORRAINE V. LOKEN

WATER INFORMATION CENTER, INC.
1099 18TH STREET, SUITE 2150   DENVER CO 80202
PHONE (303) 391 8799   FAX (303) 294 1239

Founded 1959 • *Geographic Coverage* National, Global

Mission To publish books, maps and newsletters on environmental subjects as it relates to surface water and groundwater.

Publications Bimonthly *Water Newsletter* • *The Groundwater Newsletter*. Quarterly *International Water Report*. Books including The *Water Encyclopedia* • *Practical Techniques for Groundwater and Soil Remediation* • *Drainage of Agricultural Land* • *Handbook of the Principles of Hydrology* • *Waste Disposal Effects on Groundwater* • *Groundwater Treatment Technology* • *The Water Planet: A Celebration of the Wonder of Water*

Multimedia Software *AQTESOLV™* interactive, menu-driven program for analyzing aquifer tests • *ModelCad* facilitates the design of complex groundwater models by providing an interactive graphic interface for creating model data files • *QuickFlow™* user-friendly, menu-driven, analytical groundwater flow model

For more Information List of Publications

Who's Who PRESIDENT FRED L. TROISE • CONTACT DEE FARRELL

WETLANDS PRESERVE   PAGE 55
161 HUDSON STREET   NEW YORK NY 10013
PHONE (212) 966 5244   FAX (212) 925 8715

WILDLIFE MANAGEMENT INSTITUTE   PAGE 154
1101 14TH STREET, NW   WASHINGTON DC 20005
PHONE (202) 371 1808

Canada

ALBERTA IRRIGATION PROJECTS ASSOCIATION
1210 36TH STREET NORTH, P.O. BOX 278   LETHBRIDGE AB T1J 3Y7
PHONE (403) 328 3063   FAX (403) 327 1043

Founded 1946 • *Geographic Coverage* Province, National • *Cooperative Partners* Alberta Environmental Network, Canadian Water Resources Association • *Organization Members* 13

Mission To foster a healthy environment for its member districts and the encompassed region in general, by working for the most beneficial use of available water in southern Alberta entailed by this goal. The Association, representing the thirteen organized irrigation districts in southern Alberta, presents water use issues and the development of related infrastructures to various government agencies, political entities and the public at large.

Funding	Membership	Conferences, Seminars, Interests & Other
	82%	18%

Total Income $245,000

Usage	Administration	Fundraising	Programs
	40%	5%	55%

Total Expenses $235,000

Programs Annual Conference. Seminars (internal and external). Review Committee to consider new legislation (e.g., the New Alberta Environmental Protection and Enhancement Act/Water Resources Act).

Publications Semiannual newsletter *Mainstream*. Brochures including *Because Every Drop Counts* • *Irrigation Impact Study*. Seven-volume report by UMA Engineering Consultants

Multimedia Video *Because Every Drop Counts*

Who's Who PRESIDENT KEITH FRANCIS • VICE PRESIDENTS BILL MORTENSON, DEAN ANDERSON • SECRETARY VERNA WHITNEY • EXECUTIVE DIRECTOR STAN C. KLASSEN

ALBERTA WILDERNESS ASSOCIATION
BOX 6398, STATION "D"   CALGARY AB T2P 2E1
PHONE (403) 283 2025

Founded 1965 • *Geographic Coverage* Province • *Other Field of Focus* Wildlife - Animal & Plant • *Chapters* 3

Mission To promote sound ideas for conserving wilderness; to work with government and industry, individuals and organizations to encourage careful management of Alberta's natural lands and wild rivers; to do research on Alberta's wildlands.

Annual Fees

Regular	Student/Senior	Families	Supporting	Contributing
$18	$10	$23	$25	$50

Other Fees *Institution* $45 • *Sustaining* $100 • *Lifetime* $1,000

Programs Represents its members at public hearings and planning sessions involving wilderness issues. Currently working to protect the Rumsey area as the best of the province's remaining aspen parkland, to gain recognition of the unique Milk River and Suffield grasslands, and to set aside the western Swan Hills as an outstanding boreal forest area and grizzly habitat. The Association also sponsors workshops and conferences on wilderness issues.

Publications Quarterly newsletter *Wildlands Advocate*. Seven guides to Alberta wildlands. Action alerts. Numerous books and other publications focusing on a variety of wildland proposals and wild and recreational rivers

Multimedia Audio-visual program *Why Wilderness?* (16 min.) available in video, 16-mm or slide-tape versions

For more Information Library

Who's Who PRESIDENT **CLIFF WALLIS** • VICE PRESIDENTS **ANNE ROBERTS, MIKE JUDD, KEVIN VAN TIGHEM** • EXECUTIVE DIRECTOR **AL BRAWN** • CONSERVATION DIRECTOR **DIANE PACHAL** • MANAGING EDITOR **BROOKE CAMPBELL**

BOW VALLEY NATURALISTS   PAGE 255

P.O. BOX 1693	BANFF AB T0L 0C0
PHONE (403) 762 4160	FAX (403) 762 4160

BURKE MOUNTAIN NATURALISTS   PAGE 281

BOX 52540, 2929 BARNET HIGHWAY, SUITE 1102	COQUITLAM BC V3B 7J4
PHONE (604) 463 3744	

CANADIAN NATURE FEDERATION

1 NICHOLAS STREET, SUITE 520	OTTAWA ON K1N 7B7
PHONE (613) 562 3447	FAX (613) 562 3371

Founded 1939 as Canadian Nature, became Canadian Nature Federation in 1971 • *Geographic Coverage* National, Latin and North America • *Cooperative Partners* IUCN The World Conservation Union, Birdlife International, Advisory Committee on Environmental Protection, Whitehorse Mining Initiative, World Wildlife Fund • *Organization Members* 2,500 • *Individual Members* 11,000

Mission To promote the understanding, awareness and enjoyment of nature, and to conserve the environment so that the integrity of natural ecosystems is maintained.

Annual Fees

Regular	Families	School or Library	Affiliate
$30	$35	$25	$35

Other Fees *Lifetime* $750

Funding

Membership	Corporations	Foundations
40%	10%	34%

Other Sources *Contracts & Conservation Projects* 12% • *Advertising* 4%

Total Income $1,020,000

Usage

Administration	Fundraising	Programs	Magazine Publication
16%	24%	33%	27%

Total Expenses $1,031,500

Programs In the area of the environment and the economy, the Federation participates in forums bringing decision makers together to develop solutions to environmental and economic problems. The Federation continued to support the work of the National Round Table on the Environment and Economy in 1992/93. As part of its Wildlife and Habitat Conservation program, the Federation created the Wildlife and Habitat Envelope which addresses endangered species, wildlife policy and legislation, various wildlife management issues, and the conservation of habitat required to maintain Canada's biodiversity. The Federation initiated the Endangered Plants and Invertebrates in Canada Programme in 1992. Partner in World Wildlife Fund's Endangered Spaces Programme, working to ensure the preservation of at least 12% of Canada's lands and waters, and completion of the national park system by the year 2000. Its Public Awareness and Education Programme disseminates information through publications.

Publications Quarterly magazine *Nature Canada*. Quarterly newsletter *Nature Alert*

For more Information Annual Report, Library, List of Publications

Who's Who PRESIDENT **ROBERT BALLANTYNE** • VICE PRESIDENT **LETHA MacLACHLAN** SECRETARY **EDITH WILLIAMS** • TREASURER **GLEN McCALLUM** • EXECUTIVE DIRECTOR **JULIE GELFAND** • DIRECTORS **B. T. ANISKOWICZ, KEVIN McNAMEE, BARBARA STEVENSON, LESLEY MacGREGOR** • LIBRARIAN **CENDRINE HUEMER**

CANADIAN WATER QUALITY ASSOCIATION

151 FROBISHER DRIVE, SUITE A-201	WATERLOO ON N2V 2C9
PHONE (519) 885 3854	FAX (519) 747 9124

Founded 1975 • *Geographic Coverage* National

Mission To promote the individual right to quality water, educate water quality professionals, promote the growth of the water quality improvement industry, serve as a unified voice in government and public relations, and provide a role in educating consumers on quality water.

Programs Annual Convention. Water Quality Association Convention/ Trade Show. Public relations program. Consumer Education Programme.

Publications Newsletters. Bulletins. Membership directory

CERCLES DES JEUNES NATURALISTES (LES)   PAGE 255
THE YOUNG NATURALISTS SOCIETY
4101 RUE SHERBROOKE, EST   MONTRÉAL PQ H1X 2B2
PHONE (514) 252 3023   FAX (514) 252 3023

CONSERVATION COUNCIL OF NEW BRUNSWICK
CONSEIL DE LA CONSERVATION DU NOUVEAU-BRUNSWICK
180 ST. JOHN STREET   FREDERICTON NB E3B 4A9
PHONE (506) 458 8747   FAX (506) 458 1047

Founded 1969 • *Geographic Coverage* Province, Regional, National *Cooperative Partners* Friends of the Earth Canada, Canadian Environmental Network, Environmental Liaison Centre International, Huntsman Marine Science Centre

Mission To promote ecological awareness and advocate rational solutions to the earth's environmental problems.

Annual Fees	*Regular*	*Student/Senior*	*Families*	*Organization*	*Patron*
	$25	$10	$35	$50	$100

Other Fees *Lifetime* $500

Funding	*Membership*	*Donations*	*Contracts*	*Special Events*	*Other*
	9%	46%	16.5%	13%	15.5%

Total Income $98,986

Usage	*Wages & Benefits*	*Maintenance & Utilities*	*Other*
	62.5%	15%	22.5%

Total Expenses $105,471

Programs The Tula Project encompasses the Council's efforts to enlist New Brunswickers to support ecologically and economically viable farming communities in the province. Its activities include the operation of a sustainable agriculture education center at Tula Farm on Keswick Ridge and the provision of an educational outreach program aimed at consumers. The Bay of Fundy Project focuses on the loss of undeveloped coastal lands and protection of sensitive coastal ecosystems. Activities include development of the "Zero Loss of Salt Marsh Campaign", the "Lighthouse Lands Preservation Committee", and the Black Beach Headlands Park. Ocean dumping and the hazards of plastic debris in the marine environment are the focus of the "Clean the Bay Campaign".

Publications Bimonthly bulletin *EcoAlert*. Booklet *The Global Warming Primer*

For more Information Annual Report, Library

Who's Who PRESIDENT **JANICE HARVEY** • VICE PRESIDENTS **MICHAEL CLOW, LOUISE BOLDON** • SECRETARY **SHIRLYN COLEMAN** • TREASURER **JANE EDGETT** • EXECUTIVE

DIRECTOR **MERREDITH BREWER** • POLICY DIRECTOR **DAVID COON** • ADMINISTRATIVE ASSISTANT **MARY ANNE POLLACK** • PROJECT COORDINATORS **ALISON HOWELLS, NANCY REID**

CONSERVATION COUNCIL OF ONTARIO (THE)
489 COLLEGE STREET, SUITE 506   TORONTO ON M6G 1A5
PHONE (416) 969 9637   FAX (416) 960 8053

Founded 1951 • *Geographic Coverage* Province • *Organization Members* 33 • *Affiliate Members* 200 including individuals, corporations and organizations

Mission To seek environmentally sustainable economic and social development in the province, within a political process that respects human rights and democratic choice. Through dialogue and debate, the Council strives to understand and solve problems connected with the uses of land, rivers and forests, and with urban and population growth.

Annual Fees	*Regular*	*Organization*	*Corporation*
	$25	$150	$100

Funding	*Membership*	*Foundations*	*Special Project Revenue*	*Research Revenue*	*Other*
	13.4%	11.8%	60.1%	13.4%	1.3%

Total Income $510,825

Usage	*Administration*	*Programs*	*Salaries*	*Other*
	7%	74%	13.8%	5.2%

Total Expenses $539,232

Programs The Council's Research Programme serves as a forum for interdisciplinary examination of relevant issues, presents advice to governmental, corporate, volunteer, and academic sectors of the community, encourages governmental policy approaches which integrate environmental concerns into all decision making, and promotes policy coordination between municipal, provincial, and federal levels. The Community Action Programme supports the environmental initiatives of individuals and local organizations throughout Ontario, promotes partnerships between provincial and federal organizations, governments, corporations, and others, that support action by individuals and communities, and develops educational and support materials promoting a conservation perspective. The Council's Special Projects Programme investigates environmental problems in detail, attempts to demonstrate new ideas, techniques, and technology in environmental management and resource conservation, and works with other organizations and governmental agencies for the conservation, restoration, and appropriate development of natural resources.

Publications Bimonthly newsletter *Ontario Conservation News*. Books including resource manuals *Green Communities: A Guide to Citizen Action* • *Yes In My Backyard: A Guide To Rehabilitating Urban Streams* • *Community Action for the Environment: How To*

Organize Your Community • Greening Canada: A Guide To Community Tree-Planting Projects. Various reports and brochures

For more Information Annual Report, List of Publications

Who's Who PRESIDENT DUNCAN J. MAC DONALD • VICE PRESIDENTS MACKLIN HANCOCK, KENNETH MACKAY • SECRETARY DOROTHY BROWN • TREASURER I. H. TONY JENNINGS • EXECUTIVE DIRECTOR CHRIS WINTER • OFFICE MANAGER DAVID LAKER • PROGRAM DIRECTOR MIMI KEENAN

ECOLOGY ACTION CENTRE

3115 VEITH STREET, THIRD FLOOR   HALIFAX NS B3K 3G9
PHONE (902) 454 7828   FAX (902) 454 4766

Geographic Coverage Province • *Cooperative Partners* Canadian and Maritime Environmental Networks • *Individual Members* 2,000

Mission To promote conservation and protection of Nova Scotia's wilderness, plants, animals and fish. Since over 70% of Nova Scotia's forested land is privately owned, the Centre believes protecting wilderness in the province must rely on cooperative efforts that include landowners, government, and wilderness advocates.

Annual Fees	Regular	Student/Senior	Contributing	Supporting	Sustaining
	$25	$15	$50	$75	$120

Programs Provides information and workshops for teachers and their students. The Centre presents development options to government, which prioritize protection of the environment. It also participates in advisory boards, task forces and policy conferences related to environmental issues.

Publication Quarterly newsletter *Between The Issues*, circulation 2,000

For more Information Library

Who's Who CONTACT HOWARD EPSTEIN

ENVIRONMENTAL COALITION OF PRINCE EDWARD ISLAND

126 RICHMOND STREET   CHARLOTTETOWN PEI C0A 1C0
PHONE (902) 566 4696   FAX (902) 566 4037

Founded 1989 • *Geographic Coverage* Province • *Other Field of Focus* Wildlife - Animal & Plant • *Cooperative Partners* Prince Edward Island Environmental Network, Canadian Environmental Network *Individual Members* 100

Mission To enhance and protect the environment for all living things.

Annual Fees	Regular	Corporation
	$10	$100

Publication Bimonthly newsletter *Eco-News*, circulation 1,200

For more Information Library

Who's Who SECRETARY HEDWIG KALESZAR • TREASURER RUTH RICHMAN • COORDINATORS SHARON LABCHUK, GARY SCHNEIDER

FEDERATION OF BRITISH COLUMBIA NATURALISTS (THE)
PAGE 256

1367 WEST BROADWAY, SUITE 321   VANCOUVER BC V6H 4A9
PHONE (604) 737 3057

FEDERATION OF ONTARIO NATURALISTS

355 LESMILL ROAD   DON MILLS ON M3B 2W8
PHONE (416) 444 8419   FAX (416) 444 9866

Founded 1931 • *Geographic Coverage* Province • *Other Fields of Focus* Environmental Education / Careers / Information / Networks, Quality of Life / Outdoor Activities, Wildlife - Animal & Plant

Mission To improve understanding of Ontario's natural areas and wildlife, to conserve and protect Ontario's biodiversity and quality of life, and to help in the restoration of important natural habitats and endangered wildlife.

Annual Fees	Regular	Student/Senior	Families	Library	Supporting
	$31	$25	$38	$25	$131

Other Fees *Lifetime* $900

Funding	Membership	Government Support	Corporations	Foundations
	21%	13%	4%	5%

Other Sources *Trips, Tours & Camps* 25% • *Individual Donations* 17% *Merchandise Royalties* 6% • *Other* 9%

Total Income $1,583,775

Usage	Administration	Fundraising & Membership	Programs	Other
	16%	12%	64%	8%

Total Expenses $1,515,254

Programs Ontario Rare Breeding Bird Programme is Canada's largest research project on rare, threatened, and endangered species. Ontario Mammal Atlas Project, designed to map the past and present distribution of Ontario's 85 mammal species. Wildlife Protection Programme. Forest Management Programme, to reform forestry practices in Ontario through the participation in the Class Environmental Assessment on Timber Management on Crown Land. Members' Trips and Nature Tours.

Publications Quarterly magazine *Seasons*, and a four-page *Seasons' Children's Supplement*. Quarterly newsletter *Around Ontario*. Various books including *Carolinian Canada Teacher's Guide* • *Hands-on Nature Series* • *Habitats*

For more Information Annual Report, Library, List of Publications

Who's Who PRESIDENT JOHN R. CARTWRIGHT • VICE PRESIDENTS ADAM THOMSON, ROBERT MILNE • SECRETARY SANDY GAGE • TREASURER BILL CAULFIELD-BROWNE EXECUTIVE DIRECTOR JOHN LOUNDS • PROGRAM COORDINATORS MADELINE AUSTEN, PAMELA BERTON, NANCY CROOME-MAKOWSKI, JON SANDY DOBBYN • MEMBER SERVICES COORDINATOR BOB ALEXANDER • DIRECTOR OF DEVELOPMENT JUDY EISING DIRECTOR OF ENVIRONMENTAL AFFAIRS MARION TAYLOR • EDITOR SEASONS GAIL MUIR

FRIENDS OF NATURE CONSERVATION SOCIETY   PAGE 85

P.O. BOX 281   CHESTER NS B0J 1J0
PHONE (902) 275 3361

FRIENDS OF THE STIKINE SOCIETY

1405 DORAN ROAD   NORTH VANCOUVER BC V7K 1N1
PHONE (604) 985 4659   FAX (604) 988 5887

Founded 1981 • *Geographic Coverage* Province • *Cooperative Partners* Canadian Parks and Wilderness Society, West Canada Sierra Club, Canadian Nature Federation, Friends of Clayoquot Sound Valhalla Society, British Columbia Environmental Network, Outdoor Recreation Council • *Chapter* 1 • *Organization Members* 5 • *Individual Members* 350

Mission To educate the public concerning the advantages of keeping the Stikine River free-flowing. One of the Society's objectives is the designation of the River as a "Heritage River".

Annual Fees	Regular	Student/Senior	Organization	Renewal
	$27	$17	$27	$15

Funding	Membership	Government Support	Corporations	Foundations	Sales
	14%	10%	5%	30%	40%

Total Income $14,500

Usage	Administration	Fundraising	Programs	Other
	35%	18%	40%	7%

Total Expenses $13,610

Publications Newsletters

For more Information Library

Who's Who CHAIR MAGGIE PAQUET • VICE CHAIR JOHN CHRISTIAN • SECRETARY KAREN HODSON • TREASURER MAY G. MURRAY

HUNTSMAN MARINE SCIENCE CENTRE   PAGE 57

BRANDY COVE ROAD   ST. ANDREWS NB E0G 2X0
PHONE (506) 529 1200   FAX (506) 529 1212

MUSKOKA FIELD NATURALISTS   PAGE 257

220 LORNE STREET   GRAVENHURST ON P1P 1C8
PHONE (705) 687 8766

NATURE TRUST OF BRITISH COLUMBIA (THE)   PAGE 99

100 PARK ROYAL SOUTH, SUITE 808   WEST VANCOUVER BC V7T 1A2
PHONE (604) 925 1128   FAX (604) 926 3482

OCEAN RESOURCE CONSERVATION ALLIANCE   PAGE 57

ORCA
BOX 1189   SECHELT BC V0N 3A0
PHONE (604) 885 7518   FAX (604) 885 2518

OCEAN VOICE INTERNATIONAL, INC.   PAGE 57

2883 OTTERSON DRIVE   OTTAWA ON K1V 7B2
PHONE (613) 990 2207   FAX (613) 521 4205

ONTARIO SOCIETY FOR ENVIRONMENTAL MANAGEMENT   PAGE 299

136 WINGES ROAD, UNIT 15   WOODBRIDGE ON L4L 6C4
PHONE (905) 850 8066   FAX (905) 850 7313

RAWSON ACADEMY OF AQUATIC SCIENCE (THE)   PAGE 88

1 NICHOLAS STREET, SUITE 404   OTTAWA ON K1N 7B7
PHONE (613) 563 2636   FAX (613) 533 4758

SIERRA CLUB OF CANADA

1 NICHOLAS STREET, SUITE 620   OTTAWA ON K1N 7B7
PHONE (613) 233 1906   FAX (613) 233 2292

Founded 1985 • *Geographic Coverage* National • *Other Field of Focus* Wildlife - Animal & Plant • *Cooperative Partners* Sierra Club USA, Sierra Club of Western Canada, Sierra Club of Eastern Canada *Individual Members* 5,000

Mission To explore, enjoy and preserve the country's forests, waters, wildlife and wilderness.

Annual Fees	Regular	Student/Senior	Families	Contributing
	$35	$15	$15	$100

Other Fees *Lifetime* $750

Programs The Clayoquot Express Cross-Canada Train, to support preservation of the ancient forests of Clayoquot Sound.

Who's Who EXECUTIVE DIRECTOR ELIZABETH E. MAY

SIERRA CLUB OF EASTERN CANADA

517 College Street, Suite 303   Toronto ON M6G 4A2
Phone (416) 960 9606   Fax (416) 960 0020

Founded 1970 • *Geographic Coverage* Regional • *Other Field of Focus* Wildlife - Animal & Plant • *Cooperative Partners* Sierra Club of Western Canada, Sierra Club of Canada, Sierra Club USA • *Individual Members* 1,900

Mission see Sierra Club of Canada

Annual Fees see Sierra Club of Canada

Programs Engaged in programs to preserve wilderness for South Moresby, Meare's Island and Stikine River, BC. Involved in advocacy with provincial governments to manage the forests responsibly. Programs focusing on park, wildlife, wilderness, forestry, clean air, clean water, and hydro power and nuclear issues.

Publications Newsletter. Other materials available through Sierra Club USA

For more Information List of Publications

Who's Who Executive Director MOLLY McKIECHAN • Treasurer MARK BARKER

SOCIETY PROMOTING ENVIRONMENTAL CONSERVATION

2150 Maple Street   Vancouver BC V6J 3T3
Phone (604) 736 7732   Fax (604) 736 7115

Founded 1969 • *Geographic Coverage* Province, National • *Cooperative Partner* Canadian Coalition for Nuclear Responsibility • *Chapters* 3 • *Organization Members* 17 • *Individual Members* 2,800

Mission To promote responsible management strategies that conserve and protect natural resources and contribute to an ecologically sustainable society, to act as an environmental steward promoting responsible community, corporate, and government decision making.

Annual Fees	Regular	Student/Senior	Families	Corporation
	$20	$10	$30	$250

Other Fees *Friend of SPEC* $50 • *Patron* $100 • *Benefactor* $500

Funding	Membership	Government Support	Corporations
	70%	20%	10%

Usage	Administration	Programs
	20%	80%

Programs Education in Action (EIA) - Rethinking Our Urban Environment is a comprehensive urban environment workshop series designed to educate and empower participants to become involved in community-based environmental activities, on issues such as air quality, waste manage-

ment, recycling, and water conservation. The Greater Vancouver Regional District Water Management program deals with general air pollution and solid waste management issues.

Publications Quarterly newsletter *SPECtrum*. Books including *SPEC Enviro Shoppers Guide* • *SPEC Guide to Home Energy Conservation* • *Economic Instruments in Action* • *The Environmentally Sound Office*. Various campaign pamphlets and SPEC alerts

For more Information Database, Library, List of Publications

Who's Who President LENORE HERB • Vice President PAUL HUNDEL • Secretary ALICE COPPARD • Treasurer FRANCO FERRARI • Executive Director DERMOT FOLEY Library Coordinator REBECCA HANFORD

UNION QUÉBÉCOISE POUR LA CONSERVATION DE LA NATURE
QUÉBEC UNION FOR NATURE CONSERVATION

160 76eme Rue, Est   Charlesbourg PQ G1H 7H6
Phone (418) 628 9600   Fax (418) 626 3050

Founded 1981 • *Geographic Coverage* Global • *Cooperative Partners* IUCN The World Conservation Union, World Wildlife Fund *Organization Members* 112 • *Individual Members* 5,000

Mission To provide a forum for individuals and associations working in the fields of environmental and natural sciences, and to create means for education in order to promote thoughtful use of natural resources.

Annual Fees	Regular	Organization
	$20	$40

Other Fees *Lifetime* $500

Funding	Membership	Government Support	Foundations	Contracts
	7%	28%	9%	35%

Other Sources *Sales, Subscriptions & Advertising* 21%

Total Income $734,202

Total Expenses $729,135

Publication Bimonthly magazine *Franc-Vert*

For more Information Library

Who's Who President ANDRÉ DESROCHERS • Vice Presidents PIERRE GOSSELIN, MANON LACHARITÉ, DESNEIGE PERREAULT, GILLES GAUTHIER, LUCE BALTHAZAR, YVES BÉDARD, LOUIS GAGNÉ, PIERRE GRAVEL, DONNA ROBERTS, RENÉ VEZINA, FRANKLIN GERTLER • Treasurer CLAUDE DONTIGNY • Executive Director CHRISTIAN SIMARD

VALHALLA SOCIETY (THE)

Box 224   New Denver BC V0G 1S0
Phone (604) 358 2333   Fax (604) 358 7950

Geographic Coverage National • *Other Fields of Focus* Human Rights & Environment, Wildlife - Animal & Plant • *Cooperative Partner* Great Bear Foundation

Mission The Valhalla Society is involved in a multitude of important environmental issues which touch upon wilderness preservation, forest management, energy conservation, wildlife protection, and the resolution of aboriginal land claims.

Annual Fees *Regular* $20

Programs The Endangered Wilderness Project worked to advance a comprehensive BC Endangered Wilderness Map specifying the creation of an additional 122 new park and wilderness areas in British Columbia. Canada's Future Forest Alliance. The Bear Conservation Programme has maintained the lead role in establishment of the proposed Khutzeymateen grizzly sanctuary on the north coast of British Columbia. Energy Conservation Programme.

Publications Newsletter *The Valhalla Society*. 35-page report on the state of Canada's forests

Multimedia Video *Vanishing Wildlands* (13 min.)

Who's Who CHAIRPERSON COLLEEN McCRORY • DIRECTORS WAYNE McCRORY, GRANT COPELAND, CRAIG PETTIT, ANNE SHERROD

WATER ENVIRONMENT ASSOCIATION OF ONTARIO

63 HOLLYBERRY TRAIL   NORTH YORK ON M2H 2N9
PHONE (416) 502 1440   FAX (416) 502 1786

Founded 1971 • *Geographic Coverage* Province, Global • *Cooperative Partner* Water Environment Federation • *Individual Members* 1,600

Mission To preserve and enhance water quality worldwide. The Association is dedicated to the transfer of information and concepts regarding all areas of the water environment. It provides a network for those involved in pollution abatement.

Annual Fees *Regular* $25

Funding	Membership	Newsletter Sponsor Fees	Conferences	Other
	51.2%	23.2%	21.8%	3.8%

Total Income $55,138

Usage	Administration	Programs
	31%	69%

Total Expenses $81,075

Programs Seminars, workshops, annual conference. Great Lakes

Water Quality Teleconference.

Publications Bimonthly newsletter. Directory of the Association's committees, activities, personnel and membership

For more Information Annual Report, Database, Library, List of Publications

Who's Who PRESIDENT JIM B. GREENSHIELDS • VICE PRESIDENT BRIAN EVANS • EXECUTIVE ADMINISTRATOR SANDY PICKETT • EDITOR SANDRA DAVEY

WATERCAN • EAUCAN

323 CHAPEL STREET   OTTAWA ON K1N 7Z2
PHONE (613) 230 5182   FAX (613) 237 5969

Founded 1987 • *Geographic Coverage* National, Global • *Organization Members* 15

Mission To sensitize Canadians to the need for clean water around the world, and to raise funds to support communities of the developing world in providing themselves with simple low cost water and sanitation systems along with hygiene education. WaterCan is a coalition of non-profit organizations.

Total Income $296,076

Programs Offers training and advice services to affiliated organizations. Provides a technical advisory service to member agencies to provide them with necessary information on technical and programming issues.

Who's Who EXECUTIVE DIRECTOR NICOLE BOSLEY

WESTERN CANADA WILDERNESS COMMITTEE

20 WATER STREET   VANCOUVER BC V6B 1A4
PHONE (604) 683 8220   FAX (604) 683 8229

Founded 1980 • *Geographic Coverage* Regional, National, Global *Other Field of Focus* Wildlife - Animal & Plant • *Chapters* 7 • *Individual Members* 30,000

Mission To teach and promote wilderness values and preservation, to lend support to similar activities of other organizations and agencies, and to sell products which reflect these values.

Annual Fees	Regular	Families
	$35	$50

Other Fees *Lifetime* $500

Funding	Membership & Donations	Foundations & Grants	Product Sales
	50%	20%	30%

Total Income $1,800,000

Usage

	Administration	Programs	Products
	20%	60%	20%

Programs Research stations in the Boreal Forest, Kitlope Valley, Carmanach Valley, Clayoquot Valley for the public to enjoy and scientists worldwide to visit.

Publications Educational reports including *Save Series* • *The Status of Vancouver Island's Threatened Old Growth Forests* • *The Faceless Ones: Environmental Issues - Candidate Questionnaire Results* • *The West Coast Trail Rainforest, A Proposal for the Completion of the West Coast Trail Unit of Pacific Rim National Park Reserve* • *Carmanach: Artistic Visions of an Ancient Rainforest* • *Clayoquot: On The Wild Side.* Proceedings of the Wild Regional Mapping Conference

Multimedia Online information service 1-800-661-9453. Educational slide shows

For more Information Database, Library, List of Publications

Who's Who FOUNDER PAUL GEORGE • INTERNATIONAL CAMPAIGNS COORDINATOR ADRIANNE CARR • NATIONAL CAMPAIGNS COORDINATOR JOE FOY CONTACT SUE FOX

YUKON CONSERVATION SOCIETY

P.O. BOX 4163   WHITEHORSE YT Y1A 3T3
PHONE (403) 668 5678

Founded 1968 • *Geographic Coverage* Province • *Cooperative Partners* Canadian Parks and Wilderness Society - Yukon Chapter, Yukon College

Mission To ensure the sound management of the Yukon's natural resources through advocacy, education and research. To encourage change that is sensitive to the uniquely fragile northern environment.

Annual Fees	Regular	Student/Senior	Families	Subscribing	Supporting
	$15	$10	$25	$25	$50

Programs Conservation education. Guided nature appreciation hikes. School programs. Public meetings. Ted Parnell Scholarship for students pursuing any aspect of environmental studies

Publication Quarterly newsletter

For more Information List of Publications

Who's Who CONTACT SHELLEY MATHEWSON

wildlife
animal & plant

CHAPTER 9

A Call for the Wild, by Laura L. Klure

HUMANS SHARE THIS PLANET WITH between 5 and 10 million plant and animal species, only about 40,000 of which are vertebrates. Preserving these millions of living things and approaching a sustainable way of life are perhaps the greatest challenges we face today. The International Union for Conservation of Nature and Natural Resources (IUCN The World Conservation Union) lists over 1,000 species of threatened or endangered mammals and birds. However, the vast majority of disappearing - but not generally listed - species are small, non-glamorous insects, plants, and other organisms. These living things are, nonetheless, vital parts of the food chain and possible sources of useful compounds. The US Endangered Species Act includes invertebrates and plants, but public sympathies are easier to arouse for large or "cute" animals. Wildlife preservation efforts have shifted in recent years from a focus on single endangered species to broader efforts aimed at maintaining biological diversity (or biodiversity) by saving habitats or whole ecosystems. Scientists and conservationists have recognized that it is not possible to save a species without preserving a

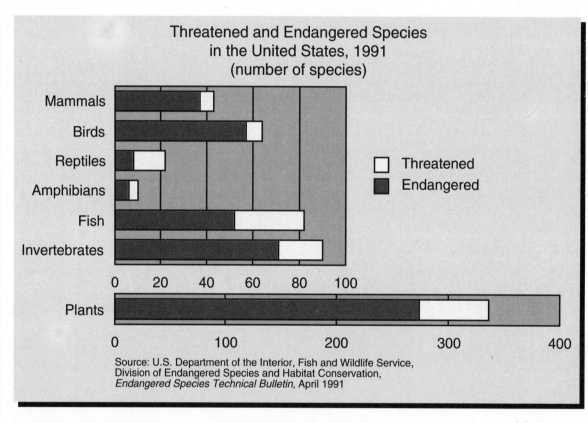

Threatened and Endangered Species in the United States, 1991 (number of species)

Threatened
Endangered

Source: U.S. Department of the Interior, Fish and Wildlife Service, Division of Endangered Species and Habitat Conservation, *Endangered Species Technical Bulletin*, April 1991

place for it to live. The 1992 annual report of the National Science Foundation noted that "the world's biodiversity, both plants and animals, is on a rapid decline, and many researchers suggest that the increased rate of extinction is equal to mass extinctions of the past". In a 1993 issue of Wildlife Monographs, 12 scientists maintained that the conventional

"species by species and threat by threat" approach to maintaining biodiversity is not adequate, and results in "gaps". They suggested that cohesive natural ecosystems, or biological diversity management areas, are necessary for maintenance of native species. All of today's sophisticated research techniques and computer modeling methods play vital roles in defining

conservation problems, but wildlife is only saved if the follow-up actions are appropriate.

AN EXAMPLE OF AN ALREADY partially successful habitat protection and restoration effort is the establishment of wetlands preserves in the Southeastern United States. Measures there are being coordinated to simultaneously protect habitats for a variety of birds, reptiles, and swamp flora. The American alligator has increased in number as a result, and has recovered from near-extinction. Ecologist Paul Erlich wrote in his 1991 book The Endangered Kingdom that "although many North American wildlife species have returned from the brink of extinction, and public awareness of the plight of non-human organisms is ►*page 156*

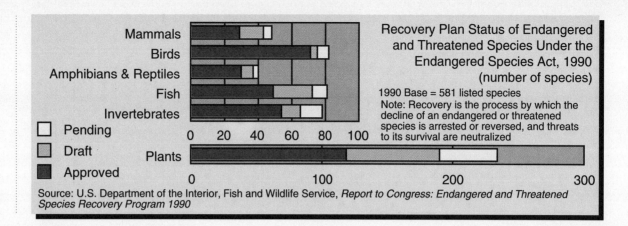

Mammals
Birds
Amphibians & Reptiles
Fish
Invertebrates

☐ Pending
☐ Draft
■ Approved

Plants

0   20   40   60   80   100

0   100   200   300

Recovery Plan Status of Endangered and Threatened Species Under the Endangered Species Act, 1990 (number of species)

1990 Base = 581 listed species
Note: Recovery is the process by which the decline of an endangered or threatened species is arrested or reversed, and threats to its survival are neutralized

Source: U.S. Department of the Interior, Fish and Wildlife Service, *Report to Congress: Endangered and Threatened Species Recovery Program 1990*

United States

AFRICAN WILDLIFE FOUNDATION

1717 MASSACHUSETTS AVENUE, NW   WASHINGTON DC 20036
PHONE (202) 265 8394   FAX (202) 265 2361

Founded 1961 • *Geographic Coverage* Africa • *Cooperative Partners* World Wildlife Fund, Fauna and Flora Preservation Society, Wildlife Conservation Society, The Biodiversity Support Program, IUCN The World Conservation Union, South Africa's Marine Mammal Institute

Mission To increase the sustainable contribution of natural resources to local and national economies and to promote the sound protection and management of these resources by the people of Africa, by working to build the capacity of African individuals and institutions to effectively manage their natural resources, especially wildlife and wildlife habitats.

Annual Fees

Regular	Sustaining	Contributing
$25	$50	$100

Funding

Membership	Contributed Services	Dividends	Other
65.3%	30.5%	2.6%	1.6%

Total Income $5,634,374 *

Usage

Administration	Fundraising	Programs
8.2%	5.8%	86%

Total Expenses $5,460,434

Programs Training of professionals, public education, institutional strengthening, and scientific research. Programs and activities in protected areas management, environmental awareness, policy development and implementation, conservation science, support for species and habitats of prime ecological significance, and community-based approaches to conservation. Neighbors as Partners Program works to ensure that local people and communities adjacent to parks and other protected areas derive some tangible benefit from their proximity. Conservation of

Biodiverse Resource Areas works to implement this five-year project and help Kenya Wildlife Service establish a Community Wildlife Service unit to implement and coordinate community-based programs. Protected Area Conservation Strategy. IUCN The World Conservation Union Meetings. Mweka College of African Wildlife Management. International Gorilla Conservation Program. Amboselli Elephant Research Project. Planning and Assessment for Wildlife Management.

Publications Quarterly briefs on selected projects and activities in Africa and the USA. Quarterly newsletter *Wildlife News*

For more Information Annual Report

Who's Who CHAIR PAUL T. SCHINDLER • VICE CHAIR JENNIFER E. INSKEEP • SECRETARY JOAN DONNER • TREASURER STUART T. SAUNDERS • DEVELOPMENT ASSISTANT MICHELLE LEASE

ALLIANCE FOR THE WILD ROCKIES   PAGE 39

P.O. BOX 8371   MISSOULA MT 59807
PHONE (406) 721 5420   FAX (406) 721 9917

AMERICAN ASSOCIATION OF BOTANICAL GARDENS AND ARBORETA

786 CHURCH ROAD   WAYNE PA 19087
PHONE (215) 688 1120   FAX (215) 293 0149

Founded 1940 • *Geographic Coverage* North America • *Organization Members* 350 • *Individual Members* 1,650

Mission To support North American botanical gardens and arboreta, public horticultural organizations, and their staffs and trustees by promoting the value of these organizations, by setting, promoting and recognizing professional standards, and by facilitating the exchange of information.

Annual Fees

Regular	Student/Senior	Associate Member	Library Subscriber
$50	$25	$50	$50

Other Fees *Corporate Affiliate* $250 • *Corporate* $500

Programs Resource Center provides a wide variety of information on public gardens and public horticulture. Workshops.

Publications Quarterly magazine *The Public Garden*. Monthly *AABGA Newsletter*. Numerous technical reports, surveys, directories and other publications focusing on botanical gardens, arboreta and general environmental issues

For more Information Library

Who's Who PRESIDENT **JUDITH ZUK** • VICE PRESIDENT **G. SHANNON SMITH**
SECRETARY **JONATHAN SHAW**

132

AMERICAN CETACEAN SOCIETY

P.O. BOX 2639   SAN PEDRO CA 90731-0943
PHONE (213) 548 6279

Founded 1967 • *Geographic Coverage* Global • *Cooperative Partner* International Whaling Commission • *Chapters* 9 • *Individual Members* 2,200

Mission To protect whales, dolphins, porpoises and their environments through research, education and conservation.

Annual Fees	Regular	Student/Senior	Patron
	$35	$25	$75

Funding	Membership	Foundations	Other
	15%	35%	50%

Total Income $300,000

Usage	Administration	Programs
	33%	67%

Programs Whalewatching trips. Educational programs.

Publication Journal *Whalewatcher*

For more Information Library

Who's Who PRESIDENT **KATY CASTAGNA** • VICE PRESIDENT **TOM LEWIS** • SECRETARY **CAROL BALL**

AMERICAN HORSE PROTECTION ASSOCIATION, INC.

1000 29TH STREET, NW, SUITE T-100   WASHINGTON DC 20007
PHONE (202) 965 0500

Founded 1966 • *Geographic Coverage* National • *Individual Members* 1,000

Mission To protect horses, both wild and domestic, by promoting the benefits and obligations of proper horse care to horse owners, industry representatives, and the general public; to ensure the enforcement of laws protecting equines; to improve federal, state and local laws regulating the treatment of horses; to advocate the protection and preservation of America's wild horses and burros.

Annual Fees	Regular	Student/Senior	Organization
	$20	$10	$25

Other Fees *Junior Member (Age 6 to 17)* $5 • *Lifetime* $750

Programs Monitors and provides input on legislation at the national and state levels. Annual hands-on training seminar for humane workers in equine cruelty investigations, rescue, and horse care. Educational program provides expertise and support to horse enthusiasts across America working to rid their communities of horse abuse and neglect.

Publications Quarterly newsletter *AHPA News*. Alerts and bulletins on crucial horse-related issues

Who's Who PRESIDENT **DOROTHY C. SAMSON** • VICE PRESIDENT **NANCY A. MURRAY** • SECRETARY **GENE C. LANGE** • EXECUTIVE DIRECTOR **ROBIN C. LOHNES**

AMERICAN ORNITHOLOGISTS' UNION
ORNITHOLOGICAL SOCIETIES OF NORTH AMERICA
P.O. BOX 1897   LAWRENCE KS 66044-8897

Founded 1883 • *Geographic Coverage* North America • *Cooperative Partner* The Cooper Ornithological Society • *Individual Members* 4,000

Mission The American Ornithologists' Union is the oldest and largest organization in North America devoted to the scientific study of birds. It supports individual research projects, provides funds for graduate students to attend annual meetings, and makes several annual awards for excellence in research.

Annual Fees	Regular	Student/Senior
	$35	$18

Other Fees *Lifetime* $1,050

Programs Annual meetings provide opportunities for meeting other people with an interest in birds. Many attendees present the results of scientific research in paper sessions, and there are plenary lectures, films, workshops, exhibits, field trips, and social events. Many members also attend quadrennial international congresses.

Publications Bimonthly *Ornithological Newsletter*. Quarterly journal *The Auk*. Book *The Check-List of North American Birds*

Who's Who PRESIDENT **F. LOHRER** • SECRETARY **STEPHEN K. RUSSELL** • TREASURER **MARION A. JENKINSON**

ASSOCIATION OF FIELD ORNITHOLOGISTS
C/O ALLEN PRESS, INC.
P.O. BOX 1897   LAWRENCE KS 66044

Geographic Coverage Global • *Cooperative Partners* Cornell Laboratory of Ornithology, US Fish and Wildlife Service

Mission The Association is dedicated to the study and conservation of birds and their habitats.

	Regular	Student/Senior	Institution	Supporting	Patron
Annual Fees	$21	$15	$45	$50	$1,000

Other Fees *Lifetime* $650

Programs Ornithological meetings. Annual meeting. Ongoing studies.

Publications Quarterly *Journal of Field Ornithology.* Annual *Bird Count Supplement.* Bimonthly *Ornithological Newsletter*

AUDUBON SOCIETY OF RHODE ISLAND

12 SANDERSON ROAD   SMITHFIELD RI 02917
PHONE (401) 231 6444

Founded 1897 • *Geographic Coverage* State • *Individual Members* 4,000

Mission Areas of focus include natural history, habitats, birds, solid waste, water, and wetlands.

	Regular	Patron
Annual Fees	$25	$100

BAT CONSERVATION INTERNATIONAL, INC.

P.O. BOX 162603   AUSTIN TX 78716-2603
PHONE (512) 327 9721   FAX (512) 327 9724

Founded 1982 • *Geographic Coverage* National, Global • *Cooperative Partner* US National Park Service

Mission To promote conservation of bats and their habitats worldwide, and to educate the public about the vital ecological and economic roles of bats, as part of the more general goal of preserving the diversity and health of life on earth.

	Regular	Student/Senior	Friend of BCI	Supporting	Contributing
Annual Fees	$30	$25	$35	$50	$100

Other Fees *Patron* $250 • *Sustaining* $500 • *Founder's Circle* $1,000

Programs North American Bat House Research Project sets up bat houses and makes careful observations to learn more about bat roosting requirements. Adopt-A-Bat Program.

Publications Quarterly *BATS Magazine.* Books *America's Neighborhood Bats* • *Bat House Builder's Handbook* • *Bats: A Natural History.* Other publications

Multimedia Video *The Secret World of Bats.* Other videos and slide shows (available in Spanish)

Who's Who PRESIDENT MICHAEL L. COOK • VICE PRESIDENTS JOHN D. MITCHELL, WILHELMINA R. MORIAN • SECRETARY PEGGY PHILLIPS • TREASURER MARK T. RITTER EXECUTIVE DIRECTOR MERLIN D. TUTTLE

BEAVER DEFENDERS (THE)

UNEXPECTED WILDLIFE REFUGE, P.O. BOX 765   NEWFIELD NJ 08344
PHONE (609) 697 3541

Founded 1968 • *Geographic Coverage* North America • *Individual Members* 200

Mission To maintain an inviolate sanctuary for wildlife and to ensure the protection and conservation of the beaver, through a strategy of promoting humane education and disseminating informative literature.

	Membership	Foundations
Funding	25%	75%

Total Income $10,000

Usage *Programs* 100%

Programs Disseminates informative/educational literature. Provides ongoing maintenance of the refuge. Guides visitors to the refuge.

Publications Quarterly newsletter *The Beaver Defenders.* Books *Beaversprite* • *Best of the Beaver Defenders*

Who's Who PRESIDENT WILLIAM R. BEY • VICE PRESIDENT LAURANCE SAWYER SECRETARY HOPE BUYUKMIHCI

BILLFISH FOUNDATION (THE)

2051 11TH STREET, NW   MIAMI FL 33125
PHONE (305) 649 8930

Founded 1986 • *Geographic Coverage* Global • *Organization Members* 100 • *Individual Members* 5,000

Mission To promote the conservation of billfish worldwide through research, education, and advocacy. The Billfish Foundation is the world's leading billfish conservation organization, delivering the scientific data required to rebuild the ocean's billfish stocks.

	Regular	Student/Senior
Annual Fees	$25	$15

	Membership	Corporations	Foundations
Funding	60%	10%	30%

Total Income $390,000

Usage	Administration	Fundraising	Programs
	30%	5%	65%

Programs Global Tagging Program. Certificate Program. Youth Education Program. "No-Marlin on the Menu" Program. Worldwide research projects.

Publication Quarterly newsletter *Billfish*

Who's Who PRESIDENT **WINTHORP P. ROCKEFELLER** • VICE PRESIDENT **STEPHEN SLOAN** • TREASURER **DON TYSON** • EXECUTIVE DIRECTOR **JOHN B. SPENCE**

BIRDLIFE INTERNATIONAL

P.O. BOX 57242   WASHINGTON DC 20037-7242
PHONE (202) 778 9563   FAX (202) 293 9342

Founded 1922 • *Geographic Coverage* Global • *Cooperative Partners* World Wildlife Fund, World Pheasant Association

Mission To prevent the extinction of any bird species in the wild, monitor the conservation status of all bird species and important bird habitats worldwide, identify and secure adequate conservation of critically important sites for the conservation of bird diversity, and promote worldwide interest in, and concern for, the conservation of birds and the environment.

Programs Field action programs based on research, to identify the threats to birds and their habitats. Conservation program in the Palas Valley in Pakistan to protect the Western Trapogan pheasant and its habitat. Conservation at Kao Nor Chuchi in southern Thailand to protect the Gurney's Pitta. Conservation program in Europe which covers around 30 countries, combining international activities with national campaigns and actions, and working under a unified strategy. Conservation programs in Ghana, Turkey, Madeira, Cameroon, Spain, and Nigeria.

Publications Quarterly magazine *World Birdwatch*. Newsletter *BirdLife International Pan American Bulletin*. *Red Data Books*. Technical publications covering a wide range of avian conservation issues. Directory *Important Bird Areas in Europe*

For more Information Database, List of Publications

Who's Who PRESIDENT **DONAL C. O'BRIEN** • SECRETARY **KIMBERLEY YOUNG** • TREASURER **STEPHEN D. ECCLES**

BROOKS BIRD CLUB, INC. (THE)

707 WARWOOD AVENUE   WHEELING WV 26003
PHONE (304) 547 5253

CACTUS AND SUCCULENT SOCIETY OF AMERICA

1535 REEVES STREET   LOS ANGELES CA 90035
PHONE (310) 556 1923   FAX (310) 286 9629

Founded 1929 • *Geographic Coverage* Global • *Organization Members* 80 • *Individual Members* 4,000

Mission To foster and benefit the hobby of growing cactus and succulents by education and scientific research.

Annual Fees *Regular* $30

Funding *Membership* 100%

Publications Bimonthly *CSSA Newsletter*. Bimonthly *Cactus and Succulent Journal*. Annual scientific journal *Hazeltonia*

For more Information Library

Who's Who PRESIDENT **GERALD BARAD** • PRESIDENT-ELECT **MARY JO GUSSETT** • VICE PRESIDENT **LARRY MITICA** • SECRETARY **SEYMOUR LINDEN** • TREASURER **MINDY FUSARO** LIBRARIAN **CHUCK EVERSON** • CONTACT **WILLIAM GLOVER**

CALIFORNIA TROUT, INC.

870 MARKET STREET, SUITE 859   SAN FRANCISCO CA 94102
PHONE (415) 392 8887   FAX (415) 392 8895

Founded 1971 • *Geographic Coverage* State • *Chapters* 4 *Organization Members* 20 • *Individual Members* 4,500

Mission To protect and restore wild trout, native steelhead, and their habitat, and to provide high quality angling opportunities for the public to enjoy.

Annual Fees *Regular* $30

Publications Newsletter *Streamkeepers Log*. Various publications focusing on miscellaneous projects

For more Information Database, Library, List of Publications

Who's Who PRESIDENT **RICHARD MAY** • VICE PRESIDENT **JIM EDMONSON** • SECRETARY **BILL POST** • EXECUTIVE DIRECTOR **TOM HESSELDENZ** • CONTACT **DAVE BAKER**

CALIFORNIA WILDERNESS COALITION

2655 PORTAGE BAY EAST, SUITE 5   DAVIS CA 95616
PHONE (916) 758 0380

CENTER FOR MARINE CONSERVATION

1725 DESALES STREET, NW   WASHINGTON DC 20036
PHONE (202) 429 5609   FAX (202) 872 0619

CENTER FOR PLANT CONSERVATION

MISSOURI BOTANICAL GARDEN, P.O. BOX 299   ST. LOUIS MO 63166-0299
PHONE (314) 577 9450   FAX (314) 664 0465

Founded 1984 • *Geographic Coverage* National • *Cooperative Partner* The Plant Conservation Fund • *Organization Members* 25 botanical gardens and arboreta

Mission To prevent the extinction of native plants, by working for the creation of a systematic, comprehensive national program of plant conservation, research and education.

Programs National office provides coordination and support services. Participating institutions perform field and horticultural work, and maintain the National Collection of Endangered Plants, which is central to the Center's conservation programs.

Publication Newsletter *Plant Conservation*

For more Information Database

Who's Who PRESIDENT ANNE B. FORDYCE • SECRETARY PHEBE S. MINER • TREASURER ROBERT W. BLUCKE • EXECUTIVE DIRECTOR DONALD A. FALK • MANAGER CONSERVATION PROGRAMS PEGGY OLWELL • CONSERVATION PROJECTS COORDINATOR MARIE M. BRUEGMANN • INFORMATION SYSTEMS COORDINATOR JEANNE A. CABLISH • COMMUNICATIONS MANAGER SHEILA S. KILGORE

COALITION TO PROTECT ANIMALS IN PARKS AND REFUGES

P.O. BOX 26   SWAIN NY 14884-0026
PHONE (607) 545 6213

Founded 1983 • *Geographic Coverage* North America • *Other Field of Focus* National Parks - Land Use / Conservation / Acquisition *Organization Members* 46 • *Individual Members* 2,000

Mission To help stop the killing of wild animals in Parks and National Wildlife Refuges.

Annual Fees *Regular* $3

Programs Education programs.

Publications Newsletters Coalition to Protect Animals in Parks & Refuges • The Civil Abolitionist (in the process of combining both publications under one name)

Who's Who CONTACT BINA ROBINSON

COOPER ORNITHOLOGICAL SOCIETY LOS ANGELES

1100 GLENDON AVENUE, SUITE 1400   LOS ANGELES CA 90024
PHONE (213) 472 7868

Founded 1893 • *Geographic Coverage* National • *Individual Members* 2,200

Mission To advance the knowledge of birds through observation and study, encouragement of bird study, conservation of birds and wildlife, and publication of ornithological materials.

Annual Fees	*Regular*	*Student/Senior*	*Families*
	$23	$15	$25

Other Fees *Lifetime* $600

Who's Who PRESIDENT JIM JENNINGS

COOPER ORNITHOLOGICAL SOCIETY (THE)
C/O ORNITHOLOGICAL SOCIETIES OF NORTH AMERICA

P.O. BOX 1897   LAWRENCE KS 66044-8897
PHONE (913) 843 1221   FAX (913) 843 1274

Founded 1893, incorporated in 1934 • *Geographic Coverage* Global *Cooperative Partners* Ornithological Societies of North America, American Ornithologists' Union

Mission To advance the knowledge of birds and their habitats. The Society's objectives include the observation and cooperative study of birds, the encouragement and spread of interest in bird study, the conservation of birds and wildlife in general, and the publication of ornithological knowledge.

Annual Fees	*Regular*	*Student/Senior*	*Families*	*Sustaining*
	$30	$15	$35	$40

Other Fees *Lifetime* $800 • *Emeritus* $15 • *Patron* $1,000

Programs Annual meeting, at which the scientific program is arranged into paper and poster sessions wherein researchers present findings from their recent avian studies.

Publications Bimonthly *Ornithological Newsletter* published jointly by the COS and three other ornithological societies. Quarterly journals *The Condor* • *Journal of Field Ornithology* • *The Wilson Bulletin* • *The Auk*. Series *Studies in Avian Biology* (formerly *Pacific Coast Avifauna*)

For more Information List of Publications

CORNELL LABORATORY OF ORNITHOLOGY

159 SAPSUCKER WOODS ROAD   ITHACA NY 14850
PHONE (807) 254 2473

Founded 1917 • *Geographic Coverage* Global • *Individual Members* 14,000

Mission To promote the study, appreciation, and conservation of birds. The Lab provides up-to-date ornithological data to scientists as well as to radio, television, newspaper, and magazine journalists the world over. The Lab provides scientists and conservationists the tools they need to study and manage birds effectively: information on bird populations, sound recordings for use in bird censusing, and behavioral studies.

Annual Fees	Regular	Contributing	Guardian	Patron
	$30	$70	$100	$250

Other Fees *Sponsor* $500 • *Benefactor* $1,000

Funding	Membership	Corporations	Foundations	Other
	29%	3%	10%	58%

Total Income $2,300,000

Usage	Administration	Fundraising	Programs	Other
	15%	7%	72%	6%

Programs Project FeederWatch. Project Tanager. Project PigeonWatch. Bioacoustics Research Program. Home study course in ornithology.

Publications Newsletter *Birdscope*. Magazine *Living Bird*

Multimedia *BirdWatch* daily radio program about birds, broadcast coast-to-coast on commercial and public radio

For more Information Library

Who's Who PRESIDENT **CHARLES WALCOTT** • SECRETARY **KATHY GARRETT** • EXECUTIVE DIRECTOR **SCOTT SUTCLIFFE**

COUSTEAU SOCIETY, INC. (THE)   PAGE 17

870 GREENBRIER CIRCLE, SUITE 402   CHESAPEAKE VA 23320-2641
PHONE (804) 523 9335   FAX (804) 523 2747

DEFENDERS OF WILDLIFE

1244 19TH STREET, NW   WASHINGTON DC 20036
PHONE (202) 659 9510   FAX (202) 833 3349

Founded 1947 • *Geographic Coverage* National • *Other Field of Focus* Ecosystem Protection / Biodiversity • *Individual Members* 80,000

Mission To further a comprehensive approach to habitat protection that will preserve intact wildlife communities which support a wide variety of plant and animal life. The Defenders are committed to the belief that this conservation principle, known as biological diversity, is the framework upon which all environmental protection strategies must be built.

Annual Fees	Regular	Student/Senior
	$20	$15

Funding	Membership	Contributions	Legacies & Bequests	Other
	24.5%	39%	26.5%	10%

Total Income $5,226,576

Usage	Administration	Fundraising	Programs	Membership Development
	10.1%	13.2%	61.2%	15.5%

Total Expenses $4,441,799

Programs Protection and restoration of endangered species. Protection of marine mammals. Preservation of biological diversity. Banning the importation of wild-caught birds. Promotion of watchable wildlife viewing areas.

Publications Bimonthly magazine *Defenders*. Quarterly newsletter *Wildlife Advocate*

For more Information Annual Report

Who's Who PRESIDENT **RODGER SCHLICKEISEN** • VICE PRESIDENT **ANITA GOTTLIEB** SECRETARY **ROBERT R. LARSEN** • TREASURER **ALAN W. STEINBERG** • EXECUTIVE ASSISTANT **SHALOM TAZEWELL** • DIRECTOR OF ADMINISTRATION **MARY M. HESSMAN** DIRECTOR OF MEMBERSHIP **KATE MATHEWS** • EDITOR DEFENDERS **JAMES G. DEANE** DIRECTOR OF MEDIA RELATIONS **JOAN MOODY**

DELTA WATERFOWL FOUNDATION   PAGE 44
NORTH AMERICAN WILDLIFE FOUNDATION
102 WILMOT ROAD, SUITE 410   DEERFIELD IL 60015
PHONE (708) 940 7776   FAX (708) 940 3739

DESERT FISHES COUNCIL   PAGE 44
P.O. BOX 337   BISHOP CA 93514
PHONE (619) 872 8751

DESERT TORTOISE COUNCIL
P.O. BOX 1738   PALM DESERT CA 92261
PHONE (619) 341 8449

Founded 1976 • *Geographic Coverage* Regional • *Individual Members* 300

Mission To assure the continued survival of viable populations of the desert tortoise throughout its existing range.

Annual Fees	Regular	Student/Senior	Patron
	$12	$8	$55

Funding *Membership* 100%

Total Income $35,000

Usage	Administration	Programs
	10%	90%

Programs Desert Tortoise Annual Symposium. Desert Tortoise Survey Techniques Workshop.

Publications Proceedings from *Desert Tortoise Symposium*

Who's Who PRESIDENT **MARC GRAFF** • VICE PRESIDENT **TOM DODSON** • SECRETARY **TERRIE CORRELL**

DOLPHIN DATA BASE
321 High School Road, NE, Box 344 Bainbridge Island WA 98110

Founded 1986 • *Geographic Coverage* Global • *Individual Members* 5,000

Mission To provide an information clearinghouse on marine mammal research, conservation, and education, and to provide a listing of resources and opportunities related to marine mammals.

Publications Newsletter *Dolphin Data Base News*. Directory *Dolphin Data Base International*

Who's Who President Toni Frohoff • Vice President James Frohoff • Secretary Lilliana Zoymel

DOLPHIN RESEARCH CENTER
P.O. Box 522875   Marathon Shores FL 33052-2875
Phone (305) 289 1121

Geographic Coverage Local

Mission To promote a greater understanding and appreciation of marine mammals through research, education, and first-hand experience with dolphins at the Grassy Keys facility in Florida.

Annual Fees

Regular	Student/Senior	Families	"Dolfriend"
$30	$15	$50	$15

Other Fees *Sponsor* $100 • *"Adopt-A-Dolphin"* $200

Programs Educational walking tours of the facility. 7-day "Dolphinlab" offers seminars and lab workshops. Dolphin Outreach educates schools and clubs. Dolphin/ Child Program involves dolphins in teaching disabled children. Dolphin Encounter. Adopt-A-Dolphin program. The Land Fund Drive. "DolphInsight". Dolphin Critical Care Unit. Florida Keys Marine Animal Rescue Team. Intern and volunteer programs.

Publication Bimonthly newsletter *Dolphin Society*

Who's Who President Jayne Shannon-Rodriguez • Government Affairs Manager Karen J. Roberts

DUCKS UNLIMITED, INC.   PAGE 107
1 Waterfowl Way   Memphis TN 38120
Phone (901) 754 4666   Fax (901) 753 2613

EAST AFRICAN WILDLIFE SOCIETY
P.O. Box 82002   San Diego CA 92138
Phone (619) 225 1233   Fax (619) 226 4003

Founded 1962 • *Geographic Coverage* East Africa • *Individual Members* 20,000 worldwide

Mission To save the endangered wildlife, habitats, and other natural places in East Africa. The organization's main areas of focus currently include working for the conservation of the Black Rhino and for a halt to the poaching of elephant ivory.

Annual Fees *Regular* $35

Funding

Membership	Corporations	Foundations
20%	20%	60%

Publications Bimonthly magazine *SWARA* (Antelope in Swahili) from Kenya. Annual *The African Journal of Ecology*

Who's Who Contact Keith Tucker

ELEPHANT RESEARCH FOUNDATION
106 East Hickory Grove Road   Bloomfield Hills MI 48304
Phone (313) 540 3947

Founded 1977 • *Geographic Coverage* Global • *Organization Members* 100 • *Individual Members* 350

Mission To promote interest in and to increase the scientific knowledge of elephants, and to collect and disseminate information needed for education, research, and conservation of elephants.

Annual Fees *Regular* $20

Funding

Membership	Foundations
90%	10%

Usage

Administration	Fundraising	Programs
10%	10%	80%

Publication Journal *Elephant*

Who's Who President Jeheskel Shoshani • Vice President William L. Thompson • Secretary Sandra Lee L. Shoshani

ENDANGERED SPECIES COALITION
666 Pennsylvania Avenue, SE   Washington DC 20003
Phone (202) 547 9009   Fax (202) 547 9022

Founded 1981 • *Geographic Coverage* National • *Organization Members* 82

Mission The Endangered Species Coalition is an alliance of 82 environmental, scientific, and animal welfare organizations collectively representing more than five million citizens dedicated to a strong Endangered Species Act.

Publications Monthly newsletters. Fact sheets. Position papers

For more Information Database

FOUNDATION FOR THE NORTH AMERICAN WILD SHEEP

720 ALLEN AVENUE   CODY WY 82414-3402
PHONE (307) 527 6261   FAX (307) 527 7117

Geographic Coverage North America • *Cooperative Partners* Arizona Desert Bighorn Society, Rocky Mountain Bighorn Society, Elko Nevada Bighorn Society, Fallon Nevada Bighorn Unlimited, Fraternity of the Desert Bighorn, Grand Slam Club, Texas Bighorn Sheep Society *Chapters* 8 • *Individual Members* 5,000

Mission To promote and enhance increasing populations of indigenous wild sheep on the North American continent, to safeguard against the decline or extinction of such species, and to fund programs for professional management of these populations.

Annual Fees	Regular	Families	Corporation	Sustaining
	$45	$80	$200	$200

Other Fees *Lifetime* $1,000

Programs Annually funds wide variety of projects, with some major areas of consideration being: biological studies and research projects, buffer land acquisition, wild sheep transplants and the re-establishment of wild sheep populations into suitable historic habitat, wildlife habitat enhancement, prudent wild sheep management, safeguarding the environment, repressing poaching and fostering sportsmen's rights. Holds annual meeting and convention.

Publication Quarterly periodical *Wild Sheep*

Who's Who PRESIDENT **CRAIG JOHNSON** • VICE PRESIDENTS **JOHNNY DRIFT, LELAND SPEAKES, JR.** • SECRETARY **PETE CIMELLARO** • TREASURER **PHYLLIS CARLSON** • EXECUTIVE DIRECTOR **KAREN WERBELOW** • CONTACT **PAULA KARRES**

FOUNDATION FOR THE PRESERVATION AND PROTECTION OF THE PRZEWALSKI HORSE

ANIMAL AND DAIRY SCIENCE DEPARTMENT
LIVESTOCK / POULTRY BUILDING UGA   ATHENS GA 30602
PHONE (706) 542 3000

Geographic Coverage Global • *Focused Country* Mongolia

Mission To provide educational materials on the Przewalski horse, and to reintroduce the Przewalski horse into the Hustain Nuruu steppe preserve in Mongolia, which is one of the few countries of the world with expansive steppes.

Programs None in the US. Many partners in the Netherlands working on the reintroduction project.

Publication Book *Przewalski Horse*

Who's Who CONTACT **JULIA MCCONN**

FRIENDS OF THE SEA LION

MARINE MAMMAL CENTER
20612 LAGUNA CANYON ROAD   LAGUNA BEACH CA 92651
PHONE (714) 494 3050

Founded 1971 • *Geographic Coverage* Local • *Focused Region* Orange County, CA

Mission To rescue and provide medical care and treatment for sick and injured marine mammals along the coast of Orange County, California. To perform research and education on the causes of diseases and injuries among marine mammals.

Total Income $100,000

Usage	Direct Animal Care	Capital Improvements & Other
	65%	35%

Total Expenses $100,000

Programs Workers at the Center provide direct care to rescued sea mammals, and engage in research and educational activities.

Publications Newsletter *Friends of the Sea Lion*. Information booklets

For more Information Library

Who's Who EXECUTIVE DIRECTOR **JUDI JONES** • ASSISTANT DIRECTOR **LORI GENETIVE**

FRIENDS OF THE SEA OTTER

P.O. BOX 221220   CARMEL CA 93922
PHONE (408) 373 2747   FAX (408) 373 2749

Founded 1968 • *Geographic Coverage* Local • *Chapter* 1

Mission To aid in the protection of a rare and threatened species, the Southern sea otter, and its habitat from any and all threats, including but not limited to oil spills, toxic pollution, adverse fishing activities, and attacks by mankind.

Annual Fees	Regular	Student/Senior	Sponsor	Patron	Benefactor
	$25	$15	$50	$100	$500

Other Fees *Lifetime* $200

Funding	Membership	Foundations	Sales	Other
	27.7%	29.6%	38.8%	3.9%

Total Income $249,137

Usage	Programs	Supporting Services	Other
	48.5%	29%	22.5%

Total Expenses $273,102

Programs Assists California Fish & Game and the US Fish & Wildlife Service in taking the sea otter census and reviewing environmental impact reports and permits. Represents the sea otters at public meetings and hearings. Coordinates recruitment, coordination, and training of volunteers in development of an oil spill response plan. Conducts educational programs and distributes literature to schools and the public. Operates The Otter Center, an educational/retail center located in the Crossroads Shopping Center in Carmel Valley, CA. Operates an otter spotting program to help visitors watch the activities of sea otters along the shores of Monterey Bay.

Publications Newsletters *The Otter Raft* • Semiannual *The Otter Pup*

For more Information Annual Report, Library

Who's Who PRESIDENT **ARTHUR W. HASELTINE** • VICE PRESIDENT **SCOTT HENNESSY** SECRETARY **ANN WOODWARD** • EXECUTIVE DIRECTOR **DINA STANSBURY** • SCIENTIFIC, EDUCATION DIRECTOR **ELLEN FAUROT-DANIELS** • MEMBERSHIP DIRECTOR **JULIE PAYNE**

GORILLA FOUNDATION (THE)

BOX 620-640   WOODSIDE CA 94062
PHONE (415) 851 8505

Founded 1976 • *Geographic Coverage* Global • *Individual Members* 65,000

Mission To promote the protection, propagation, and preservation of gorillas and to learn more about their physical and emotional needs. The Gorilla Foundation has conducted the longest uninterrupted interspecies communication study of gorillas.

Annual Fees	Regular	Student/Senior	Sustaining	Corporation
	$25	$20	$50	$5,000

Other Fees *Sponsor* $100 • *Donor* $500 • *Patron* $1,000

Funding	Membership	Foundations	Sales & Royalties	Interest
	63%	19%	12%	6%

Total Income $917,453

Usage	Administration	Fundraising	Programs
	19%	3%	78%

Total Expenses $692,043

Programs Collects data on the sign language skills of Koko, a female lowland gorilla, and Michael, a male lowland gorilla. Participates in the Species Survival Plan, to ensure the propagation of gorillas in captivity. Developing a gorilla preserve in Hawaii.

Publications Semiannual journal *Gorilla*. Various books including *The Education of Koko* • *Koko's Kitten* • *Koko's Story* • *With Love From Koko*

For more Information Annual Report

Who's Who PRESIDENT **FRANCINE G. PATTERSON** • VICE PRESIDENTS **RONALD H. COHN**, **EVE G. ANDERSON** • SECRETARY **MARY CAMERON STANFORD**

HAWKWATCH INTERNATIONAL, INC.

1420 CARLISLE BOULEVARD, NE
SUITE 100, P.O. BOX 35706   ALBUQUERQUE NM 87176-5706
PHONE (505) 255 7622   FAX (505) 255 7832

Founded 1986 • *Geographic Coverage* Regional, North America
Focused Region Mexico, US western states • *Chapter* 1 • *Organization Members* 150 • *Individual Members* 3,000

Mission To protect the nation's hawks, eagles, and falcons and their habitats, through monitoring programs, scientific research, education, and conservation action. The organization provides scientific data of benchmark quality from which the human impact on the environment, as well as the health of raptor populations, can be determined.

Annual Fees *Regular* $25

Funding	Membership	Foundations	Government Contracts	Other
	52.5%	14.3%	20.2%	13%

Total Income $226,232

Usage	Administration	Fundraising	Programs	Membership Services
	11.4%	13.8%	67.4%	7.4%

Total Expenses $225,690

Programs HawkWatch field biologists annually monitor the health and movements of birds of prey in eight western states and Mexico. The organization coordinates the largest raptor banding study in western North America. Live-Raptor Programs teach important lessons in predator-prey relationships, human ecology, and global environmental problems. Adopt-A-Hawk Program.

Publication Quarterly newsletter *Raptor Watch*

Multimedia Online information service 1-800-726-HAWK

For more Information Database

Who's Who PRESIDENT **STEPHEN W. HOFFMAN** • VICE PRESIDENT **ROBERT TERRAGNO** SECRETARY **DAVID NIMKIN** • DIRECTORS **CAROLYN CHASE, DAWN SEBESTA** • DIRECTOR OF DEVELOPMENT **EDWARD HAMILTON** • ADMINISTRATIVE DIRECTOR **JENNIFER DOYLE**

INTERNATIONAL ASSOCIATION
FOR BEAR RESEARCH AND MANAGEMENT

333 RASPBERRY ROAD   ANCHORAGE AK 99518-1599
PHONE (907) 344 0541

Founded 1968 • *Geographic Coverage* Global • *Individual Members* 400

Mission To support the scientific management of bears through research and distribution of information. The Association, consisting of several hundred members from over 20 countries, is open to professional biologists, wildlife managers, and others dedicated to the conservation of all species of bears.

Annual Fees	Regular	Student/Senior
	$10	$7

Funding	Membership	Foundations	Book Sales
	20%	20%	60%

Total Income $20,000

Usage *Programs* 100%

Programs Provides grants for research. Sponsors a Triennial International Conference on all aspects of bear biology, ecology, and management. Sponsors conferences and workshops.

Publications Quarterly newsletter *International Bear News*. Peer-reviewed scientific paper series *Bears: Their Biology and Management* (proceedings from triennial international conference)

Who's Who PRESIDENT MICHAEL PELTON • VICE PRESIDENT IVAR MYSTERUD • SECRETARY STERLING MILLER • OTHER GARY ALT, PUOTR DANILOV, KATE KENDALL, AL LECOUNT • EDITOR TERESA DELORENZO

INTERNATIONAL CARNIVOROUS PLANT SOCIETY

BIOLOGY DEPARTMENT, CSUF   FULLERTON CA 92634
PHONE (703) 980 6379

Founded 1980 • *Geographic Coverage* Global • *Chapters* 3
Organization Members 10 • *Individual Members* 800

Mission To promote communication among people interested in carnivorous plants, be they amateur naturalists or professional botanists.

Annual Fees	Regular	Outside US & Canada
	$15	$20

Funding *Membership* 100%

Publication *Carnivorous Plant Newsletter*

Who's Who EDITORS D. E. SCHNELL, J. A. MAZRIMAS, LEO SONG

INTERNATIONAL CRANE FOUNDATION

E-11376 SHADY LANE ROAD   BARABOO WI 53913
PHONE (608) 356 9462

Founded 1973 • *Geographic Coverage* Global • *Focused Countries*
Australia, Canada, China, Russian Federation, USA, Vietnam

Mission To preserve the world's cranes and their wetland and grass-

land habitats through a wide range of education and conservation activities directed toward the many countries where cranes exist.

Annual Fees	Regular	Families	Canadian/Foreign	Associate
	$20	$30	$25	$100

Other Fees *Sponsor* $500 • *Patron* $1,000

Funding	Contributions	Grants & Awards	Revenues
	18%	59%	23%

Total Income $1,237,729

Usage	Administration	Fundraising	Programs
	21%	5%	74%

Total Expenses $1,289,393

Programs Captive propagation and restocking efforts. Tours of the Foundation headquarters in Baraboo, WI.

Publication Quarterly newsletter *The ICF Bugle*

For more Information Annual Report

Who's Who PRESIDENT MARY WICKHEM • EXECUTIVE DIRECTOR GEORGE ARCHIBALD EDUCATION ASSISTANT ROB NELSON

INTERNATIONAL PRIMATE PROTECTION LEAGUE

P.O. DRAWER 766   SUMMERVILLE SC 29484
PHONE (803) 871 2280   FAX (803) 871 7988

Founded 1973 • *Geographic Coverage* National, Global • *Chapter* 1, in England • *Individual Members* 14,000

Mission To conserve and protect "non-human primates".

Annual Fees	Regular	Student/Senior	Sustaining	Patron
	$20	$10	$50	$100

Funding	Membership	Foundations	Other
	90%	8%	2%

Total Income $255,000

Usage	Administration	Fundraising	Programs	Overseas Grants
	20%	10%	65%	5%

Programs Ongoing programs to investigate and prevent illegal trafficking in endangered and trade-threatened primates, to investigate the treatment of "non-human primates" in research laboratories, and to care for injured "non-human primates" in the League's sanctuary.

Publications Newsletter *IPPL News*. Books *Baboon Orphan* • *Among the Orangutans*

For more Information Database, List of Publications

INTERNATIONAL SOCIETY FOR THE PROTECTION OF MUSTANGS AND BURROS

6212 EAST SWEETWATER AVENUE   SCOTTSDALE AZ 85254
PHONE (602) 991 0273   FAX (602) 991 2920

Founded 1960 • *Geographic Coverage* Global • *Individual Members* 10,000

Mission To influence global attitudes and catalyze actions for the protection, preservation, and understanding of wild horses and burros and their habitat. The Society is concerned with wild free roaming horses and burros nationally and internationally, their habitat, biotic needs, protection, and preservation.

Annual Fees	Regular	Student/Senior	Families	Contributing
	$25	$15	$35	$50

Other Fees *Sponsor* $100 • *Sustaining* $500 • *Benevolent* $1,000

Total Income $26,000

Usage	Administration	Programs
	25%	75%

Programs Wild Horse and Burro Heritage Center. Operation Wild Horse and Burro Rescue. Center for Wild Horse and Burro Research. Compliance Program. Wild Horses of America Registry.

Publication Newsletter *Wild Horse and Burro Diary*

Who's Who PRESIDENT KAREN A. SUSSMAN • VICE PRESIDENT MARY ANN SIMONDS • SECRETARY TRACY CONNER

INTERNATIONAL WILD WATERFOWL ASSOCIATION

7 JAMES FARM ROAD   LEE NH 03824
PHONE (603) 659 5442

Founded 1958 • *Geographic Coverage* Europe, North America
Individual Members 400

Mission To preserve and protect the waterfowl of the world through habitat preservation and to use captive breeding as a conservation tool.

Annual Fees *Regular* $25
Other Fees *Lifetime* $300

Funding	Membership	Foundations	Sales
	50%	34%	16%

Total Income $12,600

Usage	Administration	Programs	Newsletter
	8%	52%	40%

Total Expenses $11,400

Programs Habitat preservation. Captive breeding. Education.

Publication Quarterly *IWWA Newsletter*

For more Information Library

Who's Who PRESIDENT WALTER B. STURGEON • VICE PRESIDENTS ED ASPER, PAUL DYE • TREASURER WILLIAM LOWE • SECRETARY NANCY COLLINS

INTERNATIONAL WILDERNESS LEADERSHIP FOUNDATION

PAGE 111

211 WEST MAGNOLIA   FORT COLLINS CO 80521
PHONE (303) 498 0303   FAX (303) 498 0403

INTERNATIONAL WILDLIFE COALITION

634 NORTH FALMOUTH HIGHWAY,
P.O. BOX 388   NORTH FALMOUTH MA 02536-0388
PHONE (508) 564 9980   FAX (508) 563 2843

Founded 1983 • *Geographic Coverage* National, Global • *Chapters* 2, in United Kingdom, and Canada • *Individual Members* 250,000

Mission To conduct and support life-saving rescue, rehabilitation, and protection projects around the world.

Annual Fees	Regular	Rescuer	Protector	Benefactor
	$17	$35	$100	$500

Funding	Membership	Foundations	Merchandise Sales
	4%	83%	13%

Total Income $2,090,391

Total Expenses $3,057,036

Programs Public education programs. Legal actions. Product boycotts. Letter-writing campaigns. Scientific research. Elephant Care Facility. Whale Patrol Project. Cape Cod Stranding Network. Whale Adoption Project. Campaign to end commercial whaling. Convention on Trade in Endangered Species. Campaign to End the Ivory Trade. Project Swims Teacher Education Program. Campaign to End the Kangaroo Massacre. Around the World: International Wildlife Coalition - Brazil Wildlife Rescue and Rehabilitation Center. Tanzanian Wildlife Ranger Scholarship Fund. West Norfolk Seal Rescue Centre. Kangaroo Protection Cooperative Orphanage. David Sheldrick Trust Orphanage. Orenda Wildlife Trust Rehabilitation Center. Prince Edward Island Marine Mammal Stranding Network.

Publications Newsletters *Whalewatch* • *Wildlife Watch*. Booklet *Wildlife and You*. Teacher kit *Whales of the World*

For more Information Annual Report

Who's Who PRESIDENT **DAN MORAST** • VICE PRESIDENTS **DONNA HART, STEPHEN BEST** • CONTACT **TRICIA FINAMORE**

INTERNATIONAL WILDLIFE REHABILITATION COUNCIL

4437 CENTRAL PLACE, SUITE B-4   SUISUN CA 94585
PHONE (707) 864 1761   FAX (707) 864 3106

Founded 1972 • *Geographic Coverage* Global • *Cooperative Partner* National Wildlife Rehabilitation Association • *Organization Members* 169 • *Individual Members* 1,300

Mission To promote professional networking and continuing education to persons actively working in the field of wildlife rehabilitation, including administration, conservation, management, education, research, humane work, or veterinary or allied professional practice. The Council provides up-to-date rehabilitation information and hands-on training in wildlife rehabilitation.

Annual Fees	Regular	Families	Organization	Corporation	Affiliate
	$38	$48	$48	$500	$100

Other Fees *Canada, Mexico add* $4 • *Other Foreign Countries add* $6
Lifetime $1,000

Funding	Membership	Seminars, Publications, Conferences & Other
	32%	68%

Total Income $119,267

Usage	Administration	Programs	Publications & Other
	17%	50%	33%

Total Expenses $134,308

Programs Sponsors skills seminars, conferences, and oil symposiums. Minimum Standards & Accreditation Program.

Publications *The Journal of Wildlife Rehabilitation*. Membership directory. Journal reprints. Numerous other books, research papers and booklets

For more Information List of Publications

Who's Who PRESIDENT **CHRIS MIHULKA** • EXECUTIVE DIRECTOR **JAN WHITE**

IZAAK WALTON LEAGUE OF AMERICA (THE)   PAGE 112

1401 WILSON BOULEVARD, LEVEL B   ARLINGTON VA 22209-2318
PHONE (703) 528 1818   FAX (703) 528 1836

JANE GOODALL INSTITUTE (THE)

P.O. BOX 41720   TUCSON AZ 85717
PHONE (602) 325 1211   FAX (602) 325 0220

Founded 1977 • *Geographic Coverage* Africa • *Focused Countries* Angola, Burundi, Congo, Ivory Coast, Sierra Leone, Tanzania, Uganda, Zaire, Zambia • *Cooperative Partners* ChimpanZoo, The Jane Goodall Institute Canada • *Chapter* 1, in Canada

Mission To support and expand field research on wild chimpanzees, to assist studies of captive chimpanzees, and comparative studies of captive and free living chimpanzees, and to support conservation projects and educational programs which promote the physical and psychological well-being of "non-human primates".

Annual Fees	Regular	Student/Senior
	$30	$20

Programs The Institute currently sponsors three major programs: field research activities at the Gombe Stream Research Centre in Tanzania, the ChimpanZoo study of captive chimpanzees in the United States, and conservation activities targeted to both wild and captive chimpanzees, including those used in biomedical research laboratories. The Institute also contributes to an ongoing research project on wild chimpanzees living in the Tai National Park, Ivory Coast, and the initiation of a research project at Ishasha in Eastern Zaire.

Publications Semiannual *The Jane Goodall Institute Membership Report*. Annual newsletter *The Jane Goodall Institute Photo Newsletter*. Semiannual report *A Letter from Jane Goodall*

Multimedia Online information service 1-800-999-CHIMP

Who's Who SECRETARY **KATHLEEN FRACHLEY** • TREASURER **NICHOLAS LEON** • EXECUTIVE DIRECTOR **ROBERT EDISON** • PROGRAM DIRECTOR **VIRGINIA I. LANDAU**

LOS ANGELES AUDUBON SOCIETY

7377 SANTA MONICA BOULEVARD   WEST HOLLYWOOD CA 90046
PHONE (213) 876 0202   FAX (213) 876 7609

Founded 1910 • *Geographic Coverage* Local • *Cooperative Partner* National Audubon Society • *Individual Members* 3,700

Mission Dedicated to the conservation, especially the study, the appreciation and protection of birds and their habitats.

Programs Preservation of natural habitats, conservation of natural resources, and wildlife protection are the organization's main areas of expertise. Mono Lake Conservation Program. California Condor Conservation Program. Malibu Lagoon Restoration Program. Peregrine Falcon and Bald Eagle Conservation Program. Western Regional Conference at Asilomar. Research Grants. Scholarships.

Publications Newsletter *The Western Tanager* published 10 times per year. Book *The Birds of Southern California*

For more Information Library, List of Publications

Who's Who PRESIDENT **FRED HEATH** • VICE PRESIDENTS **PAT LITTLE, PETER SHEN**
SECRETARY **MILLIE NEWTON** • TREASURER **RICHARD EPPS** • EDITOR **JEAN BRANDT**

MAINE ATLANTIC SEA RUN SALMON COMMISSION (THE)

650 STATE STREET, BMHI COMPLEX   BANGOR ME 04401-5654
PHONE (207) 941 4449   FAX (207) 941 4443

Founded 1948 • *Geographic Coverage* State • *Cooperative Partner*
US Fish and Wildlife Service

Mission To undertake research, planning, management, restoration,
and propagation of the Atlantic sea run salmon in Maine. The Commission has authority to adopt and amend regulations to promote the
conservation and propagation of Atlantic salmon in Maine waters.

Who's Who CHAIR **WILLIAM J. VAIL**

MANOMET BIRD OBSERVATORY   PAGE 49

P.O. BOX 1770   MANOMET MA 02345
PHONE (508) 224 6521   FAX (508) 224 9220

MARINE MAMMAL CENTER (THE)

MARIN HEADLANDS
GOLDEN GATE NATIONAL RECREATION AREA   SAUSALITO CA 94965
PHONE (415) 289 7325

Founded 1975 • *Geographic Coverage* Global • *Focused Regions*
Coastal areas • *Individual Members* 35,000

Mission To rescue and treat ill or injured marine mammals and return
them to the wild; to increase the scientific knowledge of marine mammals through research and to disseminate this information to the world
scientific community; and to increase public knowledge of the marine
environment and public awareness of its importance to the health and
survival of all life, through public education programs.

Annual Fees	Regular	Student/Senior	Patron
	$25	$10	$50

Funding	Membership	Bequests, Services & Fees	Other
	56%	35%	9%

Total Income $2,175,849

Usage	Administration	Fundraising	Programs
	9%	11%	80%

Total Expenses $1,828,877

Programs The Center's Medical Program operates as part of the National Marine Fisheries Service's Stranding Network. Their Science Program, fosters scientific investigations that contribute to the rehabilitation
process. Educational programs in marine mammal natural history, ocean
environment and marine ecology.

Publications Newsletter *The Release Public*. Educational brochure
Myths and Facts. Numerous scientific papers

For more Information Annual Report

Who's Who PRESIDENT **JOHN ZIVNUSKA** • SECRETARY **JOSEPH ROGERS** • EXECUTIVE
DIRECTOR **PEIGIN BARRETT** • CONTACT **DENIZE SPRINGER**

MAX McGRAW WILDLIFE FOUNDATION

P.O. BOX 9   DUNDEE IL 60118
PHONE (708) 741 8000

Founded 1962 • *Geographic Coverage* Local • *Cooperative Partners* Kane County Audubon Society, US Soil Conservation Service, US
Fish and Wildlife Service, Illinois Department of Conservation

Mission To further management and conservation of wildlife and fisheries resources through programs of research, education, and cooperation
with other agencies. To maintain and increase habitat diversity, demonstrate wildlife habitat improvement techniques, and preserve natural areas
on the Foundation's land.

Programs Farmland wildlife studies. Foundation Game Farm. George
V. Burger Research Center. Fisheries Research Center. Wildlife Plant
Materials Demonstration area. Undergraduate wildlife and fisheries
intern program. Graduate student program. Research grants.

Publications Series of management notes including *Flowering Shrubs* •
Basic Small Pond and Lake Management • *Pheasants* • *Wood Ducks* •
Gravel Pit Reclamation • *Checklist of Birds Observed on the Foundation*.
Over 160 papers and reports

For more Information Library

Who's Who EXECUTIVE DIRECTOR **STANLEY W. KOENIG** • DIRECTOR OF RESEARCH
JOHN D. THOMPSON

MEMORIAL WILDLIFE FEDERATION   PAGE 26

P.O. BOX 240   HOLLBROOK NY 11741
PHONE (516) 567 0031

MINNESOTA HERPETOLOGICAL SOCIETY

JAMES FORD BELL MUSEUM OF NATURAL HISTORY
UNIVERSITY OF MINNESOTA
10 CHURCH STREET, SE,   MINNEAPOLIS MN 55455-0104
PHONE (612) 626 2030

Founded 1981 • *Geographic Coverage* National • *Organization Members* 10 • *Individual Members* 350

Mission To promote education on the care, captive propagation, and ecological role of reptiles and amphibians, and to promote their study and conservation.

Annual Fees	Regular	Institution	Patron
	$15	$25	$30 to 60

Funding *Membership* 100%

Total Income $3,000

Usage *Programs* 100%

Programs Educational programs for school groups, in conjunction with zoos. Monthly membership meeting with speakers.

Publication Newsletter *Minnesota Herpetological Society*

Who's Who PRESIDENT GLEN M. JACOBSEN • VICE PRESIDENT JOHN LEVELL SECRETARY CONNIE DELLES

NATIONAL AUDUBON SOCIETY (THE)   PAGE 50
700 BROADWAY   NEW YORK NY 10003-9562
PHONE (212) 979 3000   FAX (212) 979 3188

NATIONAL COALITION FOR MARINE CONSERVATION PAGE 115
5105 PAULSEN STREET, SUITE 243   SAVANNAH GA 31405
PHONE (912) 354 0441   FAX (912) 354 0234

NATIONAL FOUNDATION TO PROTECT AMERICA'S EAGLES
P.O. BOX 1325   PIGEON FORGE TN 37868
PHONE (615) 847 4171

Founded 1985 • *Geographic Coverage* National

Mission To save, restore, and protect America's national symbol by supporting eagle and environmental recovery programs nationwide.

Annual Fees	Regular	Student/Senior
	$15	$10

Total Income $385,000

Programs Eagle and environmental education. Eagle rehabilitation, breeding and research.

Publication *American Eagle News*

Who's Who PRESIDENT AL LOUIS CECERE • VICE PRESIDENT BOBBY HALLIBURTON SECRETARY STEVE COMPTON

NATIONAL OPOSSUM SOCIETY, INC.
P.O. BOX 3091   ORANGE CA 92665
PHONE (714) 998 4924

Founded 1986 • *Geographic Coverage* National • *Individual Members* 180

Mission To share information with wildlife experts on all aspects of proper care of opossums, to educate the public concerning the beneficial nature of the opossum in the environment, and to work with various local government and private agencies to improve the management and handling of opossums in the environment.

Annual Fees	Regular	Families
	$30	$30

Funding *Membership* 100%

Usage *Programs* 100%

Programs Environmental literature distribution.

Publications Quarterly newsletter. Bulletin *Action-Alert!*

Who's Who PRESIDENT ANITA HENNESS • VICE PRESIDENT DENNIS HOGAN • TREASURER MARILYN ANDERSON

NATIONAL WILDFLOWER RESEARCH CENTER
2600 FM 973, NORTH   AUSTIN TX 78725
PHONE (512) 929 3600   FAX (512) 929 0513

Founded 1982 • *Geographic Coverage* National • *Individual Members* 19,000

Mission To preserve and reestablish native flora. The center promotes the use of native plants in landscaping as a means to create a desirable environment for future generations.

Annual Fees *Regular* $25

Programs Education programs provide materials and speakers for schools, garden clubs, and professional associations. The Center also has a very active volunteer program.

Publications Newsletter *Wildflower*. Semiannual journal

Who's Who EXECUTIVE DIRECTOR DAVID K. NORTHINGTON

NATIONAL WILDLIFE FEDERATION
1400 16TH STREET, NW   WASHINGTON DC 20036
PHONE (202) 797 6800   FAX (202) 797 6646

Founded 1936 • *Geographic Coverage* National • *Other Field of*

Focus Ecosystem Protection / Biodiversity • *Chapters* Nationwide network of affiliate organizations • *Individual Members* 5,000,000

Mission To educate, inspire, and assist individuals and organizations of diverse cultures to conserve wildlife and other natural resources while protecting the earth's environment and to promote a peaceful, equitable, and sustainable future.

Annual Fees *Regular* $16

Total Income $92,000,000

Usage	Administration & Fundraising	Programs	Other
	10%	68%	22%

Programs Class Project. Naturequest Program. Leadership training. Nature Scope Guides. Nature Scope Workshops. Teen Adventure. Wildlife Camp.

Publications Magazines *National Wildlife* • *International Wildlife* • *Ranger Rick* for children • *Big Backyard* for preschoolers

Multimedia Online information service 1-800-432-6564

Who's Who PRESIDENT **JAY D. HAIR** • VICE PRESIDENT **WILLIAM W. HOWARD**

NATIONAL WILDLIFE REFUGE ASSOCIATION   PAGE 93
10824 FOX HUNT LANE   POTOMAC MD 20854
PHONE (301) 983 1238

NEW ENGLAND WILD FLOWER SOCIETY, INC.
GARDEN IN THE WOODS
180 HEMENWAY ROAD   FRAMINGHAM MA 01701-2699
PHONE (617) 237 4024

Founded 1922 • *Geographic Coverage* Regional • *Focused Region* New England • *Individual Members* 4,000

Mission To promote the conservation of native plants, through research and education in botany, horticulture, and ecology, as well as through active conservation programs. For example, through Task Forces in each state the Society has designated the rare and endangered plants in each state, collected seed from these plants, banked some in the event of a disaster in the wild, and propagated some.

Annual Fees	Regular	Families
	$35	$35

Programs New England Plant Conservation Program, comprised of 68 organizations throughout New England. Offers more than 150 courses in native plants studies throughout the year.

Publications Newsletter published three times per year. Books *Nursery*

Sources List • *Wild Flowers Notes*

Who's Who PRESIDENT **DAVID LONGLAND**

NEW JERSEY AUDUBON SOCIETY
P.O. BOX 125, 790 EWING AVENUE   FRANKLIN LAKES NJ 07417-9982
PHONE (201) 891 1211

Founded 1897 • *Geographic Coverage* State • *Other Field of Focus* Ecosystem Protection / Biodiversity • *Cooperative Partner* Highlands Coalition • *Chapters* 5

Mission To foster environmental awareness and a conservation ethic among New Jersey citizens; to protect New Jersey's birds, mammals, other animals and plants, especially endangered and threatened species; and to promote preservation of New Jersey's valuable natural habitats. The organization has a particular interest and expertise in research on migratory birds.

Annual Fees	Regular	Families	Sustaining	Supporting	Goldfinch Club
	$25	$30	$50	$100	$250

Other Fees *Lifetime* $1,000

Funding	Membership	Foundations	Program Fees	Merchandise Sales
	23%	32%	27%	12%

Other Sources *Investment Income* 6%

Usage	Administration	Programs	Membership Development
	14%	75%	11%

Programs Education programs for children. Teacher education. Urban Outreach. Greenway/Tributaries projects. Visiting scholar/intern program. *Bird Atlas* to be completed in 1996.

Publications Newsletters *Peregrine Observer* • *Green Gram*. Quarterly *Records of New Jersey Birds*. Quarterly magazine *New Jersey Audubon*. Books including *Bridges to the Natural World*, natural history guide for teachers of grades Pre-K through 6 • *New Jersey at the Crossroads of Migration*

For more Information Annual Report, List of Publications

Who's Who PRESIDENT **MILTON A. LEVY** • VICE PRESIDENTS **A. RICHARD TURNER, CHARLES F. WEST** • SECRETARY **RANDOLPH S. LITTLE** • TREASURER **JOHN A. DEMARRAIS** • EXECUTIVE DIRECTOR **THOMAS J. GILMORE** • COUNSEL **ALAN H. BERNSTEIN**

NEW YORK TURTLE AND TORTOISE SOCIETY (THE)
163 AMSTERDAM AVENUE, SUITE 365   NEW YORK NY 10023
PHONE (212) 459 4803

Founded 1970 • *Geographic Coverage* Global • *Individual Members* 2,500

Mission To conserve and preserve habitat and to promote proper husbandry and captive propagation of turtles and tortoises. The Society emphasizes the education of its members and the public in all areas relevant to the appreciation of these unique animals.

Annual Fees *Regular* $20

Funding *Membership* 100%

Usage	*Administration*	*Fundraising*	*Programs*
	5%	5%	90%

Programs A 24 Hour-Turtle Hotline which answers all questions about turtle care and conservation. Annual scientific turtle all-day seminar. Annual Turtle Show. Production of educational materials for classroom use. Turtle Adoption Program. Wildlife Rehabilitation Program.

Publications Quarterly newsletter *NYTTS NewsNotes*. Semiannual journal *The Plastron Papers*. Directories *The Turtle Help Network* • *The NYTTS Vet List* national directory of veterinarians

Who's Who PRESIDENT SUZANNE DOHM • VICE-PRESIDENT ALLEN FOUST • SECRETARY PHIL PUCCIU

NORTH AMERICAN BLUEBIRD SOCIETY
P.O. BOX 6295   SILVER SPRING MD 20916-6295
PHONE (301) 384 2798

Founded 1978 • *Geographic Coverage* North America

Mission To increase the population of bluebirds in North America and to educate people about the importance of preserving this species in its natural habitat.

Annual Fees	*Regular*	*Student/Senior*	*Families*	*Corporation*	*Sustaining*
	$15	$10	$25	$100	$30

Other Fees *Supporting* $50 • *Contributing* $100 • *Donor* $250 *Lifetime* $500

Programs The Society works to research and disseminate findings on obstacles impeding bluebird recovery, to promote ideas and actions which might reduce the effect of those obstacles, and to obtain more complete knowledge about bluebird ecology.

Publication Quarterly journal *SIALA*

NORTH AMERICAN NATIVE FISHES ASSOCIATION
123 WEST MOUNT AIRY AVENUE   PHILADELPHIA PA 19119
PHONE (215) 247 0384

Founded 1972 • *Geographic Coverage* North America • *Members* 350 including organizations

Mission To bring together people interested in fishes native to this conti-

nent for scientific purposes or aquarium study, to encourage increased scientific, conservation, and aquarian appreciation of native fishes through observation, study, and research, and to assemble and distribute information on native fishes.

Annual Fees	*Regular*	*Organization*	*Outside North America*
	$11	$11	$14

Funding *Membership* 100%

Publications Newsletter *Darter* published approximately 6 times per year. Quarterly magazine *American Currents*. News about aquaristics, laws, the environment, scientific literature and developments

For more Information Library, List of Publications

Who's Who PRESIDENT RAYMOND KATULA • TREASURER ROBERT E. SCHMIDT • EXECUTIVE DIRECTOR BRUCE GEBHARDT • LIBRARIAN PHIL NIXON

NORTH AMERICAN WOLF SOCIETY
P.O. BOX 82950   FAIRBANKS AK 99708
PHONE (907) 474 7741

Founded 1973 • *Geographic Coverage* North America • *Cooperative Partners* IUCN The World Conservation Union, Wolf Specialist Group, Wolf!, The International Wolf Center

Mission To work for the stewardship of the wolf and other wild canids of North America, by providing information which can be used to form reasonable, practical opinions regarding the future of wild canids and the habitat upon which they depend.

Funding *Foundations* 100%

Usage *Programs* 100%

Programs Education & information. Data collection. The Portland International Wolf Symposium, a meeting held in conjunction with IUCN The World Conservation Union - Wolf Specialist Group.

Publications Numerous books focusing on wolves and their history. Educational materials. Annual summary of major activities involving North American canids. Bibliographies

Multimedia Films. Educational slide-tape shows

Who's Who PRESIDENT ANNE K. RUGGLES

PACIFIC WHALE FOUNDATION
101 NORTH KIHEI ROAD, SUITE 21   KIHEI, MAUI HI 96753-8833
PHONE (808) 879 8860   FAX (808) 879 2615

Founded 1980 • *Geographic Coverage* Pacific • *Focused Countries*

Australia, Canada, Fiji, Japan, New Zealand, USA, Tonga • *Cooperative Partners* Community Work Day, The State Office of Litter Control • *Chapter* 1 satellite office in Brisbane - Australia • *Individual Members* 4,500

Mission To protect the world's oceans and all endangered marine life, by serving as a center for marine research, conservation, and education. Since 1980 the Foundation has carried out in-depth studies of humpback whales, developed marine education programs, and assisted in developing conservation plans and policies.

Annual Fees	*Regular*	*Student/Senior*	*Families*	*Foreign*	*Institution*
	$25	$20	$30	$40	$50

Other Fees *Supporting* $100 • *Contributing* $250 • *Patron* $500

Funding	*Membership*	*Corporations*	*Foundations*
	8%	10%	82%

Total Income $700,000

Usage	*Administration*	*Fundraising*	*Programs*
	35%	15%	50%

Programs Projects of the Ocean Outreach Program include Adopt-a-Whale Program, Whale Watches for Maui Schoolchildren, Educational Marine Tourism, the Ocean Van. Public awareness activities include Whales and Friends Lecture Series, Whale Day/Earth Day, Get the Drift and Bag it (Beach Clean-up), The Great Whale Count. Internship Program.

Publications Annual newsletters *Soundings* for Adopt-a-Whale parents • *Whale One Dispatch*. Quarterly journal *Fin & Fluke Report*. Book *Hawaii's Humpback Whales: A Complete Whalewatchers Guide*. Catalog *Humpback Whales of Australia*. Brochure *Pacific Whale Foundation Whalewatching Guide*

Multimedia Online information service 1-800-WHALE11. Numerous documentary films

Who's Who PRESIDENT GREGORY D. KAUFMAN • VICE PRESIDENT PAUL H. FORESTELL • SECRETARY DIXIE BONGOLAN • OTHER MERYL KAUFMAN, ERIC BROWN, MARISHA CLEARY, MEGAN JONES

PELICAN MAN'S BIRD SANCTUARY, INC.

1708 KEN THOMPSON PARKWAY   SARASOTA FL 34236
PHONE (813) 388 4444

Founded 1985 • *Geographic Coverage* Local, National • *Individual Members* 7,000

Mission To provide a bird sanctuary to house and care for America's many injured birds; to serve as an educational center to increase public awareness of their needs and of the importance of maintaining a healthy environment for birds as well as for human beings.

Annual Fees	*Regular*	*Student/Senior*	*Families*	*Member Spouse*	*Friend*
	$15	$10	$30	$25	$50

Other Fees *Supporting* $100 • *Patron* $250 • *Sponsor* $500 *Lifetime* $1,000

Programs The Sanctuary's staff is engaged in continual efforts to rescue, treat, and release pelicans and other wild birds in the region. The Sanctuary is open to public free of charge.

Who's Who PRESIDENT DALE SHIELDS • EXECUTIVE DIRECTOR MONA SCHONBRUNN CONTACT MAUREEN STOETZEL

PEREGRINE FUND (THE)

5666 WEST FLYING HAWK LANE   BOISE ID 83709
PHONE (208) 362 3716   FAX (208) 362 2376

Founded 1970 • *Geographic Coverage* National, Global • *Cooperative Partners* The Santa Cruz Predatory Bird Research Group, US Fish and Wildlife Service, Texas Parks and Wildlife Department, The Mauritius Wildlife Appeal Fund, Jersey Wildlife Preservation Trust, Belize Audubon Society, Programme for Belize, World Wildlife Fund, The Xerces Society, Conservation International • *Members* 4,500 including organizations

Mission To prevent the extinction of the Peregrine Falcon and restore this species throughout its former range within the United States.

Annual Fees	*Regular*	*Contributing*	*Sponsor*	*Conservator*	*Benefactor*
	$25	$50	$100	$250	$500

Funding	*Membership*	*Corporations*	*Foundations*	*Grants & Contracts*	*Sales*
	32%	2%	28%	32%	1%

Other Sources *Special Events* 3% • *Interest* 1%

Total Income $2,136,329

Usage	*Administration*	*Fundraising*	*Programs*	*Other*
	5%	6%	86%	3%

Total Expenses $1,894,023

Programs Educational Programs through the Velma Morrison Interpretive Center. Species Restoration Programs - Peregrine Falcon, California Condor, Hawaiian 'Alala, Aplomado Falcon, Mauritius Kestrel. The Fund's World Center for Birds of Prey is a unique facility with many functions, including captive breeding, public education, research, archives, library, raptor food production. World Programs include The Maya Project, which uses raptors as an environmental focus for conservation of tropical forests and for building local capacity for conservation in Latin America; The Harpy Eagle Conservation Program, The Pan Africa Raptor Conservation Program, Philippine Eagle Conservation.

Publications Semiannual newsletter *The Peregrine Fund, World Center for Birds of Prey*, circulation 8,000. Semiannual catalog, circulation

8,000. Various program reports

For more Information Annual Report, Database, Library, List of Publications

Who's Who PRESIDENT **WILLIAM A. BURNHAM** • VICE PRESIDENT **J. PETER JENNY** SECRETARY **ROBERT S. COMSTOCK** • TREASURER **HENRY M. PAULSON**

PROJECT WOLF USA

168 GALER STREET   SEATTLE WA 98109
PHONE (206) 283 1957

Founded 1980 • *Geographic Coverage* Global • *Individual Members* 1,000

Mission To stop wolf killings wherever they occur.

Who's Who PRESIDENT **WAYNE JOHNSON**

QUAIL RIDGE WILDERNESS CONSERVANCY   PAGE 95

25344 COUNTY ROAD 95   DAVIS CA 95616-9735
PHONE (916) 758 1387   FAX (916) 758 1316

RAPTOR RESEARCH FOUNDATION, INC.

12805 ST. CROIX TRAIL   HASTINGS MN 55033
PHONE (612) 437 4359

Founded 1966 • *Geographic Coverage* Global • *Cooperative Partner* National Wildlife Federation • *Organization Members* 200 *Individual Members* 1,000

Mission To stimulate the dissemination of information concerning raptorial birds among interested persons worldwide and to promote a better public understanding and appreciation of the value of birds of prey; to provide a forum for biologists and others who explore the nature of raptor ecology and the critical connection between predatory birds and ecosystems.

	Regular	Student/Senior	Organization	Corporation	Sustaining
Annual Fees	$24	$13	$30	$50	$100

Other Fees *Lifetime* $700

	Membership	Corporations	Foundations
Funding	50%	20%	30%

Total Income $60,000

	Administration	Programs	Journal
Usage	25%	25%	50%

Total Expenses $60,000

Programs Grants for research. Organizes an annual fall meeting which allows communication among members, other related conservation organizations, students, and the general public. This meeting provides a forum for scientific papers, poster presentations, special symposia workshops, open business meetings, and informal gatherings.

Publications Newsletter *WINGSPAN*. Quarterly *Journal of Raptor Research*. Reviews published under the Foundation's *Raptor Research Report Series*. Periodic workshop and symposia proceedings. Annual membership directory *The Kettle*

Who's Who PRESIDENT **RICHARD CLARK** • EXECUTIVE DIRECTOR **DAVID BIRD** • SECRETARY **BETSY HANCOCK**

RHINO RESCUE USA, INC.

P.O. BOX 33064   WASHINGTON DC 20036
PHONE (202) 293 5305   FAX (202) 223 0346

Founded 1985 • *Geographic Coverage* Africa, Indian Sub-continent *Focused Countries* Kenya, Nepal, Zimbabwe

Mission To help educate the American public and raise the funds necessary to ensure the rhino's survival.

Programs Undertaking a study on the effects and feasibility of dehorning rhinos as a deterrent to poachers. Has purchased a lorry to translocate a competing giraffe population out of a successful private rhino sanctuary in Kenya. Sponsored the recent International Conference on Rhinoceros Biology and Conservation in San Diego, California

Who's Who PRESIDENT **THOMAS J. SCHNEIDER**

SAN FRANCISCO BAY BIRD OBSERVATORY

1290 HOPE STREET, P.O. BOX 247   ALVISO CA 95002
PHONE (408) 946 6548

Founded 1991 • *Geographic Coverage* Local • *Chapter* 1 *Organization Members* 130 • *Individual Members* 350

Mission To conduct research on avian species in the San Francisco Bay National Wildlife Refuge and the surrounding area, to make this research available for publication, and to promote environmental education.

	Regular	Student/Senior	Families	Contributing	Sustaining
Annual Fees	$15	$10	$20	$100	$200

Other Fees *Lifetime* $400 • *Corporation* $500

	Membership	Government Support	Local Agencies
Funding	28%	12%	60%

Total Income $52,000

	Administration	Programs
Usage	12%	88%

Total Expenses $54,000

Publication Quarterly newsletter *The Stilt*

For more Information Library

Who's Who President **Virginia Becchine** • Vice President **Tom Esperson** Secretary **Terry Hart-Lee** • Treasurer **Richard Carlson** • Executive Directors **Pat Carlson, Janet Hanson**

SANTA BARBARA BOTANIC GARDEN

1212 Mission Canyon Road   Santa Barbara CA 93015
Phone (805) 682 4726   Fax (805) 563 0352

Founded 1926 • *Geographic Coverage* State • *Cooperative Partners* American Association of Museums, American Association of Botanic Gardens and Arboretum, University of California at Santa Barbara, Channel Island National Park • *Chapter* 1 • *Organization Members* 5 *Individual Members* 2,700

Mission Dedicated to the display, study and conservation of the native flora of California.

Annual Fees	Regular	Families	Organization	Corporation
	$40	$40	$50	$50

Funding	Membership	Government Support	Foundations	Investments & Progam Fees
	14%	5.5%	4.5%	76%

Total Income $1,329,000

Usage	Administration	Fundraising	Programs
	23%	8.5%	68.5%

Total Expenses $1,801,000

Programs Botanical and environmental education for adults and children. Research in Flora of California Islands and Structural Botany. Display of California flora. Propagation and sale of native plants. Floristic survey.

Publications Newsletter *Ironwood Quarterly*. Books including *Seed Propagation* • *Nature Loves a Detective Trail Guide* • *California Plants to Color*. Informational bulletins

For more Information Library

Who's Who President **Robert M. Jones** • Vice President **Richard Rogers** Secretary **Eric Hvoboll** • Treasurer **Gunnar Bergman** • Executive Director **Edward Schneider** • Librarian **Rebecca Eldridge** • Contact **Anne Steiner**

SAVE THE WHALES, INC.

1426 Main Street, P.O. Box 2397   Venice CA 90291
Phone (310) 392 6226   Fax (310) 392 8968

Founded 1977 • *Geographic Coverage* National, Global • *Individual Members* 2,000

Mission To educate children and adults alike about marine mammals, their environment, and their preservation. The organization's main areas of focus are ocean pollution causing cancer in whales and degrading their habitat, captivity issues, and resumption of commercial whaling.

Annual Fees	Regular	Student/Senior
	$20	$10

Programs Whales On Wheels (WOW) is an educational program which brings the marine environment, including whales' and dolphins' skeletal parts, to the classroom and other groups. Beach cleanups and other events.

Publications Quarterly newsletters *Save the Whales* • *The Orca Club*

Multimedia Online information service 1-800-WHALE-65

Who's Who President **Maris Sidenstecker I** • Vice President **Michele Levin** Secretary **Richard Kossow**

SEA SHEPHERD CONSERVATION SOCIETY

1314 Second Street   Santa Monica CA 90401
Phone (310) 394 3198   Fax (310) 394 0360

Founded 1977 • *Geographic Coverage* Global • *Chapter* 1, in Canada • *Individual Members* 25,000

Mission To protect marine mammal wildlife through the enforcement of international laws, treaties, and regulations. The organization focuses on the combined use of direct action, film documentation, and media. The purpose of 1993 campaigns is to further enforce IWC regulations in the Bering Sea and Antarctica against the illegal whale killing operations of Russia and Japan.

Funding	Supporters	Corporations	Foundations
	97%	1%	2%

Total Income $500,000

Usage	Administration	Programs
	6%	94%

Programs The Society's Volunteer Programs fall under the division called O.R.C.A. Force (Oceanic Research Conservation Action Force). Positions include crewing aboard ships during campaigns, Field Agents, Active Agents, and general office help.

Publication Quarterly periodical *Sea Shepherd Log*

Who's Who President **Paul Watson** • Secretary **Peter Brown** • Contact **Lisa Distefano**

SINAPU
COLORADO WOLF TRACKS
P.O. Box 3243   Boulder CO 80307
Phone (303) 494 3710

Founded 1991 • *Geographic Coverage* State • *Individual Members* 200

Mission To restore a healthy, flourishing population of Gray Wolves in Colorado.

Annual Fees	Regular	Student/Senior	Sustaining	Patron	Sponsor
	$35	$15	$75	$100	$500

Funding	Membership	Other
	70%	30%

Total Income $6,000

Usage	Programs	Other
	80%	20%

Programs Public education, research, advocacy.

Publication Quarterly newsletter *Colorado Wolf Tracks*

Who's Who Secretary Mary Link • Executive Director Michael Robinson Education Director Maureen Gaffney

SOCIETY FOR THE PRESERVATION OF BIRDS OF PREY
P.O. Box 66070   Los Angeles CA 90066
Phone (213) 397 8216

Founded 1966 • *Geographic Coverage* National • *Individual Members* 900

Mission To educate the public of the value of predatory birds and to stress the need for strict raptor protection laws, to disseminate information and promote communication among raptor enthusiasts, to oppose the harvesting of raptorial birds and the selling and trading of birds of prey and their parts and offspring, to oppose the proliferation of captive raptor breeding and the use of the resulting progeny for recreational purposes, to urge reasonable and biologically sound pest control methods, and to advocate the use of live traps and relocating for the taking of depredating birds in the event that damage is documented.

Biannual Fees *2-year Membership* $47 • *2-year Mailing List Placement* $5

Programs The Society engages in outreach programs to educate the public and advocate for the preservation of birds of prey. Also provides financial support to programs which the society feels will further its goals.

Publication Newsletter *The Raptor Report*

For more Information Library, List of Publications

Who's Who President J. Richard Hilton

SONORAN ARTHROPOD STUDIES, INC.
P.O. Box 5624   Tucson AZ 85703
Phone (602) 883 3945

Founded 1986 • *Geographic Coverage* National • *Organization Members* 50 • *Individual Members* 800

Mission To promote interest, understanding, and appreciation of arthropods and their vital interrelationships with plants and other animals, and to promote public interest in natural history through the study and interpretation of the vital roles arthropods play in the natural environment.

Annual Fees	Regular	Contributing	Sustaining	Patron	Benefactor
	$35	$100	$250	$500	$1,000

Other Fees *Contributing Corporation* $500 • *Patron Corporation* $2,000 *Benefactor Corporation* $5,000

Funding	Membership	Contributions	Sales & Fees	Other
	22%	52%	23%	3%

Total Income $92,687

Usage	Administration	Programs	Rent
	38%	49%	13%

Total Expenses $89,166

Programs Outreach to local schools. Field research. Training for educators. Laboratory. Volunteers programs. Discovery Scope™. Annual dinner. Arthropod Discovery Center in Tucson Mountain Park. Allocation for educational workshops and programs focusing on the arthropods and their roles in the natural environment.

Publications Quarterly magazine *Backyard Bugwatching*. Newsletter *The Instar*. Books including *Butterflies of Southeastern Arizona* • *Exploring Arthropods with Discovery Scope™*

For more Information Annual Report, Library

Who's Who President Steve Prchal • Vice President Vince Lazara • Secretary Anne Gondor

SOUTHERN UTAH WILDERNESS ALLIANCE   PAGE 121
1471 South 1100 East   Salt Lake City UT 84105-2423
Phone (801) 486 3161   Fax (801) 486 4233

TENNESSEE CITIZENS FOR WILDERNESS PLANNING

130 Tabor Road   Oak Ridge TN 37830
Phone (615) 482 2153

PAGE 121

THEODORE PAYNE FOUNDATION (THE)

10459 Tuxford Street   Sun Valley CA 91352
Phone (818) 768 1802

Founded 1960 • *Geographic Coverage* State • *Organization Members* 100 • *Individual Members* 900

Mission To acquire and disseminate knowledge of California's native flora, preserve its natural habitat, and encourage its propagation and use; to help California's growing population and its native plants live together in harmony. The Foundation encourages Californians to grow native plants.

Annual Fees

Regular	Student/Senior	Corporation	Patron
$30	$20	$5,000	$500

Other Fees *Supporting* $100 • *Sustaining* $250 • *Lifetime* $1,000

Funding

Membership	Foundations	Other
9%	12%	79%

Total Income $300,000

Programs Flowerhill-Demonstration Garden for Native Wildflowers. The Wildflower Hotline makes information available during spring months for 24 hours, giving locations of wildflower blooms. Native Plant Nursery.

Publications Quarterly newsletter *Poppy Print*. Book *Gardener's Guide to California Wildflowers*

Who's Who President **Kathryn Cerra** • Vice President **Tom Bigliones** • Secretary **Halla Speaker**

TROUT UNLIMITED, INC.

800 Follin Lane, Suite 250   Vienna VA 22180
Phone (703) 281 1100   Fax (703) 281 1825

Founded 1959 • *Geographic Coverage* National • *Chapters* 430, 35 councils, 10 regions • *Individual Members* 65,000

Mission To conserve, protect, and restore wild trout and salmon and their habitat.

Annual Fees

Regular	Student/Senior	Families	Organization
$25	$15	$30	$25

Other Fees *Corporation* $100 • *Conservator* $250 • *Lifetime* $500
Family Lifetime $600

Funding

Membership	Foundations	National Banquet Program	Other
49%	20.4%	18.7%	1.9%

Other Sources *Trout Magazine Advertising & Sales* 6% • *Books, Accessories & Other Sales* 4%

Total Income $2,821,795

Usage

Administration	Fundraising	Programs	Chapters	Other
11.8%	8.4%	67.7%	10.4%	1.7%

Total Expenses $2,751,023

Publications Quarterly magazine *Trout*, circulation 75,000. Monthly newsletter *Lines to Leaders*, circulation 600. Quarterly youth newsletter *The Emerger*. Numerous books and accessories

Multimedia Videos

Who's Who President **Charles F. Gauvin** • Vice President **Doug McClelland** Secretary **Frank S. Smith** • Treasurer **Douglas Henderson** • Contact **Peter Rafle, Jr.**

TRUMPETER SWAN SOCIETY (THE)

3800 County Road 24   Maple Plain MN 55359
Phone (612) 476 4663

Founded 1968 • *Geographic Coverage* North America • *Chapter* 1, in Washington state • *Organization Members* 25 • *Individual Members* 450

Mission To maintain existing wild Trumpeter Swan populations and to restore the Trumpeter to as much of its original range as possible, by promoting research, advancing the science and art of Trumpeter Swan management, assembling known Trumpeter Swan data, coordinating the exchange of knowledge, and providing a common meeting ground for all those interested in the Trumpeter Swan.

Annual Fees

Regular	Student/Senior	Families	Organization	Corporation
$25	$15	$30	$35	$1,000

Other Fees *Supporting* $100 • *Contributing* $250 • *Lifetime* $500

Funding

Membership	Foundations	Merchandise Sales	Other
46%	30.5%	21%	2.5%

Total Income $15,635

Programs Sponsors school and other group education. Organizes a biannual conference.

Publications Bimonthly *Trumpetings*. Semiannual newsletter. Semiannual conference proceedings. Various brochures on Swan identification and biology

Who's Who President **Laurence N. Gillette** • Vice President **Ruth E. Shea** Secretary **David K. Weaver**

WESTERN FOUNDATION OF VERTEBRATE ZOOLOGY

439 Calle San Pablo
Phone (805) 388 9944

Camarillo CA 93010
Fax (805) 388 8663

Founded 1956 • *Geographic Coverage* Global

Mission To acquire, integrate, and preserve systematic ornithological collections, support original research on birds, promote the conservation of birds, and publish scientific findings. Ornithology, conservation biology, neotropical ecology, contaminant effects, and vertebrate collection care and management are the Foundation's main areas of expertise.

Funding	*Contracts*	*Endowment Income*
	34%	66%

152 *Total Income* $557,215

Usage	*Administration*	*Programs*
	30%	70%

Total Expenses $709,538

Programs Recovery of the California Condor. Recovery of San Clemente Island Loggerhead Shrike. Nests and eggs of Ecuadorian birds. Survey of endangered species of birds on San Nicolas Island and Pt. Mugu NWS. Research on effects of DDT on Channel Islands birds. Maintenance of 8th largest bird collection in the world.

Publications WFVZ occasional papers. WFVZ proceedings series established in 1963

For more Information Database, Library, List of Publications

Who's Who President **Ed N. Harrison** • Secretary **Glen Hiatt** • Treasurer **Julia L. Kiff** • Executive Director **Lloyd F. Kiff** • Librarian **Jon Fisher**

WHALE CONSERVATION INSTITUTE

191 Weston Road
Phone (617) 259 0423

Lincoln MA 01773
Fax (617) 259 0288

Founded 1986 • *Geographic Coverage* Global • *Chapter* 1, in United Kingdom

Mission To improve the state of knowledge about whales and ocean environments, to educate the public and to enable students to make informed decisions concerning the environment, and to support and develop substantive conservation efforts.

Annual Fees	*Regular*	*Associate*	*Vanguard*	*Sponsor*
	$25	$50	$100	$250

Programs The Institute's ongoing research program investigating the characteristics and behaviors of whales, as well as on the threats facing them. Their education program includes published information, partner-

ships with educators, and mass media projects. The Institute also operates a public advocacy program.

Publication Quarterly newsletter *Critical Habitat*

Multimedia Videos *In the Company of Whales* • *Watching the Whales*. Cassettes and compact discs *Songs of the Humpback Whale* • *Whales Alive*

For more Information Library

Who's Who President **Roger Payne** • Executive Director **Charlton Reynders** Operations Consultant **Cynthia Hillier**

WHITTIER AUDUBON SOCIETY

6231 Gregory Avenue
Phone (213) 691 9251

Whittier CA 90608-0548

Founded 1970 • *Geographic Coverage* Local, Global • *Other Field of Focus* Ecosystem Protection / Biodiversity • *Cooperative Partner* National Audubon Society • *Individual Members* 750

Mission To conserve and restore natural ecosystems, with an emphasis on birds and other wildlife. Locally, the Society is working to extend Whittier Hills Wilderness Park.

Annual Fees *Regular* $35

Funding	*Membership*	*Other*
	90%	10%

Total Income $10,000

Programs Sponsors field trips in grade schools and other programs.

Publication Monthly newsletter *The Observer*

Who's Who President **Tim Bulmer** • Vice President **Carmen Diaz** • Treasurer **Judy Stabile** • Conservation Chair **Linda Oberholtzer**

WHOOPING CRANE CONSERVATION ASSOCIATION, INC.

1007 Carmel Avenue
Phone (318) 234 6339

Lafayette LA 70501

Founded 1961 • *Geographic Coverage* North America • *Chapters* 3 *Individual Members* 700

Mission To promote the conservation and protection of whooping cranes throughout North America.

Annual Fees *Regular* $7.50
Other Fees *Lifetime* $150

Programs Canada and US Whooping Crane Recovery Program.

Publications Quarterly newsletter. Educational materials

For more Information Library, List of Publications

Who's Who PRESIDENT JEROME PRATT • VICE PRESIDENT LORNE SCOTT • LIBRARIAN BRIAN JOHNS

WILD CANID SURVIVAL AND RESEARCH CENTER
WOLF SANCTUARY

P.O. BOX 760
PHONE (314) 938 5900

EUREKA MO 63025
FAX (314) 939 6490

Founded 1972 • *Geographic Coverage* North America, Western Europe *Individual Members* 3,000

Mission To contribute to the survival of the wild canids of the world by providing a focal point for the interest in and study of these species and, through education and other means, generate further interest and study. The Center is currently working to establish and maintain gene pools of selected species and subspecies of wild canids, to facilitate the reintroduction of wild canids into appropriate wilderness areas, to contribute to data banks on captive canids throughout the world, to maintain a library on wild and captive canids, to conduct and sponsor studies of its captive stock of wild canids and to encourage and support field research.

Annual Fees	Regular	Student/Senior	Families	Supporting	Contributing
	$25	$15	$35	$75	$125

Other Fees *Sponsor* $250 • *Lifetime* $1,000

Who's Who PRESIDENT RACHEL CRANDELL • EXECUTIVE DIRECTOR SUSAN LYNDAKER LINDSEY

WILD DOLPHIN PROJECT

21 HEPBURN AVENUE, SUITE 20
PHONE (407) 575 5660

JUPITER FL 33458
FAX (407) 575 5681

Founded 1986 • *Geographic Coverage* Global • *Focused Regions* Bahamas, Atlantic Ocean • *Individual Members* 500

Mission To protect dolphins in the Bahamas and the Atlantic Ocean.

Publication Semiannual newsletter *Notes From the Field*

For more Information Database

WILDLIFE CONSERVATION SOCIETY (THE)
C/O NEW YORK ZOOLOGICAL SOCIETY

185TH STREET & SOUTHERN BOULEVARD
PHONE (212) 220 5100

BRONX NY 10460

Founded 1895 • *Geographic Coverage* Global • *Other Field of Focus* Ecosystem Protection / Biodiversity • *Individual Members* 95,000

Mission To work for the better understanding and protection of endangered species and ecosystems, through an innovative combination of the resources of wildlife parks with the world's largest staff of non-governmental field scientists.

Annual Fees	Regular	Patron
	$25	$1,250

Total Income $53,100,000

Usage	Administration	Fundraising	Programs	Other
	6%	4%	81%	9%

Programs The Society operates 5 wildlife parks (4 zoos and 1 aquarium) in New York area, and 150 international conservation projects in 45 countries. Friends of Zoos Program - the Nairobi office supervises African programs. Educational programs.

Publication Bimonthly *Wildlife Conservation Magazine*

Who's Who PRESIDENT WILLIAM CONWAY • VICE PRESIDENTS JOHN ROBINSON, JOHN McKEW, JAMES MEEUWSEN • SECRETARY R. W. JOHNSON IV • CONTACT JANET ROSE

WILDLIFE DAMAGE REVIEW

P.O. BOX 2541
PHONE (602) 882 4218

TUCSON AZ 85702-2541

Founded 1991 • *Geographic Coverage* National

Mission To substantially alter the mission of the United States government's Animal Damage Control program, under which widespread killing of wildlife on public lands occurs.

Programs The Review works for change in the US government's Animal Damage Control (ADC) program by disseminating information about the widespread killing of wildlife on public lands carried out under the ADC program; by challenging environmental assessments prepared by public agencies prior to action; by mobilizing citizen activists to write their legislators, asking them to cut ADC appropriations; and by working to establish a committee that would develop legislation to substantially alter ADC's mission.

Publication Newsletter *Wildlife Damage Review*

Who's Who STAFF OFFICERS CLARKE ABBEY, MARIAN BAKER-GIERLACH, LISA PEACOCK, NANCY ZIERENBERG

WILDLIFE HABITAT ENHANCEMENT COUNCIL

1010 WAYNE AVENUE, SUITE 920
PHONE (301) 588 8994

SILVER SPRING MD 20910
FAX (301) 588 4629

Founded 1988 • *Geographic Coverage* Global • *Focused Countries* Australia, Canada, Mexico, Spain • *Organization Members* 13 conservation groups and 85 corporate organizations

Mission To support the enhancement and preservation of wildlife habitat and to broaden understanding of wildlife values, by providing assistance to large landholders, particularly corporations, in the management of their unused lands in an ecologically sensitive manner for the benefit of wildlife.

Annual Fees	*Regular*	*Corporation*	*Sustaining*	*Benefactor*
	$25	$1,650 to 3,750	$250	$500

Funding	*Corporations*	*Foundations*	*Program Assistance*	*Other*
	31.2%	43.3%	22.8%	2.7%

Total Income $459,700

Usage	*Administration*	*Fundraising*	*Programs*
	14%	4%	82%

Total Expenses $429,000

Programs The Wildlife at Work Project helps individual sites develop programs enhancing their lands for wildlife. The Waterways for Wildlife Project works to promote biodiversity, and develop community involvement and education. The Wastelands to Wildlands program designs creative management options for habitat enhancement. Neotropical Networks. Wildlands Conference.

Publications Quarterly newsletter *Wildlife in the News*. Books including *Perspective in Wildlife Management* • *A How-To for Corporate Lands* • *Fur, Feathers and the Bottom Line* • *Prairies, Predators, and Profits* • *Birds, Business and Biodiversity* • *The Economic Benefits of Wildlife Habitat Enhancement on Corporate Lands*

For more Information Annual Report, Database

Who's Who PRESIDENT **PHILIP X. MASCIANTONIO** • VICE PRESIDENT **JACK LORENZ** SECRETARY **MICHAEL P. LAWLOR** • EXECUTIVE DIRECTOR **JOYCE M. KELLY** • OTHER **HUGH RIECKEN, DARLENE PAIS, BRIDGET COWLIN** • CONTACT **JANICE M. WAGNER**

WILDLIFE MANAGEMENT INSTITUTE

1101 14TH STREET, NW   WASHINGTON DC 20005
PHONE (202) 371 1808

Founded 1911 • *Geographic Coverage* North America • *Other Field of Focus* Natural Resources / Water - Conservation & Quality *Chapters* 2 field representatives

Mission Dedicated to the restoration, sound management, and thoughtful use of natural resources in North America. The Institute strives to gain greater accommodation of wildlife in an ever growing society, and to maintain sufficient, suitable habitats for all wildlife species in North America.

Annual Fees	*Student/Senior*	*Supporting*	*Professional*	*Associate*
	$15	$35	$100	$500

Other Fees *Lifetime* $1,000

Publications Books including *Ecology and Management of the Mourning Dove* • *White-tailed Deer: Ecology and Management* • *Ducks, Geese and Swans of North America*. Booklets and brochures including *The American Landscape: 1776-1976, Two Centuries of Change* • *Placing Wildlife in Perspective* • *Wildlife, The Environmental Barometer* • *The Farmer and Wildlife*

Who's Who PRESIDENT **ROLLIN D. SPARROWE** • VICE PRESIDENT **LONNIE L. WILLIAMSON** • SECRETARY **RICHARD E. McCABE** • CONSERVATION POLICY COORDINATOR **DONALD F. McKENZIE** • WILDLIFE PROGRAM COORDINATOR **ROBERT L. BYRNE**

WILDLIFE PRESERVATION TRUST INTERNATIONAL, INC.

3400 WEST GIRARD AVENUE   PHILADELPHIA PA 19104-1196
PHONE (215) 222 3636   FAX (215) 222 2191

Founded 1971 • *Geographic Coverage* Global • *Cooperative Partner* International Training Center for the Conservation and Captive Breeding of Endangered Species

Mission To support the propagation of rare and endangered species in captivity, the reintroduction of rare and endangered species to their native habitats and the restoration of these habitats, research on these species in captivity and in the wild, the education of all persons (particularly those from developing countries living in close association with rare and endangered species) concerning the value of wildlife, the professional training of zoologists and conservation biologists, particularly those from the developing countries of the world, and the formulation of strategies and policy activities for the conservation of endangered species and their habitats.

Annual Fees	*Regular*	*Student/Senior*	*Families*	*Sustaining*	*Sponsor*
	$25	$15	$35	$50	$100

Other Fees *Conservator* $250 • *Benefactor* $500 • *Patron* $1,000

Funding	*Membership*	*Government Support*	*Foundations*	*Other*
	54%	2%	23%	21%

Total Income $689,757

Usage	*Administration*	*Fundraising*	*Programs*	*Other*
	17%	1%	72%	10%

Total Expenses $707,185

Programs The Trust has ongoing conservation programs underway in different areas, including Madagascar, Mauritius, Brazil, Columbia, Central America, and the United States. Also assists in the operation of the International Training Center for the Conservation and Captive Breeding of Endangered Species, which trains conservation workers. It also holds annual members luncheons in different cities, and offers membership tours of different regions of the world in which the group is active.

Publications Newsletter *On The Edge* published three times per year. Numerous children's books, fiction, informational books and scientific studies

For more Information Annual Report, List of Publications

Who's Who PRESIDENT G. PALMER LEROY • VICE PRESIDENT CHARLES H. WATTS II SECRETARY MRS. MURRAY S. DANFORTH, JR. • TREASURER JAMES K. FERGUSON MEMBERSHIP DIRECTOR JOANNE GULLIFER

WILDLIFE REFUGE REFORM COALITION

P.O. BOX 18414   WASHINGTON DC 20036-8414
PHONE (202) 778 6145

Founded 1988 • *Geographic Coverage* National • *Cooperative Partners* Conservation Endowment Fund, The Humane Society of the United States, the Massachusetts Society for the Prevention of Cruelty to Animals, Friends of Animals, the American Humane Association *Organization Members* 89

Mission To restore integrity to the management of the National Wildlife Refuge System. In the short term, the Coalition is focusing on the passage of HR 330, the Refuge Wildlife Protection Act, a comprehensive bill which would prohibit recreational hunting and commercial trapping on National Wildlife Refuges.

Publications Fact sheets

Who's Who DIRECTOR AMY WEINHOUSE

WILDLIFE SOCIETY (THE)

5410 GROSVENOR LANE   BETHESDA MD 20814-2197
PHONE (301) 897 9770   FAX (301) 530 2471

Founded 1937 • *Geographic Coverage* North America • *Chapters* 7 geographic sections in North America, 50 chapters and 60 student chapters within these divisions • *Organization Members* 8,900 in over 40 countries

Mission To enhance the scientific, technical, managerial, and educational capability and achievement of wildlife professionals in conserving diversity and sustaining productivity of wildlife resources for the benefit of society; to develop and promote sound stewardship of wildlife resources and the environments upon which wildlife and humans depend; to undertake an active role in preventing human-induced environmental degradation; to increase awareness and appreciation of wildlife values; and to seek the highest standards in all activities of the wildlife profession.

Annual Fees	*Regular*	*Student/Senior*
	$37	$19

Programs Working Groups, forums for members of the Society with common professional interests to network and exchange information. Working Groups include Biological Diversity, College and University Wildlife Education, Geographic Information Systems and Remote Sensing, Habitat Restoration, Native Peoples' Wildlife, Population Ecology and Management, Sustainable Use of Ecosystem Resource, Wildlife Damage Management, Wildlife Economics, Wildlife Toxicology.

Publications Quarterly *The Journal of Wildlife Management.* Quarterly *Wildlife Society Bulletin,* a scientific journal. Bimonthly newsletter *The Wildlifer.* Various books including *Checklist of North American Plants for Wildlife Biologists* • *Readings in Wildlife Conservation* • *Waterfowl Ecology and Management: Selected Readings* • *Wildlife Conservation Principles and Practices* • *Wildlife Management Techniques Manual.* List of universities and colleges offering curricula in wildlife conservation

For more Information Library, List of Publications

WILLIAM HOLDEN WILDLIFE FOUNDATION

P.O. BOX 67981   LOS ANGELES CA 90067-0981
PHONE (310) 274 3169

Founded 1982 • *Geographic* Coverage Global • *Focused Country* Kenya • *Organization Members* 4 • *Individual Members* 3,000

Mission The organization focuses on specific animal conservation programs, with an emphasis on education and some international conservation efforts.

Annual Fees *Regular* $35

Funding	*Membership*	*Corporations*	*Foundations*
	10%	15%	75%

Total Income $282,370

Usage	*Fundraising*	*Programs*
	15%	85%

Programs Scholarships. Pen Pac International Network.

Publication Newsletter

Who's Who PRESIDENT STEFANIE POWERS • VICE PRESIDENT DON HUNT • SECRETARY MINI MCGUIRE

WILSON ORNITHOLOGICAL SOCIETY (THE)
C/O MUSEUM OF ZOOLOGY
THE UNIVERSITY OF MICHIGAN   ANN ARBOR MI 48104

Founded 1888 • *Geographic Coverage* Global • *Cooperative Partners* The American Ornithologists' Union, The Cooper Ornithological Society, Association of Field Ornithologists • *Individual Members* 2,200

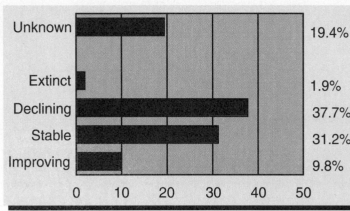

Recovery Status of all Endangered and Threatened Species Under the Endangered Species Act Recovery Program, 1990 (percentage)

Unknown	19.4%
Extinct	1.9%
Declining	37.7%
Stable	31.2%
Improving	9.8%

1990 Base = 581 listed species

Source: U.S. Department of the Interior, Fish and Wildlife Service, *Report to Congress: Endangered and Threatened Species Recovery Program 1990*

page 131 ▶ probably at an all-time high, the prognosis remains bleak". There has been a growing awareness of the need to establish "wildlife corridors", so organisms can move and exchange genetic material between preserves. This approach is being used in California to help such species as the mountain lion, desert tortoise, and kangaroo rat.

INTERNATIONAL COOPERATION IS

Mission To promote a strong working relationship among all who study birds.

Annual Fees	Regular	Student/Senior	Families	Sustaining	Patron
	$21	$15	$25	$30	$1,000

Other Fees *Lifetime* $500

Programs Sponsors an annual meeting. Organizes field trips to natural areas.

Publications Quarterly *Wilson Bulletin*. Bimonthly *The Ornithological Newsletter*. Directory of ornithologists *The Flock*

For more Information Library

WOLF PARK

NORTH AMERICAN WILDLIFE PARK FOUNDATION   BATTLE GROUND IN 47920
PHONE (317) 567 2265

Founded 1972 • *Geographic Coverage* North America • *Cooperative Partners* Institute for Environmental Learning, Wildlife Science Center, and numerous organizations dedicated to the welfare of wolves in the wild and in captivity • *Individual Members* 1,200

Mission To observe wolves' social behavior under semi-natural conditions in captivity so that the wolf can be better understood and thus protected in the wild. To demonstrate ways to improve the lives of captive wolves through proper behavior techniques designed to eliminate the stress of captivity.

Annual Fees	Regular	Families	Supporting	Adopt-A-Wolf
	$20	$35	$50	$125

Programs Park is open to visitors daily from May-November and once weekly from December-April. Adopt-A-Wolf Program. 4-week Ethology Practicum. 6-day Wolf Behavior Seminars. 24-hour Ethology Programs. Seasonal wolf-bison demonstrations.

Publication Newsletter *Wolf Park News*

Who's Who SECRETARY MARGARETA FONG • EXECUTIVE DIRECTOR ERICH KLINGHAMMER • EXECUTIVE ASSISTANT HOLLY DI MAIO

WORLD BIRD SANCTUARY

P.O. BOX 270270   ST. LOUIS MO 63127
PHONE (314) 938 6193   FAX (314) 938 9464

Founded 1977 • *Geographic Coverage* National • *Other Fields of Focus* Ecosystem Protection / Biodiversity, Environmental Education / Careers / Information / Networks

Mission To preserve the earth's biological diversity and to secure the future of threatened bird species in their natural environments.

Programs Education programs developed by the organization's Office of Wildlife Learning: Raptor Awareness Education Program spotlights birds of prey, their natural history and the problems they are facing in today's modern world; World Ecology Awareness Program uses live tropical birds, including parrots and birds of prey, and focuses on the issues confronting tropical bird species, such as the rainforest destruction and the illegal animal trade. Adopt-A-Bird Program. Internship programs.

Publication Quarterly newsletter *Mews News*

Who's Who PRESIDENT LEON P. ULLENSVANG • VICE PRESIDENT THOMAS T. COOKE SECRETARY ROBERT W. ZAK • TREASURER GEORGE F. SCHERER • EXECUTIVE DIRECTOR WALTER C. CRAWFORD, JR. • EDITOR MARION ERNST • CONTACT MAGGIE BOGART

WORLD WILDLIFE FUND

WWF
1250 24TH STREET, NW   WASHINGTON DC 20037-1175
PHONE (202) 293 4800   FAX (202) 293 9211

Founded 1961 • *Geographic Coverage* Global • *Focused Regions* Africa, Asia, Latin America • *Other Fields of Focus* Ecosystem Protec-

essential for wildlife preservation. For example, many migratory birds spend their summers in Canada, migrate through the United States, and winter in Mexico. Stretching from Alaska to South America, the "Pacific Flyway" is a series of migratory routes that are followed by vast numbers of birds. Species including the Canada goose, ducks, cranes, terns, rails, sandpipers, herons, and grebes, may depend upon habitat preservation by three or more nations. The lakes, rivers, and estuaries where migratory birds touch down to rest are also homes for amphibians, insects, water-loving plants, fish and mammals. Population pressures, changing water usage, and high land values in many places along the Flyway are threatening the existence of these mutually dependent creatures. The plight of ►

---

tion / Biodiversity, Forest Conservation / Deforestation / Reforestation
Individual Members 1,000,000

Mission To participate in the international drive to rescue endangered animals from extinction, curb illegal trade in rare species, establish and protect national parks and reserves, help meet the needs of local people without destroying natural resources, train and equip rangers, guards and anti-poaching teams, and promote scientific research to develop long-range conservation programs. Over the past three decades, WWF has sponsored more than 3,000 conservation projects in 140 wildlife-rich countries.

Annual Fees

Regular	Friend	Associate	Contributing
$15	$25	$50	$100

Other Fees *Sponsor* $250 • *Sustaining* $500 • *Partner in Conservation* $1,000

Funding

Membership	Government Support	Corporations	Foundations	Other
57%	20%	2%	6%	15%

Total Income $59,684,618

Usage

Administration	Fundraising	Programs
3%	7%	90%

Total Expenses $56,646,602

Programs The Fund's Special Rescue Program has helped stop the brutal slaughter of some of the world's most critically threatened animals, including Latin America's jaguar, the African elephant, the Asian snow leopard, and India's Bengal tiger. Their Wildlands and Human Needs Program helps people improve the quality of their lives without destroying their own natural resources. The Fund also operates Training Programs to form park rangers and anti-poaching teams, conservation educators who travel to schools, churches, markets and workplaces in Third World countries. Campaigns for major international agreements, legislation and treaties on endangered species and habitats.

Publications Bimonthly newsletter *Focus*. Frequent *Wildlife Alerts* on

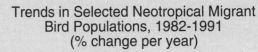

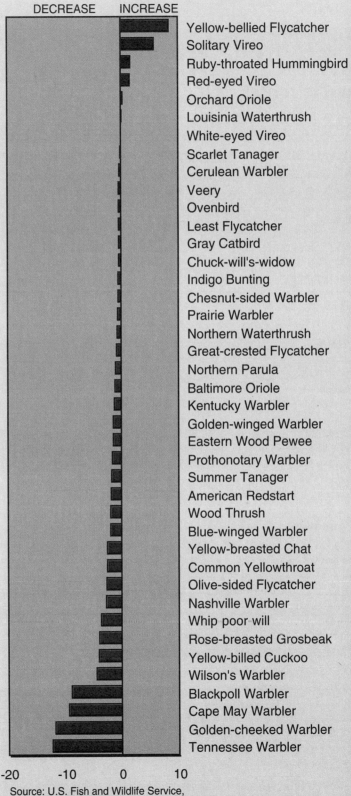

Trends in Selected Neotropical Migrant Bird Populations, 1982-1991 (% change per year)

DECREASE   INCREASE

- Yellow-bellied Flycatcher
- Solitary Vireo
- Ruby-throated Hummingbird
- Red-eyed Vireo
- Orchard Oriole
- Louisinia Waterthrush
- White-eyed Vireo
- Scarlet Tanager
- Cerulean Warbler
- Veery
- Ovenbird
- Least Flycatcher
- Gray Catbird
- Chuck-will's-widow
- Indigo Bunting
- Chesnut-sided Warbler
- Prairie Warbler
- Northern Waterthrush
- Great-crested Flycatcher
- Northern Parula
- Baltimore Oriole
- Kentucky Warbler
- Golden-winged Warbler
- Eastern Wood Pewee
- Prothonotary Warbler
- Summer Tanager
- American Redstart
- Wood Thrush
- Blue-winged Warbler
- Yellow-breasted Chat
- Common Yellowthroat
- Olive-sided Flycatcher
- Nashville Warbler
- Whip poor will
- Rose-breasted Grosbeak
- Yellow-billed Cuckoo
- Wilson's Warbler
- Blackpoll Warbler
- Cape May Warbler
- Golden-cheeked Warbler
- Tennessee Warbler

-20   -10   0   10

Source: U.S. Fish and Wildlife Service, *Breeding Bird Survey*

endangered species and WWF rescue and relocation efforts

For more Information Annual Report

Who's Who PRESIDENT KATHRYN S. FULLER • VICE PRESIDENT PAIGE K. MACDO-
NALD • SECRETARY ANNE P. SIDAMON-ERISTOFF • TREASURER HUNTER LEWIS
GENERAL COUNSEL JOHN H. NOBLE

XERCES SOCIETY (THE)

10 ASH STREET, SW, THIRD FLOOR	PORTLAND OR 97204
PHONE (503) 222 2788	FAX (503) 222 2763

Founded 1971 • *Geographic Coverage* Global • *Cooperative Partners* Smithsonian Institute, Sierra Club, National Wildlife Federation
Organization Members 200 • *Individual Members* 4,200

Mission The Xerces Society is dedicated solely to invertebrates and the
preservation of critical biosystems worldwide.

Annual Fees	*Regular*	*Student/Senior*	*Supporting*	*Friend*	*Patron*
	$25	$15	$50	$100	$250

Other Fees *Lifetime* $1,000

Funding	Membership	Foundations
	50%	50%

Usage	Administration & Fundraising	Programs
	20%	80%

Programs Volunteer and internship programs. Biodiversity research and
training in Madagascar. The Homerus Swallowtail Project in Jamaica.
Invertebrate Indicator Workshops on Conservation Survey and Monitoring. The Old Forest Project. The Monarch Project works to protect over-
wintering habitats of the Monarch butterfly in California.

Publications Semiannual magazine *Wings: Essays on Invertebrate Conservation*. Various books including *Butterfly Gardening: Creating Summer
Magic in Your Garden* • *The Common Names of North American Butterflies*

Who's Who PRESIDENT THOMAS EISNER • VICE PRESIDENT PAUL OPLER • SECRETARY
ED GROSSWILER

YOUNG ENTOMOLOGISTS' SOCIETY, INC.

1915 PEGGY PLACE	LANSING MI 48910-2553
PHONE (517) 887 0499	

Founded 1965 • *Geographic Coverage* Global • *Organization
Members* 5 • *Individual Members* 700

Mission The Society is an international organization for youth and
amateur insect enthusiasts, which works to help individuals find new
friends who have similar entomological interests, and to provide services, activities, publications and products that complement or support

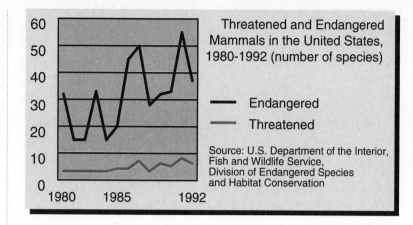

Threatened and Endangered Mammals in the United States, 1980-1992 (number of species)

Source: U.S. Department of the Interior, Fish and Wildlife Service, Division of Endangered Species and Habitat Conservation

entomological endeavors.

Annual Fees	*Regular*	*Student/Senior*	*Families*	*Institution*
	$10	$5	$10	$15

Other Fees *Donor* $100 • *Patron* $500 • *Sponsor* $1,000

Funding	Membership	Foundations
	95%	5%

Total Income $40,000

Usage	Administration	Programs
	10%	90%

Publications Bimonthly newsletters *Insect World* • *Flea Market*. Newsletter *Y.E.S. Quarterly*. Various books including *The Y.E.S. International
Entomology Resource Guide: The Insect Study Sourcebook* • *Six-Legged
Science: Insects in the Classroom* • *Buggy Books: A Guide to Juvenile
and Popular Books on Insects and their Relatives* • *The Teacher and Student Insect Identification Study Guide*

For more Information List of Publications

Who's Who EXECUTIVE DIRECTOR DIANNA K. DUNN • DIRECTOR OF EDUCATION
GARY A. DUNN

Canada

ALBERTA RECREATION, PARKS AND WILDLIFE FOUNDATION

10405 111TH STREET, HARLEY COURT BUILDING	EDMONTON AB T5K 1K4
PHONE (403) 482 6467	FAX (403) 488 9755

ALBERTA WILDERNESS ASSOCIATION

BOX 6398, STATION "D"	CALGARY AB T2P 2E1
PHONE (403) 283 2025	

marine mammals is a widely publicized example of the necessity for international cooperation. Both sea and land wildlife depend on international regulations and pollution controls, since oceans, rivers, and the atmosphere extend across borders. For instance, chemicals released in the United States can become acid rain that kills fish in Canada. One nation may serve as a reservoir for species threatened in another. The grizzly bear is one of many animals whose numbers have declined in the 48 contiguous United States. Grizzly populations remain strong only in Alaska and remote regions of Canada. Most citizens understand that animals need plants for food, but conservation efforts also must emphasize the importance of habitats for other facets of wildlife existence, such as breeding ground, protective cover, and ▶

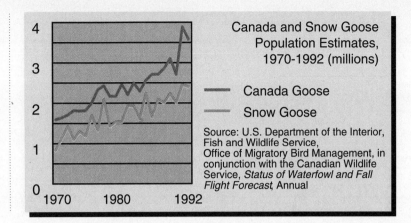

Canada and Snow Goose
Population Estimates,
1970-1992 (millions)

—— Canada Goose
—— Snow Goose

Source: U.S. Department of the Interior, Fish and Wildlife Service, Office of Migratory Bird Management, in conjunction with the Canadian Wildlife Service, *Status of Waterfowl and Fall Flight Forecast*, Annual

BOW VALLEY NATURALISTS

PAGE 255

P.O. Box 1693
Phone (403) 762 4160

Banff AB T0L 0C0
Fax (403) 762 4160

BRITISH COLUMBIA WATERFOWL SOCIETY (THE)

5191 Robertson Road
Phone (604) 946 6980

Delta BC V4K 3N2
Fax (604) 946 6980

Founded 1961 • *Geographic Coverage* Province, North America
Chapter 1 • *Individual Members* 2,150

Mission To promote the conservation of migratory waterfowl and public awareness of wetland conservation.

Annual Fees	Regular	Families
	$13.50	$27

Other Fees *Lifetime* $225

Funding	Membership	Foundations	Admission, Tours & Courses	Gift Shop
	20%	10%	40%	30%

Total Income $250,000

Usage	Programs	Sanctuary Improvements
	63%	30%

Other Usage *Bird Feed, Fundraising, Publicity & Concession Costs 7%*

Total Expenses $320,000

Programs School field trips, weekend public tours.

Publication Quarterly newsletter *Marsh Notes*

For more Information Library

Who's Who President **Barney Reifel** • Vice President **George Reifel** • Secretary **Ken Hall** • Treasurer **James Morrison** • Librarian **John Ireland** • Contact **Varri Johnson**

BRITISH COLUMBIA WILDLIFE FEDERATION

6070 200th Street, Suite 102
Phone (604) 533 2293

Langley BC V3A 1N4
Fax (604) 533 1592

Geographic Coverage Province • *Cooperative Partners* British Columbia Conservation Foundation, Okanagan and Kootenay Heritage Funds, Canadian Wildlife Federation • *Individual Members* 35,000

Mission To promote conservation and thoughtful use of British Columbia's wildlife and natural resources.

Annual Fees	Regular	Sustaining
	$25	$250

Other Fees *Lifetime* $1,000

Programs Conservation and Outdoor Recreation Education Programme which works to teach the general public about outdoor resources in British Columbia. Works with schools to reach young people through programs such as National Wildlife Week and Project Wild, and provides scholarships to students studying Natural Resource Management. Wilderness Watch Programme, designed to assist federal and provincial resource enforcement agencies in their protection of British Columbia's natural environment and habitats.

CANADIAN WILDLIFE FEDERATION
FÉDÉRATION CANADIENNE DE LA FAUNE

2740 Queensview Drive
Phone (613) 721 2286

Ottawa ON K2B 1A2
Fax (613) 721 2902

Founded 1961 • *Geographic Coverage* National • *Cooperative Partners* Alberta Fish and Game Association, Yukon Fish and Game Association, provincial Wildlife Federations, Ontario Federation of Anglers and Hunters • *Chapters* 12 provincial and territorial affiliates *Individual Members* 600,000

Mission To promote the conservation of fish and wildlife, wildlife habitat, and quality aquatic environments, to foster understanding of

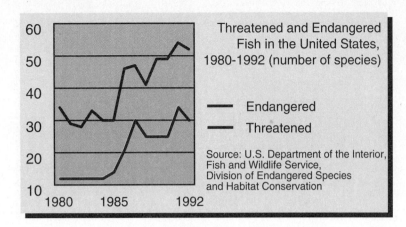

Threatened and Endangered
Fish in the United States,
1980-1992 (number of species)

— Endangered
— Threatened

Source: U.S. Department of the Interior,
Fish and Wildlife Service,
Division of Endangered Species
and Habitat Conservation

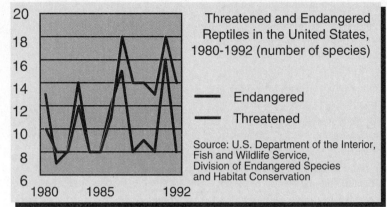

Threatened and Endangered
Reptiles in the United States,
1980-1992 (number of species)

— Endangered
— Threatened

Source: U.S. Department of the Interior,
Fish and Wildlife Service,
Division of Endangered Species
and Habitat Conservation

natural processes; to ensure adequate stocks of fish and wildlife for the use and enjoyment of all Canadians; to provide education programs and sponsor research; to cooperate with legislators, government agencies and other non-governmental agencies to achieve conservation objectives.

Annual Fees *Regular* $25

Funding

Membership	Merchandise Sales
51.7%	48.3%

Total Income $10,492,640

Usage

Administration	Programs	Membership	Merchandise	Other
9.5%	12%	31%	43.4%	4.1%

Total Expenses $12,187,497

Programs The Federation's education programs include National Wildlife Week, Project W.I.L.D., Endangered Species, and Habitat 2000. Its conservation action programs include sponsorship of the National Inquiry into Freshwater Fisheries, sponsorship of the World Conservation Strategy Conference, and leadership in the development of a new National Recreational Fisheries and Aquatic Environments Programme. Advocates on national and international conservation and environmental issues. Funds numerous research projects in a wide variety of fields. Provides numerous conservation awards.

Publications Periodicals including bimonthly *Biosphere* • Bimonthly *International Wildlife* • Monthly *Ranger Rick* • Monthly *Your Big Backyard*

For more Information Annual Report, Database, Library, List of Publications

Who's Who PRESIDENT JIM HOOK • VICE PRESIDENTS RON GLADISH, CARL SHIER, JOHN CARTER • SECRETARY YVES JEAN • TREASURER NESTOR ROMANIUK • EXECUTIVE VICE PRESIDENT COLIN MAXWELL

ECOLOGY ACTION CENTRE

3115 VEITH STREET, THIRD FLOOR   HALIFAX NS B3K 3G9
PHONE (902) 454 7828   FAX (902) 454 4766

ENVIRONMENTAL COALITION OF PRINCE EDWARD ISLAND

126 RICHMOND STREET   CHARLOTTETOWN PEI C0A 1C0
PHONE (902) 566 4696   FAX (902) 566 4037

FEDERATION OF BRITISH COLUMBIA NATURALISTS (THE)

1367 WEST BROADWAY, SUITE 321   VANCOUVER BC V6H 4A9
PHONE (604) 737 3057

FEDERATION OF ONTARIO NATURALISTS

355 LESMILL ROAD   DON MILLS ON M3B 2W8
PHONE (416) 444 8419   FAX (416) 444 9866

KENYA WILDLIFE FUND (THE)

80 "F" CENTURIAN DRIVE, SUITE 5   MARKHAM ON L3R 8C1
PHONE (416) 474 0707   FAX (416) 474 9393

Geographic Coverage East Africa • *Focused Country* Kenya
Cooperative Partner Kenya Wildlife Service

Mission To support the conservation of wildlife, with emphasis on the protection of elephants and their habitat in Kenya; to provide education and information about the plight of the Kenyan elephant; and to discourage the import and utilization of illegal ivory.

Annual Fees

Regular	Families	Young Friend	Supporting	Adopting
$25	$50	$10	$100	$250

Programs The Fund's Elephant Programme works to ensure the long-

hunting territories. Plants depend on animals for such functions as pollination, seed dispersal, and fertilization. Wildlife conservation traditionally proceeds from basic research, followed by regulatory controls and program implementation. The US government invests in wildlife research through a number of federal agencies.

The research dollars are but the tip of the iceberg, compared to the vast sums committed to implementing wildlife conservation programs in North America, by agencies of national, state, provincial, regional, and local governments.

TODAY SOME SCIENTISTS QUESTION whether research and current conservation practices can proceed fast enough to avert environmental crises and save endangered wildlife. ▶

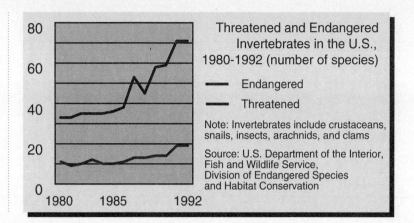

Threatened and Endangered Invertebrates in the U.S., 1980-1992 (number of species)

— Endangered
— Threatened

Note: Invertebrates include crustaceans, snails, insects, arachnids, and clams

Source: U.S. Department of the Interior, Fish and Wildlife Service, Division of Endangered Species and Habitat Conservation

term survival of biologically and touristically important elephant populations, to provide close monitoring of trends in the numbers and status of the elephant population to enable the most appropriate populations to be selected for anti-poaching and conservation efforts and provide a basis for monitoring the progress of conservation initiatives, to cooperate with other countries on international elephant conservation issues, to reconcile land-use and other conflicts between elephants and communities in areas adjoining Parks and Reserves, and to build up expertise within the Fund to deal with elephant related conservation and management issues in the long-term. The Fund works with anti-poaching groups to ensure that there is no upsurge in elephant poaching or ivory-trafficking.

Publication Quarterly newsletter *Habari*

Who's Who PRESIDENT **LOUISE CHARLTON**

LAMBTON WILDLIFE, INC.

P.O. BOX 681   SARNIA ON N7T 7J7
PHONE (519) 869 2298

Founded 1966 • *Geographic Coverage* Local • *Cooperative Partners* Federation of Ontario Naturalists, Canadian Nature Federation

Mission To promote the conservation of natural habitat, particularly in Lambton County, and to develop conservation areas and sanctuaries in the county.

Annual Fees	Regular	Student/Senior	Families	Organization	Corporation
	$16	$3	$20	$100	$100

Other Fees *Lifetime* $320

Funding	Membership	Other
	64%	36%

Total Income $4,896

Programs Educational programs in Enviro-studies and Natural History. Annual Bird Count in December.

Publication Monthly newsletter *Earthways*

For more Information Annual Report, Database

Who's Who PRESIDENT **ALF RIDER** • SECRETARY **ALICE LESTER** • TREASURER **PAUL CROSBIE** • EDITOR **CAROLE BUCK**

NORTHWEST WILDLIFE PRESERVATION SOCIETY

P.O. BOX 34129, STATION "D"   VANCOUVER BC V6J 4N3
PHONE (604) 736 8750   FAX (604) 736 9615

Founded 1987 • *Geographic Coverage* Regional • *Focused Region* Northwest North America • *Members* 250 including organizations

Mission To develop and provide educational, research, and advisory services which can advance the public's awareness and knowledge of wildlife systems in Northwest North America.

Annual Fees	Regular	Student/Senior	Families
	$20	$15	$35

Publications Periodicals including *Membernews* • *Critters* • *Focus*

For more Information Library, List of Publications

Who's Who ADMINISTRATION AND PROJECT COORDINATOR **BARBARA MEREDITH** CONTACT **VICTORIA MILES**

ONTARIO BIRD BANDING ASSOCIATION

C/O LONG POINT BIRD OBSERVATORY
BOX 160   PORT ROWAN ON N0E 1M0
PHONE (519) 586 3531

Founded 1956 • *Geographic Coverage* Province • *Cooperative Partners* Guelph Banding Group, Hawk Cliff Raptor Banding Station, Holiday Beach Bird Observatory, Long Point Bird Observatory, Ottawa Banding Group, Toronto Bird Observatory • *Individual Members* 100

Mission Bird Banding is the practice of marking birds with an identifying device in order to study their migratory behavior. The Association is dedicated to providing a network for bird-banders in Ontario, promoting good banding ethics, and publishing the results of banding studies.

Annual Fees

	Regular	*Student/Senior*	*Families*
	$15	$10	$20

Funding

	Membership	*Foundations*	*Other*
	49.5%	6.8%	43.7%

Total Income $2,365

Usage

	Administration	*Donations*	*Programs*
	5%	5.5%	89.5%

Programs Annual general meeting. Fall Band-Out. Sponsoring of young ornithologists.

Publications Annual journal *Ontario Bird Banding*. Quarterly *Ontario Bird Banding Newsletter*

For more Information Library

Who's Who PRESIDENT MARTIN K. MCNICHOLL • VICE PRESIDENTS DAVID SHEPHERD, ELIZABETH KELLOGG • TREASURER ROBERT HUBERT • DIRECTORS DAVID AGRO, PETER EWINS, ELLEN HAYAKAWA, RICHARD KNAPTON • JOURNAL EDITOR BILL MCILVEEN • NEWSLETTER EDITOR AUDREY HEAGY

PENINSULA FIELD NATURALISTS (THE) PAGE 257
P.O. BOX 23031, MIDTOWN POSTAL OUTLET
124 WELLAND AVENUE   ST. CATHARINES ON L0S 1E3
PHONE (416) 935 2913

SASKATCHEWAN WILDLIFE FEDERATION
P.O. BOX 788   MOOSE JAW SK S6H 4P5
PHONE (306) 692 8812   FAX (306) 692 4370

Established 1929, incorporated as a non-profit organization in 1954 *Geographic Coverage* Province • *Cooperative Partners* Ducks Unlimited Canada, Wildlife Habitat Canada, the Saskatchewan Government, Saskatchewan Natural History Society, Weyerhaeuser, Tree Plan Canada, Nature Saskatchewan, Prairie Farm Rehabilitation Administration *Chapters* 140 • *Individual Members* 32,000

Mission To preserve wildlife in all its natural habitats, and to restore, conserve and perpetuate Saskatchewan's natural resources.

Annual Fees *Regular* $25

Programs The Federation is involved in a wide range of conservation pro-

grams, including the Habitat Trust Programme, the Wildlife Development Fund, and the Heritage Marsh Programme (which is responsible for developing 20 marshes in Saskatchewan for waterfowl). Integrated Forest Management Programme, in collaboration with other groups, will create a computerized inventory of the Saskatchewan forest and its wildlife, to help lead to better wildlife management practices, as well as to enhance utilization of the forest.

Publication Bimonthly magazine *Outdoor Edge*

Who's Who PRESIDENT RAY PUDDICOMBE • EDITOR OUTDOOR EDGE KEN BAILEY ADMINISTRATIVE COORDINATOR DALE F. FERREL

SIERRA CLUB OF CANADA PAGE 126
1 NICHOLAS STREET, SUITE 620   OTTAWA ON K1N 7B7
PHONE (613) 233 1906   FAX (613) 233 2292

SIERRA CLUB OF EASTERN CANADA PAGE 127
517 COLLEGE STREET, SUITE 303   TORONTO ON M6G 4A2
PHONE (416) 960 9606   FAX (416) 960 0020

STEELHEAD SOCIETY OF BRITISH COLUMBIA
P.O. BOX 33947, STATION "D"   VANCOUVER BC V6J 4L7
PHONE (604) 936 9474   FAX (604) 936 5150

Founded 1970 • *Geographic Coverage* Province, Regional • *Chapters* 9 • *Individual Members* 1,000

Mission To protect and enhance wild steelhead salmon and their habitats.

Annual Fees *Regular* $25

Funding

	Membership	*Foundations*
	60%	40%

Programs The Wild Steelhead Campaign works to reduce commercial net fleet interceptions of endangered salmonids.

Publication Quarterly newsletter *The Steelhead Release*

Who's Who PRESIDENT CRAIG ORR • VICE PRESIDENT BRUCE HILL • SECRETARY MAGGIE MCCRANE • TREASURER HAROLD BAKER

VALHALLA SOCIETY (THE) PAGE 127
BOX 224   NEW DENVER BC V0G 1S0
PHONE (604) 358 2333   FAX (604) 358 7950

WESTERN CANADA WILDERNESS COMMITTEE PAGE 128
20 WATER STREET   VANCOUVER BC V6B 1A4
PHONE (604) 683 8220   FAX (604) 683 8229

► The November 1993 issue of *Ecological Applications*, a journal of the Ecological Society of America, explored the issue of sustainability, and whether science can lead us rapidly enough toward this goal. The concern is that many species and non-renewable resources may be lost before we achieve a less destructive human lifestyle. Wildlife species have little, if any, control over whether or not their environment is preserved. Humans do have a great deal of control, and a concurrent responsibility. In the book *Ecology 2000*, Mount Everest explorer Sir Edmund Hillary wrote that "the future is entirely in our hands. We can make the world what we will, a paradise for all, or a barren desolate globe spinning endlessly through space". •

Laura L. Klure

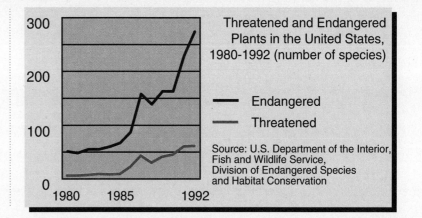

Threatened and Endangered Plants in the United States, 1980-1992 (number of species)

— Endangered
— Threatened

Source: U.S. Department of the Interior, Fish and Wildlife Service, Division of Endangered Species and Habitat Conservation

WILDLIFE FOUNDATION OF MANITOBA
FORT WHYTE CENTRE PROJECT

1961 McCreary Road, Box 124   Winnipeg MB R3Y 1G5
Phone (204) 989 8355   Fax (204) 895 4700

Founded 1966 • *Geographic Coverage* Province • *Individual Members* 6,000

Mission To provide funding and facilities for education in the art and science of keeping this planet habitable for all forms of life.

Funding	Membership	Government Support	Foundations	Program Fees
	13%	12%	18%	22%

Other Fees *General Admission* 13% • *Other* 22%

Usage	Administration	Programs
	42%	58%

Programs Public On-Site Programme with workshops, exhibits, and recreational programs. The Natural History Programme provides a basic understanding of local and global ecosystems. Sustainable Living Programmes provide insight into the environmental impact of personal everyday activities, and emphasizes positive actions towards a sustainable lifestyle. Public Off-Site Programme. School Off-Site Programme. Youth On-Site Programme.

Who's Who Chairman A. Brian Ransom

WILDLIFE HABITAT CANADA   PAGE 58

7 Hinton Avenue, North, Suite 200   Ottawa ON K1Y 4P1
Phone (613) 722 2090   Fax (613) 722 3318

ZOOCHECK CANADA

5334 Yonge Street, Suite 1830   Toronto ON M2N 6M2
Phone (416) 696 0241   Fax (416) 696 0241

Founded 1988 • *Geographic Coverage* Local, National, Global *Chapter* 1

Mission To protect animals in captivity and to participate in conservation projects which directly benefit animals in the wild.

Programs Zoo Licensing Legislative Initiative. Municipal Exotic and Performing Animal By-Laws. Elephant and Orangutan Protection. Wild Horses in Canadian West. Various Canadian Wildlife Legislative Initiatives.

Publication Annual newsletter

For more Information Database, Library

Who's Who Directors Holly Penfound, Barry Kent Mackay • Contact Rob Laidlaw

environmental **impa**

cts of human activities **part three**

"The edifice of civilization has become astonishingly complex, but as it grows ever more elaborate, we feel increasingly distant from our roots in the earth. In one sense, civilization itself has been on a journey from its foundations in the world of nature to an ever more contrived, controlled, and manufactured world of our own imitative and sometimes arrogant design."

Vice President Albert Gore, Jr., Earth in the Balance

energy
alternative & renewable
energies

CHAPTER 10

Fossil Fuels : From Blessing to Curse, by Lyn Corum

ENERGY MAKES POSSIBLE
the way of life that we now
take for granted: the ability to
light, heat, and cool our homes
and businesses, the ability to
move about in cars, the ability
to manufacture newer and
cheaper products.

An exponential increase in the
use of coal and oil in the past
century made all this possible,
but it has also created some
monumental environmental
problems. Large areas of North
America struggle with air
pollution, a byproduct of our
road vehicles. Carbon dioxide,
another byproduct of fossil-
fuel use, is increasing in the
Earth's upper atmosphere at an
alarming rate and trapping
infrared radiation; it is
warming the planet's surface
temperature and creating
changes, which, experts
suspect, may prove to be
catastrophic. Scientists predict
that if North America
continues to use coal and oil at
the rate of the past century,
temperatures could rise from
3 to 15 degrees Fahrenheit,
according to estimates.
These increases may lead to
the melting of glaciers, causing
thermal expansion of oceans
and raising sea levels by one
to four feet. It might also cause

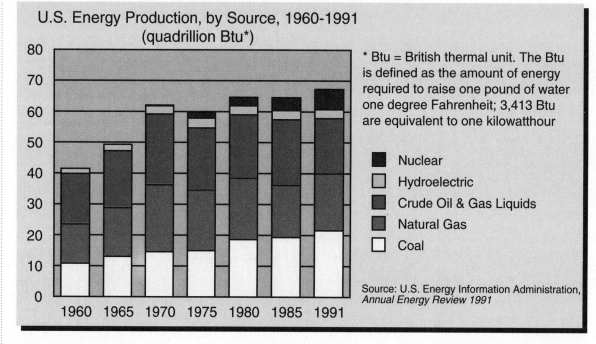

U.S. Energy Production, by Source, 1960-1991 (quadrillion Btu*)

* Btu = British thermal unit. The Btu is defined as the amount of energy required to raise one pound of water one degree Fahrenheit; 3,413 Btu are equivalent to one kilowatthour

- ■ Nuclear
- □ Hydroelectric
- ■ Crude Oil & Gas Liquids
- ■ Natural Gas
- □ Coal

Source: U.S. Energy Information Administration, *Annual Energy Review 1991*

disruptive shifts in weather
patterns. Technologies exist to
clean the air in our cities.
Unfortunately, non-fossil,
renewable resources still play
a very limited role in
electricity production and
virtually none in the
transportation sector.

THE UNITED STATES IS THE WORLD'S
second biggest energy
producer (the first is the
former Soviet Union) and
largest energy consumer - 84.4
quads in 1990. A quad is one

quadrillion (1 followed by
15 zeros) British Thermal
Units or BTUs - the standard
measure of heat energy; one
quad equals 170 million
barrels of oil. The Energy
Information Agency (EIA),
which made the estimate, says
this amount is about one
quarter of the world's energy.
Canada ranks sixth, consuming
about 10 quads. The United
States has become more energy
efficient following the two oil
shortage crises in the 1970s.
As our gross national product

rose, consumption also grew,
but less quickly. Energy
consumption, as a function of
each dollar of GNP, dropped
about 32 percent between
1970 and 1990. Forty percent
of the 84.4 quads of energy
consumed in the United States
is petroleum. Most of it is used
in the industrial and
transportation sectors; almost
none is burned in utility power
plants. Reducing oil
consumption will require
moving people from gasoline-
fueled cars to vehicles which

burn cleaner fuels like natural gas or methane or which operate using electricity. Major employers and public agencies which operate vehicle fleets are converting to various fuel-efficient vehicles. But electric car technology still remains at the research and development level. The State of California has mandated that 2 percent of the cars on its highways must be zero-emission vehicles by 1998. This edict has motivated US and foreign auto makers to increase Research and Development (R&D) efforts to produce an inexpensive electric or dual-fuel car and improve battery technology.

NATURAL GAS AND COAL ARE the other major fossil fuels which are the primary producers of electricity. Coal is by far the dirtier fuel. Its sulfur dioxide is largely responsible for the acid rain which has fallen for years in the Great Lakes region and in Canada. About 55 percent of our utilities burn coal. This number is unlikely to decrease because the United States has a 300-year supply of coal that is very cheap to mine and burn. As a result of Clean Air Act Amendments passed by the US Congress in 1990, utilities with coal-burning plants are being forced to install equipment to clean up the air. A credit program for sulfur dioxide emissions was created allowing utilities to buy and sell emissions credits, thereby rewarding those with cleaner plants which will be able to sell credits. The Department of Energy is also funding research to make coal cleaner to burn. ▶

United States

ALTERNATIVE ENERGY RESOURCES ORGANIZATION

PAGE 284

25 SOUTH EWING, SUITE 214   HELENA MT 59601
PHONE (406) 443 7272

AMERICAN COUNCIL FOR AN ENERGY-EFFICIENT ECONOMY

1001 CONNECTICUT AVENUE, NW, SUITE 801   WASHINGTON DC 20036
PHONE (202) 429 8873   FAX (202) 429 2248

Founded 1980 • *Geographic Coverage* National • *Chapter* 1

Mission To support greater energy efficiency by evaluating and disseminating information and by supporting the adoption of comprehensive new policies for increasing energy efficiency.

	Corporations	Foundations	Publications & Conferences
Funding	30%	40%	30%

Total Income $1,700,000

	Administration	Programs
Usage	18%	82%

Programs Conducts studies, publishes books and reports, provides expert testimony, and organizes conferences to facilitate information exchange between individuals developing new techniques in energy efficiency and those who can put new ideas to work. The Council's National Energy Policy details programs for increasing energy efficiency.

Publications Various pamphlets including *Guide to Energy-Efficient Office Equipment* • *Transportation and Global Climate Change* • *State-of-the Art of Energy Efficiency: Future Directions* • *Consumer Guide to Home Energy Savings*

Who's Who PRESIDENT **CARL BLUMSTEIN** • TREASURER **JON VEIGEL** • EXECUTIVE DIRECTOR **HOWARD GELLER** • DEPUTY DIRECTOR **MARC LEDBETTER** • DIRECTOR OF PUBLICATIONS **GLEE MURRAY**

AMERICAN SOLAR ENERGY SOCIETY, INC.

2400 CENTRAL AVENUE, SUITE G-1   BOULDER CO 80301
PHONE (303) 443 3130   FAX (303) 443 3212

Founded 1954 • *Geographic Coverage* National • *Chapters* 19
Individual Members 6,000

Mission To advance the use of solar energy for the benefit of US citizens and the global environment.

	Regular	Student/Senior	Subscription to Magazine
Annual Fees	$50	$25	$25

	Membership	Foundations	Program Fees & Publications
Funding	30%	30%	40%

Total Income $725,000

	Programs	Other
Usage	79%	21%

Programs National Solar Energy Conference. Solar Action Network.

Publications Bimonthly magazine *Solar Today* • Quarterly *Sun World*. Semiannual newsletter *ISES News*. Annual book *Advances in Solar Energy*. White papers written by experts in the field

Who's Who PRESIDENT **PAUL NOTARI** • VICE PRESIDENT **DONALD W. AITKEN** SECRETARY **HARRY T. GORDON** • TREASURER **REBECCA VORIES** • EXECUTIVE DIRECTOR **LARRY SHERWOOD** • EDITOR **MAUREEN MCINTYRE**

► RENEWABLE RESOURCES are the most plentiful resource in the United States, but existing technology and present costs make them hard to exploit. They actually contribute just 12 percent to the electric power fuel market, with hydroelectric resources producing 10 percent - the lion's share. Hydroelectric dams have been a power resource for over a century in

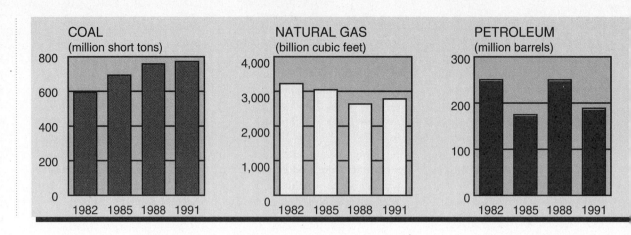

COAL (million short tons): 1982, 1985, 1988, 1991

NATURAL GAS (billion cubic feet): 1982, 1985, 1988, 1991

PETROLEUM (million barrels): 1982, 1985, 1988, 1991

AMERICAN WIND ENERGY ASSOCIATION

777 NORTH CAPITOL STREET, SUITE 805   WASHINGTON DC 20002
PHONE (202) 408 8988

Founded 1974 • *Geographic Coverage* National, Global • *Organization Members* 163 • *Individual Members* 542

Mission To promote wind energy as an economically and technically viable alternative technology capable of playing a major role in providing clean energy for growing electricity needs throughout the world. The Association is oriented toward a variety of audiences including state and federal policy makers, regulatory agencies, the media, the electric utility industry, international interests and the general public.

Annual Fees	*Regular*	*Corporation*	*Associate*	*Utility*
	$35	$600 to 3,500	$300	$500

Funding	*Membership*	*Contracts*	*Legislative*	*Conference*	*Publications*
	8%	64%	14%	11%	3%

Total Income $1,830,845

Programs Government contracts. Workshops. Legislative programs. Public awareness programs.

Publications Numerous books and technical publications focusing on alternative energies, especially wind energy

For more Information List of Publications

BIOMASS ENERGY RESEARCH ASSOCIATION

1825 "K" STREET, NW, SUITE 503   WASHINGTON DC 20006
PHONE (202) 785 2856   FAX (202) 223 4625

Founded 1982 • *Geographic Coverage* National

Mission To further the use of biomass energy by encouraging public

and private sector research, information exchange, education, and international cooperation in biofuels research, and by facilitating technology transfer from the laboratory to industry.

Annual Fees	*Regular*	*Organization*	*Corporation*
	$25	$300	$300

Programs Educates the general public about the potential of biomass energy. Enhances information exchange and coordination of research priorities within the technical and business communities. Monitors federal biomass activities and participates in deliberations concerning research funding needs. Encourages expansion of domestic and international biofuels markets through activities designed to increase the public and private sector's understanding and acceptance of biomass energy. Holds bimonthly "Capitol Hill Luncheons" in Washington, DC. Operates Consultants' Clearinghouse and Speakers' Bureau.

Publication Annual position statement on federal funding of biofuels research

CALIFORNIA SOLAR ENERGY INDUSTRIES ASSOCIATION

900 FULTON AVENUE, SUITE 210   SACRAMENTO CA 95825
PHONE (916) 488 8770   FAX (916) 488 8447

Founded 1978 • *Geographic Coverage* State • *Cooperative Partners* Branches of the Solar Energy Industries Association • *Chapters* 4
Members 450 including organizations

Mission To support the solar energy field in California.

Annual Fees *Regular* $295 to 650

Funding	*Membership*	*Other*
	25%	75%

Total Income $120,000

Programs Legislative advocacy. Golf tournament. Air quality consulting.

North America. Canada is the leading producer of hydroelectric power and accounts for 15 percent of world production.

The development of wind turbines, solar photo voltaic technology, and geothermal and biomass power plant technology began with the passage of the Public Utility Regulatory Policy Act in 1978 by the US Congress. The Act mandated that utilities buy power from independent cogeneration and small power plants. The most efficient geothermal, wind, biomass, and waste-to-energy plants can now produce electricity for almost the same price as electric utility power plants.

Geothermal and wind resources are limited by geography. Located primarily in California, Nevada, Utah and Hawaii, geothermal resources are costly to extract for the heated water, liquid or vapor which is extricated to generate electricity. Development of wind farms is constrained by the uncertainty of wind occurrences and intensity and the distance of the wind resource from electric power demands.

Wind farms also compete with other users for land. ▶

Publication Bimonthly newsletter *Solar Energy Report*, circulation 450

For more Information Database

Who's Who PRESIDENT LES MELSON • VICE PRESIDENT DAVE HARRIS • SECRETARY CHUCK WOODLEY • TREASURER ED MURRAY • EXECUTIVE DIRECTOR CATHY MURNIGHAM

CENTER FOR CLEAN AIR POLICY
PAGE 34

444 NORTH CAPITOL STREET, SUITE 602   WASHINGTON DC 20001
PHONE (202) 624 7709   FAX (202) 508 3829

CONSUMER ENERGY COUNCIL OF AMERICA
RESEARCH FOUNDATION

2000 "L" STREET, NW, SUITE 802   WASHINGTON DC 20036
PHONE (202) 659 0404   FAX (202) 659 0407

Founded 1973 • *Geographic Coverage* Global

Mission To help ensure reliable and affordable energy for all sectors of the nation, with proper regard for environmental values, by serving as a national resource for information analysis and technical expertise on a wide variety of energy initiatives.

Programs Specializes in developing public policy in the consumer interest. The Council is currently involved in studies on incorporating environmental externalities into utility planning, the economics of conservation versus conversion for home heating, and transmission siting and certification issues, including electromagnetic field effects.

Publication Monthly newsletter *The Quad Report*

For more Information List of Publications

Who's Who PRESIDENT MELVYN LESHINSKY • EXECUTIVE DIRECTOR ELLEN BERMAN DIRECTOR OF ADMINISTRATION JOAN VON DREHLE

FLORIDA SOLAR ENERGY CENTER

300 STATE ROAD 401   CAPE CANAVERAL FL 32920
PHONE (407) 783 0300

Founded 1974 • *Geographic Coverage* State

Mission To conduct research on alternative energy technologies, to ensure the quality of solar energy equipment in Florida, and to educate Floridians about their energy options. The Center operates within the state university system under the University of Central Florida.

Programs The Center's Photovoltaics R&D program focuses on the development and integration of solar electric systems into utility, residential and stand-alone applications. The Center's R&D program also focuses on a number of other areas, including advances in housing technologies to increase quality, efficiency and affordability; solar-hydrogen production, storage and utilization; alternative transportation fuels, including hythane, natural gas and methanol; solar-related technologies for detoxifying hazardous wastes; the refinement of solar water heating systems for both institutional and residential applications; and the development of computer software to aid energy research. Education and training of students and professionals.

Publications Newsletter *Solar Collector* published three times per year, circulation 47,000. Various fact sheets focusing on energy and solar energy issues, as well as global environmental concerns. Numerous publications for energy consumers as well as the academic, research and governmental sectors

Multimedia FSEC documents, including *Solar Collector* are accessible through computer modems

For more Information Annual Report, Library

Who's Who PRESIDENT R. A. BOB LAVETTE • VICE PRESIDENT STEVEN K. GORMAN EXECUTIVE DIRECTOR DAVID L. BLOCK • DIRECTOR INSTITUTIONAL AFFAIRS COLLEEN KETTLES • EDITOR CAROLYN KING BURNS

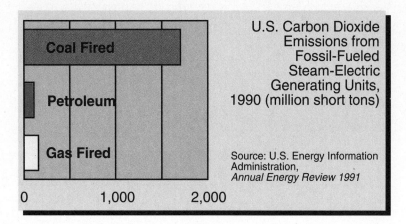

U.S. Carbon Dioxide Emissions from Fossil-Fueled Steam-Electric Generating Units, 1990 (million short tons)

Source: U.S. Energy Information Administration, *Annual Energy Review 1991*

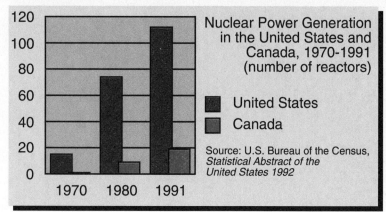

Nuclear Power Generation in the United States and Canada, 1970-1991 (number of reactors)

Source: U.S. Bureau of the Census, *Statistical Abstract of the United States 1992*

GE STOCKHOLDERS' ALLIANCE

P.O. BOX 22753   ST. PETERSBURG FL 33742-2753
PHONE (813) 576 7750   FAX (813) 576 5070

Founded 1980 • *Geographic Coverage* National, Global • *Focused Regions* Wherever GE has influence • *Other Field of Focus* Pollution / Radiations

Mission To pressure General Electric (GE) to close its nuclear power operations and convert to radiation cleanup technologies; to terminate weapons contracts and convert to socially useful consumer products; to halt production of toxic and radioactive wastes and clean up all sites for which it is responsible; to promote and market energy efficiency and renewable energy systems. The Alliance believes that a Sustainable National Energy Policy is the foundation of a healthy domestic economy, that conversion of the militarized US society to production of socially useful and environmentally sound consumer products will help restore the country to economic and social health, and that environmental responsibility is essential for a sustainable future.

Annual Fees *Regular* $25

Programs Submits stockholder proposals for GE's annual meeting. Meets privately with GE management to discuss issues of energy, weapons and environmental pollution. Meets with institutional GE stockholders to discuss need for greater GE responsibility and leadership. Works for local, state and federal legislation for safe energy, conversion, and pollution control and prevention.

Who's Who PRESIDENT **PATRICIA T. BIRNIE**

INSTITUTE FOR ENERGY AND ENVIRONMENTAL RESEARCH

6935 LAUREL AVENUE   TAKOMA PARK MD 20912
PHONE (301) 270 5500   FAX (301) 270 3029

Founded 1985 • *Geographic Coverage* National, Global • *Coope-*

rative Partner Institut fur Energie und Umweltforschung e.V. - Heidelberg, West Germany

Mission To bring scientific excellence to public policy issues, to promote the democratization of science and a healthier environment, and to provide citizens and policy makers with sound scientific information. The organization produces technical studies on a wide range of policy issues of importance to the protection and restoration of the environment, and offers technical training and consultation to make scientific materials more accessible to activists and policy makers.

Programs The Institute's Project on the Nuclear Weapons Complex researches the health, technical and economic issues related to military and civilian nuclear fuel facilities. Project on Protection and Restoration of the Ozone Layer. Municipal solid waste management. Global climate change. Energy conservation. Third World energy policy.

Publications Books including *Plutonium: Deadly Gold of the Nuclear Age* • *Mending the Ozone Hole* • *High Level Dollars* • *Low Level Sense: A Critique of Present Policies for the Management of Long-Lived Radioactive Wastes and Discussion of an Alternative Approach* • *Radioactive Heaven and Earth: The Health and Environmental Effects of Nuclear Weapons Testing In, On, & Above the Earth*

For more Information Library, List of Publications

Who's Who PRESIDENT **ARJUN MAKHIJANI** • EXECUTIVE DIRECTOR **BERND FRANKE** LIBRARIAN **LOIS CHALMERS**

INSTITUTE FOR LOCAL SELF-RELIANCE (THE)

2425 18TH STREET, NW   WASHINGTON DC 20009-2096
PHONE (202) 232 4108   FAX (202) 332 0463

Founded 1974 • *Geographic Coverage* National • *Other Field of Focus* Waste - Management / Disposal / Treatment / Recycling

Mission To promote environmentally sound development through perti-

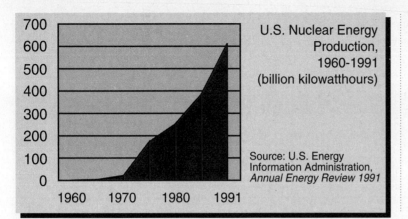

U.S. Nuclear Energy
Production,
1960-1991
(billion kilowatthours)

Source: U.S. Energy
Information Administration,
Annual Energy Review 1991

► The recent development of variable-speed wind turbines will further reduce the costs to produce electricity and increase their use. These allow operators to take advantage of shifting and wind intensities that stymied older turbines. Solar energy also faces technological barriers. It is a very dispersed resource, making for costly electricity generation. The best applications are local, apart from a utility power grid.

THE EIA PREDICTS THAT THE USE of renewable resources will continue to grow, but its share of the increasing electricity supply will stay at about 12 percent through the year 2010. However, renewable resources could make more substantial contributions if their costs to generate electricity should ►

Chapter 10 • Energy • Alternative & Renewable Energies

nent research and technical assistance. The Institute's goals include achieving a dramatic reduction in the US per capita consumption of raw materials, and a shift from US dependence on fossil fuels to a reliance on renewable resources (such as solar energy and biomass). The Institute's main focus is on the economic development of recycling related industries, particularly locally based manufacturing operations, and development of renewable sources of energy, particularly ethanol and plant-matter based production.

Funding

Foundations	Other
85%	15%

Total Income $1,039,959

Usage

Administration	Fundraising	Programs
13.5%	9%	77.5%

Programs Recycling programs.

Publications Various monographs, books and studies including *In-Depth Studies of Recycling and Composting Programs: Designs, Costs, Results* • *Co-Collection of Recyclables and Mixed Waste: Problems and Opportunities* • *Beyond 40 Percent: Record-Setting Recycling and Composting Programs* • *Waste Reduction, Recycling, and Composting for Camden County, New Jersey*. Directory *Waste Utilization Technologies in Europe and the United States*. Numerous publications focusing on waste management, renewable resources, and self-reliance related issues

For more Information Database, Library, List of Publications

Who's Who PRESIDENT **NEIL N. SELDMAN** • VICE PRESIDENT **DAVID MORRIS** • TREASURER **JAN SIMPSON** • CONTACT **INGRID KOMAR**

INTERNATIONAL INSTITUTE FOR ENERGY CONSERVATION

750 FIRST STREET, NE, SUITE 940
PHONE (202) 842 3388

WASHINGTON DC 20002
FAX (202) 842 1565

Founded 1984 • *Geographic Coverage* Global • *Focused Countries* Thailand, and Chile specifically • *Cooperative Partners* Thailand's National Energy Administration, Energy Conservation Center of Thailand, Chilean National Energy Commission, Natural Resources Defense Council, Tata Energy Research Institute - New Delhi, Comision Nacional para el Ahorro de Energia - Mexico • *Chapters* 2, in Bangkok - Thailand, and Santiago - Chile

Mission To accelerate global adoption of energy-efficiency policies, technologies, and practices in order to enable economic and ecologically sustainable development. The Institute's activities focus on industrializing countries, including those in central and eastern Europe. Global warming, energy efficiency, and transportation issues are the Institute's main areas of focus.

Funding

Foundations	Interest & Other
97%	3%

Total Income $2,064,320

Usage

Administration	Fundraising	Programs
1%	1%	98%

Total Expenses $2,021,824

Programs Demand-Side Management Program assists in the development of policies, legislation, and information that promote energy efficiency. Private Sector Initiatives Program. Transportation program. Training and information. Provides advisors to multilateral development banks. Serves as the secretariat for the Global Energy Efficiency Initiative.

Publications Quarterly newsletters *E-Notes* • *Banknote*. Reports on various topics. Numerous publications focusing on transportation and energy efficiency

For more Information Annual Report, Database, List of Publications

Who's Who PRESIDENT **DEBORAH LYNN BLEVISS** • VICE PRESIDENT **PATRICK J. KEEGAN** • CHAIRPERSON **ROBERT L. PRATT** • TREASURER **JAMES W. O'BRIEN** • PUBLIC RELATIONS MANAGER **KRISTIN RALFF**

fall below the generating costs of coal and natural gas. Technological advances and regulatory changes will require increased investments. This means higher energy costs - and in the current economic climate, American political leaders are unlikely to let this happen. But as the need for a clean and green environment gains strength as a cultural value, the people who are becoming our political and industrial leaders will be motivated by that value and find the funds to create cleaner, more energy-efficient transportation and industrial processes. This transition will be evolutionary, not revolutionary and it will be measured in decades - unless a passionate electorate demands more rapid change and is willing to pay for that change. •

Lyn Corum

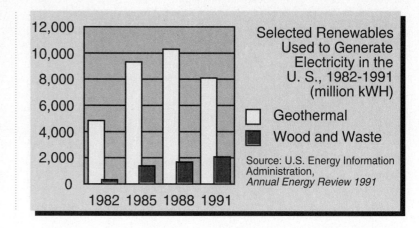

Selected Renewables Used to Generate Electricity in the U. S., 1982-1991 (million kWH)

☐ Geothermal
■ Wood and Waste

Source: U.S. Energy Information Administration, *Annual Energy Review 1991*

NATIONAL CENTER FOR APPROPRIATE TECHNOLOGY

3040 CONTINENTAL DRIVE, BOX 3838   BUTTE MT 59702
PHONE (406) 494 4572

Founded 1976 • *Geographic Coverage* National • *Other Field of Focus* Sustainable Development / Agriculture - Environmental Technologies *Cooperative Partners* US Department of Energy, The Montana Power Company, US Department of Health and Human Services, US Department of Interior

Mission To develop and promote energy efficiency and renewable energy technologies. The Center's energy program strives to synthesize often complex technical information so that it can be easily applied by a wide range of audiences. The organization operates NATAS, a program that provides technical and commercialization assistance services, under contract to the US Department of Energy.

Programs NATAS (National Appropriate Technology Assistance Service) provides support to projects in the US that use renewable energy and energy efficient technologies. ATTRA (Appropriate Technology Transfer for Rural Areas) helps farmers reduce dependence on chemical fertilizers, prevent soil erosion, and conserve water.

Publications Numerous publications focusing on energy conservation and superinsulation, mobile home weatherization, solar heating for home and harvest, independent power production, farm energy, waste recovery, and energy education

Multimedia Online information services 1-800-428-2525 • in Montana 1-800-428-1718

For more Information List of Publications

Who's Who CONTACT GEORGE EVERETT

NORTHERN CALIFORNIA SOLAR ENERGY ASSOCIATION

P.O. BOX 3008   BERKELEY CA 94703
PHONE (510) 869 2759

Founded 1974 • *Geographic Coverage* Local • *Cooperative Partner* American Solar Energy Association

Mission To promote and provide education about solar and renewable energy.

Annual Fees	Regular	Student/Senior	Corporation	Small Business
	$20	$15	$100	$50

Publication Quarterly newsletter

NUCLEAR FREE AMERICA   PAGE 185

325 EAST 25TH STREET   BALTIMORE MD 21218
PHONE (410) 235 3575   FAX (410) 235 5457

PACIFIC ENERGY INSTITUTE

101 YESLER WAY, SUITE 606   SEATTLE WA 98104
PHONE (206) 628 0460   FAX (206) 628 0953

Founded 1982 • *Geographic Coverage* Regional • *Chapter* 1

Mission The Institute focuses on education concerning resource conservation projects, such as waste reduction, recycling, and energy efficiency.

Funding	Foundations	Fees for Services
	14%	86%

Total Income $350,000

Usage	Administration	Fundraising	Programs
	10%	5%	85%

Total Expenses $345,000

Publication Quarterly newsletter

For more Information Database, Library, List of Publications

PUBLIC CITIZEN
CRITICAL MASS ENERGY PROJECT

215 PENNSYLVANIA AVENUE, SE   WASHINGTON DC 20003
PHONE (202) 546 4996   FAX (202) 547 7392

Founded 1974 • *Geographic Coverage* National • *Individual Members* 140,000

Mission To decrease reliance on nuclear and fossil fuels and to promote safe, economical, and environmentally sound energy alternatives, by preparing and disseminating reports, lobbying Congress, and acting as a watchdog over key energy regulatory agencies. The organization takes its name from founder Ralph Nader's observation that "a critical mass of people can make the critical difference" in winning a sustainable energy future.

Annual Fees *Regular* $20

Funding

Membership	Foundations
90%	10%

Total Income $6,363,641

Usage

Administration	Fundraising	Programs	Other
13%	15.5%	60.9%	10.6%

Programs Health research group. Litigation group. Congress Watch. Buyers Up. Critical Mass.

Publications Numerous publications focusing on energy issues

Who's Who PRESIDENT JOHN CLAYBROOK • DIRECTOR CRITICAL MASS PROGRAM BILL MAGAVERN

REDWOOD ALLIANCE

P.O. BOX 293   ARCATA CA 95521
PHONE (707) 822 7884

Founded 1978 • *Geographic Coverage* Local, Regional, National • *Individual Members* 5,200

Mission The Redwood Alliance is a community-based social and environmental organization whose main focus is advocacy and education to promote safe and efficient energy use and development. The Alliance is currently working on a wide range of issues, including nuclear waste and renewable energy.

Funding

Corporations	Foundations	Direct Mail & Events
5%	40%	55%

Total Income $35,000

Usage

Administration	Fundraising	Programs
30%	10%	60%

Programs Ward Valley Nuclear Waste Dump. Renewable Energy Computer Communications System. Photovoltaic Demo Center.

Publication Quarterly newsletter *Nuclear Free Times*

For more Information Library

Who's Who CONTACT MICHAEL WELCH

RENEWABLE ENERGY DEVELOPMENT INSTITUTE

733 SOUTH MAIN STREET   WILLITS CA 95490
PHONE (707) 459 1256   FAX (707) 459 0366

Founded 1993 • *Geographic Coverage* National, Global • *Cooperative Partners* Electrathon America, Rocky Mountain Institute, Solar Electric Industry Association, American Hydrogen Association • *Chapter* 1

Mission The Institute promotes and advocates research on renewable energy, demonstration, education, and application.

Funding

Membership	Corporations	Foundations	Special Events
50%	20%	20%	10%

Total Income $50,000

Usage

Administration	Fundraising	Programs
10%	10%	80%

Programs Solar Industry Conference. Solar Electric Exposition. REDI Education/Demonstration Center.

For more Information Database, Library

Who's Who PRESIDENT KEITH RUTLEDGE • VICE PRESIDENT WAYNE ROBERTSON SECRETARY PHIL JERGENSON • TREASURER DAVE LEVERETT • EXECUTIVE DIRECTOR JANET ORTH • LIBRARIAN THEO FERGUSON • CONTACT BIRDIE WILSON

SOLAR ENERGY INDUSTRIES ASSOCIATION

777 NORTH CAPITOL STREET, NE   WASHINGTON DC 20002-4226
PHONE (202) 408 0660   FAX (202) 408 8536

Founded 1974 • *Geographic Coverage* National, Global • *Cooperative Partner* Solar Energy Research and Education Foundation *Organization Members* 350

Mission To promote the use and development of solar energy.

Programs Sponsored Solar Energy Forum, the largest solar energy conference held in the US during the past decade. A variety of renewable energy events allowed entrepreneurs, engineers, technicians, government officials, and academics to meet and discuss present and future solar energy programs.

Publications Quarterly *Solar Industry Journal.* Various books including *Solar Industry Green Plan, A Call for Action* • *Solar Energy Uses in the Utility Sector* • *Building for the Caribbean Basin and Latin America* • *Active Solar Heating Systems Design Manual* • *Private Financing for the Power Sector: the Renewable Energy Option* • *Improving the Quality of Life with Renewable Energy: Highlights of U.S. Private Sector Applications in USAID-Assisted Countries* • *Directory of the U.S. Solar Thermal Industry*

For more Information List of Publications

Who's Who PRESIDENT BARRY L. BUTLER • VICE PRESIDENT WALTER HESSE • SECRETARY FREEMAN FORD • EXECUTIVE DIRECTOR SCOTT SKLAR

SOLARTHERM, INC.

1315 APPLE AVENUE   SILVER SPRING MD 20910
PHONE (301) 587 8686

Founded 1977 • *Geographic Coverage* Global

Mission To develop, apply, research, and implement solar energy systems on an international basis. The organization has developed products which offer a potential breakthrough in the use of solar energy for practical applications (solar cell-electric panel, solar-powered generats). Currently, Solartherm is focusing on photovoltaic systems, solar coal desulfurization systems, and solar reactors using Fresnel lenses.

Who's Who PRESIDENT CARL SCHLEICHER

Canada

CANADIAN WIND ENERGY ASSOCIATION

2415 HOLLY LANE   OTTAWA ON K1V 7P2
PHONE (613) 737 0524   FAX (613) 736 8938

Founded 1985 • *Geographic Coverage* National • *Cooperative Partners* American Wind Energy Association, Solar Energy Society of Canada • *Organization Members* 55 • *Individual Members* 170

Mission To promote wind energy and the wind energy industry in Canada.

Annual Fees	Regular	Student/Senior	Organization	Corporation
	$50	$30	$100	$300

Publications Quarterly bulletin. Source directory. Conference proceedings

For more Information Database, Library

Who's Who PRESIDENT MIKE BOURNS • VICE PRESIDENT BERNARD SAULNIER SECRETARY ROB BRANDON • TREASURER PAUL LIDDY • LIBRARIAN CHI LE

ENERGY PROBE RESEARCH FOUNDATION

225 BRUNSWICK AVENUE   TORONTO ON M5S 2M6
PHONE (416) 964 9223   FAX (416) 964 8239

Founded 1980 • *Geographic Coverage* National • *Other Field of Focus* Sustainable Development / Agriculture - Environmental Technologies

Mission To educate Canadians about the benefits of sound resource use; to promote the democratic process by encouraging individual responsibility and accountability; to provide business, government, and the public with information on energy, environmental, and related issues; and to help Canada contribute to global harmony and prosperity.

Funding	Foundations	Contributed Services & Materials	Other
	35%	30%	8.5%

Other Sources *Recovery of Costs of Hearings & Court Challenges* 26.5%

Total Income $2,149,251

Usage	Administration	Programs
	59%	41%

Total Expenses $2,061,772

Programs The Foundation is comprised of distinct divisions, Energy Probe, Probe International, Environment Probe, and the Margaret Laurence Fund - established to celebrate the accomplishments of one of the Foundation's most celebrated directors and ensure the continuation of her work at the Foundation.

Publications Numerous publications focusing on radiation health risks, energy and utility reform, nuclear power, nuclear waste, reactor safety, economics of nuclear power, alternative energy and conservation, energy policy and utility reform, global warming, transportation, reactors exports and weapons proliferation, water resource policy, electricity exports and pricing, rainforests, foreign aid, hydro dams, energy issues, resettlement

Multimedia Recorded material. Series of 90-second radio programs

For more Information Annual Report, List of Publications

Who's Who PRESIDENT WALTER PITMAN • SECRETARY ANNETTA TURNER • EXECUTIVE DIRECTOR PROBE INTERNATIONAL PATRICIA ADAMS • EXECUTIVE DIRECTOR ENVIRONMENT PROBE LAWRENCE SOLOMON • OFFICE MANAGER SANDRA CHANNER

NATIONAL ENERGY CONSERVATION ASSOCIATION

P.O. BOX 3214   WINNIPEG MB R3C 4E7
PHONE (204) 783 1273   FAX (204) 774 6702

Founded 1983 • *Geographic Coverage* National, Global • *Chapters* 10

Mission To champion and foster energy conservation in order to ease the strain put on the environment.

Annual Fees	Regular	Organization	Corporation
	$60	$250	$250

Funding	Membership	Corporations	Consulting Fees
	7.2%	21.4%	71.4%

Total Income $1,400,000

Usage	Administration	Programs	Other
	5.7%	92.8%	1.5%

Total Expenses $1,400,000

Programs Training. Technical Research. Program Development.

Publications Quarterly newsletter. Magazine. Technical reports

For more Information Database, Library

Who's Who PRESIDENT PETER ETHERINGTON • VICE PRESIDENT TONY WOODS • EXECUTIVE DIRECTOR LAVERNE DANGLEISH

PLANETARY ASSOCIATION FOR CLEAN ENERGY, INC.
100 BRONSON AVENUE   OTTAWA ON K1R 6G8
PHONE (613) 236 6265   FAX (613) 235 5876

Founded 1976 • *Geographic Coverage* Global • *Cooperative Partner* National Research Council of Canada • *Individual Members* 3,600

Mission To develop an international, interdisciplinary network of scientists, other individuals, and organizations to research, develop, demonstrate, and evaluate "clean energy systems" for eventual implementation on a planetary-wide scale with the guidance of the Association.

Annual Fees	Regular	Student/Senior	Families	Organization
	$45	$30	$75	$300

Other Fees *Lifetime* $500 • *Corporation* $1,000 • *Supporting* $100 • *National Affiliate* $450

Publications New releases include *Plasma Systems With Separated Electrical Charges* • *Bioenergetic Phenomena: Their Physics and Modeling*. Newsletter published at least four times per year. Various publications focusing on emerging science, electromagnetic hygiene, built environment, and subtle energy

For more Information Database, List of Publications

Who's Who PRESIDENT A. MICHROWSKI

SMALL POWER PRODUCERS ASSOCIATION OF ALBERTA
BOX 58   CLARESHOLM AB T0L 0T0
PHONE (403) 625 2127

Founded 1985 • *Geographic Coverage* Province • *Organization Members* 15 • *Individual Members* 90

Mission To produce electric power from environmentally friendly renewable sources.

Annual Fees	Regular	Corporation
	$25	$1,000

Funding *Membership* 100%

Publication Annual newsletter

Who's Who PRESIDENT ORRIN HART • SECRETARY STEVE SEARS • TREASURER DAVID MULHOLLAND

SOLAR ENERGY SOCIETY OF CANADA, INC.
72 ROBERTSON ROAD   NEPEAN ON K2H 9R6
PHONE (613) 596 1067   FAX (613) 596 1120

Founded 1973 • *Geographic Coverage* National • *Chapters* 8
Members 1,100 including organizations

Mission To promote solar and other renewable energy sources to the general public.

Annual Fees	Regular	Student/Senior	Corporation	Library	Supporting
	$45	$20	$125	$75	$1,000

Funding	Membership	Government Support	Corporations	Foundations
	6%	58%	5%	15%

Other Sources *Conference Fees & Publication Sales* 16%

Total Income $330,542

Usage	Administration	Programs
	55%	45%

Total Expenses $389,088

Programs Great Canadian Solar Race. Bolton Scholarship Fund. Youth Science Foundation Fairs.

Publications Bimonthly magazine *SOL Magazine*, circulation 2,000. Guide *Photovoltaic Systems: A Buyer's Guide*. Annual conference proceedings

For more Information Database, Library

Who's Who PRESIDENT CHRISTIAN OUELLET • VICE PRESIDENT EZRA AUERBACH SECRETARY RICHARD KADULSKI • TREASURER MARC SAUVÉ • EXECUTIVE DIRECTOR SOL MAGAZINE DON RUTHERFORD • CONTACT KELLY DOUGLAS

food • pesticides consumerism & safety

CHAPTER 11

The Poison on our Plate : The Future of Pesticides, by Joel Grossman

FEW PEOPLE WILL ARGUE AGAINST the need for a safe food supply. Safety means keeping harmful pesticides in check and keeping consumer goods secure for people and the environment. However, the task of analyzing the risks to human health and the environment seems to be fraught with more questions than answers. For example, what constitutes an acceptable risk? How much weight should we give the benefits associated with a risky yet protective technology? Do we divide risks that can be voluntarily chosen, such as cigarette smoking, from risks over which we have no control, such as exposure to secondary smoke or unlabeled pesticide residues in food? How do we deal with a chemical in the food supply that is a hazard only to selected groups, such as children, the elderly, or people with a specific gene or those with weakened immune systems? With limited budgets, how should we prioritize which risks to study, limit or remedy? Questions such as these are propelling risk assessment to the forefront of environmental discussions on food, pesticides, consumerism, and safety.

RISK ASSESSMENT INVOLVES FIRST identifying the nature, source,

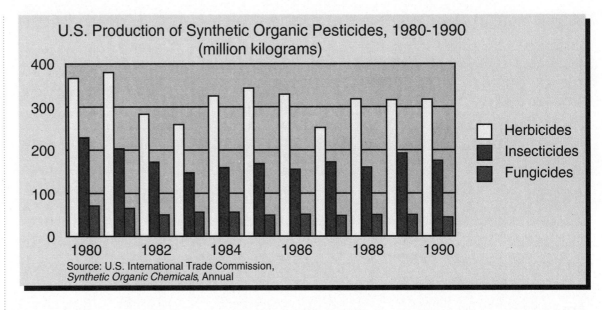

U.S. Production of Synthetic Organic Pesticides, 1980-1990 (million kilograms)

Legend: Herbicides, Insecticides, Fungicides

Source: U.S. International Trade Commission, *Synthetic Organic Chemicals*, Annual

action mechanism, and potential adverse consequences of the risk factor. Next, the source of the risk must be described, including the intensity, frequency and duration of human or environmental exposure to the risk agent. The relationship between dosage of the risk agent and the health or environmental consequences must be discerned and all data must be integrated in order to uncover the overall risk. Even in the case of long-used pesticides, there are many data gaps which make risk assessment incomplete. What's more, much data on older pesticides is

unreliable due to human and scientific failures. But even when information is available, it is not well disseminated. Consumers are typically provided no point-of-purchase information, and, thus, have little choice or control over the pesticides in their food supply. Often, this sets the stage for consumer activism. Registering a new pesticide with the US Environmental Protection Agency (EPA) under the Federal Insecticide, Fungicide, and Rodenticide Act (FIFRA) typically requires more than two dozen tests. These procedures use non-target species to study

the effects and environmental fate of oral and dermal transmission of subchronic and chronic toxic substances. Canadian laws and health concerns are similar to those in the United States. The 1988 Canada-United States Trade Agreement led the two countries to form joint working groups to ensure that the health pesticide standards and regulatory systems of their environmental agencies will be synchronized and equivalent. Deficiencies in the Delaney Amendment to the Federal Food, Drug, and Cosmetic Act (FDCA), which prohibits carcinogenic food additives, illustrates the current food safety regulatory morass and the need for reform.

UNDER DELANEY, PESTICIDES sprayed on fruits and vegetables which are consumed raw are not classified as additives; they can be carcinogenic under the current law. In contrast, pesticides in canned or processed commodities are considered food additives, and cannot legally be carcinogenic. The rules and regulations also make for bizarre cases. At Arrowhead Mills in Texas, the Food and Drug Administration (FDA) seized silos of organic grain because the company controlled granary pests with beneficial insects, a prohibited additive, instead of approved pesticides. After national media attention and almost three years of discussions between ►

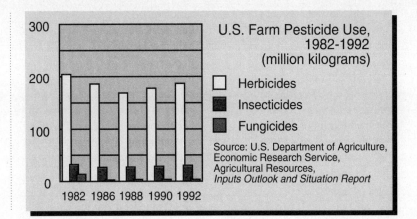

U.S. Farm Pesticide Use, 1982-1992 (million kilograms)

□ Herbicides
■ Insecticides
■ Fungicides

Source: U.S. Department of Agriculture, Economic Research Service, Agricultural Resources, *Inputs Outlook and Situation Report*

1982 1986 1988 1990 1992

United States

BEE MOUNTAIN COMMUNITY

THE FIR, TOWER HOUSE   WEITCHPEC CA 95546

Founded 1979 • *Geographic Coverage* Local • *Cooperative Partners* Californians for Alternatives to Toxic Sprays, Environmental Protection and Information Center, Northcoast Environmental Center • *Individual Members* 80

Mission To prevent herbicide applications to the surrounding forestlands.

BIO-INTEGRAL RESOURCE CENTER (THE)

P.O. BOX 7414   BERKELEY CA 94707
PHONE (510) 524 2567   FAX (510) 524 1758

Founded 1978 • *Geographic Coverage* Global

Mission To help reduce pesticide use by providing practical information and services in the area of "least-toxic" pest control, also known as Integrated Pest Management (IPM).

Annual Fees	Regular	Student/Senior	Corporation	Patron
	$30	$30	$50	$100

Funding	Membership	Foundations	Other
	26%	21%	53%

Total Income $371,273

Publications Technical journal *The IPM Practitioner* published 10 times per year. *Common Sense Pest Control Quarterly* featuring "How-to" articles. Several small publications on least-toxic pest management methods

Multimedia Various slide shows, videos and audiotapes on pest management

For more Information Database, Library, List of Publications

Who's Who PRESIDENT IRENE JUNIPER • SECRETARY GRACE RICO-PENA

CALIFORNIANS FOR ALTERNATIVES TO TOXICS

860 1/2 11TH STREET   ARCATA CA 95521
PHONE (707) 822 8497   FAX (707) 822 8497

Founded 1981 • *Geographic Coverage* State • *Chapter* 1 • *Organization Members* 200 • *Individual Members* 3,500

Mission To give Californians greater choice and control over what they are exposed to in the environment, through a program centered around providing education and information on alternatives to toxic pesticides.

Annual Fees *Regular* $5

Funding	Membership	Government Support	Foundations	Other
	10%	12.7%	13.4%	1.9%

Other Sources *Volunteer In-kind Donations* 62%

Total Income $78,570

Usage	Administration	Fundraising	Programs	Other
	12.8%	12.4%	60%	14.8%

Total Expenses $70,140

Programs Methyl Bromide/Ozone Depletion Program. Forest Spraying Program. Caltrans Spraying Program. Community Outreach Program.

Publications Quarterly newsletter *The Drift Dodger*. Report *Into the Sunlight: Exposing Methyl Bromide's Threat to the Ozone Layer*

For more Information Database, Library

Who's Who PRESIDENT CAROL WILLIAMS • VICE PRESIDENT KAYE GALLAGHER SECRETARY MIKE MANETAS • TREASURER ROBERT HITCHCOCK • EXECUTIVE DIRECTOR PATRICIA CLARY • PROGRAM ASSISTANT ELAINE WEINREB • ADMINISTRATIVE ASSISTANT CATHERINE LEACH

► the US Department of Agriculture (USDA), the EPA and the FDA, beneficial insects were finally approved as a pesticide alternative for stored grains. The FDA, along with the Public Health Service and National Marine Fisheries Service share Agricultural Marketing Act authority over seafood inspection, which is voluntary and virtually nonexistent. The USDA, which inspects eggs, poultry, and meat for pathogens such as Salmonella, was unable in 1993 to prevent fast-food restaurant hamburger deaths from meat contaminated with E. coli. Food safety is clearly a major issue needing more attention. Even with abundant statutory authority, regulatory agencies often must be compelled by the courts to enforce the law to protect the food supply.

For example, only a 1993 US Supreme Court ruling could prod the EPA and FDA to enforce the often-ignored 1958 Delaney Amendment to the Federal Food, Drug, and Cosmetic Act, which prohibits food additives that cause cancer. However, as part of a 1994 broad reform policy for pesticides and food safety, legislation designed to reduce pesticide risks for infants and children is expected to officially eliminate the ignored Delaney Amendment. In its place will be a cost-benefit risk analysis already in use.

NEW FOOD SAFETY ISSUES ARE emerging with technological advances such as irradiated and genetically engineered food products, which are designed to boost production and improve shelf life. The technologies have their opponents. Chefs have

178

CENTER FOR SCIENCE INFORMATION, INC.
63 HOMESTEAD STREET SAN FRANCISCO CA 94114
PHONE (415) 861 4908

Founded 1982 • *Geographic Coverage* Global

Mission To educate decision makers and journalists, and through them reach the wider public on the various issues created or influenced by biotechnology. Areas of concern include food, genetic diversity, and agriculture.

Funding

Foundations	Publications Sales
80%	20%

Publications Various books including *Biotechnology Microbes and the Environment* - 1990 • *Biotechnology and Genetic Diversity* - 1985

Who's Who PRESIDENT STEVEN C. WITT • VICE PRESIDENT PAMELA W. KELLY

COMMUNITY ALLIANCE WITH FAMILY FARMERS PAGE 288
P.O. BOX 464 DAVIS CA 95617
PHONE (916) 756 8518 FAX (916) 756 7857

ENVIRONMENTAL HAZARDS MANAGEMENT INSTITUTE PAGE 202
10 NEWMARKET ROAD, P.O. BOX 932 DURHAM NH 03824
PHONE (603) 868 1496

ENVIRONMENTAL HEALTH COALITION PAGE 265
1717 KETTNER BOULEVARD, SUITE 100 SAN DIEGO CA 92101
PHONE (619) 235 0281

FARM ANIMAL REFORM MOVEMENT PAGE 216
FARM
P.O. BOX 30654 BETHESDA MD 20824
PHONE (301) 530 1737 FAX (301) 530 5747

FOOD ANIMALS CONCERNS TRUST, INC. PAGE 217
P.O. BOX 14599 CHICAGO IL 60614
PHONE (312) 525 4952

GREEN SEAL
1250 23RD STREET, NW, SUITE 275 WASHINGTON DC 20037-1101
PHONE (202) 331 7337 FAX (202) 331 7533

Founded 1990 • *Geographic Coverage* National

Mission To identify and promote environmentally friendly products and services, enabling consumers to identify and purchase environmentally preferable products. The organization focuses on environmental labeling of consumer products to identify those least harmful to the environment.

Funding *Foundations* 100%

Who's Who PRESIDENT NORMAN L. DEAN

MOTHERS AND OTHERS FOR A LIVABLE PLANET PAGE 266
40 WEST 20TH STREET, 11TH FLOOR NEW YORK NY 10011
PHONE (212) 727 4474 FAX (212) 675 6481

NATIONAL COALITION AGAINST THE MISUSE OF PESTICIDES
701 "E" STREET, SE WASHINGTON DC 20003
PHONE (202) 543 5450

Founded 1981 • *Geographic Coverage* National

Mission To further pesticide safety and the adoption of alternative pest management strategies which reduce or eliminate a dependency on toxic chemicals, by serving as a national network committee, and by working to affect change by supporting local action, assisting individuals and community-based organizations to stimulate discussion on the hazards of toxic pesticides, while providing information on safe alternatives.

organized against genetically engineered foods; and dairy-state family farmers, particularly in Wisconsin, protest against genetically engineered bovine growth hormone (BGH). They are calling for labels on BGH milk products to allow consumer choice. On the political side, farmers are questioning the use of BGH to boost milk production when the government is spending millions of dollars

buying up huge surpluses of dairy products. Marketers of genetically engineered foods often argue against labeling, saying that their food is safe, but that people would be scared by the label. However, some companies indicate that they will label their genetically engineered product to allow consumer choice in the marketplace. Some supermarket chains are independently ▶

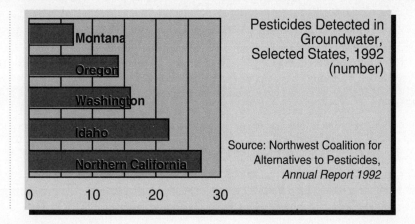

Pesticides Detected in Groundwater, Selected States, 1992 (number)

Source: Northwest Coalition for Alternatives to Pesticides, *Annual Report 1992*

Annual Fees	Regular	Student/Senior	Volunteer Organization	Public Interest Group
	$25	$15	$30	$50

Programs Disseminates information on pesticides as widely as possible. Advocates for changes in public policy related to pesticide use. Sponsors an annual National Pesticide Forum.

Publications Newsletter *Pesticides and You (PAY)* published 5 times per year. Monthly news bulletin *Technical Report*. Various books including *Unnecessary Risks: The Benefit Side of the Risk-Benefit Equation • Safety at Home: A Guide to the Hazards of Lawn and Garden Pesticides and Safer Ways to Manage Pests*. Numerous brochures and packet profiles focusing on different chemical pesticides, pesticide alternatives, and general pesticide issues. Various testimonies including *Children & Pesticides • Institutionalizing Cancer/Negligible Risks • Lawn Care Chemicals*

For more Information List of Publications

Who's Who EXECUTIVE DIRECTOR **JAY FELDMAN** • CONTACT **MARIA WASHINGTON**

NATIONAL PESTICIDE TELECOMMUNICATIONS NETWORK
TEXAS TECHNICAL UNIVERSITY HEALTH CENTER

DEPARTMENT OF PREVENTIVE MEDICINE   LUBBOCK TX 79430
PHONE (800) 858 7378

Founded 1984 • *Geographic Coverage* National, Indian Sub-continent *Other Fields of Focus* Environmental Education / Careers / Information / Networks, Public / Environmental Health

Mission To serve as a contact to the general public, medical professionals, industry, for information on pesticides. Information available includes health and chemical data as well as environmental information.

NORTHWEST COALITION FOR ALTERNATIVES TO PESTICIDES (THE)
P.O. BOX 1393   EUGENE OR 97440
PHONE (503) 344 5044

Founded 1977 • *Geographic Coverage* Regional • *Focused Region* US Pacific Northwest • *Organization Members* 100 • *Individual Members* 1,600

Mission To promote sustainable resource management, prevention of pest problems, use of alternatives to pesticides, and the right to be free from pesticide exposure. The organization strives to substantially reduce or eliminate the use of pesticides as a preferred method of pest control in the Northwest and elsewhere.

Annual Fees	Regular	Student/Senior	Associate	Sustaining
	$25	$15	$50	$100

Funding	Membership	Foundations	Sales
	59%	16%	25%

Total Income $200,000

Usage	Administration	Programs
	14%	86%

Total Expenses $215,000

Programs Inert ingredient identity disclosure. Groundwater protection. Forestry without pesticides. Sustainable agriculture. School pest control without pesticides.

Publications Quarterly magazine *The Journal of Pesticide Reform*, circulation 1,800. Numerous publications focusing on pesticide issues

For more Information Annual Report, Database, Library, List of Publications

Who's Who EXECUTIVE DIRECTOR **NORMA GRIER** • EDITOR **CAROLINE COX** • LIBRARIAN **KAY RUMSEY** • INFORMATION SERVICES COORDINATOR **CARRIE SWADENER**

PESTICIDE ACTION NETWORK
NORTH AMERICAN REGIONAL CENTER

116 NEW MONTGOMERY, SUITE 810   SAN FRANCISCO CA 94105
PHONE (415) 541 9140   FAX (415) 541 9253

► testing fresh fruits and vegetables to certify that the produce meets certain pesticide residue standards. Consumer choice is proliferating as more certified organic produce grown without synthetic pesticides or fertilizers enters mainstream commerce. On the hardgoods side, many producers and manufacturers are turning out energy efficient light bulbs, computers and appliances, organic cotton clothing, recycled commodities and renewable resources from the rainforest - to name a few. Some companies rebate cash to the nations and indigenous cultures whose resources they harvest for sale. In Canada and the United States, many consumers are voting with their money to send the message that going "green" is good business. •

Joel Grossman

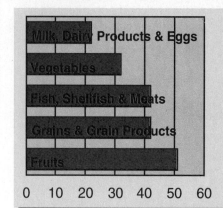

Pesticide Residues in Domestic Foods in the United States, 1991 (percentage of samples with residues found)

Source: U.S. Food & Drug Administration, Pesticide Program Residues in Foods

Founded 1982 • *Geographic Coverage* North America, Global *Chapters* 5, in Palmira - Colombia, Penang - Malaysia, Dakar - Senegal, Nairobi - Kenya, and London - England • *Organization Members* 300

Mission To promote and advocate adoption of ecologically sound practices in place of pesticide use, to increase the number and effectiveness of groups in Canada, Mexico and the USA working on local and global issues, and to promote development of an activist, international pesticide reform movement through people's initiatives.

Annual Fees *Organization* $50

Programs The Network monitors and disseminates information on pesticide use, and works to attack the root causes of pesticide dependence, and to increase the emphasis on lasting alternatives. International Pesticide Clearinghouse works to help meet the information needs of individuals and organizations as they address specific pesticide-related problems in the USA and internationally.

Publications Quarterly newsletter *Global Pesticide Campaigner*. Pesticide action alerts. Numerous publications focusing on biotechnology and pesticides

Multimedia Weekly online news *PAN North America Update Service*

For more Information Database, Library, List of Publications

Who's Who CONTACT MONICA MOORE

RACHEL CARSON COUNCIL

8940 JONES MILL ROAD   CHEVY CHASE MD 20815
PHONE (301) 652 1877

Founded 1965 • *Geographic Coverage* Global • *Cooperative Partners* United Nations Environment Programme, National Coalition Against the Misuse of Pesticides

Mission To educate the public, promote an interest in the environment, encourage conservation measures, and serve as a clearinghouse of information for the general public and the scientific community. The Council's major focus remains chemical contamination - in particular, the pesticide issue. The Council's current projects include publications on cancer and pesticides, and pets and garden pesticides.

Annual Fees *Regular* $15

Funding	*Government Support*	*Foundations*
	76%	24%

Total Income $111,000

Usage	*Administration*	*Fundraising*	*Programs*
	10%	3%	87%

Publications Newsletter. Books Rachel Carson's *Silent Spring* • *Basic Guide to Pesticides 1992*

Who's Who PRESIDENT DAVID B. MCGRATH • VICE PRESIDENT CLAIRE P. SMITH SECRETARY MARJORIE SMIGEL • TREASURER HOWARD WHITLOW • EXECUTIVE DIRECTOR DIANA M. POST

Canada

MACDONALD CAMPUS, MCGILL UNIVERSITY
21111 LAKESHORE ROAD   STE. ANNE DE BELLEVUE PQ H9X 3V9
PHONE (514) 398 7771   FAX (514) 398 7621

P.O. BOX 577   KEREMEOS BC V0X 1N0
PHONE (604) 499 2550   FAX (604) 499 2388

pollution radiations

CHAPTER 12

At What Risk Progress? by Carolyn L. Davis

FLYING INTO LOS ANGELES International Airport, passengers are first treated to a view of spectacular canyons, award-winning architecture, and smog. Lots of smog. To many people, air pollution like that found in Southern California skies is the most toxic form of industrial hazard in the country. Air pollution, however, is just one of the many environmental hazards facing the world today. It may be the most talked about and the most regulated, but hazardous and solid waste, groundwater, noise, and nuclear pollutions share in the destruction of the quality of life and health. There is another form of pollution that's gotten much less attention than industrial wastes. This pollution plays no favorites - it equally affects big-city dwellers and their rural counterparts. It's everywhere, it can't be seen by the human eye, it is the least regulated, and it is the least understood and least studied form of environmental hazard. It is radiation.

IF RECENT EPIDEMIOLOGIC STUDIES are shown to be correct, pollution from radiation waves may be one of the most deadly

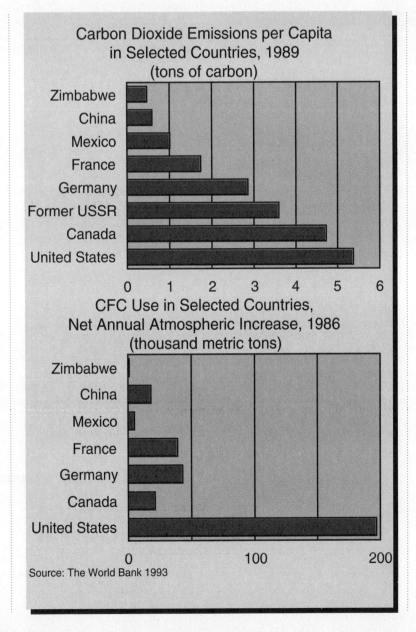

Carbon Dioxide Emissions per Capita in Selected Countries, 1989 (tons of carbon)

Zimbabwe, China, Mexico, France, Germany, Former USSR, Canada, United States — 0 1 2 3 4 5 6

CFC Use in Selected Countries, Net Annual Atmospheric Increase, 1986 (thousand metric tons)

Zimbabwe, China, Mexico, France, Germany, Canada, United States — 0 100 200

Source: The World Bank 1993

environmental hazards facing the world. And, as people buy more convenience devices to make their lives easier, and engage in activities to make themselves look healthier, the effects of radiation grow. Consider this scenario: the alarm clock radio wakes you at 6 a.m. You stumble out of bed, turn on the coffee maker, jump in the shower. Still in your towel, you blow dry and curl your hair in front of your make-up mirror. For breakfast, you pop a frozen breakfast into the microwave, drop a couple of pieces of bread into the toaster, and sit down for a few minutes in front of your television to see the weather and traffic reports. Once in your car, you check in with your secretary on the cellular phone, then turn up the volume on the car stereo. At the office, you work in front of the video display terminal. That afternoon, you leave the office early and head for the beach to spend a couple of hours working on your tan. Typical?

For many people, the answer is yes. Deadly? Growing scientific evidence indicates that radiation, in its many forms, is making us sick and certainly could be killing us. ▶

► MOST PEOPLE ASSOCIATE THE term "radiation" with radioactive waste, the kind identified with the Chernobyl tragedy in the former Soviet Union, or the Three Mile Island incident in Pennsylvania. To be sure, nuclear power's radioactive waste and the consequences of accidents are a global concern. But, in reality, the volume of radioactive waste in the United States has actually

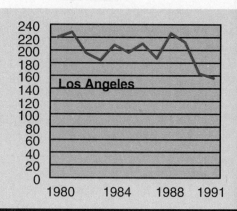

Air Quality in Selected U.S. Cities, 1980-1991 (number of PSI* days greater than 100)

* PSI = Pollutant Standards Index.
The PSI index integrates information from many pollutants across an entire monitoring network into a single number which represents the worst daily air quality experienced in the urban area. PSI index ranges and health effect descriptor words are as follows: 0 to 50 (good); 51 to 100 (moderate); 101 to 199 (unhealthful); 200 to 299 (very unhealthful); and 300 and above (hazardous). The chart shows the number of days when the PSI was greater than 100

Source: U.S. Environmental Protection Agency, Office of Air Quality Planning and Standards, *National Air Quality and Emissions Trends Report 1990*

182

United States

ABALONE ALLIANCE
SAFE ENERGY CLEARINGHOUSE
2940 16TH STREET, SUITE 310   SAN FRANCISCO CA 94103
PHONE (415) 861 0592

Founded 1977 • *Geographic Coverage* State, National, Global *Cooperative Partners* Don't Waste California, Bay Area Nuclear Waste Coalition, People's Earth Day Coalition • *Individual Members* 250

Mission To work for a permanent halt to the construction and operation of nuclear power plants in California, and to encourage the alternatives of conservation and safe, clean, and renewable sources of energy. The Alliance opposes nuclear power production and weapon proliferation, and favors sustainable development using renewable resources, conservation, and local control.

Annual Fees	Regular	Student/Senior	Families	Organization
	$25	$10	$20	$15

Other Fees *Lifetime* $500 • *Patron* $100

Funding	Membership	Foundations
	25%	75%

Total Income $8,500

Usage	Fundraising	Programs
	20%	80%

Programs People's Earth Day Celebration. Nuclear Day Dump Opposition. Computer Bulletin Board System Development.

Publications Quarterly newsletter *Ward Valley Alert*. Various information tracts on issues related to nuclear power, waste and safety

Multimedia Videos *Wake up California* • *A Question of Power*

For more Information Database, Library

Who's Who STAFF OFFICERS ROGER HERRIED, DON L. EICHELBERGER

ACID RAIN FOUNDATION, INC. (THE)   PAGE 34
1410 VARSITY DRIVE   RALEIGH NC 27606
PHONE (919) 737 3311

AIR CHEK, INC.
570 BUTLER BRIDGE ROAD   FLETCHER NC 28732
PHONE (800) 247 2435   FAX (704) 684 8498

Founded 1985 • *Geographic Coverage* National

Mission To provide the finest and fastest service to the radon testing professional, by offering a selection of do-it-yourself and laboratory-analyzed tests to help people detect and measure the presence of radon - a radioactive gas produced by the natural breakdown of uranium in the soil, which readily seeps from the ground through tiny cracks in a building's floor, foundation, or basement walls.

Publications Books including *Radon: Risk and Remedy* • *Radon: A Homeowner's Guide to Detection and Control / Radon Free*

Who's Who PRESIDENT B. V. ALVAREZ • VICE PRESIDENT JUDY ALVAREZ

ASBESTOS VICTIMS OF AMERICA   PAGE 263
P.O. BOX 559   CAPITOLA CA 95010
PHONE (408) 476 3646

CENTER FOR CITIZEN INITIATIVES
ENVIRONMENTAL PROGRAM   PAGE 104
3268 SACRAMENTO STREET   SAN FRANCISCO CA 94115
PHONE (415) 346 1875   FAX (415) 346 3731

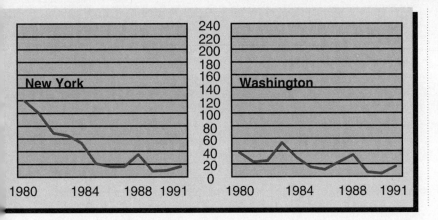

declined in the past 10 years, according to the Nuclear Regulatory Commission. Nuclear utilities and other generators are implementing innovative programs to minimize waste generation, are recycling when possible, and are using decontamination procedures or reduced radioactive volume when feasible. Public pressure and an increased awareness of the environment have prompted the nuclear industry to develop new technologies in radioactive waste disposal.

However, other forms of radiation are growing - most notably the electromagnetic and ultraviolet kind. In 1971, a council of US radiation experts noted there was a "distressing lack of data" on the possible "subtle, long-term, and cumulative effects" of low-level electromagnetic radiation. ▶

CENTER FOR SHORT-LIVED PHENOMENA (THE)

P.O. Box 199, Harvard Square Station   Cambridge MA 02238
Phone (617) 491 5100   Fax (617) 492 3312

Founded 1968 • *Geographic Coverage* Global

Mission To collect information about oil spills around the world including details of the sites, sources, particular substances, amounts, causes, clean-up actions, and environmental impacts.

Publications Biweekly newsletters *Golob's Oil Pollution Bulletin* • *Hazardous Materials Intelligence Report*

Multimedia Online information service 1-800-345-1301

Who's Who Vice President **Roger B. Wilson, Jr.** • Executive Director **Richard Golob**

COALITION FOR CLEAN AIR

122 Lincoln Boulevard, Suite 201   Venice CA 90291
Phone (310) 450 3190   Fax (310) 399 0769

Founded 1971 • *Geographic Coverage* Local • *Focused Region* Southern California

Mission To serve as a watchdog over government agencies and legislators, particularly the South Coast Air Quality Management District, to make sure they are enforcing the strict rules and regulations for air quality in the region; and to educate the public about air pollution through the speakers bureau.

Annual Fees	Regular	Student/Senior	Families	Sponsor	Patron
	$25	$15	$50	$100	$500

Programs Letter Writing Campaign. Speakers Bureau which educates the general public through presentations and literature. Office Angels Program. Annual Clean Air Awards. Conferences. Fundraisers.

Publication Quarterly newsletter *Clearing the Air*

Multimedia Slide show

Who's Who President **Tom Soto** • Vice Presidents **Jan Chatten-Brown**, **Ralph Perry** • Treasurer **Abby Arnold**

COMMITTEE FOR NUCLEAR RESPONSIBILITY, INC.

P.O. Box 421993   San Francisco CA 94142
Phone (415) 776 8299   Fax (415) 776 8299

Founded 1971 • *Geographic Coverage* National, Global • *Other Field of Focus* Public / Environmental Health

Mission To provide an independent analysis of the health effects from ionizing radiation. The Committee seeks to demonstrate that it is scientifically reasonable to use higher risk estimates than those offered by government sources.

Publications Books (available in Japanese, Chinese and Russian) *Radiation and Human Health* • *Radiation-Induced Cancer from Low-Dose Exposure* • *Radiation and Chernobyl: This Generation and Beyond.* Various short publications including *What About Reviving Nuclear Power* • *For Want of a Nail... the Rider Was Lost: A Big Flag of Warning from the Radiation Issue* • *The Greening of Nuclear Power and the De-regulating of Nuclear Waste: Four Key Facts Which Need Attention*

For more Information List of Publications

Who's Who President **John W. Gofman**

COUNCIL FOR A LIVABLE WORLD   PAGE 17

110 Maryland Avenue, NE, Suite 409   Washington DC 20002
Phone (202) 543 4100   Fax (202) 543 6297

ENVIRONMENTAL ACTION   PAGE 20

6900 Carroll Avenue, Suite 600   Takoma Park MD 20912
Phone (301) 891 1100   Fax (301) 891 2218

Today, electromagnetic radiation still receives little attention. So far, most studies have focused on extremely low frequency (ELF) electromagnetic fields created by electricity transmission. This form of radiation is transmitted from products we use every day: cordless and cellular phones, hair dryers, baby monitors, toasters, pencil sharpeners, electric shavers... The list is endless. ELF is also found in power lines.

IN 1992, TWO LONG-TERM STUDIES from Sweden showed links between exposure to ELF fields and certain forms of cancer. One study found an increase in brain cancer and leukemia in men exposed to ELF fields in several work situations. The other study found a three-times-higher-than-normal rate of leukemia in children who live near power lines. The most frightening of the studies' conclusions was that harm resulted from relatively little exposure - only a few times more than most people experience every day from appliances in their homes and offices. In January 1993, Sweden's Radiation Protection Institute became the first in the world to officially recommend taking steps to reduce the fields "where such countermeasures can be made at reasonable cost". The government institute offered examples such as moving beds away from the corner of rooms where electrical lines enter homes. Sweden remains the only country to make official recommendations.

For US workers, the dangers of computer terminal radiation are becoming better understood. Several studies in the ▶

ENVIRONMENTAL RESEARCH FOUNDATION PAGE 202
P.O. BOX 5036 ANNAPOLIS MD 21403-7036
PHONE (410) 263 1584 FAX (410) 263 8944

GE STOCKHOLDERS' ALLIANCE PAGE 170
P.O. BOX 22753 ST. PETERSBURG FL 33742-2753
PHONE (813) 576 7750 FAX (813) 576 5070

GLOBAL RESPONSE
ENVIRONMENTAL ACTION NETWORK
P.O. BOX 7490 BOULDER CO 80306-7490
PHONE (303) 444 0306

Founded 1990 • *Geographic Coverage* Global • *Organization Members* 400 • *Individual Members* 4,500

Mission Global Response is an international letter-writing network focusing on the transfer of pollution or polluting technologies between countries and the exploitation of resources by multinational companies. Each monthly *G.R. Action* highlights a specific environmental threat, recommends action to take, and gives the names and addresses of the corporations responsible.

Annual Fees *Regular* $12

Funding	Membership	Foundations
	20%	80%

Usage	Administration	Fundraising	Programs
	45%	5%	50%

Publications Monthly *Global Response Action* • *Young Environmentalist's Action* for students. *Action Status*

Who's Who PRESIDENT ROY YOUND • VICE PRESIDENT ERIC LOMBARDI • SECRETARY WALTER KINGSBERY

GRASS ROOTS ENVIRONMENTAL ORGANIZATION, INC. PAGE 227
P.O. BOX 289 HOPE NJ 07844
PHONE (908) 841 9512

GREENPEACE, INC. PAGE 23
1436 "U" STREET, NW WASHINGTON DC 20009
PHONE (202) 462 1177 FAX (202) 462 4507

HEAL THE BAY PAGE 110
1640 FIFTH STREET, SUITE 112 SANTA MONICA CA 90401
PHONE (310) 394 4552 FAX (310) 395 6878

LABOR COMMUNITY STRATEGY CENTER PAGE 195
3780 WILSHIRE BOULEVARD, SUITE 1200 LOS ANGELES CA 90010
PHONE (213) 387 2800 FAX (213) 387 3500

NATIONAL ASSOCIATION OF NOISE CONTROL OFFICIALS
53 CUBBERLY ROAD TRENTON NJ 08690
PHONE (609) 984 4161

Founded 1978 • *Geographic Coverage* National, Global • *Individual Members* 35

Mission To provide a mechanism and opportunity for information exchange, discussion, and cooperative study for members, to promote laws to control noise, to sponsor use of best measurement analysis, and to cooperate with industry and the scientific community to reduce noise.

Annual Fees	Regular	Student/Senior
	$30	$15

Funding *Membership* 100%

Usage *Programs* 100%

Publication Periodical *Vibrations* published 4 to 6 times per year

Who's Who President **Frank Gomez** • Vice President **Ronald Buege** • Administrator **Edward J. Di Polvere**

NATIONAL COUNCIL ON RADIATION PROTECTION AND MEASUREMENT

7910 Woodmont Avenue, Suite 800   Bethesda MD 20814
Phone (301) 657 2652

Founded 1928 • *Geographic Coverage* National

Mission To collect, analyze, develop, and disseminate in the public interest information and recommendations about protection against radiation, and radiation measurements quantities and units, particularly those concerned with radiation protection.

Funding	Corporations	Contributions	Other
	20%	40%	40%

Total Income $1,600,000

Publications Over 100 NCRP reports, lectures, proceedings, commentaries, and statements

Who's Who President **Charles B. Meinhold** • Vice President **S. James Adelstein** • Secretary **W. Roger Ney**

NUCLEAR FREE AMERICA

325 East 25th Street   Baltimore MD 21218
Phone (410) 235 3575   Fax (410) 235 5457

Founded 1983 • *Geographic Coverage* National, North America *Other Field of Focus* Energy - Alternative / Renewable Energies

Mission To promote a nuclear free America.

Annual Fees *Subscription* $15

Publications Newsletter *The New Abolitionist*. Data on nuclear weapons makers. Publications *Nuclear Free Zone Organizing Packets* • *NFZ Information and Statistics*

For more Information Database, Library, List of Publications

Who's Who President **Rick Torgerson** • Vice President **Eugene McDowell** Executive Director **Chuck Johnson**

NUCLEAR INFORMATION AND RESOURCE SERVICE

1424 16th Street, NW   Washington DC 20036
Phone (202) 328 0002   Fax (202) 462 2183

Founded 1978 • *Geographic Coverage* National • *Other Field of Focus* Environmental Education / Careers / Information / Networks *Organization Members* 1,000 • *Individual Members* 4,000

Mission To serve as a networking and information clearinghouse for grassroots environmental movement, in the areas of nuclear power, radioactive waste, radiation, and sustainable energy.

Annual Fees	Regular	Student/Senior
	$35	$20

Funding	Membership	Foundations
	20%	80%

Total Income $300,000

Usage	Administration	Fundraising	Programs	Other
	11%	2%	82%	5%

Publications Biweekly newsletter *Nuclear Monitor*. Book *Energy Audit Manual*. Various reports and brochures

Who's Who Executive Director **Michael Mariotte**

PACIFIC ALASKA NETWORKING   PAGE 203

56250 Glenn Road   Homer AK 99603-9525
Phone (907) 235 7112   Fax (907) 235 7128

PHYSICIANS FOR SOCIAL RESPONSIBILITY

1000 16th Street, NW, Suite 810   Washington DC 20036
Phone (202) 785 3777   Fax (202) 785 3942

Founded 1961 • *Geographic Coverage* Global • *Cooperative Partner* The International Physicians for the Prevention of Nuclear War • *Chapters* 120 • *Individual Members* 20,000

Mission The organization, whose membership includes health professionals and supporters works to protect the environment and prevent nuclear war.

Annual Fees	Doctor	Non-Doctor
	$90	$35

Programs Department of Energy Health and Safety. Nuclear Testing Moratorium. Great Lakes Initiative. Polish Enviro Health Initiative. Lead Campaign. Military Spending to Human Needs. Global Environmental Task Force.

Publications *The PSR Quarterly: A Journal of Medicine and Global Survival*. Quarterly *PSR Reports*. Periodic *PSR Monitor*. Books including *Covering the Map: A Survey of Military Pollution Sites in the US* • *Dead Reckoning: A Critical Review of the Department of Energy's Epidemiologic Research*.

For more Information Database, Library

United States, Canada, and Finland have shown evidence of problems from prolonged exposure - specifically for pregnant women.

The radiation of computer video display terminals (VDT) routinely emit 3 milligauss (mG) units. Researchers in Finland found that women exposed to more than 3 mG from a VDT had more than three times as many miscarriages as those exposed to less than 1 mG.

MANY SCIENTISTS ARE STILL studying how radiation affects people. ELF and higher radio frequency (RF) signals, such as those emitted by cellular phones and many cordless phones, carry very little energy. No consensus exists on how exposure to a non-thermal electromagnetic field, which does not "heat", could affect living cells or threaten health. Laboratory research is sketchy due to the complexity of factors that come into play: wavelength, intensity, duration of exposure, time of day, interaction with the Earth's magnetic field, and other fields which could affect an experiment, including the lab's lighting. Experiments haven't been repeated because of the difficulty in precisely duplicating previous work. Because the effects of subtler forms of radiation take years to appear, it may be difficult to convince the public that danger exists. In the summer, the beaches are still filled with sunbathers, despite dire warnings of ultraviolet radiation's effects. Would people stop turning on the television if they learned it could make them physically sick? Only time will tell. •

Carolyn L. Davis

Who's Who PRESIDENT BETH BOWEN • EXECUTIVE DIRECTOR JULIA A. MOORE CONTACT EMILY K. GREEN

STATE AND TERRITORIAL AIR POLLUTION PROGRAM ADMINISTRATORS
ASSOCIATION OF LOCAL AIR POLLUTION CONTROL OFFICIALS

444 NORTH CAPITOL STREET, NW   WASHINGTON DC 20001
PHONE (202) 624 7864   FAX (202) 624 7863

Founded 1980 • *Geographic Coverage* Local, State • *Cooperative Partner* US Environmental Protection Agency • *Chapter* 1 *Organization Members* 250

Mission State and local air pollution control officials formed both organizations to improve their effectiveness as managers of air quality programs. The associations serve to encourage the exchange of information among air pollution control officials, to enhance communication and cooperation among federal, state, and local regulatory agencies, and to promote good management of air resources.

Funding *Membership* 100%

Publications Various books including *STAPPA - ALAPCO Alternative Proposed Federal Transportation Conformity Regulation* • *Operating Permits Under the Clean Air Act: State and Local Options* • *Controlling Emissions of Nitrogen Oxides from Existing Utility Boilers* • *Air Quality Permits: A Handbook for Regulators & Industry* • *Summary of the Clean Air Act Amendments* • *Air Permit and Emissions Fees.* Membership directory

For more Information Library, List of Publications

Who's Who EXECUTIVE DIRECTOR S. WILLIAM BECKER

THREE MILE ISLAND ALERT, INC.
315 PEFFER STREET   HARRISBURG PA 17102
PHONE (717) 233 7897

Founded 1977 • *Geographic Coverage* Local • *Individual Members* 450

Mission In the last ten years the organization has been an active intervener in hearings before the Nuclear Regulatory Commission on safety, managerial, and technical issues relating to the operation of Three Mile Island Nuclear generating station. The organization has also served as a regional clearinghouse on a broad spectrum of issues related to nuclear power generation. The group has provided information, research, and educational materials.

Annual Fees	Regular	Student/Senior	Sustaining	Patron	Club Member
	$15	$5	$50	$100	$200

Funding *Membership* 100%

Total Income $10,000

Usage	Administration	Programs
	50%	50%

Publications Monthly newsletter *Three Mile Island Alert.* Quarterly *Island Updates*

Who's Who PRESIDENT DEBBIE BAKER • SECRETARY KAY PICKERING

Canada

CANADIAN INSTITUTE FOR RADIATION SAFETY
555 RICHMOND STREET, WEST, SUITE 1106   TORONTO ON M5V 3B1
PHONE (416) 366 6565   FAX (416) 366 3551

Founded 1980 • *Geographic Coverage* National • *Cooperative Partners* National Laboratories Centre for Public Education, Programme for the Early Detection and Treatment of Lung Cancer.

Mission To promote radiation safety in homes and schools, the workplace, and the environment.

Programs Radon monitoring and measurements in private homes and schools. Public education and information programs. Development of training module in radiation safety for Canadian mines.

Publications Handbook *All About Radiation*. Various fact sheets and other publications focusing on radiation in the home, in schools, in the workplace and in the environment

For more Information List of Publications

Who's Who PRESIDENT **FERGAL I. NOLAN** • CHIEF SCIENTIST, DIRECTOR **ERNEST BECKER** • SENIOR STAFF SCIENTIST AND COORDINATOR **REZA MORIDI** • STAFF SCIENTIST **KAI KALETSCH** • INFORMATION OFFICER **TINA DE GEUS**

CANADIAN NATIONAL ASBESTOS COUNCIL PAGE 269

1 SPARKS AVENUE	WILLOWDALE ON M2H 2W1
PHONE (416) 499 4000	FAX (416) 499 8752

ENVIRONMENTAL COMPENSATION CORPORATION PAGE 232
SOCIÉTÉ D'INDEMNISATION ENVIRONNEMENTALE

2300 YONGE STREET, P.O. BOX 2382	TORONTO ON M4P 1E4
PHONE (416) 323 4826	FAX (416) 323 2754

GREENPEACE CANADA PAGE 31

185 SPADINA AVENUE, SUITE 600	TORONTO ON M5T 2C6
PHONE (416) 435 8404	FAX (416) 345 8422

INSTITUT DE L'AMIANTE PAGE 270
THE ASBESTOS INSTITUTE

1002 RUE SHERBROOKE, OUEST	MONTRÉAL PQ H3A 3L6
PHONE (514) 844 3956	FAX (514) 844 1381

POLLUTION PROBE

12 MADISON AVENUE	TORONTO ON M5R 2S1
PHONE (416) 926 1907	FAX (416) 926 1601

Founded 1969 • *Geographic Coverage* National, North America, Western Europe • *Individual Members* 45,000

Mission To define environmental problems through research, to promote understanding through education, and to press for practical solutions through advocacy.

Annual Fees

Regular	Student/Senior
$40	$20

Funding

Membership	Government Support	Corporations	Foundations
59%	3%	5%	2%

Other Sources *Sales, Honoraria & Project Royalties* 31%

Total Income $1,725,241

Usage

Administration	Fundraising	Programs
12.5%	33.8%	53.7%

Total Expenses $1,697,988

Programs Advocacy of Environmental Bill of Rights. Business Education Programme. Ecology Park. Numerous other advocacy and education programs. Participation on various panels, advisory boards, and committees.

Publications Newsletter *Probe Abilities* published three times per year, circulation 20,000. Book *Canadian Green Consumer Guide*

For more Information List of Publications

Who's Who PRESIDENT **EDWARD BABIN** • VICE PRESIDENT **MARJORIE LAMB** • SECRETARY **GREGORY KING** • EXECUTIVE DIRECTOR **JANINE FERRETTI** • CONTACT **LISA MACKINNON**

transportation • systems, impacts, alternatives

CHAPTER 13

IN ITS VASTNESS AND COMPLEXITY, the US transportation system is truly dynamic. Its network of roads, transit systems, railroads, airports, and waterways provides us the means to constantly move people and goods around the country. Maintaining this mobility, however, accounts for over 25 percent of energy consumed in America. Over two-thirds of petroleum use is attributable to transportation. Such demands over the years have resulted in increased congestion and increased air pollution that threaten human health and the environment. In the 1990s, transportation planners must be aggressive in developing programs to help preserve the quality of the environment. To that end, the US Department of Transportation (DOT) has been working vigorously to create programs and guidelines towards achieving this goal. In addition, legislation to combat air pollution includes the 1991 Intermodal Surface Transportation Efficiency Act (ISTEA), the 1990 Clean Air Act Amendments, and the Oil Pollution Act of 1990. In 1992, the United States became the first nation to ratify the International Convention on Oil Preparedness, Response and Cooperation (OPRC). ISTEA has provided over

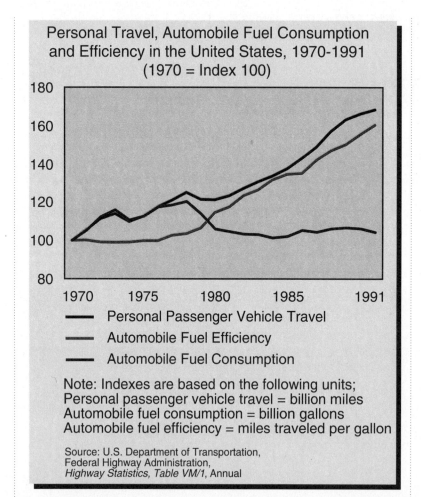

Personal Travel, Automobile Fuel Consumption and Efficiency in the United States, 1970-1991 (1970 = Index 100)

Personal Passenger Vehicle Travel
Automobile Fuel Efficiency
Automobile Fuel Consumption

Note: Indexes are based on the following units;
Personal passenger vehicle travel = billion miles
Automobile fuel consumption = billion gallons
Automobile fuel efficiency = miles traveled per gallon

Source: U.S. Department of Transportation, Federal Highway Administration, *Highway Statistics, Table VM/1*, Annual

$800 million for air quality and over $350 million for transportation enhancement, which includes historic preservation, green ways, bicycle lanes, and protecting scenery and water quality. But consideration must

still be given to use of land space. Efforts must be made to maximize the efficiency of existing systems - not necessarily to the creation of new ones. Building more roads removes available land and threatens to disrupt the balance

of delicate ecosystems.

AMENDMENTS TO THE CLEAN AIR ACT will provide positive changes in transportation planning. Some changes include improved public transit, high-occupancy-vehicles (HOV) roadway lanes for carpools and passenger buses, and incentive programs so employees will use alternative transportation. Pollution will be controlled when fuel consumption is controlled. This requires innovative mass transit programs, alternative fuels, and energy-efficient high-speed rail. A 1993 study even assessed the benefits of bicycling and walking and how federal, state and local governments can encourage citizens to consider these forms of transportation. To discourage "solo commuting", employers can cooperate with federal and local governments to offer incentives to employees who use public transportation, carpools or vanpools. Equally important are the social and institutional changes that would drastically reduce problems caused by traffic congestion. To achieve a balanced utilization of existing capacity, solutions include decentralized workplaces, staggered four-day work weeks, flexible work hours, and telecommuting. Increases are expected in the future use of automotive alternative fuels such as compressed natural gas, ethanol, propane, and electricity. In 1992, the Comprehensive National Energy Policy Act, currently known as the Energy Bill, was signed into law. One of its energy-saving/energy-producing goals includes replacing the federal automotive fleet with alternatively fueled vehicles. By the year 2000, 75 percent of the federal fleet will be fueled by

alternative means. In 1991, the US Advanced Battery Consortium was approved. Through this four-year $260 million joint venture, the federal government and major auto makers are working together to develop advanced batteries to greatly increase the range of high-performance electric vehicles. Improvement of inter-city transportation through magnetically levitated (or maglev) trains is under study by the

National Maglev Initiative, formed in 1990 through the DOT. The Urban Mass Transportation Administration (UMTA) formed the Advanced Public Transportation Systems Program to undertake Research and Development of advanced navigation, information and communication technologies as part of the overall DOT initiative in Intelligent Vehicle Highway Systems (IVHS). The Technical Assistance Program under UMTA

addresses regional mobility problems. In 1990 the Airport Noise and Capacity Act was passed for the transition to quieter aircraft fleets. One year later, the Federal Aviation Administration approved rules to phase out noisier aircraft by the end of 1999.

EVEN IN CANADA, WITH A LOWER density population than the United States, the transportation industry is responsible for about ▶

United States

BICYCLE FEDERATION OF AMERICA

1506 21ST STREET, NW   WASHINGTON DC 20036
PHONE (202) 463 6622

Founded 1977 • *Geographic Coverage* North America • *Cooperative Partner* European Cyclists Federation • *Chapters* 3

Mission To promote the increased safe use of bicycling and walking for transportation and recreation.

Funding	*Membership*	*Foundations*	*Contracts*
	18%	40%	42%

Total Income $1,000,000

Usage	*Administration*	*Programs*	*Miscellaneous*
	8%	84%	8%

Total Expenses $1,000,000

Programs National Bicycle and Pedestrian Advocacy Campaign.

Publications Monthly newsletter *Pro Bike News*, circulation 1,000. Books *Bicycling Reference Book*, diffusion 10,000 • *Bicycle Advocates Action Kit*, diffusion 10,000

For more Information Database, List of Publications

Who's Who PRESIDENT TEDSON MEYERS • EXECUTIVE DIRECTOR BILL WILKINSON

BICYCLE NETWORK (THE)

P.O. BOX 8194   PHILADELPHIA PA 19101
PHONE (215) 222 1253

Founded 1979 • *Geographic Coverage* National, Global • *Coopera-*

tive Partners International Bicycle Fund, League of American Wheelmen *Organization Members* 300 • *Individual Members* 200

Mission To monitor new developments in human powered transit and pedal technology.

Annual Fees	*Regular*	*Organization*	*Corporation*
	$25	$35	$50

Funding	*Membership*	*Foundations*
	90%	10%

Total Income $3,500

Usage	*Administration*	*Phone, Print & Postage*
	33%	66%

Publication Newsletter *Network News*

For more Information Database, Library

Who's Who PRESIDENT JOHN DOWLIN

CAMPAIGN FOR NEW TRANSPORTATION PRIORITIES

900 SECOND STREET, NE, SUITE 308   WASHINGTON DC 20002
PHONE (202) 408 8362   FAX (202) 408 8287

Founded 1986 • *Geographic Coverage* North America • *Organization Members* 50 non-profit environmental labor and consumer groups throughout the USA form the network affiliated with the National Association of Railroad Passengers which hosts the Campaign for New Transportation Priorities

Mission The Campaign is a coalition of 50 national and local groups dedicated to increasing the use of urban mass transit, inter-city passenger rail, bicycling and other clean, energy-efficient alter-

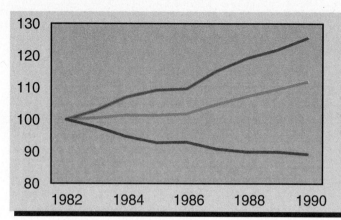

Average Fuel Consumption and Efficiency for Passenger Cars in the United States, 1982-1990 (1982 = Index 100)

— Miles per Gallon
— Miles Driven
— Gallons Consumed

Note: 1982 bases are as follows;
Miles driven = 9,428   Gallons consumed = 566
Miles traveled per gallon = 16.65

Source: U.S. Energy Information Administration, *Annual Energy Review 1991*

25 percent of the country's energy consumption. Since the fuel crisis of the 1970s, Canadians have been more cautious in planning their transportation needs. National highways are under-utilized and problems with intercity passenger travel are virtually nonexistent in Canada, but problems exist in the movement of people in and around Canada's major cities.

There are 24 metropolitan areas

natives to driving, by educating policy makers, the public and media on the need for and benefits of these alternatives and by working for increased funding, where appropriate, for these alternatives.

Annual Fees No fees, only agreement with CNTP's goals and objectives

Publications Policy papers on key transportation issues. Periodic bulletin *Tracking Transportation*

For more Information Database, Library, List of Publications

Who's Who CONTACT **HARRIET PARCELLS**

CENTER FOR CLEAN AIR POLICY   PAGE 34
444 NORTH CAPITOL STREET, SUITE 602   WASHINGTON DC 20001
PHONE (202) 624 7709   FAX (202) 508 3829

COMMITTEE FOR BETTER TRANSIT, INC. (THE)
BOX 3106   LONG ISLAND CITY NY 11103
PHONE (718) 728 0091

Founded 1962 • *Geographic Coverage* Regional • *Other Field of Focus* Urban Environment • *Chapter* 1 • *Organization Members* 20 *Individual Members* 380

Mission To promote improved public transit in the New York-New Jersey metropolitan area. Urban and suburban transit, planning, and auto restraint are the organization's main areas of focus.

Annual Fees	Regular	Student/Senior	Families	Supporting	Sponsor
	$16	$12	$25	$40	$100

Funding	Membership	Corporations	Foundations
	80%	5%	15%

Total Income $4,000

Usage	Administration	Fundraising	Programs
	5%	10%	85%

Publications Various papers including *Notes from Underground* • *Task Force Report*

Who's Who PRESIDENT **STEPHEN DOBROW** • VICE PRESIDENT **BARRY DRUSS** • SECRETARY **MARILYN ARNEIT**

INTERNATIONAL BICYCLE FUND
4887 COLUMBIA DRIVE, SOUTH   SEATTLE WA 98108-1919
PHONE (206) 628 9314   FAX (206) 628 9314

Founded 1983 • *Geographic Coverage* Global • *Focused Region* Africa

Mission To promote bicycle transportation and international understanding in the fields of transportation planning, economic development, safety education, cross-cultural education, and environmental quality.

Funding *Foundations* 99%

Total Income $10,000

Usage	Administration	Programs
	5%	95%

Programs Provides technical, material and financial support for start up bike programs around the world.

Publications Semiannual newsletter *IBF News*, circulation 5,000. Books *Bicycling in Africa* • *The Bicyclist's Dilemma in African Cities* • *Transportation, Bicycles and Development in Africa: Progression or Regression* • *Transportation Patterns in Nairobi* • *Selecting & Preparing*

with populations of over 100,000 people - over half of the country's population - and this is expected to double in the next 20 years. Like the United States, Canada is trying to reduce traffic in urban areas during morning and evening commuting hours when over 3.5 million people are driving the streets and highways; only about one-third of Canadians use public transportation.

Some Canadian cities are actively implementing programs such as bus-only highway lanes and "park-and-pool" lots. Many others are returning to surface or subway rail transit, an alternative that is more feasible and economical than expanding streets and freeways. Moving freight is another transportation demand in Canada. Until the late 1930s, rails carried 75 percent of all freight. After the completion of the Trans-Canada highway in 1962, trucking because of its speed, flexibility, availability and door-to-door service, soon took over the market for transporting freight.

Today, renewed efforts aim at making railway systems more economically and environmentally attractive. Certainly one of the most significant developments in Canada's rail efficiency was changing from steam to diesel. Marine freight is transported via vessels on Canada's waterways, which encompasses the Great Lakes, the St. Lawrence Seaway, canals, and coastal waters. However, one of the biggest disadvantages of ships propelling efficiently through water is the structure of their underwater hull surface. Ongoing research is taking place on coating hulls to protect them from corrosion and minimize resistance to water, thereby requiring the use of less energy. ▶

a Bicycle for Travel in Remote Areas • Language in Cross-Cultural Understanding

Who's Who VICE PRESIDENT **JOANNE DUFOUR** • SECRETARY **JOANNE DOWLIN** EXECUTIVE DIRECTOR **DAVID MOZER**

INTERNATIONAL HUMAN POWERED VEHICLE ASSOCIATION, INC.

P.O. BOX 51255   INDIANAPOLIS IN 46251
PHONE (317) 876 9478

Founded 1974 • *Geographic Coverage* Global • *Individual Members* 2,500

Mission To promote improvement, innovation and creativity in the design and development of human-powered transportation, and to encourage public interest in physical fitness and good health through exercise.

Annual Fees	Regular	Outside North America
	$25	$30

Funding *Membership* 100%

Usage	Administration	Programs
	30%	70%

Publications Quarterly journal *Human Power*. Bimonthly newsletter *HPV News*. Proceedings of scientific symposia

Who's Who PRESIDENT **MARTI DAILY** • VICE PRESIDENT **DAVID GORDON WILSON** SECRETARY **ADAM ENGLUND**

LEAGUE OF AMERICAN WHEELMEN

190 WEST OSTEND STREET, SUITE 120   BALTIMORE MD 21230-3755
PHONE (301) 944 3399

Founded 1880 • *Geographic Coverage* National • *Chapters* 475 affiliated Bicycle Clubs • *Organization Members* 500 • *Individual Members* 23,000

Mission To protect and advance the rights of bicyclists and encourage the use of the bicycle as an alternative mode of transportation. The League is focusing on "intermodalism" - the organization is striving to influence the creation of a transportation system that completely accommodates bicycles so cyclists have options available to them. This includes access to storage facilities at all public transportation facilities.

Annual Fees	Regular	Families	Library	Sustaining
	$25	$30	$19	$50

Other Fees *Individual Lifetime* $425 • *Family Lifetime* $525

Funding	Membership	Foundations
	80%	20%

Total Income $900,000

Usage	Administration	Fundraising	Programs
	51%	4%	45%

Programs Effective Cycling Program. Police Certification Program. National Coalition of Bicyclists.

Publications *Bicycle USA Magazine* published 8 times per year. Bimonthly newsletters *Bicycle Advocacy Bulletin* • *International Police Mountain Bike Association Newsletter*. Various how-to guides including *How To Commute to Work* • *How To Gain Access to Bridges*

Multimedia Online information service 1-800-288-BIKE

For more Information Library

Who's Who PRESIDENT **JOHN TOROSIAN** • VICE PRESIDENT **STEVE GOTTLIEB** • PUBLISHER **GILBERT M. CLARK**

►THE POPULATION OF NORTH America will continue to grow. Consequently, heavier demands will be placed on the transportation industry to keep moving people and goods from city to city and from coast to coast.

It is essential, therefore, that population growth not further impact our delicate environment.

With government and individual citizens constantly working together - keeping air-polluting vehicles off the roads, increasing use of alternative fuels and battery-powered cars, and eliminating traffic congestion through ridesharing and mass transit programs - we will see continual improvement towards better air quality and, in turn, healthier and more sustainable living. •

Athena F. Lucero

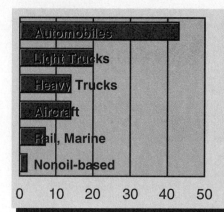

Carbon Dioxide Emissions in the U. S., by Transportation Type, 1991 (percentage)

Source: U.S. Congress, Office of Technology Assessment, *Changing by Degrees: Steps to Reduce Greenhouse Gases*, February 1991

NATIONAL ASSOCIATION OF RAILROAD PASSENGERS

900 SECOND STREET, NE, SUITE 308   WASHINGTON DC 20002
PHONE (202) 408 8362

Founded 1967 • *Geographic Coverage* National • *Cooperative Partners* Several independent state associations of railroad passengers *Individual Members* 11,000

Mission To educate public officials, the media, and the general public about the benefits of improved rail passenger service of all types - local commuter and intercity - both corridor and long-distance. Current goals include improving the quality and quantity of Amtrak service and funding for same, and encouraging realization of the 1991 highway transit authorization's potential to improve public transportation.

Annual Fees	*Regular*	*Student/Senior*	*Patron*
	$24	$12	$60

Funding	*Membership*	*Foundations*
	95%	5%

Total Income $369,974

Publications Newsletter published 11 times per year. Occasional letters mailed to members. Monthly *NARP News*. *Citizen Guide To ISTEA: Transit and Rail Funding and Public Participation Requirements*

Who's Who PRESIDENT JOHN R. MARTIN • VICE PRESIDENT EUGENE K. SKOROPOWSKI • SECRETARY ROBERT W. GLOVER

urban environment

CHAPTER 14

Ecocities : The Renewed Frontier, by David Drum

IN 1790, WHEN THE US AND Canadian economies were primarily based on agriculture, only 5 percent of the population lived in urban areas. By 1970, 75 percent of the population lived in cities. Today, 70 percent of the US population lives on only 2 percent of the land. The growing of food has long been separated from employment and daily life. Worldwide, 75 percent of the population in industrialized countries and 50 percent of developing countries live and work in urban areas.

Through the ages, as people migrated from the countryside, they encountered both high stress levels and greater opportunities for bettering their lot in the rude elbowing crowds. Concentrating people on small areas of city land created an enormous centralization of work and leisure.

Urban educational and commercial institutions allowed for great leaps forward in civilization and standards of living, but cities also created huge drains on available resources, particularly in this century. Cities obviously accelerate the pace of living.

Air Quality Trends in Major U.S. Urban Areas, 1991 (number of PSI* days greater than 100)

Atlanta, Boston, Denver, Chicago, New York, Washington, Philadelphia, Houston, Los Angeles

0   100   200

* PSI = Pollutant Standards Index. The PSI index integrates information from many pollutants across an entire monitoring network into a single number which represents the worst daily air quality experienced in the urban area. PSI index ranges and health effect descriptor words are as follows: 0 to 50 (good); 51 to 100 (moderate); 101 to 199 (unhealthful); 200 to 299 (very unhealthful); and 300 and above (hazardous). The chart shows the number of days when the PSI was greater than 100

Source: U.S. Environmental Protection Agency, Office of Air Quality Planning and Standards, *National Air Quality and Emissions Trends Report 1990*

On one hand, city planners created huge suburbs of single-family houses surrounded by small plots of grass and trees, islands of idyllic privacy and leisure. On the other hand, today's densest inner cities have the reputation of being huge impersonal and increasingly uninhabitable jungles.

PROBLEMS WITHIN CITIES INCLUDE providing adequate living conditions while maintaining adequate quality of life. We also must learn how to lessen the enormous impact of these vital centers on the local and global environment. One thing is certain: people continue to flock into major cities for the job opportunities and benefits, simultaneously adding to the environmental problems of crowded cities. Overcrowding creates an uncomfortable psychological ambiance. The environment is stressed by air, water and noise pollution,

traffic, congestion, graffiti and crime - problems associated with city rather than country life. The environmental infrastructure of urban areas involves an overlapping series of systems which deliver clean water, energy, sanitation, drainage, and solid waste management - systems which help cities protect their citizens, increase overall productivity, maintain public health and ultimately even alleviate poverty. ▶

► While the tree-laden, low-density suburbs appear to be environmentally friendly, the suburban concept may not prove to be ecologically sound. Systems of roads, pipes, and power lines must be built and maintained to connect the suburbs with the cities. The future may belong to the cities because of the ecological efficiencies that compactness allows.

RICHARD REGISTER, PRESIDENT OF Urban Ecology, San Francisco, calls the automobile "an agent of social disintegration" because cars use enormous amounts of energy and pollute the environment at an unprecedented scale. Before World War II, automobile use was largely recreational. Today, millions of North Americans commute to work from the suburbs. In the United States, the net impact of 190 million automobiles traveling more than 2 trillion miles a year is an unprecedented stress on the environment and human health. The US Environmental Protection Agency (EPA) attributes half of all human cancers to automotive air pollution. The US Public Health Service estimates that air pollution costs $6 billion a year due to effects from bronchitis, tuberculosis and lung cancer. More than half the US population is said to suffer unhealthy air quality.

Water quality and waste water disposal become huge problems when people are concentrated into cities because staggering demands are made on existing water resources. Local water tables are drawn down lower and lower, leaving many cities, such as Los Angeles,

United States

COMMITTEE FOR BETTER TRANSIT, INC. (THE) PAGE 190
Box 3106   LONG ISLAND CITY NY 11103
PHONE (718) 728 0091

COSANTI FOUNDATION
6433 DOUBLETREE RANCH ROAD   SCOTTSDALE AZ 85253
PHONE (602) 948 6145

Founded 1965 • *Geographic Coverage* Local, State, Regional, National
Cooperative Partners Arizona State Land, Eldershostel - Wakefield, MA

Mission To support environmentally sound urban planning through the development and promotion of "Arcology" - an approach which integrates architecture with ecology, combines natural and man-made environments to produce more habitable living conditions, and deals with urban problems, such as crowding and pollution.

Funding	*Corporations*	*Other*
	75%	25%

Programs Construction of Arcosanti, a prototype for an energy-efficient town combining architectural and ecological concepts. Agriculture Program. Construction Workshop. School Credit Program. Various conferences.

Who's Who CHAIRPERSON MEL ROMAN • PRESIDENT PAOLO SOLERI • SECRETARY MARY HOADLEY

COUNCIL FOR A GREEN ENVIRONMENT PAGE 106
1330 21ST STREET, SUITE 101   SACRAMENTO CA 95814
PHONE (916) 442 7195   FAX (916) 442 7198

EAST BAY CONSERVATION CORPS PAGE 75
1021 THIRD STREET   OAKLAND CA 94607
PHONE (415) 891 3900

ENVIRONMENTAL ACTION COALITION PAGE 201
625 BROADWAY, SECOND FLOOR   NEW YORK NY 10012
PHONE (212) 677 1601

ENVIRONMENTAL MANAGEMENT AGENCY
300 NORTH FLOWER STREET, P.O. BOX 4648   SANTA ANA CA 92702-4048
PHONE (714) 834 2300

Founded 1975 • *Geographic Coverage* Local • *Focused Region* Orange County, CA

Mission To serve the Orange County Community by protecting and improving the physical environment. To provide recreational opportunities and relief within the urban environment, preserve the integrity of the facilities, and protect natural, cultural and historical resources. To provide financial assistance to property owners for rehabilitation and upgrading in older, low and moderate income areas of Orange County. To analyze, develop, and present for decision and implement plans, programs and regulations for the development and conservation of the County's physical resources. To plan, schedule, design and maintain a system of public works - highway, trails, flood control and drainage facilities.

Total Income $635,000,000

Usage	*Administration*	*Programs*
	43%	57%

Total Expenses $369,000,000

Programs The Harbors, Beaches and Parks Division acquires, develops, operates, and manages the organization's administered recreational facilities. The Housing and Redevelopment Division develops affordable housing throughout the county with private developers and non-profit organizations. The Planning Division incorporates all feasible means of mitigating significant adverse impacts on the physical environment and recognizes the need for informed public involvement in the

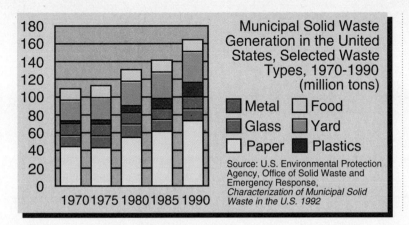

Municipal Solid Waste Generation in the United States, Selected Waste Types, 1970-1990 (million tons)

Metal ☐ Food
Glass ☐ Yard
☐ Paper ■ Plastics

Source: U.S. Environmental Protection Agency, Office of Solid Waste and Emergency Response, *Characterization of Municipal Solid Waste in the U.S. 1992*

increasingly reliant on imported water. The Environmental Protection Agency reports that raw sewage flows into 1,200 US rivers and harbors. Infrastructures are deteriorating in many North American cities because their huge networks of bridges, streets and sewer systems are not being maintained. "We need political courage and creativity in sensing what our cities ought to look like, to meet our genuine needs and to live within the resource constraints we'll face in the years ahead", Earth Day director Denis Hayes told the First International Ecocity Conference in 1990.

PLANS FOR ENVIRONMENTALLY friendly "ecocities" are beginning to appear. Ecocities aim to bring humans and ▶

planning process. The Public Works Division administers and inspects the quality of County funded and private construction of public works and recreation facilities. The Regulation Division approves development projects, which include the processing of tentative subdivision maps, plan checking subdivision improvements, processing Subdivision Committee use permits and administering the County Master Plan of Drainage.

For more Information Annual Report

Who's Who EXECUTIVE DIRECTOR **MICHAEL M. RUANE** • CHIEF DEPUTY DIRECTOR **JOHN SIBLEY** • ADMINISTRATION FUNCTION DIRECTOR **RONALD J. NOVELLO** • HARBORS, BEACHES AND PARKS FUNCTION DIRECTOR **ROBERT G. FISHER** • HOUSING AND REDEVELOPMENT FUNCTION DIRECTOR **BOB PUSAVAT** • PLANNING FUNCTION DIRECTOR **THOMAS B. MATHEWS** • PUBLIC WORKS FUNCTION DIRECTOR **WILLIAM L. ZAUN** REGULATION FUNCTION DIRECTOR **ROBERT F. WINGARD** • TRANSPORTATION FUNCTION DIRECTOR **KEN R. SMITH**

EXPERIMENTAL CITIES, INC.

P.O. BOX 731   PACIFIC PALISADES CA 90272-0731
PHONE (310) 276 0686   FAX (310) 274 7401

Founded 1972 • *Geographic Coverage* Global • *Individual Members* 50,000

Mission To seek positive solutions to social and environmental problems causing urban deterioration.

Funding	*Individual Grants*	*Government Support*	*Corporations*	*Foundations*
	25%	25%	25%	25%

Total Income $200,000

Usage *Programs* 100%

Publications Bimonthly newsletter *The New Relationships*. Books including *Experimental City I* • *Dialog I*

Multimedia TV series *The New Relationships* • *A Flash of Genius*

Who's Who PRESIDENTS **GENEVIEVE G. MARCUS**, **ROBERT L. SMITH** • SECRETARY **STEVEN J. BARLEVI**

LABOR COMMUNITY STRATEGY CENTER

3780 WILSHIRE BOULEVARD, SUITE 1200   LOS ANGELES CA 90010
PHONE (213) 387 2800   FAX (213) 387 3500

Founded 1987 • *Geographic Coverage* Local • *Other Fields of Focus* Human Rights & Environment, Pollution / Radiations • *Chapters* 2 *Individual Members* 550

Mission The Center is a multiracial "think tank-act-tank" organizing in low income communities of color to promote a broad-based social movement for corporate accountability and community controlled economic development. Its membership arm, the Labor Community Watchdog, is a county-wide organization promoting grassroots leadership development through public health organizing and advocacy in the areas of air pollution and the provision of mass transit.

Annual Fees *Regular* From $10 to 50

Funding	*Membership*	*Foundations*
	20%	80%

Usage	*Administration*	*Programs*
	20%	80%

Publications Various books including *L.A.'s Lethal Air* • *Fear At Work* • *Occupied America: A History of Chicanos* • *Workers, Communities, Toxics* • *Apartheid in an American City* • *In Struggle: SNCC and the Black Awakening of the 1960s*

For more Information Library, List of Publications

Who's Who CONTACT **GEORGIA HAYASHI**

► nature into harmonious balance and create an urban lifestyle oriented away from automotive travel and toward walking, biking or the use of mass transit. Some urban planners foresee "garden cities" which incorporate trees, pastures, and gardens into small communities also surrounded with greenbelts. Some want to blend residential and commercial use in communities which also grow their own food and recycle. The city of Cerro Gordo, Oregon, is one such futuristic development. "New traditional small towns" are popping up, based on pedestrian-friendly American and European 19th-century designs. More than 100 years ago, in *The Origin of the Species*, biologist Charles Darwin first recognized the interdependence of plant and animal groups occupying the same habitat. Urban planners are rediscovering this idea now. Within North American cities, the "urban forest" movement seeks to plant more psychologically comforting, carbon dioxide-absorbing trees along city streets. A mature tree absorbs about 13 pounds of carbon annually, they note, throwing off huge quantities of pure oxygen as it cleans the air of carbon dioxide and other greenhouse gases. Other organizations are working to create more wildlife sanctuaries within cities and towns, creating greater harmony with nature.

New forms of energy such as solar, hydrogen, and wind are being perfected. New forms of work such as telecommuting hold great promise for reducing automobile traffic. The best

PLANET DRUM FOUNDATION

P.O. Box 31251, Shasta Bioregion   San Francisco CA 94131
Phone (415) 285 6556

Founded 1973 • *Geographic Coverage* Global • *Organization Members* 200 • *Individual Members* 1,000

Mission To provide an effective bioregional grassroots approach to ecology that emphasizes sustainability, community self-determination, and regional self-reliance through publications, speakers, workshops, and performances. Planet Drum developed the concept of bioregion, a distinct area with coherent and interconnected plant and animal communities, often defined by a watershed.

Annual Fees

Regular	*Outside North America*
$20	$25

Programs Green City Project recommends changes in urban sustainability policies - comprehensive platform for issues ranging from renewable energy and recycling to neighborhood empowerment and smart transportation. Farm City Exchange. Green City Volunteer Network.

Publications Semiannual newsletter *Raise The Stakes*. Books *A Green City Program for the San Francisco Bay Area and Beyond* • *Reinhabiting a Separate Country: A Bioregional Anthology of Northern California* • *Green City Calendar*, volunteer opportunities, walks, events • *Youth Volunteer Directory*. NABC Congress proceedings

For more Information Library

Who's Who Contact Judy Goldhaft

SCENIC AMERICA

PAGE 279

21 Dupont Circle, NW   Washington DC 20036
Phone (202) 833 4300   Fax (202) 833 4304

TREEPEOPLE

12601 Mulholland Drive   Beverly Hills CA 90210
Phone (818) 753 4600   Fax (818) 753 4625

Founded 1973 • *Geographic Coverage* Local • *Other Field of Focus* Forest Conservation / Deforestation / Reforestation • *Individual Members* 20,000
,

Mission To inspire the people of Los Angeles to take personal responsibility for improving their immediate environment, by supporting the planting and care of trees, providing educational tools for environmental stewardship, serving as a catalyst for cooperative action among L.A.'s diverse population, and communicating the importance of the concept of the "urban forest".

Annual Fees *Regular* $25

Funding

Membership	*Corporations*	*Foundations*	*Other*
50%	25%	7%	18%

Usage

Administration	*Fundraising*	*Programs*
8%	17%	75%

Programs Citizen Forester Training Program. Community tree planting projects led by trained citizen foresters. Campus Forestry School Program.

Publications Newsletters bimonthly *Seedling News* • semiannual *Tree-Talk* for children

Who's Who President **Andy Lipkis** • Vice President **Katie Lipkis** • Secretary **Barbara Gonzalez**

Canada

CONSERVER SOCIETY OF HAMILTON AND DISTRICT, INC.

255 West Avenue North   Hamilton ON L8L 5C8
Phone (416) 628 3168

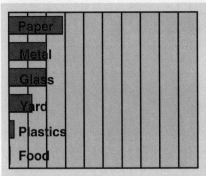

Municipal Solid Waste Recovery in the U. S., by Waste Type, 1990 (percent of generation recovered)

Paper
Metal
Glass
Yard
Plastics
Food

0 10 20 30 40 50 60 70 80 90 100

Source: U.S. Environmental Protection Agency, Office of Solid Waste and Emergency Response, *Characterization of Municipal Solid Waste in the U.S. 1992*

days of urban ecology may be to come - spurred by individual effort. The clues may be in the ways we view the land.

"WE ABUSE LAND BECAUSE WE regard it as a commodity belonging to us. When we see land as a community to which we belong we may begin to use it with love and respect", wrote Aldo Leopold in *The Land Ethic*. His words ring true today. Despite their shortcomings, cities may have a significant effect on improving the environment because they concentrate people into areas where needs can be efficiently served. The challenge of the future is to regulate the development of cities, to control expansion, and to minimize the impact of cities on the global environment. •
David Drum

Founded 1983 • *Geographic Coverage* Local • *Chapters* 5
Organization Members 3 • *Individual Members* 200

Mission To inform and involve the public in initiatives to help the environment through public meetings, community displays, public speaking, and various printed or audio-visual materials, to conduct research on environment matters; to provide liaison between members and all levels of government; and to cooperate with other groups, unions, businesses, and individuals concerned with enhancing and protecting the environment.

Annual Fees	Regular	Student/Senior	Families	Organization
	$20	$10	$30	$40

Funding	Membership	Government Support	Foundations	Interest
	20%	20%	45%	15%

Total Income $21,000

Usage	Administration	Fundraising	Programs	Chapters
	10%	10%	60%	20%

Total Expenses $13,500

Programs Trust Grants to other groups. Preserve Red Hill Valley Committee. Art and Environment Committee. Reuse Center. "Environmentalist of the Year" Award.

Publication Quarterly newsletter *The Environment Advocate*

Who's Who PRESIDENT **PETER HUTTON** • VICE PRESIDENT **KEN BALA** • SECRETARY **ANDREJS SUILPIS** • TREASURER **GORDON SNELLING**

INTERNATIONAL COUNCIL FOR LOCAL ENVIRONMENTAL INITIATIVES
EAST TOWER, CITY HALL, 100 QUEEN STREET, WEST   TORONTO ON M5H 2N2
PHONE (416) 392 1462   FAX (416) 392 1478

Founded 1990 • *Geographic Coverage* Local, Global • *Members* 124 including organizations

Mission To promote local environmental initiatives.

Annual Fees	Regular	Organization	Corporation
	$50 to 175	$100 to 350	$100 to 7,000

Publication Newsletter

For more Information Database, Library, List of Publications

Who's Who CHAIR **PETER HELLER** • VICE CHAIR **M. NDUBIWA** • SECRETARY **JAMES E. BRUGHMANN** • LIBRARIAN **EFFIE MICHAILIOIS** • CONTACT **MICHAEL MANOLSON**

PITCH-IN CANADA
PAGE 206
1676 MARTIN DRIVE, SUITE 200   WHITE ROCK BC V4A 6E7
PHONE (604) 538 0577   FAX (604) 538 3497

WOMEN AND ENVIRONMENTS EDUCATION AND DEVELOPMENT FOUNDATION (THE)
PAGE 27
736 BATHURST STREET   TORONTO ON M5S 2R4
PHONE (416) 516 2600   FAX (416) 531 6214

waste management, disposal, treatment, recycling

CHAPTER 15

From Prevention to Control, Is Waste Manageable? by Lyn Corum

OVER THE PAST 30 YEARS, the environmental movement in North America and the resulting state, provincial, regional, and national laws have had a profound effect on how we manage our garbage - municipal solid waste and hazardous or toxic wastes.

The United States has doubled the amount of waste produced in that same time while population has increased by only one-third. The percentage of waste sent to landfills has increased slightly, from 62.5 percent to 66.6 percent while recycling has increased from 6.7 percent to 15 percent. Remaining waste was burned until 1960 when the Clean Air Act forced most incinerators to shut down.

A technology called "waste-to-energy" burns trash and generates electricity and has replaced incineration, but it only burns 15 percent of municipal solid waste.

Landfills are reaching capacity, but the public resists building new ones. As a result, local, regional, and state laws have encouraged or mandated recycling programs. But recycling will not deliver us from trash. The US Environmental Protection Agency predicts that by the year

Hazardous Waste Sites, Ten First American States on the National Priority List, 1991 (number of sites)

Source: U.S. Environmental Protection Agency 1991

2000 recycling will divert just 25 percent of our trash with another 25 percent to be burned in waste-to-energy plants. Half of the expected 216 million tons will have to go to landfills. Canada is requiring many of the same changes.

In 1992, Canada recycled 20 percent of the 32 million tons of solid waste annually generated. In 1989, federal and provincial ministers of environment set a goal of diverting half of Canada's garbage from landfills by the end of this decade.

RECYCLING FACES MAJOR PROBLEMS in spite of its popularity and efforts to increase it. Markets for recycled newspaper, glass, plastic, construction materials, and yard waste are developing slower than the supply. Some states have made efforts to boost market development.

The cost to recycle materials is also an issue. A study conducted for the National Solid Wastes Management Association, a trade group of private trash haulers, found that the cost of processing recycled materials in a recovery

plant is $50 a ton, while the market value is $30.

This discrepancy will diminish as markets improve. Legislation could be introduced in the US Senate in 1994 to require manufacturers to include the cost of disposal in a product's price, or levy a tax on manufacturers to pay for recycling. Manufacturers are likely to mount a powerful fight against such a bill. A myriad of federal, state, and local laws and regulations already control hazardous waste management. The complexity of regulations and the bans have created a new and profitable industry in transport, recovery, destruction and dumping for the hundreds of chemicals that qualify as hazardous waste. Thousands of abandoned hazardous waste sites around the country were mandated for cleanup by a series of laws under the Comprehensive Environmental Response, Compensation and Liability Act first passed in 1980. The laws required that the parties responsible for dumping the hazardous waste had to pay the costs of cleaning.

These became known as Superfund sites.

A recent study by the Rand Corporation revealed that of the

1,275 hazardous waste sites placed on the national priority list since 1981, only 80 sites have actually been cleaned and removed from the list. Recycling of hazardous materials and reducing their use at the source has become a priority for more and more companies due to the increased costs of complying with federal, state, and local laws. Source reduction is also used to replace hazardous materials with non-hazardous materials in manufacturing. In Canada, a priority substance list has been developed that will eventually identify 100 substances that require priority assessment under the law. After a lengthy analysis and review process, two toxic materials - dioxins and furans - were banned. The Canadian government began a five-year program in 1989 to clean up abandoned, contaminated land sites and to develop new clean-up technologies.

STORAGE AND DISPOSAL OF NUCLEAR waste, both low level or high-level radioactive waste, also represent major areas of concern.

Low level radioactive waste, (LLRW), is a catch-all phrase for material that is neither high-level waste produced by nuclear power plants nor waste from uranium mining and nuclear weapons production.

It includes material that decays to natural background levels rapidly - after about 12 years - and that which breaks down more slowly - after about 100 years. LLRW is usually produced by university, hospital, and other research labs, and includes radioactive lab equipment and unused ▶

United States

AIR AND WASTE MANAGEMENT ASSOCIATION

P.O. Box 2861
Phone (412) 232 3444

Pittsburgh PA 15230
Fax (412) 232 3450

Founded 1907 • *Geographic Coverage* Global • *Chapters* 51
Organization Members 30 • *Individual Members* 15,000

Mission To provide international leadership in the environmental field, promote a safe and clean environment, and to promote a sense of environmental responsibility; to educate professionals, policy makers and the public about practical environmental management; to provide a neutral forum where all viewpoints of an environmental management issue - technical, scientific, economic, social, political and public health can be presented.

Annual Fees	*Regular*	*Student/Senior*	*Affiliate Member (under 27 years of age)*
	$85	$20	$42.50

Programs Annual meeting and exhibition to exchange technical, regulatory, and managerial information, and to enhance professional knowledge and skills. International and specialty conferences, workshops, courses and satellite seminars.

Publications Monthly *Journal of Air & Waste Management.* Newsletter *News & Views.* Books *Air Pollution Engineering Manual* • *Permitting for Clean Air - A Summary Guide* • *The Annual Directory and Resource Book.* Series include *Transactions* • *Specialty Proceedings* • *VIP*

Multimedia Videos

For more Information List of Publications

Who's Who PRESIDENT **DOUGLAS FOX** • VICE PRESIDENT **ANTHONY BUONICORE** SECRETARY **JON FEDORKA**

AMERICAN PUBLIC WORKS ASSOCIATION

106 West 11th Street, Suite 1800
Phone (816) 472 6100

Kansas City MO 64105-1806
Fax (816) 472 1610

Founded 1894 • *Geographic Coverage* National • *Other Field of Focus* Natural Resources / Water - Conservation & Quality • *Cooperative Partners* Canadian Public Works, International Public Works Associations, Associated General Contractors of America, American Society of Civil Engineers, National Association of Schools of Public Affairs and Administration, National Safety Council • *Individual Members* 28,000

Mission To conduct and disseminate the results of research on solid waste and water resources issues. Through its information services, the Association provides comprehensive information on management and maintenance of streets, highways, drainage, flood control, water supply, underground utilities, buildings, grounds, solid wastes, equipment, administration, and other civil engineering topics.

Annual Fees	*Regular*	*Student/Senior*	*Retired*	*Associate*
	$70	$10	$17	$85

Programs Council on Solid Waste. Council on Water Resources. Annual North American Snow Conference. Annual meeting.

Publications Monthly journal *APWA Reporter*. Periodic directory. Various books, manuals, and special reports focusing on solid waste collection and disposal

Multimedia Videos

For more Information Annual Report, Library

Who's Who EXECUTIVE DIRECTOR **RICHARD SULLIVAN**

CALIFORNIANS AGAINST WASTE

926 "J" Street, Suite 606
Phone (916) 443 8317

Sacramento CA 95814
Fax (916) 443 3912

► chemicals. A 1993 law requires that universities, hospitals, and businesses in 39 states store their own low-level radioactive wastes instead of shipping them to the nation's only three licensed LLRW disposal sites. These are located in South Carolina, Nevada and Washington. The law requires that by 1996, every state have its own disposal site or long-term access to one.

The reality is that most states won't meet that deadline. Thus, low level radioactive waste must be stored several years at facilities where it was generated. Approximately 100 nuclear power reactors in the United States produce about 30,000 highly radioactive spent fuel rods annually. Spent fuel rods, which have a half-life of thousands of years, must remain in interim storage until a high-level nuclear

waste repository is completed in Yucca Mountain, Nevada. The US Department of Energy originally planned for completion by 1997, but the project is 10 years behind schedule. Nuclear power plants are finding new ways to store waste. These include packing spent fuel rods more densely in cooling pools and storing them in huge steel casks. If interim solutions are not enough, some reactors will

have to shut down by the year 2000.

THE NATIONAL SOLID WASTES Management Association predicts that the 1990s are likely to represent a new era in waste management. Responsibilities for reducing the amount and toxicity of our trash, and safely disposing of the remainder, will be shared by many groups - manufacturers, retailers, consumers, ►

200

Part Three

GreenWorld's Almanac & Directory '94

Founded 1977 • *Geographic Coverage* Local, State • *Cooperative Partners* Californians Against Waste Foundation, Californians Against Waste Political Action Committee

Mission To promote and support the idea of a recycling economy. The organization advocates policy initiatives at both the state and local levels.

Programs The organization's Buy Recycled Campaign provides consumers, businesses and government with listings of recycled products available in California.

Publications Consumer guides *The Shopper's Guide to Recycled Products* • *The Guide to Recycled Printing and Office Paper* • *Buy Recycled! The Business and Government Buyer's Guide to Recycled Products for government procurement officers and businesses*

CLEAN SITES, INC.

1199 NORTH FAIRFAX STREET, SUITE 400 ALEXANDRIA VA 22314
PHONE (703) 683 8522 FAX (703) 548 8773

Founded 1984 • *Geographic Coverage* National

Mission To encourage, contribute to, and bring about the cleanup of hazardous waste sites in the USA. The organizations main areas of focus are technical/site management services, policy programs/analysis, and the State Superfund Network.

Funding	Corporations	Foundations	Reimbursements
	22%	7%	71%

Total Income $5,636,330

Usage	Administration	Fundraising	Programs
	19%	6%	75%

Publications Forum newsletter. Several reports focusing on Superfund cleanups and hazardous waste sites

Multimedia Video *Succeeding in Superfund*

Who's Who PRESIDENT EDWIN H. CLARK, II • VICE PRESIDENT ROBIN ROBINSON SECRETARY MARY CLARK • OTHER JAMES KOHANEK, ANDREW J. KRONE, NANCY NEWKIRK, SANDRA RENNIE, RICHARD SOBEL

COALITION FOR RESPONSIBLE WASTE INCINERATION

1113 CONNECTICUT AVENUE, NW, SUITE 1200 WASHINGTON DC 20036
PHONE (202) 775 9839 FAX (202) 775 2395

Founded 1987 • *Geographic Coverage* National, Global • *Organization Members* 35

Mission To improve the safety and efficiency of hazardous waste treatment through incineration.

Annual Fees *Organization* $25,000

Funding *Membership* 100%

Total Income $400,000

Usage	Administration	Programs
	25%	75%

Programs Legislative Programs. Public Relations Program. Operator Training Program. Metals Trials Burn Program. Site Visit Program. Conferences.

Publication Quarterly *Coalition for Responsible Waste Incineration*

Who's Who PRESIDENT JOHN PILNEY • VICE PRESIDENT JAY BIZARRO • SECRETARY STEPHEN MARGA

CORNELL WASTE MANAGEMENT INSTITUTE PAGE 17
CENTER FOR THE ENVIRONMENT
425 HOLISTER HALL ITHACA NY 14853
PHONE (607) 255 8444

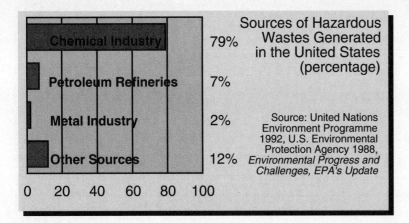

Sources of Hazardous Wastes Generated in the United States (percentage)

Chemical Industry	79%
Petroleum Refineries	7%
Metal Industry	2%
Other Sources	12%

Source: United Nations Environment Programme 1992, U.S. Environmental Protection Agency 1988, *Environmental Progress and Challenges, EPA's Update*

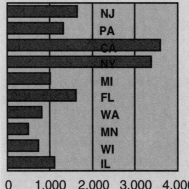

State and Local Government Expenditures for Solid Waste Management and Sewerage, Ten First American States on the National Priority List, 1990 (million dollars)

NJ PA CA NY MI FL WA MN WI IL

Source: U.S. Bureau of the Census, *Governmental Finances 1989-1990*

EAST BAY DEPOT FOR CREATIVE REUSE

1027 60TH STREET   OAKLAND CA 94608
PHONE (510) 547 6470

Founded 1980 • *Geographic Coverage* Local

Mission To gather reusable scraps from industry and individuals and make these materials available for artists, art agencies, schools, and youth groups.

Funding *Foundations* 100%

Total Income $24,000

Usage

Administration	Rent, Energy & Phone
80%	20%

Publication Quarterly newsletter

For more Information Database, Library

Who's Who CONTACT RAE HOLZMAN

ECOLOGY CENTER (THE)

2530 SAN PABLO AVENUE   BERKELEY CA 94702
PHONE (510) 548 2220

Founded 1969 • *Geographic Coverage* Local, National • *Individual Members* 1,800

Mission The Center is an education and recycling organization working to further the development of a more responsible society by identifying environmentally destructive practices and demonstrating sound alternatives. It operates the oldest ongoing recycling program in California as well as a comprehensive environmental information service. The Center offers a mix of services to the area and maintains relationships with hundreds of other environmental groups across the country.

Annual Fees

Regular	Student/Senior	Low Income
$25	$15	$15

Other *Membership Categories* from $40 to 250

Programs Major environmental information clearinghouse. Experienced staff and volunteers respond to questions on a wide range of environmental matters including recycling, household toxics, water quality, and current events. An up-to-date referral file allows staff to direct callers to other organizations, agencies, or individuals when appropriate. Curbside Recycling Program in Berkeley to help the city move toward its goal of recycling 50% of Berkeley's solid waste. Ecology Center Store. Classes.

Publication Monthly *Ecology Center Terrain*

For more Information Library

ENVIRONMENTAL ACTION   PAGE 20

6900 CARROLL AVENUE, SUITE 600   TAKOMA PARK MD 20912
PHONE (301) 891 1100   FAX (301) 891 2218

ENVIRONMENTAL ACTION COALITION

625 BROADWAY, SECOND FLOOR   NEW YORK NY 10012
PHONE (212) 677 1601

Founded 1970 • *Geographic Coverage* State • *Other Field of Focus* Urban Environment • *Individual Members* 1,500

Mission The organization specializes in recycling education, solid waste management, and urban forestry.

Annual Fees

Regular	Families	Sponsor	Sustaining	Patron
$20	$25	$50	$100	$500

Other Fees *Benefactor* $1,000

Publications Newsletters *Cycle* • *Eco-News*, for children. Interdisciplinary curriculum guides including *Plant A Tree For Arbor Day* •

local governments, and the waste industry.
This means that, as it should be, disposal costs will become as much a part of the price of a product as manufacturing and distribution. When disposal becomes fully represented in a product price, traditional market forces will reduce the size and cost of the element that eventually becomes trash. However, nuclear wastes will remain a separate, highly politicized and costly problem. Many Nevadans resist making Yucca Mountain a repository for high-level nuclear waste and activists throughout the country are stymieing the development of LLRW disposal sites.
The result will likely be above ground storage of nuclear wastes at sites close to urban centers for decades to come. •
Lyn Corum

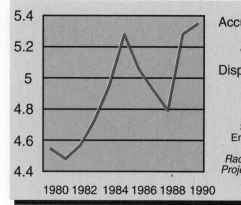

Accumulated Radioactivity of Nuclear Low-level Wastes at Commercial Disposal Sites, 1980-1990 (million curies)

Source: U.S. Department of Energy, *Integrated Data Base for 1991: Spent Fuel and Radioactive Waste Inventories, Projections, and Characteristics*

Don't Waste Waste • *Woods and Water*. Research papers including *Plastics: America's Packaging Dilemma* • *Source Separation Recycling in New York City Apartment Buildings* • *Waste Household Battery Management*

For more Information Library, List of Publications

Who's Who PRESIDENT TERENCE MEEHAN • VICE PRESIDENT CAROLYN KONHEIM SECRETARY GINA INGOGLIA WEINER • TREASURER STEPHEN BATTY • EXECUTIVE DIRECTOR NANCY WOLF • LIBRARIAN JENNIE TICHENOR

ENVIRONMENTAL HAZARDS MANAGEMENT INSTITUTE

10 NEWMARKET ROAD, P.O. BOX 932   DURHAM NH 03824
PHONE (603) 868 1496

Founded 1977 • *Geographic Coverage* Global • *Other Field of Focus* Food / Pesticides / Consumerism & Safety

Mission To serve individuals, municipalities, government, industry, and others involved in environmental management and education by providing unique, non-partisan, educational products and services. The organization researches the latest environmental information and disseminates it worldwide through EHMI slide charts, book covers, publications, information systems, and public outreach programs.

Funding

	Corporations	Foundations
	95%	5%

Programs The Critical Link program, a qualitative and quantitative study of the effect of recycling education on recycling program success. Project Automobile Care For The Environment, an education program for driver education students on proper auto fluid management.

Publications *EHMI Re: Source* • *EHMI Earth Express*

Who's Who PRESIDENT ALAN JOHN BORNER

ENVIRONMENTAL RESEARCH FOUNDATION

P.O. BOX 5036   ANNAPOLIS MD 21403-7036
PHONE (410) 263 1584   FAX (410) 263 8944

Founded 1980 • *Geographic Coverage* Local, National • *Other Field of Focus* Pollution / Radiations

Mission To perform and circulate the results of research focused on hazardous materials and hazardous technologies, particularly landfills, incinerators, toxic heavy metals, and organochlorine compounds.

Programs Provides a rapid-response information service for grassroots environmental activists. Operates Remote Access Chemical Hazards Electronic Library (RACHEL), an online computerized database of information. Student intern program.

Publications Weekly newsletter *Rachel's Hazardous Waste News*. Book *What Chemicals Each Industry Uses*. Numerous other writings, reports, resource guides and fact sheets

Multimedia Computerized database *RACHEL* accessible to the public by calling (410) 263 8903, with modem set at 8-N-1

For more Information Library, List of Publications

Who's Who CONTACT PETER MONTAGUE

HOUSEHOLD HAZARDOUS WASTE PROJECT

1031 EAST BATTLEFIED, SUITE 214   SPRINGFIELD MO 65807
PHONE (417) 889 5000   FAX (417) 889 5012

Founded 1987 • *Geographic Coverage* Local, Regional, National, Global • *Other Field of Focus* Public / Environmental Health *Cooperative Partners* University of Missouri Extension System, Environmental Improvement and Energy Resources Authority • *Chapter* 1

Mission To develop and promote education and action concerning the

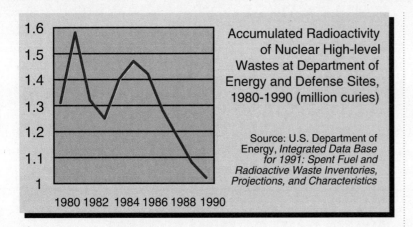

Accumulated Radioactivity of Nuclear High-level Wastes at Department of Energy and Defense Sites, 1980-1990 (million curies)

Source: U.S. Department of Energy, *Integrated Data Base for 1991: Spent Fuel and Radioactive Waste Inventories, Projections, and Characteristics*

identification, safe use, storage, and proper disposal of hazardous house-hold products and the selection of safer alternatives. The organization works with a broad range of communities to establish local programs, and attempts to foster cooperation among groups addressing health, waste disposal, water protection, air protection, fire safety, recycling, and poison prevention.

Funding

Government Support	Training Programs, Honoraria & Sales of Materials
88%	12%

Total Income $177,000

Usage *Programs* 100%

Total Expenses $177,000

Programs The Project provides training, consultation, educational materials, and an information service for concerns regarding household hazardous products and waste. The Project's day-long workshop/training course, "From Awareness to Action!", covers such topics as health and environmental concerns, product labeling requirements, household safety procedures and equipment and tools for educating the public, and trains individuals to serve as community educators and resources. Other educational projects include the Stored Waste Abatement Program, What Your Home Has: A Household Hazardous Waste Game, and Home Hazardous Product Survey, Tools for The Environmental Teacher.

Publications *Guide to Hazardous Products Around the Home* explains product ingredients, health and safety issues, disposal, recycling outlets, safer product alternatives. Guide sheets help answer commonly asked questions about household hazardous products and provide guidelines for safe use, storage and disposal.

For more Information Database, Library, List of Publications

INSTITUTE FOR LOCAL SELF-RELIANCE (THE) PAGE 170
2425 18TH STREET, NW WASHINGTON DC 20009-2096
PHONE (202) 232 4108 FAX (202) 332 0463

NUCLEAR RECYCLING CONSULTANTS
P.O. BOX 819 PROVINCETOWN MA 02657
PHONE (508) 487 1930

Founded 1983 • *Geographic Coverage* National, Global

Mission To preserve facilities of the nuclear fuel cycle and redesign them for community use. The organization is primarily a volunteer organization with consultants working on various projects.

Programs Research of incomplete nuclear power sites. Documentation of sites.

Who's Who PRESIDENT JAY CRITCHLEY

PACIFIC ALASKA NETWORKING
56250 GLENN ROAD HOMER AK 99603-9525
PHONE (907) 235 7112 FAX (907) 235 7128

Geographic Coverage Pacific • *Focused Regions* Alaska, Pacific Rim, Russian Federation • *Other Fields of Focus* Environmental Education / Careers / Information / Networks, Pollution / Radiations • *Cooperative Partners* Pan Pacific Nuclear Free Zone Association, Nuclear Free America, Nuclear Guardian Ship Project, Albert Einstein Institute, Greenpeace, Alaska Conservation Foundation

Mission To facilitate communication and networking throughout the Pacific Rim, focusing on responsible storage of radioactive materials and local and regional nuclear free zone legislation.

Who's Who EXECUTIVE DIRECTOR DENNIS SPECHT

PENNSYLVANIA RESOURCES COUNCIL
P.O. BOX 88 MEDIA PA 19063-0088
PHONE (215) 565 9131 FAX (215) 892 0504

Founded 1939 • *Geographic Coverage* National • *Organization Members* 120 • *Individual Members* 600

Mission The Council's areas of focus include environmental shopping, waste reduction, recycling, air pollution, household hazardous waste, and billboard control.

Annual Fees

Regular	Student/Senior	Families
$30	$30	$40

Funding

Membership	Corporations	Grants & Contracts
5.8%	7%	87.2%

Total Income $318,133

Usage

Administration	Fundraising	Programs
20.7%	5.5%	73.8%

Programs Environmental Shopping Program. Behavior for a Green America Program. Billboard Control Program. Environmental Living Program - a lifestyle analysis program.

Publications Numerous booklets focusing on educational subjects

Multimedia Video *Practical Guide to Environmental Shopping*. Automated fax mailing service

For more Information List of Publications

Who's Who President **F. Austin Fiore** • Vice Presidents **Barbara O'Brien, David Mc Corkle, Thomas Embich** • Secretary **Dorothy Hermani**

SOLID WASTE ASSOCIATION OF NORTH AMERICA

8750 Georgia Avenue, P.O. Box 7219   Silver Spring MD 20910
Phone (301) 585 2898

Founded 1961 • *Geographic Coverage* North America • *Chapters* 40 • *Individual Members* 5,100

Mission To advance the practice of economically and environmentally sound municipal solid waste management.

Annual Fees	Public	Private
	$100	$250

Funding	Membership	Other
	50%	50%

Total Income $1,500,000

Publication Monthly newsletter *Municipal Solid Waste News*

Who's Who President **N. C. Vasucki**

WORK ON WASTE USA, INC.

82 Judson Street   Canton NY 13617
Phone (315) 379 9200   Fax (315) 379 0448

Founded 1988 • *Geographic Coverage* National, Western Europe

Mission To do research on all aspects of incineration, including municipal, hazardous, and medical waste incineration; to document supporters of dioxin-emitting industries - federal and state regulatory agencies, consultants, major newspapers and other media.

Annual Fees	Regular	Student/Senior	Organization	Corporation
	$40	$35	$50	$125

Funding *Membership* 100%

Total Income $27,000

Program The First Citizens' Conference.

Publication Weekly newsletter *Waste Not*

Multimedia Videos of The First Citizens' Conference on Dioxin

For more Information Library

Who's Who Executive Director **Paul Connett** • Editor **Ellen Connett**

Canada

ALBERTA WASTE MATERIALS EXCHANGE

6815 8th Street, NE, Suite 350   Calgary AB T2E 7H7
Phone (403) 297 7505   Fax (403) 297 7548

Founded 1984 • *Geographic Coverage* Province • *Cooperative Partners* Alberta Research Council, Alberta Environmental Protection Agency • *Members* 1,000 including organizations

Mission To put users of waste material in contact with waste producers, who list materials of potential value with exchange.

Annual Fees *Subscription to Bulletin* $35

Funding	Government Support	Subscriptions
	80%	20%

Usage	Administration	Programs	Publication of Bulletin
	40%	10%	50%

Programs Provincial Waste Exchange and Information Clearinghouse.

Publication Quarterly *Alberta Waste Materials Exchange Bulletin*, circulation 1,000

For more Information Database, Library

Who's Who Manager **George W. Thorpe** • Coordinator **Cindy S. Jensen**

ASSOCIATION OF MUNICIPAL RECYCLING COORDINATORS

147 Wyndham Street, North, Suite 405   Guelph ON N1H 4E9
Phone (519) 823 1990   Fax (519) 823 0084

Founded 1987 • *Geographic Coverage* National

Mission To facilitate the sharing of municipal waste reduction, reuse, composting, and recycling information and experience among municipalities. The Association provides a forum which allows its members to work together in overcoming commonly shared obstacles to responsible and cost-effective waste reduction and recycling initiatives. It also allows member municipalities to act as a unified voice in promoting progressive waste reduction and recycling alternatives.

Programs Four general meetings annually. One Day Workshops/ Seminars, which provide coordinators with more detailed coverage of important program trends and issues. Advanced Recycling Coordinators Workshops, which focuses on developing the tools and programs necessary for meeting the province's 50% waste diversion goal. Waste Audit Training Workshops, designed for those putting together a waste diversion master plan, either as a separate initiative or as part of a waste management plan.

Publications Quarterly newsletter *For R Information*. Reports and manuals

For more Information Database, Library, List of Publications

Who's Who EXECUTIVE ASSISTANT CYNTHIA HYLAND • OTHER LINDA VARANGU, BEN BENNETT

CITIZENS' CLEARINGHOUSE ON WASTE MANAGEMENT

R.R. 2 CAMERON ON K0M 1G0
PHONE (705) 887 1553 FAX (705) 887 4401

Founded 1989 • *Geographic Coverage* Province • *Cooperative Partners* Ontario Environmental Network, Canadian Environmental Network • *Organization Members* 100 • *Individual Members* 30

Mission To promote responsible waste management and to provide waste management and reduction information and related services to individuals, citizens' groups, and local government in Ontario and elsewhere. The organization is concerned with solid waste, commercial, industrial, and institutional waste, household and industrial hazardous waste, and radioactive waste.

Annual Fees	Regular	Corporation	NGO	Governmental Agency
	$25	$40	$25	$40

Funding	Membership	Foundations	Subscriptions	Other
	47%	39%	2%	12%

Total Income $53,374

Usage	Administration	Salaries
	41%	59%

Total Expenses $49,187

Programs Waste Management Information Service. Community Waste Watch, a method for conducting a waste audit using a one-week diary kept by individual volunteers. Offers Waste Reduction Action Kits, complete plans for conducting short-term local projects focused on waste reduction, reuse, or recycling.

Publication Quarterly newsletter *Waste Less Times*

Multimedia Numerous videos focusing on environment and waste management

For more Information Annual Report, Database, Library, List of Publications

CLEAN NOVA SCOTIA FOUNDATION (THE)

1675 BEDFORD ROW, P.O. BOX 2528 HALIFAX NS B3J 3N5
PHONE (902) 420 3474 FAX (902) 424 5334

Founded 1987 • *Geographic Coverage* Province • *Cooperative Partners* Nova Scotia Environmental Network, Canadian Environmental Network • *Individual Members* 700

Mission To serve the people of Nova Scotia in their pursuit of environmental rejuvenation and preservation. The Foundation's key objectives are to develop and support community based environmental improvement programs, promote a pro-environment attitude among the public, and promote constructive partnerships between government, business, and other groups concerned with the environment.

Annual Fees	Regular	Families	Organization	Corporation	Governmental Agency
	$20	$30	$100	$75 to 200	$100

Funding	Membership	Government Support	Corporations	Foundations	Interest & Sales
	6%	52%	35%	2.5%	4.5%

Total Income $341,946

Usage	Administration	Programs	Other
	72%	24%	4%

Total Expenses $338,827

Programs Waste Reduction Week, a province-wide community-based effort to involve citizens, schools, towns, organizations, and businesses in a variety of activities to raise awareness of waste reduction. Moosehead Maritime Beaches Sweep, the largest per capita coastal cleanup project in North America. The Great Nova Scotia Pick-Me-Up is a province-wide spring cleanup, picking up litter from schoolyards, parks, downtown areas, and a variety of other sore spots. EnviroTowns is a comprehensive community-based approach to caring for the environment. Organized in individual municipalities by an EnviroTowns Task Force, the program is designed to assist community members develop cooperative improvement strategies. EnviroShow is a mobile set of displays, with focused information on the 3 "Rs" and the development of a conserver society.

Publications Quarterly newsletter *Briefly*. Quarterly newsmagazine *Nova Scotia Renews*. Numerous other publications focusing on waste and recycling issues

For more Information Database, Library, List of Publications

Who's Who PRESIDENT ALAN PARISH • VICE PRESIDENT ANNE COSGROVE • SECRE-

COMPOSTING COUNCIL OF CANADA (THE)

200 MacLaren Street	Ottawa ON K2P 0L6
Phone (613) 238 4014	Fax (613) 238 7559

Founded 1991 • *Geographic Coverage* National • *Organization Members* 100 • *Individual Members* 50

Mission To advocate composting as a means of municipal and industrial waste management for a sustainable society.

Annual Fees	Regular	Organization	Corporation	Small Business	Sustaining Member
	$75	$350	$2,500	$1,000	$5,000

Funding	Membership	Other
	54%	46%

Total Income $280,000

Programs Research program. National and regional conferences.

Publication Newsletter

For more Information Database

Who's Who PRESIDENT **BILL GOODINGS** • VICE PRESIDENT **LAMBERT OTTEN** SECRETARY **GORDON OWEN** • EXECUTIVE DIRECTOR **PETER MEYBOOM** • PUBLIC RELATIONS OFFICER **SUSAN ANTLER**

ENVIRONMENTALLY SOUND PACKAGING COALITION OF CANADA

2150 Maple Street	Vancouver BC V6J 3T3
Phone (604) 736 3644	Fax (604) 736 7822

Founded 1987 • *Geographic Coverage* Local, Regional, National *Cooperative Partners* Consumer's Association of Canada, Pitch-In Canada, British Columbia Wildlife Federation, Federation of British Columbia Naturalists, Recycling Council of British Columbia • *Chapter* 1 *Organization Members* 5

Mission To advocate the development and use of packaging which has minimal impact on the environment; to promote, in cooperation with industry, government and the public, the reduction, reuse, and recycling of all packaging materials.

Publications Newsletter published one or two times per year. Fact sheets. Reports

Who's Who PRESIDENT **RUTH LOTZKAR** • VICE PRESIDENT **DIANNE VAN DE BERG** SECRETARY **ADA BROWN** • TREASURER **DICK McCARTHY**

PITCH-IN CANADA

1676 Martin Drive, Suite 200	White Rock BC V4A 6E7
Phone (604) 538 0577	Fax (604) 538 3497

Founded 1967 • *Geographic Coverage* Local, Regional, National, Global • *Other Field of Focus* Urban Environment • *Cooperative Partner* Clean World International - United Kingdom

Mission To carry out promotional, educational, and action programs aimed at reducing, reusing, recycling, and the proper management and disposal of waste - solid waste in particular; to initiate cleanup and beautification programs to clean up and enhance Canada's streams, wilderness, and urban areas; to instill among Canadians a sense of pride in their community; to promote the use of the Pitch-In symbol; to secure the support of all levels of government, industry, the media, other public sector organizations, and the public for Pitch-In Canada's objectives and to encourage active participation by the public in its programs.

Annual Fees Minimum donation of $15

Programs The Civic Pride Programme is designed to help local governments and community leaders to address the need to properly manage waste before it becomes litter. Pitch-In Week is held annually during the second week of May, to help make individuals aware of the amount of mismanaged waste. Pitch-In Canada's Media Programme uses a public service advertising campaign to distribute promotional and advertising materials to print and electronic media on an ongoing basis. The organization's Educational Programme provides educational materials to help develop an environmental ethic and an acceptance of personal responsibility towards the environment, with a concentration on elementary schools and community organizations. The Clean Beaches Programme is a long-term project to curb the improper disposal of waste in oceans and along Canada' shorelines. Clean Rivers Programme. Adopt-A-Highway Programme. Clean-Up The World Programme.

Publications Semiannual newsletter *Pitch-In News*. Educational textbooks *Re-Think*, grades K - 3 • *The Yukkie Colouring Book*, grades K - 2 • *The Kids Can Activity Book*, grades 3 - 5 • *Re-Think Activity Book*, grades K - 3

Multimedia Various videos including *Action Projects to Improve the Environment: Composting, Reduce - Reuse - Recycle* • *Cleaning Up the World Starts at Home* • *Pitch-In Week: The World's Largest Clean-Up* • *Programmes to Cleans Up the Environment* • *The National Marine Debris Surveillance Programme*

For more Information Library, List of Publications

Who's Who PRESIDENT **ALLARD VAN VEEN** • CONTACT **VALÉRIE THOM**

RECYCLING COUNCIL OF MANITOBA, INC.

330 Portage Avenue, Suite 1812	Winnipeg MB R3C 0C4
Phone (204) 942 7781	Fax (204) 942 4207

Founded 1985 • *Geographic Coverage* Province • *Cooperative Partners* Canadian Environmental Network, National Recycling Coalition • *Organization Members* 75 • *Individual Members* 150

Mission The Council acts as a resource for Manitobans who seek to protect the environment by reducing waste. It works to establish networks of communication and support for waste minimization initiatives between citizens, industry, government, and environment groups; to educate and disseminate information on the stewardship ethic and waste minimization practices; to research and analyze policy in support of waste minimization objectives; and to do demonstrations of waste minimization projects and market development for recyclable materials.

Annual Fees

	Regular	Student/Senior	Organization	Corporation
	$25	$10	$25	$100

Other Fees *Small Business & Municipality* $50

Funding

Membership	Government Support	Corporations	Foundations	Other
5%	75%	5%	10%	5%

Usage

Administration & Fundraising	Programs
25%	75%

Programs Manitoba Waste Exchange. Green Works for Small Business. Speaker's Bureau. Public Information Line.

Publications Quarterly newsletter *R Report*. Various books including *Green Works for Small Business* • *Waste Product Recycling in Manitoba* • *Container Recycling for Manitoba* • *Depot Demonstration Project*

For more Information Database, Library

Who's Who PRESIDENT **RICK REUNER** • VICE PRESIDENT **BARB SPURWAY** • SECRETARY **GINI LOUDER** • TREASURER **DAVE BRICKWOOD**

RECYCLING COUNCIL OF ONTARIO

489 COLLEGE STREET, SUITE 504 ·   TORONTO ON M6G 1A5
PHONE (416) 960 1025   FAX (416) 960 8053

Founded 1978 • *Geographic Coverage* Province

Mission To offer information on all aspects of waste reduction, from backyard composting to industrial waste recycling. The Council operates Ontario's most extensive reference library on waste reduction.

Programs Yearly Conference in fall attended by representatives from all 3 levels of government, business, industrial and non-governmental organizations.

Publications Quarterly newsletter *Ontario Recycling Update*. Directories. Research reports. Information kits. Fact sheets

Multimedia Online information service 1-800-263-2849

For more Information Library

Who's Who EXECUTIVE DIRECTOR **JOHN HANSON** • ASSOCIATE EXECUTIVE DIRECTOR **CHRISTOPHER BAINES** • CONTACT **MASHI KARUMANCHIRI**

SASKATCHEWAN ASSOCIATION OF REHABILITATION CENTRES
SARCAN RECYCLING DIVISION
140 AVENUE "F", NORTH   SASKATOON SK S7L 1V8
PHONE (306) 933 0616   FAX (306) 653 3932

Founded 1968 • *Geographic Coverage* Province • *Cooperative Partners* Saskatchewan Environment and Resource Management, Saskatchewan Environment and Public Safety • *Organization Members* 35

Mission To facilitate growth and meaningful employment for people with disabilities in Saskatchewan through social integration, support of local initiatives, business development, job placements, technological aids, communications, education, training, and member services. SARCAN Recycling, begun in 1988 as the recycling division of the organization, has opened 63 recycling depots throughout the province.

Annual Fees *Organization* $500

Funding

Government Support	Recycling Division
1.4%	98%

Total Income $9,826,200

Usage

Administration	Processing	Non-Member Centres	Member Centres
7%	17%	22%	36%

Other Usage *Transportation* 8% • *Other* 10%

Total Expenses $6,955,936

Programs SARCAN operates three processing centers (in Saskatoon, Regina, and Biggar), which densify salvaged containers for cost-effective shipment to market. The organization employs more than 180 people with disabilities, and strong public support is reflected by the high return rates of containers distributed in Saskatchewan - 82% for aluminum, 77% for plastic, and 54% for glass.

Publications Newsletter. Various promotional literature

For more Information Database, Library

Who's Who PRESIDENT **JULIAN BODNAR** • VICE PRESIDENT **BERNIE BRIGIDEAR** SECRETARY **DON WICKENS** • TREASURER **JOHN HARDER** • CONTACT **PHIL WRNBLESKI**

human **responses** t

environmental challenges

"To defend and improve the environment for present and future generations

part four

has become an imperative goal of mankind - a goal to be pursued together with, and in harmony with, the established and fundamental goals of peace and of worldwide economic and social development."

United Nations Conference on the Human Environment. The Stockholm Declaration, 1972

animal welfare & protection

CHAPTER 16

Animals Have Rights Too, by Pamela S. Leven

THE ACTIVIST SPIRIT OF THE SIXTIES protest era is alive and well in the Nineties and living within the hearts of animal rights activists - for better and for worse. Animals in labs, on farms, and in captivity deserve the same rights and the same protection from exploitation as humans of all races and both sexes, insisted animal rights advocate Peter Singer in his landmark 1975 book *Animal Liberation*, which helped launch the popular movement of animal welfare and protection.

The pleasure and pain of animals are comparable to the pleasure and pain of humans, he argued. For that reason, humans are obliged to consider these civil rights factors in their treatment of animals. Moreover, because animal welfare cannot be ensured by relying on the good behavior of humans, animal advocates must take responsibility for enforcing animal rights.

"Responsible human action" represents the contrasting opinion. Adherents reject the notion that animals have externally granted natural and inalienable rights. They claim that humans must only observe internal codes of behaving ethically toward animals and

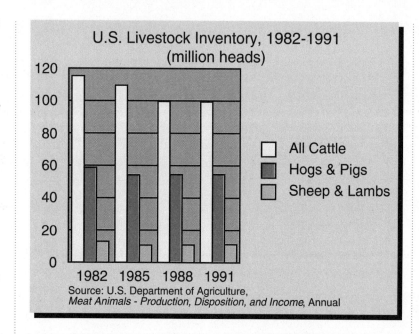

U.S. Livestock Inventory, 1982-1991 (million heads)

Legend:
- All Cattle
- Hogs & Pigs
- Sheep & Lambs

Source: U.S. Department of Agriculture, *Meat Animals - Production, Disposition, and Income*, Annual

treating them humanely and with respect. But, as often the case, the zealots grab the headlines and set the agenda.

THE START OF THE US ANIMAL RIGHTS movement is generally traced to the late 1970s with the emergence of the Animal Liberation Front (ALF). Founded in England, members believe all life is sacred and reject any use of animals by humans. They advocate veganism, a life style that includes a diet of only plant-derived foods and excludes wearing leather, silk and wool. ALF, a militant underground group, gained notoriety for its violence against animal research laboratories. It publicizes its activities by sending photos of lab destruction and pronouncements of responsibility to People for the Ethical Treatment of Animals (PETA), a moderate group founded in 1980. Distancing itself from ALF, PETA's executive director once said "we have chosen to ask people to change society through persuasion and through dissemination of information. We will go as far as civil disobedience. But that's it". But PETA recognizes that ALF,

despite its lawlessness, touches a nerve among animal lovers. PETA attracts members and raises money by decrying animal experimentation and filling its literature with graphic photos of test animals.

PETA is now the largest American animals rights group with more than 400,000 dues-paying members and annual income of nearly $10 million. Even the tamer Doris Day Animal League, founded in 1987, bases its legislature agenda on lobbying to outlaw toxicity tests on animals for cosmetics and consumer goods. Modern activists support more proactive animal protection efforts than offered by mainstream groups such as the Humane Society and the American Society for the Prevention of Cruelty to Animals (ASPCA).

Those long-standing groups say they disapprove of unnecessary or needlessly cruel animal experimentation but acknowledge that some testing is needed for the foreseeable future.

ACTIVISTS HAVE WON IMPORTANT victories. In 1991 the US Departmentof Transportation abolished testing corrosives on rabbits. Traditional tests evaluated hazardous materials by measuring the time they took to burn through a rabbit's skin. The new chemical process uses no animals. That 1991 law marked the first time a government agency approved an alternative to animal testing. Additionally, a number a major cosmetics firms have adopted test-tube research and eliminated the Draize test in which substances are inserted into eyes of live rabbits to test irritation levels. By attacking animal experimentation on a wholesale level, however, animal activists pit themselves against a formidable array of adversaries who are increasingly willing to retaliate with equal force.

The National Association for Biomedical Research, formed in the early 1980s by medical research and pharmaceutical interests, counters arguments of animal rights activists. Efforts by this and other groups led to the Animal Enterprise Protection Act of 1992, which criminalized all attacks on laboratories, livestock facilities, aquariums, zoos, circuses, and rodeos on the federal level.

PETA'S RISE MARKED THE START of a spiraling public emergence of groups and counter-groups associated with the animal welfare. Animal Rights Mobilization, Inc. (ARM!), started in 1981 as Trans-Species Unlimited - its name changed in 1990, declared the day after Thanksgiving as "Fur Free Friday", marking the occasion annually with nationwide anti-fur demonstrations.

The Fur Information Council of America (FICA) fights back with pro-fur billboards, advertorials and statements from ▶

United States

ACTORS AND OTHERS FOR ANIMALS

5510 CAHUENGA BOULEVARD   NORTH HOLLYWOOD CA 91601-9971
PHONE (818) 985 6263

Founded 1971 • *Geographic Coverage* National

Mission To promote the humane treatment of animals. Spaying and neutering are the organization's main areas of focus.

Publication Newsletter

Who's Who PRESIDENT EARL HOLLIMAN • EXECUTIVE VICE PRESIDENT JACKIE JOSEPH EXECUTIVE SECRETARY JODIE MANN • TREASURER PATRICIA BERCEL • EXECUTIVE DIRECTOR CATHY SINGLETON

AMERICAN FUND
FOR ALTERNATIVES TO ANIMAL RESEARCH

175 WEST 12TH STREET, SUITE 16-G   NEW YORK NY 10011-8275
PHONE (212) 989 8073   FAX (212) 989 8073

Founded 1977 • *Geographic Coverage* National, Global • *Cooperative Partners* Beauty Without Cruelty USA, World Society for the Protection of Animals, New York State Humane Association, Center for Advanced Training in Cell and Molecular Biology • *Individual Members* 6,000

Mission The organization raises funds from the public and uses these to provide financial support for biomedical research to develop, validate and disseminate information concerning non-animal replacements for animals.

Annual Fees *Regular* $20

Total Income $56,159

Usage	Administration	Programs
	5%	95%

Total Expenses $66,356

Programs The Fund provides support for 3 sections of a course for HS students and teachers on tissue culture and in vitro toxicology at the Center for Advanced Training in Cell and Molecular Biology, Catholic University, Washington, DC ($20,000). It also provides co-support for the MEIC Validation project for 200 non-animal product tests ($40,000), and for a Russian alternative laboratory run by an animal protection society at the Moscow University.

Publication Newsletter *News Abstract* published three times per year

For more Information List of Publications

Who's Who PRESIDENT ETHEL THURSTON • VICE PRESIDENT GEORGIANA MORRISON SECRETARY RUTH SEPPALA • TREASURER JOAN SACHS • OTHER LINDA ARNONE, TERRI DIELI, ELIZABETH FARNUM, JULIE LEE, MARGE PIATAK

AMERICAN HUMANE ASSOCIATION

63 INVERNESS DRIVE, EAST   ENGLEWOOD CO 80112-5117
PHONE (303) 792 9900   FAX (303) 792 5333

Founded 1877 • *Geographic Coverage* National • *Other Field of Focus* Public / Environmental Health • *Individual Members* 61,100

Mission Dedicated to building an aware and caring society, the Association focuses on finding and fighting the causes of social apathy and neglect which result in the abuse and suffering of children and animals. The Association is composed of a Children's Division and an Animal Protection Division.

Annual Fees *Regular* $15

Funding	Contributions & Grants	Bequests	Royalties	Other
	42.8%	49%	6.9%	1.3%

Total Income $5,462,666

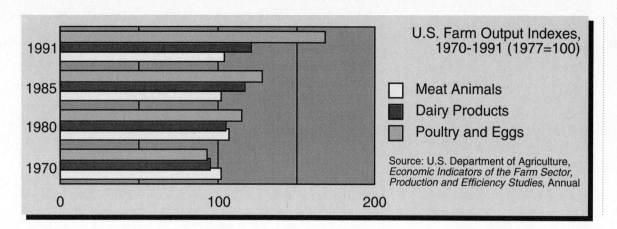

U.S. Farm Output Indexes, 1970-1991 (1977=100)

☐ Meat Animals
■ Dairy Products
☐ Poultry and Eggs

Source: U.S. Department of Agriculture, *Economic Indicators of the Farm Sector, Production and Efficiency Studies*, Annual

▶ well-known fashion designers. Putting People First was launched by a mother who thought her children were being indoctrinated with animal rights rhetoric in school. The group represents "the average American who eats meat and drinks milk, benefits from medical research, wears leather, wool and fur, hunts and fishes, owns a pet, and visits zoos". The Scientists' Center for Animal

Usage	Administration	Fundraising	Programs	Central Services
	4.3%	13.3%	73.5%	8.8%

Total Expenses $5,088,550

Programs The Association's Standards of Excellence Program helps shelters throughout America provide quality care and good homes for unwanted animals. When animals are used in TV programs and motion pictures, the Association's Los Angeles office is on the set to ensure the animals' safety and well-being. Emergency Animal Relief Program provides financial assistance to agencies, along with essential medicines and food when natural disasters strike. The Association's National Horse Abuse Investigators Training Program helps humane officers learn the skill needed to educate owners or to prosecute abuses. In order to create a broader awareness of the vulnerability of children and families to abuse and neglect, Association staff began an active effort to educate and mobilize communities in the struggle against child maltreatment. Successful passage of the Child Abuse Prevention and Treatment Act. Ninth National Conference on Child Abuse and Neglect.

Publications Quarterly magazine *Advocate*, circulation 77,900. *SHOPTALKs*, circulation 25,200

For more Information Annual Report, List of Publications

Who's Who PRESIDENT JOHN F. JONES • VICE PRESIDENT CHARLES M. GRANOSKI, JR. TREASURER HAROLD F. DATES • EXECUTIVE DIRECTOR DIANE ALLEVATO

AMERICAN SOCIETY FOR THE PREVENTION OF CRUELTY TO ANIMALS
424 EAST 92ND STREET   NEW YORK NY 10128
PHONE (212) 876 7700

Founded 1866 • *Geographic Coverage* National • *Chapters* 2 *Individual Members* 350,000

Mission To work for the prevention of cruelty to animals throughout the

United States by helping to provide effective means for meeting this end. The principles and beliefs that motivate the work of the Society encompass companion animals, animals in research and testing, animals raised for food, wild animals, entertainment and work animals, and animals in education.

Annual Fees	Regular	Supporting	Sustaining	Founder's Society Friend
	$25	$50	$100	$500

Other Fees *Founder's Society Associate* $1,000 • *Founder's Society Benefactor* $5,000

Funding	Membership	Program Income	Bequests	Investment Income	Other
	63%	17%	8.5%	6%	5.5%

Total Income $14,048,106

Usage	Administration	Membership Development & Fundraising	Programs
	10%	26%	64%

Total Expenses $13,510,771

Programs Education department advocates reform in the ways humans view and interact with animals. Legislation program to protect the rights of animals.

Publication Quarterly magazine *Animal Watch*

For more Information Annual Report

Who's Who PRESIDENT ROGER A. CARAS • SENIOR VICE PRESIDENTS MARYANN DOHERTY, HAROLD FINKELSTEIN, STEPHEN L. ZAWISTOWSKI, HERMAN N. COHEN SENIOR DIRECTORS JOANNE LAWSON, JULIE MORRIS, JOAN PAYLO, ANGEL ROSADO, DAVID VICTOR • EDITOR CINDY A. ADAMS

ANIMAL LEGAL DEFENSE FUND (THE)
1363 LINCOLN AVENUE   SAN RAFAEL CA 94901
PHONE (415) 459 0885   FAX (415) 459 3154

Welfare was formed to promote scientific education. Members say that if children relate everything they learn about animals with dogs and cats at home, they will believe biomedical research is evil and cruel and will turn their backs on science. But researchers also fear losing their abilities to perform valuable experimentation on live animals when their opponents advocate medical research ►

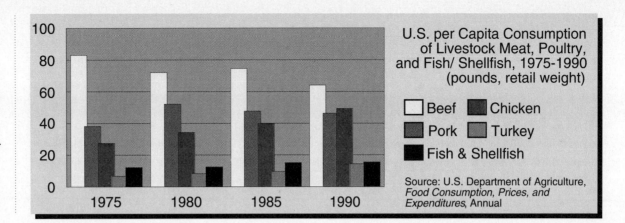

U.S. per Capita Consumption of Livestock Meat, Poultry, and Fish/ Shellfish, 1975-1990 (pounds, retail weight)

☐ Beef ■ Chicken
■ Pork ■ Turkey
■ Fish & Shellfish

Source: U.S. Department of Agriculture, *Food Consumption, Prices, and Expenditures*, Annual

---

Founded 1981 • *Geographic Coverage* National • *Individual Members* 50,000

Mission To fight animal abuse and provide long-term protection for animals, through a strategy of direct, legal action.

Annual Fees	Regular	Student/Senior
	$20	$10

Funding	Foundations	Other
	93%	7%

Total Income $1,175,637

Usage	Administration	Programs	Membership Development	Other
	10%	60%	28.8%	1.2%

Total Expenses $1,155,730

Programs Works to enforce amendments to the Animal Welfare Act mandating exercise for dogs and physical environments which promote the well-being of primates in laboratories. Works to enhance the legal status of companion animals. Filed suit against the National Marine Fisheries Service to stop the illegal "gray market" in dolphins and other marine mammals.

Publication Quarterly newsletter *The Animals' Advocate*

For more Information Annual Report

Who's Who PRESIDENT STEVEN M. WISE • VICE PRESIDENT STEVE ANN CHAMBERS SECRETARY KENNETH D. ROSS • TREASURER DAVID S. FAVRE • EXECUTIVE DIRECTOR JOYCE TISCHLER • COMMUNICATIONS DIRECTOR LAURA WILENSKY • PUBLIC OUTREACH COORDINATOR JENNIFER HOLDT

ANIMAL PROTECTION INSTITUTE OF AMERICA

2831 FRUITBRIDGE ROAD, P.O. BOX 22505   SACRAMENTO CA 95822
PHONE (916) 731 5521   FAX (916) 731 4467

Founded 1968 • *Geographic Coverage* North America

Mission To work for the education of the public regarding the alleviation of cruelty toward animals, the preservation of animal lives in a natural environment, and the alleviation of problems connected with an overpopulation of unwanted pets and abandoned and neglected animals and wildlife.

Annual Fees	Regular	Contributing	Sustaining	Sponsoring	Patron
	$20	$25	$50	$100	$500

Other Fees *Benefactor* $1,000

Funding	Contributions	Bequests	Other
	70%	27.3%	2.7%

Total Income $2,065,408

Usage	Administration	Fundraising	Programs
	24%	10%	66%

Total Expenses $2,049,537

Programs Special investigations into institutional and other forms of animal abuse. Actions to promote and support vital animal protection legislation. National education programs. Representation at international decision making forums - e.g., the International Whaling Commission, the Convention on International Trade in Endangered Species. Ethics in Experimentation Campaign. Summer for Animals Campaign. Dear City Manager Campaign.

Publications Quarterly magazine *Mainstream*. Action alerts, books, and brochures

Multimedia Online information service 1-800-348-PETS

For more Information Annual Report

Who's Who CHAIRMAN KENNETH E. GUERRERO • VICE CHAIRMAN DUF FISCHER

methods such as tissue cultures, mathematical models, and computer models.

ANIMAL ACTIVISTS ALSO TARGET farms. Farm Sanctuary, an abused animal refuge, contends that a vast majority of farm animals are raised in intensive confinement systems, are genetically altered, and fed artificial diets designed to maximize reproduction.

The counterpoint Livestock Conservation Institute represents animal industries and tries to protect the economic interests of its members. In Canada, codes of practice for the treatment of swine, veal calves, poultry, dairy cattle, and fur-bearing animals are voluntary and established under auspices of the Canadian Federation of Humane Societies. But the Federation successfully

lobbied for tough animal protection laws.
For example, farmers who mistreat animals are subject to fines up to $10,000.
Canada also hosts the Centre for the Study of Animal Welfare, the only North American institution founded to improve the lives of human-use animals. It seeks ways to assess pain in animals and fosters the development of alternatives to

animal use in teaching, testing and research.
The Centre shares its findings with animal users, concerned parties, government agencies, and the public.
Even with progress, controversy will always remain on the basic issue of human responsibility toward animals. And for that reason alone, animal rights activism will likely continue. •
Pamela S. Leven

SECRETARY **SUSAN LOCK** • TREASURER **LUANA GRIMLEY** • EXECUTIVE DIRECTOR **DAVID J. BERKMAN**

ANIMAL RIGHTS COALITION, INC.

P.O. BOX 20315   BLOOMINGTON MN 55420
PHONE (612) 822 6161   FAX (612) 822 0469

Founded 1981 • *Geographic Coverage* National

Mission To work for the end of all exploitation and institutionalized cruelty to all animals.

Annual Fees	Regular	Student/Senior	Families	Sustaining	Sponsor
	$15	$10	$25	$50	$100

Other Fees *Benefactor* $500

Programs Supports humane legislation. Presents workshops, seminars, and conferences. Provides information and referrals. Networks with other animal, environmental, and civic groups. Active Speakers' Bureau that can be contacted for presentations to schools, churches, or civic groups.

Publication Quarterly newsletter *Animal Rights Coalition News*

Multimedia Online information service 1-612-866-6604

Who's Who PRESIDENT **MARY BRITTON CLOUSE** • VICE PRESIDENT **HEIDI GREGER** SECRETARY **JOAN HARP** • TREASURER **JOANNE MURPHY** • FOUNDER **VONNIE THOMAS-BERG** • SPEAKER'S BUREAU COORDINATOR **JUDY NIEMCZYK** • NEWSLETTER EDITOR **CHARLOTTE COZZETTO** • OFFICE COORDINATOR **BARBARA STASZ**

ANIMAL RIGHTS MOBILIZATION
ARM!
P.O. BOX 6989   DENVER CO 80206
PHONE (303) 388 7120

Founded 1981 • *Geographic Coverage* North and South America

Cooperative Partners Animal Rights Mobilization Networks with over 300 grassroots and national organizations in the USA, South America, Canada, Australia, and England • *Chapter* 1 • *Organization Members* 25 • *Individual Members* 17,500

Mission To eliminate animal abuse and exploitation. ARM! evolved out of Trans-Species Unlimited, an action organization involved in the animal rights movement.

Annual Fees	Regular	Student/Senior	Corporation
	$20	$10	$250

Total Income $94,983

Usage	Administration	Fundraising	Programs
	25%	5%	70%

Total Expenses $96,897

Programs Cornell Cat Campaign. Fur-Free America Campaign.

Publications Quarterly newsletter *ARM!*. Magazine *Movement Mag*

Multimedia Online information service 1-800-CALL-ARM

For more Information Annual Report, Database, Library, List of Publications

Who's Who PRESIDENT **ROBIN DUXBURY** • VICE PRESIDENT **JUDY BROWNSTONE** SECRETARY **MARY ROBBINS**

ANIMAL RIGHTS NETWORK, INC.
P.O. BOX 345   MONROE CT 06468
PHONE (203) 452 0446

Founded 1979 • *Geographic Coverage* National, Global

Mission To promote animal rights and welfare.

Red Meats Slaughtering in the United States, 1991 (million heads)

Lamb and Mutton	
Veal	
Pork	
Beef	

0 20 40 60 80 100

Source: U.S. Department of Agriculture, *Livestock and Meat Statistics*

Publication Bimonthly magazine *The Animals' Agenda*

ANIMAL WELFARE INSTITUTE

P.O. Box 3650   Washington DC 20007
Phone (202) 337 2332

Founded 1951 • *Geographic Coverage* National, Global • *Cooperative Partner* Society for Animal Protective Legislation

Mission To prevent needless suffering of animals. To work for the humane treatment of laboratory animals and the development and use of non-animal testing methods; a ban on steel jaw traps and reform of other cruel methods for controlling wildlife populations; the prevention of trade in wild-caught exotic birds, and regulation of shipping conditions for all animals; the preservation of species threatened by extinction; the reform of cruel treatment of food animals, such as intensive confinement in factory farms; the encouragement of humane science teaching and the prevention of painful experiments on animals by high school students.

Annual Fees	Regular	Student/Senior	Supporting	Friend	Patron
	$25	$5	$50	$100	$500

Other Fees *Benefactor* $1,000

Funding	Membership	Foundations	Other
	1.7%	95.7%	2.6%

Total Income $1,165,111

Usage	Administration	Fundraising	Programs
	13.2%	2.5%	84.3%

Total Expenses $723,023

Programs Ongoing activities and programs on laboratory animals, trapping, the wildlife trade, whales (Save the Whales Campaign), and farm animals. Ongoing publishing and education program.

Publications Magazine *AWI Quarterly*. Numerous books and other publications focusing on appreciation and protection of animals, wildlife under threat, trapping laboratory animals, factory animals, saving the whales, and humane education

Multimedia Videos including *Where Have All The Dolphins Gone?* • *The Earthtrust Driftnet Expedition* • *America's Shame* • *Down on the Factory Farm* • *Laboratory Dogs*. PSA video *Gregory Peck Speaks Against Leghold Traps* (available to TV stations only)

For more Information Annual Report, Library, List of Publications

Who's Who President **Christine Stevens** • Vice President **Cynthia Wilson** Secretary **Freeborn G. Jewett, Jr.** • Treasurer **Roger L. Stevens** • Executive Director **Cathy Liss**

BEAUTY WITHOUT CRUELTY USA

175 West 12th Street, Suite 16-G   New York NY 10011-8275
Phone (212) 989 8073   Fax (212) 989 8073

Founded 1972 • *Geographic Coverage* Global • *Cooperative Partners* American Fund for Alternatives to Animal Research, World Society for the Protection of Animals, New York State Humane Association *Individual Members* 7,000

Mission To inform the public about the massive suffering of many species of animals used by the fashion and cosmetics industries; to provide information about substituting improved fashions which do not involved the suffering, confinement, or death of any animal.

Annual Fees	Regular	Student/Senior
	$15	$10

Other Fees *Lifetime* $150

Funding	Membership	Other
	98%	2%

Total Income $15,183

Usage	Administration	Programs	Other
	46%	37%	17%

Total Expenses $11,692

Publications Quarterly newsletter *Action Alert*. Leaflet published 3 times per year *The Compassionate Shopper*. Pamphlet *Please Excuse Me For Approaching You* describes the suffering involved in fur production (available in 4 languages)

For more Information Library, List of Publications

Who's Who President **Ethel Thurston** • Vice President **Gene Salinas** Secretary **Marion Friedman** • Treasurer **Joan Sachs** • Other **Linda Arnone, Marge Piatak, Terri Dieli, Elizabeth Farnum, Bonnie Hess-Rose, Julie Lee**

CENTER FOR RESPECT OF LIFE AND ENVIRONMENT

2100 "L" Street, NW   Washington DC 20037
Phone (202) 778 6133

Founded 1986 • *Geographic Coverage* National • *Cooperative Partner* The Humane Society of the United States

Mission To foster an ethic of compassion toward all sentient beings and respect for the integrity of nature, and to promote a humane and sustainable future for all members of the earth community.

Annual Fees *Regular* $20

Programs The Academic Institutions in the Earth Community program encourages colleges to develop curricula, campus-wide programs, and outreach services on the environment. The Religion in the Ecological Age program considers implications of the environmental crisis for theology and religious ethics, and seeks to develop a core curriculum for seminary education. The Land Ethics in the Land Professions program seeks to promote sustainable land use ethics to guide the management of human settlements, farm lands, and natural areas. The Arts and the Earth program emphasizes the central role of the arts in creating the images and inspiration for an earth community. The Animal Protection and the Environment program seeks to broaden the scope of environmental education to include animal protection issues.

Publication Quarterly periodical *Earth Ethics*

Who's Who Presidents Robert Welborn, John A. Hoyt • Secretary Paul G. Irwin

DORIS DAY ANIMAL LEAGUE

227 Massachusetts Avenue, NE, Suite 100   Washington DC 20002
Phone (202) 842 3325

Founded 1987 • *Geographic Coverage* National • *Individual Members* 85,000

Mission To reduce the pain and suffering of "non-human animals", to encourage the spaying and neutering of companion animals, and to increase the public's awareness of its responsibility toward "non-human animals" through legislative initiatives, public education, and programs to require the enforcement of statutes and regulations which have already been enacted to protect animals.

Annual Fees *Regular* $10

Funding *Membership* 100%

Total Income $1,860,867

Usage	*Administration*	*Fundraising*	*Programs*
	11%	8%	81%

Programs Ongoing lobbying for federal, state and local legislation promoting humane care and treatment of animals and controls on animal overpopulation. Public Awareness Program, to increase the public's awareness concerning cruel treatment of animals, animal overpopulation, toxicity tests, and animal rights.

Publications Quarterly newsletter *Animal Guardian*, circulation 150,000. Booklets on the Consumer Products Safe Testing Act

Who's Who President Doris Day • Vice President Terry Melcher

FARM ANIMAL REFORM MOVEMENT

FARM
P.O. Box 30654   Bethesda MD 20824
Phone (301) 530 1737   Fax (301) 530 5747

Founded 1981 • *Geographic Coverage* National • *Other Field of Focus* Food / Pesticides / Consumerism & Safety • *Individual Members* 10,000

Mission To alleviate and end animal abuse and other destructive impacts of intensive animal agriculture on consumer health, food resources, and environmental integrity.

Annual Fees	*Regular*	*Student/Senior*	*Supporting*	*Sponsor*	*Patron*
	$20	$10	$35	$100	$500

Other Fees *Benefactor* $1,000

Funding *Membership* 100%

Total Income $120,000

Usage	*Administration*	*Fundraising*	*Programs*
	10%	5%	85%

Total Expenses $130,000

Programs "Great American Meatout" seeks to alert American people to the impacts of meat consumption and production and asks them to "kick the meat habit" on March 20th. National Veal Ban Action. World Farm Animals Day. "Adopt-A-McDonald's" Campaign mobilizes activists to visit their McDonald's asking customers to reduce their beef consumption and management to reduce beef production and promote a meatless burger. "Vegetarian Express" Campaign. "Chicken Out" Campaign. Sponsors annual Summer conferences "Vegetarian Summerfest '93", North American Vegetarian Congress, "A New Generation For Animal Rights" for college students and teachers. Education and training programs.

Publications Quarterly newsletter *FARM Report*. Numerous fact sheets, brochures

For more Information Database, Library

Who's Who President Alex Hershaft • Vice President Melinda Marks

FARM SANCTUARY

P.O. Box 150 — WATKINS GLEN NY 14891
PHONE (607) 583 2225

Founded 1986 • *Geographic Coverage* National • *Chapters* 2
Individual Members 20,000

Mission To rescue and protect farm animals. The current focus of the organization is the passage of the Downed Animal Protection Act in the Senate, House of Representatives, and in several states.

Annual Fees *Regular* $15

Funding	Membership	Foundations
	85%	5%

Total Income $745,000

Usage	Administration	Fundraising	Programs
	8%	6%	86%

Programs Internship program at New York and California sanctuaries.

Publication Quarterly newsletter

Who's Who PRESIDENT **LORRI BAUSTON** • VICE PRESIDENT **GENE BAUSTON** • SECRETARY **LAURIE HENSLEY**

FOCUS ON ANIMALS

106 BOOTH HILL ROAD — TRUMBULL CT 06611
PHONE (203) 377 1116

Founded 1983 • *Geographic Coverage* National • *Cooperative Partners* The Geraldine R. Dodge Foundation, The Marian Rosenthal Koch Fund

Mission To increase the understanding of human/non-human animal interaction by producing videotapes on a wide variety of issues relating to animals and the environment, distributing the best films and videotapes available on animal abuse and exploitation, creating teaching guides for classroom use, and working with teachers and administrators nationwide to encourage a more compassionate student population.

Funding *Foundations* 100%

Total Income $10,000

Usage *Programs* 100%

Multimedia Videos *We Are All Noah* • *Voices I Have Heard* • *Breaking Barriers* • *Dog Lab* • *The Silver Spring Monkey* • *Unnecessary Fuss* *Britches* • *Inside Biosearch* • *Suffer the Animals* • *Kiss the Animals Goodbye* • *Among the Wild Chimpanzees*

Who's Who PRESIDENT **E. R. MECHLU** • VICE PRESIDENT **M. ROSENTHAL** • SECRETARY **N. ROBERTS**

FOOD ANIMALS CONCERNS TRUST, INC.

P.O. Box 14599 — CHICAGO IL 60614
PHONE (312) 525 4952

Founded 1982 • *Geographic Coverage* National • *Other Field of Focus* Food / Pesticides / Consumerism & Safety • *Cooperative Partner* Nest Eggs, Inc. is FACT's wholly-owned subsidiary and works with farmers on the East Coast and in the Midwest to produce NEST EGGS® brand eggs • *Individual Members* 20,000

Mission To promote better care for farm animals and improved farming methods to produce safer food. The Trust is pursuing a solution to the problem caused by factory farming through comprehensive public information programs and hands-on farm programs that demonstrate workable alternatives.

Funding	Membership	Bequests	Interests & Dividend Income
	25.3%	70.6%	4.1%

Total Income $1,058,559

Usage	Administration	Fundraising	Programs
	10%	20%	70%

Total Expenses $385,005

Programs Information research and dissemination to regulators. Model Farm Program contracts with farmers who follow safe and humane standards. Information programs focus on food safety problems that arise from crowding animals under stressful conditions.

Publication Quarterly newsletter *Fact Acts*

For more Information Annual Report

Who's Who PRESIDENT **ROBERT A. BROWN** • VICE PRESIDENT **KEVIN L. MORRISSEY** SECRETARY **LINDA A. SHIROISHI** • RESEARCH ASSOCIATE **LOUISE B. RISK** • ASSISTANT **LINDA A. FRIGHETTO**

FRIENDS OF ANIMALS

P.O. Box 1244 — NORWALK CT 06856
PHONE (203) 866 5223 — FAX (203) 853 9102

Founded 1957 • *Geographic Coverage* Global • *Focused Regions* Africa, Europe, Israel • *Cooperative Partner* No Dog Track Coalition of Bridgeport • *Chapters* 3, in the US - Florida, New York, DC, and 1 in Jerusalem, Israel • *Individual Members* 120,000

Mission To promote a compassionate ethic in the treatment of all animals worldwide and to prevent the birth of unwanted dogs and cats. Current fields of focus include the overpopulation of dogs and cats, wildlife issues - hunting, trapping, fur, and marine mammal issues.

Annual Fees	Regular	Student/Senior	International	Sustaining	Sponsor
	$20	$10	$30	$50	$100

Other Fees *Patron* $1,000

Funding	Foundations	Spay/Neuter Fees	Publications	Investments
	36%	59%	2%	3%

Total Income $3,518,876

Usage	Administration	Fundraising	Programs
	13%	9%	78%

Total Expenses $4,458,438

Programs National low cost spay/neuter program. Anti-fur campaign. National Wildlife Refuges and public lands. Marine mammal protection. Elephant and rhino protection. Committee for Humane Legislation. Anti-poaching efforts in Africa. Wolf protection. Walrus protection.

Publication Quarterly magazine *ActionLine*

Multimedia Online information service 1-800-312-PETS

For more Information Annual Report

Who's Who PRESIDENT PRISCILLA FERAL • VICE PRESIDENT SARAH SEYMOUR SECRETARY SALLY MALANGA • DIRECTOR OF ADMINISTRATION DIANNE FORTHMAN

FUND FOR ANIMALS, INC. (THE)

200 WEST 57TH STREET   NEW YORK NY 10019
PHONE (212) 246 2096   FAX (212) 246 2632

Founded 1967 • *Geographic Coverage* National

Mission The organization is dedicated to protecting animals.

Annual Fees	Regular	Student/Senior	Families	Special	Extra-Special
	$20	$10	$25	$50	$100

Other Fees *VIP* $1,000

Programs Wolf Conservation Program in Alaska. Bear Conservation Program. Mountain Lion Conservation Program. Backs federal legislation to create national park lands in California.

Publications Newsletter *The Fund for Animals*. Numerous fact sheets including *Factory Farming: Misery on the Menu* • *An Overview of Killing for Sport* • *The Bloody Business of Fur*

HUMANE SOCIETY OF THE UNITED STATES (THE)

2100 "L" STREET, NW   WASHINGTON DC 20037
PHONE (202) 452 1100   FAX (202) 778 6132

Founded 1954 • *Geographic Coverage* National, Global *Cooperative Partners* EarthKind, Humane Society International - International Division, National Association for Humane and Environmental Education - Youth Education Division, Center for Respect of Life and Environment - Higher Education Section • *Chapters* 10 regional offices in the US

Mission To prevent mistreatment, abuse and neglect of animals wherever animals need protection, to abolish cruel and unnecessary activities such as the killing of animals for their fur, dogfighting, cockfighting, and whaling, to address critical environmental issues in terms of their impact on animals, and to protect wildlife habitat.

Annual Fees	Regular	Families	Donor	Supporting	Sustaining
	$10	$18	$25	$50	$100

Other Fees *Sponsor* $500 • *Patron* $1,000

Funding	Membership	Bequests	Invested Income	Sales & Other
	49%	44%	5%	2%

Total Income $27,362,199

Usage	Administration	Fundraising	Programs	Membership Development
	10%	8%	69%	12%

Total Expenses $19,789,543

Programs Works through a wide variety of educational, legislative, investigative and legal means.

Publications Quarterly newsletters *HSUS News* • *Animal Activist Alert* • *Shelter Sense*. Periodic *Close-Up Report*. Numerous publications focusing on companion animals, wildlife and the environment, animal exploitation, and humane education

Multimedia Numerous public service announcements and audio-visuals focusing on public education, wildlife, farm animals and bioethics - available for rent or purchase

For more Information Annual Report, List of Publications

Who's Who PRESIDENT K. WILLIAM WISEMAN • VICE PRESIDENT O. J. RAMSEY SECRETARY AMY FREEMAN LEE • TREASURER PAUL G. IRWIN

INTERNATIONAL FUND FOR ANIMAL WELFARE

411 MAIN STREET, P.O. BOX 193   YARMOUTH PORT MA 02675
PHONE (508) 362 4944   FAX (508) 362 5841

Founded 1969 • *Geographic Coverage* Global • *Individual*

Members 1,000,000

Mission To promote and ensure the just and kind treatment of animals as sentient beings. Includes improving the quality of the lives of animals and their environment, preserving animals from extinction, and preventing and abolishing animal cruelty.

Annual Fees No set fee. One-year membership granted with any donation

	Membership	Government Support	Corporations
Funding	98%	1%	1%

Total Income $19,400,000

	Administration	Fundraising	Programs
Usage	14%	20%	67%

Program Cape Cod Stranding Network.

Who's Who CHIEF EXECUTIVE OFFICER BRIAN DAVIES • EXECUTIVE DIRECTOR RICHARD MOORE

INTERNATIONAL SOCIETY FOR ANIMAL RIGHTS, INC.

421 SOUTH STATE STREET   CLARKS SUMMIT PA 18411
PHONE (717) 586 2200   FAX (717) 586 9580

Founded 1959 • *Geographic Coverage* Global • *Cooperative Partner* Institute for Animal Rights Law

Mission Believing in principle that, because of their sentient nature, animals have rights, the Society works to expose and seeks to end the injustice of the exploitation of animals and the suffering inflicted on them.

	Regular	Voting Members
Annual Fees	$15	$50

	Membership	Foundations	Bequests	Financial Income	Other
Funding	30%	35%	29%	5%	1%

Total Income $420,644

	Administration	Fundraising	Membership Development	Programs
Usage	15%	5%	5%	75%

Total Expenses $586,090

Programs Disseminates published information. Works to bring about unity among organizations concerned with animal suffering. Sponsors national and international symposia. Sponsors public campaigns over animal rights issues.

Publications Quarterly newsletter *ISAR Report.* Numerous books, guides, fact sheets, pamphlets and booklets

Multimedia Numerous videos

For more Information Annual Report

Who's Who PRESIDENT HELEN JONES • VICE PRESIDENT REVEREND ALVIN VAN PELT HART • SECRETARY JEAN LAW

JEWS FOR ANIMAL RIGHTS

255 HUMPHREY STREET   MARBLEHEAD MA 01945-1645
PHONE (617) 631 7601

Founded 1985 • *Geographic Coverage* Global

Mission To publish books and ritual material on Judaism and animal rights, and Judaism and vegetarianism.

	Regular	Student/Senior
Annual Fees	$12	$6

Publications Books *Judaism and Animal Rights: Classical and Contemporary Responses* • *Judaism and Vegetarianism* • *Autobiography of a Revolutionary: Essays on Animal and Human Rights*

Who's Who PRESIDENT ROBERTA KALECHOFSKY

LAST CHANCE FOR ANIMALS

18653 VENTURA BOULEVARD, SUITE 356   TARZANA CA 91356
PHONE (310) 271 6096   FAX (310) 271 1409

Founded 1985 • *Geographic Coverage* National, North America *Chapters* 7 • *Individual Members* 40,000

Mission To abolish vivisection and exploitation of animals. Animal rights and anti-vivisection actions are the organization's main areas of focus.

Funding *Foundations* 100%

Total Income $290,492

Total Expenses $280,233

Programs Educational Workshops - 2nd and 4th Thursdays of the month. Speakers Bureau. Outreach Program - includes tabling.

Publications Quarterly newsletter. Brochures including *Fur* • *Pet Theft* • *Product and Cosmetic Testing.* Guide *Cruelty Free*

For more Information Library

Who's Who PRESIDENT CHRIS DEROSE • VICE PRESIDENT MARY MACDONALD LEWIS SECRETARY JENNIE ALVARADO • NATIONAL DIRECTOR AARON LEIDER • CONTACT MARLENE GOODMAN

NATIONAL ASSOCIATION FOR HUMANE AND ENVIRONMENTAL EDUCATION (THE)

67 NORWICH, ESSEX TURNPIKE   EAST HADDAM CT 06423-0362
PHONE (203) 434 8666   FAX (203) 434 9579

Founded 1974 • *Geographic Coverage* National • *Cooperative Partner* The Association is the youth education division of the Humane Society of the United States

Mission To promote kindness to people, animals, and the Earth through the publication of *KIND News*.

Annual Fees *Teacher "adoption" fee for KIND News* $18

Program Adopt a Teacher Program - when a teacher is "adopted," children in the classroom receive monthly issues of *KIND News* from September through May - thus far, 500,000 teachers have been "adopted".

Publications Newspaper published from September to May in 6 versions: *KIND News Primary* for grades 1 - 2 • *KIND News Junior* for grades 3 - 4 • *KIND News Senior* for grades 5 - 6 • *SNN (Student Network News)* • *SAG (Student Action Guide)* for grades 7 - 12 • *KIND News Internacional* (Spanish version of *KIND News Primary*)

For more Information Library, List of Publications

Who's Who COORDINATOR SPECIAL PROGRAMS LAURIE HOLLIN

PEOPLE FOR THE ETHICAL TREATMENT OF ANIMALS

P.O. BOX 42516   WASHINGTON DC 20015-0016
PHONE (301) 770 7382   FAX (301) 770 8969

Founded 1980 • *Geographic Coverage* National, Global • *Individual Members* 400,000

Mission The organization is dedicated to exposing and eliminating all animal abuse, and to establishing and defending the rights of all animals.

Annual Fees *Regular* $15

Funding	Membership	Merchandise & Other Sales	Interest Dividends & Royalties
	87%	11%	2%

Total Income $9,835,103

Usage	Administration	Fundraising	Programs
	12%	13%	75%

Total Expenses $8,697,999

Programs Operates a number of ongoing programs in the areas of outreach, education, lifestyle, research and investigations, communications and publications, cruelty-free merchandise, and animal rescue.

Publications Quarterly newsletter *PETA News*. Various books including *The Compassionate Cook* • *Shopping Guide for Caring Consumers* - Annual Guide • *Kids Can Save the Animals* • *Free the Animals*. Various brochures including *Take a Step Toward Compassionate Living* • *Animal Rights: Why Should It Concern Me* • *Pocket Shopping Guide*. Various mini-guides including *Animals and the Meat Industry* • *Animals and Product Testing* • *Animals in the Entertainment Industry*

Multimedia Videos including *Silver Springs Monkey* • *Unnecessary Fuss* • *Breaking Barriers* • *Getting Away With Murder* • *Exporting Cruelty* • *Don't Kill the Animals* • *Britches Dog Lab* • *Inside Biosearch*

For more Information Library, List of Publications

Who's Who PRESIDENT ALEX PACHECO • CHAIRPERSON INGRID E. NEWKIRK SECRETARY LINDA TYRELL • EXECUTIVE DIRECTOR JEANNE ROUSCH • LIBRARIAN KAREN PORRECA • CONTACT DAN MATHEWS

SOCIETY FOR ANIMAL PROTECTIVE LEGISLATION

P.O. BOX 3719, GEORGETOWN STATION   WASHINGTON DC 20007
PHONE (202) 337 2334

Founded 1955 • *Geographic Coverage* National

Mission To lobby for the protection and well-being of animals.

Funding	Contributions	Other
	75%	25%

Total Income $200,000

Usage	Administration	Fundraising	Programs	Other
	13.9%	5.8%	55%	25.3%

Who's Who PRESIDENT MADELEINE BEMELMANS • VICE PRESIDENT JOHN F. KULLBERG • SECRETARY CHRISTINE STEVENS

SPAY USA

14 VANDERVENTER AVENUE   PORT WASHINGTON NY 11050
PHONE (203) 375 6627

Founded 1990 • *Geographic Coverage* National • *Individual Members* 500

Mission To promote and facilitate spaying and neutering of pets.

Total Income $75,000

Publication *Spay USA Today*

Who's Who PRESIDENT MYRON GOULD

WORLD SOCIETY FOR THE PROTECTION OF ANIMALS

29 PERKINS STREET, P.O. BOX 190   BOSTON MA 02130-9904
PHONE (617) 522 7000   FAX (617) 522 7077

Founded 1959 • *Geographic Coverage* Global • *Chapters* 4 world-wide • *Organization Members* 341 • *Individual Members* 1,000

Mission To alleviate animal suffering throughout the world, to preserve endangered species from extinction, and to promote a humane ethic in the relationships between people and animals.

Annual Fees	Regular	Student/Senior	Families
	$20	$10	$40

Other Fees *Lifetime* $500

Funding	Membership	Contributions & Grants	Legacies
	3.7%	26%	55%

Other Fees *Net Gain on Sale of Investments* 5% • *Other* 10.3%

Total Income $6,136,504

Programs Hands-on campaigns to help animals worldwide. Disaster Relief Fund for animal victims of war and natural disasters. Educational programs and animal welfare legislation in less developed countries. Anti-fur campaign. Anti-bullfighting campaign. International bear protection campaign.

Publication Magazine *Animals International*

For more Information Annual Report

Who's Who PRESIDENT **SIR CAMERON RUSBY** • VICE PRESIDENTS **JOHN A. HOYT, GUS THORNTON** • SECRETARY **MURDAUGH S. MADDEN** • TREASURER **ROBERT S. CUMMINGS** • EXECUTIVE DIRECTOR **ANDREW DICKSON**

Canada

ASSOCIATION FOR THE PROTECTION OF FUR-BEARING ANIMALS

2235 COMMERCIAL DRIVE   VANCOUVER BC V5N 4B6
PHONE (604) 255 0411   FAX (604) 888 5817

Founded 1944 • *Geographic Coverage* North America, Western Europe

Mission To make people aware of the cruelty involved in trapping animals for fur.

Annual Fees	Regular	Patron
	$5	$25

Other Fees *Lifetime* $100

Programs Educational programs aimed at increasing the public's awareness about trapping. The society is sought out on all issues dealing with the state of trapping in Canada today.

Publication Newsletter *The Fur Bearers*

Multimedia Films including *Time To Care* • *America's Shame*

Who's Who EXECUTIVE DIRECTOR **GEORGE V. CLEMENTS** • PUBLICISTS **CATHERINE LEACH, JANET BRIDGERS** • ASSISTANT EXECUTIVE DIRECTOR **MICHELLE CLAUSIUS**

CANADIAN FEDERATION OF HUMANE SOCIETIES

30 CONCOURSE GATE, SUITE 102   NEPEAN ON K2E 7V7
PHONE (613) 224 8072   FAX (613) 723 0252

Founded 1957 • *Geographic Coverage* National • *Individual Members* 230

Mission The Federation is a national body comprised of animal welfare organizations and individuals working to promote compassionate and humane treatment for all animals.

Annual Fees	Regular	Student/Senior	Families	Corporation
	$35	$10	$50	$1,000

Funding	Membership	Corporations	Foundations	Investment Income	Other
	7%	3%	66%	19%	5%

Usage	Administration	Fundraising	Programs
	32%	6%	62%

Programs Ongoing efforts in the areas of humane education, animals in entertainment, experimental animals, farm animals, humane trapping, wildlife, marine mammals, and pet population.

Publications *Animal Welfare in Focus* • *Whale Kind* • *Caring for Animals* • *Political Animal News*

For more Information Database, Library

Who's Who PRESIDENT **ELEANOR DAWSON** • SECRETARY **BOB VAN TONGERBO** TREASURER **SANDRA BOND** • EXECUTIVE DIRECTOR **FRANCES RODENBURG** • PROGRAM DIRECTOR **SHELAGH MACDONALD** • LIBRARIAN **GAIL DELLAIRE**

LIFEFORCE FOUNDATION

P.O. BOX 3117, MAIN POST OFFICE   VANCOUVER BC V6B 3X6
PHONE (604) 299 2822

Geographic Coverage North America • *Cooperative Partner* Stanley Park - Vancouver, BC

Mission To raise public awareness of the interrelationship of human, animal, and environmental problems. Lifeforce urges society to address and solve problems by taking into consideration the long-term effects on all parts of the ecosystem. The Foundation focuses upon three major areas in which human, animal, and environmental rights are violated — the three "Es: Eating, Experimenting, and Entertaining".

Annual Fees

Regular	Student/Senior	Families	Corporation
$15	$10	$25	$100

Publications *Stanley Park Nature & History Walk* brochures

Multimedia Various videos including *Behind Laboratory Doors* • *Pound Seizure* • *Broken Promises*

WORLD SOCIETY
FOR THE PROTECTION OF ANIMALS

55 UNIVERSITY AVENUE, SUITE 902   TORONTO ON M5J 2H7
PHONE (416) 369 0044   FAX (416) 369 0147

Founded 1953 • *Geographic Coverage* National, Global • *Organization Members* 360 • *Individual Members* 1,000

Mission To promote effective means for the protection of animals, for the prevention of cruelty to animals, and for the relief of animals suffering in any part of the world.

Annual Fees *Regular* $35

Programs International Disaster Relief. Liberty Campaign for Bears. Anti-bull fighting campaign. NO-FUR campaign.

Publication Quarterly newsletter *Animals International*

Who's Who EXECUTIVE DIRECTOR **ANDREW DICKSON** • CONTACT **SILIA COIRO-SMITH**

environmental law & consulting

CHAPTER 17

Litigating for the Planet, by John Vargo

THERE ONCE WAS A TIME WHEN IT was inconceivable that our actions could damage the planet. Our dependence on the Earth was different.
We sought to feed, clothe and shelter ourselves,
and our numbers were too insignificant for the requisite harvesting to have a serious impact on any single ecosystem. Industry's effects were negligible until this century.
Early environmental law
(a set of common-law acts passed by Parliament in medieval England) existed only to protect one's health or enjoyment of property. Lawsuits heard under these acts were referred to as "nuisance" cases and they were considered adequate for their purposes.
Grounds of nuisance became limited in their effectiveness when population growth, industrial growth, land and consumer consumption began affecting the environment.
It became clear that the Earth's resources were not unlimited; the planet's capacity to heal itself from the assaults of progress was evidently much slower than the pace of the damage.
By the 1970s, laws designed to protect the environment were being passed with regularity.

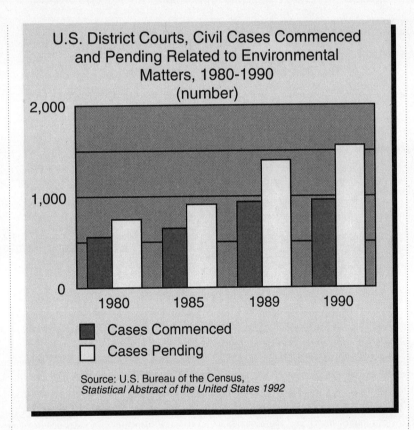

U.S. District Courts, Civil Cases Commenced and Pending Related to Environmental Matters, 1980-1990
(number)

■ Cases Commenced
□ Cases Pending

Source: U.S. Bureau of the Census,
Statistical Abstract of the United States 1992

IN THE UNITED STATES, environmental law is generally regulated on the state and local levels. Citizens and industry lock horns over issues as diverse as combating air pollution, noise pollution and zoning disputes.
The federal government regulates all environmental impacts that concern its processes.
For example, issues concerning a nuclear facility, which is federally licensed, are heard in federal courts. The Departments of Defense, Interior and Labor, the Food and Drug Administration and the Nuclear Regulatory Commission all have some authority regarding environmental matters. But most administration of federal policies and statutes in this area are the responsibility of the Environmental Protection Agency (EPA). The EPA was formed in 1970 when ecological problems began to gain the attention and interest of the American people. It had become apparent that a government agency was needed to control violations against the earth.
The formation of the EPA was preceded by the National Environmental Policy Act (1969), which requires all federal agencies to consider environmental impacts on their major decisions.

COMMON LAW IS STILL A VIABLE pursuit in environmental law. Generally, there are three areas of common law: nuisance, negligence and strict liability. Nuisance cases of the kind employed in medieval England weigh the harm to the general public against the economic benefit to a community.
For example, a court can decide for a polluting factory if that factory is also the economic backbone of the area.
For litigation to succeed in nuisance cases, an individual must often show a "distinct harm" separate from the rest of the community. Negligence cases can be brought against companies that have failed to provide proper controls and cause harm to their employees or neighbors. ▶

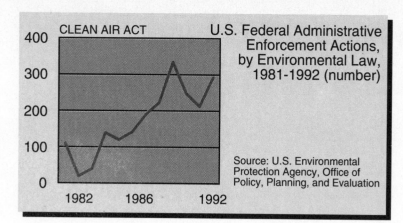

CLEAN AIR ACT — U.S. Federal Administrative Enforcement Actions, by Environmental Law, 1981-1992 (number)

Source: U.S. Environmental Protection Agency, Office of Policy, Planning, and Evaluation

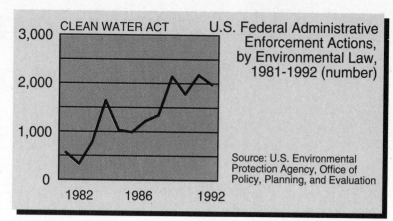

CLEAN WATER ACT — U.S. Federal Administrative Enforcement Actions, by Environmental Law, 1981-1992 (number)

Source: U.S. Environmental Protection Agency, Office of Policy, Planning, and Evaluation

United States

ASBESTOS VICTIMS OF AMERICA
PAGE 263
P.O. Box 559
Phone (408) 476 3646
Capitola CA 95010

CENTER FOR INTERNATIONAL ENVIRONMENTAL LAW

1621 Connecticut Avenue, NW
Phone (202) 332 4840
Washington DC 20009-1076
Fax (202) 332 4865

Founded 1989 • *Geographic Coverage* Global • *Cooperative Partners* Greenpeace International, Defenders of Wildlife, IUCN The World Conservation Union, Sierra Club, The Peace Research Centre of the Australian National University, Washington College of Law at the American University

Mission To bring the energy and experience of the public interest environmental law movement in the United States to the critical task of strengthening and developing international and comparative environmental law, policy, and management throughout the world. Specific goals include incorporating fundamental principles of ecology and democracy into international law, strengthening national environmental law systems and public interest movements throughout the world, educating and training public-interest-minded environmental lawyers, and improving the effectiveness of law in solving environmental problems.

Programs The Center's work is organized under seven substantive areas: Trade and the Environment, International Institutions and Sustainable Development, Biodiversity and Wildlife, Global Warming and Ozone Depletion, Oceans Conservation, State of Environmental Law, and Education. The Biodiversity Action Network (BioNet), a joint effort of environmental NGOs initiated and coordinated by the Center and the Sierra Club, supports NGOs in their efforts to use law and policy to protect biodiversity.

Publications Books *Freedom for the Seas in the 21st Century: Ocean Governance and Environmental Harmony* • *Trade and the Environment: Law, Economics and Policy* • *Annual State of Environmental Law.* Recent publications include *Trade, Environment and Sustainable Development: A Primer* • *Report Technology Transfer, Global Change, and Intellectual Property.* Country reports and annual *State of Environmental Law* special issue reports

For more Information Annual Report, List of Publications

Who's Who President Durwood J. Zaelke • Vice President Barbara L. Shaw • Senior Attorney David B. Hunter • Attorneys David Downes, Donald M. Goldberg, Robert F. Housman, Chris Wold • Contact Denise McCormick

CONSERVATION LAW FOUNDATION

62 Summer Street
Phone (617) 350 0990
Boston MA 02110-1008
Fax (617) 350 4030

Founded 1966 • *Geographic Coverage* Regional • *Focused Region* New England • *Chapters* 2 • *Individual Members* 6,000

Mission To improve the management of natural resources and protect the environment and public health throughout New England, through legal means. The organization has been instrumental in defining and advancing critical regional environmental interests, and works to conserve natural habitats, open space, and agricultural lands, improve urban environments, protect marine resources, reduce environmental threats to human health, prevent water and air pollution, and develop environmentally sound and economically efficient regional energy, water-use, and transportation policies.

Annual Fees	Regular	Student/Senior	Contributing	Supporting	Patron
	$30	$15	$50	$100	$250

Funding	Membership	Foundations	Endowment Income	Other
	21%	74.6%	3.2%	1.2%

Total Income $2,448,358

Under this area of law, businesses are required to exercise reasonable care in the protection of the community. Strict liability laws apply to any company engaged in ultra-hazardous activities. Often applied to companies dealing with radiation and toxic waste, strict liability holds that businesses are liable for any injuries caused by their activities. The injured party is not required to prove that the business did not use reasonable care.

WHILE COMMON LAW CAN BE APPLIED in certain cases, widespread environmental problems are dealt with through myriad federal statutes. The Rivers and Harbors Act (1886) was designed to keep refuse from navigable waterways. The Federal Water Pollution Control Act (1948) was meant to eliminate the discharge of material into navigable waters. In this law, the word material is synonymous with pollutant. In the Endangered Species Act (1973), all federal agencies must ensure they do not jeopardize endangered species or their habitats. Other statutes which cover environmental concerns are the Atomic Energy Act (1954), Clean Air Act (1963), Noise Control Act (1972), Safe Drinking Water Act (1974), Toxic Substances Control Act (1976), Low Level Radioactive Waste Policy Act (1980) and the Nuclear Waste Policy Act (1982). Fines are imposed against companies that violate the tenets of these acts. In 1992, Rockwell International agreed to pay $18.5 million after pleading guilty to mishandling poisonous waste at its Rocky Flats nuclear plant. Also in 1992, Dexter Corporation of Connecticut was fined $4 million in criminal penalties and $9 million ▶

Chapter 17 • Environmental Law • Consulting

Usage

Administration	Membership Development	Programs
4.5%	9.1%	86.4%

Total Expenses $2,304,357

Programs Current objectives include passing a lead paint law in Vermont, and winning funds to "de-lead" housing throughout New England, making sure highway projects throughout New England offer environmental as well as automotive benefits; forcing New England's electricity system to be the most efficient in the world; fighting for development of modern rail service to New York, reducing pollution and eliminating the need for a second major Massachusetts airport; cleaning up Connecticut's air - ranked among the most smog-filled in the US; and restoring New England's fisheries and cleaning up its harbors.

Publications Quarterly newsletter. Ecological Innovations catalog

For more Information Annual Report, Library

Who's Who PRESIDENT CHARLES C. CABOT, JR. • VICE PRESIDENT JOHN M. TEAL SECRETARY DAVID F. CAVERS, JR. • TREASURER CAROLYN G. MUGAR • EXECUTIVE DIRECTOR DOUGLAS I. FOY • SENIOR ATTORNEYS ARMAND COHEN, STEPHANIE POLLACK, PETER SHELLEY • SENIOR SCIENTIST EMILY BATESON • STAFF ATTORNEY STEVE BURRINGTON • STAFF SCIENTISTS ELLIE DORSEY, RENEE J. ROBINS • MEMBERSHIP COORDINATOR KIMBERLY COPPENRATH • LIBRARIAN ANN FRIEND

ENVIRONMENTAL DEFENSE CENTER

906 GARDEN STREET, SUITE 2   SANTA BARBARA CA 93101
PHONE (805) 963 1622

Founded 1977 • *Geographic Coverage* Local • *Focused Region* South-central coast of California

Mission The Center, public interest environmental law firm, provides free legal advice and counseling to local conservation groups, enabling these groups to be more effective. When citizens' objections can't stop an action that will significantly harm the environment, the organization provides free legal representation and litigation services in court.

Programs The Center's attorneys counsel groups on how to effectively participate in the decision making process, how to insure that laws are applied correctly, and how to preserve their legal right of appeal when the law is not followed. When legal action is the only remaining option, the Center's attorneys represent these groups, free of charge, in court.

Publication Newsletter *Public Interest Environmental Law and Education*

Who's Who PRESIDENT PAUL TEBBEL • VICE PRESIDENT DAVID LANDECKER • SECRETARY ELLEN BOUGHER • TREASURER SELMA RUBIN • CHIEF COUNSEL MARC CHYTILO STAFF ATTORNEY LINDA KROP • DEVELOPMENT COORDINATOR GREG HELMS

ENVIRONMENTAL DEFENSE FUND   PAGE 21

257 PARK AVENUE, SOUTH   NEW YORK NY 10010
PHONE (212) 505 2100   FAX (212) 505 2375

ENVIRONMENTAL EXCHANGE (THE)

1718 CONNECTICUT AVENUE, NW   WASHINGTON DC 20009
PHONE (202) 387 2182   FAX (202) 588 9422

Founded 1991 • *Geographic Coverage* National

Mission To provide environmental organizations, government, and businesses with information on effective environmental initiatives. Transportation alternatives and toxic waste issues are the organization's main areas of focus.

Annual Fees

Regular	Patron
$25	$100

Funding

Membership	Corporations	Foundations
10%	5%	85%

Total Income $110,000

Usage	Administration	Fundraising	Programs
	15%	5%	80%

Programs Information clearinghouse. Local environmental activist network.

Publications *What Works* reports. *What Works* Bulletin. *Transportation Exchange Update*

Who's Who PRESIDENT RICHARD WILES

ENVIRONMENTAL LAW INSTITUTE

1616 "P" STREET, NW, SUITE 200   WASHINGTON DC 20036
PHONE (202) 328 5150   FAX (202) 328 5002

Founded 1969 • *Geographic Coverage* National, Global • *Cooperative Partners* Case Western Reserve University School of Law, American Law Institute, American Bar Association, Smithsonian Institution, Growth Management Institute, US Environmental Protection Agency, Fish and Wildlife Service, IUCN The World Conservation Union's Center for Environmental Law, Clean Sites, Inc. • *Organization Members* 3,000

Mission To enhance the expertise of the environmental profession. Through its information services, training courses and seminars, research programs, and policy recommendations, the Institute activates a broad constituency of environmental professionals in government, industry, the private bar, public interest groups, and academia.

Annual Fees	Regular	Student/Senior
	$75	$50

Funding	Membership	Government Support	Corporations	Foundations	Other
	7%	41%	4%	15%	33%

Total Income $5,262,601

Total Expenses $4,807,877

Programs Center for Public Health and Law. Center for State, Local, and Regional Environmental Programs. Environmental Program for Central and Eastern Europe. Inter-American Center for Environmental Policy. Middle East Program. Professional and Corporate Associates Programs. Wetlands Program. Courses, workshops, conferences, and seminars in environmental law and management. State Superfund Network.

Publications Periodicals *The Environmental Forum* • *Environmental Law Reporter* • *National Wetlands Newsletter*. Books including *Environmental Law and Practice* • *Sustainable Environmental Law*. Numerous other books, monographs, treatises and research reports

For more Information Annual Report, Library, List of Publications

Who's Who PRESIDENT J. WILLIAM FUTRELL • LIBRARIAN LINDA LARSEN • CONTACT LISA PELSTRING

ENVIRONMENTAL SUPPORT CENTER (THE)

1825 CONNECTICUT AVENUE, NW   WASHINGTON DC 20009
PHONE (202) 328 7813   FAX (202) 265 9419

Founded 1990 • *Geographic Coverage* National

Mission To strengthen the environmental community by helping groups develop effective organizations. Since the Center was created, it has assisted several hundred groups with managerial and administrative needs, such as the establishment or upgrading of financial systems, finding needed equipment, developing media strategies, and improving relations between board and staff.

Funding	Foundations	Interest
	97.6%	2.3%

Total Income $540,000

Usage	Administration	Fundraising	Programs
	22%	2%	76%

Total Expenses $680,000

Programs The Center operates a Training and Technical Assistance program to boost the fundraising, strategic planning, organizational, and financial management capabilities of environmental groups. Equipment and Software Acquisition/Distribution. Federated Fundraising for Environmental Groups.

For more Information Annual Report

Who's Who PRESIDENT BILL DAVIS • VICE PRESIDENT LOIS GIBBS • SECRETARY PAT BRYANT • EXECUTIVE DIRECTOR JAMES W. ABERNATHY • OTHER LYNN BOCK, LOUISA CLARK, MELISSA HIPPLER, DONNA M. MUÑOZ, MIDGE TAYLOR

ENVIRONMENTAL TECHNICAL INFORMATION SYSTEM
DEPARTMENT OF URBAN AND REGIONAL PLANNING

1003 WEST NEVADA STREET   URBANA IL 61801
PHONE (217) 333 1369   FAX (217) 244 1717

Founded 1973 • *Geographic Coverage* National • *Other Field of Focus* Environmental Education / Careers / Information / Networks

Mission To provide planners, economists, decision makers, and environmental specialists with current environmental information through a collection of environmental databases, producing increased efficiency due to substantial savings in time.

Annual Fees *Computer online service subscription* $200 plus $15 per additional login plus $90 per hour connect time • *Staff assistance* $25 per hour

Programs Economic Impact Forecast System, a database with socio-economic data for all US counties, allowing assessment of impact on

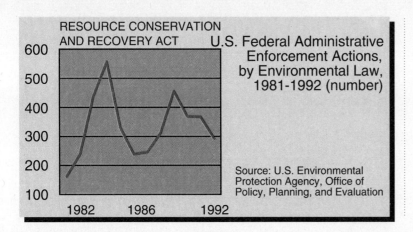

RESOURCE CONSERVATION AND RECOVERY ACT

U.S. Federal Administrative Enforcement Actions, by Environmental Law, 1981-1992 (number)

Source: U.S. Environmental Protection Agency, Office of Policy, Planning, and Evaluation

▶ in civil penalties for violating the Clean Water Act. Mobil Oil Corporation agreed to pay a $950,000 fine for violating the Clean Air Act.

STILL, FEDERAL STATUTES DO NOT exist without challenge. In 1992, Interior Secretary Manual Lujan called the spotted owl debate "a big headache" and claimed the Endangered Species Act was too stringent. He was suggesting that as more species dwindle in numbers, more confrontation between industry and environmental protection is inevitable. Human concern for the future of the planet has lead to all the legislation. The role of the environmental activists and their organizations has been to publicize dangers and force lawmakers to establish environmental guidelines for businesses and government agencies. Through persistent ▶

local economies of proposed activities using several economic models. Computer-aided Environmental Legislative Data System, a database with abstracted federal and state environmental regulations and standards. Soils Systems, a database which allows easy access to SCS data by soils series name or by entering a combination of desired soil characteristics. Environmental Impact Computer System, an interactive system which enables user to determine how any activity may affect various aspects of the environment.

Publication Quarterly newsletter

For more Information Database, Library

Who's Who LIBRARIAN **ELIZABETH G. DENNISON**

GRASS ROOTS ENVIRONMENTAL ORGANIZATION, INC.

P.O. BOX 289   HOPE NJ 07844
PHONE (908) 841 9512

Founded 1985 • *Geographic Coverage* National • *Other Field of Focus* Pollution / Radiations • *Chapters* 3 • *Organization Members* 35

Mission To provide organizing and technical assistance, as well as legal referral, to grassroots citizen's groups fighting toxic chemical pollution problems.

Funding	*Membership*	*Foundations*
	5%	95%

Total Income $25,000

Usage	*Administration*	*Programs*
	50%	50%

Programs Environmental Ribbon for Environmental Justice - A Fight Against Environmental Racism.

Publications Periodicals *GrassRoots Environmental Organization Newsletter* • *GrassRoots Environmental Organization Action Bulletin*

Who's Who PRESIDENT **MATT KRAUTHEIM** • VICE PRESIDENT **MARK LOBHAUER** SECRETARY **CHERYL VOGEL**

INFORM, INC.

381 PARK AVENUE, SOUTH   NEW YORK NY 10016-8806
PHONE (212) 689 4040   FAX (212) 447 0689

Founded 1974 • *Geographic Coverage* National • *Individual Members* 1,000

Mission To further the protection of natural resources and public health, through the identification, development and sharing of practical methods to meet these ends. Inform's research attempts to contribute in a constructive way to environmental debates, and is used by federal and state legislators, by national and local conservation groups, and by business leaders who are shaping environmental policies and programs. Hazardous waste reduction, garbage management, air pollution, alternative vehicle fuels, and irrigation are the organization's main areas of focus.

Annual Fees	*Regular*	*Friend*	*Contributing*	*Supporting*	*Donor*
	$25	$50	$100	$250	$500

Other Fees *Associate* $1,000 • *Benefactor* $5,000

Funding	*Grants*	*Contributions*	*Book Sales, Royalties & Subscriptions*	*Other*
	60.2%	34.4%	4.4%	1%

Total Income $1,500,000

Usage	*Administration*	*Fundraising*	*Programs*
	15.1%	9.7%	75.2%

Programs Provides internships, grassroots workshops, conferences.

Publications Quarterly newsletter *INFORM Reports.* Reports *Cutting*

Chemical Waste • Reducing Office Paper Waste • Burning Garbage in the US • Toxics in Our Air • Trading Toxics Across State Lines • Promoting Hazardous Waste Reduction • Drive for Clean Air • A Citizen's Guide to Promoting Toxic Waste Reduction. Book Environmental Dividends

For more Information Annual Report, List of Publications

Who's Who CHAIR **CHARLES A. MORAN** • VICE CHAIR **KIKU HOAGLAND HANES** PRESIDENT **JOANNA D. UNDERWOOD** • DIRECTOR OF RESEARCH AND PUBLICATIONS **SIBYL R. GOLDEN**

INVESTOR RESPONSIBILITY RESEARCH CENTER, INC.

1755 MASSACHUSETTS AVENUE, NW   WASHINGTON DC 20036
PHONE (202) 234 7500   FAX (202) 332 8570

Founded 1972 • *Geographic Coverage* National, Global • *Organization Members* 500

Mission To provide institutions with reliable, objective information on contemporary social and business policy and practice issues. The Center's Environmental Information Service addresses corporate environmental performance of 500 companies through its *Profile Directory*, which is designed to enable investors to select companies based on a comparison of their environmental attributes.

Funding	Corporations	Foundations	Subscriptions
	10%	10%	80%

Total Income $4,000,000

Usage	Administration	Programs
	59%	41%

Programs Subscription services. Proxy program.

Publications Newsletters including monthly *News for Investors* • Bimonthly *Corporate Governance Bulletin* • Bimonthly *Investor's Environmental Report* • Quarterly *Global Shareholder* • Quarterly *South Africa Reporter*. Various books including *Trash to Cash, New Business Opportunities in the Post-Consumer Waste Stream* • *Tropical Deforestation* • *The Greenhouse Gambit, Industry Responses to Climate Change* • *The Greenhouse Effect, Investment Implications and Opportunities* • *Power Plays, Profiles of America's Leading Renewable Electricity Developers*

For more Information Annual Report

Who's Who SECRETARY **SHIRLEY CARPENTER** • TREASURER **SCOTT FENN** • EXECUTIVE DIRECTOR **MARGARET CARROLL** • CONTACT **JONATHAN S. NAIMON**

LAND AND WATER FUND OF THE ROCKIES (THE)

2260 BASELINE ROAD, SUITE 200   BOULDER CO 80302
PHONE (303) 444 1188   FAX (303) 786 8054

Founded 1989 • *Geographic Coverage* Regional • *Cooperative Partners* The Wilderness Society, Natural Resources Defense Council, National Wildlife Federation • *Chapters* 7 • *Individual Members* 250

Mission To provide free legal aid and increase the effectiveness of local, state, and regional environmental organizations by providing legal counseling, litigation services, and a pro bono network of volunteer attorneys and technical experts. Public lands, water and toxics, energy efficiency and related environmental issues in law are the organization's main areas of expertise.

Annual Fees	Regular	Student/Senior	Dues & Contributions
	$25	$15	$50 to 1,000

Funding	Membership	Foundations
	10%	90%

Total Income $698,000

Usage	Administration	Fundraising	Programs
	7%	5%	89%

Programs Water and Toxics Program. Energy Project. Adopt A Forest. Public Lands Program which works to address federal lands issues. Pro bono program.

Who's Who PRESIDENT **FRANCES M. GREEN** • SECRETARY **KATHY P. REIMER**

LEGAL ENVIRONMENTAL ASSISTANCE FOUNDATION

1115 NORTH GADSEN STREET   TALLAHASSEE FL 32303-6327
PHONE (904) 681 2591

Founded 1979 • *Geographic Coverage* Regional • *Focused Region* Alabama, Florida, and Georgia • *Organization Members* 4 • *Individual Members* 300

Mission To protect humans and the environment from pollution by providing legal services, free of charge to citizens. Particular areas of focus include the protection of human health from toxic contaminants, groundwater and surface water protection, energy conservation and efficiency.

Annual Fees	Regular	Special Contribution	Patron
	$25	$15	$100

Funding	Membership	Foundations
	10%	90%

Total Income $500,000

Usage	Administration	Fundraising	Programs
	8%	8%	84%

Programs The Foundation operates ongoing programs on the issues of

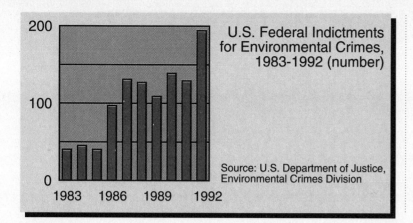

U.S. Federal Indictments for Environmental Crimes, 1983-1992 (number)

Source: U.S. Department of Justice, Environmental Crimes Division

200

100

0

1983   1986   1989   1992

challenges and litigation, environmental groups have structured the foundations which support the governing of environmental concerns.
They continue to shape and define environmental policy by mustering solid, unified fronts against practices that spoil the Earth and its atmosphere. Despite the extraordinary power that environmental law offers those dedicated to protecting the Earth,

employing environmental law is not a remedy for a polluted, ailing planet. Statutes set guidelines which regulate the amount of waste that industry is allowed to introduce and methods for its disposal.

BUT LAWS DO NOT PROVIDE complete protection. A palpable "us against them" notion maintains a breach between those motivated by profit and those who are ▶

---

pollution prevention and reduction, justice and empowerment and energy advocacy.

Publications Quarterly newsletter *Leaf-Briefs*. Over 50 educational documents

Who's Who PRESIDENT **B. SUZI RUHL** • VICE PRESIDENT **CYNTHIA VALENCIC** SECRETARY **BOB KUEHN**

NATURAL RESOURCES DEFENSE COUNCIL

40 WEST 20TH STREET   NEW YORK NY 10011
PHONE (212) 727 2700

Founded 1970 • *Geographic Coverage* Local, National, Global *Focused Countries* Canada, the Caribbean, Chile, Russian Federation, USA • *Cooperative Partners* Russian Center for Environmental Law, Yale Law School, The Nature Conservancy of Hawaii, Northwest Conservation Act Coalition, Federation of American Scientists, Sequoia Group • *Chapters* 4

Mission To use the power of law, science and people to defend the environment, and to defend people's rights to unpolluted air, clean water and unspoiled public lands through the courts, legislation, regulatory agencies, and the public arena.

Annual Fees *Membership through contributions* of $10, $15, $25, or $50

Funding	Membership	Foundations	Fees, Contracts & Other Revenues
	59%	32%	9%

Total Income $17,967,795

Usage	Administration	Fundraising	Membership Development	Programs
	11%	9%	3%	77%

Total Expenses $16,452,386

Programs Working on a variety of issues including global warming, ozone depletion, the James Bay Wilderness, nuclear waste and nuclear weapons, the Farm Bill, national forests, global energy efficiency, California wildlife, protecting the Chilean Wilderness, strengthening the Clean Water Act, and numerous other issues of global, national and local significance. Clean Air Network. Hakalau Forest National Wildlife Refuge reforestation project.

Publications Quarterly magazine *Amicus*. Book *50 Simple Things You Can Do To Save The Earth*. Reports *Testing The Waters* • *Safety at Bay*

For more Information Annual Report

Who's Who EXECUTIVE DIRECTOR **JOHN H. ADAMS** • ASSOCIATE DIRECTOR FOR MEMBERSHIP **MARIE WEINMANN**

NORTHWEST RENEWABLE RESOURCES CENTER PAGE 117

1411 FOURTH AVENUE, SUITE 1510   SEATTLE WA 98101
PHONE (206) 623 7361   FAX (206) 467 1640

SCIENTIFIC CERTIFICATION SYSTEMS

1611 TELEGRAPH AVENUE, SUITE 1111   OAKLAND CA 94612-2113
PHONE (510) 832 1415   FAX (510) 832 0359

Founded 1984 • *Geographic Coverage* National

Mission To spur the private and public sectors toward more environmentally sustainable policy planning, product design, management, and production through programs based on sound scientific principles. In pursuit of this goal, the organization has applied the tools of analytical science to launch research and certification initiatives in variety of areas.

Programs Forest Conservation Program works to identify forestry management practices which most successfully sustain timber resources while maintaining the ecological viability of the forest and benefiting the larger community. Environmental Claims Certification Program works to verify specific environmental claims. Environmental Report Card provides a complete environmental profile of products and packaging based on "cradle-to-grave" analysis. Food Inspection and Certification Program. NutriClean Program, which is the first ever third party certification system for testing pesticide residues in fresh produce.

Multimedia Online information service 1-800-ECO-PACTS

Who's Who PRESIDENT STANLEY P. RHODES • CONTACT JIM DUFFY

SIERRA CLUB LEGAL DEFENSE FUND

180 MONTGOMERY STREET   SAN FRANCISCO CA 94104-4209
PHONE (415) 627 6700   FAX (415) 627 6740

Founded 1971 • *Geographic Coverage* National, Global • *Cooperative Partner* Sierra Club USA • *Chapters* 7 • *Individual Members* 150,000 of the Sierra Club's 570,000 members

Mission To ensure that government agencies enforce existing environmental laws, and that private industries obey them; to use legal strategies in protecting threatened places and creatures; and to advise citizen groups, state legislatures, and Congress on proposals for useful new laws.

Annual Fees *Tax-deductible contributions over* $10

	Membership	Foundations	Court-Awarded Attorneys' Fees
Funding	75%	15%	10%

Total Income $10,446,354

	Administration	Fundraising	Programs
Usage	5%	14%	81%

Total Expenses $10,068,807

Programs The Ancient Forests, Pacific Northwest Program has protected thousands of acres of remnant old-growth forest in Oregon and Washington from destruction by clearcutting. The Huaorani Indians project works to address the situation of these Indians of the Ecuadorian Amazon, who face massive oil development on traditional lands. The "Save Yellowstone Now!" project is an effort to save Yellowstone National Park from resource extraction and land development projects in the areas surrounding the park. Many other active cases throughout the United States dealing with wildlife and habitat, national forest planning, coasts and wetlands, clean air, clean water, and public water rights. Pooled Income Fund: high yield investment opportunity.

Publication Quarterly newsletter *In Brief*

For more Information Annual Report

Who's Who VICE PRESIDENT SPECIAL PROJECTS JOANNE C. MAY KLIEJUNAS • EXECUTIVE DIRECTOR VAWTER PARKER • DIRECTOR OF DEVELOPMENT LESLIE ANN FOX

SOUTHERN ENVIRONMENTAL LAW CENTER

201 WEST MAIN STREET   CHARLOTTESVILLE VA 22902-5065
PHONE (804) 977 4090   FAX (804) 977 1483

Founded 1986 • *Geographic Coverage* Regional • *Focused Region* US South • *Individual Members* 2,000

Mission To protect the natural resources of the South through legal advocacy.

	Membership	Foundations	Interest	Other
Funding	25%	71%	2%	2%

Total Income $1,413,848

	Administration	Fundraising	Programs
Usage	7%	9%	84%

Total Expenses $1,145,922

Programs The Center operates a number of programs to defend the South's natural resources, including a Public Lands Project, a Coastal and Wetlands Project, a Clean Water Project, a Billboard and Sign Control Project and an Energy Project.

Publication Quarterly newsletter *Southern Resources*

For more Information Annual Report

Who's Who EXECUTIVE DIRECTOR RICK MIDDLETON • LEGAL SECRETARY LAURIE A. MILLER

WASHINGTON ENVIRONMENTAL COUNCIL

5200 UNIVERSITY WAY, NE   SEATTLE WA 98105
PHONE (206) 527 1599   FAX (206) 527 1693

Founded 1967 • *Geographic Coverage* State • *Cooperative Partner* Earth Share of Washington • *Organization Members* 100 • *Individual Members* 100

Mission To inform, unite and empower Washington citizens to protect and restore the state's environment. The Council works with its member groups to encourage strong environmental laws, "watchdog" the enforcement of existing laws, encourage citizen involvement in policy decisions and educate the public about environmental issues. Fields of focus include wetlands and wilderness, solid and hazardous wastes, wildlife, pesticides, open space and public recreation, forest practices, endangered species, air and water pollution control, transportation planning and land use and growth management.

	Regular	Families	Living Lightly	Sponsor	Centennial Club
Annual Fees	$25	$35	$15	$50	$100 to 450

Other Fees *Major Donor* $500+

Programs Advocacy of environmental laws, including drafting legisla-

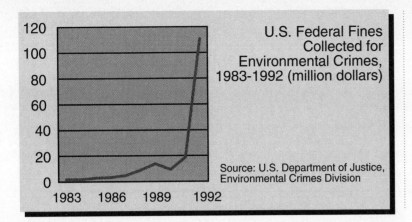

U.S. Federal Fines Collected for Environmental Crimes, 1983-1992 (million dollars)

Source: U.S. Department of Justice, Environmental Crimes Division

environmentally sensitive. Controls are expensive. They limit resources. They limit production. They drive up product costs. Consequently, industry often finds it difficult to consider regulations as necessary. Yet the relentless march of progress continues to threaten a seriously damaged planet. The ability of the Earth to continue to absorb significant waste is suspect. And the human race has long exceeded the planet's capacity to provide the natural essentials of food and shelter.

Our appetite for consumption continues to accelerate. And despite the great strides we have made in enacting policy and legislation, it is clearly evident (more so than in the days when the EPA was designed) that the scope of the problem is much more immense than a debate over profit and the environment. •

John Vargo

tion, testifying at hearings, serving on advisory committees, holding an annual "Legislative Workshop", conferences, media events, and wetlands tours.

Publications Newsletters *Alert!* • *Voices*

Who's Who PRESIDENT **DARLENE MADENWALD** • VICE PRESIDENT **JOAN THOMAS** TREASURER **JOHN ANDERSON** • EXECUTIVE DIRECTOR **TOM ROBINSON** • CONTACT **MEGAN M. DAHL**

Canada

CANADIAN ENVIRONMENTAL DEFENCE FUND

347 COLLEGE STREET   TORONTO ON M5T 2V8
PHONE (416) 323 9521   FAX (416) 323 9301

Founded 1985 • *Geographic Coverage* National • *Chapter* 1 *Individual Members* 6,500

Mission To help citizens pursuing nationally significant and precedent-setting environmental law cases.

Annual Fees *Regular* $25

Programs Some causes assisted by the Fund include Save Kelly's Mountain Society on Cape Breton Island, The New Foundland Inshore Fisherman's Association, Maisie Shiell at Cluff Lake, Time to Respect Earth's Ecosystems in Manitoba, Okanagan Save Our Lakes in British Columbia, Stop Construction of the Rafferty/Alameda Project in Saskatchewan, Assuring Protection for Tomorrow's Environment in Ontario, and the Save Richmond Farmland Society in British Columbia.

Publication Annual newsletter

Who's Who PRESIDENT **MURRAY KLIPPENSTEIN** • VICE PRESIDENT **RON PUSCHAK** SECRETARY **PETER PICKFIELD** • TREASURER **STUART MULCAHY** • EXECUTIVE DIRECTOR **DAVID DONNELLY**

CANADIAN ENVIRONMENTAL LAW ASSOCIATION

517 COLLEGE STREET, SUITE 401   TORONTO ON M6G 4A2
PHONE (416) 960 2284   FAX (416) 960 9392

Founded 1970 • *Geographic Coverage* Province, National • *Cooperative Partners* Canadian Institute for Environmental Law and Policy, Canadian Environmental Defence Fund, Great Lakes United, Canadian Environmental Network, Pollution Probe, Friends of the Earth, Federation of Ontario Naturalists, West Coast Environmental Law Association of Vancouver, Environmental Law Centre of Edmonton • *Individual Members* 600

Mission To provide effective legal assistance on issues of environmental law to those otherwise unable to afford representation. To promote, through legal channels, standards and objectives that will ensure the maintenance of environmental quality in Ontario and throughout Canada. To preserve Canada's environmental heritage and to encourage the sound management of energy and resources by: (1) encouraging thorough planning, to ensure all interests have been represented and all concerns considered; (2) increasing awareness of and responsibility towards the environment in all sectors of society; (3) fostering the protection of significant and strategic natural areas; (4) making the law work for citizens with environmental concerns, and (5) undertaking research into the ways of preserving and improving the quality of the environment.

Annual Fees *Regular* $20

Funding *Government Support* 99%

Total Income $591,586

Usage	*Administration*	*Programs*
	20%	80%

Total Expenses $581,337

Programs The Association has focused its attention on the problems posed by toxic and hazardous wastes and the legal aspects of their control. It continues to take legal action on cases regarding air and water pollution, timber management, landfill sites, development of wetlands, toxic waste disposal, or land contamination. The Association also makes law reform recommendations and participates in the development of new legislation.

Publications Bimonthly newsletter *The Intervener.* Various briefs focusing on major environmental issues

For more Information Annual Report, Database, Library, List of Publications

Who's Who PRESIDENT **GRAHAM REMPE** • SECRETARY **KATHY COOPER** • TREASURER **KATHLEEN MCPHERSON** • EXECUTIVE DIRECTOR **MICHELLE SWENARCHUK** • COUNSELS **RICK LINDGREN, ZEN MAKUCH, BARBARA RUTHERFORD** • EDITOR **JILL CAMERON** LIBRARIAN **MARY VISE**

CANADIAN INSTITUTE OF RESOURCES LAW
INSTITUT CANADIEN DU DROIT DES RESSOURCES
THE UNIVERSITY OF CALGARY
FACULTY OF LAW, BIO SCIENCES BUILDING   CALGARY AB T2N 1N4
PHONE (403) 220 3200   FAX (403) 282 6182

Founded 1979 • *Geographic Coverage* National • *Cooperative Partners* The University of Calgary, The Alberta Law Foundation, the Canadian Government, The Centre for Natural Resources Law at the University of Melbourne - Australia, The Energy Law Center - Salt Lake City, The International Institute for Energy Law - Leiden, The Japan Energy Law Research Institute - Tokyo, The Rocky Mountain Mineral Law Foundation - Denver

Mission To undertake and to promote research, education, and publication on the law relating to Canada's renewable and non-renewable natural resources. The Institute's objectives are to contribute to a better understanding of how legal systems and laws deal with natural resources, to analyze whether such laws accomplish their policy objectives, and to propose reforms; to analyze the techniques by which resources policies are developed and implemented, to assess the appropriateness of such techniques, and to make suitable recommendations; to disseminate the results of its research through educational activities and publications; to complement the responsibilities of existing legal education institutions by providing a pool of expertise in resources law.

	Membership	Government Support	Corporations	Foundations
Funding	9%	25%	8%	44%

Other Sources *Sales & Seminars* 14%

Total Income $648,396

	Administration	Fundraising	Programs
Usage	45%	2%	53%

Total Expenses $641,286

Programs The Institute's ongoing research program includes studies on mining, forestry, environmental, petroleum, water, and international trades law. The Institute also sponsors conferences and short courses on topical aspects of resources law, and a variety of workshops and seminars, dealing with topics such as environmental law for practitioners, resource development and aboriginal land rights, agricultural trade, interjurisdictional water management, and offshore oil and gas law.

Publications Quarterly newsletter *Resources,* circulation 5,500. Various books including *Canadian Law of Mining* • *Environmental Protection: Its Implications for the Canadian Forest Sector* • *Alberta's Wetlands: Legal Incentives and Obstacles to Their Conservation* • *Instream Flow Protection and Alberta's Water Resources Act: Legal Constraints and Consideration Reforms* • *Energy Conservation Legislation for Building Design and Construction*

For more Information Library, List of Publications

Who's Who CHAIR **HUGH GAUDET** • VICE CHAIR **JAMES HOPE-ROSS** • SECRETARY **NANCY MONEY** • EXECUTIVE DIRECTOR **OWEN SAUNDERS** • LIBRARIAN **EVANGELINE CASE**

CONSULTING FORESTERS OF BRITISH COLUMBIA
890 WEST PENDER STREET   VANCOUVER BC V6C 1K4
PHONE (604) 687 5500   FAX (604) 687 1327

Geographic Coverage Province, Regional • *Focused Region* Pacific Northwest • *Other Field of Focus* Forest Conservation / Deforestation / Reforestation • *Organization Members* 50 • *Individual Members* 15

Mission Professional association promoting the practice of forestry consulting.

	Regular	Corporation
Annual Fees	$85	$550

For more Information Database

Who's Who PRESIDENT **STUART MACPHERSON** • VICE PRESIDENT **DAVE ORMEROD** SECRETARY **JOHN FULLER** • TREASURER **GREG TAYLOR**

ENVIRONMENTAL COMPENSATION CORPORATION
SOCIÉTÉ D'INDEMNISATION ENVIRONNEMENTALE
2300 YONGE STREET, P.O. BOX 2382   TORONTO ON M4P 1E4
PHONE (416) 323 4826   FAX (416) 323 2754

Founded 1985 • *Geographic Coverage* National • *Other Field of Focus* Pollution / Radiations

Mission The Corporation is an Ontario Crown Corporation created to help fulfill the third goal set forth by the 1985 Environmental Protection Act - "to compensate those who have suffered a loss as a result of a spill". The Corporation provides compensation to those who have suffered as a result of a spill but are unable to obtain satisfactory compensation from their insurance company or the party responsible for the damage. When a pollutant is spilled, those who own or control it have a legal duty to deal with others' losses and property cleanup. The Corporation provides compensation to victims of spills and to owners or controllers of pollutants that were spilled but who are not at fault for the spill.

Funding *Government Support* 100%

Total Income $358,600

Total Expenses $363,548

Program Spill Victim Compensation Programme.

Publications Guides *A Spill Victim's Guide* • *A Guide for Owners and Controllers of Pollutants*

For more Information Annual Report

Who's Who PRESIDENT MARJORY LOVEYS • EXECUTIVE DIRECTOR GEOFFREY T. G. SCOTT • DIRECTORS ROBERT W. MACKENZIE, JOHN G. W. MANZIG, MARIANNE LINES

ENVIRONMENTAL LAW CENTRE ALBERTA SOCIETY
10350 124TH STREET   EDMONTON AB T5N 3V9
PHONE (403) 482 4891   FAX (403) 488 6779

Founded 1981 • *Geographic Coverage* Province

Mission To provide public information and assistance on environmental law and policy; to ensure the existence of effective laws to protect the environment, and of a procedure for public participation in regulatory and law making processes.

Funding	*Foundations*	*Alberta Law Foundation*	*Contracts & Grants*
	4%	71.8%	12.7%

Other Sources *Publication Sales* 3.4% • *Other* 8.1%

Total Income $581,138

Usage	*Administration*	*Programs*
	26.6%	73.4%

Total Expenses $565,956

Programs Public Information and Assistance Programme responds to public requests for assistance with information on environmental law, conducts public seminars and workshops, and speaks to citizen and community groups, professional and business organizations. Legal Research Programme undertakes research on important topics in environmental law where reliable information is lacking, publishes research papers, articles, citizen guides and handbooks, and accepts contracts for research in the area of environmental law where appropriate. Monitoring and Reform Programme monitors and comments upon law and policy relating to the environment, provides recommendations for legislative reform, encourages decision makers to improve environmental laws and legal processes, and participates in legal reform as members of committees, review panels and advisory boards.

Publications Quarterly newsletter *NEWS BRIEF. Journal of Environmental Law Practice* published two to three times per year. Various books and research papers including *Good Riddance: Waste Management in Alberta* • *Underground Storage Tanks: A Legal Review* • *The Price of Pollution: Environmental Litigation in Canada* • *Demystifying Forestry Law: An Alberta Analysis.* Conference proceedings including *Into the Future: Environmental Law and Policy for the 1990s* • *Environmental Protection and the Canadian Constitution* • *Environmental Enforcement: Proceedings of the National Conference on the Enforcement of Environmental Law*

Multimedia Online information service 1-800-661-4238. Video *Peoples' Guide to Energy Projects*

For more Information Annual Report, Database, Library, List of Publications

Who's Who PRESIDENT RONALD M. KRUHLAK • VICE PRESIDENTS JUDITH HANEBURY, DENNIS R. THOMAS • SECRETARY WILLIAM A. FULLER • EXECUTIVE DIRECTOR DONNA TINGLEY • LIBRARIAN DOLORES NOGA

PLANNING, RESEARCH AND ANALYSIS SERVICE
10 WELLINGTON STREET   HULL PQ K1A 0H3
PHONE (819) 953 9739   FAX (819) 953 6789

Geographic Coverage National, Global • *Cooperative Partner* Greenplan Partners

Mission To help decision makers deal with sustainable development issues by informing them about public opinion and media coverage, and handling specific requests.

environmental education, careers, information environmental networks

CHAPTER 18

Educating the People : Reading, Writing and Recycling, by Laura L. Klure

FOR A HUMAN BEING SPENDING a lifetime on this planet, environmental education can be a lifelong process. People of all ages benefit from learning more about the Earth, its flora and fauna, and our relationship to other living things. Environmental education begins at home, where small children learn from concerned parents the importance of conserving, reusing, recycling, and shopping wisely. Good examples set at home can be reinforced at school, if the curriculum includes teaching respect for nature. A 1993 report from the American Association for the Advancement of Science (AAAS) stressed that science education in schools needs to emphasize understanding, rather than rote memorization. Franklyn G. Jenifer of the AAAS contends that "just to be good citizens, young people are going to have much more comprehensive understanding of the world around them".

STEPS TOWARD IMPROVING students' grasp of ecology and complex interactions in nature have already been taken in many schools in North America. For example, the newly developed science curriculum in

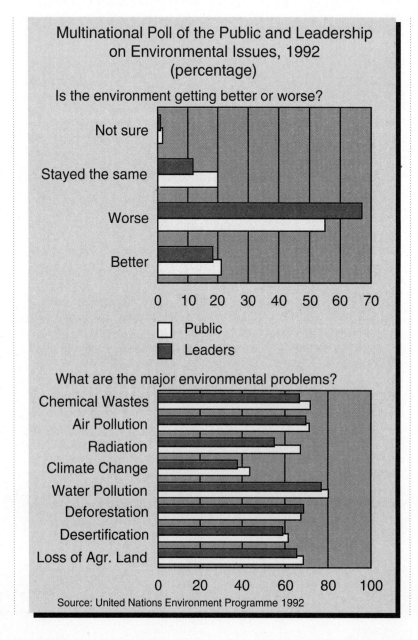

Multinational Poll of the Public and Leadership on Environmental Issues, 1992 (percentage)

Is the environment getting better or worse?

- Not sure
- Stayed the same
- Worse
- Better

0 10 20 30 40 50 60 70

☐ Public
■ Leaders

What are the major environmental problems?

- Chemical Wastes
- Air Pollution
- Radiation
- Climate Change
- Water Pollution
- Deforestation
- Desertification
- Loss of Agr. Land

0 20 40 60 80 100

Source: United Nations Environment Programme 1992

California takes an integrated, interactive approach to education. In this approach, concepts are reinforced by hands-on experience, and children actively investigate how multiple factors can influence situations. The emphasis is on comprehending the "big picture", or the major themes in science. The Kindergarten-12th Grade California State Science Framework, adopted in 1990 with advice from the National Science Teachers Association (NSTA), is not merely a change in what is being taught. It involves a paradigm shift in teaching methods. New, less autocratic methods encourage children to explore ideas cooperatively, to question standard assumptions, and to develop novel solutions to problems. Teaching children to appreciate the environment and cultivating their problem-solving skills means creating new generations of citizens and leaders who will be able to face the environmental challenges of the coming millennium. Colleges and universities continue the task started in grade schools. In addition to offering science ►*page 257*

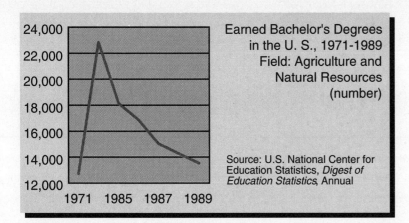

Earned Bachelor's Degrees in the U. S., 1971-1989 Field: Agriculture and Natural Resources (number)

Source: U.S. National Center for Education Statistics, *Digest of Education Statistics*, Annual

Earned Bachelor's Degrees in the U. S., 1971-1989 Field: Parks and Recreation (number)

Source: U.S. National Center for Education Statistics, *Digest of Education Statistics*, Annual

United States

Environmental Education, Careers, Information

ALLIANCE FOR ENVIRONMENTAL EDUCATION

51 MAIN STREET, P.O. BOX 368   THE PLAINS VA 22171
PHONE (703) 253 5812   FAX (703) 258 5811

Founded 1972 • *Geographic Coverage* National • *Cooperative Partners* Biopolitics International Organization, Network for Environmental Education, EcoNet Network • *Chapters* 7 • *Organization Members* 300

Mission To help further the vision of an educated society working to sustain a quality environment, by providing a neutral forum for the exchange of scientifically and technologically accurate information on the environment.

	Organization	Corporation	Sustaining	Sponsor
Annual Fees	$125	$250 or 1,000	$2,500	$10,000

Programs Annual conference. Offers programs to develop materials and services to improve environmental education nationwide.

Publications Bimonthly newsletter *The Network Exchange*. Periodic bulletin *The Messenger*. Annual membership directory. *Education Resource Catalog*. "Saddlebag" mailings distributed four times per year, containing the latest news, information and resources offered by members

Multimedia Computer network *EcoNet* which maintains seven online conferences for members

For more Information Database, Library

Who's Who PRESIDENT **DUANE A. COX**

AMERICAN NATURE STUDY SOCIETY

5881 COLD BROOK ROAD   HOMER NY 13077
PHONE (607) 749 3655

Founded 1908 • *Geographic Coverage* North America • *Organization Members* 80 • *Individual Members* 700

Mission To further environmental education by providing assistance to educators and others working in this field.

	Regular	Student/Senior	Library
Annual Fees	$15	$10	$18

	Membership	Foundations
Funding	96%	4%

Total Income $10,955

	Administration	Fundraising	Programs
Usage	5%	5%	90%

Publication Quarterly *ANSS Newsletter*

For more Information Library

Who's Who PRESIDENT **JOY FINLAY** • VICE PRESIDENT **TRACY KAY** • SECRETARY **BETTY MCKNIGHT**

AMERICAN SOCIETY FOR ENVIRONMENTAL HISTORY

NEW JERSEY INSTITUTE OF TECHNOLOGY   NEWARK NJ 07102
PHONE (201) 596 3270

Founded 1976 • *Geographic Coverage* Global • *Individual Members* 800

Mission To promote the interdisciplinary study of past environmental change.

	Regular	Student/Senior	US Institution	Non-US Institution
Annual Fees	$24	$12	$30	$38

Other Fees *Contributing* $100 • *Patron* $300

Funding *Membership* 100%

Publications Quarterly journal *Environmental History Review*. Periodical *Environmental History Newsletter*

Who's Who PRESIDENT **WILLIAM CROWN** • VICE PRESIDENT **SAM HAYS** • SECRETARY **CHRISTINE THOMAS** • EDITOR **JOHN OPIE**

ASSOCIATION FOR ENVIRONMENTAL AND OUTDOOR EDUCATION

HI-HILL SCHOOL, STAR ROUTE   LA CANADA CA 91011
PHONE (818) 797 3892

Founded 1954 • *Geographic Coverage* Local, State • *Focused Region* Southern California • *Other Field of Focus* Quality of Life / Outdoor Activities • *Chapters* 2 • *Organization Members* 4 *Individual Members* 200

Mission To promote the conservation of natural resources; to awaken interest in environmental and outdoor education; to acquire and disseminate accurate information and materials on environmental and outdoor education; to encourage, sponsor, conduct and participate in conferences, workshops and other meetings concerned with environmental outdoor education; and to promote and foster programs of leadership and teacher training for environmental and outdoor educators.

Annual Fees	Regular	Student/Senior	Organization
	$12	$6	$25

Other Fees *Lifetime* $100

Funding	Membership	Foundations	Conferences
	33%	12%	55%

Programs The Association's Fall and Spring conferences bring together environmental and outdoor educators for sharing, communication and growth opportunities. It also sponsors research studies.

Publication Newsletter published three times per year

Who's Who PRESIDENT **KATHEEN MITCHELL** • TREASURER **DONALD BEAVER** CONTACT **BERNIE LEMM**

BALTIMORE JOBS IN ENERGY PROJECT

28 EAST OSTEND STREET   BALTIMORE MD 21230
PHONE (410) 727 7837   FAX (410) 539 2087

Founded 1981 • *Geographic Coverage* Local • *Other Field of Focus* Human Rights & Environment

Mission To help develop the capacity of low income communities to rebuild their economy in the context of environmental work.

Funding	Government Support	Foundations	Fees for Services
	60%	10%	30%

Total Income $500,000

Who's Who EXECUTIVE DIRECTOR **DENNIS LIVINGSTON**

CALIFORNIA INSTITUTE OF PUBLIC AFFAIRS

517 19TH STREET, P.O. BOX 189040   SACRAMENTO CA 95818
PHONE (916) 442 2472   FAX (916) 442 2478

Founded 1969 • *Geographic Coverage* Global • *Cooperative Partners* The Claremont Graduate School, Sierra Club, Environmental Defense Fund, California Senate Office of Research, IUCN The World Conservation Union

Mission To convene discussions of leaders and scholars, conduct policy research, and publish descriptive directories of organizations and information sources. To understand the character, problems, and future possibilities of California and to promote sustainable development and the protection of natural resources. To promote communication and cooperation across academia, government agencies, and the business community.

Programs Organizer of California Forum on Hazardous Materials (1985-88), a collaborative policy forum. The Institute is currently working on a number of comprehensive projects that include convening discussions of leaders and experts, studies and analyses, public outreach, and actively following up to bring results to those who make decisions.

Publications Directories including *California Environmental Directory: A Guide to Organizations and Resources* - Fifth Edition, 1993 • *World Directory of Environmental Organizations* - Fourth Edition, 1992. Other publications include *California Information Guides Series* • *Environmental Studies Series* • *California Handbook: A Comprehensive Guide to Sources of Current Information and Action*

Who's Who PRESIDENT **THADDEUS C. TRZYNA** • VICE PRESIDENT **PAUL F. SMITH** SECRETARY **DAVID W. HENSON** • TREASURER **LAWRENCE W. STEWART** • OTHER **JULIE DIDION, JULIA K. ROELOF, DANIEL A. MAZMANIAN, MICHAEL R. ETON**

CHEWONKI FOUNDATION (THE)

R.R. 2, BOX 1200   WISCASSET ME 04578
PHONE (207) 882 7323   FAX (207) 882 4074

Founded 1963 • *Geographic Coverage* Local

Mission To foster personal growth through group interaction in the context of the natural world.

Funding	Foundations	Tuition
	10%	90%

Total Income $1,650,000

Usage

Fundraising	Programs
12%	88%

Programs Natural history education wilderness trips. Adventure programming.11th Grade interdisciplinary study. Environmental issues investigation. Camp Chewonki and Wilderness expeditions. Environmental education center. Maine Coast Semester - 11th Grade Students. Teacher's resource center.

Publications Quarterly newsletter *Chewonki Chronicle*. Miscellaneous reports

Who's Who PRESIDENT **ROBERT L. ELMORE** • SECRETARY **WARREN M. LITTLE** • TREASURER **WARREN BELL** • EXECUTIVE DIRECTOR **DON HUDSON**

CHULA VISTA NATURE CENTER

1000 GUNPOWDER POINT DRIVE   CHULA VISTA CA 91910-1201
PHONE (619) 422 2481   FAX (619) 422 2964

Founded 1987 • *Geographic Coverage* Local • *Focused Region* Southern California • *Other Field of Focus* Natural Resources / Water- Conservation & Quality • *Cooperative Partner* US Fish and Wildlife Service • *Chapter* 1 • *Individual Members* 205

Mission The Nature Center offers a view into the natural history and ecology of California wetlands. The organization serves the public with educational programs and exhibits and leads the way in the restoration, preservation, and enhancement of the surrounding wetlands. The Nature Center is home to a wide variety of creatures, some common in San Diego Bay and others rare in the world.

Annual Fees

Regular	Student/Senior	Families	Corporation
$25	$12 to 20	$40	$1,000

Other Fees *Active Volunteer* $10 • *Supporting Volunteer* $30 *Lifetime* $250

Funding

Membership	City Support	Other
10%	80%	10%

Total Income $505,000

Usage

Administration	Programs
11%	89%

Total Expenses $500,000

Programs Moons and Tides Exhibit. Clapper Rail Exhibit. Public programs.

Publications Monthly *Bayfront Byline*, circulation 500. Quarterly *Event Brochure*, circulation 2,000

For more Information Database, Library

Who's Who EXECUTIVE DIRECTOR **STEPHEN NEUDECKER** • DIRECTOR OF VOLUNTEER AND PUBLIC PROGRAMS **BARBARA COFFIN MOORE**

CLEARING MAGAZINE
ENVIRONMENTAL EDUCATION PROJECT
P.O. BOX 5176   OREGON CITY OR 97045
PHONE (503) 656 0155   FAX (503) 656 0155

Founded 1978 • *Geographic Coverage* Regional, National • *Individual Members* 2,500 subscribers

Mission To provide information, activities, and resources to teachers of environmental education in grades K-12.

Annual Fees

Regular	Organization
$15	$25

Funding

Subscriptions	Sales of Other Publications
95%	5%

Usage

Administration	Programs
35%	65%

For more Information Library

Who's Who LIBRARIAN **L. BEUTLER** • CONTACT **MARK DUBOIS**

COALITION FOR
EDUCATION IN THE OUTDOORS (THE)
S.U.N.Y. COLLEGE AT CORTLAND
BOX 2000   CORTLAND NY 13045
PHONE (607) 753 4971

Founded 1987 • *Geographic Coverage* National, Global • *Other Field of Focus* Quality of Life / Outdoor Activities • *Organization Members* 80

Mission To support the broad purposes of education in, for, and about the outdoors, through a program centered around assisting its affiliates in the identification of networking needs, and on efforts to meet those needs.

Annual Fees

Regular	Organization	Educational Institution	Business
$25	$50 to 100	$50	$125 to 250

Funding

Membership	Foundations
95%	5%

Total Income $6,000

Usage *Programs* 100%

Programs Networking. Sponsors conference on research.

Publication Quarterly newsletter *Taproot*

Who's Who EXECUTIVE COORDINATOR **BRUCE MATTHEWS**

CONCERN, INC.
1794 Columbia Road, NW   Washington DC 20009
Phone (202) 328 8160

Founded 1970 • *Geographic Coverage* National, Global

Mission To broaden public participation in the protection of the environment and promote environmental literacy and action by supplying citizens with the information they need to be effective community advocates for policies and programs that improve environmental quality and public health. Concern, Inc. believes that change begins with the individual, that protection of the environment should be a core principle governing community decision making, and that prevention should take precedence over remedial solutions.

238

Programs Provides individuals and organizations in the private and public sectors with information on a range of issues including recycling, pollution prevention, safe pest management, water resource protection, and energy efficiency. Sustainable Communities Project works to help communities achieve environmental and economic health and social equity through comprehensive, inclusive, long-term planning.

Publications Numerous guides including *Pesticides in our Communities: Choices for Change* • *Global Warming and Energy Choices* • *Household Waste: Issues and Opportunities* • *Waste: Choices for Communities* • *Drinking Water: a Community Action Guide* • *Farmland: a Community Issue* • *Building Sustainable Communities*

For more Information List of Publications

COOLIDGE CENTER
FOR ENVIRONMENTAL LEADERSHIP (THE)
1675 Massachusetts Avenue   Cambridge MA 02138
Phone (617) 864 5085   Fax (617) 864 6503

Founded 1983 • *Geographic Coverage* Global

Mission To promote environmental awareness and leadership, with a new emphasis on North-South and South-South liaisons and issues, following the UNCED Conference held in Rio de Janeiro in June 1992.

For more Information Library

EARTH FIRST! JOURNAL
P.O. Box 1415   Eugene OR 97440
Phone (503) 741 9191   Fax (503) 741 9192

Founded 1983 • *Geographic Coverage* Global • *Chapters* 107 local contacts

Mission To accurately report on the Earth First! movement. This includes information regarding threatened ecosystems, species, and habitats as well as information about what people can do and what others have

done in the past and will do in the future. Earth First! is not a centralized organization, the movement is composed of a number of fully autonomous local groups.

Annual Fees	*Regular*	*Organization*
	$20	$25

Other Fees *Lifetime* $500

Programs A listing of local Earth First! groups is offered in the back of each *Earth First! Journal*, circulation over 7,000.

EARTHSHARE OF CALIFORNIA
116 New Montgomery Street   San Francisco CA 94105
Phone (415) 882 9330   Fax (415) 882 4571

Founded 1982 • *Geographic Coverage* State • *Chapters* 3
Organization Members 82

Mission Earth Share of California represents 82 environmental organizations in workplace fundraising campaigns and provides important outreach and education to audiences not traditionally reached by environmental groups.

Funding	*Membership*	*Foundations*
	14.5%	85.1%

Total Income $2,034,489

Programs Field trip program with donors. Educational programs in workplaces throughout California to present information about the work of the organization's affiliates. Fundraising programs (in 1992, Earth-Share of California raised $1,291,729 for its affiliates).

Publications Quarterly newsletter *Bear Tracks*. Brochures

Multimedia Online information service 1-800-368-1819. Videos

For more Information Database

Who's Who President **Wick Kenney** • Vice President **Steve Katz** • Secretary **Sue Liskovec** • Treasurer **David McDonald** • Executive Director **Nancy Snow** Program Director **Sung Baik** • Campaign Managers **Tim Duff**, **Friday Forsthoff** • Contact **Catherine Carroll**

EARTHWATCH   PAGE 19
680 Mount Auburn Street, P.O. Box 403-N   Watertown MA 02272
Phone (617) 926 8200   Fax (617) 926 8532

EARTHWATCH CALIFORNIA
100 Wilshire Boulevard, Suite 800   Santa Monica CA 90401
Phone (310) 451 0327   Fax (310) 393 0616

Founded 1972 • *Geographic Coverage* State, Global

Mission To improve human understanding of the planet, the diversity of its inhabitants, and the processes that affect the quality of life on earth. Earthwatch is a coalition of citizens and scientists working to sustain the world's environment, monitor global change, conserve endangered habitats and species, explore the vast heritage of all peoples, and foster world health and international cooperation.

Annual Fees *Regular* $25

Programs Each year Earthwatch sponsors numerous projects around the world - 165 in 1993, and recruits volunteers to serve in an environmental EarthCorps. Projects include Understanding the Earth, Threatened Habitats, Strategies for Survival, Human Impacts, Managing the Planet.

For more Information Database, Library

Who's Who CONTACT LINDA KNIGHT

EDUCATIONAL COMMUNICATIONS

P.O. BOX 351419   LOS ANGELES CA 90035-9119
PHONE (310) 559 9160

Founded 1958 • *Geographic Coverage* Local, Regional, National, Global • *Cooperative Partner* The Ecology Center of Southern California • *Chapters* 3

Mission To facilitate and further communication and education about all environmental issues, from the local to the international level, by providing services such as a speaker's bureau, award-winning public service announcements, radio and television programs, and input into the decision making process.

Annual Fees	*Regular*	*Student/Senior*	*Families*	*Sustaining*	*Donor*
	$20	$15	$25	$30	$50

Other Fees *Sponsor* $100

Programs Disseminates information through *Econews* television series, *Environmental Directions* and *Environmental Viewpoints* radio series, and *Ecoview* newspaper articles.

Publications Bimonthly *The Compendium Newsletter: Your Guide to the World's Environmental Crisis*. Book *The Directory of Environmental Organizations* - Eighteenth Edition, 1993

Multimedia 1,000 *Econews* videos. Audiotapes *Environmental Directions*. *Directory of Environmental Organizations* on PC Diskettes - ASCII Format

For more Information Database, Library, List of Publications

Who's Who PRESIDENT CHARLES CAREY • SECRETARY PAUL KORETZ • EXECUTIVE PRODUCER AND EDITOR NANCY PEARLMAN • ASSOCIATE DIRECTORS LYNN CASON, ANNA HARLOWE • LIBRARIAN LESLIE LEWS

ELMWOOD INSTITUTE (THE)

2522 SAN PABLO AVENUE   BERKELEY CA 94702
PHONE (510) 845 4595   FAX (510) 845 1439

Founded 1984 • *Geographic Coverage* Global • *Chapter* 1
Individual Members 1,200

Mission To support the goal of making ecological literacy, defined as systems thinking, knowledge of the principles of ecology, and the practice of ecological values, the central organizing principle in business and education. Based on the vision and values of deep ecology, the Institute applies systems thinking to the understanding and solution of current social, economic, and environmental problems, and, in particular, to issues where significant institutional change is likely, and to programs that communicate widely.

Annual Fees *Regular* $30

Funding	*Membership*	*Programs*
	57%	42%

Total Income $317,748

Usage	*Administration*	*Fundraising*	*Programs*
	22%	19%	58%

Total Expenses $331,354

Programs Ecoliteracy Program. Ecomanagement Program. Disseminates information through "Deep Ecology Dialogues", a regular series of dialogues, lectures, and seminars for the purpose of teaching the theoretical framework of deep ecology and applying the deep ecology approach to current issues.

Publications Quarterly *Elmwood Newsletter*,- circulation 1,000. Semiannual *Global File Monitor*. Book *EcoManagement: The Elmwood Guide to Ecological Auditing and Sustainable Business*

For more Information Database, List of Publications

Who's Who PRESIDENT FRITJOF CAPRA • EXECUTIVE DIRECTOR ZENOBIA BARLOW PROJECT DIRECTOR LENORE GOLDMAN • EDITOR CRAIG COMSTOCK • LIBRARIAN LEE SUMMERELL

ENVIRO-ED

9730 MANITOU PLACE   BAINBRIDGE ISLAND WA 98110
PHONE (206) 456 1854

Founded 1983 • *Geographic Coverage* North and central America
Focused Region The Caribbean

Mission To promote environmental education on the issues of wildlife, natural resources, waste reduction and recycling.

Funding	Membership	Contracts, Agencies & Schools
	10%	90%

Total Income $100,000

Usage	Administration	Programs
	20%	80%

Total Expenses $100,000

Programs Environmental Education Teacher Workshops on the topics of watersheds, water quality monitoring, wildlife habitat enhancement, environmental stewardship projects, waste reduction and recycling. Also offers Adult Education on watershed stewardship, wildlife habitat enhancement. Grant proposals.

Publications Interpretive material production of signs and brochures

Multimedia Slide and video presentations

Who's Who EXECUTIVE DIRECTOR LAURIE E. USHER

ENVIRONMENTAL CAREERS ORGANIZATION (THE)

286 CONGRESS STREET, THIRD FLOOR   BOSTON MA 02210-1009
PHONE (617) 426 4375

Founded 1972 • *Geographic Coverage* National • *Chapters* 5

Mission To protect and enhance the environment through the development of environmental professionals, the promotion of careers in the environmental field, and by working to inspire individuals into action.

Funding	Corporations	Foundations
	50%	50%

Total Income $5,625,952

Usage	Administration	Fundraising	Programs
	9%	1%	90%

Programs Offers paid short-term environmental positions for senior undergraduate, graduate and doctoral students, recently graduated men and women, and other entry-level environmental job-seekers. Operates environmental placement services, career services, career products, research and consulting. Minority Opportunities Program.

Publications Books *The New Complete Guide to Environmental Careers* • *Beyond the Green: Redefining & Diversifying the Environmental Movement* • *Becoming an Environmental Professional*

Who's Who PRESIDENT JOHN R. COOK, JR. • VICE PRESIDENT MICHAEL RODRIGUES SECRETARY LAWRENCE M. BEALS

ENVIRONMENTAL DATA RESEARCH INSTITUTE, INC.

1655 ELMWOOD AVENUE, SUITE 225   ROCHESTER NY 14620-3426
PHONE (716) 473 3090   FAX (716) 473 0968

Founded 1989 • *Geographic Coverage* National, Global

Mission To compile, analyze, and disseminate information on environmental funding. All environmental fields are included in the Institute's analyses of funding.

Funding	Foundations	Sales
	40%	60%

Total Income $300,000

Publication Directory *Environmental Grantmaking Foundations* - 400 independent, community and corporate foundations that give grants for environmental programs

For more Information Database

Who's Who PRESIDENT EDITH C. STEIN • PROJECT MANAGER ALLEN KRUSENSTJERNA RESEARCH AND ADMINISTRATION ASSISTANT CORINNE SZYMKO

ENVIRONMENTAL MEDIA CORPORATION

P.O. BOX 1016   CHAPEL HILL NC 27514
PHONE (919) 933 3003   FAX (919) 942 8785

Founded 1987 • *Geographic Coverage* State, National

Mission To design, produce, and distribute media to support environmental education for children and adults.

Programs The organization works with colleagues among education, Public TV and other public and private organizations who are committed to environmental education. Through low-cost distribution of its programs on Public TV and videocassette, the organization ensures equity by all educators, parents and children.

Multimedia Online information service 1-800-ENV-EDUC

Who's Who PRESIDENT BILL PENDERGRAFT

ENVIRONMENTAL OPPORTUNITIES

P.O. BOX 747   MENDOCINO CA 95460
PHONE (707) 937 1529

Founded 1982 • *Geographic Coverage* National

Mission To provide subscribers/readers with a comprehensive list of positions open primarily in private sector areas of environmental employment and environmental groups throughout the USA.

Annual Fees *Regular* $44

Funding *Membership* 100%

Usage

Administration	Programs
15%	85%

Publication Book *Environmental Opportunities*

Who's Who PRESIDENT SANFORD BERRY • VICE PRESIDENT MARTHA VINEYARD

ENVIRONMENTAL TECHNICAL
INFORMATION SYSTEM
DEPARTMENT OF URBAN AND REGIONAL PLANNING
1003 WEST NEVADA STREET
PHONE (217) 333 1369

PAGE 226

URBANA IL 61801
FAX (217) 244 1717

FEDERATION OF ENVIRONMENTAL TECHNOLOGISTS, INC.
P.O. BOX 185
PHONE (414) 251 8163

MILWAUKEE WI 53201

Founded 1981 • *Geographic Coverage* National • *Chapters* 5
Organization Members 150 • *Individual Members* 1,200

Mission To foster and promote environmental education to increase compliance with environmental regulations.

Annual Fees

Regular	Student/Senior	Patron
$80	$15	$120

Total Income $292,500

Programs Annual conference and exhibition. Seminars. Workshops. Training courses.

Publication Monthly newsletter

Who's Who PRESIDENT CATHRINE MCCONNELL • VICE PRESIDENT RICK FULK
SECRETARY HIRAM BUFFINGTON

FOUNDATION FOR FIELD RESEARCH
10633 ROSELLE STREET, SUITE B
PHONE (619) 445 9264

SAN DIEGO CA 92121

Founded 1981 • *Geographic Coverage* National, Global • *Chapters* 2, in Grenada, and the West Indies

Mission To coordinate scientific research expeditions for amateurs and scientists in the fields of anthropology, archaeology, conservation, and ecology.

Annual Fees *Regular* $20

Total Income $700,122

Usage

Administration	Programs
17%	83%

Programs Projects include studies of sea turtle and monkey conservation, marine biology and underwater archaeology, folklore and archaeology of prehistoric sites as well as more recent ones, ornithology and etymology, solar energy conservation, and pre-historic rock art.

Publication Bulletin *Explorer News*

Who's Who PRESIDENT THOMAS J. BANKS • VICE PRESIDENT FRANKLIN BANKS
SECRETARY ALEX PEAL

FOUR CORNERS SCHOOL
OF OUTDOOR EDUCATION
P.O. BOX 1029
PHONE (801) 587 2156

MONTICELLO UT 84535

Founded 1984 • *Geographic Coverage* Regional • *Individual Members* 400

Mission To increase participants' awareness and sensitivity to the physical and cultural heritage of the Colorado Plateau by providing outdoor educational and environmental opportunities within this 160,000 square mile region. It promotes knowledge of outdoor skills, natural sciences, and land stewardship by creating a community of individuals who share their interests through informal experiences.

Annual Fees *Regular* $25

Programs Offers educational programs in archaeology adventures, environmental studies, wilderness advocacy, cultural studies, photography and writing, natural history, of the Plateau.

Publication Semiannual newsletter *Voices From The Four Corners*

Who's Who PRESIDENT REID ROSS • SECRETARY KEN OLSON

GLEN HELEN OUTDOOR EDUCATION CENTER
1075 ROUTE 343
PHONE (513) 767 7648

YELLOW SPRINGS OH 45387
FAX (513) 767 1891

Founded 1956 • *Geographic Coverage* Global • *Focused Countries* Brazil, England, Germany • *Other Field of Focus* Quality of Life / Outdoor Activities

Mission To provide environmental education for school children and a training program for graduate students interested in working with children in the outdoors. The Center provides a balance among natural history, environmental problem solving, pioneer heritage activities, and interpersonal skills.

Funding	Camper Fees	Other
	84%	16%

Total Income $329,683

Programs Operates Eldershostel Ecocamps - Summer, school camps, Raptor Rehabilitation Program at The Raptor Center. Also sponsors Extension Naturalist, a credit-bearing internship program for undergraduate and graduate students.

Publication Quarterly newsletter *The Wingbeat*

For more Information Library

242 GREEN LIBRARY, INC.

P.O. Box 11284   BERKELEY CA 94701
PHONE (415) 841 9975   FAX (415) 841 9996

Founded 1986 • *Geographic Coverage* North America, Global *Focused Countries* Canada, New Guinea, Poland, Ukraine, USA *Chapters* 3, in Poland, Sweden, and Latvia

Mission To promote the development and establishment of environmental libraries.

Funding	Membership	Corporations	Foundations
	10%	10%	80%

Usage	Administration	Fundraising	Programs
	20%	20%	60%

Programs Environmental library program. Publishing program.

Publication *Green Library Journal*

Who's Who PRESIDENT **JACEK PURAT** • VICE PRESIDENT **KATHLEEN MANGOTICH** SECRETARY **MARIEL LIVINGSTONE**

HAWAII NATURE CENTER

2131 MAKIKI HEIGHTS DRIVE   HONOLULU HI 96822
PHONE (808) 955 0100   FAX (808) 955 0116

Founded 1981 • *Geographic Coverage* Pacific • *Focused Region* Hawaiian Islands • *Other Field of Focus* Natural Resources / Water - Conservation & Quality • *Chapter* 1 • *Individual Members* 300

Mission To foster awareness, appreciation, and understanding of the environment, and to encourage sound stewardship of the Hawaiian Islands in the future. The Center provides hands-on environmental education field experiences for elementary school children, families, and the public in order to foster a personal appreciation of the unique Hawaiian environment.

Annual Fees	Regular	Families	Contributing	Steward
	$25	$50	$250	$1,000

Funding	Membership	Corporations	Foundations	Other
	12%	20%	32%	36%

Total Income $759,836

Usage	Administration	Fundraising	Programs
	12%	10%	78%

Programs The Center offers school programs which focus on outdoor education. In addition, weekend programs include interpretive hikes, sensory explorations of forests and streams, earth care projects, and an array of educational classes.

Publication Quarterly newsletter *The Steward*

Who's Who PRESIDENT **WARREN G. HAIGHT** • VICE PRESIDENT **OSWALD K. STENDER** • SECRETARY **JEAN C. MARCHANT** • TREASURER **R. E. WHITE, JR.** • EXECUTIVE DIRECTOR **TAMAR CHOTZEN**

HULBERT OUTDOOR CENTER   PAGE 277

R.R. 1, BOX 1031   FAIRLEE VT 05055
PHONE (802) 333 9840   FAX (802) 333 9216

INSTITUTE FOR CONSERVATION LEADERSHIP

2000 "P" STREET, NW, SUITE 413   WASHINGTON DC 20036
PHONE (202) 466 3330   FAX (202) 659 3897

Founded 1988 • *Geographic Coverage* National

Mission To further the protection and conservation of the Earth's environment through training and empowering volunteer leaders and building volunteer organizations The institute is committed to broadening the base of environmental protection as well as the depth of commitment.

Programs Offers training for conservation leadership in the areas of board development, individual leadership training, building volunteer organizations, network conferences, long-range planning, executive director training, and training for trainers. A list of organizations served is available.

For more Information Database

Who's Who CONTACT **MARY TUTMAN**

INSTITUTE FOR EARTH EDUCATION (THE)

CEDAR COVE   GREENVILLE WV 24945-0115
PHONE (304) 832 6404

Founded 1974 • *Geographic Coverage* Global • *Chapters* Branches in Australia, Britain, Canada, France, Germany, Italy, Japan, and the US • *Members* 1,200 including organizations

Mission To help people cultivate an understanding of, appreciation for, and harmony with the earth and its life, by developing and disseminating educational programs.

Annual Fees

Regular	Professional	Affiliate	Sponsor
$25	$35	$50	$100

Funding

Membership	Workshops, Conferences & Sales of Materials	Other
12%	80%	8%

Total Income $231,000

Programs Earthkeepers™. Sunship Earth™.

Publications Various books including *Earth Education: A New Beginning* • *The Earth Speaks* • *EarthKeepers* • *Sunship Earth* • *Acclimatization* • *Earth Walks* • *Conceptual Encounters I and II*. Seasonal journal *Talking Leaves*. Pamphlet *The Earth Education Sourcebook*

Who's Who PRESIDENT STEVE VAN MATRE • OTHER BRUCE JOHNSON, MIKE MAYER, LAURIE FARBER

INSTITUTE FOR ENVIRONMENTAL EDUCATION

18554 HASKINS ROAD   CHAGRIN FALLS OH 44023
PHONE (216) 543 7303   FAX (216) 543 7160

Founded 1971 • *Geographic Coverage* National, Global

Mission To improve the environmental quality of life through education. Known for its hands-on approach, the Institute provides program development and consulting services on environmental education and training to schools, businesses, and the general public.

Funding

Membership	Government Support	Corporations	Foundations	Book Sales
25%	10%	40%	20%	5%

Total Income $100,000

Usage

Administration	Programs
20%	80%

Total Expenses $100,000

Programs The Institute's school-based Waste Minimization and Education Program trains teams of teachers, administrators, students, and employees, who return to their districts and work with students and personnel to set up the program, thus helping schools to develop an effective in-house program to cut waste disposal costs, bring the school into compliance with Ohio law, and educate students and staff. Pollution prevention for small businesses. Cleveland's Teacher Internship Program. Environmental Education Guide Series. Environmental education workshops. Land-Use Manual.

Publications *Common Groundwork: A Practical Guide to Protecting Rural and Urban Land*. Various solid waste and recycling publications including

Administrator's Manual • *K - 12 Curriculum Manual, Closing the Loop: Integrated Waste Management Activities for School and Home*. Various publications focusing on waste minimization and education programs, integrating environmental studies into a three-year program in terrestrial ecology, pollution prevention and protection of sensitive lands

Multimedia Online information service 1-800-484-7949

For more Information Library, List of Publications

Who's Who PRESIDENT JOSEPH H. CHADBOURNE • VICE PRESIDENT MARY CHADBOURNE

INSTITUTE FOR SOCIAL ECOLOGY

P.O. BOX 89   PLAINFIELD VT 05667
PHONE (802) 454 8493

Founded 1974 • *Geographic Coverage* Global

Mission The Institute was established for the purpose of research, education, and outreach in the field of social ecology. The mission of the Institute is the creation of educational programs that enhance people's understanding of their relationship to the natural world and to each other. Their focus on people's relationship to the natural world integrates studies in the Social Sciences, Arts, Humanities, and the Natural Sciences.

Funding

Foundations	Tuition
10%	90%

Usage

Administration	Programs
40%	60%

Programs Sponsors conferences on Social Ecology, Design and Sustainable Communities, Ecology and Community, Women and Ecology. Sponsors a study tour of India.

Publications *The Newsletter of the Institute for Social Ecology*. International political ecology journal *Society and Nature*

For more Information List of Publications

ISLAND INSTITUTE   PAGE 277

4004 58TH PLACE, SW   SEATTLE WA 98116
PHONE (206) 938 0345   FAX (206) 932 2341

ISLAND PRESS

CENTER FOR RESOURCE ECONOMICS
1718 CONNECTICUT AVENUE, NW   WASHINGTON DC 20009
PHONE (202) 232 7933   FAX (202) 234 1328

Founded 1984 • *Geographic Coverage* North America, Western Europe, Pacific • *Cooperative Partners* Yale School of Forestry and Environmental Studies, The Aspen Institute, The Chesapeake Bay Foundation, Trust for Public Land, The Wilderness Society, World Wildlife Fund, National Toxics Campaign, Earthscan - London, UK

Mission To develop and produce books that fill gaps in current environmental information. Moreover, the publisher increases the exposure, distribution, and readership of materials developed by other non-profit organizations and professional associations that do excellent research and policy development, but may lack an effective marketing apparatus.

Funding	Foundations	Sales
	51%	49%

Total Income $3,482,049

Usage	Administration	Fundraising	Programs
	11%	2%	87%

Total Expenses $3,674,114

Programs Research and publication. Marketing and distribution. Technical assistance. UN program. Policy studies.

Publications Publishes 32 books annually focusing on all major environmental issues including *The New Complete Guide to Environmental Careers* • *Choosing a Sustainable Future, the Report of the National Commission on the Environment* • *Compass and Gyroscope, Integrating Science and Politics for the Environment* • *Environmental Strategies for Industry: International Perspectives on Research Needs and Policy Implications* • *For the Wild Places: Profiles in Conservation* • *California's Threatened Environment: Restoring the Dream* • *The Wild and Scenic Rivers of America*

For more Information List of Publications

Who's Who CHAIR SUSAN SECHLER • PRESIDENT CHARLES C. SAVITT • VICE PRESIDENT CHRISTINE GODSON

JOB SEEKER (THE)

ROUTE 2, BOX 16   WARRENS WI 54666
PHONE (608) 378 4290   FAX (608) 378 4290

Founded 1987 • *Geographic Coverage* National

Mission To provide a job listing service for the environmental and natural resource fields.

Fees *Summer Jobs Special* $10 • *6 month-Subscription* $36 *1 year-Subscription* $60 • *Organization* $84

Publications Books *The Job Seeker* • *Summer Jobs Special* published from December 6 through April 6 lists great summer and seasonal opportunities with non-profit, private, local, state, and Federal employers

Who's Who PRESIDENT BECKY POTTER

KEEWAYDIN
ENVIRONMENTAL EDUCATION CENTER

R.D. 1, BOX 88   SALISBURY VT 05769
PHONE (802) 352 4247

Founded 1973 • *Geographic Coverage* State

Mission To provide residential environmental education programs for school groups. The Center mainly focuses on the natural and local history of Vermont and the adaptation of plants and animals to winter.

Programs 2-5 day programs for school groups - some programs conducted in school classroom.

Who's Who DIRECTOR MS. BARRY SCHULTZ KING

LAKE ERIE NATURE AND SCIENCE CENTER

28728 WOLF ROAD   BAY VILLAGE OH 44140
PHONE (216) 871 2900

Founded 1950 • *Geographic Coverage* Local • *Other Field of Focus* Natural Resources / Water - Conservation & Quality • *Chapter* 1 *Individual Members* 700

Mission To increase awareness, respect, enjoyment, and responsibility among people of all ages who will serve as advocates of the environment, through the efforts of a well trained and dedicated staff, incorporating hands-on experience with a unique natural setting.

Annual Fees	Regular	Families	Contributing	Sponsoring	Sustaining
	$20	$40	$50	$100	$500

Other Fees *Patron* $1,000

Funding	Membership	Corporations	Foundations	Other
	3%	5%	33%	59%

Total Income $273,000

Usage	Administration	Fundraising	Programs
	20%	15%	65%

Programs Wildlife rehabilitation. Teacher training.

Publication Newsletter *Erie Views*

Who's Who PRESIDENT JOHN CAVALIER • VICE PRESIDENT VALERIE KOEHLER SECRETARY DEAN BRENNAN

MEEMAN ARCHIVE (THE)
SCHOOL OF NATURAL RESOURCES AND ENVIRONMENT

UNIVERSITY OF MICHIGAN
430 EAST UNIVERSITY   ANN ARBOR MI 48109-1115
PHONE (313) 763 1312

Founded 1982 • *Geographic Coverage* National

Mission To preserve and make accessible to the public outstanding journalism concerning conservation, natural resources, and the environment. This service is now available to any individuals and organizations needing information in the field of natural resource use.

Funding *Foundations* 100%

Total Income $15,000

Programs Partial sponsor of Annual Environmental Journalism Conference.

Publications Books *The Best From the Meeman Archive, 1987* • *Toxic Substances,1990-91.* Each book is a selection of environmental news stories.

Who's Who PRESIDENT **PAUL F. FRANK** • EXECUTIVE DIRECTOR **MICHAEL NEMEC**

MESSENGER ENVIRONMENTAL JOURNAL
CITIZENS ENERGY COUNCIL
P.O. BOX U   HEWITT NJ 07421
PHONE (201) 728 7835   FAX (201) 728 7664

Founded 1986 • *Geographic Coverage* National • *Cooperative Partners* Greenpeace, Public Citizen, Society of Environmental Journalists • *Individual Members* 200

Mission To work for greater awareness of local, national and global environmental problems, and for the development of solutions to these problems, by serving as a source of information for the public.

Annual Fees *Regular* $10

Funding	Membership	Advertising
	15%	85%

Total Income $12,000

Publication *The Messenger Environmental Journal*

For more Information Library

Who's Who CONTACT **KARIN WESTDYK**

MOUNTAIN WEST ENVIRONMENTAL OPTIONS
2257 SOUTH ZENOBIA STREET   DENVER CO 80219
PHONE (303) 936 0270

Founded 1990 • *Geographic Coverage* Regional • *Chapter* 1

Mission To promote environmental, outdoor, and recreation oriented employment opportunities in the western United States, through the publication of three regional environmental employment newsletters, twice a

month, covering the Rocky Mountains west to the Pacific.

Funding *Membership* 100%

Usage	Administration	Programs
	15%	85%

Publications Regional employment newsletters *Southwest Edition* - CO, UT, NV, AZ, NM • *Northern Edition* - WY, MT, ID • *Pacific Edition* - OR, WA, CA. Directories of newspapers, environmental agencies and marketplace environmental companies for each state. Guides *US Government Summer Employment* • *Resume Preparation Guide*

Who's Who CONTACT **NANCY L. KEHOE**

NATIONAL ASSOCIATION FOR INTERPRETATION
P.O. BOX 1892   FORT COLLINS CO 80522
PHONE (303) 491 6434   FAX (303) 491 2255

Founded 1961 • *Geographic Coverage* Local, Regional, National, Global • *Chapters* 10 • *Organization Members* 300 • *Individual Members* 2,800

Mission To support the work of interpretative professionals, communicators who combine an understanding of natural or cultural history with a love for sharing knowledge and feeling with others, who are involved in discovering and communicating the meanings and relationships between people and their natural, historical, and cultural world.

Annual Fees	Regular	Student/Senior	Families	Organization	Corporation
	$65	$25	$75	$165	$225

Other Fees *Supporting* $1,000 • *Lifetime* $850

Funding	Membership	Corporations
	85%	15%

Total Income $300,000

Programs Employment opportunities service (Dial-A-Job, Dial-An-Internship, Printed Listings, Information for Employers). Professional development training. Networking among individuals and organizations. Provides research, trend, and services information. Recognition and support of the interpretation profession. Works for corporate, fiscal, and administrative efficiency. Sponsors National Interpreters Workshop.

Publications Bimonthly journal *Legacy*, circulation 3,300. Quarterly newsletter *Regional*, circulation 200 to 500. Books *Preparing for the 21st Century: Solving Management Problems Through Interpretation* • *Interpreter's Green Pages.* Directory of colleges and universities *Interpretation: A Resource and Curricula Guide for the United States and Canada.* Conference proceedings

Multimedia Video *The Art of Interpretation* produced for NAI by the National Park Service's Harper's Ferry Interpretive Design Center

For more Information Annual Report, Database, Library

Who's Who PRESIDENT **ANN WRIGHT** • VICE PRESIDENT **NEIL HAGADORN** • SECRETARY **KARIN HOSTETTER** • EXECUTIVE DIRECTOR **BOBBIE GALLUP** • EDITOR **ALAN LEFTRIDGE** • OFFICE MANAGER **PHILIP B. TEDESCO**

NATIONAL ASSOCIATION OF PROFESSIONAL ENVIRONMENTAL COMMUNICATORS

P.O. BOX 61-8352   CHICAGO IL 60661-8352
PHONE (312) 661 1721

Founded 1990 • *Geographic Coverage* National • *Chapters* 11

Mission To open new pathways of communicating in the environmental field, to share the wide-ranging perspectives and issues represented by those involved in communicating and using environmental information, to define effective methods for communicating environmental information and ways to evaluate the success of these methods, to evaluate the effectiveness of existing environmental communication programs and how these programs can be incorporated into the process of environmental decision making, and to recognize outstanding contributions to the profession and examples of innovative and effective communication of environmental information.

Annual Fees	*Regular*	*Student/Senior*	*Organization*
	$50 to 90	$25	$150 to 525

Other Fees *Non-US add* $25

Programs Mentor Program, helps students and new professionals get the advice and information they need to find jobs, enhance their environmental communication skills, obtain access to professional resources, and handle problems on the job.

Publications Newsletters *NAPEC Quarterly* • *NAPEC News.* Annual membership directory

NATIONAL AUDUBON SOCIETY EXPEDITION INSTITUTE

P.O. BOX 365   BELFAST ME 04915
PHONE (207) 338 5859

Founded 1978 • *Geographic Coverage* National

Mission The Institute uses mobile classrooms to bring students in direct contact with learning experiences throughout North America. Since its inception, over 600 students have experienced first-hand how they can take effective personal action to preserve the ecological and cultural diversity of the earth.

NIZHONI SCHOOL FOR GLOBAL CONSCIOUSNESS

R.R. 14, BOX 203   LA CIENEGA NM 87505
PHONE (505) 473 4848   FAX (505) 438 2002

Founded 1987 • *Geographic Coverage* Global

Mission To prepare students of all ages to be personally accountable, to be in touch with their own spirituality and with universal spirituality, and to be powerful global beings.

Programs Elementary/middle school, high school, college level academics.

For more Information Library

Who's Who PRESIDENT **ROBERT SAMANIEGO** • VICE PRESIDENT **MARTHA MCLAY** TREASURER **LOU SCHREIBES** • OTHER **CHRIS GRISCOM, LILIAN CORVISON**

NORTH AMERICAN ASSOCIATION FOR ENVIRONMENTAL EDUCATION

P.O. BOX 400   TROY OH 45373
PHONE (513) 339 6835

Founded 1971 • *Geographic Coverage* North America • *Cooperative Partners* Montana Environmental Education Association, Western Regional Environmental Education Council • *Organization Members* 75 • *Individual Members* 1,450

Mission To promote environmental education and support the work of environmental educators around the world. The Association is an integrated network of professionals in the field of environmental education with membership throughout North America and in 25 additional countries.

Annual Fees	*Regular*	*Student/Senior*	*Institution*
	$35	$20	$150

Programs Annual conference of the North American Association for Environmental Education. Pathways to Partnership Program. Coalition for Environmental Education.

Publication Bimonthly magazine *Environmental Communicator*

For more Information Database

Who's Who EXECUTIVE DIRECTOR **EDWARD J. MCCREA**

NUCLEAR INFORMATION AND RESOURCE SERVICE PAGE 185

1424 16TH STREET, NW, SUITE 601   WASHINGTON DC 20036
PHONE (202) 328 0002   FAX (202) 462 2183

ORANGE COUNTY OUTDOOR SCIENCE SCHOOL

1833 MENTONE BOULEVARD   MENTONE CA 92359
PHONE (909) 794 1988   FAX (909) 794 4362

Founded 1974 • *Geographic Coverage* Local • *Cooperative Partner* Orange County Department of Education

Mission To provide a classroom setting in the San Bernardino Mountains for 5th and 6th graders, with an emphasis on natural sciences and environmental education.

Funding

Government Support	Fundraising
3%	97%

Total Income $2,800,000

Usage

Administration	Fundraising	Programs
3%	1%	96%

Total Expenses $2,800,000

For more Information Library

Who's Who CONTACT DAN LEINBACH

PAUL BABLADELIS EBERSILE CENTER

3400 SECOND STREET   WAYLAND MI 49348
PHONE (616) 792 9294

Founded 1977 • *Geographic Coverage* Local

Mission To help individuals gain an understanding and appreciation of the natural world and develop an understanding of other people; and to promote self-growth through new experiences.

Programs Variety of environmental educational programs for children of all ages.

Publication *Earthbeat* published seasonally

POCONO ENVIRONMENTAL EDUCATION CENTER

R.D. 2, BOX 1010   DINGMANS FERRY PA 18328
PHONE (717) 828 2319

Established 1972, restructured in 1986 • *Geographic Coverage* National, eastern Europe • *Focused Countries* Russian Federation, USA *Cooperative Partners* US National Park Service, Vodlozero Russian Park, Elderhostel • *Organization Members* 700 • *Individual Members* 4,350

Mission To advance environmental awareness, knowledge, and skills through education in order that those who inherit the planet may better understand the complexity of natural and human designed environments. The Center is committed to the education of individuals, minorities, people with special needs, and social communities.

Annual Fees

Regular	Student/Senior	Families	Patron
$20	$15	$25	$50

Funding

Membership	Corporations	Visitors User Fees
16%	2%	82%

Usage

Administration	Fundraising	Programs
10%	3%	87%

Programs Sponsors Russian cooperative eco-vacations. Provides internships for professionals in environmental education and journalism. Senior American programs. Minority youth and youth at risk programs. Bird Watching Program. Family Camp and Holiday Program. Arts and Recreation Program, Photography Weekends Program. In-service credit workshops.

Publication Quarterly newsletter *PEEC Seasons*

Who's Who PRESIDENT JOHN PADALINO

PROJECT LEARNING TREE
C/O AMERICAN FOREST FOUNDATION

1250 CONNECTICUT AVENUE, NW   WASHINGTON DC 20036
PHONE (202) 463 2462

Geographic Coverage Local • *Cooperative Partners* American Forest Foundation, American Tree Farm System

Mission To help students in grades K-12 become aware of their presence in their environment, their impact upon it, and their responsibility for it, and to develop the skills and knowledge to make informed decisions regarding the use and management of the environment, and the confidence to take action on their decisions.

Programs Project Learning Tree is an environmental education program designed for teachers and other educators working with students in kindergarten through grade 12. It uses the forest as a "window" into the natural world, helping young people gain an awareness and knowledge of the world around them, as well as their place within it. It is a source of interdisciplinary instructional activities and provides workshops and in-service programs for teachers, foresters, park and nature center staff, and youth group leaders.

RENE DUBOS CENTER
FOR HUMAN ENVIRONMENTS, INC. (THE)

100 EAST 85TH STREET   NEW YORK NY 10028
PHONE (212) 249 7745   FAX (212) 772 2033

Founded 1975 • *Geographic Coverage* National, Global • *Cooperative Partners* United Nations Environment Programme, Massachusetts Institute of Technology's Center for Educational Computing Initiatives, New York Academy of Medicine

Mission To help complement the defensive efforts of the environmental movement with a program emphasizing the creative, positive interventions into nature. The Center performs research and education to assist in the development of creative policies for the resolution of environmental conflicts and to help decision makers and the general public formulate new environmental values. Provides facilities and opportunities for different sectors of society to interact, free of existing constraints and priorities.

Programs Organizes and conducts national and international forums, workshops and related meetings. Launched "The Decade of Environmental Literacy" in 1990 to improve environmental literacy in schools, the workplace, and the community.

Publications Books including *The World of Rene Dubos: A Collection from His Writings* • *The Encyclopedia of the Environment*

Multimedia *Think Globally, Act Locally*™ interactive multimedia series for computer applications

For more Information Library

SAN DIEGO COUNTY OFFICE OF EDUCATION

6401 Linda Vista Road   San Diego CA 92111-7399
Phone (619) 292 3500   Fax (619) 292 5648

Founded 1946 • *Geographic Coverage* Local • *Individual Members* 12,000

Mission To provide environmental and outdoor education to children in San Diego County, with a focus on appreciation of nature, understanding of science concepts, and developing a commitment to take actions to protect the environment.

Annual Fees *Regular* $150.75

Funding	Membership	Other
	90%	10%

Total Income $3,100,000

Usage	Administration	Programs
	20%	80%

Programs Operates an outdoor education program for sixth grade children, involving a five-day, four-night residential outdoor school experience in the mountains studying natural science and the environment.

Publications Guides *Curriculum Guide* • *Classroom Teacher Guide*

Who's Who Executive Director Daniel R. Baker • Other C. Smith, Greg Scherett, Mary Ann Sardina

SAVE THE PLANET SOFTWARE

P.O. Box 45   Pitkin CO 81241
Phone (303) 641 5035

Founded 1989 • *Geographic Coverage* Global • *Organization Members* 6,000 • *Individual Members* 1,000

Mission To provide the environmental community with high quality, low cost, user-friendly software which offers education about climate change - global warming and ozone depletion - that is understandable and current, and encourages environmental activism that can effectively deal with these problems.

Multimedia Software including *Save The Planet* • *EcoMap*, global view of major terrestrial ecosystems and human impact • *UV B-Ware*, UV calculator and ozone depletion trend database

Who's Who Presidents Roger Cox, Kathy Cox

SLIDE RANCH

2025 Shoreline Highway   Muir Beach CA 94965
Phone (415) 381 6155

Founded 1970 • *Geographic Coverage* Local

Mission Slide Ranch is an education center in a small coastal farming center, which provides hands-on experiences teaching respect for the human role in the web of life. Through participation in Slide Ranch programs, Bay Area residents can make personal choices which are ecologically and agriculturally informed, take actions supporting the sustainable use of natural resources, and feel nourished by the natural world.

Programs Multicultural outreach. Homeless program. Programs for physically challenged and developmentally delayed participants.

Who's Who President Rodger Faulkner • Secretary Suzanne Marr

SOCIETY OF ENVIRONMENTAL JOURNALISTS

7904 Germantown Avenue   Philadelphia PA 19118
Phone (215) 247 9710   Fax (215) 247 9712

Founded 1990 • *Geographic Coverage* National • *Individual Members* 850

Mission To enhance the quality and accuracy of environmental reporting. A further aim is to raise awareness on the importance of environmental reporting itself among editors and other key decision makers in the media.

Programs National Conference of the Society of Environmental Journalists. Regional Seminars. Mentoring and Networking services through SEJ membership database and directory. Outreach and education targeted to leadership and decision making groups in the journalism community.

Publications Quarterly newsletter *SEJournal*. Annual membership directory

Multimedia *The SEJ Forum*, electronic bulletin board operated through America Online. Audiotapes of the National Conference

Who's Who President Jim Detjen • Vice President Rae Tyson • Secretary Kevin P. Carmody • Treasurer Noel Grove • Executive Director Beth Parke

STUDENT CONSERVATION ASSOCIATION, INC.

P.O. Box 550   Charlestown NH 03603
Phone (603) 543 1700   Fax (603) 543 1828

Founded 1957 • *Geographic Coverage* North America, including Mexico • *Cooperative Partners* US Forest Service, National Park Service, Bureau of Land Management, US Fish and Wildlife Service, Garden Club of America, Trout Unlimited • *Individual Members* 1,500

Mission To foster lifelong stewardship of the environment by offering opportunities for education, leadership, and personal development, while providing public service in conservation.

Funding

Membership	*Gifts & Grants*	*Program Income*	*Investments & Other*
14%	21%	62%	3%

Total Income $5,594,314

Usage

Administration	*Membership Development*	*Programs*
12%	9%	79%

Total Expenses $5,580,524

Programs Educational programs work for high school, adult and minority development (ages 16-23). New Hampshire Conservation Corps.

Publication Magazine *Earth Work*

For more Information Annual Report

Who's Who President **Scott Izzo** • Executive Vice President **Valerie Shand** Chairperson **Kathleen Selz** • Vice Chairperson **Nicholas S. Lamont** • Secretary **Marylin Armstrong** • Treasurer **B. Jane Sherwin**

TERRENE INSTITUTE

1717 "K" Street, NW, Suite 801   Washington DC 20006
Phone (202) 833 8317   Fax (202) 296 4071

Founded 1990 • *Geographic Coverage* National, Global • *Cooperative Partners* The Clean Lakes Clearinghouse for the US Environmental Protection Agency, Alliance for Environmental Education, Water Quality 2000

Mission To link the corporate with the governmental and the academic worlds in the effort to improve the total environment that all must share. The Institute's research and educational activities related to the environment focus on peer reviewed research on environmental topics and distribution of educational materials.

Funding

Foundations	*Other*
98%	2%

Total Income $1,500,000

Usage

Programs	*Other*
90%	10%

Programs Terrene facilitates organizational development as part of its citizen outreach program, which includes seminars, workshops, and print

and audiovisual materials. Up to 12 programs that focus primarily on non-point source and water issues.

Publications Citizen handbooks *Handle With Care: Your Guide to Preventing Water Pollution* • *Urban Runoff and Stormwater Management Handbook* • *Your ABC Guide to the Environment* • *Lake Maintenance Handbook* • *Decision maker's Stormwater Handbook.* Technical proceedings *Remote Sensing and GIS Applications to Nonpoint Source Planning* • *Reducing Risk in Paint Stripping.* Various liming manuals including *International Lake and Watershed Liming Practices* • *Practical Guide to Managing Acidic Surface Waters and their Fisheries*

Multimedia Audio-visual materials

For more Information Database, Library, List of Publications

Who's Who President **William Funk** • Vice President **Judith Taggart** • Secretary **James E. Fraser**

TREE HILL, INC.
JACKSONVILLE'S NATURE CENTER

7152 Lone Star Road   Jacksonville FL 32211
Phone (904) 724 4646   Fax (904) 724 4646

Founded 1971 • *Geographic Coverage* Local • *Cooperative Partners* Duval Environmental Educators Network, Duval County School Board, Jacksonville Electric Authority, University of North Florida, Museum of Science and History • *Chapters* 3 • *Organization Members* 50 • *Individual Members* 200

Mission To preserve the Tree Hill properties in Arlington, Mandarin, and the Westside; to provide environmental and energy education programs; and to promote environmental awareness in the Greater Jacksonville community.

Annual Fees

Regular	*Student/Senior*	*Families*	*Organization*	*Corporation*
$25	$10	$25	$100	$250

Other Fees *Lifetime* $500

Funding

Membership	*Corporations*	*Foundations*	*Contracts*
30%	10%	10%	50%

Usage

Administration	*Fundraising*	*Programs*	*Property Operations*
40%	10%	40%	10%

Programs Environmental and energy education programs for grades K-6, teacher workshops, science day camps, scout camp-ins, adult workshops, lectures, outreach programs.

Publication Quarterly newsletter *Tree Lines*, circulation 1,000

For more Information Database, Library

Who's Who President **William Brinton** • Vice President **Mary Ann Southwell**

SECRETARY GARDNER DAVIS • TREASURER DREW THEONI • EXECUTIVE DIRECTOR LUCILLE G. HEINE • EDUCATION COORDINATOR CHRIS MORLOCK • OFFICE MANAGER ESMÉ LEE

TREES FOR TOMORROW, INC.

611 SHERIDAN STREET, P.O. BOX 609   EAGLE RIVER WI 54521
PHONE (715) 479 6456

Founded 1944 • *Geographic Coverage* Regional • *Cooperative Partners* Wisconsin Department of Natural Resources, US Forest Service, University of Wisconsin • *Organization Members* 255 • *Individual Members* 221

Mission Originally founded by nine Wisconsin-based paper companies to encourage reforestation, the organization works towards the goal of providing a natural resources education which presents a balanced variety of perspectives on natural resource topics so that participants can develop informed decisions about sound resource management.

Annual Fees	Regular	Student/Senior	Sustaining	Patron	Associate
	$30	$5	$50	$100 to 200	$500

Other Fees *Executive* $1,000

Funding	Membership	Corporations	Scholarships
	20%	20%	60%

Total Income $50,000

Usage	Administration	Fundraising	Programs
	20%	5%	75%

Programs Forestry program. Water program. Wildlife program. Cross-country skiing program.

Publications Quarterly *Northbound* • *Hey Teacher!*

Multimedia *Introducing Trees for Tomorrow Student Workshops*, orientation video (16 min.). Numerous films and other videos focusing on the organization's programs

Who's Who PRESIDENT MILES BENSON • SECRETARY PATRICK SCHRICKEL • EXECUTIVE DIRECTOR HENRY HASKELL

UNIVERSITY RESEARCH EXPEDITIONS PROGRAM

UNIVERSITY OF CALIFORNIA   BERKELEY CA 94720
PHONE (510) 642 6586

Founded 1976 • *Geographic Coverage* Global • *Other Field of Focus* Quality of Life / Outdoor Activities

Mission To provide educational research expeditions worldwide for interested members of the public, with an emphasis on environmental and cultural studies. Environmental studies and tropical forests studies are the organization's main areas of expertise.

Annual Fees	Regular	Friend	Associate	Supporting	Patron	Sponsor
	$35	$50	$100	$250	$500	$1,000

Funding *Foundations* 100%

Total Income $500,000

Usage	Administration	Fundraising	Programs
	15%	5%	80%

Programs Volunteer research projects/expeditions programs include Archaeology - Hawaii, Ireland, Benin, South Pacific, California; Environmental Studies - Kenya, Ecuador, Costa Rica, Belize, Hawaii; Paleontology - Russia, California; Social Sciences - Guatemala, South Pacific, Scotland, Honduras, Mali.

Publication Annual catalog of expeditions

Who's Who EXECUTIVE DIRECTOR JEAN G. COLVIN

VIDEO PROJECT (THE)

5332 COLLEGE AVENUE, SUITE 101   OAKLAND CA 94618
PHONE (510) 655 9050   FAX (510) 655 9115

Founded 1982 • *Geographic Coverage* Global • *Individual Members* 350

Mission To provide the public with affordable videos on a variety of environmental issues not available through mainstream channels.

Annual Fees	Regular	Producers' Circle	Directors' Circle
	$35	$150	$250

Publication Annual catalog

Multimedia Extensive supply of videos focusing on environmental issues

For more Information List of Publications

Who's Who PRESIDENT VIVIENNE VERDON-ROE • SECRETARY IAN THIERMANN • EXECUTIVE DIRECTOR STEVE LADD

WILDERNESS EDUCATION ASSOCIATION

20 WINONA AVENUE, BOX 89   SARANAC LAKE NY 12983
PHONE (518) 891 2915

Founded 1978 • *Geographic Coverage* National • *Organization Members* 40 • *Individual Members* 1,900

Mission To promote the educated use and conservation of wilderness lands. Through a network of affiliate organizations and programs, the Association certified instructors teach a field-based curriculum providing participants with the training and experience necessary to lead safe and enjoyable backcountry expeditions while minimizing the impact on the wilderness resource.

Annual Fees

	Regular	Student/Senior	Families	Corporation	Sustaining Organization
	$30	$15 to 20	$45	$250	$100

Other Fees *Supporting* $500 • *Steward* $1,000 • *Lifetime* $1,000

Funding

Membership	Corporations	Foundations	Other
40.4%	6.2%	5.6%	47.8%

Total Income $80,500

Usage

Administration	Fundraising	Programs	Other
84.5%	3.7%	1.2%	10.6%

Total Expenses $80,500

Programs The foundation of the Association's program is a college level course developed by several of the nation's top outdoor education professionals. Called the National Standard Program, this 28-35 day expedition is offered in wilderness areas across North America. Successful graduates of the program receive Outdoor Leadership Certification from the Association.

Publications Quarterly newsletter *The WEA Legend*. Books *WEA Affiliate Handbook* • *Backcountry Classroom: Lesson Plans for Teaching in the Wilderness* • *Wilderness Educator: The WEA Curriculum Guide*

Multimedia WEA Job Referral Service, computerized listing of outdoor recreation positions

For more Information Library

Who's Who PRESIDENT **JACK K. DRURY** • VICE PRESIDENT **MITCHELL SAKOFS** SECRETARY **DAVID COCKRELL** • TREASURER **WILLIAM W. FORGEY** • EXECUTIVE DIRECTOR **CATHERINE E. PALMER** • ADMINISTRATIVE ASSISTANT **DUANE GOULD**

WILDERNESS SOUTHEAST

711 SANDTOWN ROAD   SAVANNAH GA 31410
PHONE (912) 897 5108

Founded 1973 • *Geographic Coverage* Regional, Central America *Focused Regions* Georgia, Florida, Bahamas, Belize, Virgin Islands, Costa Rica, Brazilian Amazonian rainforest

Mission To foster a sense of earth stewardship through environmental and natural history education.

Programs Environmental Tours to Great Smokies Basecamp, Coastal Georgia, Cumberland Island Basecamp, Okefenokee Swamp, Florida Springs, The Everglades 10,000 Islands, Bahamas, Belize/Tikal, Costa Rica, and the Amazon/Pantanal Basin

Who's Who PRESIDENT **TED WESEMANN** • PROGRAM DIRECTORS **BRUCE LOMBARDO, KIM POWELL, MARILYN COMPTON**

WILDLAND STUDIES

3 MOSSWOOD CIRCLE   CAZADERO CA 95421
PHONE (707) 632 5665

Founded 1979 • *Geographic Coverage* National, Global • *Cooperative Partner* San Francisco State University

Mission Wildland Studies is an educational institution offering environmental classes in a natural setting. Participants can earn 9-14 college units from San Francisco State University. The organization strives to minimize its impact on the land during every outing.

Funding *Tuition* 100%

Total Income $250,000

Programs Worldwide Environmental Field Study offers programs throughout the term. Wolf Habitats: The Canadian Corridor Project. Marine Mammal Survival: The St. Lawrence Whale. Wildlife Survival: The Yellowstone Endangered Species Project. Preserving Ancient Forests: The Washington Endangered Habitats Projects. Preserving Wildland Habitats: The Idaho Wilderness Ecology Project. Critical Canadian Environments: The Vancouver Island Project. Tropical Rain of Sulawesi: The Indonesia Wildland Program. Wolves, Grizzlies, and Wilderness. The Environment of Nepal: The Himalayan Ecosystems Program. New Environmental Frontiers: The Russian Far East Wildland Program. Culture and Environment: The Mexico Program.

For more Information List of Publications

Who's Who EXECUTIVE DIRECTOR **CRANDALL BAY**

WISCONSIN ASSOCIATION
FOR ENVIRONMENTAL EDUCATION

7290 COUNTY MM   AMHERST JUNCTION WI 54407
PHONE (715) 346 2796

Founded 1972 • *Geographic Coverage* State • *Cooperative Partners* Wisconsin Center for Environmental Education, Wisconsin Department of Natural Resources, Wisconsin Department of Public Instruction, University of Wisconsin at Stevens Point, Wisconsin Environmental Protection Agency *Organization Members* 45 • *Individual Members* 1,800

Mission To promote responsible environmental action through education in the classroom and in the community. The Association is a statewide professional organization composed of people interested in learning about and helping others learn about environmental issues, including teachers at all levels, environmental professionals, college students, and community educators.

Annual Fees

	Regular	Student/Senior	Families	Organization	Corporation
	$15	$8	$25	$50	$100

Other Fees *Lifetime* $300

Funding *Membership* 100%

Total Income $45,000

Usage	*Administration*	*Fundraising*	*Programs*
	16%	2%	82%

Programs The Association's annual Fall Conference in October features presentations on critical environmental issues and new teaching techniques, field trips, and hands-on workshops. The Winter Workshop in January offers educational speakers and sessions, as well as recreational activities exploring the world of winter and providing time to get to know other members. At the Spring Adventure in Outdoor Education in May, participants learn outdoor skills, such as canoeing, nature photography, and orienteering. The organization also cosponsored the Midwest Environmental Education Conference held August 10-13, 1993, in Stevens Point, Wisconsin.

Publications Quarterly newsletters *The Bulletin* • *EE News*

For more Information Database

Who's Who PRESIDENT CYNDI MAY • VICE PRESIDENT PAT MARINAC • TREASURER DEAN SAUERS • OTHER CLAYTON RUSSELL, SUSAN GILCHRIST, TERRIE COOPER, TIM BYERS, JOE PASSINEAU, ELIZABETH JANVRIN, RUTH OPPEDAHL, DIANE DALTON, JUDY KLIPPEL • CONTACT META REIGEL

WORLD BIRD SANCTUARY

PAGE 156

P.O. BOX 270270
PHONE (314) 938 6193

ST. LOUIS MO 63127
FAX (314) 938 9464

WORLD ENVIRONMENT CENTER

419 PARK AVENUE, SOUTH, SUITE 1800
PHONE (212) 683 4700

NEW YORK NY 10016
FAX (212) 683 5053

Founded 1974 • *Geographic Coverage* Global

Mission To strengthen industrial and urban environmental, health and safety policy and practices by promoting partnerships and information exchange among industry, government and non-governmental organizations. The Center provides training and technical cooperation programs staffed by volunteer and other experts from industry, government, academia, non-governmental organizations and the general public.

Programs Sponsors the International Environment Forum (IEF), a group of 60 major multinational manufacturing corporations based in eight countries which meets quarterly for discussions of environmental, health, safety and resource management issues. The Center's International Environment and Development Service (IEDS) provides pro bono assistance to enhance industrial and urban environmental, health and safety management policy and practices. Sponsors Annual World Environmental Center Gold Medal for International Corporate Environmental Achievement.

Publications Quarterly newsletters *WEC Network News* • *WEC IEDS Review*

Who's Who PRESIDENT ANTHONY G. MARCIL • MANAGER CORPORATE PROGRAMS

ANN VENARDOS

YELLOWSTONE ASSOCIATION FOR NATURAL SCIENCE, HISTORY, & EDUCATION, INC. (THE)

P.O. BOX 117
PHONE (307) 344 7381

YELLOWSTONE NATIONAL PARK WY 82190

Founded 1976 • *Geographic Coverage* Regional, National • *Other Field of Focus* National Parks - Land Use / Conservation / Acquisition- *Cooperative Partner* The Yellowstone Institute

Mission To educate the general public about Yellowstone Park and its surrounding ecosystem, including both natural processes and the roles that humans play.

Total Income $175,000

Programs The Association offers a number of educational opportunities, including Summer field courses, nature study vacations, winter courses, environmental classes. The Yellowstone Institute offers short courses in cultural history, natural history, and humanities topics.

Publications Numerous books, maps, and pamphlets about Yellowstone National Park

Who's Who PRESIDENT DON NELSON

YOSEMITE NATIONAL INSTITUTE

GOLDEN GATE NATIONAL RECREATION AREA
BUILDING 1033
PHONE (415) 332 5771

SAUSALITO CA 94965

Founded 1971 • *Geographic Coverage* Regional • *Other Field of Focus* National Parks - Land Use / Conservation / Acquisition • *Chapters* 3

Mission Guided by the belief that protection and preservation of the earth's environmental integrity is among the most significant legacies that can be passed to future generations, the Institute is calling for the mounting of a thoughtful, sustained commitment to environmental education focusing on a global imperative for the prudent use and balanced preservation of America's natural resources.

Programs Annual three week International Seminar on Environmental Education.

Publication Quarterly newsletter *Nature's Classroom*

Who's Who PRESIDENT GARRY MITCHELL

YOUTH FOR ENVIRONMENTAL SANITY

THE YES! TOUR
706 FREDERICK STREET
PHONE (408) 459 9344

SANTA CRUZ CA 95062
FAX (408) 458 0255

Founded 1990 • *Geographic Coverage* National • *Cooperative Partners* EarthSave Foundation, YES! Australia • *Chapter* 1, in Australia

Mission To educate, inspire, and empower students to take positive action for the Earth and its future; to help students to become conscious of their impact, and to make thoughtful choices, assisting them in making their community and world more healthy, happy, and supportive.

Annual Fees

Regular	Student/Senior	Seed Funder	Angel	Super Pal
$25	$15	$100	$500	$2,000

Other Fees *Awesome Person* $5,000

Programs The YES! Tour, a national speaking tour reaching 150,000 students annually. Follow-up Program. Summer training camps. Ozone Campaign, an effort to boycott major CFC producers.

Publications Newsletter *Action Update*. Manual *Tour Action Guide*

Environmental Networks

CARRYING CAPACITY NETWORK

1325 "G" STREET, NW
PHONE (202) 879 3044

WASHINGTON DC 20005-3104
FAX (202) 879 3019

Founded 1989 • *Geographic Coverage* National • *Other Field of Focus* Sustainable Development / Agriculture - Environmental Technologies • *Organization Members* 460 • *Individual Members* 400

Mission To further the cause of a healthy environment and sustainable development by facilitating cooperation and disseminating information among organizations working on carrying capacity and sustainable development issues. "Carrying capacity" refers to the number of individuals who can be supported without degrading the natural, cultural, and social environment, i.e. without reducing the ability of the environment to sustain the desired quality of life for present and future generations. The Network feels that the concept provides a unifying perspective recognizing the interrelated nature of environmental protection, population stabilization, resource conservation, growth control, and quality of life issues.

Annual Fees

Regular	Student/Senior	Government Organization
$30	$15	$100

Other Fees *Organization <15,000 Members* $60 • *>15,000 Members* $85

Funding

Membership	Corporations	Foundations
1%	2%	97%

Total Income $798,384

Usage

Administration	Fundraising	Programs
13%	9%	78%

Programs Provides its participants with a Resource Bank of car-

rying capacity contacts, statistics, and reports. Speakers/Writers Bureau. Sponsors the Annual National Carrying Capacity Issues Conference.

Publications Monthly newsletter *Clearinghouse Bulletin*. Quarterly journal *FOCUS*

Multimedia Online information service 1-800-466-4866

Who's Who PRESIDENT **DAVID DURHAM** • VICE PRESIDENT **VIRGINIA ABERNETHY** SECRETARY **K. R. HAMMOND** • EXECUTIVE DIRECTOR **MONIQUE MILLER**

ENVIRONMENTAL INFORMATION NETWORKS

119 SOUTH FAIRFAX STREET
PHONE (703) 683 0774

ALEXANDRIA VA 22314
FAX (703) 683 3893

Founded 1981 • *Geographic Coverage* National, Global • *Other Field of Focus* Atmosphere & Climate / Global Warming

Mission To track world news on climate change and related issues, including energy taxes, CO_2 emissions controls and standards, atmospheric and oceanographic studies, and related industrial initiatives; to track world news on stratospheric ozone depletion, the Clean Air Act and related local, national and international issues, and alternative fuels and transportation. Ozone depletion, clean air, air toxics, and emissions are the organization's main areas of focus.

Fees Vary from $25 to 150 per month, depending on type of service

Programs On a daily basis, the organization's editors review over 30 major newspapers and over 50 wire services, and publish daily summaries of world news on environmental issues specific to the Clean Air Act and the National Energy Policy Act. Each month over 600 magazines, periodicals, specialized journals, and press releases are scanned for relevant news.

Publication *Month-In-Review* bound set of the month's daily newsletters

Multimedia Daily fax service. Online service available through computer modems over ordinary telephone lines or *Internet*

For more Information Database, Library

FOREST ECOSYSTEM RESCUE NETWORK (THE)   PAGE 76

7781 LENOX AVENUE

JACKSONVILLE FL 32221

GLOBAL ACTION INFORMATION NETWORK

GAIN
575 SOQUEL AVENUE
PHONE (408) 457 0130

SANTA CRUZ CA 95062
FAX (408) 457 0133

Geographic Coverage Global

Mission To support its members' actions for sustainability by providing them with reliable and current information on a variety of sustainability issues, including ideas and opportunities for action on many fronts.

Annual Fees *Regular* $25
Other Fees *Gain-On-EcoNet* $15 per year plus $10 per month and connect time

Programs Database of Successful Approaches to Sustainable Development, contains models of successful actions that have been undertaken and presents them in format designed for easy retrieval.

Publication Journal *Gaining Ground* published three times per year

Multimedia *Gain-On-EcoNet* computer network. Information provided to members through *EcoNet* includes up-to-the-minute news on bills in Congress, background data and analysis on legislation, action alerts, organizational resources, addresses and phone numbers of Congress members, Cabinet officials, and other agencies. Members of *Gain-On-EcoNet* also get access to *EcoNet's* other conferences and electronic mail services such as *PeaceNet*, and *ConflictNet*

Who's Who EXECUTIVE DIRECTOR **BILL LELAND** • LEGISLATIVE COORDINATOR **JANE LOONEY** • LEGISLATIVE ASSISTANT **KATHERINE SILVERTHORNE** • COMMUNICATIONS COORDINATOR **TERRY TEITELBAUM**

INTERNATIONAL CLEARINGHOUSE ON THE ENVIRONMENT
PAGE 24
1601 CONNECTICUT AVENUE, NW, SUITE 301   WASHINGTON DC 20009
PHONE (202) 387 3034   FAX (202) 667 3291

INTERNATIONAL ENVIRONMENTAL NEGOTIATION NETWORK (THE)
MIT-HARVARD PUBLIC DISPUTES PROGRAM
513 POUND HALL, HARVARD LAW SCHOOL   CAMBRIDGE MA 02138
PHONE (617) 495 1684   FAX (617) 495 7818

Founded 1990 • *Geographic Coverage* Global • *Chapter* 1
Individual Members 700

Mission To improve the process of environmental treaty making through informal consensus-building, information exchange, workshops, training, and the dissemination of educational materials. Its primary goals are to improve the negotiating capacity of representatives of governments and NGOs who are or will be involved in environmental treaty making, to build support for a variety of institutional reforms that will help ensure that global and regional environmental negotiations are conducted more efficiently and fairly while achieving outcomes that are scientifically informed, and to provide information and materials that will enhance the chances of negotiating meaningful agreements following the 1992 United Nations Conference on Environment and Development.

Fees *Regular* $25 one-time fee for members from OECD countries, no fee otherwise

Funding

Membership	Foundations
5%	95%

Total Income $10,500

Usage *Publications* 100%

Publication Newspaper *Concordare* published three times per year, worldwide circulation 3,500

For more Information Database

Who's Who ADMINISTRATOR **ADIL NAJAM** • SECRETARIAT COORDINATOR **LAWRENCE E. SUSSKIND** • MANAGING EDITOR **DONNA L. MCDANIEL**

NATIONAL PESTICIDE TELECOMMUNICATIONS NETWORK
PAGE 179
TEXAS TECHNICAL UNIVERSITY HEALTH CENTER
DEPARTMENT OF PREVENTIVE MEDICINE   LUBBOCK TX 79430
PHONE (800) 858 7378

PACIFIC ALASKA NETWORKING
PAGE 203
56250 GLENN ROAD   HOMER AK 99603-9525
PHONE (907) 235 7112   FAX (907) 235 7128

RIVER NETWORK
PAGE 118
P.O. BOX 8787   PORTLAND OR 97207-8787
PHONE (503) 241 3506   FAX (503) 241 9256

SACRED EARTH NETWORK (THE)
267 EAST STREET   PETERSHAM MA 01366
PHONE (508) 724 3443   FAX (508) 724 3436

Founded 1985 • *Geographic Coverage* National, Global • *Focused Countries* Former USSR, USA • *Cooperative Partner* Socio-Ecological Union - Moscow Golubka, Russian Federation • *Organization Members* 160 • *Individual Members* 500

Mission To empower and enable people to work in defense of the biosphere by providing training and support in the use of inexpensive telecommunications technologies and in environmental leadership skills.

Annual Fees *Newsletter Subscription* $25

US CLIMATE ACTION NETWORK
PAGE 36
1350 NEW YORK AVENUE, NW, SUITE 300   WASHINGTON DC 20005
PHONE (202) 624 9360   FAX (202) 783 5917

Environmental Education, Careers, Information

ACADIA ENVIRONMENTAL SOCIETY

P.O. Box 1269   WOLFVILLE NS B0P 1X0
PHONE (902) 542 2287   FAX (902) 542 3901

Founded 1989 • *Geographic Coverage* Local • *Cooperative Partners* Acadia Students' Union, Acadia University, Canadian Environmental Network, Canadian Unified Student Environmental Network

Mission The Society works to provides a service to the Acadia community by providing an information resource on environmental issues; providing a medium through which students may voice concerns regarding the environment in Acadia; providing an organizational structure that facilitates action by students on environmental issues; encouraging and helping the Acadia community to adopt and maintain environmentally sound and sustainable practices; and encouraging members of the Acadia community to cherish and respect the natural world.

Programs Composting Program at Acadia University. Organization and promotion of major events for Earth Day '90 and '91. Volunteer Recycling Initiative which helped expose the need for the "Blue Bag" Program. Beach cleaning. Workshops and student activities for personal development.

Who's Who PRESIDENTS MANDI WISWELL, CINDY UNDERHILL

BOW VALLEY NATURALISTS

P.O. Box 1693   BANFF AB T0L 0C0
PHONE (403) 762 4160   FAX (403) 762 4160

Founded 1967 • *Geographic Coverage* Regional, National • *Other Fields of Focus* Natural Resources / Water - Conservation & Quality, Quality of Life / Outdoor Activities, Wildlife - Animal & Plant • *Cooperative Partners* Alberta Wilderness Association, Federation of Alberta Naturalists, Canadian Nature Federation • *Chapter* 1 • *Individual Members* 100

Mission To acquire and disseminate knowledge of natural history; stimulate interest in the appreciation of nature; work for the protection and preservation of wildlife, wilderness areas, parks and natural ecosystems; and inform members and the public about environmental issues.

Annual Fees *Regular* $5

Programs Monthly meetings from September through May (except for December) on the fourth Wednesday of each month. Guest speakers invited to speak on natural history topics and environmental issues. Summer outings, Christmas bird counts, May species counts, cleanup projects.

Publications Seasonal newsletters published three times per year. Statements and briefs on National Parks and provincial environmental issues

For more Information Library

Who's Who PRESIDENT GERRY WILKIE • VICE PRESIDENT SHELLY ALEXANDER • SECRETARY DIANE MCIVOR • TREASURER MARC RICHARDSON • CONTACT MIKE MCIVOR

BURKE MOUNTAIN NATURALISTS   PAGE 281

Box 52540, 2929 BARNET HIGHWAY   COQUITLAM BC V3B 7J4
PHONE (604) 463 3744

CALGARY ECO CENTRE

1019 FOURTH AVENUE, SW   CALGARY AB T2P 0K8
PHONE (403) 263 8228   FAX (403) 263 8229

Founded 1990 • *Geographic Coverage* Province, Local, Regional, National • *Cooperative Partner* Alberta Environmental Network *Individual Members* 250

Mission To promote ecological awareness and channel environmental concerns into positive community action towards a sustainable, healthy future.

Annual Fees	Regular	Families	Organization
	$15	$30	$35

Funding	Membership	Government Support	Corporations	Foundations	Other
	3.7%	22.2%	42.6%	5.6%	25.9%

Total Income $54,000

Programs EcoHelp Line. School visits.

Publication Quarterly newsletter *Solar Cycle*

For more Information Database, Library

Who's Who CHAIRS TREVOR BORDEN, DENISE GRANEN • TREASURER BRENDA OSLOWSKI

CERCLES DES JEUNES NATURALISTES (LES)
THE YOUNG NATURALISTS SOCIETY

4101 RUE SHERBROOKE, EST   MONTRÉAL PQ H1X 2B2
PHONE (514) 252 3023   FAX (514) 252 3023

Founded 1957 • *Geographic Coverage* Province, North America *Other Fields of Focus* Natural Resources / Water - Conservation & Quality, Quality of Life / Outdoor Activities • *Chapters* 7 • *Organization Members* 90 • *Individual Members* 2,500

Mission To encourage young people aged 8 to 17 to benefit from natural science related activities. The organization's objectives are to develop young people's capacity to discover and understand nature through

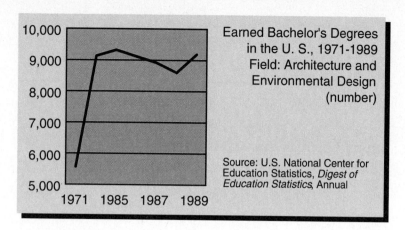

Earned Bachelor's Degrees
in the U. S., 1971-1989
Field: Architecture and
Environmental Design
(number)

Source: U.S. National Center for
Education Statistics, *Digest of
Education Statistics*, Annual

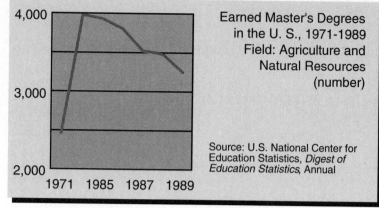

Earned Master's Degrees
in the U. S., 1971-1989
Field: Agriculture and
Natural Resources
(number)

Source: U.S. National Center for
Education Statistics, *Digest of
Education Statistics*, Annual

the natural sciences, to increase their observation skills and capabilities for leadership and communication in a group, to increase the level of environmental awareness among young people, and to encourage them to protect and restore their environment.

Annual Fees

Regular	Student
$35	$10

Total Income $188,422

Programs Outdoor activities, birdwatching, cleanup projects, research activities.

Publications Newsletters *Les Naturalistes* published quarterly • *Les Feuillets du Naturaliste*

Multimedia Slide shows *Ecolothèque*

For more Information Library, List of Publications

Who's Who PRESIDENT **ROBERT BÉLANGER** • VICE PRESIDENT **MICHEL LORD** • TREASURER **PAUL RIVERIN** • EXECUTIVE DIRECTOR **CLAUDE OUELLET**

FEDERATION OF BRITISH COLUMBIA NATURALISTS (THE)
1367 WEST BROADWAY, SUITE 321   VANCOUVER BC V6H 4A9
PHONE (604) 737 3057

Geographic Coverage Province • *Other Fields of Focus* Natural Resources / Water - Conservation & Quality, Quality of Life / Outdoor Activities, Wildlife - Animal & Plant • *Chapters* Federation of 38 local clubs of naturalists

Mission To promote the understanding and enjoyment of nature by education through field trips, camps, lectures and publications; to encourage the establishment of protected areas within the province, with special attention to preservation of endangered and threatened habitats; to defend the integrity of existing wildlife sanctuaries; to promote and engage in funding and research needed to protect the integrity of natural

ecosystems; and to encourage and engage in the protection and restoration of threatened and endangered species with special attention to the preservation of essential habitats.

Annual Fees

Regular	Subscription
$15	$15

Other Fees *Lifetime* $400

Programs Organized walks, hikes and other outings in local clubs. Summer camps. Symposia and local roundtable discussions to initiate action on environmental issues.

Publication Newsletter *The B.C. Naturalist*

FEDERATION OF ONTARIO NATURALISTS   PAGE 125
355 LESMILL ROAD   DON MILLS ON M3B 2W8
PHONE (416) 444 8419   FAX (416) 444 9866

HARMONY FOUNDATION OF CANADA   PAGE 31
FONDATION HARMONIE DU CANADA
560 JOHNSON STREET, SUITE 209   VICTORIA BC V8W 3C6
PHONE (604) 380 3001   FAX (604) 380 0887

KOOTENAY LAKE
ENVIRONMENTAL EDUCATION CENTRE SOCIETY
BOX 20   CRAWFORD BAY BC V0B 1A0
PHONE (604) 227 9555   FAX (604) 227 9505

Geographic Coverage Local • *Cooperative Partner* British Columbia Environmental Network • *Chapter* 1

Mission To promote environmental education.

Funding

Government Support	Foundations
74%	26%

page 234 ► and various programs related to the environment, many universities have courses to help non-scientists understand ecology, pollution, and other topics. These courses help produce knowledgeable conscientious voters and consumers.

SOLVING ENVIRONMENTAL problems requires teamwork among people with advanced degrees in a wide variety of subjects, including biological and physical sciences, social science, economics, political science, geography, and related disciplines. For listings of colleges offering advanced degrees in ecology, environmental science, and other pertinent subjects, see the current edition of *Peterson's Annual Guide to Graduate Study*. The section covering Biological and Agricultural Sciences lists over 4,500 graduate programs in 42 disciplines at universities in the United States and Canada. For example, Pennsylvania State University has a large interdisciplinary graduate program in Ecology, which draws on the expertise of 52 faculty members from 14 academic departments. More than 100 master and doctorate students have received degrees in that program. Community college and university extension programs often give adults a chance to continue their education about the environment on a more casual basis. Special seminars and field trips, sometimes co-sponsored by conservation organizations, offer unique opportunities for citizens to study nearby or distant natural habitats. For retired ►

Total Income $38,000

Usage

	Administration	Other
	53.6%	46.4%

Programs Environmental Resource Library. Planning and Development Issue Reports. Recycling Information Guide.

For more Information Library

Who's Who PRESIDENT **PATTY KELLY** • SECRETARY **SUSAN HULLAND** • TREASURER **DONNA WHITTA** • EXECUTIVE DIRECTOR **LUANNE ARMSTRONG**

MUSKOKA FIELD NATURALISTS

220 LORNE STREET   GRAVENHURST ON P1P 1C8
PHONE (705) 687 8766

Founded 1980 • *Geographic Coverage* Regional • *Other Fields of Focus* Natural Resources / Water - Conservation & Quality, Quality of Life / Outdoor Activities • *Cooperative Partners* Federation of Ontario Naturalists, Long Point Bird Observatory, Seniors for Nature, Canadian Nature Federation • *Individual Members* 180

Mission To develop member's understanding of and interest in nature, promote thoughtful use of resources, and advance public knowledge of nature.

Funding

	Membership	Foundations
	75%	25%

Total Income $4,000

Publication Newsletter *The Wakerobin*

For more Information Database

Who's Who PRESIDENT **DANIEL BURTON** • SECRETARY **LINDA BOON** • TREASURER **MEREDITH COATES** • LIBRARIAN **CYRIL FRY**

PEMBINA INSTITUTE (THE)

BOX 7558   DRAYTON VALLEY AB T0E 0M0
PHONE (403) 542 6272   FAX (403) 542 6464

Founded 1984 • *Geographic Coverage* Province, National • *Cooperative Partners* Alberta Environmental Network, Canadian Environmental Network, Alberta Ecotrust Foundation, Canadian Adult Educators Association, Canadian Peace Educators Network, Canadian Peace Alliance *Individual Members* 35

Mission To support and encourage formal education about environmental and global issues; to research, develop, and promote public awareness of policies and programs that lead to environmental protection, resource conservation, and environmentally sound and sustainable resource management and development.

Programs Environmental Education and Publishing. Research, Development and Promotion of Environmental Policy. Information and Networking Services. Community Environmental Programs.

Publications Directories including *The Canadian Environmental Education Catalogue* • *Who's Who in Environmental Education: A Directory of Organizations and Agencies* • *The Alberta Environmental Directory, an Annotated Guide to Alberta's Environmental Organizations and Agencies* • *The Green List (La Liste Verte)*, bilingual directory of Canadian environmental organizations

For more Information Library

Who's Who PRESIDENT **WALLY HEINRICHS** • EXECUTIVE DIRECTOR **ROB MACINTOSH** MARKETING MANAGER **GRACE MITCHELL** • DIRECTOR OF EDUCATIONAL PROGRAMS **THOMAS MARR-LAING** • LIBRARIAN **DONN BAKER**

PENINSULA FIELD NATURALISTS (THE)

P.O. BOX 23031
124 WELLAND AVENUE   ST. CATHARINES ON L0S 1E3
PHONE (416) 935 2913

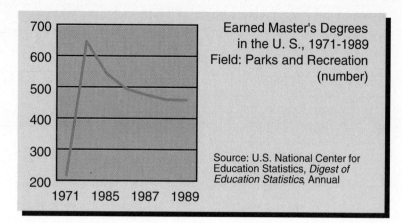

Earned Master's Degrees
in the U. S., 1971-1989
Field: Parks and Recreation
(number)

Source: U.S. National Center for
Education Statistics, *Digest of
Education Statistics*, Annual

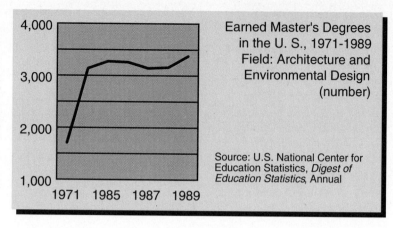

Earned Master's Degrees
in the U. S., 1971-1989
Field: Architecture and
Environmental Design
(number)

Source: U.S. National Center for
Education Statistics, *Digest of
Education Statistics*, Annual

Founded 1954 • *Geographic Coverage* Local • *Other Fields of Focus* Quality of Life / Outdoor Activities, Wildlife - Animal & Plant *Cooperative Partner* Federation of Ontario Naturalists • *Individual Members* 177

Mission To preserve wildlife and protect its habitat; to promote public interest in and a knowledge of the natural history of the area; to promote, encourage, and cooperate with other organizations with similar objectives.

Annual Fees	*Regular*	*Families*
	$12	$15

Programs Regular meetings. Field outing

YOUNG NATURALIST FOUNDATION (THE)

56 THE ESPLANADE, SUITE 302   TORONTO ON M5E 1A7
PHONE (416) 868 6001   FAX (416) 868 6009

Founded 1975 • *Geographic Coverage* National

Mission To specialize in the publishing of magazines and books for children that emphasize nature, science, and the environment and encourage children to participate in and discover the world around them.

Programs The Hoot Club, for children. Hoot Club Awards recognize young people who are working to improve their environment. The Foundation's National Trust offers OWL checking and savings accounts for children.

Publications Magazines published ten times per year *OWL* • *Chickadee*

Multimedia Software programs for classroom use *Build-a-Land Bird* and *Build-a-Shore Bird*. The OWL Centre for Children's Film and Television. OWL/TV

For more Information List of Publications

Who's Who PRESIDENT ANNABEL SLAIGHT • VICE PRESIDENT DIANE DAVY • DIRECTOR OF MARKETING PHYLLIS YAFFE • PUBLIC RELATIONS MANAGER JANE WEEKS

Environmental Networks

ALBERTA ENVIRONMENTAL NETWORK

10511 SASKATCHEWAN DRIVE   EDMONTON AB T6E 4S1
PHONE (403) 433 9302   FAX (403) 439 5081

Founded 1979 • *Geographic Coverage* Province • *Cooperative Partners* Canadian Environmental Network, and nine other provincial networks in Canada • *Organization Members* 150

Mission To support networking, communication, and resource sharing among environmental NGOs to facilitate common action and initiatives.

Annual Fees *Organization* $20 to 150

Funding	*Membership*	*Government Support*	*Fees for Services*
	1.6%	32.8%	65.6%

Total Income $122,000

Publications Bimonthly newsletter *Environment Network News*. Annual *Alberta Environmental Directory*, over 400 environmental organizations in Alberta

For more Information Database

Who's Who PRESIDENT JUDY HUNTLEY • TREASURER HOWARD SAMOIL • CONTACTS GEORGE NEWTON, CHRISTINE HAGG

BRITISH COLUMBIA ENVIRONMENTAL NETWORK

1672 EAST 10TH AVENUE   VANCOUVER BC V5N 1X5
PHONE (604) 879 2279   FAX (604) 879 2272

► people, studying and working to conserve the environment can be intellectually stimulating as well as a way to participate in leaving a better world for future generations. Elderhostel programs include many mini-courses on nature and environmental issues. The American Association for Retired Persons (AARP) occasionally includes environmental articles in its journal *Modern Maturity*.

INFORMAL READING AT HOME IS AN easy way for people of all ages to improve their knowledge about vital ecological issues. Magazines such as the National Wildlife Federation's *Ranger Rick* helps children discover the fascinating world of wildlife. By subscribing to one or more of the many worthwhile environmental publications, or by simply selecting ecology oriented topics from mainstream media, readers can keep abreast of current developments. Television programs, especially on public-supported stations, play a major role in educating the public about such problems as declining whale populations. Continued support is necessary to sponsor TV programming that educates, rather than merely entertains. Public and private museums, aquariums, zoos, parks, and botanical gardens are important vehicles for environmental education, especially in large urban areas. Well-designed museum displays can give city dwelling visitors multisensory experiences simulating distant or past natural environments. Examples of very educational and appealing natural history ►

Founded 1979 • *Geographic Coverage* Province, Regional, North America • *Focused Region* British Columbia, Pacific Northwest, Canada, USA • *Cooperative Partners* Canadian Environmental Network, and nine other provincial networks in Canada • *Organization Members* 250 • *Individual Members* 30 associates

Mission To network the British Columbia environmental community.

Annual Fees

Regular	Organization
$25	$25 to 50

Funding

Membership	Federal Support	Provincial Support
20%	40%	40%

Total Income $80,000

Usage

Administration	Programs
40%	60%

Programs Networking through caucus structure. Caucuses are comprised of representatives delegated by environmental groups to come together and work on strategies of common concern.

Publications *British Columbia Environmental Report* published 5 times per year. *British Columbia Environmental Directory: A Directory of Environmental, Peace, Union and Native Organizations* published every 2 years

For more Information Database, Library

Who's Who CHAIR LLOYD MANCHESTER • TREASURER MICHAEL RODGERS • EXECUTIVE DIRECTOR ANNE-MARIE SLEEMAN

CANADIAN ENVIRONMENTAL NETWORK

P.O. BOX 1289, STATION "B"   OTTAWA ON K1P 5R3
PHONE (613) 563 2078   FAX (613) 563 7236

Geographic Coverage National • *Cooperative Partners* Canadian International Development Agency, ten other provincial networks in Canada *Organization Members* 2,000

Mission To provide a way for environmental organizations of diverse size, mandate, and membership to have organized input into national policy discussions while sharing and improving their knowledge and expertise.

Programs The Network organizes environmentalists in a variety of forums, conferences and consultations, provides referrals and responses to inquiries about environmental groups and their activities, holds an annual conference which brings together environmentalists across Canada, coordinates the Environment and Development Support Program for environmental groups working with Southern partners, to facilitate and fund environmental initiatives with the goal of encouraging global thinking on environmental problems and supporting undertakings that will contribute to resolving the environmental crisis. It hopes to establish working relationships between Southern and Canadian environmental NGOs, and between Canadian environmental NGOs and development NGOs to encourage institutional cooperation.

Publications Quarterly newsletter *CEN Bulletin*. Directory *The Green List: a Guide to Canadian Environmental Organizations and Agencies*

For more Information Database

Who's Who INFORMATION COORDINATOR LESLEY CASSIDY • OTHER EVA SCHACHERL, CRAIG BOLJKOVAC, STEFAN OCHMAN, BEV MCBRIDE, ELAINE WHITTAKER, VANORA MILLAR, JANICE ASTBURY, VICKI FRASER

CANADIAN NETWORK FOR ENVIRONMENTAL EDUCATION AND COMMUNICATION (THE)

P.O. BOX 1514   ANTIGONISH NS B2G 2L8
PHONE (902) 863 5984   FAX (902) 863 9481

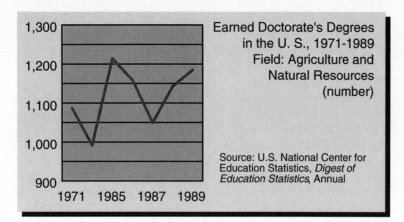

Earned Doctorate's Degrees in the U. S., 1971-1989 Field: Agriculture and Natural Resources (number)

Source: U.S. National Center for Education Statistics, *Digest of Education Statistics*, Annual

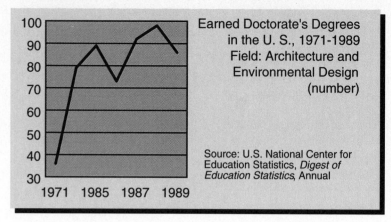

Earned Doctorate's Degrees in the U. S., 1971-1989 Field: Architecture and Environmental Design (number)

Source: U.S. National Center for Education Statistics, *Digest of Education Statistics*, Annual

260

Founded 1993 • *Geographic Coverage* Regional, National, North America • *Cooperative Partners* Canadian Forestry Association, UNESCO Canada, Environmental Youth Alliance, Association Québécoise pour la Promotion de l'Education Relative à l'Environnement - Québec Association for the Promotion of Environmental Education, Canadian Teacher's Federation, Sierra Club of Western Canada

Mission To encourage communication and information exchange among Canadians involved in environmental education; to improve environmental education in Canada; to develop a greater awareness of environmental education; to facilitate discussion of environmental education issues in local, national, and international contexts; and to strengthen and expand the network to make it more effective.

Annual Fees	Regular	Organization	Corporation
	$30	$150 to 500	$250

Multimedia *National Electronic and Paper Newsletter. Guide to E-Mail for Environmental Educators*

For more Information Database

Who's Who PRESIDENT ANNE CAMOZZI

MANITOBA ECO-NETWORK, INC.

P.O. Box 3125   WINNIPEG MB R3C 4E6
PHONE (204) 956 1468   FAX (204) 949 9052

Geographic Coverage Province • *Cooperative Partners* Canadian Environmental Network, and nine other provincial networks in Canada

Mission To encourage cooperation and communication between citizen's environmental groups and between these groups and government.

NEW BRUNSWICK ENVIRONMENTAL NETWORK
RÉSEAU ENVIRONNEMENTAL DU NOUVEAU-BRUNSWICK

R.R. 4   SUSSEX NB E0E 1P0
PHONE (506) 433 6101   FAX (506) 433 6101

Founded 1991 • *Geographic Coverage* Province • *Cooperative Partners* Canadian Environmental Network, and nine other provincial networks in Canada • *Organization Members* 64

Mission see Manitoba Eco-Network, Inc.

Annual Fees *Organization* $10

For more Information Database

Who's Who CONTACT MARY ANN COLEMAN

NORTHERN ENVIRONMENTAL NETWORK

P.O. Box 4163   WHITEHORSE YT Y1A 3T3
PHONE (403) 668 5678   FAX (403) 668 5678

Geographic Coverage Province • *Cooperative Partners* Canadian Environmental Network, and nine other provincial networks in Canada

Mission see Manitoba Eco-Network, Inc.

NOVA SCOTIA
ENVIRONMENTAL NETWORK

P.O Box 223   PICTOU NS B2A 3L8
PHONE (902) 794 9849

Geographic Coverage Province • *Cooperative Partners* Canadian Environmental Network, and nine other provincial networks in Canada

Mission see Manitoba Eco-Network, Inc.

► exhibits include those at the New Mexico Museum of Natural History in Albuquerque and the Aquarium of the Americas in New Orleans. The botanic garden at the University of British Columbia in Vancouver is an example of an extensive, research-based garden with collections of both common and unusual native and cultivated plants.

INTERNATIONALLY, EFFORTS TO support and promote education of all types in Third World countries can help raise environmental awareness in those areas. Hungry, uneducated people cannot be expected to value conserving the global environment more than they value finding their next meal. Even affluent, educated people in developed nations are often ignorant of the impact of their actions and choices on distant environments.

Governmental agencies, responsible corporations and most of the organizations listed in other sections of this publication participate in environmental education in numerous ways: distributing brochures, publishing newsletters or magazines, holding educational meetings, offering lectures, creating displays or booths in public places, and supporting other educational activities. Environmental activists hope that all these educational efforts, in all sectors of society, will total enough collective wisdom to ensure that both humans and the rest of the environment will survive and thrive. Some of the necessary choices and lifestyle modifications may not be easy, and they are possible only if an educated public is convinced of their importance. •

Laura L. Klure

261

ONTARIO ENVIRONMENTAL NETWORK

PARK MALL
2 QUÉBEC STREET, SUITE 201-C   GUELPH ON N1H 2T3
PHONE (519) 837 2565   FAX (519) 836 4191

Geographic Coverage Province • *Cooperative Partners* Canadian Environmental Network, and nine other provincial networks in Canada

Mission see Manitoba Eco-Network, Inc.

PRINCE EDWARD ISLAND ENVIRONMENTAL NETWORK

126 RICHMOND STREET   CHARLOTTETOWN PEI C1A 1H9
PHONE (902) 566 4170   FAX (902) 566 4037

Founded 1990 • *Geographic Coverage* Province • *Cooperative Partners* Canadian Environmental Network, and nine other provincial networks in Canada

Mission To promote communication and cooperation among environmental organizations, and between environmental organizations and the government.

Annual Fees *Organization* $5

Publication Bimonthly newsletter *The Networker*, circulation 250

For more Information Database, Library

Who's Who CHAIRS IRENÉ NOVACZEK, JEREMY STILES

RÉSEAU QUÉBÉCOIS DES GROUPES ÉCOLOGISTES QUÉBEC ENVIRONMENTAL NETWORK

C.P. 1480, SUCC. PLACE D'ARMES   MONTRÉAL PQ H2Y 3K8
PHONE (514) 982 9444   FAX (514) 844 1446

Geographic Coverage Province • *Cooperative Partners* Canadian Environmental Network, and nine other provincial networks in Canada

Mission see Manitoba Eco-Network, Inc.

SASKATCHEWAN ECO-NETWORK

219 22ND STREET , EAST, SUITE 103   SASKATOON SK S7K 0G4
PHONE (306) 665 1915   FAX (306) 665 2128

Founded 1980 • *Geographic Coverage* Province • *Cooperative Partners* Canadian Environmental Network, and nine other provincial networks in Canada • *Organization Members* 25

Mission To facilitate communication and cooperation among environmental organizations and to increase public awareness of these organizations within Saskatchewan.

Annual Fees *Organization* $ 20 to 40

Funding

Membership	Government Support
5%	95%

Programs Meetings. Working Groups on Environmental Issues.

Publication Bimonthly newsletter

Who's Who PRESIDENT LARRY MORRIS • EXECUTIVE DIRECTOR LYNN BROWN

public &
environmental health

CHAPTER 19

Public Health : Our Foremost Concern, by Deborah Brown

As THE WORLD FINDS ITSELF IN the throes of an industrial and technological revolution, there's no question that advances in sanitation, medicine, and agriculture have led to an increase in life expectancy and quality of life for people throughout the planet.

Yet, conversely, introduction of foreign substances or processes to the Earth's delicate, interlocking ecosystems can lead to eventual endangerment of public and environmental health - be it physical, psychological, spiritual or economic in nature. Such threats can be relatively "minor" - people may feel tense and anxious as green open spaces turn into concrete jungles - or gravely serious, as exposure to toxic substances can lead to birth defects, debilitating diseases and death. Some public dangers are immediate while others are cumulative - taking 10 to 40 years before the effects are fully known.

While usage of substances such as asbestos, lead, and polychlorinatedbiphenyl (PCB) is now under careful scrutiny, reports continue to implicate many others which may be problematic. Common household carpeting was added to a long list of items under investigation.

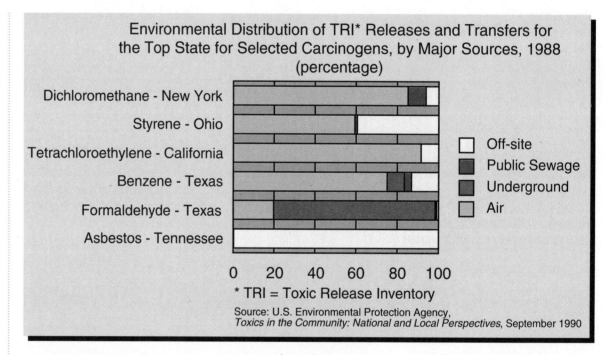

Environmental Distribution of TRI* Releases and Transfers for the Top State for Selected Carcinogens, by Major Sources, 1988 (percentage)

Dichloromethane - New York
Styrene - Ohio
Tetrachloroethylene - California
Benzene - Texas
Formaldehyde - Texas
Asbestos - Tennessee

0   20   40   60   80   100

* TRI = Toxic Release Inventory

Off-site
Public Sewage
Underground
Air

Source: U.S. Environmental Protection Agency, *Toxics in the Community: National and Local Perspectives*, September 1990

A CONTROVERSIAL STUDY REPORTS that lab mice, when exposed to air blown over a variety of carpet samples, became ill or died. In addition, chlorine has come under fire, as some activist organizations claim it may have links to breast cancer. Alleged health risks from exposure to electromagnetic charges emitted from cellular car phones, power lines, and other sources have also been hotly debated in the news. In addition, worries persist over a relatively new disorder - "environmental illness", sometimes known as Multiple Chemical Sensitivity (MCS). An article published by Green Media Group claims MCS is usually brought on by an initial heavy chemical exposure. The reaction progresses to a point where the person can develop a sensitivity to hundreds of chemicals in perfumes, soap, tobacco smoke, plastics, etc. leading to allergy-like symptoms, skin reactions, headaches, depression, and weakness.

As of yet, the best defense is to avoid prolonged chemical exposure.

SMOKING CONTINUES TO BE ONE of the longest-running public health issues. A US Environmental Protection Agency study revealed that "second-hand smoke" is responsible for 3,000 lung cancer deaths each year in non-smoking adults, and impairs the respiratory health of hundreds of thousands of children.

The American Lung Association claims an estimated 168,000

new cases of lung cancer were discovered in 1992. As a result, strong anti-smoking sentiment is prevailing in public places, such as restaurants and airlines, with a similar situation in Canada. "People still smoke, but you don't see it as much. It's possible to go for days without encountering a smoke-filled environment", observes Mary Turner of the International Institute of Concern for Public Health in Toronto, Ontario.

PESTICIDES AND HERBICIDES ARE a growing public health concern as "organically" grown foods become the preference of more consumers. Groups such as Mothers and Others for a Livable Planet educate the public about various dangers of pesticides, particularly as they pertain to children's health.

They advocate agricultural practices that emphasize organic and integrated pest management practices rather than chemical intensive farming.

Recent "scares" included a 1991 US Geological Survey report that altrazine, a toxic herbicide, was discovered in 146 water samples from the Mississippi River, exceeding EPA standards for drinking water in 27 percent of the samples. In a related issue regarding the safety of food we eat, Ellen Schwartzel of Toronto's Pollution Probe notes that Ontario regularly publishes a guide to specific fish and waterways that are safe for human consumption. Advice is based on the level of toxic pollutants found in the fish. Numerous waterside communities in the ▶

United States

AMERICAN HUMANE ASSOCIATION   PAGE 132

63 INVERNESS DRIVE, EAST   ENGLEWOOD CO 80112-5117
PHONE (303) 792 9900   FAX (303) 792 5333

AMERICANS FOR NONSMOKERS' RIGHTS

2530 SAN PABLO AVENUE, SUITE J   BERKELEY CA 94702
PHONE (510) 841 3032   FAX (510) 841 7702

Founded 1976 • *Geographic Coverage* National • *Cooperative Partner* American Nonsmokers' Rights Foundation • *Chapter* 1, in Washington, DC

Mission To protect the right of non-smokers to smoke-free air in the workplace, restaurants, public transportation and other public places by pursuing a program of legislative and legal activities.

Annual Fees	*Regular*	*Fixed Income*	*Contributing*
	$25	$15	$35

Funding	*Membership*	*Foundations*	*Other*
	34%	54%	12%

Total Income $291,897

Usage	*Administration*	*Fundraising*	*Programs*
	16%	7%	77%

Total Expenses $300,417

Programs Ongoing efforts to enact legislation to protect non-smokers in public settings. National Resource Center provides information on passive smoking, tobacco, and the tobacco industry to government agencies, local advocates and the media.

Publications Quarterly newsletter *UPDATE.* Curriculum Guides *Death in the West* • *Secondhand Smoke.* Pamphlet *Tobacco Smoke and the Nonsmoker.* Frequent *Action Alert* bulletins. Other publications include *A Smoke-free Workplace* • *Legislative Approaches to a Smoke-free Society*, Volumes 1 & 2 • *National Matrix of Local Smoking Ordinances*

For more Information Annual Report, List of Publications

Who's Who PRESIDENT BILL ROTHBARD • VICE PRESIDENT ANNE-MARIE O'KEEFE SECRETARY MERRILL J. MATCHETT • TREASURER DOROTHY RICE • EXECUTIVE DIRECTORS JULIA CAROL, MARK PERTSCHUK • MANAGER LEGISLATIVE PROGRAMS KEVIN GOEBEL MANAGER EDUCATIONAL PROGRAMS PATRICIA BRAZIL

ASBESTOS VICTIMS OF AMERICA

P.O. BOX 559   CAPITOLA CA 95010
PHONE (408) 476 3646

Founded 1981 • *Geographic Coverage* National • *Other Fields of Focus* Environmental Law / Consulting, Pollution / Radiations • *Individual Members* 19,000

Mission To provide education about asbestos hazards and exposure, and to provide direct client services, including counseling.

Annual Fees	*Asbestos Victim*	*Non-Victim*
	$10	$25

Funding	*Membership*	*Corporations*	*Foundations*
	10%	10%	80%

Total Income $150,000

Usage	*Administration*	*Fundraising*	*Programs*
	10%	10%	80%

Programs Community training program. National Education Services publications.

Who's Who PRESIDENT ROBERT MEYER

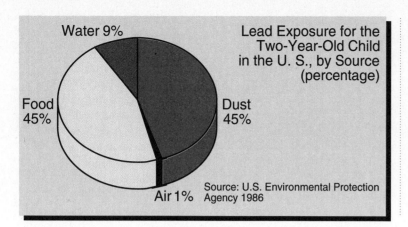

Lead Exposure for the
Two-Year-Old Child
in the U. S., by Source
(percentage)

Water 9%

Food 45%

Dust 45%

Air 1%

Source: U.S. Environmental Protection Agency 1986

United States offer similar advisories.

THE DESTRUCTION OF THE OZONE layer is also gaining more attention. Scientists believe that exposure to ultraviolet radiation weakens the human immune system and could lead to an increase in skin cancer, cataracts, and a greater susceptibility of infectious diseases. According to the *Environmental Almanac*, the highest levels of ozone-destroying compounds ever measured over Canada were detected in February 1992. To combat this problem, the US Environmental Protection Agency issued a mandate that any product processed after May 15, 1993 containing Class I or II ozone-depleting substances must bear warning labels about endangering public health and

CALIFORNIA
ENVIRONMENTAL HEALTH ASSOCIATION

2211 WESTCHESTER DRIVE

SAN JOSE CA 95124

PHONE (408) 356 7574

FAX (408) 358 1712

Founded 1930 • *Geographic Coverage* State • *Cooperative Partner* National Environmental Health Association • *Chapters* 8 throughout the state of California • *Organization Members* 25 • *Individual Members* 1,500

Mission To improve the quality of life and health through environmental education and protection. The Association is the oldest association of environmental health professionals in the United States and the largest and strongest affiliate of the National Environmental Health Association.

Annual Fees	*Regular*	*Student/Senior*	*Corporation*
	$30	$10.50	$200

Funding	*Membership*	*Special Events*
	45%	55%

Total Income $120,000

Usage	*Administration*	*Fundraising*	*Programs*	*Chapters*	*Other*
	20%	5%	25%	10%	40%

Total Expenses $100,000

Programs The Association has established an organized network of professionals involved in diverse program areas that together make up the broad field of environmental health. Technical dissections exist in the areas of Disaster Preparedness, Food Protection, Hazardous Materials, International Environmental Health, Solid Waste Control, and Vector Control.

Publications *Journal of Environmental Health*. Newsletters

For more Information Database, Library

Who's Who PRESIDENT DONALD GOMSI • PRESIDENT-ELECT SUSAN STRONG • VICE PRESIDENT STEVE DURHAM • SECRETARY LORI BRAUNSREITHER • TREASURER ALBILIU LOPEZ • EXECUTIVE SECRETARY LINDA SPANGLER

CITIZENS
FOR A BETTER ENVIRONMENT

407 SOUTH DEARBORN, SUITE 1775

CHICAGO IL 60605

PHONE (312) 939 1530

Founded 1971 • *Geographic Coverage* Regional • *Chapters* 4 *Individual Members* 30,000

Mission To prevent and fight environmental health threats through research, advocacy, public education, and citizen empowerment. The organization's central areas of focus currently include solid waste and toxic pollution.

Annual Fees *Regular* $25

Funding	*Membership*	*Foundations*
	90%	10%

Total Income $1,500,000

Usage	*Administration*	*Fundraising*	*Programs*
	10%	25%	65%

Publication Quarterly *The Environmental Review*

Who's Who PRESIDENT BILL DAVIS • VICE PRESIDENT MARTY WOCJIK • SECRETARY MARILYN GORIS

COMMITTEE
FOR NUCLEAR RESPONSIBILITY, INC.

PAGE 183

P.O. BOX 421993

SAN FRANCISCO CA 94142

PHONE (415) 776 8299

FAX (415) 776 8299

the environment.

PERHAPS THE MOST HIDEOUS specter to public health is the toxic waste or nuclear accident. Environmentalists claim the battle over the proposed placement of a radioactive waste dump in Ward Valley, California, near the Colorado River represents a "moment of truth" for the nuclear industry, as there is no known, safe way to dispose

of radioactive wastes.

Opponents to the site claim that radioactive materials could leak into an underlying aquifer and contaminate the Colorado - a major drinking and irrigation water source for the Southwest. Other "test case" battles rage across continent. Near Savannah River, South Carolina, many workers at a bomb factory which made tritium claim they developed rare cancers and ▶

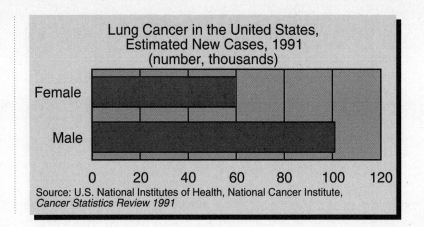

Lung Cancer in the United States,
Estimated New Cases, 1991
(number, thousands)

Source: U.S. National Institutes of Health, National Cancer Institute,
Cancer Statistics Review 1991

EARTH SHARE

3400 INTERNATIONAL DRIVE, NW, SUITE 2-K   WASHINGTON DC 20008
PHONE (202) 537 7100   FAX (202) 537 7101

ENVIRONMENTAL COMMISSION OF
THE DEMOCRATIC SOCIALISTS OF AMERICA

1608 NORTH MILWAUKEE, FOURTH FLOOR   CHICAGO IL 60647
PHONE (312) 384 0327   FAX (312) 702 0090

ENVIRONMENTAL HEALTH COALITION

1717 KETTNER BOULEVARD, SUITE 100   SAN DIEGO CA 92101
PHONE (619) 235 0281

Geographic Coverage Regional • *Other Field of Focus* Food / Pesticides / Consumerism & Safety

Mission To develop customized programs for education on urban runoff, to provide in-service training or classroom presentations on watershed protection, and to provide consultation on establishing an Integrated Pest Management (IPM) program for locations that typically add pesticides to the pollutant loading in urban runoff - such as school districts, park and recreation departments, public or private golf courses, and mortuaries.

Annual Fees	Regular	Student/Senior	Families	Friend	Supporting
	$25	$15	$40	$100	$250

Other Fees *Toxic Avenger* $500

Programs The School Pesticide Use Reduction (S.P.U.R.) Campaign promotes integrated pest management policies mandating that toxic pest controls be used only as a last resort, and informs the public about ecosystem management and alternatives to toxic pest controls.

Publications Quarterly newsletter *Toxinformer*. Educational materials including *How To Create A Storm Water Pollution Prevention Campaign* • *Watershed Protection Kits* • *Best Management Practices: Good For*

Business, Good for the Environment. Guides including *S.P.U.R.* • *Ecological Buying Guide*

Multimedia *S.P.U.R.* slide show

For more Information List of Publications

Who's Who PRESIDENT **BEATRIZ BARRAZA-ROPPÉ** • VICE PRESIDENT **MICHAEL SHAMES** • TREASURER **TONY PETTINA** • EXECUTIVE DIRECTOR **DIANE TAKVORIAN** • FUND DEVELOPMENT DIRECTOR **SONYA HOLMQUIST** • OFFICE MANAGER **ADEN NARDONE**

GLOBAL 2000, INC

THE CARTER CENTER, ONE COPENHILL   ATLANTA GA 30307
PHONE (404) 872 3848   FAX (404) 874 5515

GROUP AGAINST SMOKERS' POLLUTION

GASP®, INC.
P.O. BOX 632   COLLEGE PARK MD 20741-0632
PHONE (301) 459 4791

Founded 1971 • *Geographic Coverage* National • *Chapters* 30, throughout the US • *Individual Members* 13,000

Mission To protect non-smokers from involuntary exposure to environmental tobacco smoke and to reverse the social acceptability of smoking, through disseminating information in a broad educational campaign, supporting the enactment of public policy measures, and encouraging non-smokers to assert their rights.

Annual Fees	Regular	Patron
	$10	$50

Programs Provides posters, buttons, literature, non-smokers neckties, an anti-smoking board game - *Smokers Wild*, and other materials. Provides information for those who wish to find or form a local chapter of GASP®.

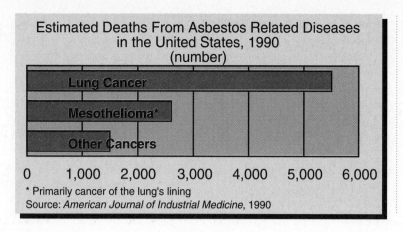

Estimated Deaths From Asbestos Related Diseases in the United States, 1990
(number)

Lung Cancer	
Mesothelioma*	
Other Cancers	

0   1,000   2,000   3,000   4,000   5,000   6,000

* Primarily cancer of the lung's lining
Source: *American Journal of Industrial Medicine*, 1990

other serious disorders. Further, the issue of hazardous waste disposal via incineration continues to cause concern. In May 1993, the EPA announced it would spend the next 18 months ensuring that incinerators and industrial boilers operating under interim federal approval are performing safely before the agency considers proposals to add capacity. The EPA will also introduce emission standards for dioxin, which has been identified as a cancer-causing toxic, and implement more stringent controls on emission of particulates. Ironically, while government and industry have created a significant share of hazardous wastes, some of the worst offenders may be average consumers. Many people don't realize that numerous household items are considered hazardous waste - from roach spray and

Publications Various pamphlets and manuals including *The Nonsmoker's Liberation Guide* • *GASP® Chapter Kit* • *The Spitting Image of Smoking* • *Model Local Smoking Ordinance and State Clean Indoor Act* • *Smoking Policy: Questions and Answers* • *Involuntary Smoking: Risks for Non-smokers* • *Smoking in the Workplace*

Who's Who PRESIDENT CLARA L. GOUIN • SECRETARY WILLARD K. MORRIS

HOUSEHOLD HAZARDOUS WASTE PROJECT PAGE 202

1031 EAST BATTLEFIED, SUITE 214 SPRINGFIELD MO 65807
PHONE (417) 889 5000 FAX (417) 889 5012

MOTHERS AND OTHERS
FOR A LIVABLE PLANET

40 WEST 20TH STREET, 11TH FLOOR NEW YORK NY 10011
PHONE (212) 727 4474 FAX (212) 675 6481

Founded 1989 • *Geographic Coverage* North America, Western Europe • *Focused Countries* Canada, United Kingdom, USA • *Other Field of Focus* Food / Pesticides / Consumerism & Safety • *Cooperative Partner* Natural Resources Defense Council • *Individual Members* 15,000

Mission To serve as a resource for parents and other caretakers concerned with their children's health, well being, and their right to a safe future. Through its public education programs, organizing, and advocacy work, the organization reaches out to the community in addressing issues such as pesticides and pesticide residues in children's food.

Annual Fees *Regular* $15

Funding	Membership	Foundations	Other
	4%	65%	31%

Usage	Administration	Fundraising	Programs
	18%	7%	75%

Programs A major consumer education campaign to focus consumer demand on safer food for their families, to foster market opportunities for foods grown using sustainable methods, to work to form a coalition of organizations including various sectors of the food industry, consumer and community groups, environmental groups, public health institutions.

Publications Quarterly newsletter *Mothers & Others Action: News for a Livable Planet.* Consumer guide *For Our Kids Sake: How To Protect Your Child Against Pesticides in Food.* Book *The Way We Grow: Good-Sense Solutions for Protecting Our Families from Pesticides in Food*

Who's Who EXECUTIVE DIRECTOR KATE ROTH • SECRETARY BETSY LYDON • PROGRAM DIRECTOR AND CO-FOUNDER WENDY GORDON

NATIONAL ENVIRONMENTAL HEALTH ASSOCIATION

720 SOUTH COLORADO BOULEVARD, SUITE 970 DENVER CO 80222
PHONE (303) 756 9090

Founded 1937 • *Geographic Coverage* National • *Chapters* 50 state chapters • *Individual Members* 5,700

Mission To advance anyone working in the environmental field. The Association is involved in many environmental issues including air pollution, hazardous waste, food, vector control, on-site waste management, occupational safety and health.

Annual Fees	Regular	Student/Senior
	$60	$25

Total Income $1,400,000

Usage	Administration	Programs
	10%	90%

Programs Conferences, continuing education, credentials, networking.

Publication *Journal of Environmental Health*

empty aerosol cans to used batteries and motor oil - and should not be discarded with normal trash.
According to estimates, illegally discarded motor oil in the United States equals 24 to 36 "Exxon oil spills" each year. Fortunately, legislation is being introduced in various areas to mandate localities to provide for free hazardous household waste disposal.

ENVIRONMENTAL HEALTH AND public health are obviously intertwined: if the environment is abused and sickly, the human population is likely to be at risk. It is in the vital interests of public health, as well as the interests of all the living things that co-inhabit our planet, that human beings become more aware of the environmental impact their actions have on themselves as well as on others. •
Deborah Brown

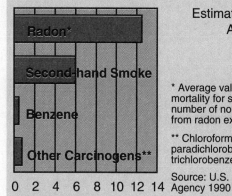

Estimated Deaths From Indoor Air Pollution in the U. S., by Pollutant, 1990 (number, thousands)

* Average value based on estimated mortality for smokers exposed to radon; the number of non-smokers estimated to die from radon exposure each year is 3,000

** Chloroform, carbon tetrachloride, paradichlorobenzene, tetrachloroethylene, trichlorobenzene

Source: U.S. Environmental Protection Agency 1990

Who's Who PRESIDENT CHRIS WIANT • VICE PRESIDENT JOHN BARRY • EXECUTIVE DIRECTOR NELSON E. FABIAN

NATIONAL PESTICIDE TELECOMMUNICATIONS NETWORK

PAGE 179

TEXAS TECHNICAL UNIVERSITY HEALTH CENTER

DEPARTMENT OF PREVENTIVE MEDICINE   LUBBOCK TX 79430

PHONE (800) 858 7378

SOCIETY FOR OCCUPATIONAL AND ENVIRONMENTAL HEALTH

6728 OLD MCLEAN VILLAGE DRIVE   MCLEAN VA 22101

PHONE (703) 556 9222   FAX (703) 556 8729

Founded 1972 • *Geographic Coverage* National

Mission To serve as a forum for the presentation of scientific data and exchange of information among occupational and environmental health professionals in government, industry, labor and academia with the aim of reducing the risks of occupational and environmental hazards.

	Regular	Student/Senior
Annual Fees	$60	$30

Programs Organizes Annual Conference. Sponsors research on Free Trade in North America: The Occupational and Environmental Health Impact.

Publications Bimonthly journal *Archives of Environmental Health*. Quarterly *SOEH Bulletin*. Guide *Protecting Workers and Their Communities from Hazards Related to Lead-Based Paint Abatement*

Who's Who PRESIDENT JOSEPH LADOU • PRESIDENT-ELECT RONALD D. DOBBIN VICE PRESIDENTS GENEVIEVE MATANOSKI, DIANE WAGENER, BRUCE A. FOWLER SECRETARY DOROTHY CANTER • EXECUTIVE DIRECTOR MARGE DEGNON

SOUTHWEST RESEARCH AND INFORMATION CENTER

105 STANFORD, SE, P.O. BOX 4524   ALBUQUERQUE NM 87106

PHONE (505) 262 1862   FAX (505) 262 1864

Founded 1971 • *Geographic Coverage* Regional, National, Eastern Europe • *Other Field of Focus* Human Rights & Environment

Mission To help protect natural resources, promote citizen participation, and ensure environmental and social justice now and for future generations, by providing timely, accurate information to the public on matters that affect the environment, human health, and communities, and by providing technical assistance, policy analysis, and skills development.

	Membership	Government Support	Foundations
Funding	25%	10%	65%

Total Income $425,000

	Administration	Fundraising	Programs	Other
Usage	15%	1%	80%	4%

Programs Nuclear Waste Safety Project. Puerto River Education Project. Resource Management Policy Project. Citizens' Mining Information Network. Community Water Quality Program. Radiation, Toxics, and Health Program. Citizen's Action. National Citizens' Network on Oil and Gas Wastes. Solid Waste Action Project. Health Information Project.

Publication Quarterly magazine *The Workbook*

For more Information Library

Who's Who PRESIDENT DAVID BENAVIDES • VICE PRESIDENT KATHERINE MONTAGUE SECRETARY BARBARA MCANENY • EXECUTIVE DIRECTOR DON HANCOCK • EDITOR KATHY CONE • LIBRARIAN ANNETTE AGUAYO

STOP TEENAGE ADDICTION TO TOBACCO

121 LYMAN STREET, SUITE 210   SPRINGFIELD MA 01103
PHONE (413) 732 7828

Founded 1985 • *Geographic Coverage* National

Mission The organization works to decrease and prevent youth tobacco addiction, decrease and eliminate sales of tobacco products to youth, and prevent unethical tobacco company advertising, through a combination of community projects, advocacy, public education, information, and policy research.

Annual Fees *Regular* $25

Publications Quarterly newsletter *Tobacco Free Youth Reporter. Speaker's Guide* and slide collection. *STAT Community Organizer's Manual*

Who's Who PRESIDENT JOE B. TYE

TOXNET
DEPARTMENT OF HEALTH AND HUMAN SERVICES
SPECIALIZED INFORMATION SERVICE DIVISION
NATIONAL LIBRARY OF MEDICINE, 8600 ROCKVILLE PIKE   BETHESDA MD 20894
PHONE (301) 496 6531

Founded 1985 • *Geographic Coverage* National

Mission To make publicly accessible online databases related to toxicology, hazardous chemicals, and the environment.

Fees *Average online cost* $18 per hour

Programs Integrated Risk Information System. Hazardous Substances Data Bank. Toxic Chemical Release Inventory. Toxicology Information Program.

Multimedia Online databases

For more Information Library

WORLD RESEARCH FOUNDATION

15300 VENTURA BOULEVARD, SUITE 405   SHERMAN OAKS CA 91403
PHONE (818) 907 5483   FAX (818) 907 6044

Founded 1984 • *Geographic Coverage* Global • *Chapters* 4
Individual Members 40,000

Mission To collect and disseminate information on traditional and nontraditional therapies for all major diseases and on environmental issues affecting health.

Annual Fees	*Regular*	*Student/Senior*	*Patron*	*Supporting Donor*
	$40	$15	$100	$250

Other Fees *Patron Donor* $500 • *Sponsoring Donor* $1,000
Honored Donor $5,000

Funding	*Membership*	*Corporations*	*Foundations*
	10%	10%	80%

Usage	*Administration*	*Fundraising*	*Programs*
	30%	20%	50%

Programs Sponsors the biannual International Health and Environmental Congress. Organizes local bimonthly lectures in the Los Angeles area.

Multimedia Monthly TV and radio shows. Computer searches. Videos and audiotapes

For more Information Library, List of Publications

Who's Who PRESIDENT STEVEN A. ROSS • VICE PRESIDENT ROSS LAVERNE BOECKMAN

Canada

ADVOCACY GROUP
FOR THE ENVIRONMENTALLY SENSITIVE
1887 CHAINE COURT   ORLEANS ON K1C 2W6
PHONE (613) 830 5722   FAX (613) 834 6699

Founded 1985 • *Geographic Coverage* North America • *Other Field of Focus* Human Rights & Environment • *Cooperative Partners* Canadian Environmental Network, Franco-Ontario Coalition on Housing *Chapter* 1 • *Organization Members* 30 • *Individual Members* 300

Mission To help people who have suffered from injuries caused by environmental disasters. Advocacy, social services, individual litigation appeals, and counseling are the organization's main areas of expertise. The association is the only Canadian bilingual organization that personally assists disabled individuals with all problems they face when made ill, especially by the environment and the workplace.

Annual Fees	*Regular*	*Organization*	*Corporation*
	$25	$30	$35

Other Fees *Lifetime* $300

Funding	*Membership*	*Other*
	90%	10%

Total Income $1,500

Usage	*Administration*	*Fundraising*	*Programs*	*Other*
	30%	5%	60%	5%

Programs Educational programs. Individual counseling. Nutrition. Housing. Health. Legal representation/appeals. Litigation. Social services.

Publications Quarterly bilingual magazine, circulation 300. Literature pamphlets

For more Information Library, List of Publications

Who's Who PRESIDENT **MARIE LAURIN** • VICE PRESIDENT **CLAUDETTE F. GUIBORD** SECRETARY **GISELE SANTERRE** • TREASURER **LOUISELLE BARRETTE** • OTHER **DIANE DOYLE, JOSEPH ROBERTS, ANNIE MCCALLUM**

AIRSPACE NON-SMOKERS' RIGHTS SOCIETY

P.O. BOX 27001   VANCOUVER BC V5R 6A8
PHONE (604) 540 9112   FAX (604) 535 9451

Founded 1985 • *Geographic Coverage* National • *Chapter* 1
Individual Members 200

Mission To prevent exposure to environmental tobacco smoke, a class A carcinogen responsible for approximately one-third of the occupational diseases associated with chemical exposure.

Annual Fees	*Regular*	*Families*	*Corporation*
	$25	$30 to 175	$45

Other Fees *Lifetime* $150

Programs The Society has ongoing programs working to prevent kids from starting to smoke, inform people of how tobacco companies promote smoking in third world countries, and inform people of how many trees are cut down to cure tobacco - 2 million acres of rainforest each year in countries without alternative fuel sources.

Publications Quarterly newsletter. Books including *Breathers' Dining Guide*, list of 325 completely smoke-free eateries • *Hazards of Involuntary Smoking* • *Benefits of a Smoke-Free Restaurant*

For more Information Database

Who's Who SECRETARY **NANCY UNGER** • TREASURER **MARC ANDER** • EXECUTIVE DIRECTOR **DEBORAH WOTHERSPOON**

ALBERTA LUNG ASSOCIATION

BOX 4500   EDMONTON AB T6E 6K2
PHONE (403) 492 0354   FAX (403) 492 0362

Founded 1939 • *Geographic Coverage* Province • *Chapters* 7
Individual Members 2,500

Mission To improve respiratory health in Alberta through fundraising, research, health education, and professional education.

Annual Fees *Regular* $20

Publications Quarterly periodicals *Second Wind* • *Clean Air Views*, circulation 700 • *Asthma Network*, circulation 1,000

For more Information Database

Who's Who PRESIDENT **NAVIN DAVE** • VICE PRESIDENT **BRENT BUCHANAN** SECRETARY **AL MACLEAN** • EXECUTIVE DIRECTOR **GARY LATHAN** • CONTACT **DAWN LEROHL**

ASSOCIATION POUR LA SANTÉ PUBLIQUE DU QUÉBEC
QUÉBEC PUBLIC HEALTH ASSOCIATION

3958 RUE DANDURAND   MONTRÉAL PQ H1X 1P7
PHONE (514) 593 9939   FAX (514) 593 4554

Founded 1943 • *Geographic Coverage* Province • *Organization Members* 125 • *Individual Members* 350

Mission To build a non-partisan forum for all players in the field of public health and to help them develop new alliances and partnerships.

Annual Fees	*Regular*	*Student/Senior*	*Organization*	*Community*
	$40	$10	$125	$50

Programs Seminars and workshops.

Who's Who PRESIDENT **JEAN-PIERRE BÉLANGER**

CANADIAN NATIONAL ASBESTOS COUNCIL

1 SPARKS AVENUE   WILLOWDALE ON M2H 2W1
PHONE (416) 499 4000   FAX (416) 499 8752

Founded 1988 • *Geographic Coverage* National • *Other Field of Focus* Pollution / Radiations • *Organization Members* 22

Mission To disseminate information and provide education concerning asbestos and other building environmental health hazards to construction workers, maintenance employees, and occupants of buildings, industrial sites, and other facilities. To promote uniformity in all provincial and federal regulations dealing with the handling, maintenance, or abatement of these hazards.

Annual Fees	*Regular*	*Corporation*
	$175	$300

Programs Yearly One-day Seminar on a topical issue. Scientific Conference and Trade Show every two years. Changes to the asbestos Variance Approvals Program.

Publications *CAN NAC Newsletter* published two or three times per year

Multimedia Videos and audiotapes

Who's Who PRESIDENT **PETER BERRY** • PRESIDENT-ELECT **BILL DENAULT** • VICE PRESIDENT **BOB WYLDE** • SECRETARY **GLENN SMITH** • TREASURER **DAVID SOLOMON** • ASSOCIATE MANAGER **MARY THORBURN**

INSTITUT DE L'AMIANTE
THE ASBESTOS INSTITUTE

1002 Rue Sherbrooke, Ouest   Montréal PQ H3A 3L6
Phone (514) 844 3956   Fax (514) 844 1381

Founded 1984 • *Geographic Coverage* National • *Other Field of Focus* Pollution / Radiations • *Cooperative Partners* Asbestos International Association, Mining Association of Canada

Mission To encourage the implementation and enforcement of effective regulations, standards, work practices, and techniques for the safe use of asbestos; to participate in international missions by providing information, consultation, or training of a technical, medical, and scientific nature for processors and users in other countries; and to gather and disseminate medical, scientific, and technical data about asbestos and substitute fibers; to provide advice and information to the public, media, government regulators, workers, and special interest groups about the relative risks of all breathable fibers.

Funding	*Government Support*	*Corporations*
	45%	55%

Programs Research and Development program, supports research on the biological effects of asbestos and other breathable fibers, works to improve the quality of existing asbestos products, to develop new products, to improve technologies to facilitate safety in the use of asbestos, and to provide technical assistance, information, and advice to asbestos producing and consuming industries.

Publications Quarterly newsletter. Various technical publications

For more Information Database, Library, List of Publications

Who's Who President **Michel Graton** • Executive Director **Claude Dugas** Librarian **Jacques Dunnigan**

INTERNATIONAL INSTITUTE
OF CONCERN FOR PUBLIC HEALTH
INSTITUT INTERNATIONAL DE LA SANTÉ PUBLIQUE

830 Bathurst Street   Toronto ON M5R 3G1
Phone (416) 533 7351   Fax (416) 533 7879

Founded 1984 • *Geographic Coverage* North America, Global *Focused Countries* Argentina, Canada, India, Kazakhstan, Ukraine, USA

Mission To engage in advocacy on health issues; to assist in health promotion and health protection for people in their work and residential settings; and to provide expertise in health, scientific, and environmental issues.

Funding	*Membership*	*Foundations*	*Honoraria & Earned Income*
	28%	16%	56%

Total Income $144,000

Programs Participation in Ontario Hydro's Environment Assessment hearings. Health 2000.

Publications Annual journal *International Perspectives in Public Health*. Newsletter

For more Information Annual Report, Database, Library, List of Publications

Who's Who President **Rosalie Bertell** • Secretary **Mary Ruddy** • Treasurer **Ross Waddingham** • Resource Coordinator **Mary Turner**

NATIONAL CLEARINGHOUSE ON TOBACCO AND HEALTH

170 Laurier Avenue, West, Suite 1202   Ottawa ON K1P 5V5
Phone (613) 567 3050   Fax (613) 567 2730

Founded 1989 • *Geographic Coverage* National • *Cooperative Partner* Canadian Council on Smoking and Health

Mission To provide information and networking services relevant to tobacco use prevention and reduction programs, projects, resources, and advocacy initiatives with the objective of contributing to the goal of a tobacco-free Canada. Works in cooperation with the National Strategy to Reduce Tobacco Use in Canada in providing access to information and support for citizen action.

Funding	*Membership*	*Contract Projects*
	93%	7%

Total Income $305,778

Usage	*Administration*	*Programs*
	5%	95%

Total Expenses $300,059

Programs Information on all aspects of tobacco and health activities and resources in Canada. Access and referrals to tobacco and health networks. School smoking prevention.

Publications Newsletter *Clearinghouse Connection* published three times per year. Fact sheets including *Youth and Tobacco* • *Smoke Free Schools* • *The Tobacco Industry in Canada*. Clearinghouse brochures

Multimedia Online information service 1-800-267-5234

For more Information Annual Report, Database, Library

Who's Who President **Gerry Bonham** • Executive Director **Brenda Wagman** Program Coordinators **Bill Howard**, **Barbara Lewis**, **Brenda Mitchell**

NON-SMOKERS' RIGHTS ASSOCIATION

344 Bloor Street, West, Suite 308   Toronto ON M5S 3A7
Phone (416) 928 2900   Fax (416) 928 1860

Founded 1975 • *Geographic Coverage* National • *Cooperative Partner* Smoking and Health Action Foundation • *Chapter* 1

Mission Dedicated to fighting environmental tobacco smoke (ETS) exposure or passive smoking, and to decreasing active smoking. The Association believes the key to prevention related to ETS is the implementation of policies and the enactment of laws to keep ETS out of indoor environments, and the elimination of child and adolescent starters joining the tobacco market. Fewer smokers means less ETS being produced and less illness caused by both ETS and active smoking.

Annual Fees	*Regular*	*Student/Senior*	*Institution*
	$29	$18	$47

Other Fees *Lifetime* $36

Funding	*Membership*	*Government Support*	*Other*
	19.5%	77.3%	3.2%

Total Income $303,900

Usage	*Administration*	*Programs*
	7%	93%

Total Expenses $48,755

Programs The Association's research program assembles information on ETS and all aspects of the tobacco industry, which is then disseminated through the Association's public education program which prepares reports and recommends policies on ETS and tobacco issues to federal, provincial and municipal governments and makes the information available to the wider public via the Association's publications and media coverage. As part of their legal reform program, the Association led the national campaign for the landmark Tobacco Products Control Act and played a leadership role in the passage of the Non-smokers' Health Act.

Publications Brochures and fact sheets focusing on tobacco issues

For more Information Annual Report, Database, List of Publications

Who's Who MEMBERSHIP DIRECTOR **SHARON E. HEENAN**

PHYSICIANS FOR A SMOKE-FREE CANADA
P.O. BOX 4849, STATION "E" OTTAWA ON K1S 5J1
PHONE (613) 233 4878 FAX (613) 567 3730

Founded 1985 • *Geographic Coverage* National • *Cooperative Partner* National Health Community • *Individual Members* 1,500

Mission To reduce tobacco use and prevent tobacco caused diseases.

Annual Fees	*Regular*	*Student/Senior*	*Affiliate*
	$80	$20	$50

Note Individual, Student and Senior fees apply to physicians only

Publication Newsletter

For more Information Database

WOMEN AND ENVIRONMENTS EDUCATION AND DEVELOPMENT FOUNDATION (THE) PAGE 32
736 BATHURST STREET TORONTO ON M5S 2R4
PHONE (416) 516 2600 FAX (416) 531 6214

quality of life
outdoor activities

CHAPTER 20

Discovering a Healthy Playground, by Deborah Brown

AS THE DECADE PROGRESSES and we peer over the horizon into the millennium, it's evident that North Americans are taking to the great outdoors in record numbers. With the lingering recession requiring a lowering of conspicuous consumption, and an increasing public awareness of both environmental and health/fitness issues, people have rediscovered the simple pleasures and rewards of a walk in the woods, an invigorating bike ride or a relaxing day at the fishing hole. In fact, "ecotourism" is a growing phenomenon as people eschew traditional "tourist" areas and luxuries for genuine wilderness experiences such as camping, boating, or bird-watching in remote, unspoiled areas. The American Hiking Society, for example, actually offers "Volunteer Vacations" for participants to build and maintain hiking trails during work trips. In addition, a Conservation International report claims that more than 5,000 tour operators offer nature or adventure travel expeditions.

ACCORDING TO CHARLIE HARDY, operations manager of the Outdoor Department at the National Sierra Club, participation in outings for hikes, backpacking, kayaking,

biking, and other outdoor activities has been steadily increasing by 150 to 200 people per year, with 4,400 embarking on such excursions as of mid-November 1993. Hardy believes some of the rise in attendance

could be due to better marketing on the part of the club, but he also notes these adventures tend to be fun, family-oriented, and affordable. The US National Park Service shows a similar upward pattern with attendance.

America's 367 national parks now cover 80,663,217 acres. Visits to these sites have jumped from 268 million visitors in 1991 to 275 million visitors in 1992, the latest figures available. This dramatic increase points to a greater

interest in these landmark sites and reflects the fact that new protected areas spotlighting the country's natural beauty and resources have been added to the system. One such area is Marsh-Billing National Historical Park in

Woodstock, Vermont - a site which includes the boyhood home of George Perkins March, author of *Man & Nature*, the ground-breaking 1864 book on conservation which is credited with laying the foundation of today's ecological movement.

IT'S IMPORTANT TO NOTE THAT while America's national park system may be thriving, the same cannot be said for the whole of the country's wilderness areas. While America's 120 national forests offer even more rugged recreational opportunities for those who enjoy mountain climbing, hiking, and camping, many of these sites continue to be threatened by logging, mining and cattle grazing interests.
To the north, organizations such as the Western Canada Wilderness Society see a similar threat, and continue to fight to preserve its nation's forests for their ecological significance as well as their recreational use.
Wetlands - ecologically crucial havens for at least 45 percent of America's endangered wildlife - also provide unique fishing, bird-watching, photography and boating opportunities for thousands of North Americans. Perhaps the most famous of these disappearing areas is the Florida

> "Ecotourism" is a growing phenomenon as *people eschew traditional "tourist" areas and luxuries for genuine wilderness experiences* such as camping, boating, or bird-watching in remote, unspoiled areas.

Everglades, also known as "The River of Grass".

THOUGH EXHIBITING A WILLINGNESS to travel hundreds and thousands of miles for the consummate outdoor experience, most North Americans find ways to enjoy the rejuvenation and beauty of the outdoors without venturing far from home. *Time Magazine* reported in September 1993 that the US mountain states -

Colorado, Wyoming, Montana, Idaho, Utah and New Mexico - are enjoying boom years as more and more Americans give up high-powered jobs in the nation's most sophisticated urban areas for the serenity of majestic mountains, cool streams, and lakes. Newcomers are also attracted to the overall quality of life - relative freedom from urban violence and congestion, as well as the myriad of family-oriented

recreational opportunities these areas afford. The lure and liberating power of nature is not lost on big business. Corporations throughout the continent are spending significant amounts of money to send employees on wilderness retreats or "adventure camps" where they jump off cliffs, balance precariously atop swaying poles, and perform other feats of "daring do" in natural settings. The idea is to build teamwork

among co-workers and empower people with a sense that if they can overcome physical challenges, they can do virtually anything - including "sell, sell, sell" in a down economy.

MOST OBSERVERS AGREE THAT AT least partial credit for the recent wide-spread appreciation for the outdoors and related environmental issues can be traced to a flurry of education ▶

United States

AMERICAN BIRDING ASSOCIATION, INC.

2812 WEST COLORADO, P.O. BOX 6599   COLORADO SPRINGS CO 80934-6599
PHONE (719) 578 9703   FAX (719) 578 1480

Founded 1969 • *Geographic Coverage* National • *Cooperative Partners* International Council for Bird Preservation, Partners in Flight, Wildlife Habitat Enhancement Council, US Forest Service, Bureau of Land Management • *Individual Members* 10,650

Mission To promote recreational birding, to contribute to the development of bird identification and population study, and to help foster public appreciation of birds and their role in the environment.

Annual Fees	*Regular*	*Student/Senior*	*Families*
	$30	$15	$37

Other Fees *Lifetime* $1,000 • *Non-US and Non-Canada* slightly higher

Funding	*Membership*	*Corporations*	*Foundations*	*Other*
	49%	16%	18%	17%

Total Income $740,000

Usage	*Administration*	*Fundraising*	*Programs*
	25%	8%	67%

Total Expenses $658,000

Publications Monthly newsletter *Winging It*. Bimonthly magazine *Birding*. Books *Lane Series* of Birdfinding Guides

For more Information Library, List of Publications

Who's Who PRESIDENT **ALLAN R. KEITH** • VICE PRESIDENT **WILLIAM J. GRABER III** SECRETARY **DAPHNE GEMMILL** • TREASURER **STAN R. LINCOLN** • EXECUTIVE DIRECTOR **GREG BUTCHER** • BUSINESS MANAGER **BOB BERMAN** • DEVELOPMENT DIRECTOR **LANGDON STEVENSON**

AMERICAN CAMPING ASSOCIATION, INC.

5000 STATE ROAD 67, NORTH   MARTINSVILLE IN 46151-7902
PHONE (317) 342 8456   FAX (317) 342 2065

Founded 1910 • *Geographic Coverage* National • *Chapters* 32 *Individual Members* 5,300

Mission To enhance the quality of the camp experience for youth and adults; to promote high professional practices in camp administration; to convey the values of camping to the public.

Annual Fees	*Regular*	*Student/Senior*
	$170	$42

Total Income $2,593,918

Usage	*Administration*	*Programs*	*Other*
	18%	67%	15%

Total Expenses $2,464,692

Programs Accreditation of summer camps. Conference and retreat centers. Certification of camp directors. Annual educational conference. Outdoor Living Skills Instructor Education Program.

Publications Bimonthly magazine *Camping*. Various books including *Acclimatization* • *Basic Camp Management* • *Basic River Canoeing* • *Camp Compensation Survey* • *Creative Crafts* • *Decentralized Camping* • *Easy Green: Earth-Smart Activities and Operating Procedures for Youth Programs* • *Fifty Years of Outdoor Education* • *Marketing and Communications Strategies for Camps* • *Nature's Classroom*

For more Information List of Publications

Who's Who PRESIDENT **CONNIE COUTELLIER** • VICE PRESIDENT **HELEN BALDWIN** EXECUTIVE VICE PRESIDENT **JOHN A. MILLER** • PUBLIC RELATIONS MANAGER **GARY ABELL**

AMERICAN CANAL SOCIETY, INC.
PAGE 101

809 RATHTON ROAD

YORK PA 17403

PHONE (717) 843 4035

AMERICAN RIVER
TOURING ASSOCIATION, INC.

STAR ROUTE 73

GROVELAND CA 95321

PHONE (800) 323 2782

Founded 1963 • *Geographic Coverage* Regional

Mission To promote a sense of involvement and fulfillment and foster an appreciation of the wilderness by conducting river trips.

Total Income $825,000

Who's Who PRESIDENT STEVE WELCH • VICE PRESIDENT BILL BJORGE • SECRETARY NELSON MATHEWS

AMERICAN RIVERS
MANAGEMENT SOCIETY
PAGE 102

P.O. BOX 621911

LITTLETON CO 80162-1911

PHONE (614) 265 6460

AMERICAN WHITEWATER AFFILIATION
PAGE 102

P.O. BOX 85

PHOENICIA NY 12464

PHONE (914) 688 5569

APPALACHIAN TRAIL CONFERENCE
PAGE 87

WASHINGTON & JACKSON STREETS, P.O. BOX 807 HARPERS FERRY WV 25425

PHONE (304) 535 6331

ASSOCIATION FOR ENVIRONMENTAL
AND OUTDOOR EDUCATION
PAGE 256

HI-HILL SCHOOL, STAR ROUTE

LA CANADA CA 91011

PHONE (818) 797 3892

BROOKS BIRD CLUB, INC. (THE)

707 WARWOOD AVENUE

WHEELING WV 26003

PHONE (304) 547 5253

Founded 1932 • *Geographic Coverage* National • *Other Field of Focus* Wildlife - Animal & Plant • *Cooperative Partners* Non-Game Wildlife Fund, West Virginia Department of Natural Resources • *Individual Members* 1,000 from 12 countries

Mission To promote the study and enjoyment of birds and the rest of the natural world, by encouraging preservation and conservation, and by keeping its members informed on environmental issues.

Annual Fees	Regular	Student/Senior	Families	Corresponding	Sustaining
	$17	$5	$20	$13	$30

Other Fees *Lifetime* $300

Programs Variety of annual activities, including bird-watching field trips. Scientific studies related to birds.

Publications Quarterly newsletter *The Mail Bag*. Quarterly publication *The Redstart*. Books *Birds of West Virginia* • *The List of West Virginia Birds* • *Birds of North America* • *Field Guide to Birds' Nests* • *Dozen Birding Hot Spots* • *The Backyard Bird Watcher* • *The Birds of Winter*

Who's Who PRESIDENT CARL SLATER • VICE PRESIDENT THOMAS R. FOX SECRETARIES JANE ANDERSON, DOROTHY BROEMSEN • TREASURER GERALD A. DEVAUL

COALITION FOR EDUCATION
IN THE OUTDOORS (THE)
PAGE 237

BOX 2000, S.U.N.Y. COLLEGE AT CORTLAND CORTLAND NY 13045

PHONE (607) 753 4971

COLORADO MOUNTAIN CLUB (THE)

710 10TH STREET, SUITE 200

GOLDEN CO 80401

PHONE (303) 279 5643

FAX (303) 279 9690

Founded 1912 • *Geographic Coverage* State • *Other Field of Focus* Natural Resources / Water - Conservation & Quality • *Chapters* 19 groups • *Individual Members* 8,500

Mission To promote mountain activities across Colorado as well as conservation programs that focus on wilderness and natural resources preservation.

Annual Fees	Regular	Student/Senior	Families
	$53	$32	$71

Programs Every fall-winter, the Club schedules events for members which include mountain hikes, ice climbing, winter camping, ice skating, and skiing. In spring-summer, these events include mountain hikes, climbs, technical rock climbs, bicycle tours, backpacking trips. Educational activities. The Club is also involved in conservation and environmental issues. It was involved in the establishment of Rocky Mountain National Park and Dinosaur National Monument. It is currently involved in issues affecting wilderness preservation, water and timber management, and access to public lands.

Publications Monthly magazine *Trail and Timberline*. Monthly newsletter *Mile High Mountaineer*

Multimedia Online information service 1-800-633-4417

Who's Who CONTACT MARILYN PETERSON

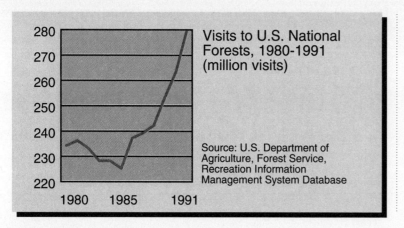

Visits to U.S. National Forests, 1980-1991 (million visits)

Source: U.S. Department of Agriculture, Forest Service, Recreation Information Management System Database

▶ programs, particularly those aimed at children. The National Park Foundation, a non-profit agency based in Washington, DC, has teamed with the National Parks Service on a new program, "Parks as Classrooms". Project director Pat Reilly notes that 200 US national parks have such a program, which is developed locally in parks, community groups, and schools. Activities include junior ranger programs, in which children study birds and plants, as well as more advanced curriculums for older students who study ecological concepts then pass on their knowledge to younger children. Another approach, "individual accountability" for the environment, comes from Committee Future, an organization headquartered in Vancouver, British Columbia and in Frankfurt, Germany. Notes ▶

CONTINENTAL DIVIDE TRAIL SOCIETY

P.O. Box 30002   Bethesda MD 20824-0002
Phone (301) 493 4080

Founded 1978 • *Geographic Coverage* Regional • *Other Field of Focus* National Parks - Land Use / Conservation / Acquisition • *Individual Members* 200

Mission To promote development and enjoyment of the Continental Divide Natural Scenery Trail as a "silent trail." Current area of concern is the development of the trail corridor.

Annual Fees *Regular* $7.50

Publications Books *Guide to the Continental Divide Trail* - 5 volumes. Semiannual newsletter *DIVIDEnds*

Who's Who PRESIDENT JAMES R. WOLF

EARTHSAVE

706 Frederick Street   Santa Cruz CA 95062-2205
Phone (408) 423 4069

Founded 1988 • *Geographic Coverage* National

Mission To raise awareness about how a diet rich in animal products can contribute to some of today's environmental problems, including rainforest destruction, ocean and freshwater pollution and overuse of fresh water supplies, rampant topsoil erosion, and global warming.

Annual Fees	Regular	Student/Senior	Families	Sustaining	Benefactor
	$35	$20	$50	$500	$1,000

Programs Youth for Environmental Sanity (YES!) educational outreach program tours high schools, weekend workshops and summer training camps. The Action and Support Groups program fosters the formation of local groups of EarthSave members to provide outreach at the local level. The Role Model Project presents celebrities in public service announcements. The Health People Healthy Planet program works with schools nationwide to provide wholesome lunches and updated nutritional and environmental curricula.

Publications Quarterly newsletter *EarthSave*. Pamphlet *Realities for the 90s*. Numerous books focusing on nutrition, the environment, lifestyles and personal awareness. Cookbooks

Multimedia VHS videos *Diet for a New America* • *A Diet for All Reasons* • *The YES! Tour - Working for Change* • *Our Diet and the Future of Life: the Windstar Video*. Audiotape *John Robbins in Chicago*. Software *VegieCard - Educational Software for the Mac* • *Save the Planet Software*. Online information service 1-800-362-3648

For more Information List of Publications

Who's Who PRESIDENT SHAMS KAIRYS • FOUNDER JOHN ROBBINS • EXECUTIVE DIRECTOR PATRICIA CARNEY

EAST BAY REGIONAL PARK DISTRICT

CRABE COVE VISITOR CENTER
ROBERT CROWN MEMORIAL STATE BEACH
1252 McKay Avenue   Alameda CA 94501
Phone (510) 521 6887

Founded 1934 • *Geographic Coverage* Local • *Other Field of Focus* National Parks - Land Use / Conservation / Acquisition *Chapters* 47 parks • *Organization Members* 100 • *Individual Members* 2,500

Mission To acquire, maintain and provide open space for the public's use. To present a variety of environmental education activities to the public.

Annual Fees	Regular	Student/Senior	Contributing	Sponsoring	Supporting
	$50	$20	$100	$250	$500

Other Fees *Patron* $1,000

Programs Environmental education activities of various types, including hikes, talks, lectures, workshops, campfires, backpacking programs, and pre-school and elementary school programs.

Publication Monthly newsletter

For more Information Library

Who's Who GENERAL MANAGER PAT O'BRIEN

FEDERATION OF WESTERN OUTDOOR CLUBS

512 BOYLSTON AVENUE, EAST   SEATTLE WA 98102
PHONE (206) 322 3041

Founded 1932 • *Geographic Coverage* Regional • *Focused Region* Western US states and British Columbia • *Other Field of Focus* National Parks - Land Use / Conservation / Acquisition • *Organization Members* 45 • *Individual Members* 300

Mission To promote the proper use, enjoyment, and protection of America's scenic wilderness and outdoor recreation resources. The Federation is concerned with all matters related to the environment of the American West.

Annual Fees	Regular	Student/Senior	Patron
	$10	$5	$25

Funding *Membership* 100%

Total Income $5,000

Program Annual convention.

Publication *Outdoors West*

Who's Who PRESIDENT WINCHELL HAYWARD • SECRETARY MARY MASON

FLORIDA TRAIL ASSOCIATION, INC.

P.O. BOX 13708   GAINESVILLE FL 32604-1708
PHONE (904) 378 8823

Founded 1966 • *Geographic Coverage* State • *Other Field of Focus* National Parks - Land Use / Conservation / Acquisition *Chapters* 12 • *Individual Members* 5,000

Mission To develop and maintain the Florida Trail, designated as a National Scenic Trail in 1986, which will take hikers through adjacent undeveloped areas including swamps, prairies, river banks and sandy beaches. The goal is to create and maintain 1,300 miles of continuous footpaths throughout the state. Currently 1,100 miles have been completed.

Annual Fees	Regular	Families	Sustaining	Contributing	Supporting
	$25	$30	$50	$100	$150

Other Fees *Lifetime* $400 • *Family Lifetime* $600

Funding	Dues	Contributions & Grants	Merchandise Sales
	65.9%	15.8%	5.7%

Other Sources *Conference Income* 2.2% • *Other* 10.4%

Total Income $109,385

Usage	Administration	Programs
	61.8%	38.2%

Total Expenses $97,617

Programs Annual regional and statewide conferences. Year-round program of outdoor activities including backpacking expeditions, day hikes, and canoeing trips.

Publications Bimonthly newsletter *Footprint*. Guides including *Hiking Guide to the Florida Trail* • *Florida Hiking Trails: The Official Guide to the Florida Trail on Public Lands*

For more Information Annual Report, List of Publications

Who's Who PRESIDENT ETHEL PALMER • VICE PRESIDENT PAM HALE • SECRETARY DARYL WELLS • TREASURER SUNNY PISKURA • VICE PRESIDENT MEMBERSHIP VAN TAYLOR • VICE PRESIDENT TRAILS WILEY DYKES, SR. • VICE PRESIDENT PUBLIC RELATIONS DICK SCHULER

GLEN HELEN OUTDOOR EDUCATION CENTER PAGE 241

1075 ROUTE 343   YELLOW SPRINGS OH 45387
PHONE (513) 767 7648   FAX (513) 767 1891

GLOBAL ACTION PLAN

84 YERRY HILL ROAD   WOODSTOCK NY 12498
PHONE (914) 679 4830   FAX (914) 679 4834

Geographic Coverage National • *Chapters* 5 community affiliates in Minneapolis, MN; Bend, OR; Newton, MA; Manhattan Beach, CA; Portland, ME • *Individual Members* 1,831 households in the USA, 3,912 worldwide

Mission To develop a strategy that addresses the need for a well conceived behavior change program and a mass media campaign that galvanizes America's imagination and desire to participate in environmentally sustainable lifestyle practices.

Annual Fees *Regular* $35

Programs Household Eco Team Program, a behavior change methodology that empowers individuals to create environmentally sustainable lifestyles. Average household participating in feedback part of the program

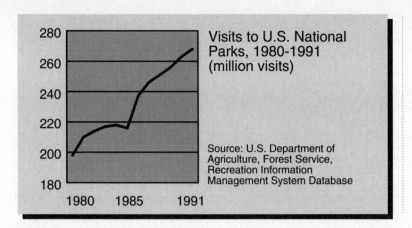

Visits to U.S. National Parks, 1980-1991 (million visits)

Source: U.S. Department of Agriculture, Forest Service, Recreation Information Management System Database

▶ founder Chris Alexander, "we have to market social responsibility in order to instill a sense of personal accountability... using all the creativity, sophistication, commercialism, and financial commitment that a major soft-drink manufacturer would use to market its product. It's a deliberate, long-term proposition". Buoyed by environmental education and a desire to escape the fast-pace and congestion of urban life, the outdoor renaissance is alive and well. The more people know about and experience the outdoors, the more they seem to appreciate and want to protect nature.

The beauty and wonder of nature, and the myriad of enriching recreational experiences it affords, continues to be an invaluable part of the lives of millions of North Americans. •

Deborah Brown

sent 39% less garbage to the landfill, used 26% less water, cut 18% of their CO_2 output, used 16% less fuel for transportation and saved $403. The National Mass Media Campaign works to develop broad-based awareness of the planet's need for Americans to live environmentally sustainable lifestyles, to stir the imagination of the American public to participate in the organization's national lifestyle campaign, and to maintain momentum in the national campaign by reporting its progress.

Publications Quarterly *EcoTeam Newsletter*. Book *Household EcoTeam Workbook, A Six-Month Program to Bring Your Household Into Environmental Balance*. Media materials in the form of releases, brochures and position papers

Who's Who PRESIDENT **DAVID GERSHON** • EXECUTIVE DIRECTOR **PATRICIA GOODWIN** COMMUNITY AFFILIATE MANAGER **DAVID KREGER** • ECOTEAM SUPPORT MANAGER **EVE BAER** • OFFICE MANAGER **PAMELA ADAMS**

HULBERT OUTDOOR CENTER

R.R. 1, Box 1031   FAIRLEE VT 05055
PHONE (802) 333 9840   FAX (802) 333 9216

Founded 1978 • *Geographic Coverage* National • *Other Field of Focus* Environmental Education / Careers / Information / Networks *Cooperative Partner* The Aloha Foundation

Mission To offer year-round outdoor and environmental education programs for groups of all ages. Personal growth, community responsibility, and environmental awareness are the essence of Hulbert's programs.

Programs School Outdoors. Eldershostel. TeamWorks (management training courses). Wilderness medicine. Nature photography. Wilderness trips. Natural History Weekends. Family camps. Weekend workshops.

Publication Occasional newsletter

Who's Who PRESIDENT **ANDREW WILLIAMS**

ISLAND INSTITUTE

4004 58TH PLACE, SW   SEATTLE WA 98116
PHONE (206) 938 0345   FAX (206) 932 2341

Founded 1989 • *Geographic Coverage* Regional • *Focused Region* Pacific Northwest • *Other Field of Focus* Environmental Education / Careers / Information / Networks • *Cooperative Partner* Western Washington University • *Chapter* 1

Mission The Institute promotes the development of outdoor activities and environmental education.

Programs Summer camps. Custom designed programs for groups throughout the year.

For more Information Library

Who's Who PRESIDENT **JANE O. HOWARD**

NATIONAL GARDENING ASSOCIATION

180 FLYNN AVENUE   BURLINGTON VT 05401
PHONE (802) 863 1308

Founded 1972 • *Geographic Coverage* North America • *Individual Members* 210,000

Mission Guided by the belief that gardening adds joy and health to living while improving the environment and encouraging the proper stewardship of the earth, the Association works to help people be successful gardeners at home, in community groups, and in institutions. The Association's fields of focus include backyard gardening - vegetables, fruits and flowers, and education programs involving children with gardening.

Annual Fees *Regular* $18

Publications Periodicals *Growing Ideas Newsletter* • *Gardens For All*

Newsletter • *National Gardening Magazine*. Gardening books and curriculums

Who's Who PRESIDENT DAVID ELS

NATIONAL RECREATION AND PARK ASSOCIATION PAGE 93
2775 SOUTH QUINCY STREET, SUITE 300   ARLINGTON VA 22206-2204
PHONE (703) 820 4940

NATIONAL SPELEOLOGICAL SOCIETY, INC.
2813 CAVE AVENUE   HUNTSVILLE AL 35810-4431
PHONE (205) 852 1300   FAX (205) 851 9241

Founded 1941 • *Geographic Coverage* National • *Other Field of Focus* Ecosystem Protection / Biodiversity • *Chapters* 200 • *Organization Members* 250 • *Individual Members* 11,000

Mission To work for the preservation of caves, by encouraging self-discipline among cavers, performing research and education on the causes and prevention of cave damage, and by undertaking special projects, including cooperation with other groups similarly dedicated to the conservation of natural areas.

Annual Fees	*Regular*	*Student/Senior*	*Institution*	*Sustaining*
	$25	$18	$50	$70

Other Fees *Individual Lifetime* $450
For additional Family Members *Regular* $5 • *Sustaining* $27.50
Lifetime $225

Programs National Cave Rescue Commission. Photo salon. Cave mapping salon. Cave Ballad Contest. Museum of Speleology. Legal committee. Federal Agencies and Commercial Cave Liaison. Youth Groups Liaison. Annual convention.

Publications Monthly magazine *NSS News*. Semiannual *NSS Bulletin* devoted to scientific cave-related articles. *Speleo Digest*. Books *Cave Basics* • *On Rope* • *Cumberland Cavers* • *US Cave Rescue Manual*

Multimedia Audio-visual library

Who's Who PRESIDENT JEANNE GURNEE • EXECUTIVE VICE PRESIDENT TOM REA • ADMINISTRATIVE VICE PRESIDENT WAYNE MARSHALL • SECRETARY BILL STRINGFELLOW

NATURAL HYGIENE, INC.
P.O. BOX 2132   HUNTINGTON STATION CT 06484
PHONE (203) 929 1557

Founded 1983 • *Geographic Coverage* National, Western Europe, Southern Africa • *Focused Countries* Germany, Italy, South Africa, Switzerland, USA • *Individual Members* 3,000

Mission To teach and learn to create the conditions for health, that is to say eat close to Earth - organically grown food, adhere to nature's laws, and avoid the use of pesticides.

Annual Fees *Regular* $17

Funding	*Membership*	*Foundations*
	95%	5%

Usage	*Administration*	*Fundraising*	*Programs*
	83%	2%	15%

Programs Two major conferences per year.

Publications Bimonthly educational journal. Numerous books focusing on natural living and health

Multimedia Numerous videos and audiotapes. Two weekly radio programs

Who's Who PRESIDENT JO WILLARD • VICE PRESIDENT HEIDI WETYEL • SECRETARY BERYL GARBOW

NEW ENGLAND TRAIL CONFERENCE
33 KNOLLWOOD DRIVE   EAST LONGMEADOW MA 01028
PHONE (413) 525 7052

Founded 1916 • *Geographic Coverage* Regional • *Focused Regions* New England and New York State • *Other Field of Focus* National Parks - Land Use / Conservation / Acquisition • *Organization Members* 45

Mission To be a clearinghouse for information on trails, shelters, camping, and backpacking. The organization consists of some 45 hiking and outdoor clubs in New England and New York State, which share a common interest in trail maintenance, construction, and conservation.

Annual Fees No assessed dues; most clubs donate $10 to 50 per year

Funding *Membership* 100%

Usage	*Administration*	*Programs*
	50%	50%

Programs Annual meeting each spring open to the public.

Publications Guides including *New England Trails* • *Hiking Trails of New England*

For more Information Annual Report

Who's Who PRESIDENT VIRGINIA DOWD • SECRETARY FORREST E. HOUSE

QUÉBEC-LABRADOR FOUNDATION

PAGE 118

ATLANTIC CENTER FOR THE ENVIRONMENT

39 SOUTH MAIN STREET   IPSWICH MA 01938
PHONE (508) 356 0160

RAILS-TO-TRAILS CONSERVANCY

1400 16TH STREET, NW, SUITE 300   WASHINGTON DC 20036
PHONE (202) 797 5400   FAX (202) 797 5411

Founded 1985 • *Geographic Coverage* National • *Other Field of Focus* National Parks - Land Use / Conservation / Acquisition *Chapters* 6, in Florida, Illinois, Michigan, Ohio, Pennsylvania, and Washington state • *Individual Members* 55,000

Mission To help convert America's abandoned railroad corridors into multifaceted trails for public use. Through a nationwide network of contacts in the recreation, transportation and conservation communities, the organization notifies trail advocates and local governments of upcoming railroad abandonments; assists public and private agencies in the legalities of trail corridor acquisition; provides technical assistance to private citizens as well as trail planners and managers on trail design, development and protection; and publicizes rails-to-trails issues throughout the country.

Annual Fees

Regular	Families	Patron	Benefactor	Advocate
$18	$25	$50	$100	$500

Other Fees *Trailblazer Society* $1,000

Programs Information on specific rail-trail projects is available upon request.

Publications Quarterly newsletter *Trailblazer*. Numerous fact sheets and studies focusing on general topics, corridor acquisition, trail development, impacts on local communities, impacts on adjacent properties, technical and legal issues

For more Information List of Publications

Who's Who PRESIDENT DAVID BURWELL

SCENIC AMERICA

21 DUPONT CIRCLE, NW   WASHINGTON DC 20036
PHONE (202) 833 4300   FAX (202) 833 4304

Geographic Coverage Regional • *Other Field of Focus* Urban Environment • *Cooperative Partners* Scenic Tennessee, Scenic North Carolina, Scenic Minnesota, Scenic Kentucky, Scenic Connecticut, Scenic Rhode Island, Scenic Illinois, Scenic Colorado, Ohio Roadside Council, Scenic Texas, Scenic Georgia, Scenic Birmingham, New Jersey Roadside Council, Citizens for A Better Clearwater, Scenic Missouri, Scenic Louisiana • *Organization Members* 50

Mission To preserve and enhance the scenic character of America's

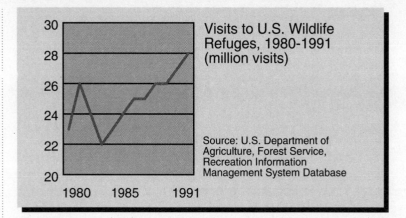

Visits to U.S. Wildlife Refuges, 1980-1991 (million visits)

Source: U.S. Department of Agriculture, Forest Service, Recreation Information Management System Database

communities and countryside, with a focus on the goals of controlling billboards along highways, helping local governments enact effective strategies to protect community appearance, controlling signs, preserving trees, protecting special landscapes and views, and establishing a coast-to-coast network of scenic highways.

Annual Fees

Regular	Organization	Associate	Contributing	Sponsor
$20	$50 to 100	$35	$60	$100

Funding

Membership	Foundations	Program Revenue	Other
14%	75%	8%	3%

Total Income $415,096 in 1991

Usage

Administration	Fundraising	Membership Services	Programs
11%	9%	10%	70%

Total Expenses $413,963 in 1991

Programs Education programs focusing on providing information and technical assistance on ways to protect and restore the visual quality of America's natural beauty. Research programs designed for citizen activists to help them promote scenic resource protection agendas.

Publications Quarterly newsletter *Viewpoints*. Various books including *Visual Pollution and Sign Control: A Legal Handbook on Billboard Control* • *Aesthetics and Land Use Controls* • *Citizen's Action Handbook on Alcohol and Tobacco Billboard Advertising*. Technical bulletins

Multimedia Various videos including *Signs: The Economic and Environmental Benefits of Community Sign Control* • *The Gift of the Journey: America's Scenic Roadways*

For more Information Annual Report, List of Publications

Who's Who PRESIDENT SALLY G. OLDHAM • ACTING POLICY DIRECTOR ROBERT BONNIE • POLICY CONSULTANT HAL HIEMSTRA • DEVELOPMENT ASSOCIATE FRANK VESPE • OFFICE MANAGER CARMEN D. HUNT

TRANET

P.O. Box 567   RANGELEY ME 04970
PHONE (207) 864 2252

Founded 1976 • *Geographic Coverage* Global • *Cooperative Partner* Gaian Cultural Transition • *Organization Members* 300 • *Individual Members* 1,500

Mission Tranet is a transnational network of, by, and for people who are changing the world by changing themselves, by creating and adopting new world views, social institutions, technologies, and lifestyles. Tranet is involved in the educational, economic, legal, environmental, and other aspects of ecological breakdown.

Annual Fees	*Regular*	*Patron*
	$30	$1,000

Funding *Membership* 100%

Total Income $30,000

Usage	*Administration*	*Fundraising*	*Programs*
	15%	5%	80%

Publications Bimonthly newsletter/directory compendium of abstracts from over 1,000 publications, papers, projects, and people who are active in the Gaian Cultural Transition

UNIVERSITY RESEARCH
EXPEDITIONS PROGRAM   PAGE 250

UNIVERSITY OF CALIFORNIA   BERKELEY CA 94720
PHONE (510) 642 6586

VEGETARIAN SOCIETY (THE)
SAVE THE RAINFOREST ACTION COMMITTEE

P.O. Box 34427   LOS ANGELES CA 90034
PHONE (310) 281 1907

Founded 1948 • *Geographic Coverage* National • *Other Field of Focus* Forest Conservation / Deforestation / Reforestation • *Organization Members* 3 • *Individual Members* 600

Mission To educate the public on the benefits of a vegetarian diet and the health and environmental impact of a meat centered diet.

Annual Fees	*Regular*	*Student/Senior*	*Patron*
	$25	$18	$50

Funding	*Membership*	*Foundations*
	90%	10%

Usage	*Administration*	*Fundraising*	*Programs*
	10%	5%	85%

Publication *Vegetarian News & Views*

Who's Who PRESIDENT VICTOR C. FORSYTHE • SECRETARY JENNIFER ROBERTS

WOODSWOMEN

25 WEST DIAMOND LAKE ROAD   MINNEAPOLIS MN 55419
PHONE (612) 822 3809   FAX (612) 822 3814

Founded 1977 • *Geographic Coverage* Global • *Focused Countries* Costa Rica, Ecuador, Mexico, Nepal, New Zealand, Switzerland, Tanzania • *Chapter* 1, in Atlanta • *Individual Members* 800

Mission To offer supportive and challenging learning opportunities for women, youth, and children for the purpose of fostering individual growth, responsibility, and relationship skills. This is done in the context of safe, enjoyable outdoor and wilderness travel experiences and leadership development courses that provide healthy living options, community building activities, and new perspectives on the natural world.

Fees *Regular* $20 to 100 • *Lifetime* $5,000

Funding	*Membership*	*Participant Fees*	*Other*
	1.5%	85.4%	13.1%

Total Income $295,000

Usage	*Administration*	*Programs*
	42.6%	57.4%

Programs Sponsors environmentally conscious adventure activities for women of all ages, including horsepacking, backpacking, canoeing, rock climbing, mountaineering, dog sledding, skiing, kayaking, trekking, bicycling.

Publications Quarterly newsletter *Woodswomen News*. Annual membership directory

Multimedia Video *Song of Women Traveling*

Who's Who PRESIDENT DENISE MITTEN • ASSISTANT DIRECTOR LIZ OHLE

Canada

ALBERTA RECREATION,
PARKS AND WILDLIFE FOUNDATION

10405 111TH STREET, HARLEY COURT BUILDING   EDMONTON AB T5K 1K4
PHONE (403) 482 6467   FAX (403) 488 9755

Founded 1976 • *Geographic Coverage* Province • *Other Fields of Focus* National Parks - Land Use / Conservation / Acquisition, Wildlife - Animal & Plant • *Cooperative Partners* Ducks Unlimited, Grant Unlimited, Elk Foundation, Alberta Recreation and Parks Association, Alberta Fish and Game Association • *Chapter* 1

Mission To provide grants to any person or organization for projects which will develop or enhance recreational programs, services, and to a lesser extent, facilities; develop or enhance parks; and manage and conserve fish and wildlife.

Funding

Membership	Alberta Lottery Fund	Interest
3%	89%	7%

Total Income $6,063,845

Usage

Administration	Grants	Project Expenses
8%	84%	8%

Total Expenses $7,050,043

Programs Quarterly grant program. Active lifestyles program. Park ventures program. Youth in Action Program. Annual Association Enrichment Program.

Publication Newsletter *Our Legacy*

Who's Who SECRETARIES LAVONNE WINTERS, KAREN RIMNEY • TREASURER JANET KACHMAN • EXECUTIVE DIRECTOR CHUCK MOSER • PROGRAM DIRECTORS DAVID JOHNSTON, LLOYD BENTZ, HISKE GERDING, MARILYN COOKE

ALBERTA SPELEOLOGICAL SOCIETY

Box 2474   JASPER AB T0E 1E0
PHONE (403) 234 8829

Founded 1968 • *Geographic Coverage* Province • *Other Field of Focus* Ecosystem Protection / Biodiversity • *Chapters* 3 • *Individual Members* 70

Mission To pursue sporting, scientific, and conservation activities concerning caves and karst within the Canadian Rocky Mountains.

Annual Fees

Regular	Families
$10	$12.50

Funding

Membership	Fundraising
70%	30%

Total Income $1,000

Usage

Administration	Equipment	Newsletter Publication
20%	40%	40%

Publication Quarterly newsletter

For more Information Database, Library

Who's Who PRESIDENT DENNIS WEEKS • VICE PRESIDENT MARIA CASHIN SECRETARY IAN MCKENZIE • TREASURER DON RUMPEL • LIBRARIAN MARGARET SAUL

BOW VALLEY NATURALISTS

PAGE 255

P.O. Box 1693   BANFF AB T0L 0C0
PHONE (403) 762 4160   FAX (403) 762 4160

BRUCE TRAIL ASSOCIATION

P.O. Box 857   HAMILTON ON L8N 3N9
PHONE (905) 529 6821   FAX (905) 529 6823

Founded 1963 • *Geographic Coverage* Local • *Other Field of Focus* National Parks - Land Use / Conservation / Acquisition *Cooperative Partners* Ontario Heritage Foundation, Hike Ontario, Ontario Trails Council, Coalition on the Niagara Escarpment, Conservation Council Ontario • *Chapters* 9 clubs • *Individual Members* 7,700

Mission To establish and maintain for the use of the public the Bruce Trail along the Niagara Escarpment and the wild lands associated with it. To establish and maintain similar trails in such other areas as may be determined. To establish, maintain and operate on the Bruce Trail and other trails camps, campsites and other facilities to provide the public with access to year-round hiking, recreation, physical fitness and study. To engage in and promote conservation of wildlife and natural resources.

Annual Fees

Regular	Families	Supporting
$30	$30	$300

Other Fees *Lifetime* $600

Funding

Membership	Foundations	Sales	Interest
67%	16%	12%	5%

Total Income $349,970

Usage

Administration	Programs
34.7%	65.3%

Total Expenses $336,197

Programs Trail Maintenance programs. Landowner Relations. Hiking programs.

Publications Quarterly magazine *Bruce Trail News*, circulation 8,000. *Trail Maintenance Handbook* published every 2 years, circulation 500. *Annual Bed & Breakfast Guide*, circulation 200

For more Information Annual Report, Database, Library

Who's Who PRESIDENT KENNETH A. W. GANSEL • VICE PRESIDENT BRUCE CALVERT SECRETARY EVELYN M. CARLETON • TREASURER CHARLES STEARNS • EXECUTIVE DIRECTOR JACQUELINE WINTERS

BURKE MOUNTAIN NATURALISTS

Box 52540, 2929 BARNET HIGHWAY   COQUITLAM BC V3B 7J4
PHONE (604) 463 3744

Founded 1989 • *Geographic Coverage* Local • *Other Fields of Focus* Environmental Education / Careers / Information / Networks, Natural Resources / Water - Conservation & Quality *Cooperative Partner* Federation of British Columbia Naturalists *Organization Member* 1 • *Individual Members* 400

Mission To promote the enjoyment of nature; to foster an interest in and an appreciation of the environment; to actively pursue the conservation and preservation of the natural world; and to promote the accessibility and maintenance of natural areas, particularly local areas.

Annual Fees	*Regular*	*Families*	*Organization*
	$20	$25	$25

Publications Newsletter published ten times per year. Books including *The Birds of Colony Farm* • *The Plants of Colony Farm* • *The Birds of DeBouville Slough* • *The Plants of DeBouville Slough* • *The Birds of Minnekada Regional Park and Area*

For more Information Library

Who's Who PRESIDENT **APRIL MOL** • VICE PRESIDENT **QUIRIEN MULDER**TEN **KATE** SECRETARY **ANNE HOLT**

sustainable development, agriculture environmental technologies

CHAPTER 21

Sustainability Is Mankind's Insurance, by Joel Grossman

SUSTAINABLE DEVELOPMENT MEANS harnessing appropriate technologies to meet current consumption and economic needs without depleting the environmental and ecological foundations that provide future growth and development. Higher employment is an outcome of a sustainable development approach in which patterns of production, consumption and development of natural resources minimize depletion and pollution. Historically, negative ecological effects from large-scale development projects and cumulative smaller actions have hindered development of sustainable agriculture.

For example, ancient Mesopotamian civilizations declined over the centuries as the fertile lands along the Tigris and Euphrates Rivers were transformed into crusted white salt deserts by natural salts in irrigation water. Unfortunately, planners of modern large-scale irrigation projects - in the Egyptian Nile, Australia and California's San Joaquin Valley - have ignored ancient precedents, even adding fertilizer and pesticide salts to the natural water salinity. Thus, high water tables and other symptoms of salinity are already reducing crop yields in wide areas of arid land-irrigated agriculture. Remedial technologies such as drip irrigation, water desalinization, soil management and drainage

> To meet current consumption and economic needs *without depleting the environmental and ecological foundations* that provide future growth and development.

schemes might make the agriculture sustainable, but the outcome remains to be seen.

SOIL EROSION IS ANOTHER THREAT to agricultural sustainability. Agricultural lands are losing topsoil at the rate of 0.7 percent per year; fertilizers can no longer reverse crop yield declines on severely eroded lands. Soils naturally form at the rate of only one foot per 10,000 years. For that reason, soil erosion is increased herbicide applications replacing weed control cultivations. Thus, herbicide production in the United States soared from about 100 million pounds in the early 1960s to over 800 million pounds in recent years. This resulted in new problems such as herbicide-resistant weeds, groundwater pollution, and reduced water quality. Sustainable alternatives under development include less-polluting chemicals, allopathic crops that kill weeds with natural root exudates, weed-smothering intercrops, and arthropod and microbial natural enemies of weeds. Insecticide production has now leveled at about half the tonnage of herbicides since the early 1960s. Part of the reason is the implementation of pest control philosophies such as integrated pest management (IPM). With IPM, old spray schedules based solely on the calendar are replaced by population monitoring of pests and their natural enemies. In IPM programs, fields are sprayed with the least-toxic pesticide only when monitoring indicates that economic damage will occur - and then only after using non-chemical options, such as ▶

conservation and soil-building technologies such as agroforestry, living mulches, cover crops, compost, windbreaks, strip cropping and reduced tillage are vital. The flip side of minimizing soil

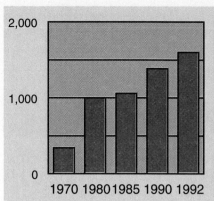

U.S. Federal Funding for Research & Development, Budget "Natural Resources and Environment", 1970-1992 (million dollars)

Source: U.S. National Science Foundation, *Federal R&D Funding by Budget Function*, Annual

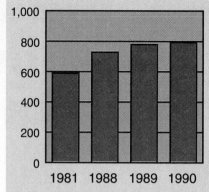

Research & Development Expenditures at U.S. Universities, Field "Environmental Sciences", 1981-1990 (million dollars)

Source: U.S. National Science Foundation, *Survey of Scientific and Engineering Expenditures at Universities and Colleges*, Annual

United States

AG ACCESS

603 FOURTH STREET   DAVIS CA 95616
PHONE (916) 756 7177   FAX (916) 756 7188

Founded 1983 • *Geographic Coverage* Global • *Cooperative Partners* Committee for Sustainable Agriculture, International Association of Sustainable Agriculture, Organic Farming and Research Foundation, International Federation of Organic Agriculture Movement, National Agriculture Library

Mission To disseminate information about agriculture, sustainable land use, horticulture, forestry and water resources.

Programs Distribution of books, videos, through catalogs and stores. Publishing program. Information service offering custom research on agricultural practices, issues, markets.

Publication Annual catalog

For more Information Database, Library, List of Publications

Who's Who PRESIDENT DAVID KATZ • TREASURER ANITA WHIPPLE • EDITOR KAREN VAN EPEN • INFORMATION SERVICES MANAGER LARRY DIETRICH • CONTACT JEFFREY HARPAIN

ALTERNATIVE ENERGY RESOURCES ORGANIZATION

AERO
25 SOUTH EWING, SUITE 214   HELENA MT 59601
PHONE (406) 443 7272

Founded 1974 • *Geographic Coverage* Regional • *Other Field of Focus* Energy - Alternative / Renewable Energies • *Members* 400 including organizations

Mission To help find ways to enhance the biological and economic sta-

bility of farming and ranching operations, and to promote communities shaped by the principles of meeting local needs with local resources to the fullest extent possible, by addressing public policy as well as practical "in-your-backyard" issues that can create opportunities for safe, sustainable energy self-reliance.

Annual Fees	*Regular*	*Student/Senior*	*Families*	*Patron*
	$25	$15	$30	$30

Other Fees *Non-Profit Organization* $35 • *Commercial* $50

Funding	*Membership*	*Foundations*
	10%	90%

Total Income $200,000

Usage	*Administration*	*Fundraising*	*Programs*
	20%	5%	75%

Programs Farm Improvement Clubs. Agricultural Task Force. Beginning Farmers Committee. Transportation Committee. Renewable Energy Task Force. Action and Support Network, conferences, drama and art.

Publications Quarterly magazines *AERO Sun Times* • *The Sustainable Farming Quarterly*. Books including *Cereal-Legume Cropping Systems: Nine Farm Case Studies in the Dryland Northern Plains, Canadian Prairies and Intermountain Northwest* • *Results from the Montana Agricultural Assessment Project Questionnaire: A Survey of Sustainable Agriculture* • *Protecting Groundwater from Agricultural Chemicals: Alternative Farming Strategies for Northwest Producers* • *AERO's Guide to Sustainable Agriculture in the Northern Rockies and Plains*

Multimedia Videos and audiotapes. Slide presentations

For more Information List of Publications

Who's Who CHAIR ZANE ZELL • VICE CHAIR HOLLY DIFANI • SECRETARY JEFF BIRKBY

► biological control of pests with predators, parasites and pathogens.

CANADA IS FOLLOWING recommendations of the Federal-Provincial Agriculture Committee on Environmental Sustainability, which were made as part of the Agri-Food Policy review. Canada is also heeding supporting initiatives, such as IPM, to make the agriculture industry more environmentally sustainable. Canadian provinces and the five-year $170 million Federal Green Plan initiative on sustainable agriculture are supporting the Land Stewardship, National Soil Conservation and other programs for environmentally sound farming and sustainable soil management. In the United States, the 1985 Food Security Act provides farmers with incentives for soil conservation. The 1985 bill also mandated the Sustainable Agriculture Research and Education program, funded at $8 million per year by the USDA and EPA, to further the use of low-input and sustainable agriculture technologies in the United States.

ENVIRONMENTALLY SUSTAINABLE development paths are needed in North America to prevent environmental deterioration from leading to economic declines that worsen environmental problems and lead to social decay and political upheaval. This may require new more ecological economic paradigms. For example, investors might be required to consider new criteria relating to sustainable development before ►

AMERICAN FARMLAND TRUST

1920 "N" STREET, NW, SUITE 400   WASHINGTON DC 20036
PHONE (202) 659 5170   FAX (202) 659 8339

Founded 1980 • *Geographic Coverage* National • *Chapters* 3 offices, in Chicago, IL; Northampton, MA; Davis, CA; 2 field offices in New York, NY; Visalia, CA • *Individual Members* 20,000

Mission To prevent the loss of productive farmland and promote farming practices that lead to a healthy environment by working with farmers, business people, legislators and conservationists to encourage sound farming practices and land use.

Annual Fees

Regular	Blue Ribbon	Silver Trophy
$20	$60	$100

Programs Agricultural land conservation programs.

Publication Quarterly magazine *American Farmland*

For more Information Annual Report

Who's Who PRESIDENT RALPH E. GROSSI • SECRETARY ALFRED H. TAYLOR, JR. SENIOR ADVISOR NORMAN A. BERG • DIRECTOR OF LAND PROJECTS DENNIS P. BIDWELL • DIRECTOR OF POLICY DEVELOPMENT DAVID R. DYER • DIRECTOR OF DEVELOPMENT AND COMMUNICATIONS KAREN B. KRESS

APROVECHO INSTITUTE

80574 HAZELTON ROAD   COTTAGE GROVE OR 97424
PHONE (503) 942 8198

Founded 1979 • *Geographic Coverage* Global • *Individual Members* 80

Mission To help people take greater control over their own lives using technologies which make the best use of their skills and resources, by performing research and education on sustainable technologies, agriculture, forestry, and community living.

Annual Fees *Regular* $30

Programs Has developed a research center land trust which is a living example of appropriate lifestyle and gives courses that demonstrate various appropriate technologies. Appropriate Technology Project provides internships (3-12 months).

Publications Various newsletters including quarterly *News from Aprovecho*

For more Information Library

Who's Who PRESIDENT LAURIE CHILDERS • SECRETARY GLENN BURKET

ASSOCIATION OF FOREST SERVICE EMPLOYEES FOR ENVIRONMENTAL ETHICS   PAGE 75

P.O. BOX 11615   EUGENE OR 97440
PHONE (503) 484 2692

CARRYING CAPACITY NETWORK   PAGE 253

1325 "G" STREET, NW, SUITE 1003   WASHINGTON DC 20005-3104
PHONE (202) 879 3044   FAX (202) 879 3019

CENTER FOR GLOBAL ENVIRONMENTAL TECHNOLOGIES

NEW MEXICO ENGINEERING RESEARCH INSTITUTE
THE UNIVERSITY OF NEW MEXICO   ALBUQUERQUE NM 87131-1376
PHONE (505) 272 7250   FAX (505) 272 7203

Founded 1990 • *Geographic Coverage* National, Global • *Other Field of Focus* Global Environmental Concerns

Mission The Center is operated by the Advanced Protection Technologies Division of the New Mexico Engineering Research Institute at the University of New Mexico and conducts research and development to solve environmental problems crossing national and regional boundaries,

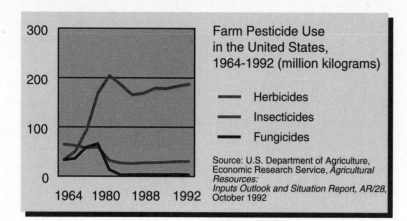

Farm Pesticide Use
in the United States,
1964-1992 (million kilograms)

— Herbicides
— Insecticides
— Fungicides

Source: U.S. Department of Agriculture,
Economic Research Service, *Agricultural
Resources:
Inputs Outlook and Situation Report, AR/28*,
October 1992

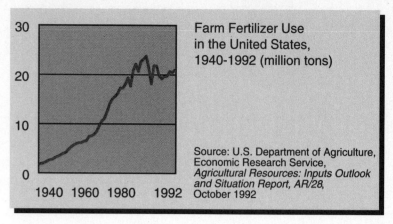

Farm Fertilizer Use
in the United States,
1940-1992 (million tons)

Source: U.S. Department of Agriculture,
Economic Research Service,
*Agricultural Resources: Inputs Outlook
and Situation Report, AR/28*,
October 1992

such as ozone depletion, global warming, transboundary air pollution, and protection of the global commons. The organization develops equipment, processes, instrumentation, new engineering approaches, and chemical substitutes to limit emissions, to mitigate impacts, and to perform remediation. Assessments of environmental characteristics, toxicity, hazards, treatment, disposal, and waste minimization are performed for existing materials having transboundary environmental impacts and for new materials introduced to mitigate those impacts.

Funding *Contracts* 100%

Total Income $1,200,000

Usage	*Administration*	*Programs*
	50%	50%

Programs Maintains databases of new technologies to address global problems and performs technology transfer and information services for the general public, industry, and government. Recent projects include the design and fabrication of a prototype halon recycling unit, assessment of the impact of international and national environmental regulations, development of new engineering approaches to reduce reliance on halons, recycling/recovery study of chemicals restricted by international regulations, assessment of CFC alternative cleaning technologies, development of alternatives to ozone-depleting chemicals, and evaluation of halon replacements in total-flood and streaming applications.

Publications Numerous scientific papers

For more Information Library, List of Publications

Who's Who DIRECTOR **ROBERT E. TAPSCOTT** • DEPUTY DIRECTOR **STEPHANIE SKAGGS**

CENTER FOR HOLISTIC RESOURCE MANAGEMENT
5820 FOURTH STREET, NW   ALBUQUERQUE NM 87107
PHONE (505) 344 9079

Founded 1984 • *Geographic Coverage* Global • *Focused Countries* Canada, Mexico, Namibia, South Africa, USA • *Chapters* 13 *Organization Members* 200 • *Individual Members* 1,500

Mission To restore communities and the natural resources upon which they depend. Restoration of biological diversity, economic prosperity, and social stability in diverse communities through a process called holistic resource management are the organization's main areas of expertise.

Annual Fees *Regular* $20

Funding	*Membership*	*Government Support*	*Foundations*	*Training Fees*
	5%	5%	20%	70%

Total Income $800,000

Usage	*Administration*	*Programs*	*Other*
	10%	80%	10%

Total Expenses $800,000

Publication Quarterly newsletter *Holistic Resource Management*

Who's Who PRESIDENT **BETSY BROWN** • SECRETARY **TERESA MAURER** • EXECUTIVE DIRECTOR **SHANNON A. HORST**

CENTER FOR RESOURCE MANAGEMENT
1104 EAST ASHTON AVENUE, SUITE 210   SALT LAKE CITY UT 84106
PHONE (801) 466 3600   FAX (801) 466 6800

Founded 1981 • *Geographic Coverage* National, Global • *Chapter* 1

Mission To promote a program of sustainable development which balances vital human needs with environmental stewardship, by helping to build alliances between the environmental, corporate, and governmental communities in a way which attempts to avoid blame and to inte-

deciding to proceed with land development projects. Profit potential would be weighed against the direct costs of eliminating or cleaning up pollution, environmental damage, deleterious health impacts, resource depletion and the future value of ecological resources. In theory, investment plans would then inherently consider the environment costs. Canadian Council of Ministers of the Environment (CCME), recognizing that 90 percent of the technology now in use will be replaced in the next 15 years, developed a pro-active agenda to integrate the environment and the economy into decision making standards that will further sustainable development strategies. The CCME gave priority to six key program areas that have international implications and require concerted national action and fundamental reassessment of current environmental policies. These are: fresh water quality, toxic chemical education and substitution, reduction of hazardous wastes and the substitution of alternative chemicals, partnerships with indigenous peoples, establishing the links between human health and the environment, and preventing overfishing on the East Coast.

THE CANADIAN MINISTERS BELIEVE that sustainable development approaches to human settlements represent the best way to mitigate climate change and prevent loss of biodiversity. Canada's National Round Table on Environment and the Economy has taken charge of a multi-stakeholder process to develop a plan for a ▶

grate environmental and economic decision making.

Programs Corporate Programs with Adolph Coors Company, Wal Mart, World Bank. Northern Forests Program. International Environmental Leadership Exchange. Haitian Charcoal Project. Environment and Native Americans. Public Interest Coalitions include Clean Air, Environmental Marketing and Advertising Council, Hot Dry Rock-WasteLink.

Publications Books *Environmental Decision Making* • *Greenhouse Glasnost: The Crisis of Global Warming*

Who's Who PRESIDENT **TERRELL MINGER** • VICE PRESIDENTS **JON LEAR, PAUL PARKER** PROGRAM MANAGER **MEREDITH MILLER** • ADMINISTRATIVE ASSISTANT **NANCY NELSON** PROGRAM ASSISTANT **ROBIN OANES** • CONTROLLER **DOUGLAS STEPHENS**

CENTER FOR RURAL AFFAIRS

101 SOUTH TALLMAN, P.O. BOX 406   WALTHILL NE 68067
PHONE (402) 846 5428

Founded 1973 • *Geographic Coverage* National

Mission To work for the achievement of social and economic justice, stewardship of the natural environment, broad distribution of wealth, and opportunity for all people to earn just incomes and own and control productive resources. The Center engages rural people in evaluating trends and policies in terms of these values and beliefs.

Funding

Foundations	Donations
80%	20%

Total Income $2,105,605

Usage

Administration	Fundraising	Programs
13%	4%	83%

Programs The Rural Economic Opportunities Program. Stewardship, Technology, and World Agriculture Program: Sustainable Agriculture Policy Project. Conservation and Environment Project. Global Warming Initiative. Research and Technology Project. World Agriculture Project.

Publications Various reports and workbooks including *Sustainable Agriculture in the National Research Initiative* • *Groundwater and Agricultural Chemicals* • *Rural Economic Development and Sustainable Agriculture*. Quarterly newsletters *The Rural Enterprise Reporter* • *The Beginning Farmer*. Monthly *The Center for Rural Affairs Newsletter*

For more Information Annual Report

Who's Who PRESIDENT **DAVID HANSEN** • VICE PRESIDENT **CLARK NICHOLS** • SECRETARY **MARIANNE ROUSE** • TREASURER **MARILYNNE BERGMAN**

CHARLES A. LINDBERGH FUND, INC. (THE)

708 SOUTH THIRD STREET, SUITE 110   MINNEAPOLIS MN 55415-1141
PHONE (612) 338 1703   FAX (612) 338 6826

Founded 1977 • *Geographic Coverage* Global • *Other Field of Focus* Global Environmental Concerns • *Individual Members* 1,200 contributors currently

Mission To support future generations in working toward meeting the need, in the words of Charles Lindbergh, "to discern nature's essential wisdom and to combine it with our scientific knowledge". The Fund works to further this vision of a balance between technology and the environment through Lindbergh Grants, the Lindbergh Award, and other educational motivational projects.

Programs Sponsors symposia and lectures. Lindbergh Grants. The Lindbergh Award.

Publication Newsletter *Of Flight and Life*

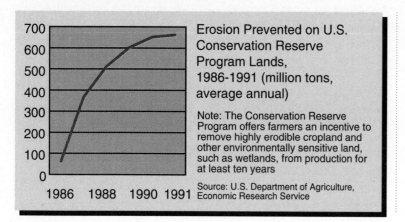

Erosion Prevented on U.S. Conservation Reserve Program Lands, 1986-1991 (million tons, average annual)

Note: The Conservation Reserve Program offers farmers an incentive to remove highly erodible cropland and other environmentally sensitive land, such as wetlands, from production for at least ten years

Source: U.S. Department of Agriculture, Economic Research Service

▶ sustainable future that makes protected ecosystems an integral part of sustainable development strategies. In the United States, the President's Council on Sustainable Development is examining how to balance environmental protection, economic growth, industrial changes, and income redistribution. Sustainable development is seen as also fostering a sense of community.

The goal of the Clinton administration is to develop a society that is both high-tech and sustainable, that conserves resources, makes best use of assets, and minimizes waste. A computer information superhighway that includes networks sharing environmental protection research may become part of the US sustainable development plan. •
Joel Grossman

Who's Who PRESIDENT SYLVIA A. EARLE • VICE PRESIDENT REEVE LINDBERGH TRIPP SECRETARY JAMES W. LLOYD

For more Information List of Publications

COALITION FOR ENVIRONMENTALLY RESPONSIBLE ECONOMIES

711 ATLANTIC AVENUE   BOSTON MA 02111
PHONE (617) 451 0927   FAX (617) 482 2028

Founded 1989 • *Geographic Coverage* Global

Mission To bring together environmental organizations and the investment community in order to promote responsible economic activity for a just, safe and sustainable future throughout the world; to focus on various ways investors could help implement environmentally and financially sound investment policies; to forge a new and forceful dialogue with corporations around the protection of the planet; and to establish a well-informed public that chooses where to invest its capital based on environmental, not just economic, performance.

Annual Fees	*Regular*	*Student/Senior*
	$25	$15

Programs Promoting the creation of a widely-accepted mechanism for corporate self-governance consistent with the principle that economic vitality and environmental responsibility go hand in hand. The "CERES Principles" is a comprehensive ten-point code - or environmental ethic - for corporations devised to encourage the development of positive programs to prevent environmental degradation, to assist corporations in setting policy and to enable investors to make informed decisions regarding environmental issues. The CERES Report provides a comprehensive corporate environmental reporting format comprising permanent criteria for the improvement of corporate environmental performance over time.

Publications Reports including *1992 Guide to the CERES Principles* • *Individual 1990 CERES Report* • *1992 CERES Report*. Membership directory

COMMUNITY ALLIANCE WITH FAMILY FARMERS

P.O. BOX 464   DAVIS CA 95617
PHONE (916) 756 8518   FAX (916) 756 7857

Founded 1977 • *Geographic Coverage* State • *Other Field of Focus* Food / Pesticides / Consumerism & Safety • *Chapters* 3 *Organization Members* 200 • *Individual Members* 800

Mission The Alliance works to bring together family farmers, rural residents and consumers in a movement to promote ecologically balanced and economically viable agriculture on small family farms, through a program of community organizing, political advocacy, and public education. Since its inception the organization has grown to become one of the most important grassroots forces working on agricultural and rural issues in California.

Annual Fees	*Regular*	*Student/Senior*	*Families*	*Organization*	*Corporation*
	$25	$15	$35	$50	$50

Other Fees *Charter Member* $75 or more

Programs The Alliance's Lighthouse Farm Campaign works to further the cause of alternative farming methods.

Publications Bimonthly newsletter *Agrarian Advocate*. Bimonthly magazine *Farmer to Farmer*. Directories *The National Directory of Organic Wholesalers*, 10th Edition • *Consumers Organic Mail-Order Directory* - 2nd Edition 1994

For more Information Library, List of Publications

Who's Who PRESIDENT GLENN ANDERSON • VICE PRESIDENT CINDY HOOPES SECRETARY SHARON McLIN • EXECUTIVE DIRECTOR TOM HALLER • DEVELOPMENT DIRECTOR INGRID WALLEN • NEWSLETTER EDITOR THOMAS NELSON • OFFICE MANAGER LINDA DEERING • CONTACT CANDACE LAMPE

CONSERVATION TECHNOLOGY INFORMATION CENTER

1220 Potter Drive, Room 170   West Lafayette IN 47906-1334
Phone (317) 494 9555   Fax (317) 494 5969

Founded 1982 • *Geographic Coverage* National • *Cooperative Partner* National Association of Conservation Districts • *Organization Members* 74 • *Individual Members* 12,500

Mission To bring together industry and government to foster transfer of information that encourages profitable and environmentally-sound agricultural and natural resource management. Water quality, crop residue management, soil and water conservation, watershed management, and pollution prevention are the organization's main areas of expertise.

Annual Fees

Regular	Organization	Corporation
$15	$100	$250 to 7,500

Other Fees *Individual Membership Outside US* $25

Programs Serves as a technology transfer resource center. Holds quarterly meetings, and disseminates conservation information through a number of media.

Publications Monthly newsletter *Conservation Impact*. Numerous fact sheets, brochures and books focusing on conservation issues

Multimedia Periodic audiotape *Conservation Update*. Computer program *Farming for MAXimum Information*

For more Information Annual Report, List of Publications

Who's Who Chair Ray Brownfield • Vice Chair Bob Williams • Secretary John Hebblethwaite • Treasurer Kurt Schenck • Executive Director Jerry Hytry

CONTEXT INSTITUTE (THE)

P.O. Box 11470   Bainbridge Island WA 98110
Phone (206) 842 0216   Fax (206) 842 5208

Founded 1979 • *Geographic Coverage* Global • *Individual Members* 8,000

Mission To explore how human society can become sustainable - i.e., able to meet the needs of the present without diminishing the prospects for the future, and serve as a catalyst for voluntary cultural change toward a more humane and sustainable future.

Annual Fees

Regular	Patron
$24	$35+

Funding

Membership	Foundations
80%	20%

Programs EcoTeam Workbook translates global goals into individual actions which small groups of homeowners and tenants can implement over a six-month period to make their consumption patterns more environmentally sustainable. Eco-Village Report looks for the kinds of supporting services and programs that are helpful to developing communities. Outreach Programs with the International Union of Architects/American Institute of Architects World Congress around the theme of "Designing for a Sustainable Future". St. Petersburg, Russian Federation Ecoville Program. Sustainable Seattle Program. Development-As-Transformation Network, a network of journals concerned with viewing development from a transformational perspective. North Seattle Community College Study Circles.

Publications Journal *In Context: A Quarterly of Humane Sustainable Culture*. Newsletter *The Sustainer*

Who's Who Director Robert Gilman • Special Projects Manager Diane Gilman • Director of Operations and Planning Jack Carlsen • Publications and Managing Editor Sarah van Gelder • Marketing Department Manager Sally Wilson • Administrative Assistant Jane Engel

E. F. SCHUMACHER SOCIETY

Box 76-A, R.D. 3 Jug End Road   Great Barrington MA 01230
Phone (413) 528 1737   Fax (413) 528 4472

Founded 1980 • *Geographic Coverage* Global • *Cooperative Partners* Authors Wendell Berry - *The Unsettling of America*, Wes Jackson - *New Roots for Agriculture*, Jane Jacobs - *Cities and the Wealth of Nations* and *Systems of Survival* • *Individual Members* 500

Mission To promote the ideas of British economist Ernst Friedrich Schumacher (1911-1977), author of *Small is Beautiful: Economics as if People Mattered* (1973), who advocated incorporating respect for human scale and the natural world into human economic activities by decentralizing and democratizing political, social and economic institutions. The Society works to realize Schumacher's vision of a sustainable economy and environment through education and the implementation of model programs.

Annual Fees *Regular* $30

Programs Annual E.F. Schumacher Lectures. SHARE (Self-Help Association for a Regional Economy) community micro-lending. Community Land Trust in the Southern Berkshires. Several local currency programs. Schumacher Education Center sponsors scholars and authors engaged in alternative economic research.

Publications Newsletter published 3 to 4 times per year. Transcripts of annual lecture series

For more Information Database, Library, List of Publications

Who's Who President Robert Swann • Executive Director Susan Witt Chairman of the Board John McClaughry

EAST-WEST CENTER

PROGRAM ON ENVIRONMENT

1777 EAST-WEST ROAD   HONOLULU HI 96848

PHONE (808) 944 7265   FAX (808) 944 7298

ECOLOGICAL SOCIETY PROJECT OF THE TIDES FOUNDATION

ROUTE 1, BOX 20   NEWBURG MO 65550

PHONE (314) 762 3423   FAX (314) 762 3302

Founded 1985 • *Geographic Coverage* National, Global

Mission As a step towards the eventual goal of realizing global sustainability and halting and reversing social and ecological degradation, the Foundation is working to ensure that all vital functions of human society can be carried out in an ecologically positive fashion through integrated ecological design applications, by serving as a focal point/information clearinghouse for the ecological movement, and providing consultative services for ecological planning and organizational development activities.

Programs Lectures, seminars, and writings on ecological theory and practice. Bioregionalism Program provides program development or organizing assistance for several bioregional organizations. Ecological Economics Program advances the theory and practice of ecological economics to ameliorate social and ecological degradation while building economic viability. Forests Program works for the protection of public forests, and to advance ecological forestry on both public and private lands. The "Meta-Program" works to develop, strengthen, and integrate 30 major movements and disciplines from around the world which the Foundation feels most fully embody ecological values and practices.

Publication Book *Clearcut, The Tragedy of Industrial Forestry*

Who's Who DIRECTOR **DAVID HAENKE**

ENVIRONMENTAL AND ENERGY STUDY INSTITUTE

122 "C" STREET, NW, SUITE 700   WASHINGTON DC 20001

PHONE (202) 628 1400

Founded 1985 • *Geographic Coverage* National, Global

Mission To promote environmentally sustainable societies through a transition to social and economic patterns that sustain people, the environment, and the natural resources upon which present and future generations depend. The Institute produces credible, timely information and innovative public policy initiatives that lead toward these transitions.

Funding	Corporations	Foundations	Publications
	10%	60%	30%

Programs Performs research and disseminates information on energy, water, international environmental issues, and the climate.

Publications Congressional legislative update *Weekly Bulletin*. Annual reference guide *Briefing Book*

ENVIRONMENTAL CENTER OF SAN LUIS OBISPO COUNTY

45 PRADO ROAD, P.O. BOX 1014   SAN LUIS OBISPO CA 93406

PHONE (805) 544 7651   FAX (805) 544 1871

Founded 1972 • *Geographic Coverage* Local • *Individual Members* 800

Mission To assist San Luis Obispo community in its pursuit of sustainability.

Annual Fees	Regular	Student/Senior	Supporting	Sustaining	Patron
	$30	$15	$45	$75	$125

Funding *Membership* 100%

Total Income $25,000

Publication *Recycled Products Guide*

For more Information Database, Library

Who's Who PRESIDENT **JOHN EWAN** • VICE PRESIDENT **ELAINE GENSCI** • SECRETARY **PATTI COLEHLO** • TREASURER **BOB WOLF** • EXECUTIVE DIRECTOR **KURT KUPPER**

ENVIRONMENTAL ENTERPRISES ASSISTANCE FUND

1611 NORTH KENT STREET, SUITE 202   ARLINGTON VA 22209

PHONE (703) 522 5928   FAX (703) 522 6450

Founded 1990 • *Geographic Coverage* Global • *Focused Countries* Developing countries, eastern Europe, Russian Federation • *Cooperative Partner* Winrock International • *Chapters* 2

Mission To promote investment in environmentally beneficial business in developing countries through the transfer of long-term risk capital and managerial assistance.

Programs Equity and quasi-equity investment capital. Managerial training.

Who's Who PRESIDENT **BROOKS H. BROWNE** • VICE PRESIDENT **HELEN CHAIKOVSKY**

GLOBAL TOMORROW COALITION

1325 "G" STREET, SUITE 1010   WASHINGTON DC 20005

PHONE (202) 628 4016

Founded 1981 • *Geographic Coverage* Global • *Cooperative Partners* United Nations agencies, several Third World NGOs, International Network for Environmental Policy • *Organization Members* 93 *Individual Members* 390

Mission To help provide for a more humane, productive global future by working to increase awareness and understanding of sustainable development issues.

Annual Fees

	Regular	Student/Senior
	$25	$15

Funding

Membership	Corporations	Foundations	Other
2%	22%	50%	26%

Usage

Administration	Fundraising	Programs	Other
6%	8%	84%	2%

Programs "Globescope" Assemblies. 21st Century Dialogues. Global Issues Forum. Processes for Sustainability program. Provides opportunities for year-round unpaid internships.

Publications Books *Sustainable Development: A New Path for Progress • The Global Ecology Handbook: What You Can Do About the Environmental Crisis.* Other publications include *Global Issues Education Set • Sustainable Development: A Guide to Our Common Future • Environmental Career Packet*

Who's Who PRESIDENT **DONALD R. LESH** • VICE PRESIDENT **DIANE G. LOWRIE**

INSTITUTE FOR AGRICULTURE AND TRADE POLICY (THE)

1313 FIFTH STREET, SE, SUITE 303   MINNEAPOLIS MN 55414-1546
PHONE (612) 379 5980   FAX (612) 379 5982

Founded 1986 • *Geographic Coverage* National, Global • *Cooperative Partners* Fair Trade Campaign, Citizens Trade Campaign

Mission To create economically and environmentally sustainable rural communities and regions. The organization's primary focus is on achieving two key objectives in the international policy making arena. First, the Institute is working to democratize the global decision making process, making international policy making institutions understandable, accessible and accountable to the public by monitoring global policy making institutions and events, researching and analyzing potential impacts of major international policy options, and educating citizens, opinion leaders, and constituency organizations about the organization's findings and conclusions. Second, the Institute works to enable public interest groups to participate effectively in the international policy making arena.

Funding *Foundations* 99%

Total Income $431,079

Usage

Administration	Fundraising	Programs	Distribution
17%	4.5%	75%	3.5%

Total Expenses $397,328

Programs The Institute has established the GATT Program to monitor the talks. The Institute's NAFTA Program convened trinational meetings among public interest advocates, environmental organizations, and farm commodity groups to develop a final agreement that would serve the needs of people and the environment in all three countries, and conveyed it to the negotiators. The UNCED Campaign was designed to develop grassroots participation in the conference through public service messages, educational materials, training, and direct organizing assistance to local and regional citizen organizations.

Publications Daily news bulletins. Numerous reports, pamphlets, studies focusing on food and agriculture, trade and environment, and the North American Free Trade Agreement (NAFTA)

Multimedia Computer-based databases on a wide range of trade, agriculture and sustainable development topics. Electronic Conferences

For more Information Annual Report, Library, List of Publications

Who's Who PRESIDENT **MARK RITCHIE** • NAFTA PROJECT COORDINATOR **KAREN LEHMAN** • UNCED PROJECT COORDINATOR **KRISTIN DAWKINS** • ADMINISTRATIVE DIRECTOR **NIEL RITCHIE** • INFORMATION COORDINATOR **MICHELLE THOM** • TRADE PUBLICATIONS EDITOR **KAI MANDER**

INSTITUTE FOR ALTERNATIVE AGRICULTURE, INC.

9200 EDMONSTON ROAD, SUITE 117   GREENBELT MD 20770
PHONE (301) 441 8777

Founded 1983 • *Geographic Coverage* Global • *Organization Members* 100 • *Individual Members* 1,100

Mission To encourage and facilitate the adoption of low-cost, resource- conserving, economically viable, and environmentally-sound farming systems. In order to advance the scientific and educational goals of alternative agriculture, the Institute works directly with government agencies, educational institutions, producer groups, and other organizations that provide agricultural research, education, and information services.

Funding

Membership	Foundations
10%	90%

Total Income $425,257

Usage

Administration	Fundraising	Programs
10.3%	10.3%	79.4%

Programs Policy research and advocacy. Annual conference. Visiting scholar program. Occasional paper series.

Publications Monthly newsletter *Alternative Agriculture News.* Quarterly *American Journal of Alternative Agriculture. Alternative Agriculture Resource Report*

Who's Who PRESIDENT **KATE CLANCY** • VICE PRESIDENT **ROBERT O. BLAKE** • SECRETARY **MICHAEL HELLER** • EXECUTIVE DIRECTOR **I. GARTH YOUNGBERG**

INSTITUTE FOR RESOURCE AND SECURITY STUDIES

27 ELLSWORTH AVENUE CAMBRIDGE MA 02139
PHONE (617) 491 5177

Founded 1984 • *Geographic Coverage* Global

Mission The Institute conducts research and education programs on environmental protection, international security, and sustainable development.

Total Income $150,000

Who's Who PRESIDENT **GORDON THOMPSON** • SECRETARY **PAULA GUTLOVE**

INSTITUTE FOR SUSTAINABLE COMMUNITIES (THE)

P.O. BOX 96, CHELSEA STREET SOUTH ROYALTON VT 05068
PHONE (802) 763 8303 FAX (802) 763 2920

Founded 1991 • *Geographic Coverage* Central and eastern Europe
Focused Countries Bulgaria, Czech Republic, Hungary, Poland, Romania, Russian Federation, Slovakia

Mission To promote sustainable development, environmental protection, and participatory democracy to communities in central and eastern Europe through training, technical assistance, and demonstration projects.

Programs Training programs: The Community Environmental Action Project, The Environmental Training Project, The Environmental Management Training Centers Project, and the Environmental Education Project. The Institute also sponsors Demonstrations Projects to provide training, funding and technical assistance to projects that serve as national models for environmental action at the community level. Their Capacity Building program provides technical assistance in organizational development, management, strategic planning, fundraising and financial strategies to enhance the effectiveness and stability of democratic institutions. Environmental Management Training Centers in Sofia, Bulgaria, and Warsaw, Poland, run hands-on workshops for policy makers, government representatives, businesses, individuals, and non-governmental organizations.

Publication Annual newsletter *The ISC Report*

Who's Who CHAIR **DOUGLAS COSTLE** • VICE CHAIR **PAMELA LINTON** • SECRETARY **JEAN RICHARDSON** • EXECUTIVE DIRECTOR **GEORGE E. HAMILTON** • EDITOR **ELLEN BUTLER**

INTERNATIONAL ALLIANCE
FOR SUSTAINABLE AGRICULTURE

UNIVERSITY OF MINNESOTA
1701 UNIVERSITY AVENUE, SE MINNEAPOLIS MN 55414-2076
PHONE (612) 331 1099 FAX (612) 379 1527

Founded 1983 • *Geographic Coverage* Global • *Cooperative Partner* United Nations Development Programme

Mission To build a strong sustainable agriculture industry and movement through organizational support and network building. The Alliance focuses on a widespread understanding of and participation in sustainable agriculture through education and information sharing, and universal adoption of governmental and institutional policies that implement sustainable agriculture.

Annual Fees	Low Income	Sustaining	Supporting	Contributing	Sponsor
	$10	$25	$50	$100	$250

Other Fees *Organization* $50 • *Benefactor* $1,000

Usage	Administration	Fundraising	Programs
	11%	6%	83%

Programs Skiers Ending Hunger Program works to support local food shelves and sustainable development projects in the Third World. Resource and Information Center. Minnesota Sustainable Agriculture Policy Group. Humane Sustainable Agriculture Project (HSAP) works to support the humane treatment of farm animals. Sponsor of the 1993 International Sustainable Agriculture Conference.

Publications Quarterly newsletter *Manna*. Books *Planting the Future, A Resource Guide to Sustainable Agriculture in the Third World* • *Humane Consumer and Producer Guide* • *Benefits of Diversity*. Directories *Minnesota Green Pages, Sustainable Agriculture, Food, and Environment* • *Healthy Harvest, A Global Directory of Sustainable Agriculture and Horticulture Organizations 1992*

Multimedia Video *Sustainable Organizations and Selves*. Slide show and video presentation *A Grain of Hope*

For more Information List of Publications

Who's Who PRESIDENT **TERRY GIPS** • EXECUTIVE DIRECTOR **BARRY COLLEY**

INTERNATIONAL SOCIETY
FOR ECOLOGICAL ECONOMICS (THE)

P.O. BOX 1589 SOLOMONS MD 20688
PHONE (410) 326 0794 FAX (410) 326 7354

Founded 1988 • *Geographic Coverage* Global • *Chapter* 1, in Russia • *Individual Members* 1,600

Mission To integrate ecology and economics in order to develop the mechanisms with which to achieve sustainable development. Ecological economics goes beyond the normal conceptions of scientific disciplines and attempts to integrate and synthesize many different disciplinary perspectives in order to achieve an ecologically and economically sustainable world.

Annual Fees *Membership fees based on income. Less than $30,000* $15

From $30,000 to 50,000 $30 • *Over $50,000* $60 • Add $35 for journal

Funding

Membership	Foundations
70%	30%

Total Income $100,000

Usage

Administration	Programs
40%	60%

Programs Sponsors conferences: past conferences have included Ecological Economics Curriculum Development - June 1991; Ecosystem Health and Environmental Management - January 1991; Free Trade and the Environment - February 1992.

Publications Bimonthly journal *Ecological Economics*. Newsletter *ISEE Quarterly*. Books *Ecological Economics: The Science and Management of Sustainability* • *Ecosystem Health: New Goals for Environmental Management* • *Principles of Ecological Economics*. Membership directory

Who's Who PRESIDENT **ROBERT COSTANZA** • SECRETARY **CARL FOLKE** • TREASURER **HERMAN DALY** • VICE PRESIDENT FOR EDUCATION AND MEMBERSHIP **FAYE DUCHIN** • VICE PRESIDENT FOR POLICY DEVELOPMENT **STEPHEN VIEDERMAN**

INVENTORS WORKSHOPS
INTERNATIONAL EDUCATION FOUNDATION

7332 MASON AVENUE
PHONE (818) 340 4258

CANOGA PARK CA 91306-2822
FAX (818) 884 8312

Founded 1971 • *Geographic Coverage* National • *Individual Members* 22,000

Mission To assist the development and commercialization of environmentally related products and services. Intellectual property protection, "Green" certification, financing and material sources, and marketing and licensing constitute the organization's main areas of focus.

Annual Fees

Regular	Student/Senior	Organization	Corporation	Renewal
$139	$75	$139	$139	$59

Funding

Membership	Foundations
80%	20%

Usage

Administration	Programs
15%	85%

Program Young Eco-Inventors Contest.

Publications Magazines *Invent!* • Bimonthly *Lightbulb*, circulation 6,000 to 20,000 depending on special events

For more Information Database, Library, List of Publications

Who's Who PRESIDENT **ALAN A. TRATNER** • SECRETARY **MAGGIE WEISBERG** OTHER **MELVIN L. FULLER, DUBRAVKA PINEDA**

IUCN THE WORLD CONSERVATION UNION PAGE 24

1400 16TH STREET, NW
PHONE (202) 797 5454

WASHINGTON DC 20036
FAX (202) 797 5461

LAND INSTITUTE (THE)

2440 EAST WATER WELL ROAD
PHONE (913) 823 5376

SALINAS KS 67401
FAX (913) 823 8728

Founded 1976 • *Geographic Coverage* Global • *Other Field of Focus* National Parks - Land Use / Conservation / Acquisition

Mission The Land Institute is a private research and education organization that is devoted to sustainable agriculture and stewardship of the earth. It looks to nature as a model for the kind of agriculture that will save the soil and support a diversity of life.

Programs Perennial polyculture research, studying the prairie, developing perennial grain crops, investigating polyculture cropping systems. The Sunshine Farm Project seeks to develop renewable energy options. Intern program seeks to educate future leaders. Public policy/education activities work to promote the marriage of ecology and agriculture.

Publications Books *A Natural History of Wolves* • *A List of Coyote Literature* • *A List of Wolf Literature* • *Red Wolves* • *Yellowstone National Park and Wolf Reintroduction* • *Wolves in Alaska* • *Wolf Recovery*

LAND STEWARDSHIP PROJECT

14758 OSTLUND TRAIL NORTH
PHONE (612) 433 2770

MARINE ON ST. CROIX MN 55047

Founded 1982 • *Geographic Coverage* National • *Cooperative Partner* Midwest Sustainable Agriculture Working Group • *Chapters* 4, all located in Minnesota

Mission To foster a renewed ethic of farmland stewardship and to promote a sustainable system of agriculture - one that is environmentally sound, profitable, family-farm based, and socially just. The organization believes a healthy rural landscape requires more people - farmers and non-farmers alike - who have a fundamental responsibility to care for the land that sustains life.

Funding

Foundations	Publications	Church Grants	Other
89%	4%	5%	2%

Total Income $900,000

Usage	Administration	Programs
	6%	94%

Programs Sustainable Agriculture Education Program works to empower citizens to address land stewardship issues and to create opportunities in agriculture for stewardship-minded farmers. Metro Farm Program. Policy Development Program. Outreach and Comprehensive Development Program. Internships occasionally available.

Publications Quarterly newsletter *Land Stewardship Letter*. Books

Multimedia Videos related to sustainable agriculture

Who's Who   CHAIR LARRY OLSON • EXECUTIVE DIRECTOR RON KROESE • MANAGING DIRECTOR GEORGE BOODY

MEADOWCREEK

1 MEADOWCREEK LANE, P.O. BOX 100   FOX AR 72051
PHONE (501) 363 4500

Founded 1979 • *Geographic Coverage* National, eastern Europe *Focused Countries* Russian Federation, USA • *Cooperative Partners* The Kerr Center for Sustainable Agriculture, Elderhostels

Mission To demonstrate sustainable technology in the areas of energy and agriculture.

Programs Internships, summer ecology programs for youth, Elderhostels, school/university programs, Russian exchanges and group retreats.

Publications Technical briefs *The Many Applications of Photovoltaics* • *Solar Water Pumping* • *Shiitake Mushroom Cultivation* • *Solar Oven Resource List* • *Photovoltaic Suppliers Resource List* • *Meadowcreek Self-Guided Tour*

Who's Who   PRESIDENT LUKE ELLIOTT

NATIONAL CENTER FOR APPROPRIATE TECHNOLOGY PAGE 172

3040 CONTINENTAL DRIVE, BOX 3838   BUTTE MT 59702
PHONE (406) 494 4572

NATIVE SEEDS SEARCH

2509 NORTH CAMPBELL, SUITE 325   TUCSON AZ 85719
PHONE (602) 327 9123

Founded 1983 • *Geographic Coverage* Regional • *Focused Region* Southwest USA, Northwest Mexico • *Individual Members* 4,000

Mission To preserve seeds of crops grown by Native Americans in Southwest USA and Northwest Mexico.

Annual Fees	Regular	Student/Senior	Patron
	$18	$10	$30

Publication Quarterly newsletter

Who's Who   PRESIDENT GARY NABHAN • VICE PRESIDENT BARNEY BURNS • SECRETARY MAHINA DREES

NEW FORESTS PROJECT   PAGE 80

731 8TH STREET, SE   WASHINGTON DC 20003
PHONE (202) 547 3800   FAX (202) 546 4784

NORTHEAST ORGANIC FARMING ASSOCIATION

411 SHELDON ROAD   BARRE MA 01005
PHONE (413) 247 9264

Founded 1980 • *Geographic Coverage* Regional • *Individual Members* 500

Mission To promote organic agriculture by farmers, gardeners, and consumers working together.

Annual Fees	Regular	Student/Senior
	$25	$15

Funding *Membership* 100%

Total Income $22,000

Usage	Administration	Programs
	50%	50%

Programs Bulk order. Certification. Summer and winter conferences.

Publications Newsletters *The Natural Farmer* • *NOFA*

Multimedia Videos

Who's Who   PRESIDENT LYNDA SIMKERIS • VICE PRESIDENT IAN ALPER • SECRETARY TONI JAKOBI

NORTHERN PLAINS SUSTAINABLE AGRICULTURE SOCIETY

P.O. BOX 36   MAIDA ND 58255
PHONE (701) 256 2424

Founded 1979 • *Geographic Coverage* Regional • *Individual Members* 230

Mission To involve farmers and friends of farmers in gathering and sharing information about sustainable agriculture systems. Members include farmers with 1 to 25 years of experience in farming organically in the Northern Plains.

Annual Fees

Regular	Patron
$25	$50

Funding

Membership	Foundations	Other
10%	75%	15%

Total Income $42,000

Usage

Administration	Fundraising	Programs
49%	1%	50%

Programs Winter conference. Summer symposium. Farmer involvement in land grant research.

Publications Quarterly newsletter. Book *Crazy Musings from the North Outback*. Booklet *Switching to a Sustainable System*

Who's Who PRESIDENT **TERRY JACOBSON** • VICE PRESIDENT **DAVID PODOLL** • SECRETARY **SHARON CLANCY** • EXECUTIVE SECRETARY **SUSANNE R. SCHILL**

RESOURCE RENEWAL INSTITUTE

FORT MASON CENTER, BUILDING A   SAN FRANCISCO CA 94123
PHONE (415) 928 3774

Founded 1983 • *Geographic Coverage* Global • *Focused Countries* Canada, Netherlands, New Zealand, USA

Mission To advocate comprehensive, integrated environmental planning at the local, regional, and national levels. The Institute's goal is to see a US "Green Plan" by the year 2000, based on the Canadian model.

Funding *Foundations* 100%

Programs Volunteer programs, internships, sponsorship of conferences and workshops on Integrated Environmental Planning.

Publications Quarterly newsletter *ECO-Z*. Book *Saving Cities, Saving Money: Environmental Strategies That Work*

Who's Who PRESIDENT **HUEY D. JOHNSON** • VICE PRESIDENT **PEGGY LAUER**

ROCKY MOUNTAIN INSTITUTE

1739 SNOWMASS CREEK ROAD   SNOWMASS CO 81654-9199
PHONE (303) 927 3851   FAX (303) 927 4178

Founded 1982 • *Geographic Coverage* Global

Mission To foster the efficient and sustainable use of resources as a path to global security. The Institute believes that people can solve complex problems through collective action and their own common sense, and that understanding interconnections between resource issues can often solve many problems at once.

Total Income $1,700,000

Usage

Administration	Fundraising	Programs
19%	2%	79%

Programs The Institute has ongoing programs in the areas of energy, transportation, Green development services, water, agriculture, economic renewal, and global security.

Publications Newsletter. Numerous publications focusing on energy, security and oil policy, water, agriculture and economic renewal issues

For more Information List of Publications

Who's Who PRESIDENT **L. HUNTER LOVINS** • VICE PRESIDENT **AMORY LOVINS**

UNION OF CONCERNED SCIENTISTS

26 CHURCH STREET   CAMBRIDGE MA 02238
PHONE (617) 547 5552   FAX (617) 864 9405

Founded 1969 • *Geographic Coverage* National, Global • *Chapters* 2, in District of Columbia and California • *Individual Members* 100,000

Mission To advance responsible public policies in areas where technology plays a critical role. UCS is currently working to encourage responsible stewardship of the global environment and life sustaining resources; to promote energy technologies that are renewable, safe and cost effective; to reform transportation policy; to curtail weapons proliferation.

Annual Fees *Suggested donation* $20

Funding

Membership	Foundations	Other
47%	40.5%	12.5%

Total Income $4,080,000

Usage

Administration	Fundraising	Programs
2.6%	20.5%	76.9%

Total Expenses $3,778,000

Programs Global Resources Program. Energy Program. Transportation Program. Arms Control Program. Nuclear Power Safety Program. Action Networks. National Educational Campaign "Renewables Are Ready".

Publications Quarterly magazine *Nucleus*. Numerous UCS educational materials, including briefing papers, books and reports available to sponsors

Multimedia Videos accessible to sponsors

For more Information Annual Report

Who's Who CHAIRMAN **HENRY KENDALL** • SECRETARY **LINDA DREYFUS** • EXECUTIVE DIRECTOR **HOWARD RIS** • EDITOR **JANET S. WAGER** • CONTACT **LORI WALKER**

WINDSTAR FOUNDATION (THE)

2317 SNOWMASS CREEK ROAD   SNOWMASS CO 81654
PHONE (303) 927 4777

Founded 1976 • *Geographic Coverage* Global • *Cooperative Partners* Windstar Connection groups • *Individual Members* 3,000

Mission To inspire individuals to make responsible choices and take direct personal actions to achieve a peaceful and environmentally sustainable future.

Annual Fees	Regular	Sustaining	Director	Patron
	$35	$100	$250	$500

Programs Annual Volunteer Work Weekend. Biodome Workshops. Sponsors Annual Choices for the Future Symposium.

Publication *Windstar Vision Newsletter*

Who's Who PRESIDENT **JOHN DENVER** • VICE PRESIDENT **STEVE BLOMEKE**

WOMEN'S ENVIRONMENT
AND DEVELOPMENT ORGANIZATION   PAGE 27
845 THIRD AVENUE, 15TH FLOOR   NEW YORK NY 10022
PHONE (212) 759 7982   FAX (212) 759 8647

WORLD RESOURCES INSTITUTE   PAGE 28
1709 NEW YORK AVENUE, NW   WASHINGTON DC 20006
PHONE (202) 662 2543   FAX (202) 638 0036

WORLDWIDE NETWORK
WOMEN IN DEVELOPMENT AND ENVIRONMENT
1331 "H" STREET, NW, SUITE 903   WASHINGTON DC 20005
PHONE (202) 347 1514   FAX (202) 347 1524

Founded 1981 • *Geographic Coverage* Global • *Focused Countries* Barbados, Brazil, Costa Rica, Kenya, Mali, Nepal, South Africa, Thailand, USA • *Chapters* 8, worldwide • *Individual Members* 350 members and 7,500 networkers

Mission To establish a worldwide network of women concerned about environmental management and protection, to educate the public and policy makers about the vital links between women, natural resources and sustainable development, promote the inclusion of women and their environmental perceptions in designing and implementing policies, and to mobilize and support women, both individually and in organizations, in environmental and natural resource programs. To encourage women from all walks of life to share information and help create solutions for environmental problems. The Network's current areas of focus are women, the environment and sustainable development.

Annual Fees	Regular	Student/Senior	Patron
	$20	$15	$250

Funding	Membership	Foundations	Other
	2%	96%	2%

Total Income $350,000

Usage	Administration	Programs
	6%	94%

Programs Volunteer internship. Global, national and regional assemblies. Forums at Duke University, and in Kenya, Nepal, South Africa, and Barbados. Encourages women to start local chapters.

Publication *Directory of Women in Environment*

Who's Who CHAIRPERSONS **HELEN FREEMAN**, **KATHRYN CAMERON PORTER** MANAGING DIRECTOR **WAAFAS OFOSU-AMAAH** • SECRETARY **SUSAN A. FLETCHER**

WORLDWISE
GRASSROOTS CAMPAIGN
FOR INTERNATIONAL DEVELOPMENT BANK REFORM
401 SAN MIGUEL WAY   SACRAMENTO CA 95819
PHONE (916) 456 9205   FAX (916) 739 6951

Founded 1990 • *Geographic Coverage* Global • *Focused Countries* Especially developing nations • *Cooperative Partners* Many NGOs located in the Third World, Friends of the Earth

Mission To support grassroots organizations, scientists, economists, and concerned individuals who are working, or ready to work, to redirect the $30 billion in loans made annually by Multilateral Development Banks away from projects that cause major environmental, social, and financial damage and towards projects which are environmentally, socially, and economically sustainable.

Funding	Membership	Foundations
	50%	50%

Publications *International Directory of Non-Governmental Organizations Working for Environmentally, Socially and Economically Sustainable Development* published in collaboration with Friends of the Earth

For more Information Database, Library

Who's Who EXECUTIVE DIRECTOR **MARK DUBOIS**

ASSOCIATION DE BIODYNAMIE DU QUÉBEC, INC.

BIO-DYNAMIC ASSOCIATION OF QUÉBEC, INC.

416 RANG 4, OUEST   BAIE DES SABLES PQ G0J 1C0
PHONE (418) 772 6574   FAX (418) 772 7865

Founded 1979 • *Geographic Coverage* Province • *Cooperative Partners* Bio-Dynamic Association of Ontario, Bio-Dynamic Association of British Columbia • *Organization Members* 17 • *Individual Members* 327

Mission To promote and foster organic farming techniques known as bio-dynamic farming.

Annual Fees *Regular* $30

Funding *Membership* 100%

Total Income $9,000

Usage	Administration	Publication of Periodicals	Other
	10%	60%	30%

Programs Quarterly conferences and workshops. Educational programs focusing on bio-dynamic farming techniques.

Publications Quarterly journal *Le Germe*. Semiannual bulletin *Le Dynamot*

For more Information Library

Who's Who PRESIDENT JEAN RAUSSEL • VICE PRESIDENT HANS BUECHELI • SECRETARY LILIANE LECHRETIEN • EXECUTIVE DIRECTOR PIERRE MOMINGUE • OTHER PATRIC LÉTOURNEAU, DIANE GONTHIER • CONTACT LISE BEAULIEU

BIO-ALTERNATIVES SOL-SANTÉ, INC.

INTERNATIONAL DOCUMENTATION CENTRE FOR ALTERNATIVES

2690 PIE IX, SUITE 1   MONTRÉAL PQ H1V 2E7
PHONE (514) 899 5752   FAX (514) 899 5753

Founded 1990 • *Geographic Coverage* Province • *Cooperative Partners* Association Québécoise de Médecine Holistique - Québec Holistic Medical Association, New York Academy of Sciences

Mission To offer pertinent information and training on all aspects of organic food production, holistic medicine, and environmental sciences.

Programs Conferences. Classes. Seminars for the public or professionals.

Publications Numerous books focusing on organic agriculture and breeding, organic nutrition, applied ecology, natural and alternative medicine

For more Information Library

Who's Who PRESIDENT JEAN CLAUDE RODET

CAMROSE INTERNATIONAL INSTITUTE

5061 50TH STREET   CAMROSE AB T4V 1R3
PHONE (403) 672 8780   FAX (403) 672 4331

Founded 1977 • *Geographic Coverage* National, Global • *Other Field of Focus* Global Environmental Concerns • *Cooperative Partners* Canadian Council of International Cooperation, South Asia Partnership, Partnership Africa Canada, Canadian Environmental Network, Development Education Coordinating Council of Alberta • *Organization Members* 6 • *Individual Members* 250

Mission To encourage equitable, ecologically sound human development in Canada and the Third World, and to make links between the people of Canada and the Third World through education and development projects.

Annual Fees	Regular	Student/Senior	Families	Organization	Corporation
	$24	$12	$30	$60	$60

Other Fees *Lifetime* $500

Funding	Programs	Projects	Other
	89%	9.7%	1.3%

Total Income $1,557,314

Total Expenses $1,580,441

Programs Prairie Decentralized Support Program. Education Program - Development and Environment. Overseas Projects.

Publication Quarterly *CII Newsletter*

For more Information Annual Report, Library

Who's Who PRESIDENT BRIAN HEIDECKER • EXECUTIVE DIRECTOR BRENDA NAYLOR ENVIRONMENT PROGRAM OFFICER RICHARD VERBISKY

CANADIAN ORGANIC GROWERS

BOX 116   COLLINGWOOD ON L9Y 3Z4
PHONE (705) 444 0923   FAX (705) 444 0380

Founded 1975 • *Geographic Coverage* National, Global • *Cooperative Partners* Several alternative agricultural groups in Canada, USA and Europe, Society for Biodynamic Farming and Gardening, Ecological Farmers Association of Ontario, Guelph Agricultural Alternatives, Organic Crop Improvement Association, Ontario Ministry of Agriculture and Food, University of Guelph • *Chapters* 10 *Organization Members* 20 • *Individual Members* 2,000

Mission To provide information about organic food while supporting and promoting organic agricultural research, encouraging decentralized, regionally based food systems, endorsing practices which promote and maintain long-term soil fertility and reduce fossil fuel use, and assisting members with how-to demonstrations, lectures, fact sheets, videos, and studies.

Annual Fees	Regular	Student/Senior	Organization	Corporation	Sustaining
	$20	$12	$30	$30	$100

Other Fees *Patron* $250

Funding	Membership	Foundations
	75%	25%

Programs Sponsors the Annual Organic Agriculture Conference in Guelph, Ontario. Mary Perlmutter Organic Scholarship. Heritage Seed Program. Regional activities including conferences, compost demonstrations, farm tours, speaker series and traveling displays.

Publications Quarterly magazine *Cognition*, circulation 3,200. Various books including *The Organic Field Crop Handbook* • *Directory of Organic Agriculture*, international sourcebook listing 500 organic growers, products and educational services • *How Does Your Garden Grow... Organically?*

Multimedia Video Field of Greens 4-part TV series on The Rogers Cable Network

For more Information Database, Library, List of Publications

Who's Who PRESIDENT ELIZABETH WHITE • VICE PRESIDENT TOMAS NIMMO SECRETARY KATHY LAMARCHE • LIBRARIAN BRIAN WOODS

CONSERVATION LEARNING CENTRE

Box 3003
800 CENTRAL AVENUE   PRINCE ALBERT SK S6V 6G1
PHONE (306) 953 2770   FAX (306) 953 2440

Founded 1993 • *Geographic Coverage* Province • *Cooperative Partners* Saskatchewan Soil Conservation Association, Ducks Unlimited Canada, Agriculture Canada - Parkland Agricultural Research Initiative *Chapter* 1

Mission To demonstrate land management techniques which focus on the optimum utilization of the landscape for annual crop and forage production, employ appropriate soil and water conservation techniques, and facilitate wildlife habitat enhancement. To provide a learning center for farmers, agrologists, students of all ages, and the general public interested in agricultural sustainability and environmental quality. To collect scientific information to evaluate the interaction of crop production and livestock-based agriculture with the environment, utilizing the landscape relief characteristic of the Parkland region of Saskatchewan. To provide a common location for the interaction of public and private interests concerned with issues related to production agriculture and resource conservation.

Publications Newsletters

For more Information Annual Report

Who's Who SECRETARY ADRIAN JOHNSON • MANAGER MS. PAT FLATEN

ECOLOGICAL FARMERS ASSOCIATION OF ONTARIO

C/O MAITLAND VALLEY CONSERVATION AUTHORITY
Box 127   WROXETER ON N0G 2X0
PHONE (519) 335 3557   FAX (519) 335 3615

Founded 1979 • *Geographic Coverage* Regional, North America *Focused Region* Central and eastern Canada, northern USA • *Cooperative Partners* Canadian Organic Growers, Ecological Agriculture Projects at McGill University, Maitland Valley Conservation Authority, Alternative Energy Resources Organization, University of Guelph • *Organization Member* 1 • *Individual Members* 500

Mission To motivate and inspire farmers to educate themselves about holistic approaches to farming, to promote an ecologically sound agriculture, to provide a support network for farmers who are adopting ecological farming practices, to research alternative farming methods, to demonstrate ecological farming practices, and to collect and evaluate data on holistic farming experiences.

Annual Fees	Regular	3-Year Membership
	$20	$50

Funding	Membership	Other
	69%	31%

Total Income $14,500

Usage	Administration	Programs	Advisory Services	Other
	50%	20%	20%	10%

Total Expenses $10,000

Programs Farm Tours - 3 to 5 times a year. Introductory Courses on Ecological Agriculture - each spring. Fall Conference. Annual general meeting. EFAO Advisory Consulting Service.

Publication Quarterly *EFAO Newsletter*

Multimedia How-to videos *Organic Field Crops* • *Sharing the Experience*

For more Information Database, Library, List of Publications

Who's Who PRESIDENT LAWRENCE ANDRES • SECRETARY PHIL BEARD • TREASURER TONI MCQUAIL • EXECUTIVE DIRECTOR TED ZETTEL • CONTACT RON STROME

ENERGY PROBE RESEARCH FOUNDATION   PAGE 174

225 BRUNSWICK AVENUE   TORONTO ON M5S 2M6
PHONE (416) 964 9223   FAX (416) 964 8239

ENVIRONMENT COUNCIL OF ALBERTA

9925 109TH STREET   EDMONTON AB T5K 2J8
PHONE (403) 427 5792   FAX (403) 427 0388

Founded 1970 • *Geographic Coverage* Province • *Cooperative Partners* Alberta Environment, Water Resources Commission

Mission To work towards a sustainable future for Alberta by providing leadership and long-term strategic advice on environmental conservation to the government, based on input from knowledgeable and concerned Albertans. Its main role is to question current assumptions in the areas of sustainable development and environmental protection, and to identify future issues related to the environment in Alberta.

Programs Seeks public input, prepares and distributes information to the public, and provides secretariat services at ministerial request in areas where mandates are complementary.

Publications Various publications focusing on biodiversity and land use management, energy and natural resources, urban environment

For more Information Annual Report, Library, List of Publications

Who's Who EXECUTIVE DIRECTOR NATALIA M. KRAWETZ • LIBRARIAN ANN SCHIEBELBEIN

INTERNATIONAL INSTITUTE FOR SUSTAINABLE DEVELOPMENT

161 PORTAGE AVENUE, EAST   WINNIPEG MB R3B 0Y4
PHONE (204) 958 7700   FAX (204) 958 7710

Geographic Coverage Global • *Cooperative Partners* Institute for Research on Public Policy, Center for Trade Policy and Law, National Round Table on Environment and Economy, Department of Environment, World Resources Institute

Mission To promote sustainable development in decision making within government, business, and the daily lives of individuals. The Institute engages in policy research and communications, including a focus on international trade, business strategy, national budgets, and new institutions that support sustainable development.

Funding	*Grants*	*Interest*
	93%	6.5%

Total Income $4,623,378

Usage	*Administration & Fundraising*	*Programs*
	19%	81%

Total Expenses $4,322,922

Programs The Institute's Business and Government Program focuses on corporate accountability in response to the new pressures for sustainable development. The Earth Enterprise Project works to generate successful entrepreneurial and innovative activity that will help the environment and support sustainable development. Trade and Investment Program. Communications and Partnerships. Poverty and Empowerment Program. Agenda 21 and post-UNCED follow-up are incorporated into each program area.

Publications Periodical *Earth Negotiations Bulletin*. Report *Business Strategy for Sustainable Development: Leadership and Accountability in the 90s*. Other publications include *Trade and Sustainable Development: A Survey of the Issues and a New Research Agenda* • *Sourcebook on Sustainable Development drawing upon many international databases* • *Impoverishment and Sustainable Development: A Systemic Perspective* • *Our Responsibility to the Seventh Generation*

For more Information Annual Report, Database, List of Publications

Who's Who PRESIDENT ARTHUR J. HANSON • PROGRAMS COORDINATORS STEPHAN BARG, RICHARD BLACKHURST, NICHOLAS SONNTAG, GABRIEL RÉGALLET, ROBE KERR

JESUIT FARM PROJECT

P.O. BOX 1238   GUELPH ON N1H 6N6
PHONE (519) 824 1250

Founded 1986 • *Geographic Coverage* Central America • *Focused Country* Jamaica • *Cooperative Partners* Jesuits of Canada, Regenerative Ecological Agricultural Project, Friends of Foodland, Catholic Rural Life Conference • *Chapter* 1

Mission The organization's mission is to approach faith-justice concerning environmental and social issues in agriculture.

Funding	*Foundations*	*Book Sales*
	50%	50%

Total Income $8,000

Usage	*Programs*	*Other*
	80%	20%

Programs The organization works on subsistence farming project with a North Ontario indigenous group. Information talks. Retreats for farmers.

Publications Newsletter *Foodland Alert*. Book *Living Off the Land: Spirituality of Farming*

For more Information Database, Library

Who's Who PRESIDENT DAVID SHULIST • VICE PRESIDENT JOHN MCCARTHY • SECRETARY ZACH ZACHARIAH • TREASURER LOIS ZACHARIAH • CONTACT DIANE BATTAZ

NEW BRUNSWICK SOIL AND CROP IMPROVEMENT ASSOCIATION
ASSOCIATION POUR L'AMÉLIORATION DES SOLS ET CULTURES DU NOUVEAU-BRUNSWICK

R.R. 3   BELLEISLE CREEK NB E0G 1E0
PHONE (506) 485 2584

Geographic Coverage Province • *Chapters* 9 • *Individual Members* 700

Mission To develop, promote, and demonstrate environmentally and economically sound agricultural practices as they relate to soils and crops in New Brunswick.

Annual Fees *Regular* $15

Programs Sponsor of No-Till Forage Seeder Project. Speakers, seminars, field tours. Sponsor of research trials

Publication Occasional newsletter

Who's Who PRESIDENT **BRIAN O'NEILL** • VICE PRESIDENT **GERALD DALEY** • SECRETARY **ROGER KAYE**

ONTARIO SOCIETY FOR ENVIRONMENTAL MANAGEMENT

136 WINGES ROAD, UNIT 15   WOODBRIDGE ON L4L 6C4
PHONE (905) 850 8066   FAX (905) 850 7313

Founded 1976 • *Geographic Coverage* Province • *Other Fields of Focus* Ecosystem Protection / Biodiversity, Natural Resources / Water - Conservation & Quality • *Cooperative Partners* Ontario Healthy Communities Coalition, Conservation Council of Ontario, Natural Heritage League • *Chapters* 2 • *Individual Members* 150

Mission To promote environmental management in Ontario. As defined in the Society's Constitution, environmental management is systematic and continuing action to maintain or to enhance the quality of the environment. This is achieved by interdisciplinary application of scientific knowledge and professional skills.

Annual Fees

Regular	Student/Senior	Retired
$95	$20	$45

Funding

Membership	Programs
50%	50%

Total Income $16,000

Usage

Administration	Fundraising	Programs	Chapters
30%	5%	60%	5%

Total Expenses $17,000

Programs One day conference "Environmental and Land Use Planning for Municipalities". Liability of Environmental Professionals, Leadership of Environmental Groups and Environmental Bill of Rights (draft Ontario legislation) evening debates.

Publication Newsletter published 4 to 6 times per year

For more Information Database, Library

Who's Who PRESIDENT **P. DOUGLAS PETRIC** • VICE PRESIDENT **BOB BURDETT** • ADMINISTRATOR **SUE RUGGERO** • SECRETARY **RANDALL GOODWIN** • TREASURER **DIANNE DAMMEN** CONTACT PUBLIC RELATIONS **RICK BRADY**

PROJETS POUR UNE AGRICULTURE ECOLOGIQUE
ECOLOGICAL AGRICULTURE PROJECTS

MACDONALD CAMPUS, MCGILL UNIVERSITY
21111 LAKESHORE ROAD   STE. ANNE DE BELLEVUE PQ H9X 3V9
PHONE (514) 398 7771   FAX (514) 398 7621

Founded 1974 • *Geographic Coverage* Local, Province, National, North America • *Other Field of Focus* Food / Pesticides / Consumerism & Safety

Mission To facilitate the establishment of food systems worldwide that are nutritionally sound, socially just, humane, economically viable, and environmentally sustainable. The organization collects, organizes, and disseminates essential information, conducts research, and provides expert analysis and advice to farmers, consumers, government, academia, agribusiness, and the media.

Funding

Membership	Government Support	Foundations	Programs
5%	25%	25%	45%

Publications Quarterly bulletin *EAP News*. Numerous publications focusing on organic farming and sustainable agriculture

For more Information Database, Library, List of Publications

Who's Who EXECUTIVE DIRECTOR **STUART B. HILL** • CONTACT **JEFF MARTIN**

SIMILKAMEEN OKANAGAN
ORGANIC PRODUCERS ASSOCIATION

P.O. BOX 577   KEREMEOS BC V0X 1N0
PHONE (604) 499 2550   FAX (604) 499 2388

Founded 1986 • *Geographic Coverage* Local • *Other Field of Focus* Food / Pesticides / Consumerism & Safety • *Cooperative Partners* British Columbia Organic Alliance, Certified Organic Association of British Columbia • *Individual Members* 63

Mission To certify as organically grown the produce of organic farmers in the Similkameen and Okanagan Valleys and in British Columbia's southern interior.

Annual Fees *Regular* $115

Funding

Membership	Other
59%	41%

Total Income $12,380

Usage

Administration	Programs
15%	85%

For more Information Database

Who's Who PRESIDENT **WAYNE STILL** • VICE PRESIDENT **ROB VANDERLIP** • SECRETARY **ELAINE STEWART**

alphabetical index

index *by state* & *province*

california

colorado

connecticut

massachussets

manitoba

maryland

maine

michigan

minnesota

oregon

pennsylvania

prince edward island

québec

list of **charts**

part one

part two

part three

part four

323

324

CHAPTER 19 • public & environmental health

CHAPTER 20 • quality of life
• outdoor activities

CHAPTER 21 • sustainable development, agriculture
• environmental technologies

order *form*

LAST NAME : _____   FIRST NAME : _____

ORGANIZATION / COMPANY : _____

ADDRESS : _____

CITY : _____

STATE / PROVINCE : _____   ZIP / MAIL CODE : _____   COUNTRY : _____

TELEPHONE : (_____) _____   FAX : (_____) _____

PLEASE SEND ME _____ COPIES OF *GreenWorld's Almanac & Directory of Environmental Organizations 1994.*

THE PRICE IS *$49.95* PER COPY. PLEASE INCLUDE *$3.00* FOR SHIPPING AND HANDLING IN THE USA OR *$5.00* FOR OTHER COUNTRIES.

CALIFORNIA RESIDENTS PLEASE ADD *8.25%* SALES TAX.

❑ CHECK   MAKE CHECK PAYABLE TO *GreenWorld Environmental Publications Co.*
CHECKS MUST BE IN US DOLLARS, PAYABLE IN THE UNITED STATES. C.O.D. ORDERS ARE NOT ACCEPTED.

❑ VISA   ❑ MASTERCARD

CARD NUMBER : _____ / _____ / _____ / _____   EXPIRATION DATE : _____ / _____

NAME ON CARD : _____

AUTHORIZED SIGNATURE : _____

PHONE ORDERS (310) 815 8867   FAX ORDERS (310) 815 8868

GREENWORLD ENVIRONMENTAL PUBLICATIONS CO.

253 A 26TH STREET, SUITE 306, SANTA MONICA, CA 90402, USA

mail it *or* fax it

address
3 A 26TH Street
Suite 306
Santa Monica
CA 90402

fax
310) 815 8868

listing information *form*

IF YOU WISH TO MODIFY YOUR LISTING IN *GreenWorld's Almanac and Directory of Environmental Organizations*, PLEASE FILL OUT THE FOLLOWING.

NAME OF ORGANIZATION : _____

ADDRESS : _____

CITY : _____

STATE / PROVINCE : _____ ZIP / MAIL CODE : _____ COUNTRY : _____

TELEPHONE : ( ) _____ FAX : ( ) _____

MODIFICATIONS : _____

_____

_____

_____

_____

_____

_____

_____

_____

_____

_____

_____

GREENWORLD ENVIRONMENTAL PUBLICATIONS CO.

253 A 26TH STREET, SUITE 306, SANTA MONICA, CA 90402, USA

PHONE (310) 815 8867   FAX (310) 815 8868

if you wi
to have yo
organization
in this
publicatio
please,

contact us

at our addr
phone or f
numbers, an
will send yo
applicati
form